2004
The Supreme Court Review

2004
The

"Judges as persons, or courts as institutions, are entitled to
no greater immunity from criticism than other persons
or institutions . . . [J]udges must be kept mindful of their limitations and
of their ultimate public responsibility by a vigorous
stream of criticism expressed with candor however blunt."
—*Felix Frankfurter*

". . . while it is proper that people should find fault when
their judges fail, it is only reasonable that they should recognize the
difficulties. . . . Let them be severely brought to book,
when they go wrong, but by those who will take the trouble
to understand them."
—*Learned Hand*

THE LAW SCHOOL

THE UNIVERSITY OF CHICAGO

Supreme Court Review

EDITED BY

DENNIS J. HUTCHINSON

DAVID A. STRAUSS

AND GEOFFREY R. STONE

THE UNIVERSITY OF CHICAGO PRESS

CHICAGO AND LONDON

INTERNATIONAL STANDARD BOOK NUMBER: 0-226-36323-6

LIBRARY OF CONGRESS CATALOG CARD NUMBER: 60-14353

THE UNIVERSITY OF CHICAGO PRESS, CHICAGO 60637

THE UNIVERSITY OF CHICAGO PRESS, LTD., LONDON

© 2005 BY THE UNIVERSITY OF CHICAGO, ALL RIGHTS RESERVED, PUBLISHED 2005

PRINTED IN THE UNITED STATES OF AMERICA

The paper used in this publication meets the minimum requirements of American National Standard for Information Sciences–Permanence of Paper for Printed Library Materials, ANSI Z39.48-1984. ∞

CONTENTS

VINCENT BLASI

HOLMES AND THE MARKETPLACE OF IDEAS

At least five basic values might be served by a robust free speech principle: (1) individual autonomy; (2) truth seeking; (3) self-government; (4) the checking of abuses of power; (5) the promotion of good character. Free speech might serve one or more of these values by functioning in at least three different ways: (1) as a privileged activity; (2) as a social mechanism; (3) as a cultural force. My contention is that the conventional understanding of the most familiar metaphor in the First Amendment lexicon, the "marketplace of ideas," has had the undesirable effect of focusing attention too much on the truth seeking and self-government values and on the function of free speech as a social mechanism.

The detriment in this emphasis is threefold. First, the case for a high level of protection for free speech has been weakened by being made to depend too much on unconvincing claims regarding how the phenomenon of provocative speech followed by countervailing "more speech" produces a satisfactory process of collective delib-

Vincent Blasi is Corliss Lamont Professor of Civil Liberties, Columbia Law School, and James Madison Distinguished Professor of Law and Roy L. and Rosamund W. Morgan Research Professor, The University of Virginia.

AUTHOR'S NOTE: Drafts of this paper were vetted by colleagues and workshops too numerous to list. Their input has improved it immeasurably. I am especially indebted to Anuj Desai, Alan Hyde, Petros Mavroidis, Richard Posner, Seana Shiffrin, Kim Szurovy, Jeremy Waldron, and G. Edward White for detailed written comments; to Simon Canick and JoAnn Koob for extraordinarily helpful research assistance; and to Irene ten Cate for her insightful student work comparing the free speech philosophies of Holmes and John Stuart Mill.

eration. Second, the identification of the freedom of speech with the ideal of a well-functioning market in ideas has generated distracting and dangerous regulatory proposals that attempt to redistribute communicative power as a means of realizing that ideal. Third, as a result of viewing free speech primarily as a plebiscitary mechanism designed to produce collective understanding and political legitimacy, we have failed to appreciate how it serves as a cultural force that contributes to the control of abuses of power and the promotion of adaptive character traits.

In this article I do not attempt to defend the claims just stated. Rather, I seek to demonstrate that Justice Oliver Wendell Holmes's dissent in *Abrams v United States*,[1] the canonical opinion that gave rise to the arresting figure of the "marketplace of ideas," contains the seeds of an understanding of the First Amendment that has more to do with checking, character, and culture than with the implausible vision of a self-correcting, knowledge-maximizing, judgment-optimizing, consent-generating, and participation-enabling social mechanism. This project of looking beneath the surface of Holmes's metaphor is designed not so much to invoke the authority of his stature and eloquence as to suggest promising lines of thought concerning the value and function of free speech.

The *Abrams* dissent is remarkable on many counts. Its peroration articulates in a single paragraph a highly sophisticated if cryptic philosophical justification for the freedom of speech. Surprisingly perhaps, the paragraph begins by explaining the unassailable logic of repression:

> Persecution for the expression of opinions seems to me perfectly logical. If you have no doubt of your premises or your power and want a certain result with all your heart you naturally express your wishes in law and sweep away all opposition. To allow opposition by speech seems to indicate that you think the speech impotent, as when a man says that he has squared the circle, or that you do not care whole-heartedly for the result, or that you doubt either your power or your premises.[2]

Then suddenly Holmes switches gears, true to his celebrated observation thirty-eight years earlier, "the life of the law has not been

---

[1] 250 US 616, 624 (1919).

[2] Id at 630.

logic: it has been experience."[3] He notes how prudence born of experience should temper the "natural" and "perfectly logical" desire to extirpate disturbing ideas:

> But when men have realized that time has upset many fighting faiths, they may come to believe even more than they believe the very foundations of their own conduct that the ultimate good desired is better reached by free trade in ideas—that the best test of truth is the power of the thought to get itself accepted in the competition of the market, and that truth is the only ground upon which their wishes safely can be carried out.[4]

In perhaps his most daring move, Holmes then asserts that this prudence is embodied in the positive law of the U.S. Constitution:

> That at any rate is the theory of our Constitution. It is an experiment, as all life is an experiment. Every year if not every day we have to wager our salvation upon some prophecy based upon imperfect knowledge. While that experiment is part of our system I think that we should be eternally vigilant against attempts to check the expression of opinions that we loathe and believe to be fraught with death, unless they so imminently threaten immediate interference with the lawful and pressing purposes of the law that an immediate check is required to save the country.[5]

Next, consistent with his preference for experience over logic as the source of law, he invokes the authority of history:

> I wholly disagree with the argument of the Government that the First Amendment left the common law as to seditious libel in force. History seems to me against the notion. I had conceived that the United States through many years had shown its repentance for the Sedition Act of 1798, by repaying fines that it imposed.[6]

Finally, Holmes characterizes the First Amendment as a "sweeping command" subject to limitation only on the occasion of an "emergency that makes it immediately dangerous to leave the correction of evil counsels to time."

---

[3] Oliver Wendell Holmes, Jr., *The Common Law* 5 (1881).

[4] 250 US at 630.

[5] Id.

[6] Id.

As should be apparent, Holmes managed to pack into this paragraph an astonishingly rich set of allusions. His market metaphor is only one of many suggestive and loaded figurations. Notice, for example, his pointedly mundane account of religious devotion: "time has upset many fighting faiths"; "we have to wager our salvation upon some prophecy based upon imperfect knowledge." Or his deflating retort to the Constitution worshipers of his day: "It is an experiment, as all life is an experiment." The challenge for one who would make sense of Holmes is to avoid being swept away by any one of his seductive formulations. To that end, we must try to understand his market metaphor in the light of the observations and judgments that surround it in the *Abrams* peroration. Considering the metaphor in isolation can lead to a failure to appreciate what it has to offer, as well as an inaccurate account of Holmes's surprisingly coherent argument for a robust freedom of speech.

I. Equilibrium

"The best test of truth is the power of the thought to get itself accepted in the competition of the market."[7] This statement, together with his call for "free trade in ideas,"[8] might suggest that Holmes based his interpretation of the First Amendment on the assumption that ideas should be evaluated the way consumer goods and services are: not by any kind of political or intellectual authority but rather by an open-ended process that measures and integrates the ongoing valuations of all the individuals who comprise the relevant community. In this view, the crucial concept is "equilibrium," the balance of valuations at any given moment. The benefit of free speech is its role in generating the individual choices regarding ideas, and the public awareness of those choices, that add up to the equilibrium of the moment. In support of this interpretation, we might note that Holmes once claimed that "the function of private ownership is to divine in advance the equilibrium of social desires."[9] On another occasion he asked: "What proximate test of excellence can be found except correspondence to the actual equilibrium of

---

[7] Id.

[8] Id.

[9] Oliver Wendell Holmes, *Law and the Court*, in *Collected Legal Papers* 294 (1920).

force in the community—that is, conformity to the wishes of the dominant power?"[10]

Holmes was interested in economics. In *The Path of the Law* he famously said: "For the rational study of the law the black-letter man may be the man of the present, but the man of the future is the man of statistics and the master of economics."[11] He sprinkled his correspondence with approving references to the first-ever professional economist,[12] the statistically minded sage of scarcity and diminishing returns, T. R. Malthus. Holmes once told Harold Laski: "I am a devout Malthusian."[13] In a different letter to Laski he reported: "Fred Pollock speaks of Saint Jane (Austen). I shall speak of Saint Malthus."[14] When Laski described Adam Smith as "a very great writer and the best observer of his time; I know nothing like his book in the whole of economic literature,"[15] Holmes wrote back: "I am with you on Smith's *Wealth of Nations*. I was staggered when Marx patronized him."[16] Earlier he had complained to Laski: "I never read a socialist yet . . . and I have read a number, that I didn't think talked drool."[17] We can be confident that Holmes was

---

[10] Oliver Wendell Holmes, *Montesquieu*, in id at 250, 258.

[11] Oliver Wendell Holmes, Jr., *The Path of the Law*, 10 Harv L Rev 457, 469 (1897).

[12] See William J. Barber, *A History of Economic Thought* 57 (1967) ("*History*").

[13] Letter from Holmes to Harold J. Laski (Sept 16, 1924), in Mark De Wolfe Howe, ed, 1 *Holmes-Laski Letters* 658–59 (1953).

[14] Letter from Holmes to Laski (June 14, 1927), in 2 *Holmes-Laski Letters* at 950. See also Letter from Holmes to Laski (Dec 9, 1921), in 1 *Holmes-Laski Letters* at 385 ("In short I believe in Malthus—in the broad—not bothering about details."); Letter from Holmes to Laski (July 23, 1925), id at 762 ("But I look at men through Malthus's glasses— as like flies—here swept away by a pestilence—there multiplying unduly and paying for it."); Letter from Holmes to Lewis Einstein (Sept 2, 1914), in James Bishop Peabody, ed, *Holmes-Einstein Letters* 99 (1964) ("I was delighted with Malthus and his quiet, English, unemphatic way of expressing penetrating thought over which a modern German sociologist or Mathew Arnold would have cackled for half a volume."). See also Letter from Holmes to Laski (July 30, 1920), in 2 *Holmes-Laski Letters* at 272.

[15] 1 *Holmes-Laski Letters* at 471 (cited in note 13).

[16] Id at 474. See also id at 161.

[17] Id at 96. In a subsequent letter to Laski, Holmes expatiated further on his preference for the capitalist worldview: "I don't at all agree to describing [capitalism's] tyrannies with resentment, as coming from bad men when you gloss those on the other side. I think that most of the so-called tyrannies of capital express the economic necessities created by the pressure of population—a pressure for which capitalism is not responsible and for which communism has offered no remedy. If I praised or blamed (which I don't) either one, I should blame the communists as consciously and voluntarily contemplating their despotism whereas on the other side it is largely unconscious and the automatic result of the situation. I may add that class for class I think the one that communism would abolish is more valuable—contributes more, a great deal more, than those whom Communism exalts." 2 *Holmes-Laski Letters* at 945 (cited in note 13).

familiar with and sympathetic to the general worldview and many of the specific observations of the laissez-faire economists. But as is often the case with Holmes,[18] we know more about *which* thinkers he liked than about exactly *what* he liked in their work. Adam Smith, T. R. Malthus, David Ricardo, and their cohorts had many ideas— and many disagreements—about the virtues and limitations of markets.[19] Which, if any, might Holmes have drawn upon in formulating his understanding of the freedom of speech?

Should we, for example, read Holmes as resting his defense of free speech on the assumption that a cognitive Invisible Hand continually generates informational, critical, and rhetorical correctives that keep patterns of belief in a welfare-maximizing state of dynamic equilibrium? Someone who took this claim to be the underpinning of Holmes's marketplace theory might question whether the process by which ideas are generated, disseminated, and validated in contemporary mass culture accurately measures and fairly computes the beliefs of the individuals who constitute the society.[20]

One reason to doubt the efficacy of the market mechanism as a means of ordering beliefs derives from the concept, well recognized by economists, of market failure.[21] Except in models, markets are imperfect. Differential access to information distorts markets.[22] Collective behavior can distort markets.[23] So too can free riders: persons who are in a position to benefit from the transactions of others without having to pay the price.[24] A different type of "externality" undermines efficiency when the full quantum of social costs generated by an activity cannot practically be ob-

---

[18] See Thomas C. Grey, *Holmes and Legal Pragmatism*, 41 Stan L Rev 787, 788 (1989).

[19] See Davide Fiaschi and Rodolfo Signorino, *Consumption Patterns, Development and Growth: Adam Smith, David Ricardo and Thomas Robert Malthus*, 10 Euro J Hist Economic Thought 5 (2003).

[20] See, for example, C. Edwin Baker, *Human Liberty and Freedom of Speech* 12–17 (1989) ("*Human Liberty*"); Owen Fiss, *Liberalism Divided* 9–10, 17–20 (1996).

[21] See, for example, Alvin I. Goldman and James C. Cox, *Speech, Truth, and the Free Market for Ideas*, 2 Legal Theory 1, 19–26 (1996); Albert Breton and Ronald Wintrobe, *Freedom of Speech vs. Efficient Regulation in Markets for Ideas*, 17 J Econ Behav & Org 217 (1992).

[22] See Hal R. Varian, *Intermediate Microeconomics* 630–50 (4th ed 1996); Goldman and Cox, 2 Legal Theory at 19–23 (cited in note 21).

[23] See Varian, *Intermediate Microeconomics* at 458–79 (cited in note 22).

[24] Id at 616–18; Richard Posner, *Free Speech in an Economic Perspective*, 20 Suffolk U L Rev 1, 19–24 (1986).

served, measured, or assessed against those who engage in the activity.[25]

If the markets for goods and services are prone to such distortions, the market for ideas would seem to be especially divergent from the economists' ideal.[26] Individuals and groups who would peddle their ideas to the public enjoy enormously disparate access to the channels of mass communication. To a greater degree than is true for commodity and service markets, cultural affinities and psychological predispositions distort the way ideas are bought and sold, as does the fact that some ideas are more easily packaged than others. Differences among humans in such capacities as articulateness and comprehension also contribute to market failure: ideas that favor intelligent, well-spoken people—the priority accorded higher education might be one example—have a distinct and unfair advantage in the marketplace. In most speech settings, the audience could fairly be described as a veritable convention of free riders.[27] And as Frederick Schauer has demonstrated, the costs created by speech are seldom borne by the speakers.[28]

One can imagine a regulatory regime designed to correct or mitigate these disparities and externalities. Some reformers have found in Holmes's market metaphor a justification for various governmental interventions that would attempt to redistribute communicative opportunity.[29] Opponents of such reforms have argued that

---

[25] This disability can derive from inadequately defined property rights, see Varian, *Intermediate Microeconomics* at 561 (cited in note 22), from the fact that some social costs take the form of the loss or diminution of "goods" the very character of which prevents them from being computed or realized in the idiom of private property or revealed preferences, see Elizabeth Anderson, *Value and Ethics in Economics* 144–47 (1993) ("*Value and Ethics*"), or from physical and epistemological limitations in observing and understanding causal relationships.

[26] For an argument that in terms of economic analysis the market for ideas is probably more in need of regulation, due to greater externalities, than the market for goods, see R. H. Coase, *The Market for Goods and the Market for Ideas*, 64 Am Econ Rev: Papers & Proc 384 (1974).

[27] Judge Posner regards the free rider phenomenon to be especially important in the case of political speech. See Posner, 20 Suffolk U L Rev at 19–22 (cited in note 24). For an elaboration of the implications of viewing free speech as a public good due in part to the prevalence of audience free riders, see Daniel A. Farber, *Free Speech without Romance: Public Choice and the First Amendment*, 105 Harv L Rev 554 (1991).

[28] See Frederick Schauer, *Uncoupling Free Speech*, 92 Colum L Rev 1321 (1992).

[29] See, for example, Fiss, *Liberalism Divided* at 17–21 (cited in note 20); Cass R. Sunstein, *Democracy and the Problem of Free Speech* 16 (1993); Jerome A. Barron, *Access to the Press—A New First Amendment Right*, 80 Harv L Rev 1641 (1967); David Cole, *First Amendment Antitrust: The End of Laissez-Faire in Campaign Finance*, 9 Yale L & Policy Rev 236, 239–45 (1991); Charles Lawrence III, *If He Hollers Let Him Go: Regulating Racist Speech on Campus*, 1990 Duke L J 431, 466–73.

the intervention of government in the realm of speech is likely to take us even further from the free market ideal so far as the distribution of communicative influence is concerned.[30] However, before the concept of market failure or success is deemed to have any kind of First Amendment relevance deriving from Holmes's memorable figure of speech, we must confront the fundamental objection that ideas cannot properly be treated as consumer goods, that discussion and persuasion cannot be analogized to competitive exchange.[31] If we pursue the analogy beyond the first level, the strength of this objection can be appreciated.

Markets for goods and services generate prices and levels of output. A market for ideas generates a collection of individual beliefs and, in some sense, the production of observations and arguments. Scarcity, both of production and consumption resources, is the phenomenon that drives markets for goods and services. (For this purpose, information is better treated as a "good" than an "idea.") Scarcity of a sort also limits what ideas can be believed and communicated: a person must choose whether to believe p or not-p; she must decide which few ideas from a nearly infinite universe will command her finite attention and which of her numerous thoughts she will attempt to disseminate. Nevertheless, the generation and consumption of ideas is characterized by choices that are less stark, less categorical, less discrete—more qualified, more variegated, more continual, more reversible, more nuanced, more synergistic, more holistic—than are the choices faced by producers and consumers of most goods and services. One reason for this difference is that the process of transmitting ideas, even in the large and among strangers, has dimensions of cooperation, reciprocity, and mutual ongoing identification—a bonding, if mainly symbolic, between the sender and the receiver— that are not endemic to the phenomenon of competitive exchange in product markets, the efficiency of which is a function of their capacity to execute discrete impersonal transactions. Moreover, the production of an idea does not deplete resources available to the

---

[30] See, for example, Lillian R. BeVier, *The Invisible Hand of the Marketplace of Ideas*, in Lee C. Bollinger and Geoffrey R. Stone, eds, *Eternally Vigilant: Free Speech in the Modern Era* 232 (2002); L. A. Powe, Jr., *Mass Speech and the Newer First Amendment*, 1982 Supreme Court Review 243, 280–84; Charles Fried, *The New First Amendment Jurisprudence: A Threat to Liberty*, 59 U Chi L Rev 225, 250–53 (1992); Ronald W. Adelman, *The First Amendment and the Metaphor of Free Trade*, 38 Ariz L Rev 1125 (1996).

[31] See, for example, Anderson, *Value and Ethics* at 158–63 (cited in note 25); Margaret Jane Radin, *Contested Commodities* 164–83 (1996).

producer as occurs when production priorities are established regarding goods and services; more often the production of an idea creates additional intellectual resources that facilitate future production. Similarly, when one consumer "buys" an idea, the supply of that idea available to other consumers is not thereby diminished. In these respects, the phenomenon of scarcity does not determine how ideas are socially ordered in quite the way it determines the allocation and distribution of conventional "rivalrous" goods and services.

Nor do substitution effects, a critical component of microeconomic analysis,[32] operate in the realm of ideas the way they do in markets for goods and services. Appealing ideas do not command less assent when ideas that are almost but not quite as appealing become available at a lower price. One reason is that the very concept of "price" is problematic when the object of consumption is ideas. What is it that a person must give up in order to "consume" an idea other than the opportunity to believe conflicting ideas?[33] The forming of a belief sometimes entails costs to one's reputation, and perhaps to one's sense of personal identity, such that alternative beliefs that exact less of a price in these terms might represent a better "bargain" for the consumer. But even if available substitutes sometimes figure in the process of belief formation in this odd manner, the impact of such behavior on the aggregate demand for an idea is not something that contributes to an "efficient" outcome in the social project of truth seeking. If beliefs are considered valuable primarily for their expressive function by which persons forge identities and make interpersonal connections,[34] the choice to embrace a less costly substitute belief entails, if not conscious insincerity, at least cognitive dissonance that would seem to call into question the expressive value of the belief so chosen, assuming that it is even possible to choose to "believe" a less costly substitute. If, on the other hand, the instrumental value of a belief—its contribution to future thought and conduct—is to be emphasized, the practice of intellectual avoidance and denial is not likely to generate either the cognitive commitment or the cognitive resources that its practitioners will need to serve their personal utility functions in

---

[32] See Varian, *Intermediate Microeconomics* at 38–40, 48–52, 111–12 (cited in note 22).

[33] See Alvin I. Goldman, *Knowledge in a Social World* 203–04 (1999).

[34] For an argument that many exchanges, not only of ideas, serve such expressive purposes and for that reason ought not to be governed by market norms, see Anderson, *Value and Ethics* at 150–58 (cited in note 25).

the face of the choices with which they will be confronted by the ever-changing course of events. Whatever collective belief patterns emerge from this phenomenon of intellectual substitution cannot be considered a socially functional equilibrium analogous to the equilibrium that results when available substitutes inform producer and consumer choices in the realm of goods and services.

The analogy breaks down over the concept of price in another respect, moreover. In a commodity or service market, at a given point in time there is such a thing as a market price; participants in the market ignore that price at their peril. Possibly one could analogize a current consensus of belief, if such there be, to a market price, but can we say that participants in the market for ideas are bound to respond to the current consensus in anything like the way economic actors must respond to the market price? It is, of course, true that someone trying to "sell" an idea ordinarily will want to take into account the prevailing baseline of belief in deciding which potential buyers to address and with what kinds of appeals. Moreover, inertia probably plays as large a role in belief formation and retention as in consumption decisions regarding conventional goods and services. In fact, one could turn to Holmes for the best aphorism on this point: "property, friendship, and truth have a common root in time."[35] Nevertheless, ideas that defy the current consensus often get "consumed" in ways that are not replicated for material goods that languish on the shelves because they are priced too far above the going market rate. Such ideas can be the seeds of future intellectual, cultural, and political growth. They also can provide current value for dissident thinkers too idiosyncratic, too reticent, or too isolated to constitute even a niche market.

The analogy cannot be saved by switching the focus from the mechanism of price setting to the process of consumer choice. In a commodity or service market, consumers are expected much of the time to be self-interested in a rather narrow sense. The aggregation of individual preference-maximizing decisions provides the best available measure of what people want, and hence what ought to be and will be produced. In this regard, there is a normative dimension to the concept of a commodity or service market. I doubt that anyone would contend as a normative matter that consumer choice in the market for ideas should be self-interested to anything like the same

---

[35] Oliver Wendell Holmes, Jr., *Natural Law*, 32 Harv L Rev 40 (1918).

degree as in economic markets. We do not want listeners and readers to be looking simply for ideas that will best serve their personal needs narrowly conceived to encompass only private use. We expect them to be, in one way or another, searching for ideas that are valuable in a broader sense. In deciding what to believe, consumers of ideas should and do take into account the desires, needs, opinions, and experiences of other people. We also expect consumers of ideas to believe some things they wish were not so. The social value of ideas lies to a large extent in how their production and consumption generates benefits over time for persons other than the immediate producers and consumers. Such positive externalities are likely to be greater the less ephemeral and parochial, and hence personal to the point of being inapplicable to others, are the choices made by the immediate consumers of the ideas.

Of course, decisions to consume goods and services also are not invariably self-interested and short-sighted. Often consumers of goods and services make their selections motivated in part by focused altruism or generalized social responsibility. But that phenomenon is not really analogous to what occurs when consumers of ideas decide, sometimes reluctantly, what to believe. The fundamental difference is that even when economic consumption is not narrowly self-interested, the phenomenon of discretionary choice predominates to a degree that is not replicated in the formation of beliefs. Even if one holds that there is no such thing as a mind-independent Truth "out there," even if one believes that the measure of an idea's truth is the practical effect of adopting it, even if one thinks that reality is irreducibly a function of perspective, the experience of holding a genuine belief entails a quality of personal identification and (at least temporary) commitment that is approximated by only the most unusual of consumer purchases. Holmes put the point succinctly when he characterized his beliefs as his "can't helps,"[36] and the driving ideas of common law development as "felt necessities."[37]

---

[36] Letter from Holmes to Sir Frederick Pollock (Oct 27, 1901), in Mark D. Howe, ed, 1 *Holmes-Pollock Letters* at 100 (1941) ("all I mean by truth is the road I can't help travelling"); id at 139 ("all I mean by truth is what I can't help thinking"); Letter from Holmes to Laski (Jan 11, 1929), in 2 *Holmes-Laski Letters* at 1124 (cited in note 13) ("[W]hen I say that a thing is true I only mean that I can't help believing it—but I have no grounds for believing that my can't helps are cosmic can't helps—and some reasons for thinking otherwise. I therefore define the truth as the system of my intellectual limitations—there being a tacit reference to what I bet is or will be the prevailing can't help of the majority of that part of the world that I count.").

[37] Holmes, *The Common Law* at 5 (cited in note 3).

All the more problematic is the analogy of ideas to economic resources when the production function is taken into account. To a large extent, ideas are not generated in response to demand. Nor would we want them to be. We even have a derogatory term for the practice: pandering. (Again, notice that information is different.) The expressive reward of producing an idea makes that experience a form of socially valuable "consumption" by the author even of an idea that convinces no one. Moreover, ideas that are not selling often serve a social function precisely because they can be productively used—as foils, as partial truths to be selectively scavenged, as options available for future use as conditions change[38]—by persons who do not "buy" them at the time they are placed on the market. There are, of course, analogies in the way that economic goods and services generate value to persons who either produce them or use them for purposes other than consumption. Some entrepreneurs offer goods and services in the spirit of self-expression. Most buyers develop their consumption preferences by learning from the possibilities and pitfalls of products they decide not to purchase. But here the differences of degree are telling. The nonconsumption sources of social value are not integral to economic production in the way that the sincerity, integrity, and personal identification of the speakers and the multifarious, radiating, and delayed uses of ideas actually constitute a major part of their value.

These comparisons suggest that the sources of social value in the market for ideas are so different from those in conventional economic markets that one cannot persuasively develop a philosophy of free speech by drawing upon the insights of classical and neoclassical economics regarding the interaction of supply and demand. In a way, Holmes acknowledged this. In their extended and intellectually rich correspondence, Frederick Pollock tried repeatedly to get Holmes to read Alfred Marshall, the doyen of the neoclassical movement in economics and the writer who by working out the implications of marginal analysis put the concept of equilibrium at the center of microeconomic theory. Here is Holmes's response: "I do not get much nourishment except when the writers [on economics] become sociological (I remember getting much pleasure from Adam Smith because there he gives his

---

[38] Each of these sources of the value of ideas was emphasized by Mill. See John Stuart Mill (David Bromwich and George Kateb, eds), *On Liberty* 97–98, 103–17 (2003).

general views of life). So I have been excusing myself from reading your Marshall."[39]

II. Skepticism

If Holmes's market theory of the First Amendment does not rest upon a conception of cognitive fine-tuning via the elegant equilibrium-seeking mechanics of neoclassical economics, on what does it rest? What "general views of life" did he find in the sociology of the market? Perhaps what Holmes liked about markets is their nonprescriptive character, embodied in their designed function of enabling participants to implement their understandings and preferences whatever (within broad limits) they might be. Recall that his references quoted above[40] to the phenomenon of equilibrium were not to a supposed *cognitive* equilibrium but rather to "the equilibrium of social desires" and "the equilibrium of actual force in the community." His invocation of the market metaphor in the *Abrams* peroration may have been to make the point that truth reduces to choice. Perhaps the imagery that we should take from Holmes's figure of speech is not that of a highly structured price-determining *market* such as a stock exchange, a mechanism designed to achieve plebiscitary and transactional precision, but rather a choice-proliferating market*place*, a site for spontaneous and promiscuous browsing, comparing, tasting, and wishing, a paean to peripatetic subjectivity amid abundance.[41] Applied to ideas, the image evokes intellectual serendipity.

---

[39] Letter from Holmes to Pollock (July 28, 1911), in 1 *Holmes-Pollock Letters* at 183 (cited in note 36). On Marshall's role in developing general equilibrium theory, see Barber, *History* at 168–97 (cited in note 12).

[40] See notes 9 and 10.

[41] The second earliest reference to a "marketplace" of (or for) ideas that I have been able to discover, in either legal or popular discourse, uses the metaphor in precisely this sense. Touting the forthcoming 1939 New York World's Fair, Grover A. Whalen, the exhibition's president, boasted that conditions affecting lives in every category would be shown, together with all the possibilities existing in science, art, medicine, mechanics, education, play, and industry: "The fair, planned to entertain and delight every one with its beauty, its comfort, its magnificence, and its variegated amusements will be a market place for ideas, the birthplace of a wonderful new era." New York Times 27 (Oct 9, 1936). One year earlier, David M. Newbold wrote a letter to the *New York Times* in which he reassured readers that if neither Herbert Hoover nor William Borah, the ideal candidates, were willing to challenge President Roosevelt in the 1936 presidential election, "then their likes will issue not from a dark room at 2 o'clock in the morning, but as the result of men and ideas competing in the market place of ideas where public opinion is formed." New York Times 14 (Dec 28, 1935). So far as I can tell, Mr. Newbold deserves the prize for first transforming Holmes's "competition of the market" into a "marketplace of ideas."

Holmes certainly was a pluralist. Throughout his adult life, in a variety of intellectual endeavors, he displayed an instinctive aversion to assertions of "absolute" truth. He wrote to John Wu: "I don't believe or know anything about absolute truth."[42] He once described truth as "the majority vote of that nation that could lick all others."[43] In a law review article published the year before he wrote the *Abrams* dissent, Holmes expressed in characteristically colorful terms his utter disdain for absolutist modes of thought:

> There is in all men a demand for the superlative, so much so that the poor devil who has no other way of reaching it attains it by getting drunk. It seems to me that this demand is at the bottom of the philosopher's effort to prove that truth is absolute and of the jurist's search for criteria of universal validity which he collects under the head of natural law.[44]

His pluralism born of skepticism permeates his writings. In the critique of natural law just quoted, Holmes explained further his aversion to transcendent truth claims:

> What we most love and revere generally is determined by early associations. I love granite rocks and barberry bushes, no doubt because with them were my earliest joys that reach back through the past eternity of my life. But while one's experience thus makes certain preferences dogmatic for oneself, recognition of how they came to be so leaves one able to see that others, poor souls, may be equally dogmatic about something else. And this again means scepticism.[45]

Holmes called himself a skeptic, as did his admirers, but Grant Gilmore found that his skepticism crossed the border into cynicism:

> Put out of your head the picture of the tolerant aristocrat, the great liberal, the eloquent defender of our liberties, the Yankee from Olympus. All that was a myth, concocted principally by Harold Laski and Felix Frankfurter about the time of World War I. The real Holmes was savage, harsh, cruel, a bitter and lifelong pessimist who saw in the course of human life nothing

---

[42] Letter from Holmes to John C. H. Wu (June 16, 1923), in Harry C. Shriver, ed, *Justice Oliver Wendell Holmes: His Book Notices and Uncollected Letters and Papers* 164, 165 (1936).

[43] Holmes, *Natural Law* at 40 (cited in note 35).

[44] Id.

[45] Id at 41.

but a continuing struggle in which the rich and the powerful impose their will on the poor and weak.[46]

Alexander Meiklejohn considered Holmes's market conception of truth to be

> a fruitful source of intellectual irresponsibility and of the errors which irresponsibility brings. We Americans, when thinking in that vein, have taken the "competition of the market" principle to mean that as separate thinkers, we have no obligation to test our thinking, to make sure that it is worthy of a citizen who is one of "the rulers of the nation." That testing is to be done, we believe, not by us, but by "the competition of the market." Each one of us, therefore, feels free to think as he pleases, to believe whatever will serve his own private interests. . . . [T]he intellectual degradation which that interpretation of truth-testing has brought upon the minds of our people is almost unbelievable. . . . It has made intellectual freedom indistinguishable from intellectual license. And to that disastrous end the beautiful words of Mr. Holmes have greatly contributed.[47]

What matters here is not the proper label to be attached to Holmes's view of the world, but whether his irreverent attitude toward the concept of truth provides a discrediting key to understanding his market metaphor. However irritating may be the pretensions of self-righteous moralists and self-appointed guardians of the public interest, we cannot help but be troubled by the cognitive and normative abyss that Holmes might be understood to embrace.[48] Moreover, one must ask whether a constitutional interpretation can claim sufficient pedigree if it rests on radical premises—moral, political, or epistemological—that have never commanded much assent in the relevant political community. In this regard, the nihilism that some have discerned in Holmes's concept of truth is indeed troubling.

There is another problem with grounding a strong free speech principle on an intensely skeptical attitude toward the concept of truth. Steven Smith has shown that extreme skepticism is a double-edged sword in First Amendment analysis. Just as skepticism tends

---

[46] Grant Gilmore, *The Ages of American Law* 48–56 (1977).

[47] Alexander Meiklejohn, *Political Freedom* 70–71 (1948).

[48] A hard-hitting, detailed, and well-informed critique of Holmes in this vein is Albert W. Alschuler, *Law Without Values: The Life, Work, and Legacy of Justice Holmes* (2000).

to undercut the arguments of those who would regulate speech in the name of ideological decency, skepticism also tends to undercut the arguments of those who assert that speech is a special human activity deserving of extraordinary constitutional protection.[49] If truth really does reduce entirely to arbitrary preference and power, as Holmes seems to say in some of his saltier moments,[50] why treat speech disputes as exceptional in terms of the principles of deference and separation of powers that limit the judicial role in a constitutional democracy?

These are powerful objections, but they have purchase only if Holmes's market metaphor does indeed express an extreme form of skepticism bordering on nihilism. It does not. Recall that in his *Abrams* dissent Holmes says *two* things about truth. First, he states that the competition of the market provides the "best test of truth." Then he asserts "that truth is the only ground upon which [men's] wishes safely can be carried out."[51] This second step in the argument is crucial. Even if we could be confident that free speech leads to truth, the case for protecting speech in the face of the harms it might cause depends on the further proposition that knowing the truth is a value of overriding importance.[52] Holmes apparently believed that the pursuit of truth *is* that important. He certainly lived

---

[49] Steven D. Smith, *Skepticism, Tolerance, and Truth in the Theory of Free Expression*, 60 S Cal L Rev 649 (1987).

[50] See, for example, Holmes, *Natural Law* at 40 (cited in note 35); Letter from Holmes to Pollock (Oct 26, 1929), in 2 *Holmes-Pollock Letters* at 255–56 (cited in note 36); Letter from Holmes to Laski (April 6, 1920), in 1 *Holmes-Laski Letters* at 259 (cited in note 13).

[51] *Abrams v United States*, 250 US 616, 630 (1919) (Holmes, J, dissenting).

[52] It is possible to read Holmes's statement "that truth is the only ground upon which [men's] wishes safely can be carried out" as if the word "that" were italicized so as to shift the emphasis from "truth" to "that," thereby transforming "that" from a conjunction to a demonstrative adjective. In this reading, the "truth" he is talking about is simply his proposed test of truth, not truth in all its manifestations. The interpretative consequence would be to read Holmes as saying nothing about the priority to be accorded the activity of truth seeking, but rather as asserting that his market test of truth, as compared with alternative tests that are more transcendent or inflexible, is to be preferred on grounds of safety and efficacy. Such a reading cannot be definitively refuted by Holmes's syntax and rhetorical context. Nevertheless, it is some internal evidence against this revisionist interpretation that earlier in the same sentence, in clauses structurally parallel to the clause at issue, Holmes twice used the word "that" as a conjunction rather than an adjective: "they may come to believe . . . that the ultimate good desired . . . that the best test of truth . . . ." Moreover, Holmes's penchant for discussing metaphysical and epistemological matters in global albeit humble terms, see text at note 44 and also note 75, together with his skeptic's disinclination to label his specific controversial claims "truths," leads me to conclude that Holmes's meaning in this crucial sentence is better captured by reading it to say "that *truth*" rather than "*that* truth," and thus to be asserting the priority of truth seeking. On the importance in the overall truth-centered argument for the freedom of speech of this claim that truth seeking has a special social priority, see Frederick Schauer, *Free Speech: A Philosophical Enquiry* 29 (1982).

his life as though he did. Edmund Wilson particularly admired this quality in Holmes:

> He was not merely a cultivated judge who enjoyed dipping into belles lettres or amusing himself with speculation: he was a real concentrator of thought who had specialized in the law but who was trying to determine man's place, to define his satisfactions and duties, to try to understand what humanity is. . . . In spite of his . . . fundamental skepticism as to human convictions and systems . . . he is always alert and attentive, always inquiring and searching, to find out some further answers.[53]

One manifestation of Holmes's inquisitiveness was his fascination with science. In February of 1919 the philosopher Morris Cohen asked Holmes in a letter whether his reading of Voltaire had had an important influence on his views concerning truth.[54] Holmes answered:

> Oh no—it was not Voltaire—it was the influence of the scientific way of looking at the world—that made the change to which I referred. . . . The Origin of Species I think came out while I was in college—Herbert Spencer had announced his intention to put the universe into our pockets—I hadn't read either of them to be sure, but as I say it was in the air.[55]

Although Holmes never pursued scientific knowledge systematically, he was interested in the scientific method and the role of science in society. During the 1870s he participated in a discussion group that called itself the Metaphysical Club. The group's leader was, by all accounts, Chauncey Wright, a latter-day Socrates who wrote very little, achieved no public recognition, but persistently challenged his conversational partners with the power and probity of his mind. Wright was both a practicing scientist, trained in mathematics, biology, and physics, and a philosopher of science.[56] With

---

[53] Edmund Wilson, *Patriotic Gore: Studies in the Literature of the American Civil War* 781 (1962).

[54] Letter from Morris Cohen to Holmes (Feb 3 or 4, 1919), described in Felix Cohen, ed, *The Holmes-Cohen Correspondence*, 9 J Hist Ideas 3, 14 n 27 (1948).

[55] Letter from Holmes to Morris Cohen (Feb 5, 1919), id at 14.

[56] Wright was a fascinating character who had an important influence on Holmes. See note 62; Letter from Holmes to Laski (Nov 29, 1923), in 1 *Holmes-Laski Letters* at 565 (cited in note 13) ("It seemed to me that [Peirce] was overrated especially allowing for what he owed to Chauncey Wright . . . ."). William James also held Wright in awe: "If power of analytic intellect pure and simple could suffice, the name of Chauncey Wright

the regular participation also of William James and Charles Sanders Peirce, both trained scientists who became philosophers, the Metaphysical Club provided Holmes with an opportunity to discuss the nature and meaning of science with some of the ablest thinkers of his generation. James and Peirce, of course, were later to develop the philosophy of pragmatism, which builds on a view of truth that is derived from the scientific method.[57]

Holmes maintained an interest in science throughout his life. Save only his book *The Common Law*, probably his most ambitious publication is an article entitled "Law in Science and Science in Law," published in the *Harvard Law Review* in 1899.[58] When speaking in 1902 at the dedication of the Northwestern University Law School building, Holmes said:

> If [a university training] could give to every student a scientific point of view . . . . I should think it had more than paid for itself. . . . I cannot believe that anything else would be so likely to secure prosperity as the universal acceptance of scientific premises in every department of thought.[59]

In the last two decades of his life, Holmes conducted a regular correspondence with Morris Cohen, one of the founders of the academic discipline of philosophy of science.[60]

---

would assuredly be as famous as it now is obscure, for he was not merely the great mind of a village—if Cambridge will pardon the expression—but either in London or Berlin he would, with equal ease, have taken the place of master which he held with us. The reason why he is now gone without leaving any work which his friends can consider as a fair expression of his genius, is that his shyness, his want of ambition, and to a certain degree his indolence, were almost as exceptional as his power of thought." William James, *Chauncey Wright*, 21 The Nation 194 (1875), reprinted in Edward H. Madden, *Chauncey Wright and the Foundations of Pragmatism* 143 (1963). The best brief account of Wright's life and thought that I have found is the chapter devoted to him in Philip P. Wiener, *Evolution and the Founders of Pragmatism* 31–69 (1949, 1972) ("*Evolution*"). For a less flattering estimate of Wright's originality and influence, see Bruce Kuklick, *The Rise of American Philosophy* 63–79 (1977).

[57] For portraits of the Metaphysical Club and its participants, see Louis Menand, *The Metaphysical Club: A Story of Ideas in America* 201–32 (2001) ("*Metaphysical Club*"); Wiener, *Evolution* at 18–30 (1972) (cited in note 56); Morton White, *Science and Sentiment in America* 120–216 (1972). For perceptive accounts of Holmes's complex relationships with the leading pragmatist thinkers, see Grey, 41 Stan L Rev at 787 (cited in note 18); David A. Hollinger, *The Tough-Minded Justice Holmes, Jewish Intellectuals, and the Making of an American Icon*, in Robert W. Gordon, ed, *The Legacy of Oliver Wendell Holmes, Jr.* 216–22 (1992).

[58] 12 Harv L Rev 443 (1899).

[59] *Address of Chief Justice Holmes*, in Richard A. Posner, ed, *The Essential Holmes* 98, 99 (1992).

[60] Portions of the correspondence are reprinted in Cohen, ed, 9 J Hist Ideas (cited in note 54).

As a young man, Holmes studied the writings of John Stuart Mill, particularly his influential account of the scientific method, *A System of Logic*.[61] That book can be viewed as the culmination of the British empiricist tradition in philosophy, stretching back to Locke and Hume. A key tenet of that tradition is that all propositions are subject to perpetual testing. And that process of testing, whether it takes the form of systematic observation, controlled experiment, logical derivation, or probabilistic calculation, must always hold out at least the possibility that prior understandings will be displaced. Time, after all, has upset many scientific laws. In short, no matter how elegant and coherent the explanation and supportive the current data, we might be wrong. This guiding principle has come to be called fallibilism. Both Mill and Holmes believed in it passionately.[62] It is noteworthy that Holmes reread Mill's essay *On Liberty*, which depends heavily on the premise of fallibilism in arguing for the freedom of speech, during the early months of 1919, the year of his *Abrams* dissent.[63]

This emphasis on fallibilism puts in perspective Holmes's many breezy statements about the nature of truth. He discussed the concept of truth in several letters with two of his favorite correspondents, Sir Frederick Pollock and Harold Laski. On almost every occasion when he spoke dismissively about truth, Holmes included

---

[61] See Mark De Wolfe Howe, *Justice Oliver Wendell Holmes: The Shaping Years 1841–1870* 212–17 (1957); Patrick J. Kelley, *Was Holmes a Pragmatist? Reflections on a New Twist to an Old Argument*, 14 SIU L J 427, 436–37 (1990).

[62] See Letter from Holmes to Pollock (Aug 30, 1929), in 2 *Holmes-Pollock Letters* at 252 (cited in note 36):

> If there is anything that has been supposed to be compulsory upon us short of not affirming nonsense I should think it was that every phenomenon must have a cause. Yet I find scientific men suggesting nowadays (e.g. Eddington) that there are phenomena for which no causes can be discovered and seemingly believing that they are outside the category of cause and effect. I am far from believing with them, but I am entirely ready to believe it on proof. Chauncey Wright, a nearly forgotten philosopher of real merit, taught me when young that I must not say *necessary* about the universe, that we don't know whether anything is necessary or not.

See also Letters from Holmes to Laski (Nov 29, 1923 and July 23, 1924), in 1 *Holmes-Laski Letters* at 565, 634 (cited in note 13). For a concise and lucid explanation of Mill's theory of induction and its relationship to his premise of fallibilism, see John Skorupski, *John Stuart Mill* 5–12 (1989). See also Geoffrey Scarre, *Mill on Induction and Scientific Method*, in John Skorupski, ed, *The Cambridge Companion to Mill* 112–38 (1998).

[63] Letter from Holmes to Laski (Feb 28, 1919), in 1 *Holmes-Laski Letters* at 187 (cited in note 13).

a criticism of moral or intellectual absolutism.[64] After setting out his majority-vote-of-the-strongest-nation theory of truth in *Natural Law*, he added: "Certitude is not the test of certainty. We have been cock-sure of many things that were not so."[65] He reserved his strongest ire for persons and philosophies that were not capable of adaptation or reassessment: "When you know that you know persecution comes easy."[66] The animating idea of Holmes's book *The Common Law* is that seemingly absolute principles of law must be seen in their historical context, studied with attention to their patterns of development, and evaluated according to their adaptability to modern conditions.[67] I think Holmes would have embraced almost any test of truth that rendered the concept of an absolute principle incoherent. He associated the rejection of absolutist thinking with the scientific method.

That association may help us to unpack Holmes's bugbear. "Absolute" could refer to any of a number of properties bearing on the derivation, strength, scope, constancy, purity, singularity, contingency, fundamentality, corrigibility, or exclusivity of a proposition. Recall Holmes's identification of "the effort to prove that truth is absolute" with "demand for the superlative" and "search for criteria of universal validity."[68] One might be tempted from these formulations to enter Holmes in the lists of various modern debates over moral realism,[69] moral relativism,[70] and moral particularism.[71] While his thought can be mapped along some of these

---

[64] See, for example, Letters from Holmes to Laski (Feb 26, 1918, April 6, 1920, and Jan 11, 1929), in 1 *Holmes-Laski Letters* at 139, 259 (cited in note 13), and 2 *Holmes-Laski Letters* at 1124–25; Letter from Holmes to Lady Pollock (Sept 6, 1902), in 1 *Holmes-Pollock Letters* at 105 (cited in note 36); Letter from Holmes to Frederick Pollock (Oct 26, 1929), in 2 *Holmes-Pollock Letters* at 255–56.

[65] Holmes, *Natural Law* at 40 (cited in note 35).

[66] Letter from Holmes to Pollock (Aug 30, 1929), in 2 *Holmes-Pollock Letters* at 253 (cited in note 35).

[67] See Benjamin Kaplan, *Encounters with Oliver Wendell Holmes, Jr.*, 96 Harv L Rev 1828, 1829 (1983).

[68] See text at note 44.

[69] Compare, for example, Gilbert Harman, *The Nature of Morality* (1977), and J. L. Mackie, *Ethics: Inventing Right and Wrong* (1977), with Charles Larmore, *The Morals of Modernity* 89–117 (1996).

[70] Compare, for example, Bernard Williams, *The Truth in Relativism*, in *Moral Luck* 132 (1981), with Thomas Nagel, *The View from Nowhere* (1986).

[71] Compare, for example, Jonathan Dancy, *Moral Reasons* (1993), with Joseph Raz, *The Truth in Particularism*, in *Engaging Reason* (1999).

coordinates—he was a moral relativist and not a moral realist[72]—
Holmes's focus on fallibilism indicates that the absolutism he rejected with such vehemence is that which places certain ideas and
practices beyond the need for ongoing evaluation and modification
in the light of criticism, evidence, experience, changing conditions,
and changing "felt necessities." Stasis and certitude bothered him
more than conceptual overreach or metaphysical pretension.[73]
This aversion to intellectual rigidity, surely an attribute of all wise
persons but peculiarly central to Holmes's thought, transcends
differences over moral realism, relativism, and particularism.

Indeed, such was Holmes's broad-ranging curiosity that he even
liked to ponder elusive intimations regarding the mysteries of the
universe. Here is how he concludes *The Path of the Law*:

> The remoter and more general aspects of the law are those
> which give it universal interest. It is through them that you not
> only become a great master in your calling, but connect your
> subject with the universe and catch an echo of the infinite, a
> glimpse of its unfathomable process, a hint of the universal law.[74]

This passage is not aberrational. Addressing his Harvard classmates
on the occasion of their fortieth reunion, Holmes observed:

> Life is a roar of bargain and battle, but in the very heart of it
> there rises a mystic spiritual tone that gives meaning to the
> whole. It transmutes the dull details into romance. It reminds
> us that our only but wholly adequate significance is as parts of
> the unimaginable whole. It suggests that even while we think
> that we are egotists we are living to ends outside ourselves.[75]

---

[72] For an especially illuminating overview of Holmes's theory of value, see David Luban,
Justice Holmes and the Metaphysics of Judicial Restraint, 44 Duke L J 449, 461–88 (1994).

[73] See Holmes, 10 Harv L Rev at 466 (cited in note 11) ("certainty generally is illusion
and repose is not the destiny of man").

[74] Id at 478 (1897).

[75] Holmes, *The Class of '61*, in *The Essential Holmes* at 94, 95 (cited in note 59). See also
Holmes, *Natural Law* at 44 (cited in note 35) ("Philosophy does not furnish motives but
it shows men that they are not fools for doing what they already want to do. It opens to
the forlorn hopes on which we throw ourselves away, the vista of the farthest stretch of
human thought, the chords of a harmony that breathes from the unknown."); Holmes,
Law in Science and Science in Law at 462–63 (cited in note 58) (". . . without ideals what
is life worth? They furnish us our perspectives and open glimpses of the infinite."); Letter
from Holmes to Wu (Sept 20, 1923) at 167 (cited in note 42) ("A man's spiritual history
is best told in what he does in his chosen line. Life having thrown me into the law, I must
try to put my feeling of the infinite into that, to exhibit the detail with such hint of a
vista as I can, to show in it the great line of the universal."); Holmes, *The Profession of the*

Elsewhere he noted how absolutist patterns of thought not only stunt observation and thwart speculation but also impair action. For he associated the absolutist "demand for the superlative" with eventual disillusionment, and with the paralysis, disengagement, and despair that flows therefrom:

> If a man sees no reason for believing that significance, consciousness and ideals are more than marks of the finite, that does not justify what has been familiar in French sceptics; getting upon a pedestal and professing to look with haughty scorn upon a world in ruins. . . . Why should we employ the energy which is furnished to us by the cosmos to defy it and shake our fist at the sky? It seems to me silly.[76]

To Holmes, the challenge we all confront is to abandon comforting illusions and appreciate the limits of human understanding, and then live life to the fullest with energy, wonder, dedication, and joy in the struggle. The duty and dignity of mundane engagement was a theme that stirred his imagination:

> When it is said that we are too much occupied with the means of living to live, I answer that the chief worth of civilization is just that it makes the means of living more complex; that it calls for great and combined intellectual efforts, instead of simple, uncoordinated ones, in order that the crowd may be fed and clothed and housed and moved from place to place. Because more complex and intense intellectual efforts mean a fuller and richer life. They mean more life. Life is an end in itself, and the only question as to whether it is worth living is whether you have enough of it.[77]

Law, in *Collected Legal Papers* at 29–30 (cited in note 9) ("a man may live greatly in the law as well as elsewhere . . . there as well as elsewhere his thought may find its unity in an infinite perspective"); Holmes, *Brown University—Commencement 1897*, id at 165, 166 ("I care not very much for the form if in some way [a man] has learned that he cannot set himself over against the universe as a rival god, to criticize it, or to shake his fist at the skies, but that his meaning is its meaning, his only worth is as a part of it, as a humble instrument of the universal power . . . . not merely a necessary but a willing instrument in working out the inscrutable end."). For an interesting comparison of Holmes's observations concerning what he termed "the infinite" and "the cosmos" with those of Ralph Waldo Emerson, whom Holmes emulated as a young man, see Catherine Wells Hantzis, *Legal Innovation Within the Wider Intellectual Tradition: The Pragmatism of Oliver Wendell Holmes, Jr.*, 82 Nw U L Rev 541, 560–61 (1988).

[76] Id at 43.

[77] Holmes, *Speech to the Bar Association of Boston*, in *Collected Legal Papers* at 244, 247–48 (cited in note 9). See also Letter from Holmes to Wu (March 26, 1925) at 178 (cited in note 42), in which Holmes describes his "imaginary society of jobbists, who were free to be egotists or altruists on the usual Saturday half holiday provided they were neither while

Holmes was indeed a skeptic by temperament and self-training. But he was not a cynic or nihilist or disengaged agnostic.[78] The operational skepticism that is integral to the scientific method bears little resemblance to the skepticism of cynical withdrawal. That difference is of the essence in trying to understand Holmes's thought in general and his views about free speech in particular. He did not treat ideas, his own or those of others, as trivial play-things. To the contrary, he believed that forming and defending strong opinions—not just self-serving preferences—is the stuff of life. He considered the freedom to do so "the principle of the Constitution that more imperatively calls for attachment than any other."[79]

As is true of the law of supply and demand, the rubric of nihilism cannot elucidate Holmes's market metaphor. We might stop here and conclude that for all his brilliance and eloquence Holmes simply was not a systematic thinker, however remarkable he might have been at producing the felicitous aphorism or the penetrating apercu. At the least we might conclude that he failed to articulate a coherent argument on the occasion of the *Abrams* dissent. My project, however, is to look further, to see whether more can be gleaned from his opinion than the inadequate explanations con-sidered so far.

---

on the job. Their job is their contribution to the general welfare and when a man is on that, he will do it better the less he thinks either of himself or his neighbors, and the more he puts all his energy into the problem he has to solve." Emphasizing this existen-tialist dimension, Richard Posner has described Holmes as "the American Nietzsche." See Richard Posner, *The Problems of Jurisprudence* 239–42 (1990); Posner, *The Essential Holmes* at xviii-xx, xxviii (cited in note 59). This characterization is defended at length in Brian Leiter, *Holmes, Economics, and Classical Realism*, in Steven J. Burton, ed, *The Path of the Law and Its Influence* 285–301 (2000). It is elaborated with important qualifications in Luban, 44 Duke L J at 485–88 (cited in note 72). In an encomium to the late Chief Justice of Massachusetts, Walbridge Abner Field, Holmes gave expression to a philosophy of heroic engagement: "Our last word about the unfathomable universe must be in terms of thought. If we believe that anything is, we must believe in that, because we can go no further. We may accept its canons even while we admit that we do not know that we know the truth of truth. Accepting them, we accept our destiny to work, to fight, to die for ideal aims. At the grave of a hero who has done these things we end not with sorrow at the inevitable loss, but with the contagion of his courage; and with a kind of desperate joy we go back to the fight." See *The Essential Holmes* at 213 (cited in note 59).

[78] The *locus classicus* of the argument that "[t]o a remarkable degree Holmes simply did not care" is Yosal Rogat, *The Judge as Spectator*, 31 U Chi L Rev 213, 255 (1964). For a convincing refutation that discerns very different implications from the central role that skepticism played in Holmes's thought, see Thomas C. Grey, *The Colin Raugh Thomas O'Fallon Memorial Lecture on Law and American Culture: Holmes, Pragmatism, and Democracy*, 71 Or L Rev 521 (1992).

[79] *United States v Schwimmer*, 279 US 644, 653 (1928) (Holmes, J, dissenting).

III. Evolution

Holmes never used the phrase "marketplace of ideas." That is a paraphrase supplied by his interpreters.[80] The phrase he actually employed in the *Abrams* opinion, "competition of the market," may suggest a focus on neither the price- and output-determining, utility-maximizing characteristics of markets nor their celebration of discretionary choice, but rather on the harsh fact that economic actors and their products are pitted against one another. This interpretation gains support from Holmes's particular affinity for the work of Malthus, who emphasized scarcity and challenged some of the more ambitious claims of his fellow economists regarding inevitable market self-corrections.[81] Perhaps the key word in Holmes's phrase is not "market" but "competition." In this view, precisely because "truth is the only ground upon which their wishes safely can be carried out,"[82] what is needed for ideas is a vibrant, brutal weeding-out process analogous to the function markets for goods and services perform in killing off inefficient enterprises and forcing unproductive workers to be fired.[83] In an unsent letter to Herbert Croly, composed in the year of his *Abrams* dissent, Holmes said: "in the main I am for aeration of all effervescing convictions—there is no way so quick for letting them get flat."[84] As he put it to John Wu, one of his favorite correspondents in later life: "Every society is founded on the death of men."[85] Every society is also founded, he might have added, on the death of ideas.

---

[80] The precise phrase "marketplace of ideas" was first employed in a Supreme Court opinion in Justice Brennan's majority opinion in *Lamont v Postmaster General*, 381 US 301, 308 (1965). For a detailed survey of the Court's use of the phrase, see Haig Bosmajian, *Metaphor and Reason in Judicial Opinions* 49–72 (1992). For the earliest uses of the phrase in popular discussion, see note 41.

[81] See text at note 13; Barber, *History* at 68–72 (cited in note 12); Stefan Collini, Donald Winch, and John Burrow, *That Noble Science of Politics: A Study in Nineteenth Century Intellectual History* 80–81 (1983).

[82] See text at notes 50–51.

[83] The classic justification of economic elimination is Schumpeter's notion of "creative destruction." See Joseph Schumpeter, *The Theory of Economic Development* (1911). On the analogy between selective survival in nature and in economic markets, compare Milton Friedman, *The Methodology of Positive Economics*, in *Essays in Positive Economics* 3 (1953), with Richard R. Nelson and Sidney G. Winter, *Evolutionary Theorizing in Economics*, 16 J Econ Perspectives 23 (2002).

[84] See Letter from Holmes to Laski (May 12, 1919), in 1 *Holmes-Laski Letters* at 204 (cited in note 13).

[85] Letter from Holmes to Wu (July 21, 1925), in Max Lerner, ed, *The Mind and Faith of Justice Holmes* 427–28 (1943).

Holmes was fascinated by lethal force. As befits a soldier who was seriously wounded at Ball's Bluff, Antietam, and yet again near Fredericksburg,[86] his writings abound with military metaphors and paeans to the dignity of struggle.[87] The centrality of conflict and contest is a recurrent theme in his philosophical musings.[88] Recall his description of life as a "roar of bargain and battle."[89] After his youthful brushes with death and the carnage on a grand scale that he witnessed, it is no wonder that the subject of survival engaged his attention, or that he was intrigued by the discoveries of his fellow Malthusian, Charles Darwin.[90] Holmes considered himself a Darwinist and concentrated his scholarly energies on the question of how law evolves.[91] When Holmes was attending the meetings of the Metaphysical Club during the early 1870s, Chauncey Wright, the group's leader whom Holmes treated as a mentor,[92] was in the midst of an extended, mutually supportive correspondence with Darwin.[93]

A possible difficulty with reading into the market metaphor a

---

[86] See Liva Baker, *Justice from Beacon Hill: The Life and Times of Oliver Wendell Holmes* 114–19, 131–36, 142–43. For an account of how Holmes's experience in the Civil War had a profound influence on his thought, see Menand, *Metaphysical Club* at 23–69 (cited in note 57).

[87] See, for example, Holmes, *The Fraternity of Arms*, in *The Essential Holmes* at 73 (cited in note 59); *The Soldier's Faith*, id at 87.

[88] See, for example, Letter from Holmes to Pollock (Feb 1, 1920), in 2 *Holmes-Pollock Letters* at 36 (cited in note 36) (". . . I do think that the sacredness of human life is a purely municipal ideal of no validity outside the jurisdiction. I believe that force, mitigated so far as may be by good manners, is the *ultima ratio*, and between two groups that want to make inconsistent kinds of world I see no remedy except force"); Letter from Holmes to Einstein (Oct 12, 1914), in *Holmes-Einstein Letters* at 100–01 (cited in note 14) ("I suppose the war was inevitable . . . . it shows us that classes as well as nations that mean to be in the saddle have got to be ready to kill to keep their seat; and that the notion that all that remained for the civilized world was to sit still, converse, and be comfortable was humbug.").

[89] See text at note 75.

[90] On Darwin's considerable intellectual debt to Malthus, see Jonathan Hodge, *The Notebook Programmes and Projects of Darwin's London Years*, in *The Cambridge Companion to Darwin* 40, 60–61 (2003); Jonathan Howard, *Darwin* 14–15, 19 (1982); Ernst Mayr, *One Long Argument: Charles Darwin and the Genesis of Modern Evolutionary Thought* 75–79, 85–86 (1991).

[91] See J. W. Burrow, *Holmes in His Intellectual Milieu*, in Gordon, ed, *The Legacy of Oliver Wendell Holmes, Jr.* at 17 (cited in note 57); E. Donald Elliott, *Holmes and Evolution: Legal Process as Artificial Intelligence*, 13 J Legal Stud 113 (1984); Wiener, *Evolution* at 172–89 (cited in note 56); Jan Vetter, *The Evolution of Holmes, Holmes and Evolution*, 72 Cal L Rev 343 (1984).

[92] See text at note 56; Letter from Holmes to Pollock (Aug 30, 1929), in 2 *Holmes-Pollock Letters* (cited in note 36).

[93] See Wiener, *Evolution* at 48–60 (cited in note 56).

Darwinist concern for intellectual adaptation is that Holmes was struck by how resistant to change are the ideas that people hold dear: "One can not be wrenched from the rocky crevices into which one has grown for many years without feeling that one is attacked in one's life."[94] Much as he believed that traditional beliefs regarding population and progress had been disproved by Malthus, Holmes chafed at their resilience: "Malthus pleased me immensely—and left me sad. A hundred years ago he busted fallacies that politicians and labor leaders still live on. One thinks that an error exposed is dead, but exposure amounts to nothing when people want to believe."[95] Holmes may have welcomed the death of ideas but, given his understanding of the psychology of belief formation, one wonders how he could have considered the marketplace of ideas to be the Grim Reaper he sought.

Actually, the theory of evolution might help to explain why a robust freedom of speech can be extremely valuable even when most individuals remain stubbornly impervious to demonstrably valid refutations of their beliefs. For the engine that drives evolution is not change in the characteristics of individual creatures but rather change over time in the makeup of populations. Natural selection causes the creatures with the most adaptive traits to predominate and those with the least adaptive traits to recede within a population.[96] Applied to the realm of ideas, this selection process causes new entrants to a community who hold more adaptive beliefs to constitute over time a larger proportion of the population. The newcomers with the better-suited ideas arrive due to generational changeover and immigration. As the population changes with the infusion of new persons with different ideas, the pattern of beliefs within the community changes, even if no single individual ever embraces a new idea or discards an old one.

---

[94] Holmes, *Natural Law* at 40 (cited in note 35).

[95] Letter from Holmes to Pollock (Aug 30, 1914), in 1 *Holmes-Pollock Letters* at 219 (cited in note 36). See also Letter from Holmes to Laski (Dec 26, 1917), in 1 *Holmes-Laski Letters* at 122 (cited in note 13): ("When I read Malthus I thought he had ripped the guts out of some humbugs—but they are as alive as ever today. Humbugs have no guts—and live all the better without them.").

[96] See Howard, *Darwin* at 22 (cited in note 90) ("It is meaningless to say that individuals evolve: evolution is the change in the average constitution of a population of individuals as the generations succeed one another."); Mayr, *One Long Argument* at 43–44 (cited in note 90) ("Darwinian evolution is discontinuous because a new start is made in every generation when a new set of individuals is produced. That evolution nevertheless appears to be totally gradual is because it is populational and depends on sexual reproduction among the members of the population.").

For this dynamic to occur, however, it is essential that the new-comers not simply replicate the preexisting pattern of beliefs. In Darwinist terms, what is needed is variation. To provide that, the newcomers must have the capacity to exercise independent judg-ment and to form opinions that draw upon experiences different from those that produced the earlier pattern of beliefs. Here is where the freedom of speech comes in. A political regime that discourages and punishes free thought reduces the incidence of variation in the realm of ideas, variation both in the production of new ideas and in the embrace of previously unpopular ideas.

An unregulated marketplace of ideas encourages free thought not so much by determining the equilibrium of the moment as by keep-ing low the barriers to entry, barriers that take the form not only of coercive sanctions but also social and intellectual peer pressures toward conformity. The sheer proliferation of ideas in a free market complicates perceptions in a manner that helps to weaken such barriers. In addition, the market metaphor makes a statement about the dynamic and chronically incomplete character of understanding and the value of intellectual contest and innovation. Such a state-ment by the constitutional regime can help to legitimate dissent and discredit demands for orthodoxy, and in that way lend much needed support to newcomers whose heretical notions will almost always engender strong resistance laced with accusations of illegit-imacy if not disloyalty.

This demographic account of intellectual evolution assumes that individuals never change their minds about questions that matter to them. That, of course, is an exaggeration. Holmes was impressed by how seldom and slowly people yield to telling criticism, but he never maintained that such resistance is for most persons absolute. When ideas cease to work, whether as guides to conduct or further inquiry, they tend to be abandoned by the individuals whose projects are frustrated as a result. The process takes time and the admission of inefficacy does not come easily for most believers. Much more than rational or empirical refutation in the abstract is required. Usually pressure builds up gradually before it becomes unbearable. But changes of mind do occur, if only rarely, for all but the most refractory zealots. Whether or not it is accurate to call Holmes a pragmatist—a question that has produced a rich literature[97]—he

---

[97] Compare Posner, *The Essential Holmes* at 242–44 (cited in note 59); Wiener, *Evolution* at 172–89 (cited in note 56); Morton White, *Social Thought in America: The Revolt Against*

embraced the pragmatist tenet that ideas tend to flourish when they
work and wither when they don't. His explicit and extravagant ad-
miration for the writings of John Dewey, though never explained
by Holmes in any detail, was very likely because of what Dewey
had to say in support of a pragmatist conception of justifiable belief.
Holmes said of *Experience and Nature*, Dewey's magnum opus elab-
orating his theory of knowledge:

> although Dewey's book is incredibly ill written, it seemed to
> me after several rereadings to have a feeling of intimacy with
> the inside of the cosmos that I found unequaled. So me-thought
> God would have spoken had He been inarticulate but keenly
> desirous to tell you how it was.[98]

Formalism 59–75 (1947, 1957); Edward J. Bloustein, *Holmes: His First Amendment Theory
and His Pragmatist Bent*, 40 Rutgers L Rev 283 (1988); M. H. Fisch, *Justice Holmes, The
Prediction Theory of Law, and Pragmatism*, 39 J Philosophy 85 (1942); Grey, 41 Stan L Rev
(cited in note 18); Hantzis, 82 Nw U L Rev (cited in note 75); Luban, 44 Duke L J at
464 n 41 (cited in note 72); Note, *Holmes, Peirce, and Legal Pragmatism*, 84 Yale L J 1123,
with H. L. Pohlman, *Justice Oliver Wendell Holmes and Utilitarian Jurisprudence* 163–64
(1984); Robert Gordon, *Holmes's Common Law as Legal and Social Science*, 10 Hofstra L
Rev 719, 722–26 (1982); Hollinger, *The Tough-Minded Justice Holmes* at 217–22 (cited in
note 57); Kelley, 14 SIU L J (cited in note 61).
    Three arguments in John Stuart Mill's *On Liberty*, which as mentioned above Holmes
reread the same year he wrote the *Abrams* dissent, see text at note 63, lend support to
the effort to establish a link between Holmes and the pragmatists on the specific question
of how people change their minds. Mill had much more faith than Holmes in the power
of rational persuasion, but he did note in *On Liberty* that one of the advantages that truth
has over falsehood is that it can be continually rediscovered in different eras until eventually
conditions are ripe for its acceptance. Further signaling his recognition of how large a
part context plays in the process of belief formation, Mill claimed (implausibly) that all
the great advances in modern Western thought occurred in just three brief periods when
the society-wide level of intellectual ferment was extraordinary. And on the respective
roles of logic and experience, Mill said in *On Liberty*: "All languages and literatures are
full of general observations on life, both as to what it is, and how to conduct oneself in
it; observations which everybody knows, which everybody repeats, or hears with acquiescence, which are received as truisms, yet of which most people first truly learn the
meaning, when experience, generally of a painful kind, has made it a reality to them."
Mill, *On Liberty* at 97–98, 102–03, 110 (cited in note 38). It would be inaccurate to label
Mill a pragmatist and controversial to consider him a protopragmatist, but Mill's recognition of the importance of experience and context in how persons process ideas, articulated in a text well known to Holmes, is a further indication that Holmes did not
envision a marketplace of ideas in which the actors readily change their minds.
    [98] Letter from Holmes to Pollock (May 15, 1931), in *2 Holmes-Pollock Letters* at 287
(cited in note 36). See also Holmes's remark about Dewey in an earlier letter to Pollock:
"he is a bad writer and I found him very hard reading. Still his view of the universe came
home to me closer than any other I know." Letter from Holmes to Pollock (July 26,
1930), in id at 272. To Harold Laski Holmes wrote: "I am reading a book by John Dewey,
Experience and Nature . . . . Few indeed are the books which hold so much of life with
an even hand. If you asked me for a summary I couldn't give more than a page of ideas,
but the stimulus and the quasi-aesthetic enjoyment are great—and the tendencies those
which I agree with." Letter from Holmes to Laski (Dec 4, 1926), in *2 Holmes-Laski Letters*
at 900 (cited in note 13). In a subsequent letter to Laski, Holmes continued to rave about

The Darwinist/pragmatist strain in Holmes's thought helps to explain how he could have valued the freedom of speech highly, at least by the time of the *Abrams* dissent and thereafter,[99] while nevertheless holding that "beliefs and wishes have a transcendental basis in that their foundation is arbitrary. You can not help entertaining and feeling them, and there is an end of it."[100] Neither demographically driven changes in the pattern of beliefs nor the abandonment of ideas that are not working will occur if people do not take their beliefs seriously. Casual attitudes about belief formation and retention invite conformity, the path of least resistance. Improperly understood, the First Amendment itself can contribute to such dysfunctional conformity. Deprived by the freedom of speech of the comforts of certitude and centralized intellectual authority, people may be tempted to take their beliefs lightly. The market metaphor offers an antidote to this temptation: a powerful image that treats beliefs as significant, even self-defining, and of the highest social priority, all the while being contingent, probabilistic, and tentative. As expounded by Holmes, the market in ideas is not about intellectual gratification and whimsy. It is about important choices with practical consequences under difficult conditions of uncertainty and change. The truths that people come to by free trade in ideas are, remember, "the only ground upon which their wishes safely can be carried out."[101] Conformity, deference to authority, stasis, passivity in the realm of beliefs is not just unfortunate or unwise but *dangerous*.

The constructive, urgent role that speech can play in the evolution of beliefs under a pragmatist conception of truth insulates

---

Experience and Nature: "truly a great book . . . . he seems to me . . . more honestly to see behind all the current philosophers than any book I can think of on such themes." Letter from Holmes to Laski (Dec 15, 1926), in id at 904–05. See also Holmes's extravagant praise for *Experience and Nature* in a letter to John C. H. Wu, the friend who originally suggested to Holmes that he read the book: "I thought it great. It seemed to me to *feel* the universe more inwardly and profoundly than any book I know, at least any book of philosophy." Letter from Holmes to Wu (Jan 30, 1928), in Shriver, ed, *Justice Oliver Wendell Holmes* at 193 (cited in note 42).

[99] On whether Holmes changed his views in the direction of valuing free speech more highly on the occasion of the *Abrams* dissent, compare H. L. Pohlman, *Justice Oliver Wendell Holmes: Free Speech and the Living Constitution* (1991), Sheldon M. Novick, *The Unrevised Holmes and Freedom of Expression*, 1991 Supreme Court Review 303, 353–61, and David S. Bogen, *The Free Speech Metamorphosis of Mr. Justice Holmes*, 11 Hofstra L Rev 97 (1982) (no change), with David M. Rabban, *Free Speech in Its Forgotten Years* 346–55 (1997), Geoffrey R. Stone, *Perilous Times: Free Speech in Wartime* 198–211 (2004) ("*Perilous Times*"), and G. Edward White, *Justice Holmes and the Modernization of Free Speech Jurisprudence: The Human Dimension*, 80 Cal L Rev 391 (1992) (change).

[100] Holmes, *Natural Law* at 41 (cited in note 35).

[101] See text at note 51.

Holmes's market metaphor from some of the standard criticisms to which it is subjected. The value of free trade in ideas does not depend on the assumption that there is an objective, perdurable truth to be discovered.[102] It does not depend on the claim that personal beliefs are more or less independent of the believer's social position, psychological propensities and needs, adventitious experiences, and ideological inheritance.[103] Those assumptions might be implicit in a market metaphor that evoked a finely calibrated measurement of the equilibrium of well-grounded rational beliefs. They are not implicit in Holmes's Darwinist invocation of "the competition of the market."

Markets move quickly; evolution takes forever. Many of the pragmatists, Dewey most prominently, were reformers who sought to remake various social institutions and practices in a fundamental way and without delay.[104] They may have been inspired by Darwin, but the pace of change that one associates with biological or geological evolution was not what inspired them. If the value of a free market in ideas lies in its contribution to the evolution of adaptive beliefs, at what pace are those beliefs supposed to evolve? And does the legal immunizing of speech that is perceived by governing majorities to be subversive of political or moral authority yield the optimal rate of change? What did Holmes think about the relationship between free speech and the rate of social change?

One of Holmes's guiding convictions was that the dominant forces in the society are entitled to have their way. He took the point of political institutions to be to enable the majority to implement its (arbitrary) preferences, "the kind of world that we should like."[105] He expressed none of the concern about the tyranny of the majority that informs the political thought of Madison, Tocqueville, and Mill.[106] Louis Menand well captures this dimension of his thought:

---

[102] Compare Baker, *Human Liberty* at 6, 12–14 (cited in note 20); Stanley Ingber, *The Marketplace of Ideas: A Legitimizing Myth*, 1984 Duke L J 1, 15 (1984).

[103] Compare, Baker, id at 6–7, 14–17; Ingber, id at 15; Jonathan Weinberg, *Broadcasting and Speech*, 81 Cal L Rev 1101, 1157–62 (1993).

[104] See generally James T. Kloppenberg, *Uncertain Victory: Social Democracy and Progressivism in European and American Thought 1870–1920* 349–94 (1986); Robert B. Westbrook, *John Dewey and American Democracy* (1991).

[105] Holmes, *Natural Law* at 41 (cited in note 35).

[106] Characteristically, Holmes was no absolutist on the subject of majority rule: he saw a role for minority rights. But he did not fear majorities the way many leading political thinkers have. His dissent in *Lochner v New York*, 198 US 45, 76 (1905), expresses his enthusiasm for majority rule: "Every opinion tends to become a law. I think that the word

> The key to Holmes's civil liberties opinions is the key to all his jurisprudence: it is that he thought only in terms of aggregate social forces; he had no concern for the individual. The spectacle of individuals falling victim to dominant political or economic tendencies, when those tendencies had been instantiated in duly enacted laws, gave him a kind of chilly satisfaction. It struck him as analogous to the death of soldiers in a battlefield victory, and justified on the same grounds—that for the group to move ahead, some people must inevitably fall by the wayside.[107]

Unlike many of his privileged contemporaries, however, Holmes did not believe that the dominant forces have any moral claim to maintain their dominance. He thought that change is both inevitable and endurable. He never spelled out a theory of legitimate change—it would have been against his very nature to have done so—but his approach to constitutional interpretation depended on an attitude, if not a theory, about change.

Holmes's general approach to constitutional interpretation was to defer to legislative judgments. He was skeptical, at times even contemptuous, of much of the progressive era legislation that was challenged in the Supreme Court during his tenure, but he was loathe to hold that legislation unconstitutional.[108] He believed that when the dominant forces in the community were (regrettably) bitten by the bug of progressive reform, that preference had to be permitted to prevail. The previously dominant forces of laissez-faire capitalism were not entitled, in Holmes's view, to preserve their power indefinitely against the rise of the emergent forces of progressivism. Dominant forces emerge and recede. "Time has upset many fighting faiths."[109]

Disputes over the freedom of speech raise an interesting question for someone who respects the claims of force.[110] On the one hand, legislation restricting speech, especially speech that challenges ex-

---

liberty in the Fourteenth Amendment is perverted when it is held to prevent the natural outcome of a dominant opinion, unless it can be said that a rational and fair man necessarily would admit that the statute proposed would infringe fundamental principles as they have been understood by the traditions of our people and our law."

[107] Menand, *Metaphysical Club* at 65–66 (cited in note 57).

[108] See, for example, *Lochner v New York*, 198 US 45, 75 (1905) (Holmes, J, dissenting); *Coppage v Kansas*, 236 US 1, 26 (1915) (Holmes, J, dissenting); *Adair v United States*, 208 US 161, 190 (1908) (Holmes, J, dissenting).

[109] *Abrams v United States*, 250 US 616, 630 (1919) (Holmes, J, dissenting).

[110] See Frederick Schauer, *The Role of the People in First Amendment Theory*, 74 Cal L Rev 761 (1986).

isting social and political arrangements, can be seen as just another example of the dominant forces in the community having their way. In this view, one prerogative of political ascendancy is the authority to control the terms of debate. On the other hand, one might argue that, at least in a democracy, the dominant forces are entitled to prevail only if they are able to maintain their dominance in the face of open challenges to their authority. Political arrangements should reflect the ascendancy of forces, but new forces must have some opportunity to emerge and eventually gain ascendancy.

I may be guilty here of trying to impose on Holmes's thought a conception of procedural legitimacy that is entirely alien to his way of thinking. He was a Darwinist, he did believe in change, and he viewed society in terms of forces, but he simply did not like to think about political issues in terms of so morally tinged a notion as legitimacy. Still, a judge has to decide cases, and it is impossible to do that, I would argue, without repairing in some way to a view of legitimacy. In any event, there is reason to believe that Holmes at first thought that free speech cases are constitutionally similar to economic regulation cases in that legislatures should be given broad authority to implement their preferred policies. At least on the occasion of *Abrams*, and arguably eight months earlier,[111] Holmes seems to have shifted to the view that the dominant forces of the community do not have broad power to determine which challenges to their authority shall be heard.

There is no premise or metric internal to the theory of evolution that can determine the answer to this fundamental question of how much the dominant forces are entitled to mobilize the resources of law to extend their dominance by slowing the pace or altering the direction of inevitable change. Even in a regime that represses dis-

---

[111] *Schenck v United States*, 249 US 47 (1919); *Frohwerk in United States*, 249 US 204 (1919); *Debs v United States*, 249 US 211 (1919). These are decisions, with Holmes writing for a unanimous court, that upheld criminal convictions of various socialists for antiwar polemics that today clearly would qualify for First Amendment protection. Nevertheless, by employing the "clear-and-present-danger" test and by declining to suspend it even "[w]hen a nation is at war," *Schenck*, 249 US at 52, Holmes can be read to evince an appreciation of the value of political criticism. By insisting that First Amendment protection remains "a question of proximity and degree," not a matter of the innate tendency of the idea, Holmes implemented an approach that was, in theory at least, more protective of controversial speakers than the "bad tendency" test that previously had dominated First Amendment interpretation and that was being urged in many quarters as a justification for the widespread prosecution of war protestors. See Geoffrey R. Stone, *The Origins of the "Bad Tendency" Test: Free Speech in Wartime*, 2002 Supreme Court Review 411, 446–47. On the bad tendency test generally, see Rabban, *Free Speech in Its Forgotten Years* at 132–46 (cited in note 99).

sent systematically and without constitutional constraint, the forces of nascent displacement still can operate underground, and still have means for bringing about change ranging from anonymous protest to peaceful civil disobedience to violent revolution. Is that enough to effectuate the evolutionary process? To decide, one needs more than an understanding of variation, adaptation, and natural selection. One needs a political or constitutional theory, or a reading of history.

IV. SEDITION

Holmes realized this. Recall the passage of his *Abrams* dissent quoted earlier:

> I wholly disagree with the argument of the Government that the First Amendment left the common law as to seditious libel in force. History seems to me against the notion. I had conceived that the United States through many years had shown its repentance for the Sedition Act of 1798, by repaying fines that it imposed.[112]

This allusion to the nation's ill-fated effort during its fledgling years to enforce a political orthodoxy[113] has not received the attention it deserves.[114] The passage is not just boilerplate rhetoric; it is integral to Holmes's argument. The Espionage Act of 1918, the federal statute that the defendants in the case were charged with violating, was really a sedition act. It prohibited ideological disloyalty as much

---

[112] 250 US 616, 630 (1919) (Holmes, J, dissenting).

[113] See generally Anthony Lewis, *Make No Law: The Sullivan Case and the First Amendment* 56–66 (1991); James Morton Smith, *Freedom's Fetters: The Alien and Sedition Laws and American Civil Liberties* (1956); Stone, *Perilous Times* at 16–78 (cited in note 99).

[114] A notable exception is Robert Post, *Reconciling Theory and Doctrine in First Amendment Jurisprudence*, in Bollinger and Stone, eds, *Eternally Vigilant* at 156–61 (cited in note 30). Post marks Holmes's reference to the rejection of seditious libel as "the precise point in American constitutional history when First Amendment theory enters into the construction of First Amendment doctrine, for Holmes's bold assertion required him to explain why the First Amendment prohibited the punishment of seditious libel." Id at 156–57. Post concludes, however, that although Holmes was prompted by the issue of the constitutional status of seditious libel to develop a First Amendment theory, he "chose not to elaborate a political conception of the First Amendment" but rather "proposed the now-famous theory of the marketplace of ideas." Id at 157. My claim, to be elaborated below, is that Holmes's market metaphor does indeed embody "a political conception of the First Amendment."

as material interference with the war effort.[115] The government lawyers in the *Abrams* appeal did not shrink from this characterization but rather embraced it.[116] Their brief, written by Assistant Attorney General Robert Stewart, maintained that the First Amendment was never meant to invalidate the old crime of seditious libel. Rather, the power to punish sedition remained a prerogative of sovereignty even in the *novus ordo seclorum*. The legitimate objective of the crime of seditious libel, so the brief claimed, was to control hostile criticism in order to protect the government's reputation and thereby preserve political stability, a fragile condition in the seventeenth and eighteenth centuries, the heyday of seditious-libel prosecutions. A modern equivalent like the Espionage Act of 1918, in this view, was not constitutionally problematic, particularly in light of the need to preserve political stability in time of war.[117]

Stewart may have been goaded into making this provocative argument by a brief filed earlier that year in the case of *Debs v United States* by the noted civil liberties lawyer Gilbert Roe.[118] That brief had argued that the very purpose of the First Amendment is to protect fundamental political criticism of the sort historically punished as seditious libel. To sustain that contention, Roe constructed his brief around James Madison's *Virginia Report*, the classic challenge to the Sedition Act of 1798 by the principal author of the First Amendment.[119] In Madison's view, the distinctive "genius" of the American republic, based on the concepts of limited government, divided powers, and popular sovereignty, not to mention revolutionary heritage, is a dynamic of political opposition, ac-

---

[115] The *Abrams* defendants were convicted on four counts of violating the Espionage Act of 1918. Two of those counts clearly sound in sedition: (1) publishing "disloyal, scurrilous and abusive language about the form of Government of the United States"; and (2) publishing language "intended to bring the form of Government of the United States into contempt, scorn, contumely and disrepute." See *Abrams v United States*, 250 US 616, 617 (1919). The convictions were affirmed by the Supreme Court on the other two counts, for language encouraging resistance and curtailment of production. Id. The majority did not reach the issue of whether conviction on the first two counts standing alone would have violated the First Amendment.

[116] Brief of the United States in *Abrams v United States*, 250 US 616 (1919) (No 316), p 36. See Richard Polenberg, *Fighting Faiths: The Abrams Case, the Supreme Court, and Free Speech* 232–33 (1987).

[117] Id at 19–21, 25.

[118] Brief of Gilbert E. Roe as Amicus Curiae in *Debs v United States*, 249 US 211 (1919) (No 714), pp 32–42.

[119] James Madison, *Report on the Alien and Sedition Acts* (1800) ("*Report*"), in Jack N. Rakove, ed, *James Madison: Writings* 608–62 (Library of America, 1999).

countability, and checks and balances that makes inapplicable many English political notions, including that of seditious libel.[120]

At the time of the Court's decision in *Debs*, Roe was unable to persuade Holmes to adopt this Madisonian understanding of the First Amendment; in fact, Holmes wrote the majority opinion that upheld Debs's conviction.[121] But in the *Abrams* dissent eight months later, Holmes saw fit to state explicitly his conclusion that, whatever else the freedom of speech means in the American context, it means that dissenters cannot be punished for undermining the authority of government by disseminating seditious ideas.[122] Even his rhetoric in *Abrams* has a Madisonian ring: "we should be eternally vigilant against attempts to check the expression of opinions that we loathe and believe to be fraught with death . . . ."[123] In deciding whether, in a system committed to political evolution, the dominant forces may employ the authority of law to stifle or weaken dissent, Holmes turned to one of the premier object lessons of the nation's history and to the concept of legitimate political opposition that it spawned.

To appreciate the significance of this move, one must realize how controversial it was in Holmes's day. Many persons who conceded the value of dissent stopped short at the notion that a constitutional principle such as the freedom of speech could be invoked by persons who advocate the use of force or violence to effectuate a fundamental change of political regime.[124] In this view, the Constitution

---

[120] Id at 329–31.

[121] *Debs v United States*, 249 US 211 (1919).

[122] 250 US at 630.

[123] Id.

[124] See, for example, John H. Wigmore, *Abrams v. U.S.: Freedom of Speech and Freedom of Thuggery in War-Time and Peace-Time*, 14 U Ill L Rev 539, 559–60 (1920):

> The truth is that the constitutional guarantee of freedom of speech is being invoked more and more in misuse. It represents the unfair protection much desired by impatient and fanatical minorities—fanatically committed to some new revolutionary belief, and impatient of the usual process of rationally converting the majority. . . . Certain leaders of thought—some idealists, some materialists— see only red when their own particular doctrines are balked of immediate general acceptance. Impatient of that "free trade in ideas" which the Minority Opinion assures us will exhibit ultimately the "power of the thought to get itself accepted," these fanatical leaders invoke club-law. They call for "direct action" (this cowardly euphemism for brutal mob violence must now be familiar to all readers of recent periodical literature). And when their urgent propaganda of club-law meets lawful interference, they invoke the sacred constitutional guarantee of "freedom of

provides for change but only by the prescribed method of peaceful protest directed toward eventual success at the polls; radicals unwilling to play by those rules should not be permitted to claim the benefit of the very freedoms they seek to displace. This position was not the exclusive preserve of reactionaries. Even Learned Hand drew the line at the explicit advocacy of law violation:

> Every society which promulgates a law means that it shall be obeyed until it is changed, and any society which lays down means by which its laws can be changed makes those means exclusive . . . . If so, how in God's name can an incitement to do what will be unlawful if done, be itself lawful?[125]

Holmes, in contrast, did not believe that the Constitution should be read to lock in place an absolute procedural truth regarding the exclusive means for effectuating political change. In *Abrams* he voted to protect the speech of anarchists who had called for a general strike, never even considering whether that tactic was forbidden by law.[126] Six years later, in *Gitlow v New York*,[127] Holmes argued in dissent that the explicit advocacy of "revolutionary mass action" was entitled to First Amendment protection in the particular circumstances of the case. On that occasion, he made even more explicit his Darwinist understanding of the dynamics of political change, adopting the very position that Learned Hand considered incoherent.

Hand's view, most fully elaborated in his great opinion in *Masses Publishing Co. v Patten*,[128] was that under democratic theory incitements to law violation fall outside the ambit of the freedom of speech as a matter of principle, irrespective of whether the context indicates an imminent danger of illegal conduct by persons exposed to the speech. Hand held that view because he considered incitements to law violation not to be among the "exclusive" means laid down by a democratic society "by which its laws can be changed."

---

speech." It is simply a profanation of that term.

For a retrieval and defense of this view in the modern era, see Robert H. Bork, *Neutral Principles and Some Modern First Amendment Problems*, 47 Ind L J 1, 31 (1971).

[125] Letter from Learned Hand to Elliot Richardson (Feb 29, 1952), quoted in Gerald Gunther, *Learned Hand: The Man and the Judge* (1994).

[126] 250 US at 630.

[127] 268 US 652 (1925) (Holmes, J, dissenting).

[128] 235 F 535 (SDNY 1917), rev'd 246 F 24 (2d Cir 1917).

"Words," he explained, "which have no purport but to counsel the violation of law cannot by any latitude of interpretation be a part of that public opinion which is the final source of government in a democratic state."[129] On the other hand, "political agitation which can be shown to be apt to create a seditious temper" is indeed, so long as it falls short of the direct advocacy of law violation, a part of "that public opinion which is the final source of government," and as such deserves protection as among the proper means by which the laws of a democratic society can be changed.[130] Thus Hand, possibly influenced by another Madisonian brief filed by Gilbert Roe,[131] rejected the legitimacy of the crime of seditious libel. Notwithstanding that judgment—itself an important moment in the history of thought about the freedom of speech—Hand believed that incitement to law violation can be prohibited; he did not consider the punishment of such incitement to be precluded by the rejection of seditious libel.

Holmes declined to follow Hand in this last respect. While joining his friend in finding the crime of seditious libel to be incompatible with the First Amendment, Holmes saw no reason to exclude incitement to law violation from the protection of his imminent danger standard, no reason to exclude the explicit and impassioned advocacy of lawbreaking from the means by which political change may be brought about so long as the likely or intended effects are not imminent.[132] He put the point memorably, with pragmatist resonance, in *Gitlow*:

---

[129] Id at 540.

[130] Id.

[131] Gilbert Roe was the counsel of record for the magazine in *Masses Publishing Co. v Patten*. See 244 Fed 535, 537 (1917). I have not been able to locate the papers he submitted to Judge Hand in the District Court. It is possible, in light of Hand's reference in his *Masses* opinion to the illegitimacy of prohibiting speech on the ground that it is likely to create a seditious temper, that in arguing the case before Judge Hand Roe invoked Madison's *Virginia Report* in much the way he did twenty months later in the amicus brief he filed in the *Debs* case. See text accompanying notes 118–20. Such a speculation gains support from the fact that not long before he tried the *Masses* case in Judge Hand's courtroom, Roe testified against the Espionage Act to the House Committee on the Judiciary. See Hearings Before the House of Representatives Committee on the Judiciary, 65th Cong, 1st Sess, Hearings on HR 291 at 36–43 (Apr 9 and 12, 1917). On that occasion as well, Roe discussed the controversy over the Sedition Act of 1798. See Geoffrey R. Stone, *Judge Learned Hand and the Espionage Act of 1917: A Mystery Unraveled*, 70 U Chi L Rev 335, 351 (2003).

[132] In the *Abrams* dissent, Holmes stated that a person can be punished for speech "that produces *or is intended to produce* a clear and imminent danger." 250 US at 627 (emphasis added). A page later, he repeated his belief that a speaker's intent to create an imminent

> Every idea is an incitement. It offers itself for belief and if believed it is acted on unless some other belief outweighs it or some failure of energy stifles the movement at its birth. The only difference between the expression of an opinion and an incitement in the narrow sense is the speaker's enthusiasm for the result. Eloquence may set fire to reason.[133]

As if to underscore his differences with Hand regarding the sources and limits of political authority, Holmes added:

> If in the long run the beliefs expressed in proletarian dictatorship are destined to be accepted by the dominant forces of the community, the only meaning of free speech is that they should be given their chance and have their way.[134]

Hand understood the rejection of seditious libel to entail a rejection of the power of the state to enforce any kind of orthodoxy of acceptable political ends; he was the first judge to interpret the freedom of speech to imply a strong principle of substantive viewpoint neutrality.[135] In doing so, he anticipated an idea that has come to be the cornerstone of modern First Amendment doc-

---

danger can justify regulation even of speech that appears under the circumstances to be unlikely to have that effect. This is because such an intent "might indicate a greater danger and at any rate would have the quality of an attempt." Id at 628. In *Gitlow*, Holmes voted to protect a defendant who had engaged in abstract advocacy of revolution. He specified, however, that if the speaker had been convicted of "an attempt to induce an uprising against government at once and not at some indefinite time in the future," then the "object would have been one with which the law might deal, subject to the doubt . . . whether [the speech] was not futile and too remote from possible consequences." 268 US at 673. This last caveat indicates Holmes's recognition of a futility defense, which he had seemed to reject in *Abrams*.

The important point is that Holmes's willingness to punish speakers on the basis of their specific intentions as well as the likely effects of their speech extended only to the intention to create *imminent* harm. He did not embrace a content-based, context-independent conception of illegitimate speech akin to Learned Hand's view that the advocacy of law violation is, as a matter of democratic principle, outside the ambit of First Amendment protection. Holmes understood the rejection of seditious libel to mean that a critic of government must be free, whatever his long-term objectives, to say that a law should be violated or a regime overthrown by force, so long as the requisite connection to imminent consequences has not been established. Hand did not agree.

[133] 268 US at 673.

[134] Id.

[135] See Letter from Learned Hand to Zechariah Chafee, Jr. (Jan 8, 1920), in Gerald Gunther, *Learned Hand and the Origins of Modern First Amendment Doctrine: Some Fragments of History*, 27 Stan L Rev 719, 765 (1975) ("any State which professes to be controlled by public opinion, cannot take sides against any opinion except that which must express itself in the violation of law.").

trine.[136] Holmes went further. In addition to the rejection of an orthodoxy of ends, he took the rejection of seditious libel to entail the rejection of an orthodoxy of means, specifically the orthodoxy establishing democratic deliberation as the exclusive means of political change. Both judges knew, of course, that violence or the threat thereof has throughout history played a large role in bringing about political change, salutary and nefarious, in constitutional democracies as well as in other systems. Both judges had no qualms about punishing dissidents who themselves engage in violence. The difference between them, I believe, is that Holmes, the old soldier and proud Darwinist, thought that one of the valuable functions of dissenting speech, including speech that advocates violent revolution, is its capacity to generate some of the grievances, aspirations, and mobilizations that force political adaptation and transformation. Such energies are activated and sustained not only by respectful petition and rational persuasion but also by incitement, recruitment, and organization for collective action. Probably the most energizing contribution that the freedom of speech can make is simply to leave people free to follow their political thoughts wherever they might lead—free, that is, to think the unthinkable regarding political loyalty, consent, obedience, and violence. That no viable political community could possibly recognize a comparable freedom to act does not, in this view, render incoherent or dysfunctional a capacious freedom to disseminate heretical political ideas, including ideas about the appropriate means for bringing about change.

To understand Holmes on this point, one must appreciate how far he was from a modern procedural liberal concerned more about the right than the good, and thus how wrong it is to try to turn his marketplace of ideas into a systematic process to be evaluated according to standards of fairness, neutrality, and efficiency.[137] Holmes consistently talked about dissenting speech in terms of the energies it releases or fails to release,[138] not the quality of decisions or opportunities for participation that it makes possible. Understood

---

[136] See generally Geoffrey R. Stone, *Content Regulation and the First Amendment*, 25 Wm & Mary L Rev 189 (1983); Susan H. Williams, *Content Discrimination and the First Amendment*, 139 U Pa L Rev 615 (1991).

[137] For an otherwise interesting critique of the market metaphor that founders by making this mistake, see Stanley Fish, *Fraught with Death: Skepticism, Progressivism, and the First Amendment*, 64 U Colo L Rev 1061, 1071–73 (1993).

[138] See text at notes 84 and 133.

in these Darwinist/pragmatist terms, such speech achieves its effect mainly by influencing the culture of political struggle. This can happen when the visibility of dissenting ideas, made possible in part by legal protection, emboldens persons in the minority to hold out hope for change, to fight back when ridiculed, exploited, or ignored, perhaps to find confederates in the project of resistance. It can happen when persons who hold views currently in the ascendancy find it more difficult, due to the constitutionally sanctioned legitimacy of seditious speech, to dismiss protestors as beneath political recognition, in effect beyond the pale. It can happen when the sheer plurality of perspectives in play forces all actors to "realize that time has upset many fighting faiths" and that one's "preferences dogmatic for oneself" grew out of unique experiences such that "others, poor souls, may be equally dogmatic about something else."[139]

The cultural/intellectual/political combat facilitated by free speech is, in Holmes's vision, messy, unpredictable, often nasty, and impossible to domesticate. But it is what human flourishing in a competitive, evolving world is all about. A letter that Holmes wrote to Learned Hand the year before his *Abrams* dissent best articulates the view of life that led Holmes to see value in the speech of dissenters who refuse to play by the rules:

> You tempt me to repeat an apologue that I got off to my wife in front of the statue of Garrison on Commonwealth Avenue, Boston, many years ago. I said—If I were an official person I should say nothing shall induce me to do honor to a man who broke the fundamental condition of social life by bidding the very structure of society perish rather than he not have his way— Expressed in terms of morals, to be sure, but still, his way. If I were a son of Garrison I should reply—Fool, not to see that every great reform has seemed to threaten the structure of society,—but that society has not perished, because man is a social animal, and with every turn falls into a new pattern like the Kaleidoscope. If I were a philosopher I should say—Fools both, not to see that you are the two blades (conservative and radical) of the shears that cut out the future. But if I were the ironical man in the back of the philosopher's head I should conclude— Greatest fool of all, Thou—not to see that man's destiny is to fight. Therefore take thy place on the one side or the other, if with the added grace of knowing that the Enemy is as good a

---

[139] Holmes, *Natural Law* at 41 (cited in note 35).

man as thou, so much the better, but kill him if thou canst.[140]

When Holmes was required by his office shortly thereafter to determine what legal tools should be available for "killing" a political enemy "as good a man as thou," he gave no weight to whether the enemy was observing the prescribed procedures for cutting out the future.

Why prefer Holmes's more radical, more cultural, less procedural interpretation of the meaning of the rejection of seditious libel? The market metaphor suggests some reasons. Markets are notable for their decentralization of authority. Consumers rather than producers or planners are sovereign in that their choices ultimately determine the allocation of economic resources. The placement of authority anywhere else runs the risk of discouraging productive adaptation and innovation, and providing opportunities for inefficient corruption and the wasteful perpetuation of privilege. A conception of political sovereignty that denies to officials the legal power to enforce an ideological orthodoxy of either ends or means likewise is characterized by relatively decentralized authority. Under that constraint on officials, political subjects are given the authority to contemplate and advocate arrangements and practices that have the potential to undermine the projects, and sometimes even the very existence, of the prevailing regime. The energies latent in such an allocation of authority reduce certain risks of political ossification and abuse. In his *Virginia Report* challenging the constitutionality of the Sedition Act of 1798, Madison derived his case for the right to express seditious criticism of officials, even to the extent of undermining their authority by stirring up hatred against them, from the premise that "[t]he people, not the government, possess the absolute sovereignty."[141] Those sovereign private citizens, whose authority extends to creating and replacing particular regimes,[142]

---

[140] Letter from Oliver Wendell Holmes to Learned Hand (June 24, 1918), in Gunther, 27 Stan L Rev at 756–57 (cited in note 135).

[141] Madison, *Report* at 645 (cited in note 119).

[142] Madison noted in the *Virginia Report* that had all seditious speech been successfully censored during the years leading up to the founding of the current regime, "might not the United States have been languishing, at this day, under the infirmities of a sickly Confederation? Might they not, possibly, be miserable colonies, groaning under a foreign yoke?" Id at 647–48. In an opinion that Holmes joined, Justice Brandeis invoked the nation's revolutionary heritage in developing his argument for the First Amendment right to advocate the overthrow of an entire regime: "Those who won our independence by revolution were not cowards. They did not fear political change." *Whitney v California*, 274 US 357, 377 (1927) (Brandeis, J, concurring).

can be analogized to the sovereign consumers in a market. Pressures from below stimulate adaptation and help to contain corruption in both the political and economic realms.

An egalitarian might be tempted to run with this logic to the extent of finding in the market metaphor support for a First Amendment ideal of equal opportunity to persuade (or incite or organize collective pressure). I doubt that the sovereignty enjoyed by consumers as a whole in most markets implies any such principle of equal worth of individuals. Markets are egalitarian in that a pauper's dollar buys as much as a prince's and the division of labor that markets make possible can spread opportunity,[143] but inegalitarian in that markets greatly facilitate the leveraging of (unequally distributed) wealth and economic savvy. Perhaps an economic cooperative would be a stronger (though still problematic) source of analogical support for a conception of political equality. In any event, we can be confident that Holmes had no such egalitarian implication in mind when he invoked the competition of the market in his *Abrams* dissent. He once infamously dismissed an equal protection contention as "the usual last resort of constitutional arguments."[144] Throughout his career on the Supreme Court, "he treated the Equal Protection Clause as having virtually no effect."[145] What Holmes liked about markets so far as the role of consumers is concerned is not the way purchasing power is distributed among them, but rather the power that consumers exercise as a collective force that induces producers to adapt and innovate. The proper analogy is to the power that sovereign political subjects in combination can exert in holding officials, and even entire regimes, roughly accountable over time through the threat of disaffection, noncooperation, and resistance.

This focus on the role of force as the arbiter of political power means that the freedom of speech implied by a reliance on the market metaphor is not confined to settings where the social prerequisites for meaningful persuasion and participation are operative. Accordingly, neither the town meeting nor the philosophy seminar should be seen as the prototypical free speech situation. In this view, the First Amendment is primarily about the location of political

---

[143] For an illuminating account of the often-overlooked egalitarian dimensions of Adam Smith's thought, see Samuel Fleischaker, *On Adam Smith's Wealth of Nations* 72–80 (2004).

[144] *Buck v Bell*, 274 US 200, 208 (1927).

[145] G. Edward White, *Justice Oliver Wendell Holmes: Law and the Inner Self* 348 (1993).

authority, and more broadly about the cultural conditions that foster political accountability and adaptation. Deliberation among relatively open-minded persons plays a role in such matters, but far more is entailed by this understanding of the function of free speech than an exclusive concern for rational inquiry and debate. Communicative experiences that are important mainly in promoting solidarity among like-minded persons, or in helping individuals and groups to mark out a distinctive identity, might qualify as having First Amendment salience even if "persuasion" in the narrow sense is not what those experiences are about.[146] That the market metaphor implies the extension of First Amendment concern to some such activities leaves unresolved all sorts of difficult questions regarding the proper scope of the principle of freedom of speech.[147] It is important, nevertheless, to realize that an understanding of the First Amendment that includes protection for many communicative endeavors that bear no resemblance to the town meeting or the philosophy seminar does not represent a departure from the view of free speech that underlies Holmes's market metaphor.

That the First Amendment may be as much about political combat between ideologically committed, power-hungry actors as about disinterested inquiry and deliberation also suggests a rationale for the clear-and-present-danger test which Holmes elaborated in the *Abrams* dissent. The dominant forces of the community are not entitled to freeze themselves in power, but they *are* entitled to protect their interests as they see them. Thus, speech can be regulated when it is likely in light of the context of its dissemination to lead directly and immediately to tangible harm, as defined by what threatens the material interests of the dominant forces. Such harms are "substantive evils that Congress has a right to prevent."[148] To disallow all preemptive regulatory authority regarding them would be to deny the dominant forces the power to protect their interests. However, speech that is likely to cause harm only over

---

[146] For an important development of this line of justification for the principle of freedom of speech, see the chapter entitled "Free Expression and Personal Identification," in Joseph Raz, *Ethics in the Public Domain* 131 (1994).

[147] For sophisticated arguments that demonstrate how difficult it is to determine the proper scope of the freedom of speech, see C. Edwin Baker, *Scope of the First Amendment Freedom of Speech*, 25 UCLA L Rev 964 (1978); Frederick Schauer, *The Boundaries of the First Amendment: A Preliminary Exploration of Constitutional Salience*, 117 Harv L Rev 1765 (2004); Richard Vernon, *John Stuart Mill and Pornography: Beyond the Harm Principle* 106 Ethics 621 (1996).

[148] *Schenck v United States*, 249 US 47, 52 (1919).

time, if at all, cannot be regulated because the legitimate ongoing process of displacing preexisting dominant forces with newly emergent dominant forces requires that such nonimminent and/or nonmaterial "harms" be permitted to occur. Political evolution, like evolution in the natural world, is based on harm. Some groups, previously dominant, lose out in the struggle for existence and necessarily suffer great harm. It is not one of the prerogatives of the ascendancy of force to abort that evolutionary process.

Notice that this understanding of the clear-and-present-danger test does not depend on the far-fetched assumption that, except when the time frame is imminent, "more speech" ordinarily will reach and dissuade potential wrongdoers who otherwise would be prompted to act by the speaker's words. Holmes's position is that sometimes we have to live with those remote harms. They can be inseparable from adaptive political change. Notice also that the legitimation of fundamental political opposition manifested by the rejection of seditious libel goes far to explain the principle, explicitly stated by Holmes earlier in the *Abrams* dissent[149] and integral to the clear-and-present-danger test, that speakers cannot be punished for "the creed they avow"—that is, for their lack of commitment to the ideals, symbols, and procedures around which the political community is currently organized—but only for the material threat their speeches and writings pose to the specific endeavors of the community. The clear-and-present-danger test is not the only (or necessarily the best) doctrinal standard that one might derive from placing the rejection of seditious libel at the heart of the First Amendment, but Holmes's understanding of why the crime of seditious libel cannot be squared with the First Amendment provides the best justification for the clear-and-present-danger test.

V. Conclusion

In a lecture entitled "The Influence of Darwin on Philosophy," delivered ten years before Holmes's *Abrams* dissent, John Dewey observed:

> The conceptions that had reigned in the philosophy of nature and knowledge for two thousand years, the conceptions that had become the familiar furniture of the mind, rested on the assumption of the superiority of the fixed and final; they rested

---

[149] 250 US at 629.

upon treating change and origin as signs of defect and unreality. In laying hands upon the sacred ark of absolute permanency, in treating the forms that had been regarded as types of fixity and perfection as originating and passing away, the "Origin of Species" introduced a mode of thinking that in the end was bound to transform the logic of knowledge, and hence the treatment of morals, politics, and religion.[150]

What the theory of evolution, the legitimation of fundamental political opposition, and the renunciation of philosophical absolutes all have in common is an emphasis on change. Such emphasis is shared also by free markets. That, I believe, is why Holmes's invocation of all four phenomena in his succinct justification for the freedom of speech is more coherent, and less intellectually peripatetic, than is commonly assumed. A constitutional regime fearful of political entrenchment and dedicated to continual adaptation has every reason to accord high priority to the freedom of speech and to interpret that freedom with reference to the dynamism of free markets. In this regard, the features of markets that merit attention are those that also figure prominently in efficacious governance, scientific inquiry, and natural selection: openness to new ideas and capabilities, thirst for better information, responsiveness to changing conditions, encouragement of innovation and initiative, swift punishment of rigidity, slowness, lack of awareness, or the failure to audit. Whatever their limits and shortcomings, free markets are a powerful force against inertia. So is free speech.

This reading of the *Abrams* dissent ascribes to Holmes a justification for the freedom of speech that rests not upon highly contentious epistemological and moral premises but rather on the historical acceptance of the political principle of legitimate opposition. So interpreted, Holmes's argument is more modest, more persuasive, and of better constitutional pedigree than is often claimed. The argument is not dependent on heroic assumptions regarding human rationality or self-correcting social dynamics. It offers no support to idealists who would turn his vision of free trade in ideas into a charter for regulatory interventions designed to correct "market failures" in the domain of political and social disputation. As Holmes understood the notion, the marketplace of ideas does not offer the prospect of a just distribution of the opportunity to per-

---

[150] John Dewey, *The Influence of Darwin on Philosophy*, Popular Science Monthly (July 1909), reprinted in *The Influence of Darwin on Philosophy and Other Essays* 1 (1997).

suade. It does not offer the prospect of wisdom through mass deliberation, nor that of meaningful political participation for all interested citizens. What the marketplace of ideas does offer is a much needed counterweight, both conceptual and rhetorical, to illiberal attitudes about authority and change on which the censorial mentality thrives. It honors certain character traits—inquisitiveness, capacity to admit error and to learn from experience, ingenuity, willingness to experiment, resilience—that matter in civic adaptation no less than economic. It devalues deference and discredits certitude, and in the process holds various forms of incumbent authority accountable to standards of performance. It offers a reason to interpret the First Amendment to protect some gestures of opposition and resistance that have nothing to do with dialogue or dialectic. In these respects, Holmes's arresting metaphor serves better as a cultural statement than as a mechanism of social or intellectual ordering. So conceived, it does valuable work.

CASS R. SUNSTEIN

MINIMALISM AT WAR

The Founders intended that the President have primary responsibility—along with the necessary power—to protect the
national security and to conduct the Nation's foreign relations. . . . This Court has . . . held that the President has
constitutional authority to protect the national security and that
this authority carries with it broad discretion. . . . [I]t is crucial to recognize that *judicial* interference in these domains destroys the purpose of vesting primary responsibility in a unitary
Executive.[1]

The Constitution has never greatly bothered any wartime President.[2]

More importantly, the search for alternatives helps avoid two
extreme positions. The first says that, insofar as war is concerned, the Constitution does not really matter. That is wrong.
The Constitution always matters, perhaps particularly so in
times of emergency. The second says that, insofar as the Constitution is concerned, war or security emergencies do not really
matter. That is wrong too. Security needs may well matter,

Cass R. Sunstein is Karl N. Llewellyn Distinguished Service Professor, Law School and
Department of Political Science, University of Chicago.

AUTHOR'S NOTE: I am grateful to Jack Goldsmith, Richard Posner, Adam Samaha, Geoffrey Stone, David Strauss, and Adrian Vermeule for extremely helpful comments on a
previous draft.

[1] *Hamdi v Rumsfeld*, 124 S Ct 2633, 2675–76 (2004) (Thomas dissenting).
[2] Francis Biddle, *In Brief Authority* 219 (Doubleday, 1962).

playing a major role in determining just where the proper constitutional balance lies.[3]

I. Introduction

Many judges are minimalists; they want to say and do no more than necessary to resolve cases.[4] Judicial minimalism leads in two different directions. First, minimalists favor shallowness over depth, in the sense they seek to avoid taking stands on the most deeply contested questions of constitutional law. They attempt to reach *incompletely theorized agreements*, in which the most fundamental questions are left undecided. They prefer outcomes and opinions that can attract support from people with a wide range of theoretical positions, or with uncertainty about which theoretical positions are best. In these ways, minimalist judges avoid the largest questions about the meaning of the free speech guarantee, or the extent of the Constitution's protection of "liberty," or the precise scope of the President's authority as Commander in Chief of the Armed Forces.

Second, minimalists favor narrowness over width. Proceeding one case at a time, they seek decisions that resolve the problem at hand without also resolving a series of other problems that might have relevant differences. In the fashion of common law courts, minimalist judges prefer to focus on the particular question at issue, refusing to venture broader judgments that might turn out, on reflection, to be unwarranted.[5] With their emphasis on shallowness and narrowness, some minimalists have a particular preference for democracy-promoting decisions, certainly as compared to decisions that simply invalidate what government proposes to do. Democracy-promoting decisions are those that lead to explicit judgments by

---

[3] Stephen Breyer, *Liberty, Security, and the Courts* (April 14, 2003), online at http://www.supremecourtus.gov/publicinfo/speeches/sp_04−15−03.html (visited Dec 1, 2004).

[4] Minimalism is discussed in general terms in Cass R. Sunstein, *One Case at a Time: Judicial Minimalism on the Supreme Court* (Harvard, 1999).

[5] See Richard A. Posner, *Law, Pragmatism, and Democracy* 80 (Harvard, 2003): "The pragmatic judge tends to favor narrow over broad grounds of decision in the early stages in the development of a legal doctrine. . . . What the judge has before him is the facts of the particular case, not the facts of future cases. He can try to imagine what those cases will be like, but the likelihood of error in such an imaginative projection is great. Working outward, in stages, from the facts before him to future cases with new facts that may suggest the desirability of altering the contours of the applicable rules, the judge avoids premature generalization."

democratically accountable actors, above all Congress.[6]

Many judges distrust minimalism and prefer maximalism.[7] Maximalists reject shallowness in favor of depth. They are committed to a large-scale theory about the foundations of constitutional law. They might believe that "originalism" is the best theory of constitutional meaning, or they might think that the document should be interpreted to ensure the appropriate operation of democracy itself.[8] Typically they believe that their own theory is correct and that it reflects the right kind of judicial modesty (or, as the case may be, aggressiveness). What matters is that maximalists want to adopt a foundational account of one or another kind.

In the same vein, maximalists reject narrowness in favor of width. They believe that narrow rulings leave a great deal of unpredictability and also promote judicial discretion.[9] They think that firm, clear rules, laid down in advance, are the best way of ensuring clarity for the future—and also of simultaneously constraining and emboldening judges, encouraging them to protect liberty when the stakes are highest.[10] They add that such rules provide a highly visible background against which other branches of government can do their work.[11]

The terrorist attacks of September 11, 2001 have raised fresh questions about the places of minimalism and maximalism in American constitutional law. Those questions are especially pressing in the face of conflicts between national security and claimed violations of constitutional rights. Perhaps a form of minimalism makes particular sense for the resolution of such conflicts; perhaps some kind of maximalism is much better. In fact we can readily imagine two stylized positions: National Security Maximalism and Liberty Maximalism.[12] National Security Maximalists understand the Consti-

---

[6] This point is elaborated in Sunstein, *One Case at a Time* at 26–39 (cited in note 4).

[7] See Antonin Scalia, *A Matter of Interpretation* (Princeton, 1997).

[8] See John Hart Ely, *Democracy and Distrust* (Harvard, 1983).

[9] For an argument in favor of width, see Antonin Scalia, *The Rule of Law Is a Law of Rules*, 56 U Chi L Rev 115 (1989); the best general treatment is Adrian Vermeule, *Interpretive Choice*, 75 NYU L Rev 74 (2000)

[10] Scalia, 56 U Chi L Rev at 119 (cited in note 9).

[11] See id.

[12] For excellent and related discussions from which I have learned a great deal, see Eric A. Posner and Adrian Vermeule, *Accommodating Emergencies*, 56 Stan L Rev 605 (2003); Richard Pildes and Samuel Issacharoff, *Between Civil Libertarianism and Executive Unilateralism: An Institutional Process Approach to Right During Wartime*, 5 Theoretical Inquiries in Law (online edition), no 1, article 1 (Jan 2004), online at http://www.bepress.com/til/

tution to call for a highly deferential role for the judiciary, above all on the ground that when national security is threatened, the President must be permitted to do what needs to be done to protect the country. If he cannot provide that protection, who will? By contrast, Liberty Maximalists insist that in times of war, at least as much as in times of peace, federal judges must protect constitutional liberty.[13] Indeed, Liberty Maximalists believe that under circumstances of war, it is all the more important that federal judges take a strong stand on behalf of liberty.[14] If they do not, who will?

Of course some people reject both maximalism and minimalism in favor of an intermediate approach. They might, for example, err in the direction of presidential power without accepting National Security Maximalism, or err in the direction of freedom without accepting Liberty Maximalism. But an emphasis on the two forms of maximalism is helpful for analytic purposes; by exploring the poles, we can have a clearer sense of what might be wrong with more cautious versions as well. In addition, the poles have considerable appeal—National Security Maximalism to many federal judges as well as to the executive branch, Liberty Maximalism to many academic commentators as well as mission-oriented organizations focused on the protection of freedom. As we shall see, unmistakable forms of National Security Maximalism, rather than an intermediate approach, can be found in several places in recent years.

This article has two central purposes. The first is to reject both forms of maximalism and to specify and support a minimalist approach to intrusions on freedom amidst war. The second is to suggest that, to a remarkable degree, an identifiable form of minimalism captures the practices of the American courts when national security

---

default/vol5/iss1/art1 (visited Dec 1, 2004). National Security Maximalism is an extreme version of what Posner and Vermeule call the accommodationist view; Liberty Maximalism is akin to what they deem the strict enforcement view. Their target is the civil libertarian concern that accommodationist rulings will weaken liberty during peacetime and that during emergencies, the government will respond to unjustified public panic. Like Posner and Vermeule, I reject the strict enforcement view, and for reasons that overlap with theirs. National Security Maximalists are what Pildes and Issacharoff call Executive Unilateralists; Liberty Maximalists are what Pildes and Issacharoff call Civil Libertarians. Like Pildes and Issacharoff, and borrowing from their discussion, I stress the use of clear statement principles.

[13] See generally David Cole, *Enemy Aliens: Double Standards and Constitutional Freedoms in the War on Terrorism* (W.W. Norton, 2003).

[14] This is one reading of Geoffrey R. Stone, *Perilous Times: Free Speech in Wartime from the Sedition Act of 1798 to the War on Terrorism* (W.W. Norton, 2004).

is threatened.[15] Prominent uses of minimalism can be found during the Civil War, World War I, World War II, the Cold War, and the contemporary war on terrorism. In general, the Supreme Court has adopted a form of minimalism having three central components: a requirement of clear congressional authorization for executive action intruding on interests with a claim to constitutional protection;[16] an insistence on fair hearings, including access to courts, for those deprived of liberty; and judicial decisions that are themselves shallow and narrow and that therefore impose modest constraints on the future. The minimalist pattern unifies an extraordinary number of seemingly disparate decisions, including those in the recent past.[17] Indeed, the Court's notorious decisions involving the exclusion and detention of Japanese Americans during World War II should be seen not as blind deference to executive power, but as a tribute to minimalism—requiring clear congressional support for deprivations of liberty by the executive, and permitting those deprivations only if that support can be found.[18]

The Court's own practices help to identify serious problems with both forms of maximalism. If the nation is genuinely threatened, Liberty Maximalism runs into two difficulties. First, it is unrealistic, certainly in its most ambitious forms; judges simply will not protect liberty with the same aggressiveness when a country faces a serious threat to its survival.[19] By itself this is a large objection to Liberty Maximalism. "Ought implies can," and it is unhelpful to urge courts to adopt a role that they will predictably refuse to assume.[20] Second, Liberty Maximalism is undesirable. The government's power to intrude on liberty depends on the strength of the justifications it

---

[15] An important aspect of minimalism, requiring congressional authorization, is traced in some detail in Pildes and Issacharoff, *Civil Libertarianism* (cited in note 12).

[16] The notion of authorization raises a number of complexities, on which see Curtis Bradley and Jack Goldsmith, *Congressional Authorization and the War on Terrorism*, Harv L Rev (forthcoming 2005); I deal with some of those complexities below, see text at notes 240–43. Cass R. Sunstein, *Administrative Law Goes to War*, Harv L Rev (forthcoming 2005).

[17] See *Rasul v Bush*, 124 S Ct 2686 (2004); *Hamdi v Rumsfeld*, 124 S Ct 2633 (2004).

[18] See text at notes 204–19 below.

[19] See Lee Epstein et al., *The Supreme Silence During War* (unpublished manuscript, 2003) (offering quantitative study of judicial deference during war); William Rehnquist, *All the Laws But One* (Knopf, 1998).

[20] Of course I am using the term "can" to suggest willingness, rather than feasibility. There is nothing in the structure of the universe that would prevent courts from adopting Liberty Maximalism, and hence "can" operates, in this context, in a relatively weak sense. There is no point in asking courts to assume a posture that they will predictably refuse.

can muster on behalf of the intrusion.[21] When security is at risk, government has greater justifications than when it is not. Hence it is correct to say, with Chief Justice Rehnquist, that it "is neither desirable nor is it remotely likely that civil liberty will occupy as favored a position in wartime as it does in peacetime."[22]

None of this means that in times of war the government may proceed however it wishes or act in blatant violation of constitutional commands. Interferences with freedom of speech, for example, should be regarded with great skepticism, simply because they eliminate the principal method by which democracies correct themselves.[23] As we shall see, courts do, and should, take steps to ensure against arbitrary detentions. In American law, it cannot be said that "inter arma silent leges" (amidst war laws are silent).[24] But as a general approach for courts in wartime, Liberty Maximalism is a nonstarter. It is too broad, and too neglectful of legitimate government interests, to have a serious claim to our attention.

But its principal competitor, National Security Maximalism, runs into serious problems as well. First, its reading of the Constitution, typically emphasizing the President's role as Commander in Chief, is tendentious; some of the document's provisions can be taken to support National Security Maximalism, but they need not be read in that fashion. In fact they are more plausibly seen to ensure a shared division of authority between the President and Congress, above all because they retain the role of Congress as the nation's lawmaker. Second, National Security Maximalism neglects the fact that under many circumstances the executive branch is most unlikely to strike the right balance between security and liberty.[25] A primary task of the President is to keep the citizenry safe, and any error on

---

[21] See Breyer, *Liberty* at 3 (cited in note 3): "The value does not change; the circumstances change, thereby shifting the point at which a proper balance is struck. That is what happens in wartime when more severe restrictions may be required."

[22] Id at 224–25.

[23] See Stone, *Perilous Times* (cited in note 14); see also Aharon Barak, *A Judge on Judging: The Role of a Supreme Court in a Democracy*, 116 Harv L Rev 16, 149 (2002): "[M]atters of daily life constantly test judges' ability to protect democracy, but judges meet their supreme test in situations of war and terrorism. The protection of every individual's human rights is a much more formidable duty in times of war and terrorism than in times of peace and security. . . . As a Justice of the Israeli Supreme Court, how should I view my role in protecting human rights given this situation? I must take human rights seriously during times of both peace and conflict."

[24] Cicero, Oratio Pro Annio Milone IV; see Rehnquist, *All the Laws* at 224 (cited in note 19).

[25] For countless examples, see Stone, *Perilous Times* (cited in note 14).

that count is likely to produce extremely high political sanctions. For this reason, the President has a strong incentive to take precautions even if they are excessive and even unconstitutional. Internal deliberations within the executive branch are more likely than not to aggravate the problem, leading not to sensible checks and balances, but to a tendency toward a degree of extremism.

Of course unjustified intrusions on liberty can and do produce political retribution as well. But whether they do so depends on their incidence; and here is a further problem for National Security Maximalism. Political safeguards are most reliable if the intrusions severely burden many people at once. Such general intrusions are unlikely to be tolerated unless citizens can be convinced that they are necessary. But if the intrusions are faced by an identifiable few, political checks will not ensure that they are justified. On the contrary, political pressures might well favor them even if they are not.

In some circumstances, then, the executive is likely to adopt steps that sacrifice liberty for no adequate reason.[26] But judicial intervention is no panacea, for courts have institutional weaknesses of their own. Worst of all, they lack relevant information and hence they may not know whether an interference with liberty is actually justified. Because their historic mission is to protect individual liberty, they may give insufficient attention to the variables on the other side.[27] But none of this means that courts cannot play a productive role. I investigate here three ingredients of a minimalist approach that seems to me to have significant promise, and to represent a distillation of much of the practice of American courts over the last century and more:

1. *Clear congressional authorization.* Courts should require

---

[26] See id; Epstein et al., *Supreme Silence* (cited in note 19); and Rehnquist, *All the Laws* (cited in note 19), for many illustrations.

[27] Notably, however, there appears to be no evidence of judicial overprotection of civil liberties in the nation's long history. See Stone, *Perilous Times* (cited in note 14). Compare the use of the Precautionary Principle in environmental regulation, which calls for margins of safety to protect against harmful outcomes. See Cass R. Sunstein, *Laws of Fear: Beyond the Precautionary Principle* (forthcoming 2005), for general discussion. When national security is in danger, government officials are engaging in a form of risk management, and it should not be surprising to find that they often adopt a kind of Precautionary Principle. Stone, *Perilous Times* (cited in note 14), may be seen as a catalogue of instances in which something akin to that principle was employed to produce many unjustifiable intrusions on liberty; in this sense, it is a cousin to Aaron Wildavsky, *But Is It True: A Citizen's Guide to Environmental, Health, and Safety Issues* (Harvard, 1995), which catalogues a number of cases in which unjustifiable steps were taken in response to imagined environmental concerns.

clear congressional authorization before the executive in-
trudes on interests that have a strong claim to constitutional protection.[28] As a general rule, the executive should
not be permitted to act on its own.[29] The underlying ideas
here are twofold: a requirement of congressional authorization provides a check on unjustified intrusions on liberty,
and such authorization is likely to be forthcoming when
there is a good argument for it. A requirement of clear
authorization therefore promotes liberty without compromising legitimate security interests.[30]

2. *Hearing rights.* Courts should insist, whenever possible, on
the core principle of the Due Process Clause: Before anyone is deprived of liberty, some kind of procedure must
be put in place to ensure against erroneous deprivations.
This requirement protects against unjustified imprisonment, which counts as the most serious infringement of
civil liberty.[31]

3. *Judicial self-discipline.* Courts should discipline themselves
through narrow, incompletely theorized decisions. Such
decisions tend to ensure against dual risks: judicial overreaching, in the form of limits on executive power that
will ultimately prove unjustified; and excessive judicial
modesty, in the form of decisions that, in the heat of the
moment, lead to large-scale intrusions on liberty.[32] When
vindicating minimalist principle (2), for example, judges
can refuse to specify the precise procedure that must be
used, allowing the executive (for example) to use military
tribunals or otherwise to depart from ordinary adjudicative
procedures, so long as the rudiments of due process are
observed.

---

[28] An early version of this idea can be found in *Masses Publishing Co. v Patten*, 244 F
535 (SDNY 1917), discussed below.

[29] Complexities emerge when the President's inherent authority is plausibly involved.
See *Loving v United States*, 517 US 748 (1996).

[30] I discuss below the complex question whether clear authorization is sufficient as well
as necessary; the short version is that outside of the egregious cases, courts should ordinarily respect the shared views of Congress and the President.

[31] The hearing right is a modest one, because as I am understanding it here, it requires
a proceeding only to determine whether the executive has deprived someone of liberty
on the basis of facts that are relevant as a matter of existing law.

[32] See Epstein et al., *Supreme Silence* (cited in note 19), for details.

These three ideas can be unified under the general rubric of Due Process Writ Large. The requirement of congressional authorization provides a degree of procedural protection at the structural level. By mandating action from an institution that is both diverse and deliberative, that requirement offers a procedural safeguard against ill-considered intrusions into the domain of liberty. The requirement of a minimal hearing reflects the most familiar aspect of the due process guarantee. The requirement of narrow and shallow rulings from the courts applies due process principles to judges themselves, by ensuring that those not before the court will be provided with an opportunity to be heard.

All of these principles make sense not only for courts, but also for constitutional judgments within the executive branch and Congress in times of war. Judges are hardly the only people involved in constitutional interpretation. The executive branch, for example, would do well to seek congressional authorization for intrusions on constitutionally sensitive interests, to ensure hearings for those deprived of liberty, and to rely on narrow and incompletely theorized judgments about issues at the frontiers of constitutional law.

Of course minimalism is not always the appropriate course for federal judges or for anyone else.[33] Predictability can be extremely important, and in some contexts minimalism cannot be tolerated, simply because it sacrifices rule of law values for no sufficient reason. And of course general principles cannot resolve concrete cases; everything turns on the particular intrusion and its underlying justification. Sometimes the President is constitutionally permitted to act on his own;[34] sometimes hearings need not be held;[35] sometimes judges should rule broadly. A committed minimalist will insist on these very points, contending that it is too ambitious to insist, all of the time, on congressional authorization, hearings, and narrow and incompletely theorized rulings. But when national security and liberty are in tension, the three principles provide the best general orientation.

The remainder of this article comes in three parts. Part II sketches the role of National Security Maximalism in the war on terror. It shows that in recent years, this way of proceeding has had a prom-

---

[33] See Vermeule, 75 NYU L Rev 74 (cited in note 9).

[34] See, for example, *Johnson v Eisentrager*, 339 US 763 (1950).

[35] See id.

inent place in the Department of Justice, the Supreme Court, and federal courts of appeals. Part III outlines the problems with National Security Maximalism, including its tendentious reading of the Constitution and its failure to appreciate the relevant incentives on the part of the executive branch. Part IV sketches the minimalist alternative, with its emphasis on clear statement principles, hearing rights, and narrow, shallow judicial judgments.

II. National Security Maximalism

> We are now confronted by a profoundly disturbing trend in our national political life: the growing tendency of the judicial branch to inject itself into areas of executive action originally assigned to the discretion of the president. These encroachments include some of the most fundamental aspects of the president's conduct of the war on terrorism.[36]

> But the "law" which this prisoner is convicted of disregarding is not found in an act of Congress, but in a military order. Neither the Act of Congress nor the Executive Order, nor both together, would afford a basis for this conviction. It rests on the orders of General Dewitt.[37]

It should be unsurprising to find that in the aftermath of the attacks of 9/11, National Security Maximalism has obtained a great deal of support. To be sure, the Supreme Court has refused to accept it, at least thus far.[38] But the basic approach can be found in many places.

A.   THE DEPARTMENT OF JUSTICE

In recent years, the most visible moment for National Security Maximalism came from the Office of Legal Counsel of the Department of Justice, with its 2002 memorandum on the legality

---

[36] Attorney General John Ashcroft, quoted in Terry Frieden, *Ashcroft: "Activist" Judges Can Put Nation's Security at Risk* (Nov 12, 2004), available at http://www.cnn.com/2004/ALLPOLITICS/11/12/ashcroft.judges/index.html (visited Dec 1, 2004).

[37] *Korematsu v United States*, 323 US 214, 243 (1944) (Jackson dissenting).

[38] See, for example, *Hamdi v Rumsfeld*, 124 S Ct 2633, 2674 (2004); *Rasul v Bush*, 124 S Ct 2686 (2004).

of coerced interrogation.[39] The most remarkable aspect of the memorandum is its suggestion that as Commander in Chief of the Armed Forces, the President of the United States has the inherent authority to torture suspected terrorists, so as to make it constitutionally unacceptable for Congress to ban the practice of torture.[40] The Office of Legal Counsel emphasized that "the President enjoys complete discretion in the exercise of his Commander-in-Chief authority and in conducting operations against hostile forces."[41] In addition, the Office of Legal Counsel insisted that a core function of the Commander in Chief includes interrogation of the enemy.[42] Because of "the President's inherent constitutional authority to manage a military campaign against al Qaeda and its allies," congressional enactments "must be construed as not applying to" interrogations undertaken as part of the President's Commander in Chief authority.[43] "Any effort by Congress to regulate the interrogation of battlefield combatants would violate the Constitution's sole vesting of the Commander in Chief authority in the President."[44] Hence coercive interrogation, including torture, must be permitted if the President wants to engage in it.

The Office of Legal Counsel is part of the executive branch, and one of its major functions is to protect the constitutional prerogatives of the President, especially those prerogatives that are associated with the Commander in Chief power. Generous interpretations of the President's prerogatives should be expected

---

[39] See Office of Legal Counsel, *Memorandum for Alberto Gonzales, Counsel to the President, Re: Standards of Conduct for Interrogation under 18 USC 2340–2340A* (Aug 1, 2002) (copy on file with author). This was the most visible moment for National Security Maximalism, but perhaps not the most extreme one. In the *Padilla* case, the President claimed that, as Commander in Chief, he had the inherent power to order military authorities to seize an American citizen in the United States without any judicial approval and to hold him indefinitely, incommunicado, with no access to a lawyer, a court, family, or friends, and without even informing his family or friends what they had done with him. I discuss *Padilla* below.

[40] Id at 31.

[41] Id at 33.

[42] Id at 38.

[43] Id at 34. To be sure, the position of the Department of Justice was stated with a degree of tentativeness, with the suggestion that the congressional ban on torture "might" be unconstitutional in the context of battlefield interrogations. So phrased, the suggestion is a form of minimalism, asking for avoidance of the constitutional issue by reading the statute so as not to intrude on the President's authority as Commander in Chief. But the general impression is that the ban probably should be regarded as unconstitutional.

[44] Id at 39.

from any office within the Department of Justice, above all when national security is at risk. But in its endorsement of presidential power, the memorandum on coerced interrogation went well beyond ordinary practice. To be sure, the President has inherent authority to oversee battlefield operations, and Congress has limited power to control such operations. The President also has the inherent authority to conduct interrogations amidst war. But to say the least, it is unusual to say that this authority includes the power to torture people when Congress has expressly said otherwise. The power to command the armed forces is not easily taken to include "inherent" power to torture enemy combatants. Even if it does include that power, it is hard to contend that Congress cannot provide protection against torture.[45]

Whatever one's ultimate judgment on the merits, the memorandum of the Office of Legal Counsel provides a dramatic example of National Security Maximalism—one that may be taken to presage future understandings if that approach ultimately prevails.

B.   JUSTICE CLARENCE THOMAS IN HAMDI

In recent Supreme Court decisions involving the war on terrorism, National Security Maximalism failed to attract a majority opinion.[46] But it made a conspicuous appearance in a remarkable dissenting opinion by Justice Clarence Thomas in the *Hamdi* case.[47] I will turn to the particular facts of the case in due course. For the moment, note that Justice Thomas emphasized, very broadly, that any constitutional judgment in this domain should consider "basic principles of the constitutional structure as it relates to national security and foreign affairs."[48] In his view, the Constitution accords to the President the "primary responsibility . . . to protect the national security and to conduct the na-

---

[45] See Justice Jackson's views in *Youngstown Sheet and Tube Co. v Sawyer*, 343 US 579 (1952) ("The Steel Seizure Case"), explored below. Note that in some applications, the Commander in Chief power is more plausibly read to include the power to torture—when, for example, torture is deemed necessary to prevent an imminent attack on American troops. But even here, Congress almost certainly has the authority to forbid the practice of torture.

[46] See *Rasul*, 124 S Ct 2686 (2004); *Rumsfeld v Padilla*, 124 S Ct 2711 (2004); *Hamdi*, 124 S Ct 2633 (2004).

[47] *Hamdi*, 124 S Ct 2633, 2674 (2004).

[48] Id at 2675.

tion's foreign relations."[49] Hence judicial judgments should be made against the backdrop set by the President's inherent and broadly discretionary power to protect national security.[50]

With respect to the courts, Justice Thomas contended, "it is crucial to recognize that *judicial* interference in these domains destroys the purpose of vesting primary responsibility in a unitary Executive."[51] Judges "lack the relevant information and expertise to second-guess determinations made by the President. . . . "[52] In fact congressional grants of power should be construed generously on the President's behalf, rather than narrowly, so as to fit with institutional limits on the power of the judiciary.[53] Because the executive branch of the federal government "has an overriding interest in protecting the Nation," it can invoke that interest to justify depriving people of liberty.[54] In fact Justice Thomas argued in favor of broad constructions of congressional grants of authority partly to avoid constitutional difficulties: "Although the President very well may have inherent authority to detain those arrayed against our troops, I agree with the plurality that we need not decide that question because Congress has authorized the President to do so."[55]

Justice Thomas's opinion is a form of National Security Maximalism because of its breadth and ambition. There is no effort here to offer a cautious ruling tailored to the facts of the particular case. On the contrary, Justice Thomas speaks generally about the "primary responsibility" of the President in the domain of "national security." In addition, he adopts a kind of clear statement principle in favor of presidential authority, suggesting, at least implicitly, that statutes should be read in a way that does not conflict with the President's inherent authority. But from a reading of the Constitution alone, it would not be entirely clear whether the President or the Congress has primary responsibility in the domain of national security—an issue to which I will return. The important point is that Justice Thomas offers a distinctive vision

---

[49] Id.

[50] Id.

[51] Id at 2676.

[52] Id.

[53] Id at 2677.

[54] Id at 2685.

[55] Id at 2679.

of the constitutional structure, one that accords principal authority to the President and thus exemplifies National Security Maximalism.

In the years since the September 11 attacks, National Security Maximalism has played a large role on the lower federal courts.[56] Two circuits have decided most of the cases involving a conflict between national security and individual liberty: the United States Courts of Appeals for the District of Columbia and for the Fourth Circuit. Both have shown a remarkable tendency toward National Security Maximalism. In nearly every case in which a serious challenge was mounted to the power of the President, the President has prevailed in the courts of appeals.[57] Let us investigate the details.

1. *The D.C. Circuit.* One of the most strikingly maximalist decisions by the D.C. Circuit is *Al Odah v United States*,[58] reversed by the Supreme Court.[59] In its exceedingly ambitious ruling, the court held that aliens captured outside of the United States have no rights under the Due Process Clause. The court said that the Guantanamo Bay detainees were, in law, analogous to German prisoners captured on the battlefield in World War II. The court acknowledged that Guantanamo Bay is controlled by the United States military, but it insisted on the irrelevance of this fact because Cuba has sovereignty over the area.[60] Broadly reading Supreme Court precedents, the court ruled in favor of executive discretion.[61]

A concurring opinion by Judge Randolph (who wrote the ma-

---

[56] The principal exception is *Padilla v Rumsfeld*, 352 F3d 695 (2d Cir 2003), in which the court held that the President could not detain Padilla because he lacked the inherent authority to do so and because Congress had not authorized the detention of American citizens on American soil. Id at 712-18, 722–23. This is an example of minimalism in action, as discussed below.

[57] The only significant exception is id. The evident influence of National Security Maximalism on the lower courts may attest to the reluctance of judges on those courts to reject security-related decisions by the President of the United States; perhaps the Supreme Court, by virtue of its unique position, is bound to be more cautious about embracing National Security Maximalism.

[58] 321 F3d 1134 (DC Cir 2003).

[59] *Rasul*, 124 S Ct 2686 (2004).

[60] 321 F3d at 1143.

[61] Id.

jority opinion as well) went further still, resolving several issues that it was not necessary for him to discuss. Consider his confessedly maximalist opening sentence: "I write separately to add two other grounds for rejecting the detainee's non-habeas claims."[62] The fundamental motivation for his separate opinion seemed to be captured by his final sentence: "The level of threat a detainee poses to United States interests, the amount of intelligence a detainee might be able to provide, the conditions under which the detainee may be willing to cooperate, the disruption visits from family members and lawyers might cause—these types of judgments have traditionally been left to the exclusive discretion of the Executive Branch, and there they should remain."[63] Here is an explicit endorsement of National Security Maximalism.

Other rulings within the D.C. Circuit fall in the same category. In *Center for National Security Studies v Department of Justice*,[64] a divided court of appeals permitted an extraordinary level of secrecy from the executive branch. A number of public interest groups invoked the Freedom of Information Act (FOIA), the common law, and the First Amendment to require the government to release information about those who had been detained in the aftermath of the September 11 attacks. The requested information included names, dates of arrest and release, and reasons for detention. The disclosure request had a strong democratic justification: Evaluation of the executive's behavior could not easily come from a public not provided with this information. In ruling that disclosure was not required, the court relied on a broad interpretation of exemption 7(A) of FOIA, which exempts "records or information compiled for law enforcement purposes . . . to the extent that the production could reasonably be expected to interfere with enforcement proceedings."[65]

As Judge Tatel emphasized in dissent, the court's interpretation of this exemption was exceptionally deferential to the government's vague statements about potential harms.[66] The court was entirely aware of this point. In language that is closely linked to Justice Thomas's dissenting opinion in *Hamdi*, the court empha-

---

[62] Id at 1145.

[63] Id at 1150.

[64] 331 F3d 918 (DC Cir 2003).

[65] 5 USC § 552 (2000).

[66] 331 F3d at 924.

sized that "the judiciary owes some measure of deference to the executive in cases implicating national security, a uniquely executive purview. . . . We have consistently reiterated the principle of deference to the executive in the FOIA context when national security concerns are implicated. . . . [W]e have consistently deferred to executive affidavits predicting harm to the national security, and have found it unwise to undertake searching judicial review."[67] Indeed, the court went so far as to comment on the distinctive nature of the current threat: "America faces an enemy just as real as its former Cold War foes, with capabilities far beyond the capacity of the judiciary to explore."[68] In fact the court insisted that deference was "mandated by the separation of powers,"[69] suggesting that disclosure under FOIA would raise constitutional problems. The court left no doubt about the motivation for its action: "We are in accord with several federal courts that have wisely respected the executive's judgment in prosecuting the national response to terrorism."[70] What is most noteworthy about the decision, then, is not the outcome, but the broad pronouncements about the need to defer to the executive.

Within the District of Columbia, the district courts have shown a similar tendency to National Security Maximalism. Consider, for example, *ACLU v Department of Justice*,[71] in which organizations sought information involving the government's use of Section 215 of the Patriot Act. Section 215 gives the FBI broad power to "make an application for an order requiring production of any tangible things . . . for an investigation to obtain foreign intelligence information . . . or to protect against international terrorism."[72] In particular, the plaintiffs sought to use FOIA to find out (1) the total number of Section 215 requests received by the National Security Law Unit of the FBI and (2) any and all records relating to Section 215. Notwithstanding the fact that the Department of Justice had previously made several disclosures of its behavior under the Patriot Act, the court ruled broadly that the national security exemption of FOIA justified the failure to disclose the in-

---

[67] Id at 926.

[68] Id.

[69] Id.

[70] Id at 932.

[71] 321 F Supp 2d 24 (DDC 2004).

[72] 50 USC § 1681 (2000).

formation. It acknowledged that the "issue is hardly free from doubt," but ruled for the government "because it [was] mindful of the 'long-recognized deference to the executive on national security issues.'"[73] Thus the court deferred, not to specific explanations by the executive, but to the vague claims that release of the number of Section 215 field requests "poses the continuing potential to harm our national security by enabling our adversaries to conduct their intelligence or international terrorist activities more securely."[74] The court's willingness to embrace National Security Maximalism is best understood in light of a background principle in favor of executive power in the domain of national security.

A similar approach can be found in *Edmonds v Department of Justice*.[75] There the court gave an exceedingly broad reading to the "state secrets privilege" so as to dismiss a Privacy Act claim brought by a self-styled whistleblower at the Federal Bureau of Investigation. One of the most striking parts of the court's opinion came in a footnote, in which it addressed the possibility of staying the case rather than dismissing it: "This is due not only to the nature of the information, but also because the imminent threat of terrorism will not be eliminated anytime in the foreseeable future, but is an endeavor that will consume our nation's attention indefinitely."[76] Under FOIA, then, National Security Maximalism has been explicitly endorsed within the D.C. Circuit, in holdings that fit well with the general approach in *Al Odah*.

2. *The Fourth Circuit.* Broad rulings in favor of executive authority have also come from the Fourth Circuit.[77] The most prominent of these is *Hamdi v Rumsfeld*.[78] There the court held that enemy combatants, captured on the battlefield, could be detained indefinitely and without trial, even if they were American citizens. In so ruling, the court relied largely on the President's power as Commander in Chief, contending that this power includes "the authority to detain those captured in armed struggle" and also "to

---

[73] 321 F Supp 2d at 26.

[74] Id.

[75] 323 F Supp 2d 65 (DDC 2004).

[76] Id at 82 n 7.

[77] See, for example, *United States v Moussaoui*, 382 F3d 453 (4th Cir 2004).

[78] 316 F3d 450 (4th Cir 2003), revd, *Hamdi v Rumsfeld*, 124 US 2633 (2004).

deport or detain alien enemies during the duration of hostilities" and "to confiscate or destroy enemy property."[79]

The central question in the case involved the procedural protection, if any, that would accompany the exercise of the Commander in Chief power. The court emphasized the need to defer to the President: "The Constitution's allocation of the warmaking powers reflects not only the expertise and experience lodged within the executive, but also the more fundamental truth that those branches most accountable to the people should be the ones to undertake the ultimate protection and to ask the ultimate sacrifice from them."[80] Hence deference to the executive would be the basic rule.[81] The court was aware that in denying fair procedure, the President was doing something unusual. But changed circumstances justified this step. "As the nature of threats to America evolves, along with the means of carrying those threats out, the nature of enemy combatants may change also. In the face of such change, separation of powers does not deny the executive branch the essential tool of adaptability."[82]

Indeed the court said that the source of the detention was not a statute, but "Article II, Section 2, of the Constitution, wherein the President is given the war power."[83] (I will return to this important statement in due course.) Deference to the President stems from this explicit grant of authority. So long as a detention "is one legitimately made pursuant to the war powers," it must be respected.[84] A general statement on the part of the executive, supporting the claim that a citizen was detained in the course of war and qualified as an enemy combatant, would be sufficient.[85] The court left no doubt that this conclusion stemmed from National Security Maximalism: "The constitutional allocation of war powers affords the President extraordinarily broad authority as Commander in Chief and compels courts to assume a deferential posture."[86]

---

[79] Id at 463.

[80] Id.

[81] Id at 464. Notably, however, the court was careful to limit the reach of its ruling, in a way that suggests a form of minimalism described below. See id at 465.

[82] Id at 466.

[83] Id at 471.

[84] Id.

[85] Id at 472–73.

[86] Id at 474.

That deference required the conclusion that Hamdi could be held indefinitely, even after the end of the relevant hostilities.[87] In reaching this conclusion, the court referred to the judgments of the executive branch, without even pausing to consider what kind of authorization Congress had given it.[88]

III.   Three Problems with National Security Maximalism

> In a government of separated powers, deciding finally on what is a reasonable degree of guaranteed liberty whether in peace or war (or some condition in between) is not well entrusted to the Executive Branch of Government, whose particular responsibility is to maintain security. For reasons of inescapable human nature, the branch of Government asked to counter a serious threat is not the branch on which rests the Nation's entire reliance in striking the balance between the will to win and the cost in liberty on the way to victory. . . . A reasonable balance is more likely to be reached on the judgment of a different branch. . . . Hence the need for an assessment by Congress before citizens are subject to lockup, likewise the need for a clearly expressed congressional resolution of the competing claims.[89]

> Judges are sometimes called upon to be courageous, because they must sometimes stand up to what is generally supreme in a democracy: the popular will. Their most significant roles in our system are to protect the individual criminal defendant against the occasional excesses of that popular will, and to preserve the checks and balances within our constitutional system that are precisely designed to inhibit swift and complete accomplishment of that popular will.[90]

In the abstract, National Security Maximalism has a great deal of appeal. Far more than Congress, the President is in a position to act quickly and decisively to protect the citizenry. He is also likely to be able to acquire relevant information about what must be done and about when to do it. Because the President is

---

[87] Id at 476.

[88] Id. This is a striking contrast with the minimalist approach of the Supreme Court, explored below.

[89] *Hamdi v Rumsfeld*, 124 US 2633, 2655 (2004) (Souter, joined by Ginsburg, concurring in part, dissenting in part, and concurring in the judgment).

[90] Antonin Scalia, *The Rule of Law Is a Law of Rules*, 56 U Chi L Rev 1175, 1180 (1989).

Commander in Chief of the Armed Forces, Congress cannot override the President's judgments about how to carry out a lawful war. Justice Thomas correctly emphasizes that Alexander Hamilton defended the creation of a "unitary executive" as a means of ensuring energy, coordination, and dispatch in the presidency.[91] These qualities are relevant above all in time of war. By contrast, courts lack good tools for assessing the President's claims of military necessity.

At least equally important, judicial errors may turn out to be disastrous rather than merely harmful. To be sure, American practice suggests that judges are most unlikely to err by protecting civil liberties; in our history, it is hard to find even a single case in which judicial protection of freedom seriously damaged national security. But if Liberty Maximalism were accepted, some such errors would become far more probable. In ordinary contexts, even those that involve criminal justice, the stakes are not nearly so high. There is every reason for courts to avoid a decision that leads to freedom for terrorists, or to disclosure of information that helps those who want to kill Americans. Structural concerns, along with simple prudence, argue in favor of considerable judicial deference to presidential choices when national security is at risk. These points provide important cautionary notes; they help to explain why Liberty Maximalism is senseless. But for several reasons, National Security Maximalism should itself be rejected.

A.   TENDENTIOUS READINGS OF THE CONSTITUTION

If National Security Maximalism were mandated by the Constitution, judges would be bound to follow it. But far from requiring National Security Maximalism, the Constitution is best read to forbid it.

No one doubts that the President has considerable power in the domain of national security. I have emphasized that under Article II, he is explicitly authorized to be "Commander in Chief of the Army and Navy of the United States." He is allowed "to make Treaties," at least when two-thirds of the senators concur. He is authorized to "appoint Ambassadors" and "other public Ministers and Consuls." He "shall receive Ambassadors and other public

---

[91] See *Hamdi*, 124 S Ct at 2675–76. For general discussion, see Lawrence Lessig and Cass R. Sunstein, *The President and the Administration*, 94 Colum L Rev 1 (1994).

Ministers." But none of this supports Justice Thomas's suggestion that the President has "primary responsibility—along with the necessary power—to protect the national security and to conduct the Nation's foreign relations." Nor does anything in the document support the Fourth Circuit's suggestion that under Article II, "the President is given the war power." On the contrary, that view is a tendentious reading of the legal materials. To see why, let us turn to Article I.

Perhaps most notably, Congress, rather than the President, has the power "to declare War." [92] The Constitution also grants Congress, not the President, the power "to raise and support Armies." It authorizes Congress "to provide and maintain a Navy." In a formulation that bears on the President's supposedly inherent power to torture, and that much complicates any claims about the broad power of the Commander in Chief, the founding document permits Congress to "make Rules for the Government and Regulation of the land and naval Forces." It is Congress that is authorized to raise funds to "provide for the common Defense and general Welfare of the United States." Congress, rather than the President, is empowered to "regulate Commerce with foreign nations." Congress is also authorized to "define and punish Piracies and Felonies committed on the high Seas, and Offenses against the Law of Nations," and also to "make Rules concerning Captures on Land and Water." It is under Article I, not Article II, that the Constitution allows suspension of habeas corpus "when in Cases of Rebellion or Invasion the public Safety may require it." The fact that the Suspension Clause can be found in Article I tends to suggest that Congress, not the President, is entitled to suspend the writ.[93]

In this light, the Constitution does not repose in the President anything like the general authority "to protect the national security." On the contrary, the more natural reading of the document is that protection of national security is parceled out between Congress and the President—and that if either has the dominant role, it is the national lawmaker. To be sure, the Commander in Chief Clause does give the President the authority to direct the armed forces, an

---

[92] For treatment of some of the complexities here, with reference to the literature, see Curtis Bradley and Jack Goldsmith, *Congressional Authorization and the War on Terrorism*, Harv L Rev (forthcoming 2005).

[93] See below.

expansive authority;[94] but even that authority is subject to legislative constraints, because Congress controls the budget and because Congress can choose not to declare war. And if Congress refuses either to authorize the use of force or to declare war, the President is generally not—on the best reading of the document—entitled to commence hostilities.[95] The Commander in Chief Clause allows the President to manage wars; but it does not give him "the war power." All of this means that National Security Maximalism cannot claim a strong constitutional pedigree.

Of course, the constitutional text is hardly all there is to our constitutional tradition.[96] In the domain of separation of powers, historical practices and changes over time are highly relevant. As Justice Frankfurter contended, "It is an inadmissibly narrow conception of American constitutional law to confine it to the words of the Constitution and to disregard the gloss which life has written upon them."[97] In this context, an understanding of that "gloss" greatly favors the President. There can be no doubt that for questions of national security, the President has assumed authority that the text alone might not sanction. The power to make war is a leading example; the President has long engaged in military actions without the kind of legislative authorization that Article I appears to require.[98]

Historical "glosses" on constitutional text might well be taken to argue in the direction of National Security Maximalism. They make it plausible to contend that the President has more authority, in the domain of national security, than the document alone appears to contemplate. Undoubtedly the increasing power of the President is largely a product of functional considerations having to do with

---

[94] See *Loving v United States*, 517 US 748 (1996).

[95] The principal exception is that the President is always permitted to repel sudden attacks—a category that is not self-defining. See John Hart Ely, *Suppose Congress Wanted a War Powers Act That Worked*, 88 Colum L Rev 1379, 1388 (1988); Note, *Congress, the President, and the Power to Commit Forces to Combat*, 81 Harv L Rev 1771, 1782 (1968).

[96] The best discussion is David A. Strauss, *Common Law Constitutional Interpretation*, 63 U Chi L Rev 877 (1996).

[97] See *Youngstown Co.*, 343 US at 610–11. For general discussion, see Bradley and Goldsmith, Harv L Rev (forthcoming 2005) (cited in note 92).

[98] For relevant discussion, see Harold Koh, *The National Security Constitution: Sharing Power after the Iran-Contra Affair* 38–41 (Yale, 1990); John Hart Ely, *The American War in Indochina, Part I: The (Troubled) Constitutionality of the War They Told Us About*, 42 Stan L Rev 877 (1989); Gregory Sidak, *To Declare War*, 41 Duke L J 29 (1991); Harold Koh, *The Coase Theorem and the War Power: A Response*, 41 Duke L J 122, 127 (1991).

the rise of the United States as an international power and the growing need for energy and dispatch. But even when the document is thus glossed, it remains tendentious to contend that when the nation is at risk, the President must be in charge of the apparatus of government. To say this is to reject a constitutional accommodation that, by text and tradition, unambiguously retains Congress's role as the nation's lawmaker.

B.   THE INCENTIVES OF THE EXECUTIVE BRANCH

The second problem with National Security Maximalism is that it understates the risks of unlimited presidential authority. The executive branch perceives protection of the nation's security as one of its principal tasks, in part because political retribution will fall swiftly on any President who fails in that task. When the nation is under threat, the executive will naturally take precautionary steps to reduce the risks. So far, so good. But recall here Attorney General Biddle's suggestion: "The Constitution has never greatly bothered any wartime President."[99] The question is whether internal dynamics, or external checks, will help to ensure that the precautionary steps are optimal rather than excessive. For two reasons, National Security Maximalism is far too optimistic on that count.[100]

1. *Internal dynamics, unitariness, and group polarization.* Internal dynamics present a serious problem, precisely because the executive branch is designed so as to be neither diverse nor deliberative, certainly as compared with the national legislature. As Justice Thomas emphasized in *Hamdi*, the executive branch is "unitary" in principle;[101] it is run by a single person, and he is constitutionally entitled to fill his branch with like-minded people. And here is a real difficulty. One of the most robust findings in modern social science is that after deliberation, like-minded people tend to end up thinking a more extreme version of what they thought before deliberation began.[102] Ordinary processes within the executive branch are all too likely to produce not careful investigation of

---

[99] Biddle, *In Brief Authority* at 219 (cited in note 2).

[100] For relevant discussion, see Dominic Johnson, *Overconfidence and War: The Havoc and Glory of Positive Illusions* (Harvard, 2004).

[101] See sources cited in note 91.

[102] See Cass R. Sunstein, *Why Societies Need Dissent* (Harvard, 2003).

alternatives, but a heightened version of what executive branch officials believed in advance.[103] As a result, liberty might well be at risk.[104]

Of course a presidential disposition in favor of liberty over security[105] can alter this dynamic. Suppose, for example, that the President and his advisers believe that some national security risk is trivial while a small group within the administration disagrees. It is predictable that precautionary steps will not be taken even though they are justified.[106] Deliberative processes among like-minded people can produce excessive rather than insufficient concern for liberty.[107] In addition, a system of internal checks and balances can alter the dynamic by which groups end up amplifying their antecedent tendencies.[108] Different agencies and departments often have different agendas and interests; consider the notorious fact that the Department of State and the Department of Defense often disagree on issues of both law and policy. A President can certainly take steps to ensure a diversity of views; it is possible to structure executive branch processes so as to create internal safeguards.[109]

My only suggestion here is that there can be no assurance that the executive branch, consisting of people who work under a single president and usually seeking internal consensus, will consider the relevant factors in a way that produces sensible outcomes. If the outlook of the President and his closest advisers includes a predisposition toward aggressive steps to counteract national security risks, even at the expense of liberty, the executive branch is likely to blunder. History offers countless illustrations.[110]

As an example of a failure of deliberation within the executive branch, consider the account in the 2004 report of the Senate Select Committee on Intelligence, which explicitly accused the Central In-

---

[103] See Irving Janis, *Groupthink* (Houghton Mifflin, 1983), for many examples.

[104] Many of the findings in Stone, *Perilous Times* (cited in note 14), can be explained in part in this way.

[105] Note that such a disposition might be literally dangerous, see Posner and Vermeule, 56 Stan L Rev 605 (cited in note 12).

[106] In fact this is one view of the situation in the United States before the attack of September 11.

[107] See Adrian Vermeule, *Libertarian Panics* (unpublished draft 11/04).

[108] See Sunstein, *Why Societies Need Dissent* (cited in note 102).

[109] See Cass R. Sunstein, *Group Judgments*, NYU L Rev (forthcoming 2005).

[110] For illustrations, see Janis, *Groupthink* (cited in note 103); Stone, *Perilous Times* (cited in note 14).

telligence Agency (CIA) of groupthink, in which the agency's predisposition to find a serious threat from Iraq led it to fail to explore alternative possibilities or to obtain and use the information that it actually held.[111] In the Committee's view, the CIA "demonstrated several aspects of group think: examining few alternatives, selective gathering of information, pressure to conform within the group or withhold criticism, and collective rationalization."[112] Thus the agency showed a "tendency to reject information that contradicted the presumption" that Iraq had weapons of mass destruction.[113] Because of that presumption, the agency failed to use its own formalized methods "to challenge assumptions and 'group think,' such as 'red teams,' 'devil's advocacy,' and other types of alternative or competitive analysis."[114] Above all, the Committee's conclusions emphasize the CIA's failure to elicit and aggregate information. Through processes of this sort, it is easy to imagine that liberty could be sacrificed in favor of national security, even if there is no adequate justification for the sacrifice.

The claim of the Senate Select Committee is a remarkable and even uncanny echo of one that followed the 2003 investigation of failures at NASA, stressing that agency's similar failure to elicit competing views, including those based on information held by agency employees.[115] The Columbia Accident Investigation Board explicitly attributed the accident to NASA's unfortunate culture, one that does too little to elicit information. In the Board's words, NASA lacks "checks and balances."[116] It pressures people to follow a "party line."[117] At NASA, "it is difficult for minority and dissenting opinions to percolate up through the agency's hierarchy"[118]—even though, the Board contended, effective safety programs require the encouragement of minority opinions and bad news. Here too the unitariness of the relevant agency was a central source of the problem.

---

[111] Available at http://intelligence.senate.gov/ (visited Dec 1, 2004).

[112] Id. Conclusions at 4.

[113] Id at 6.

[114] Id at 8.

[115] NASA, 1 *Report of the Columbia Accident Investigation Board*, available at http://www.nasa.gov/columbia/home/CAIB_Vol1.html (visited Dec 1, 2004).

[116] Id at 12.

[117] Id at 102.

[118] Id at 183.

These examples of executive branch failure reflect the process known as *group polarization*, through which like-minded people often go to unjustified extremes.[119] If those within an executive agency believe that Iraq has weapons of mass destruction, that very belief is likely to be heightened after members have started to talk. And if those within the executive branch think that some abridgement of civil liberties is necessary and desirable as a precautionary measure, internal deliberations are likely to produce polarization in the direction of the antecedent belief. Of course internal deliberations will not produce a final outcome if external political checks exist; an outraged public is often able to discipline presidential choices. Sometimes political checks will ensure against unjustified intrusions on liberty. But to understand this point, we have to make a distinction.

2. *Selective denials of liberty.* Some restrictions on liberty apply to all or most—as in, for example, a general increase in security procedures at airports, or a measure that subjects everyone, citizens and noncitizens alike, to special scrutiny when they are dealing with substances that might be used in bioterrorism. Other restrictions on liberty apply to some or few—as in, for example, restrictions on Japanese Americans during World War II, racial profiling, or the confinement of enemy aliens at Guantanamo Bay.[120] When restrictions apply to all or most, it is reasonable to think that political safeguards provide a strong check on unjustified government action. If the burden of the restriction is widely shared, it is unlikely to be acceptable unless most people are convinced that there is good reason for it; and for genuinely burdensome restrictions, people will not be easily convinced unless a good reason is apparent or provided. But if the restriction is imposed on an identifiable subgroup, the political check is weakened. Liberty-reducing intrusions can be imposed even if they are difficult to justify. These are the circumstances in which political checks are unlikely to provide an adequate safeguard against unjustified presidential intrusions on liberty.[121]

---

[119] See S. Moscovici and M. Zavalloni, *The Group as a Polarizer of Attitudes*, 12 J Personality and Soc Psychol 125 (1969).

[120] See Cole, *Enemy Aliens* (cited in note 13).

[121] Of course we can imagine cases in which it is not easy to tell whether the denial is general or selective. I have suggested that intrusions on those who board airplanes, or use public spaces, are general, simply because such a heterogeneous group of people is burdened. But imagine a law that makes it a crime to advocate terrorism, or to disclose information that compromises national security. Measures of this kind burden everyone,

These claims can be illuminated by a glance at the views of Frederick Hayek about the rule of law. Hayek writes, "how comparatively innocuous, even if irksome, are most such restrictions imposed on literally everybody, as . . . compared with those that are likely to be imposed only on some!"[122] Thus it is "significant that most restrictions on what we regard as private affairs, such as sumptuary legislation, have usually been imposed only on selected groups of people or, as in the case of prohibition, were practicable only because the government reserved the right to grant exceptions."[123] Hayek urges, in short, that the risk of unjustified burdens dramatically increases if they are selective and if most people have nothing to worry about. The claim is especially noteworthy in situations in which the executive is imposing restrictions on civil liberties. People are likely to ask, with some seriousness, whether those restrictions are in fact justified *if* the result is burdensome consequences on them. But if other people face the relevant burdens, then the mere fact of "risk," and the mere presence of fear, will seem to provide a justification.

The danger of unjustified infringement is amplified when the victims of the infringement can be seen as an identifiable group that is readily separable from "us." Stereotyping of groups significantly increases when people are in a state of fear; when people are primed to think about their own death, they are more likely to think and act in accordance with group-based stereotypes.[124] Experimental findings of this kind support the intuitive idea that when people are afraid, they are far more likely to tolerate government action that abridges the freedom of members of some "out-group." And if this is the case, responses to social fear, in the form of infringements on liberties, will not receive the natural political checks that arise when majorities suffer as well as benefit from them. The simple idea here is that liberty-infringing action is most likely to be justified if those who support that action are also burdened

---

in a sense; they do not affect an antecedently identifiable group such as Japanese Americans, noncitizens, or Muslims. In practice, however, the burdens imposed by such laws would be faced by a few rather than many. Perhaps the best way to deal with the question, at least for such restrictions, is to insist on strong protection of free speech, at least when there is no imminent risk of serious harm.

[122] Friedrich A. von Hayek, *The Constitution of Liberty* 155 (Chicago, 1960).

[123] Id.

[124] See William von Hippel et al., *Attitudinal Process versus Context: The Role of Information Processing Biases in Social Judgment and Behavior*, in Joseph P. Forgas et al., eds, *Social Judgments* 251, 263 (Cambridge, 2003).

by it; in that event, the political process contains a built-in protection against unjustifiable restrictions. In all cases, it follows that free societies need some methods for ensuring against excessive reactions to unjustified intrusions on civil liberties.

Consider in this regard an argument in a famous opinion by Justice Robert Jackson.[125] In that opinion, Justice Jackson made two points. The first is that when the Court rules that some conduct cannot be regulated at all, it is intervening, in a major way, into democratic processes, making that conduct essentially "unregulable." The second is that when the Court invalidates government action on equality grounds, it requires the government to increase the breadth of its restriction, thus triggering political checks against unjustified burdens. With a modest twist on Jackson's argument, we can see a potential approach for courts faced with claims about unlawful interference with civil liberties. If the executive is imposing a burden on an identifiable subclass of people, a warning flag should go up. The courts should give careful scrutiny to that burden.

Of course these general propositions do not resolve concrete cases; everything turns on the particular nature of the legal challenge. In addition, the incidence of benefits and burdens might result, in theory, in too much liberty rather than too much security. Assume, for example, that government is asked to take steps that would provide security to an identifiable subgroup rather than to the public as a whole, whereas the burden of this step would be faced by everyone; if so, we should expect it to err in the direction of insufficient protection of security, precisely for the reasons that Jackson emphasizes.[126] The existence of selective benefits and burdens does not always show that the executive will unduly sacrifice liberty; the opposite may be true.[127] But an appreciation of the risks of selectivity suggests the problems with National Security Maximalism. Political processes are unlikely to provide an adequate check when government imposes burdens on people who are unable to

---

[125] *Railway Express Agency v New York*, 336 US 106, 112–13 (1949) (Jackson, J, concurring).

[126] For example, those concerned with the problem of "environmental justice" emphasize the failure to protect identifiable subcommunities against environmental risks. See generally Alan Boyle and Michael Anderson, *Human Rights Approach to Environmental Protection* (Oxford, 1996). This failure might easily be explained in Jacksonian terms.

[127] See Vermeule, *Libertarian Panics* (cited in note 107). I am abstracting here from obvious complexities, including the possibility that certain groups are especially well organized, enabling them to obtain measures favorable to their interests or to fend off measures that are unfavorable to those interests.

protect themselves in the political process. The legislature has some advantages over the executive on this count, simply because it is both diverse and deliberative, in a way that ought to ensure a degree of representation for identifiable groups that are at risk.

To summarize: National Security Maximalism cannot claim much support in the Constitution itself; on the contrary, the document does not give the President "the war power." The strongest claim for a maximalist approach emphasizes the Commander in Chief Clause, which does give the President some "inherent" power; but that power must be read in the light of a host of other provisions conferring broad authority on Congress. In addition, National Security Maximalism reposes excessive confidence in the President. Deliberative processes within a unitary branch are likely to lead to an amplification of preexisting tendencies, not toward a system of internal checks and balances. When deprivations of liberty are limited to an identifiable few—as they frequently are—external checks on the executive provide an insufficient safeguard of civil liberties. But Liberty Maximalism is neither feasible nor desirable. Is there anything that courts might do to help? And what does American history say about that question?

IV.   THE MINIMALIST ALTERNATIVE

> Even more important than the method of selecting the people's rulers and their successors is the character of the constraints imposed on the Executive by the rule of law.[128]

As an alternative to National Security Maximalism, we might imagine a minimalist approach. But what, precisely, is minimalism? It is easy to imagine a range of answers, simply because minimalism is relative, not absolute. Suppose that a court requires congressional authorization for presidential detentions of American citizens on American soil. That ruling is more minimalist than a decision to require congressional authorization for any and all presidential detentions; but it is less minimalist than a ruling that in the particular circumstances of a given case, the President must obtain congressional authorization to detain a particular American citizen on

---

[128] *Rumsfeld v Padilla*, 124 S Ct 2711, 2735 (2004) (Stevens dissenting).

American soil. With respect to minimalism, there is a continuum rather than a set of dichotomies.[129]

- Belonging at the minimalist extreme is a refusal to hear a case at all, as in a denial of certiorari or a jurisdictional ruling. Refusals to adjudicate offer no guidance at all. They leave everything undecided.
- Slightly less minimalist is an authoritative ruling, and therefore a holding, but one that is unaccompanied by much in the way of reasoning—as in, for example, a judgment without opinion or a ruling whose rationale is so thin and vague that it fails to give a real account of why the court ruled as it did.
- Less minimalist, but firmly within the minimalist camp, is a narrow and shallow decision, tightly tied to the facts of the particular case and avoiding broad statements about the relevant law.
- Still less minimalist, but minimalist still, is a set of established doctrines that embody a self-conscious refusal to rule ambitiously. Consider, for example, the avoidance canon—the notion that statutes should be construed so as to avoid constitutional doubts.[130] This idea is less minimalist than an insistent (stubborn? infuriating?) refusal to specify the circumstances under which statutes will and should be so construed. In its way, the avoidance canon is wide and therefore ambitious. In fact the avoidance canon could well be justified deeply rather than shallowly—by emphasizing, for example, the value of congressional rather than merely executive deliberation on constitutionally sensitive issues.[131] Nonetheless, the avoidance canon is easily taken as part of the minimalist project. The reason is that it leaves the most fundamental issues undecided; it refuses to take a stand on the contested issues of constitutional law.

In the context of war, minimalists want above all to avoid large-scale interventions into democratic processes. They do so because they know how little they know, and because they generally respect the wishes of a threatened nation, at least when Congress and the

---

[129] As discussed above, the same is true for maximalism; I use National Security Maximalism and Liberty Maximalism as endpoints on a continuum.

[130] See, for example, *Yates v United States*, 354 US 298 (1957).

[131] Cass R. Sunstein, *Nondelegation Canons*, 67 U Chi L Rev 315 (2000).

executive branch agree. Of course sensible people acknowledge that courts should strike down egregious violations of constitutional rights. But outside of the egregious cases, courts should proceed cautiously and narrowly when national security is at risk. As I understand it here, the minimalist project is built on three principles in the context of war. First, Congress should be required to authorize any interference with constitutionally protected interests; as a general rule, the executive should not be allowed to proceed on its own. Second, any deprivation of liberty, at the individual level, should be accompanied by at least minimally fair procedures. Third, judicial decisions should be narrow and incompletely theorized. As we shall see, these three principles, the cornerstones of minimalism at war, do a remarkably good job of explaining the practices of the Supreme Court amidst war. The first principle is the most complex, and it provides the place to begin.[132]

A. CLEAR STATEMENT PRINCIPLES

1. *The basic framework.* For many years, Israel's General Security Service has engaged in certain forms of physical coercion, sometimes described as torture, against suspected terrorists. According to the General Security Service, these practices occurred only in extreme cases and as a last resort, when deemed necessary to prevent terrorist activity and significant loss of life. Nonetheless, practices worthy of the name "torture" did occur, and they were not rare. Those practices were challenged before the Supreme Court of Israel on the ground that they were inconsistent with the nation's fundamental law. The government responded that abstractions about human rights should not be permitted to overcome real-world necessities so as to ban a practice that was, in certain circumstances, essential to prevent massive deaths in an area of the world that was often subject to terrorist activity. According to the government, physical coercion was justified in these circumstances. A judicial decision to the opposite effect would be a form of unjustified activism, even hubris.

In deciding the case, the Supreme Court of Israel refused to

---

[132] For valuable general discussion, see Pildes and Issacharoff, *Civil Libertarianism* (cited in note 15); for valuable discussion in the context of authorizations to use force, see Bradley and Goldmith, Harv L Rev (forthcoming 2005) (cited in note 97).

resolve the most fundamental questions.[133] It declined to say whether the practices of the security forces would be illegitimate if expressly authorized by a democratic legislature. But the Court nonetheless held those practices unlawful. The Court's principal argument was that if such coercion were to be acceptable, it could not be because the General Security Service, with its narrow agenda, said so. At a minimum, the disputed practices must be endorsed by the national legislature, after a full democratic debate on the precise question. "[T]his is an issue that must be decided by the legislative branch which represents the people. We do not take any stand on this matter at this time. It is there that various considerations must be weighed."[134]

It is worthwhile to pause over the central feature of this decision. The Supreme Court of Israel required clear legislative authorization for this particular intrusion on liberty; it insisted that executive action, under a vague or ambiguous law, would not be enough. The Court's decision stands for the general principle that even when national security is threatened, the legislative branch of government must explicitly authorize disputed infringements on civil liberty. The reason for this safeguard is to ensure against inadequately considered restrictions—and to insist that political safeguards, in the form of agreement from a diverse and deliberative branch of government, are a minimal precondition for intrusions on civil liberties. In these ways, the requirement of clear legislative statement enlists the idea of checks and balances in the service of individual rights—not through flat bans on government action, but through requiring two, rather than one, branches of government to approve.

The Office of Legal Counsel memorandum, sketched above, provides a startling and ironic contrast here. While the Supreme Court of Israel held that clear legislative *authorization* is required to permit torture, the United States Department of Justice concluded that clear legislative *prohibition* is insufficient to forbid torture. But it is reasonable to doubt whether the Supreme Court of the United States would accept this reasoning. The reason is that in a large number of cases, many involving national security, the

---

[133] *Association for Civil Rights in Israel v The General Security Service* (1999). Supreme Court of Israel: Judgment Concerning the Legality of the General Security Service's Interrogation Methods, 38 ILM 1471 (1999).

[134] Id.

Court has required a clear congressional statement before permitting the executive to intrude on an interest that has a plausible claim to constitutional protection. These decisions can be understood to create "nondelegation canons"—canons of construction ensuring that Congress and the President jointly, rather than the President alone, will make decisions on constitutionally sensitive issues.[135] In the context of threats to national security, nondelegation canons provide a cornerstone of the practice of minimalism at war.

As a leading example, consider *Kent v Dulles*,[136] decided in the midst of the Cold War. In that case, the Secretary of State, John Foster Dulles, denied a passport to Rockwell Kent, a member of the Communist Party, who sought to attend a meeting of the "World Council of Peace" in Helsinki, Finland. The State Department denied the passport on two grounds, both supported by its own regulations. First, Kent was a Communist; second, Kent had "a consistent and prolonged adherence to the Communist Party line." Under the governing statute, enacted in 1926, the Secretary of State was authorized "to grant and issue passports . . . under such rules as the President shall designate and prescribe for, and on behalf of, the United States . . . ."[137] Kent objected that the denial of the passport was unconstitutional.

The Supreme Court could have decided the case on any number of grounds. It could have said that Kent's First Amendment rights had been violated—that it was unconstitutional to deny someone a passport because of his political convictions. It could have said that the decision of the Secretary of State violated Kent's right to travel—that the Due Process Clause includes a right to leave the country and that the government needs particularly strong grounds for interfering with that right. It could have said that the grant of open-ended discretion to the Secretary of State violated the nondelegation doctrine—that under Article I, Section 1, Congress must give the Secretary some guidelines by which to decide whether to grant or to deny passports. Or it could have said that the denial of the passport was lawful—authorized by the language of the relevant statute and, as authorized, within constitutional

---

[135] See Cass R. Sunstein, 67 U Chi L Rev 315 (cited in note 131).

[136] 357 US 116 (1958).

[137] Act of July 3, 1926, ch 772, 44 Stat 887, Part 2, codified as amended at 22 USC § 211a (2000).

bounds. All of these routes would have been simple and straight-forward.

The Court did none of these things. Instead it held that the denial of the passport was beyond the statutory authority of the Secretary of State. Its analysis began with a bow in the direction of constitutional requirements. In the Court's view, the "right to travel is a part of the 'liberty' of which the citizen cannot be deprived without due process of law under the Fifth Amendment."[138] The question of statutory authority would be approached in this light. And while the statute was phrased in broad terms, the Secretary had "long exercised" his power "quite narrowly."[139] In fact passports had been refused in only two categories of cases: those in which the applicant's citizenship and allegiance to the United States were in doubt; and those in which the applicant was engaged in unlawful conduct. No one claimed that Kent fell in either of these categories. "We, therefore, hesitate to impute to Congress, when in 1952 it made a passport necessary for foreign travel and left its issuance to the discretion of the Secretary of State, a purpose to give him unbridled discretion to grant or with-hold a passport from a citizen for any substantive reason he may choose."[140] The Court was concerned that Congress had not par-ticularly authorized the executive branch to do as it did. "No such showing of extremity, no such showing of joint action by the Chief Executive and the Congress to curtail a constitutional right of the citizen has been made here."[141]

The Court left no doubt that its decision was constitutionally inspired. It drew attention to the fact that the case involved "an exercise by an American citizen of an activity included in consti-tutional protection."[142] For that reason, the Court would "not readily infer that Congress gave the Secretary of State unbridled discretion."[143] The right of exit had constitutional foundations, and if it is "to be regulated, it must be pursuant to the law-making functions of the Congress."[144] Hence the Court would "construe

---

[138] 357 US at 125.

[139] Id at 127.

[140] Id at 128.

[141] Id.

[142] Id at 129.

[143] Id.

[144] Id.

narrowly all delegated powers that curtail or dilute" those "activities and enjoyment, natural and often necessary to the well-being of an American citizen."[145] The Court explicitly linked its narrow construction with the nondelegation principle, citing cases that require any delegation to be accompanied by intelligible standards.[146] The Court emphasized that it "would be faced with important constitutional questions" if Congress "had given the Secretary authority to withhold passports to citizens because of their beliefs or associations."[147] But "Congress has made no such provision in explicit terms."[148] Proceeding in minimalist fashion, the Court left undecided the question whether Congress could constitutionally give that authority to the President. The advantage of the minimalist approach is that it reflects commendable uncertainty about difficult questions, enlisting political safeguards as the first line of defense against unjustified intrusions on freedom.

Was *Kent v Dulles* decided during war? In a sense, it was not; military forces were not engaged in 1958, and the Court was aware of that fact. The Court explicitly noted that "more restrictive measures were applied in 1918 and in 1941 as war measures," and it said that it would not "equate this present problem of statutory construction with problems that may arise under the war power."[149] But in 1958, the Cold War was at its height, and in the period many people believed that the United States was, in some sense, at war with the Soviet Union.[150]

Did *Kent v Dulles* involve the Commander in Chief Clause? That clause was not directly mentioned. But the Court's crucial citation, in *Kent v Dulles*, involved an explicit reference to a case involving the Commander in Chief power: *The Steel Seizure Case*.[151] In that case, the Court's method was exceedingly close to that used in *Kent v Dulles*. Hence *The Steel Seizure Case* is highly relevant to the question of presidential power when national security is at

---

[145] Id.

[146] Id.

[147] Id at 130.

[148] Id.

[149] Id at 128.

[150] In the First Amendment context, the Supreme Court followed a similar approach in *Yates v United States*, 354 US 298 (1957), decided only one year before *Kent v Dulles*. In *Yates*, the Court narrowly construed the Smith Act so as to protect the abstract advocacy of overthrowing the government. See below for a more detailed discussion.

[151] *Youngstown Co.*, 343 US 579 (1952).

risk. That much-discussed decision is illuminatingly seen in minimalist terms.

In 1951, the President directed the Secretary of Commerce to take possession of, and to operate, the majority of steel mills in the United States. The directive was prompted by a threatened strike in the steel industry, one that would apparently jeopardize the continued availability of steel. According to the President, national defense was at risk, because steel was indispensable as a component in nearly all weapons and war materials. The President defended his action as justified by his power as Commander-in-Chief of the Armed Forces. But the Supreme Court firmly rejected the argument. It emphasized that there "is no statute that expressly authorizes the President to take possession of the property as he did here. Nor is there any act of Congress to which our attention has been directed from which such a power can fairly be implied."[152] It stressed that lawmaking power is vested in Congress, not in the President: "The Founders of this Nation entrusted the lawmaking power to the Congress alone in both good and bad times. It would do no good to recall the historical events, the fears of power and the hopes for freedom that lay behind their choice."[153] Justice Frankfurter wrote separately, also emphasizing the need for both minimalism and checks and balances.[154] But Justice Frankfurter's opinion, and that of the Court itself, have come to be less important than the concurring opinion of Justice Jackson, who explored in some detail the central importance of a grant of authority from Congress.[155]

Jackson famously offered a tripartite division of presidential authority, suggesting that the President's "authority is at its maximum"[156] when he is acting under an authorization from Congress, and "at its lowest ebb" when the President's exercise of power is "incompatible with the expressed or implied will of Congress."[157] Less famously but also significantly, Jackson offered a narrow construction of the Commander in Chief Clause, and showed a great deal of skepticism about the idea of "inherent" presidential power.

---

[152] Id at 585.

[153] Id at 589.

[154] Id at 593 (Frankfurter concurring).

[155] Id at 634 (Jackson concurring).

[156] Id at 635.

[157] Id at 637.

The Commander in Chief Clause, he said, "undoubtedly puts the Nation's armed forces under presidential command."[158] But it could not be taken "as support for any presidential action, internal or external, involving use of force . . . ."[159] More broadly, Justice Jackson said that "no doctrine that the Court could promulgate would seem to me more sinister and alarming than that a President whose conduct of foreign affairs is so largely uncontrolled, and often even is so unknown, can vastly enlarge his mastery over the internal affairs of the country by his own commitment of the Nation's armed forces to some foreign venture."[160] Jackson challenged the "loose and irresponsible use of adjectives" that affected "much legal discussion of presidential powers," including adjectives like inherent, implied, incidental, war, plenary, and emergency.[161] Jackson expressed skepticism about these adjectives, suggesting that they amounted to an effort to "amend" the work of those who produced the Constitution.

2. *Illustrations.* Jackson's legislature-centered framework helps to organize a remarkable number of Supreme Court decisions involving civil liberty and war, many of them written before *The Steel Seizure Case*. Time and again, the Court has emphasized the importance of congressional authorization for presidential action and refused to rule that the President has the power to act on his own. In these ways, the Court has acted in good minimalist fashion, leaving many of the most fundamental questions undecided.[162]

Consider, for example, *Ex Parte Endo*,[163] in which the Court struck down the detention of concededly loyal Japanese Americans on the West Coast. The case involved a petition for a writ of habeas corpus, sought on behalf of Mitsue Endo, a loyal citizen who had been placed in a relocation center. The Court held that Endo would have to be released. In so holding, it relied on the absence of statutory authorization for her detention. "In reaching that conclusion we do not come to the underlying constitutional issues which have been argued. For we conclude that, whatever power the War Relocation Authority may have to detain other

---

[158] Id at 641.

[159] Id.

[160] Id at 642.

[161] Id at 646–47.

[162] See Pildes and Issacharoff, *Civil Libertarianism* (cited in note 15).

[163] 320 US 81 (1943).

classes of citizens, it has no authority to subject citizens who are concededly loyal to its leave procedure."[164] The Court emphasized that even in the midst of war, the President would have to identify clear statutory authorization for any such detention: "In interpreting a wartime measure we must assume that their purpose was to allow for the greatest possible accommodation between those liberties and the exigencies of war."[165] Thus the constitutional issues would be avoided in light of "the silence of the legislative history and of the Act and the Executive Orders on the power to detain."[166] The Court added that "if there is to be the greatest possible accommodation of the liberties of the citizen with this war measure, any such implied power [of the President] must be narrowly confined to the precise purpose of the evacuation program."[167]

To be sure, the Court had also held, on the same day, that the forced evacuation of Japanese Americans was acceptable as a matter of statutory and constitutional law—a holding to which I will turn in due course.[168] But as in *Kent v Dulles*, the Court emphasized that for the evacuation, "the Congress and the Chief Executive moved in coordinated action"[169]—a clear signal that the existence of simultaneous and explicit approval by both branches was both necessary and sufficient to produce judicial deference. The clarity of the signal is underlined by a pointed reference to *Endo* in *Kent v Dulles* itself, citing *Endo* to support the proposition that narrow construction of delegated powers is appropriate when "activities or enjoyment, natural and often necessary to the well-being of an American citizen, such as travel, are involved."[170]

----

[164] Id at 297.

[165] Id at 300.

[166] Id.

[167] Id at 302. Note, however, that the Court refused to decide the case until *after* Roosevelt decided to end the internment; the Court announced its decision the next day. To say the least, this was not a tribute to judicial courage.

[168] See *Korematsu v United States*, 323 US 214 (1943). The line between *Korematsu* and *Endo* was explained in this way by the Court: "The *Endo* case, post, graphically illustrates the difference between the validity of an order to exclude and the validity of a detention order after exclusion has been effected." Id at 222. For discussion, see Patrick O. Gudridge, *Remember Endo?* 116 Harv L Rev 1933 (2003); Stone, *Perilous Times* at 302–03 (cited in note 14).

[169] 357 US at 128.

[170] Id at 129.

In the same spirit is *Duncan v Kahanamoku*,[171] involving the imposition of martial law in Hawaii during World War II. Civilians in Hawaii had been imprisoned after a trial in military tribunals; the central question was whether those tribunals had the legal authority to try civilians. In its narrow ruling, the Court held that they did not. The Court concluded that the Hawaii Organic Act did allow the governor of the state to declare martial law, but it refused to agree that as a statutory matter, the governor of the state, even with presidential approval, could "close all the courts and supplant them with military tribunals."[172] The Court acknowledged that the statutory language and history were unclear and stressed, as relevant to the interpretive question, "the birth, development, and growth of our political institutions."[173] Because "courts and their procedural safeguards are indispensable to our system of government," the Court would not construe an ambiguous statute to authorize the displacement, by the executive, of ordinary courts with military tribunals.[174]

The oldest example of a minimalist approach to civil liberties can be found during the Civil War period. President Lincoln suspended the writ of habeas corpus, referring to Section 9, clause 2 of the Constitution, which says, "The Privilege of Writ of Habeas Corpus shall not be suspended, unless when in Cases of Rebellion or Invasion the public Safety may require it."[175] The Suspension Clause is phrased in the passive voice; it does not say who may suspend the great writ. Chief Justice Roger Taney ruled that the President could not suspend the writ on his own; he needed congressional authorization.[176] Chief Justice Taney was able to point to the fact that the Suspension Clause is found in Article I, which specifies the powers of Congress, rather than Article II, which deals with presidential authority. The textual argument is certainly powerful, but Chief Justice Taney's conclusion is also supported by a structural concern, to the effect that suspension of habeas corpus is a grave act, one that requires a judgment by a body that is both deliberative and diverse.

---

[171] 327 US 304 (1946).

[172] Id at 315.

[173] Id at 319.

[174] Id at 323.

[175] US Const, Art I, § 9, cl 2.

[176] See Rehnquist, *All the Laws* at 36–38 (cited in note 19).

In fact a clear statement principle, rather than the Constitution by itself, underlies one of the most celebrated free speech decisions in American history: Judge Learned Hand's in the *Masses* case.[177] At issue was an effort by the postmaster of New York to prevent the mailing of a revolutionary journal called *The Masses.* The postmaster invoked the Espionage Act of 1917. Judge Hand's opinion, issued during World War I, was animated by free speech principles, but he rested his decision on narrow reading of the Act rather than on the First Amendment. Judge Hand contended that under the Act, speech would be protected unless it expressly advocated lawless action; it could not be regulated merely because it did so indirectly or by implication.

This interpretation of the Act was hardly inevitable. By its terms, the Act banned any effort willfully "to cause or attempt to cause insubordination, disloyalty, mutiny, or refusal of duty, in the military or naval forces of the United States"; it also banned any effort willfully to "obstruct the recruiting or enlistment service of the United States."[178] These prohibitions could well have been understood to apply to the relevant issue of *The Masses,* which praised and even glorified conscientious objectors to the draft.[179] Judge Hand strained to argue that "One may admire and approve the course of a hero without feeling any duty to follow him. There is not the least implied intimation in these words that others are under a duty to follow."[180] Judge Hand's narrow construction of the Act enabled him to avoid resolution of a difficult constitutional problem.

Judge Hand's approach was followed in some of the most famous liberty-promoting dissenting opinions written in World War I, by Justices Louis Brandeis and Oliver Wendell Holmes.[181] Both Bran-

---

[177] See *Masses Publishing Co. v Patten,* 244 F 535 (SDNY 1917); see generally Stone, *Perilous Times* at 164–70 (cited in note 14), for a detailed discussion.

[178] See Geoffrey R. Stone et al., *Constitutional Law* 1088 (Little, Brown, 3d ed 1996).

[179] For example, the issue contained a poem called "Tribute," dedicated to Emma Goldman and Alexander Berkman, both in jail for opposing the war and the draft. The poem said, among other things, "Emma Goldman and Alexander Berkman/Are in prison tonight/ But they have made themselves elemental forces . . ./They are working on our destinies/ They are forging the love of the nations." This unambiguous "tribute" to lawbreakers opposing the draft could easily be taken as a willful obstruction of "the recruiting or enlistment service of the United States."

[180] 244 F at 538.

[181] *United States v Bureleson,* 255 US 407 (1921); *Abrams v United States,* 250 US 622 (1919).

deis and Holmes are now celebrated for their insistence on the constitutional protection of free speech. But their opinions have unmistakable minimalist features, arguing for narrow construction of authorization to the executive, not for invalidation on constitutional grounds. In one case, the Postmaster General revoked the mailing privileges of a newspaper because it published articles that criticized America's involvement in World War I and that therefore might be taken to obstruct military recruitment and enlistment. Refusing to interpret the Espionage Act in this way, both Brandeis and Holmes contended that the statute should not be read to grant such open-ended power to the President.[182] Justice Brandeis insisted that the real question "is one of statutory construction."[183] The Postmaster General had argued that the relevant articles violated the Espionage Act, but the statute need not be taken in that way.[184] In a manner analogous to that pursued by the majority in *Kent v Dulles*, Justice Brandeis sketched the historical practices of Congress and the executive to suggest that the Postmaster General lacked the statutory authority to exclude materials that he deemed objectionable and even unlawful.[185] And Justice Brandeis explicitly invoked a clear statement principle on behalf of his narrow construction, suggesting that "even if the statutes were less clear in this respect than they seem, I should be led to adopt that construction because of the familiar rule" that legislative enactments should be read so as to avoid constitutional doubts.[186]

Justice Holmes spoke in identical terms, insisting that "it would take very strong language to convince me that Congress ever intended to give such a practically despotic power to any one man. . . . Therefore I do not consider the limits of its constitutional power."[187] Justice Holmes's great dissenting opinion in *Abrams* did speak of the First Amendment.[188] But his initial submission was that the governing statutes should be interpreted not

---

[182] 255 US at 417 (Brandeis dissenting); id at 436 (Holmes dissenting).

[183] Id at 417.

[184] Id at 418–19.

[185] Id at 419–23.

[186] Id at 429.

[187] Id at 437.

[188] *Abrams*, 250 US at 632 (1919) (Holmes dissenting).

to cover the speech that had been subject to prosecution.[189] Of course nothing here is meant to deny the fact that Brandeis and Holmes sometimes voted simply to strike legislation down on constitutional grounds. All I am emphasizing here is that in some striking opinions, they took a more minimalist approach to intrusions on free speech amidst war.

In fact, an approach of this sort attracted the support of a majority of the Court at the height of the Cold War. Following Judge Hand and Justice Brandeis, the Court protected speech through an aggressive clear statement approach in *Yates v United States*.[190] At issue was a provision of the Smith Act, making it unlawful to "advocate, abet, advise, or teach the duty, necessity, desirability, or propriety of overthrowing or destroying any government in the United States by force or violence"; to print, sell, edit, display, or circulate written matters so advocating; and "to organize or to help to organize any group or assembly of persons who reach, advocate, or encourage overthrowing or destroying any government in the United States by force or violence."[191] The Court narrowly construed these terms, concluding that the Act does not prohibit "advocacy and teaching of forcible overthrow as an abstract principle," and that it reaches only efforts "to instigate action to that end."[192] The Court referred to the constitutional difficulty but insisted: "We need not, however, decide the issue before us in terms of constitutional compulsion, for our first duty is to construe this statute. In doing so, we should not assume that Congress chose to disregard a constitutional danger zone so clearly marked. . . ."[193]

The Court also offered a narrow construction of the term "organize," which it limited to acts entering into the initial creation of an organization, not to acts performed in carrying on its activ-

---

[189] Id at 626–27. It would be easy to imagine a slight recasting of Holmes's opinion in *Abrams* that would speak principally in statutory terms, emphasizing the constitutional backdrop as he did in *Burleson*. Notably, however, his *Abrams* opinion begins with the statute, but adds, "let me pass to the more important aspect of the case. I refer to the First Amendment of the Constitution that Congress shall make no law abridging the freedom of speech." Id at 627. Holmes thus shows some (nonminimalist) impatience with the statutory issues, in a way that suggests an intense desire to clarify the constitutional problem.

[190] 354 US 298 (1957).

[191] Smith Act, June 28, 1940, 54 Stat 670, 671. See 354 US at 300–01.

[192] Id at 318.

[193] Id at 319.

ities.[194] The Court thus refused to permit the executive to interpret the Smith Act to enter into a "constitutional danger zone," even though the language could easily have been taken to allow it to do so. What was required was clear congressional authorization.[195]

An analogous lesson emerges from the much-discussed decision in *Ex Parte Quirin*,[196] where the Court upheld the use of military commissions to try German saboteurs captured during World War II. In that case, the President asked the Court to hold that as Commander in Chief, the President had inherent authority to create and to use military tribunals. The Court refused to accept this argument: "It is unnecessary for present purposes to determine to what extent the President as Commander in Chief has constitutional power to create military commissions without the support of Congressional legislation. For here Congress has authorized trial of offenses against the law of war before such commissions."[197] Thus the Court posed the question as involving the unified position of Congress and the executive: "We are concerned only with the question whether it is within the constitutional power of the *National Government* to place petitioners upon trial before a military commission for the offenses with which they are charged."[198] The congressional grant of authority was far from unambiguous here, and hence the Court's interpretation might have been motivated, in part, by a desire to avoid ruling on the President's broad claims about his authority as Commander in Chief.[199] The crucial point is that the Court's reliance on congressional authorization gives *Quirin* an unmistakable minimalist character.

In its ruling, the *Quirin* Court followed the path set out by the concurring Justices in *Ex Parte Milligan*, which prohibited the use of military tribunals to try civilians during the Civil War.[200] Rejecting a broad constitutional ruling from the majority,[201] the con-

---

[194] Id at 310.

[195] See Gerald Gunther, *Learned Hand and the Origins of Modern First Amendment Doctrine: Some Fragments of History*, 27 Stan L Rev 719 753 (1975).

[196] 317 US 1 (1942).

[197] Id at 39.

[198] Id at 30 (emphasis added).

[199] See below; Sunstein, *Administrative Law Goes to War* (cited in note 16).

[200] 71 US 2 (1866).

[201] See id; this is one of the rare examples of Liberty Maximalism in American constitutional history.

curring Justices said, "It is for Congress to determine the question of expediency. And Congress did determine it. That body did not see fit to authorize trials by military commission in Indiana, but by the strongest implication prohibited it . . . ."[202] Avoiding the constitutional question, the concurring Justices emphasized that the President had not been authorized to use military tribunals. So too in the *Hamdi* case, to which I will turn in due course; there the Court refused to consider the President's broad claim of inherent authority to detain citizens who count as "enemy combatants." It chose instead the minimalist route of emphasizing the existence of congressional authorization for such detentions.[203]

3. *Korematsu and Hirabayashi redux: Minimalism in surprising places.* This catalogue should be sufficient to show that a primary precept of minimalism in war, requiring congressional authorization for intrusions on liberty, helps to organize a remarkable variety of judicial decisions. But I have not discussed the Supreme Court's most notorious decisions in this domain: *Hirabayashi v United States*[204] and *Korematsu v United States.*[205] In *Hirabayashi*, the Court upheld a curfew order imposed by a military commander on an American citizen of Japanese ancestry. In *Korematsu*, the Court upheld a military order excluding an American citizen of Japanese descent from San Leandro, California. It is tempting and probably even right to see both decisions as cowardly and deplorable capitulations, on the part of the Court, to intrusions on liberty that could find no justification in national security concerns.[206] It is even tempting to see both decisions as vindications of National Security Maximalism. But the Court's overall approach also has an unmistakable minimalist feature, requiring executive action to be authorized by Congress, and deferring to it only if it has been so authorized.

Hirabayashi was largely decided on institutional grounds. The Court's initial submission was that "so far as it lawfully could, Congress authorized and implemented such curfew orders as the commanding officer should promulgate pursuant to the Executive Order

---

[202] Id at 141.

[203] 124 S Ct at 2639.

[204] 320 US 81 (1943).

[205] 323 US 214 (1944).

[206] See Stone, *Perilous Times* (cited in note 14). Compare Breyer, *Liberty* at 3 (cited in note 3) ("It seems fair to say that *Korematsu* now represents the kind of constitutional decision that courts should seek to avoid.").

of the President."[207] Thus dual branch lawmaking, rather than executive unilateralism,[208] was involved: "The question then is . . . whether, acting in cooperation, Congress and the President have constitutional authority to impose the curfew restriction here complained of."[209] The Court ultimately concluded that "it was within the constitutional power of Congress and the executive arm of the Government to prescribe this curfew order for the period under consideration."[210] In fact one of Hirabayashi's principal objections was that the curfew had been an unconstitutional delegation by Congress; the Court's response was that the statute was to be read together with the executive's actions under it, so that "the standard set up for the guidance of the military commander, and the action taken and the reasons for it, are in fact recorded in the military orders."[211]

Of course the Court could have ruled otherwise, and I am not suggesting that it was right to do as it did. The Court could have concluded that the orders were unacceptable unless Congress had specifically set out the governing standards through ordinary law. A nondelegation challenge was hardly implausible; and the Court would have done better, in my view, to have proceeded as in *Kent v Dulles*, so as to find an absence of sufficient legislative authorization for an extraordinary intrusion into the domain of liberty. The general tenor of the Court's opinion might reasonably be invoked in support of National Security Maximalism: "Since the Constitution commits to the Executive and to Congress the exercise of the war power in all the vicissitudes and conditions of warfare, it has necessarily given them wide scope for the exercise of judgment and discretion in determining the nature and extent of the threatened injury or danger and in the selection of the means for resisting it. . . . [I]t is not for any court to sit in review of the wisdom of their action or substitute its judgment for theirs."[212] Note, however, that even here, the Court stressed that both Congress and the executive had concurred; the executive was not acting on its own.

In *Korematsu*, the Court similarly emphasized that the exclusion

---

[207] 320 US at 91.

[208] For the term, see Pildes and Issacharoff, *Civil Libertarianism* (cited in note 15).

[209] 320 US at 91.

[210] Id at 92.

[211] Id at 104.

[212] Id at 93.

order was based on a recent statute, making it a crime to "remain in . . . any military area of military zone" so prescribed by a competent official.[213] The exclusion order, issued by General Dewitt, was specifically authorized by an Executive Order by the President, who was in turn acting under congressional authorization. The Court stressed the institutional force behind the exclusion: "The Hirabayashi conviction and this one thus rest on the same 1942 Congressional Act and the same basic executive and military orders."[214] The Court pointedly noted that it was dealing not with the executive alone, but with "the war power of Congress and the Executive."[215]

Justice Frankfurter underlined the institutional point: "I find nothing in the Constitution which denies to Congress the power to enforce such a valid military order by making its violation an offense triable in the civil courts."[216] Justice Jackson, dissenting, also emphasized institutional factors, but saw them as cutting the other way: "[T]he 'law' of which this prisoner is convicted of disregarding is not found in an act of Congress, but in a military order. Neither the Act of Congress nor the Executive Order of the President, nor both together, would afford a basis for this conviction. It rests on the orders of General Dewitt."[217] This institutional point plainly contributed to Justice Jackson's refusal to vote to uphold the evacuation.

But let us take the Court's three decisions as a whole. If we consider *Hirabayashi* and *Korematsu* together with *Ex Parte Endo*, we can obtain a fresh perspective on what the Court was doing with the American government's acts of discrimination against Japanese Americans. In short, it was rejecting National Security Maximalism and Liberty Maximalism in favor of a distinctive form of minimalism. In none of the three cases did the Court issue a broad ruling on presidential authority. When the executive acted without congressional authorization, it lost; it survived legal attack only when Congress had specifically permitted its action. In all three cases, the Court paid exceedingly careful attention to the role of legislation, and thus refused to rule that the Commander in Chief

---

[213] Act of Mar 21, 1942, 56 Stat 173.

[214] 323 US at 217.

[215] Id.

[216] Id at 225.

[217] Id at 244.

power allowed the President to act on his own. In permitting the executive to implement a curfew and an exclusion order, the Court rejected Liberty Maximalism, indicating that it would yield to the shared judgments of the two democratically accountable branches.

Of course it would be possible to question the Court's holdings. In my view, the Court should have required greater legislative clarity in *Hirabayashi*. I have said that the Court should have ruled, in the fashion of *Kent v Dulles*, that if Japanese Americans were going to be deprived of their liberty, it must be as a result of clear and specific instructions from the national legislature.[218] And in *Korematsu*, Justice Jackson's opinion could have been recast to emphasize the absence of clear authorization from either Congress or the President. But for present purposes, the most important point lies elsewhere. *Hirabayashi*, *Korematsu*, and *Endo* reflect an emphatically minimalist approach to civil liberties in wartime—an approach that both defers to, and insists on, agreement from both of the democratically accountable branches.

From the standpoint of liberty, of course, skeptics will object that deference is unacceptable even if both branches agree. All I am suggesting here is that congressional authorization should ordinarily be required for presidential intrusion into the domain of constitutionally sensitive interests—and that outside of the egregious cases, courts will, and usually should, hesitate if such authorization is forthcoming.

4. *Clear statements and terrorism*. In the recent cases involving terrorism, clear statement principles have played a central role.

a) Hamdi. Such principles were endorsed most explicitly by Justice Souter, in his concurring opinion, joined by Justice Ginsburg, in *Hamdi*.[219] Justice Souter's central argument was that Congress had not authorized Hamdi's detention when a clear statement from Congress was required:

"In a government of separated powers, deciding finally on what is a reasonable degree of guaranteed liberty whether in peace or war (or some condition in between) is not well entrusted to the Executive Branch of Government, whose particular responsibility is to maintain security. For reasons of inescapable human nature, the branch of Government asked to counter a serious threat is not

[218] Compare *Gooding v Wilson*, 405 US 518 (1972) (using vagueness principles to strike down a restriction on speech).

[219] *Hamdi v Rumsfeld*, 124 US 2633 (2004).

the branch on which to rest the Nation's entire reliance in striking the balance between the will to win and the cost in liberty on the way to victory. . . . [A] reasonable balance is more likely to be reached on the judgment of a different branch."[220]

In making this argument, Justice Souter invoked the Non-Detention Act, which plainly states, "No citizen shall be imprisoned or otherwise detained by the United States except pursuant to an Act of Congress."[221] In his view, the Non-Detention Act ought generally to be read in accordance with its apparently "severe" terms.[222] One reason is that the Act was enacted against the background "of an interpretive regime that subjected enactments limiting liberty in wartime to the requirement of a clear statement and [Congress] presumably intended" the Act "to be read accordingly."[223] Emphasizing the cautionary examples afforded by history, and proceeding in light of the executive's incentive to favor security over liberty, Justice Souter contended that "manifest authority to detain" should be demanded "before detention is authorized."[224]

Hence Justice Souter emphasized "the need for a clearly expressed congressional resolution of the competing claims."[225] Not having found any such resolution, he concluded that the detention was unlawful. In a fashion reminiscent of Justice Jackson in *The Steel Seizure Case*, Justice Souter went on "to note the weakness of the Government's claim of inherent, executive authority" to detain people.[226] He acknowledged the possibility that the President could do this "in a moment of genuine emergency, when the Government must act with no time for deliberation."[227] But that was not the case here.

I believe that Justice Souter was entirely correct to stress the importance of requiring a clear statement from Congress before authorizing detentions of this sort by the executive. But for two different reasons, I am doubtful that Justice Souter was correct in his conclusion in *Hamdi*. First, and most fundamentally, a congressional authorization to use force is reasonably read to include

---

[220] Id at 2655.

[221] 18 USC 4001(a) (2000).

[222] 124 S Ct at 2653–54.

[223] Id at 2655.

[224] Id.

[225] Id.

[226] Id at 2659.

[227] Id.

the authority to detain those combatants who were captured during hostilities, at least for the period of those hostilities—a point to which I will return. Second, the President claimed inherent authority to detain those captured on the battlefield—a claim that was at least plausible under the Commander in Chief Clause. For this reason, the plurality's conclusion—that Congress had authorized the detention—actually helped to avoid the resolution of a serious constitutional question.

This latter point raises some real complexities for minimalism and the use of clear statement principles to limit presidential power. Such principles are justified, as in *Kent v Dulles*, as a means of avoiding constitutional questions by requiring a judgment by two branches, rather than simply one, that an invasion of liberty is justified. But in some (narrow) contexts, the President will be able to make a plausible argument that he has inherent authority to proceed with some course of action. If so, there is reason for an opposing clear statement principle, one that reads ambiguous statutory provisions as authorizing, rather than forbidding, presidential action. In fact this is an important form of judicial minimalism, and it is one reading of the Court's opinion in *Ex Parte Quirin*.[228] When the President has a strong claim of inherent power, the clear statement approach does not argue in favor of limiting his authority. But for the reasons sketched by Justice Jackson, broad claims of inherent power, made by reference to the Commander in Chief Clause, are usually not strong. On the contrary, they are usually implausible. When they are strong, the *Hamdi* plurality's approach is the right form of minimalism. When they lack plausibility, Justice Souter provides the best path for the future.

Indeed, an important aspect of the *Hamdi* plurality's own approach reflects an endorsement of Justice Souter's central idea. The government had argued that as a result of Congress's authorization of the use of force, it was permitted to detain Hamdi indefinitely.[229] The plurality rejected this argument, invoking a kind of clear statement principle, one that read the authorization to allow detention only during active prosecution of the war in Afghanistan. The plu-

---

[228] This is because in that case, the asserted statutory authorization for the President's creation of military tribunals was ambiguous; a clear statement principle would not have found it sufficient. See Jack L. Goldsmith and Cass R. Sunstein, *What a Difference Fifty Years Makes*, 19 Const Comm 621 (2002).

[229] *Hamdi*, 124 S Ct at 2641.

rality noted that "the national security underpinnings of the 'war on terror,' although crucially important, are broad and malleable."[230] A long-standing war on terror might mean that "Hamdi's detention could last for the rest of his life."[231] Congress had said nothing to allow the President to reach this conclusion. The plurality insisted, in this light, that "indefinite detention for the purpose of interrogation is not authorized."[232] It went on to conclude that detention could occur only for the duration of the hostilities in Afghanistan.[233] This conclusion, based on a narrow reading of the authorization of the use of force, is a more modest version of Justice Souter's plea for a clear statement principle in *Hamdi*.

b) Padilla. Minimalism of the same sort played the central role in the powerful decision of the court of appeals in the Padilla case.[234] At issue was the legality of the detention of Jose Padilla, an American citizen held as an enemy combatant after having been seized on American soil. The court squarely rejected the claim, urged by the executive and rooted in National Security Maximalism, to the effect that the "President has the inherent authority to detain those who take up arms against this country."[235] The court of appeals correctly emphasized that Articles I and II divide the war powers, rather than conferring them on the executive alone.[236] The court added that the grant of numerous war-related powers "to Congress is a powerful indication that, absent express congressional authorization, the President's Commander in Chief powers do not support" the confinement of an American citizen captured on American soil. It stressed that *Quirin*, the government's best precedent, rested on congressional authorization rather than on inherent presidential authority.[237]

Thus the key issue was whether such authorization could be found here. In the court's view, Congress's authorization to use "all necessary and appropriate force" to respond to the September 11 at-

---

[230] Id.

[231] Id.

[232] Id at 2641.

[233] Id at 2642.

[234] *Padilla v Rumsfeld*, 352 F3d 695 (2d Cir 2003), reversed on other grounds, *Rumsfeld v Padilla*, 124 S Ct 2711 (2004).

[235] 352 F3d at 712.

[236] Id at 713–14.

[237] Id at 716.

tacks should be understood in light of *Endo*. There the Court emphasized that "in interpreting a war-time measure we must assume that [the purpose of Congress and the Executive] was to allow for the greatest possible accommodation between those liberties and the exigencies of war."[238] Here no clear and unmistakable statement could be found; and that was what was required.[239] This decision is an unambiguous exercise in minimalism at war.

5. *What kind of authorization?* A general emphasis on the need for congressional authorization hardly answers all questions about the relationship between statutory provisions and presidential power.[240] We can group the cases discussed thus far into three categories. Sometimes Congress is required *to authorize*; the President cannot act without some grant of power from the national legislature. Sometimes Congress is required *to authorize clearly*; in the face of ambiguity, the President is not permitted to engage in a certain course of conduct. Sometimes Congress is required *to authorize both clearly and specifically*; without an express grant of authority to act in a specific way, the President is powerless. My emphasis has been on the need for clear authorization, which dominates the cases on liberty amidst war. But as the discussion thus far should suggest, the other categories are relevant as well.

When the President has inherent authority to act, legislative authorization is by hypothesis irrelevant. If, for example, prompt presidential warmaking is needed to repel a sudden attack on the United States, the best reading of the Constitution is that the President can take action whether or not Congress has authorized him to do so.[241] But suppose that the President merely has a plausible claim of inherent authority to act—and that there is a reasonable dispute about whether that authority actually exists. In such cases, the minimalist route is to require congressional authorization, and to find such authorization both necessary and sufficient whether or not it is clear. Because a constitutional question would be presented if such authorization were absent, minimalist judges reasonably rule that the authorization need not be clear. Indeed, such judges might aggressively construe the existing statutory materials to enable the President to do what (he plausibly claims) the Constitution enables

---

[238] Id at 722–23.

[239] Id at 723.

[240] See Bradley and Goldsmith, Harv L Rev (forthcoming 2005) (cited in note 92).

[241] See sources cited in note 95.

him to do on his own. *Ex Parte Quirin*, finding authorization that cannot fairly be described as clear,[242] is the most important example of this kind of minimalism.

But compare a case in which the President lacks a strong claim of constitutional power and in which some kind of liberty-based objection is mounted against his action. Here the proper course is to require a high degree of clarity. *Hamdi, Kahanamoku, Masses*, and *Yates* comfortably fall in this category. And where the liberty-based objection is especially strong, both clarity and specificity should be required. The difference between the two is usually unimportant, because clarity is usually absent without specificity. But we can see the relevance of the distinction in the disagreement between the plurality and Justice Souter in *Hamdi*. Justice Souter would have required specificity in the form of an express grant of authority to detain. By contrast, the plurality was satisfied with the general authorization for the use of force, which seemed relatively clear in light of historical understandings.[243] I will return to this dispute shortly. Note in this regard that *Kent v Dulles* is the strongest precedent for the view that congressional authorization must be both clear and specific; and *Ex Parte Endo* speaks in similar terms. The most sensible orienting point here is that the demand for specificity grows with the magnitude of the intrusion on liberty—a claim that will shortly bring us to the second component of minimalism at war.

6. *On the necessity and sufficiency of congressional authorization.* Under the law as I have reconstructed it here, congressional authorization is ordinarily both a necessary and a sufficient condition for presidential intrusions into the domain of constitutionally sensitive interests. I have also noted that in some areas, such authorization is not necessary. And many civil libertarians will argue that in many areas, such authorization is not sufficient. They will fear that in times of genuine crisis, Congress is likely to do whatever the President wants; and if the stakes are high enough, it will do so fairly automatically, capitulating to his will. Isn't it better, and in a sense more minimalist, to say that while congressional authorization is often sufficient, it should not always be, and that question must be resolved on a case-by-case basis rather than categorically?

---

[242] See Goldsmith and Sunstein, 19 Const Comm (cited in note 228).

[243] See Bradley and Goldsmith, Harv L Rev (forthcoming 2005) (cited in note 92), for detailed discussion of the history and interpretation of such authorizations.

A committed minimalist would be tempted to answer this question with an enthusiastic "Yes." In fact I have already suggested that congressional authorization is sometimes insufficient. Even if Congress and the President agree to silence political dissent during war, the First Amendment should stand in their way; and for reasons to be discussed shortly, fair hearings should generally be required even if the democratic branches want to dispense with them. But committed minimalists should also agree that outside of the egregious cases, and when Congress and the President have settled on a certain course of action, courts should be reluctant to rule against them. At the very least, American history attests to the likelihood that courts will follow this path when the stakes are high. Of course we can imagine clear constitutional violations, even outrages, in which we might expect, and certainly hope for, a degree of judicial courage.[244] Unfortunately, national experience testifies to the existence and future likelihood of such violations. The jury remains out, so to speak, on the likelihood of future judicial courage. What I am emphasizing here is that congressional authorization should be seen as the first line of defense against intrusions into the domain of constitutionally sensitive interests.

B.   MINIMALLY FAIR PROCEDURES

In one of the wisest and most important pronouncements in the history of American law, Justice Felix Frankfurter wrote, "The history of liberty has largely been the history of the observance of procedural safeguards."[245] A primary component of the minimalist program is to take this pronouncement extremely seriously, by requiring, where the legal materials are ambiguous, some kind of hearing for those who are deprived of their liberty.

Indeed, many of the cases explored thus far are centrally concerned with procedural safeguards. The clearest statement along these lines is found in *Duncan v Kahanamoku*, the martial law case from Hawaii, in which the Court narrowly construed the Hawaiian Organic Act so as to ensure that civilians would receive access to ordinary courts.[246] There the Court offered a ringing endorsement of "procedural safeguards," describing them as "indispensable to

---

[244] See Stone, *Perilous Times* (cited in note 14).

[245] *McNabb v United States*, 318 US 332, 347 (1943).

[246] 327 US 304 (1945).

our system of government" and as ensuring checks on executive absolutism.[247] *Ex Parte Endo* is best read in this general spirit. So too, Chief Justice Taney's rejection of President Lincoln's claim of authority to suspend the writ of habeas corpus endorses this aspect of minimalism at war.

The requirement of a hearing before people can lose their liberty deserves firm judicial support even when national security is at risk. Of course a general proposition of this kind does not resolve all cases; if people have been captured on the battlefield and are held beyond the territorial jurisdiction of American courts, then judges are powerless to intervene.[248] But if the legal materials can fairly be interpreted to require procedural protection, they should be so interpreted. And indeed this idea has received ringing endorsement in recent Supreme Court decisions involving the war on terrorism. Of these the more elaborately reasoned was the plurality opinion in *Hamdi v Rumsfeld*,[249] mentioned above; it is now time to explore that ruling in more detail.

Yaser Esam Hamdi, an American citizen born in Louisiana, was seized by members of the Northern Alliance in Afghanistan. From there he was transferred to Guantanamo Bay, then to a naval brig in Norfolk Virginia, and then to a brig in Charleston, South Carolina. According to the United States government, Hamdi qualified as an "enemy combatant" and hence could be held indefinitely without formal proceedings of any kind. The government urged that Hamdi had become affiliated with a Taliban military unit, received weapons training, and had an assault rifle with him at the time that he surrendered to the Northern Alliance.

The initial question was whether the executive had been authorized to detain citizens who qualify as "enemy combatants." This was an unusually complex question, for the government argued that even if Congress had not so authorized the executive, the executive "possesses plenary power to detain pursuant to Article II of the Constitution."[250] As I have noted, the plurality avoided the constitutional question by holding that Congress had authorized presidential detentions. The plurality pointed to the language of the authorization for the use of military force, which

---

[247] Id at 322.

[248] See *Johnson v Eisentrager*, 339 US 763 (1950).

[249] 124 S Ct 2633 (2004).

[250] Id at 2639.

gives the President the authority to use "all necessary and appropriate force" against "nations, organizations, or persons" associated with the terrorist attacks of September 11, 2001. The plurality concluded that the detention of "enemy combatants," at least for the duration of the conflict in which the capture occurred, "is so fundamental and accepted an incident to war as to be" an authorized exercise of "necessary and appropriate force."[251]

This was not an inevitable conclusion. As I have noted, Justice Souter contended that an explicit legislative statement should be required and that no such statement could be found. The plurality responded, plausibly, that detention to prevent return to the battlefield "is a fundamental incident of war." But we have also seen that the plurality rejected the government's claim that Congress had authorized indefinite detention by the executive. In its view, the "detention may last no longer than active hostilities."[252] As a matter of statutory interpretation, the plurality said that Congress's grant of authority to use force included the power to detain only for the duration of the relevant conflict. In good minimalist fashion, the plurality acknowledged that this "understanding may unravel" if "the practical circumstances of a given conflict are entirely unlike those of the conflicts that informed the development of the law of war."[253] But this "is not the situation we face as of this date."[254]

Having found that the detention of Hamdi was authorized, at least for the duration of the conflict, the plurality turned to the question of due process. The government contended that because Hamdi was seized in a combat zone, no fact-finding was necessary. The plurality disagreed. For Hamdi to be lawfully detained, he would have to have been part of armed forces engaged in conflict against the United States. This question was disputed and the conclusion of the executive would not be enough. The government also argued that no individual procedure was justified "in light of the extraordinary constitutional interests at stake"—or at most, that the court should ask whether "some evidence" supported the executive's determination that a citizen is an enemy combatant.[255]

---

[251] Id at 2640.

[252] Id at 2642.

[253] Id at 2641.

[254] Id at 2642.

[255] Id at 2645.

The plurality disagreed here as well. In the key passage, the plurality said that an enemy combatant must be supplied with "notice of the factual basis for his classification, and a fair opportunity to rebut the Government's factual assertions before a neutral decisionmaker."[256]

The plurality acknowledged the possibility that the constitutional requirements could be met before a military tribunal.[257] What was necessary was not any particular set of procedures, but a process that offers both notice and a chance to be heard. "We anticipate that a District Court would proceed with the caution that we have indicated is necessary in this setting, engaging in a factfinding process that is both prudent and incremental."[258]

What is noteworthy about the plurality's reasoning is its insistence on the right to a fair hearing before a deprivation of freedom, which it called one of the "essential liberties that remain vibrant even in times of security concerns."[259] Minimalists emphasize that right above all others. Of all the opinions in the Court's terrorism cases, the clearest endorsement of this point can be found in Justice Stevens's dissenting opinion in *Padilla*, where he wrote that "[u]nconstrained Executive detention for the purpose of investigating and preventing subversive activity is the hallmark of the Star Chamber," and added that the ability to retain "counsel for the purpose of protecting the citizen from official mistakes and mistreatment is the hallmark of due process," even when the nation is attempting "to resist an assault by the forces of tyranny."[260] In so saying, Justice Stevens was writing in the same spirit as the Court's majority, which has yet to question the general requirement of fair hearings.[261]

Of course that requirement has exceptions. Good minimalists cannot claim that hearings are always required; the very endorsement of hearing rights is, in its way, a departure from the minimalist reluctance to rule widely. As the Court said in *Rasul*, "there

---

[256] Id at 2651.

[257] Id.

[258] Id at 2652.

[259] Id.

[260] *Rumsfeld v Padilla*, 124 S Ct 2711, 2735 (2004) (Stevens dissenting).

[261] *Padilla* itself was decided not on the merits, but on jurisdictional grounds. See id at 2727 (ruling that Padilla was required to bring his habeas petition in South Carolina, not the Southern District of New York).

is a realm of political authority over military affairs where the judicial power may not enter."[262] If an enemy combatant is being held for a specific period in an area outside the territorial control of the United States, federal courts may not intervene.[263] It is clear that as Commander in Chief, the President can authorize the capture and detention of enemy combatants for specified periods of time, free from federal judicial oversight. But even in such situations, American courts have been careful to reject indefinite detention without trial, and have looked to ensure that some kind of procedure was available to reduce the risk of error.[264] In times of war, minimalist judges are reluctant to impose sharp constraints on the executive. But they are less reluctant to intervene when they are being asked to ensure against arbitrary or mistaken deprivations of liberty.

C.   NARROW AND INCOMPLETELY THEORIZED RULINGS

Thus far my emphasis has been on the need to restrain executive power. But there is also a need for courts to restrain themselves. In the context of war, minimalists endorse narrow, incompletely theorized rulings in order to promote two goals. First, judges ought to avoid excessive intrusions into the executive domain. Minimalist rulings help to ensure against judicial overreaching. Second, judges ought to avoid setting precedents that will, in retrospect, appear to give excessive authority to the President.[265] Minimalist rulings help to ensure against that risk as well.

Justice Frankfurter's concurring opinion in *The Steel Seizure Case* offers the most elaborate discussion of the basic point.[266] He emphasized that "[r]igorous adherence to the narrow scope of the judicial function" is especially important in constitutional cases when national security is at risk, notwithstanding the national "eagerness to settle—preferably forever—a specific problem on the basis of the broadest possible constitutional pronouncement."[267] In his view, the Court's duty "lies in the opposite di-

---

[262] *Rasul v Bush*, 124 S Ct at 2700.

[263] See id, relying on *Johnson v Eisentrager*, 339 US 763 (1950).

[264] 124 S Ct at 2700; 339 US at 777–78.

[265] On this risk, see Epstein et al., *Supreme Silence* (cited in note 19).

[266] 343 US at 594–97.

[267] Id at 594.

rection," through judgments that make it unnecessary to consider "delicate problems of power under the Constitution."[268] Thus the Court has an obligation "to avoid putting fetters upon the future by needless pronouncements today."[269] Thus he would have ruled, very narrowly, that the President had been deprived, by Congress, of the authority to engage in the seizure of the steel mills—a ruling that would have said exceedingly little about the hardest constitutional questions.[270]

We have already encountered a number of illustrations of analogous forms of judicial self-discipline. The ruling in *Kent v Dulles* left the largest constitutional questions for another day. So too, the concurring Justices in *Ex Parte Milligan* argued against a broad ruling on individual rights. In the same vein, *Ex Parte Quirin*, emphasizing congressional authorization, was a narrow ruling, simply because it left so much in legislative hands. In *Masses*, Judge Hand did not hold that Congress lacked the constitutional power to punish the relevant speech; he ruled more modestly that Congress had not seen fit to exercise whatever power it might have. The Supreme Court followed precisely the same approach in *Yates*.

The same tendency toward minimalist rulings was on fine display in 2004. In *Rasul v Bush*,[271] the Court was asked to say whether federal courts have jurisdiction to consider the detentions of foreign nationals captured and incarcerated at Guantanamo Bay. The Court chose to restrict itself to two exceedingly narrow questions. It held only that the federal habeas statute granted jurisdiction to federal courts to hear challenges by foreign nationals to their detentions, and that the Alien Tort Statute did not bar federal jurisdiction.[272] Having reached these conclusions, the Court said almost nothing else: "Whether and what proceedings may become necessary after respondents make their response to the merits of petitioners' claims are matters that we need not address now. What is presently at stake is only whether the federal courts have jurisdiction to determine the legality of the Executive's potentially

---

[268] Id at 595.

[269] Id at 596.

[270] Id at 602.

[271] 124 S Ct 2686 (2004).

[272] Id at 2698–99.

indefinite detention of individuals who claim to be wholly innocent of wrongdoing."[273]

We might compare the majority's approach here with the maximalist approaches of Justices Scalia and Thomas. Characteristically, Justice Scalia produced two opinions that were both deep and wide. In *Hamdi*, he argued that unless Congress has suspended the writ of habeas corpus, an American citizen is entitled to challenge his imprisonment and to obtain release unless and until criminal proceedings are brought.[274] The implication here is large: The President of the United States may not detain American citizens indefinitely, even if they are captured on the battlefield, unless the writ of habeas corpus has been suspended. "Many think it not only inevitable but entirely proper that liberty give way to security in times of national crisis . . . . Whatever the general merits of the view that war silences law or modulates its voice, that view has no place in the interpretation and application of a Constitution designed precisely to confront war and, in a manner that accords with democratic principles, to accommodate it."[275] Suspension of habeas corpus, or an ordinary trial-type hearing, is the rule for American citizens.

Justice Scalia's preference for a maximalist ruling fits well with one of his strongest argument on behalf of wide rather than narrow decisions: Width works not only to constrain judges but also to embolden them. "The chances that frail men and women will stand up to their unpleasant duty are greatly increased if they can stand behind the solid shield of a firm, clear principle enunciated in earlier cases."[276]

Justice Scalia urges a different but similarly wide rule for foreign nationals detained overseas by the United States military.[277] Here his rule is also clear: The federal habeas corpus statute does not apply at all, and the President can detain people free from judicial oversight. Thus Justice Scalia rejects the Court's conclusion that some kind of hearing is necessary to support detention. "For this Court to create such a monstrous scheme in time of war, and in frustration of our military commanders' reliance upon clearly

---

[273] Id at 2699.

[274] 124 S Ct 2633, 2671 (Scalia dissenting).

[275] Id at 2674.

[276] See Scalia, 56 U Chi L Rev at 1181 (cited in note 90).

[277] *Rasul v Bush*, 124 S Ct 2686 (2004).

stated prior law, is judicial adventurism of the worst sort."[278] Justice Thomas joined Justice Scalia on the point; and as we have seen, he also favors a broad rule for American citizens, permitting the President to detain enemy combatants indefinitely. For present purposes, what is noteworthy about the Scalia and Thomas opinions is that they favor both width and depth. Justice Thomas is quite explicit on this point, objecting specifically to the Court's use of a "balancing scheme" and responding, "I do not think that the Federal Government's war powers can be balanced away by this Court."[279]

Of course civil libertarians are likely to approve of Justice Scalia's approach in *Hamdi* and to reject that of Justices Scalia and Thomas in *Rasul*. But as Justice Thomas points out, Justice Scalia's liberty-protecting position in *Hamdi* creates risks simply because of its breadth.[280] If Justice Scalia or Justice Thomas were clearly right on the law, then no one could object to their plea for depth and width. But suppose that the law is not clear and that a deep or wide ruling might be confounded by unanticipated circumstances. If so, there is every reason for federal judges to issue shallow and narrow opinions, refusing to freeze the future and allowing decisions to turn on particular circumstances. Indeed, the Court's very refusal to decide the *Padilla* case on the merits, relying instead on a jurisdictional objection, can be understood as an extreme example of an insistence on shallowness and narrowness;[281] and if the underlying issues are extremely complex, then it is not hard to understand the Court's reluctance to resolve them.[282]

At this point it would be possible to object that narrow decisions, stressing particular facts, are in a sense more intrusive than those

---

[278] Id at 2711.

[279] Id at 2674.

[280] The difficulty is that it is easy to imagine cases of emergency in which the writ may not be suspended, because "Cases of Rebellion or Invasion" are not involved. 124 S Ct 2682–83. If the writ may not be suspended, then the President must hold formal trials and may not detain people—perhaps a plausible conclusion, but troublesome as well.

[281] *Rumsfeld v Padilla*, 124 S Ct 2711 (2004). The extreme case may, of course, conflict with the second feature of minimalism if it results in a failure to require a minimally fair hearing. Note, however, that there is a difference between a refusal to decide whether such a hearing is required and a ruling that such a hearing is not required; the Supreme Court's ruling in *Padilla* does not foreclose a future decision that the court of appeals was correct on the merits.

[282] See the discussion of the passive virtues in Alexander Bickel, *The Least Dangerous Branch: The Supreme Court at the Bar of Politics* (1962).

that offer greater width and depth. The reason is that narrow decisions leave the executive, and other institutions, so unclear about what they are supposed to do. This is a significant and legitimate concern about *Rasul* in particular. I have emphasized that that decision is highly minimalist, holding only that on these particular facts, these detainees are entitled to hearings. But this ruling leaves the government with very little guidance. Are those held at an air force base in Afghanistan or Iraq entitled to hearings? Does it matter if they are being held for only a few weeks, while the government explores the relevant facts, obtains a translator, and so forth? Justice Kennedy's concurring opinion appears responsive to the government's need for a measure of clarity.[283] If the Court leaves too much undecided, the government will have to proceed in the dark, in a way that might lead to a range of problems.

As evidence, consider here the distinctive problems that have emerged in the aftermath of *Rasul*. In December 2004, a federal district court "served as the stage for the beginning of what [was] expected to be a long and bruising second phase of the legal battle" over the fate of prisoners at Guantanamo Bay.[284] The administration argued for a narrow reading of *Rasul*, one that would be satisfied by a hearing at the naval base in which detainees were permitted to argue that they were not properly characterized as enemy combatants.[285] By contrast, the detainees contended that they were entitled to a lawyer and to an opportunity to see the evidence against them.[286] Because the Supreme Court did not resolve this dispute, protracted litigation was inevitable. In this light, it is reasonable to worry whether narrowness might not create unnecessary and even damaging uncertainty.

The concern is justified, and for some problems, it offers a good reason for a degree of width; but that reason is only one of a set of relevant considerations, many of them pointing toward narrow rulings in the context of war. If judges can be confident about a wider ruling, then they should issue it. By doing so, they reduce uncertainty, and they do so (by hypothesis) without compromising

---

[283] 124 S Ct at 2699-70 (Kennedy concurring in the judgment).

[284] See Neil Lewis, *Fate of Guantanamo Detainees Is Debated in Federal Court*, New York Times (Dec 2, 2004) at p 36.

[285] Id.

[286] Id.

other important values. But if judges lack confidence in a wider ruling, the costs of uncertainty may be worth incurring. The argument in *Rasul* involved the narrow questions the Court decided, not the broader ones that have arisen in the aftermath of its decision. The most that can be said is that government's need for planning provides a cautionary note about narrow and shallow rulings—suggesting the need to be minimalist, so to speak, about minimalism itself. But I hope that I have said enough to show that during war, a minimalist posture, of the sort defined by the three principles, provides the best general orientation.

Conclusion

I have attempted to outline and to evaluate three general approaches to conflicts among civil liberty and national security: Liberty Maximalism, National Security Maximalism, and minimalism. Courts are most unlikely to adopt Liberty Maximalism, and for good reason. The extent of liberty depends, in large part, on the strength and the legitimacy of the reasons for intruding on it, and when national security is genuinely at risk, the legitimate reasons for intruding on liberty are stronger. Of course courts should strike down indefensible restrictions on constitutional rights, above all freedom of speech.[287] But where the founding document leaves gaps and ambiguities, judicial caution is entirely appropriate amidst war.

By contrast, National Security Maximalism might seem highly attractive to courts, and there are appealing arguments on its behalf. More than anyone else, the President is in a strong position to protect the country, because he is uniquely well-equipped to acquire relevant information, and because he can act both in a coordinated way and with dispatch. These points are closely connected with central ideas about the executive branch in the founding era.[288] For their part, judges lack the information that would permit them to make sensible judgments about when an intrusion on liberty is justified, and the costs of judicial errors in the direction of liberty may turn out to be catastrophic. Notably, National Security Maximalism has received some strong endorsements on federal courts of appeals amidst the war on terrorism.

---

[287] See Stone, *Perilous Times* (cited in note 14).

[288] See Lessig and Sunstein, 94 Colum L Rev 1 (cited in note 91).

Notwithstanding its attractions, National Security Maximalism cannot claim much support in the Constitution itself. The founding document carefully divides authority between the President and Congress. It does not give a general "war power" to the President. With respect to war, the Constitution is easily read to give the national legislature the primary role. In addition, National Security Maximalism neglects institutional factors that create a grave risk that the executive branch will support unjustified intrusions on civil liberties. Group polarization is a significant danger, particularly for a branch specifically designed to consist of like-minded people. As a result, the executive might well support interferences with freedom that are not adequately justified by security concerns. This is especially likely if those interferences affect identifiable groups rather than the public as a whole.

In the face of the relevant risks, the best general orientation is a particular form of minimalism, with its three principal requirements, representing a kind of Due Process Writ Large. First, Congress should be required to provide clear authorization for executive intrusions on interests that have a strong claim to constitutional protection. Second, some kind of hearing should be required before the executive deprives people of their freedom. Third, courts should discipline themselves through narrow, incompletely theorized rulings. To a remarkable degree, these three ideas capture the practices of the Supreme Court in dealing with claimed violations of constitutional rights when national security has been threatened. Minimalism can find prominent endorsement during the Civil War, World War I, World War II, the Cold War, and the contemporary war on terrorism.

In numerous cases, the Court, and its most celebrated members, have adopted a form of minimalism in war. To be sure, minimalist decisions are unlikely to do all that should be done to prevent unjustified intrusions into the domain of liberty. But such decisions have the significant advantage of carving out a role that is admirably well suited to the institutional strengths and weaknesses of the federal judiciary.

GERALD L. NEUMAN

THE ABIDING SIGNIFICANCE OF LAW
IN FOREIGN RELATIONS

The foreign relations cases of the October 2003 Term provided an important opportunity to test the role that law would play in the relationship between the United States and the external world in the twenty-first century. The coming decades are certain to be marked by the ongoing trend of economic globalization, and by its shadow, transnational terrorism. Cases arising from the aftermath of September 11 reached the Supreme Court, and both in those cases and in others the Government repeatedly raised the question of how the world had changed since 2001, and whether former rules could still apply.[1]

The Supreme Court's response was moderate and nuanced. It did not reduce the law of foreign relations to the single principle of Executive discretion. Rather, it confirmed the continuing significance of law as an element of foreign relations, and the separation of powers in the sense of shared responsibility of the three branches to contribute in their own ways to managing the interactions of the United States with the international system. At a time

Gerald L. Neuman is Herbert Wechsler Professor of Federal Jurisprudence, Columbia Law School.

AUTHOR'S NOTE: I would like to thank José Alvarez, Lori Damrosch, Harold Koh, Henry Monaghan, and Kal Raustiala for comments and criticisms. All errors are my own.

[1] This article will not, however, analyze the two decisions regarding U.S. citizens held as alleged "enemy combatants," *Hamdi v Rumsfeld*, 124 S Ct 2633 (2004), and *Rumsfeld v Padilla*, 124 S Ct 2711 (2004), which are discussed in Cass R. Sunstein, *Minimalism at War*, 2004 Supreme Court Review 47.

when nothing could be taken for granted, the affirmation of continuity was a major event.

I. Four "Foreign" Cases

This section describes four major foreign affairs decisions of June 2004: three high-profile transnational individual rights cases, and an ordinary transnational commercial litigation. The former include the challenge to the law-free regime of military detention of foreign nationals at the Guantanamo Bay Naval Base, the alien tort action arising from the abduction of a Mexican doctor by the Drug Enforcement Administration, and the attempt of a U.S. citizen to recover from Austria paintings looted by the Nazis. The fourth, more "normal" case involved an antitrust action arising from a global conspiracy to fix the price of vitamins. Both the Court and the Government as amicus regarded the fourth case as within the paradigm of law-governed international cooperation. The Court treated that paradigm as at least presumptively applicable to the other three cases, and as a result rejected important positions advanced by the Government as party or amicus in those cases.

A.   GUANTANAMO[2]

The Supreme Court's grant of certiorari in *Rasul v Bush*[3] surprised many. The D.C. Circuit's holding that neither habeas corpus jurisdiction nor the "privilege of litigation" extended to foreign nationals held as enemy combatants at the Guantanamo Bay Naval Base arguably tracked World War II–era precedent. There was no live circuit conflict.[4] And the Government vigorously opposed certiorari. According to the Solicitor General, any contrary ruling would have acute potential for interference with core war powers of the President.[5] Because Guantanamo lay outside the

---

[2] I should disclose to the reader that I was an author of the Brief Amici Curiae of Former U.S. Government Officials in Support of Petitioners, *Rasul v Bush* and *Al Odah v United States*, Nos 03-334 and 03-343 (filed Jan 2003).

[3] 124 S Ct 2686 (2004).

[4] The Second Circuit's earlier decision favoring the application of constitutional rights to Haitian refugees detained at Guantanamo had been vacated as moot after the preliminary injunction it affirmed was superseded by a permanent injunction. *Haitian Centers Council, Inc. v McNary*, 969 F2d 1326 (2d Cir 1992), vacated as moot, 509 US 918 (1993).

[5] Brief for the Respondents in Opposition, *Rasul v Bush* and *Al Odah v United States*, Nos 03-334 and 03-343, *19 (filed Oct 2003).

"sovereign territory" of the United States, aliens held there had
no constitutional rights and lacked the "privilege of litigation" in
U.S. courts.[6] Moreover, the classification of foreign nationals as
enemies was a "quintessential political question" to be determined
by the Executive.[7]

On the other hand, the international outcry over the government's maintenance of a "legal black hole"[8] at Guantanamo was
intense. The fact that the detainees included numerous citizens
of European allies kept a spotlight on the issue. The government's
resistance to diplomatic overtures underlined the reality that no
external authority could constrain its actions at the base. At a
minimum, the Court may have concluded that it should decide
for itself whether the U.S. legal system would continue to incur
this reproach.

The Court granted certiorari limited to the question of federal
jurisdiction.[9] The majority opinion by Justice Stevens similarly
stressed the narrowness of the holding, although the discussion
ranged more widely. Four other Justices joined this opinion; Justice Kennedy concurred in the judgment and Justice Scalia wrote
for three dissenters. The Court rejected the effort of the Executive
to characterize Guantanamo as an extraterritorial enclave subject
to plenary U.S. authority but beyond the reach of habeas corpus.
With no bar to habeas jurisdiction, the implied barrier to other
forms of court access did not exist, either.

Part of the analysis turned on *Johnson v Eisentrager*,[10] a 1950
precedent denying access to habeas corpus to German nationals

---

[6] Id at 13, 15.

[7] Id at 14. I should note that I will follow here the convention of capitalizing the word
"Executive," regardless of whether it refers to the President in person or to others purportedly acting on behalf of the Executive Branch, although that convention presents the
risk of clouding responsibility and inducing unmerited deference. In contrast, I will cap-
italize "Government" when referring to the litigating positions taken by the Executive.

[8] See *Abbasi v Secretary of State for Foreign and Commonwealth Affairs*, [2002] EWCA Civ
1598, ¶ 64 ("[W]e do not find it possible to approach this claim for judicial review other
than on the basis that, in apparent contravention of fundamental principles recognised by
both jurisdictions and by international law, Mr. Abbasi is at present arbitrarily detained
in a 'legal black-hole'."); Johan Steyn, *Guantanamo Bay: The Legal Black Hole*, 53 Intl &
Comp L Q 1 (2004).

[9] The Court itself rewrote the question as "Whether United States courts lack jurisdiction to consider challenges to the legality of the detention of foreign nationals captured
abroad in connection with hostilities and incarcerated at the Guantanamo Bay Naval Base,
Cuba." *Rasul v Bush*, 124 S Ct 534 (2003) (granting certiorari).

[10] 339 US 763 (1950).

who had been convicted of war crimes and were being held in occupied Germany. While the Government and the dissent gave *Eisentrager* as broad a reading as its many dicta supported, the majority interpreted the case narrowly, and regarded it as largely overtaken by other legal changes. Justice Stevens quoted a passage from *Eisentrager* that identified six factors of status, process, and location that grounded its holding.[11] Moreover, the majority described *Eisentrager* as focusing primarily on a putative *constitutional* entitlement to extraterritorial habeas corpus, rather than engaging in interpretation of the federal habeas statute. The majority observed that the statutory assumptions underlying *Eisentrager*, making habeas jurisdiction depend on the location of the prisoner rather than the location of an appropriate custodian, had since been overruled.[12]

Aside from *Eisentrager*, the Government also invoked the presumption against extraterritorial application of statutes. The majority responded that that presumption did not apply to Guantanamo, which lay within, not outside, the "territorial jurisdiction" of the United States.[13] The unusual terms of the Guantanamo lease agreement gave the United States "complete jurisdiction and control" for as long as it wanted. The majority also cited English precedents that it interpreted as indicating that the degree of practical control, not formal territorial sovereignty, determined the reach of the venerable writ.

These arguments suggest that the breadth of exclusive U.S. power at Guantanamo justified a geographically defined extension of the writ to all persons in custody there, which might not reach further to less unilateral detentions in foreign countries. Justice Kennedy's concurrence placed heavy weight on this factor, con-

---

[11] 124 S Ct at 2693 (quoting *Eisentrager*, 339 US at 777). The six overlapping factors were (*a*) enemy alien status, (*b*) never having been or resided in the United States, (*c*) being captured as a prisoner of war outside the United States, (*d*) having been tried and convicted by a military tribunal outside the United States, (*e*) for offenses committed outside the United States, and (*f*) being imprisoned outside the United States. The first and fourth factors, and arguably others, were lacking in *Rasul*. The majority expressly mentioned imprisonment "in territory over which the United States exercises exclusive jurisdiction and control" as a distinguishing factor between *Rasul* and *Eisentrager*. Id.

[12] Justice Kennedy disagreed with this account, and offered an alternative analysis that preserved and distinguished *Eisentrager*. See Section IIC.

[13] 124 S Ct at 2696.

cluding that "Guantanamo Bay is in every practical respect a United States territory."[14]

But other, textual arguments intertwined in the majority opinion might suggest a broader scope. Justice Stevens emphasized that the federal habeas statute, 28 USC § 2241, draws no distinction between detention of citizens and detention of aliens, and thus gives no evidence "that Congress intended the geographical coverage of the statute to vary depending on the detainee's citizenship."[15] Yet, as the dissent pointed out, it is understood that the writ reaches U.S. citizens wherever they are detained in federal custody.[16] Justice Scalia regarded this distinction as an "atextual" interpretation of the statute designed to avoid a constitutional doubt that existed only for citizens, but the majority insisted that his interpretation would require a textual basis that it lacked.[17] Instead, the majority concluded that petitioners had alleged unlawful federal custody and that no one questioned the district court's jurisdiction over their custodians, and that "Section 2241, by its terms, requires nothing more."[18] Again, this reasoning might extend far beyond Guantanamo Bay. A similar ambiguity characterized the single footnote in which the majority spoke in passing to the merits, suggesting that the petitioners had successfully alleged violations of constitutional right.[19]

On either alternative, the *Rasul* decision strikingly repudiated the theory on which the Government had sought to exclude the rule of law from Guantanamo.

B.   THE ALIEN TORT STATUTE

Sosa v Alvarez-Machain[20] arose out of the irregular arrest and delivery to the United States of Dr. Humberto Alvarez-Machain, suspected of participation in the torture and murder of an agent

---

[14] Id at 2700 (Kennedy concurring in the judgment).

[15] Id at 2696 (majority).

[16] Id at 2708 (Scalia dissenting).

[17] Id at 2695–96 nn 9 & 10 (majority).

[18] Id at 2698 (citing *Braden v 30th Judicial Circuit Court of Kentucky*, 410 US 484, 495 (1973)). The reference to "jurisdiction" is ambiguous, and the operative notion would need to be spelled out in light of *Braden* and the majority and concurring opinions in *Rumsfeld v Padilla*, 124 S Ct 2711 (2004), decided the same day as *Rasul* but by a different majority.

[19] Id at 2698 n 15.

[20] 124 S Ct 2739 (2004).

of the U.S. Drug Enforcement Administration in Mexico. The underlying fact situation has produced two other major Supreme Court decisions.[21] Eventually, the trial judge dismissed the prosecution for lack of evidence,[22] and Alvarez brought suit against U.S. and Mexican defendants responsible for his abduction.[23] After years of litigation, the Ninth Circuit en banc found the federal government subject to suit for false arrest under the Federal Tort Claims Act, and found the Mexican abductor Jose Francisco Sosa liable for arbitrary detention in violation of international law.[24] With the encouragement of the Solicitor General, Sosa's petition for certiorari became the vehicle for a coordinated effort to end human rights litigation under the Alien Tort Statute (ATS).[25]

The ATS, a recodified provision of the 1789 Judiciary Act, gives the district courts "original jurisdiction of any civil action by an alien for a tort only, committed in violation of the law of nations or a treaty of the United States."[26] It has served as a channel for international human rights litigation by foreign nationals since the lower courts came to recognize that modern international law had

---

[21] *United States v Alvarez-Machain*, 504 US 655 (1992) (holding that abduction did not violate the U.S.-Mexico extradition treaty, and that prosecution would not be barred even if abduction violated international law); *United States v Verdugo-Urquidez*, 494 US 259 (1990) (holding that the Fourth Amendment did not restrict search of property in Mexico belonging to another suspect later convicted in the killing).

[22] See Jim Newton, *Judge Orders Camarena Case Defendant Freed*, LA Times 1a (Dec 15, 1992).

[23] I should disclose that at an earlier stage of the litigation I was a coauthor of an amicus brief for the Lawyers Committee for Human Rights, et al, in *Alvarez-Machain v United States*, 107 F3d 696 (9th Cir 1996), that addressed the extraterritorial application of the Due Process Clause to torture, as well as the retroactivity of the Torture Victims Protection Act.

[24] *Alvarez-Machain v United States*, 331 F3d 604 (9th Cir 2003), revd, 124 S Ct 2739 (2004).

[25] The United States both sought certiorari concerning its own FTCA liability and urged the Supreme Court to grant Sosa's petition. See Brief for the United States in Support of the Petition, *Sosa v Alvarez-Machain*, No 03-339 (filed Sept 2003) (US Sosa Petition Brief). The Supreme Court granted both petitions, and held that the FTCA claim was barred by the "foreign country" exception in the statute. The entire Court rejected the "headquarters doctrine" adopted by some courts of appeals, which permitted FTCA claims for foreign injuries caused indirectly by prior actions within the United States, as "threaten[ing] to swallow the foreign country exception." 124 S Ct at 2749. This holding—and Government victory—deserve greater discussion than I have room for here, but the Court justified it in terms of respect for Congress's choices in drafting the FTCA. Id at 2754.

[26] 28 USC § 1350. The original provision gave the federal district courts "cognizance, concurrent with the courts of the several States, or the circuit courts, as the case may be, of all causes where an alien sues for a tort only in violation of the law of nations or a treaty of the United States." Judiciary Act of 1789, ch 20, § 9(b), 1 Stat 79.

evolved to encompass human rights obligations owed by states to their own citizens. The Second Circuit, prompted by the Carter administration, led the way in *Filartiga v Pena-Irala*,[27] holding that the ATS provided jurisdiction for a tort action against a Paraguayan immigrant who had earlier tortured the plaintiff's son to death in Paraguay. Congress subsequently codified the cause of action for torture and extrajudicial killing, while extending it to U.S. citizens as well in the Torture Victims Protection Act (TVPA).[28]

The Government's arguments for grant of certiorari urged that the lower courts' acceptance of a private right of action under the ATS had "profound separation-of-powers implications and serious consequences for both the development and expression of the Nation's foreign policy."[29] The impact on "the actions of the Executive abroad is great and further heightened by the Nation's ongoing war against terrorism."[30] Moreover, the Ninth Circuit had enforced a norm against arbitrary detention that was based on no act of Congress or self-executing treaty, a result that was "antidemocratic."[31] The ATS could not properly be construed as empowering federal courts to pass on the legality of foreign governments' actions abroad, or the conduct of the United States and its allies in foreign lands. Such adjudication usurped the Executive's foreign affairs power. To avoid these ills, the Government asked the Court to abolish ATS litigation altogether. The ATS should be interpreted as purely jurisdictional, and courts should not be permitted to derive private rights of action from customary international law. As a fallback, the Government argued that the ATS should not be applied to extraterritorial conduct.[32] Once the Court granted review, the Government further elaborated these

---

[27] 630 F2d 876 (2d Cir 1980).

[28] Pub L 102–256, 106 Stat 73 (1992), codified at 28 USC § 1350 note.

[29] US Sosa Petition Brief (cited in note 25) at *7.

[30] Id.

[31] Id at *9 (quoting *Al Odah v United States*, 321 F3d 1134, 1148 (DC Cir 2003), revd as *Rasul v Bush*, 124 S Ct 2686 (2004)).

[32] Id at *26. Sosa himself did not make this argument, and the Court did not expressly address it, but the discussion of the history and nature of ATS litigation clearly assumes extraterritorial applicability. See 124 S Ct at 2759, 2763, 2767–68; id at 2782 (Breyer concurring) (noting comity concerns raised by adjudication of human rights claims arising abroad).

arguments in an amicus brief. Sosa argued similarly, but did not raise the issue of extraterritorial application.

Sosa prevailed, but not on the grounds that the Government preferred. The Supreme Court unanimously rejected Alvarez's international law claim, splitting six to three on the rationale. Justice Souter wrote for the majority, confirming that the Alien Tort Statute provided jurisdiction for private rights of action under federal common law to vindicate certain human rights protected by customary international law, while finally concluding that Alvarez had not demonstrated that his detention in Mexico violated a sufficiently specific international norm. Justice Breyer concurred, adding some additional thoughts on the limits of ATS actions.[33] Justice Scalia concurred in the judgment, denying judicial authority to derive private rights of action to enforce customary international law.[34]

Central to the Court's analysis was a three-fold distinction between subject matter jurisdiction, private rights of action, and substantive rules of conduct. Justice Souter first addressed whether the Alien Tort Statute itself provided a private right of action for violations of international law. After examining the history of the statute, he concluded that the ATS supplied only jurisdiction. Nonetheless, it was enacted against a background assumption that a limited category of international law violations were actionable at common law, and that others might evolve. The majority concluded that the ATS should not be viewed solely as a placeholder creating jurisdiction in case Congress should later enact legislation authorizing private suits.

The majority turned next to the question whether the federal courts retained the power to afford private rights of action for violations of customary international law, including human rights law. Sosa and the Government put forward the revisionist argument, much debated in the secondary literature,[35] that after *Erie*

---

[33] 124 S Ct at 2782 (Breyer concurring). He suggested differentiating between suits against U.S. nationals or arising from events in U.S. territory and suits against foreign nationals arising abroad. In the latter category, courts should limit the private right of action to wrongs for which an international "procedural consensus" existed concerning the propriety of exercising civil jurisdiction.

[34] Id at 2769 (Scalia, joined by Rehnquist and Thomas, concurring in part and concurring in the judgment in part).

[35] See Curtis A. Bradley and Jack L. Goldsmith III, *The Current Illegitimacy of International Human Rights Litigation*, 66 Fordham L Rev 391 (1997); Ernest Young, *Sorting Out the Debate Over Customary International Law*, 42 Va J Intl L 365 (2002).

Railroad Co. v Tompkins,[36] federal courts no longer possessed such authority. The majority rejected this revisionist attack, but accommodated some of its underlying concerns by emphasizing that the power should be exercised with caution.[37] The Court held that private rights of action for human rights violations must "rest on a norm of international character accepted by the civilized world and defined with a specificity comparable to" the actionable international norms that existed in 1789.[38] The majority concluded that Alvarez's claim of arbitrary detention, particularly given that the arbitrariness lay in its (allegedly) unauthorized character under national law, did not rest upon a "norm of customary international law so well defined as to support the creation of a federal remedy."[39]

This disposition made it unnecessary to consider other reasons for declining to entertain ATS litigation in particular cases. The majority noted the possibility of an exhaustion of remedies requirement like that codified in the TVPA.[40] In response to the example of South Africa's current objection to litigation against companies that had allegedly abetted apartheid, the majority observed that the U.S. Government's statements of interest raising case-specific foreign policy concerns might be entitled to serious weight.[41]

Justice Scalia, acerbically concurring, gave greater credence to the revisionist critique of customary international law and its enforcement. He protested that "American law—the law made by the people's democratically elected representatives—does not recognize a category of activity that is so universally disapproved by other nations that it is automatically unlawful here, and automatically gives rise to a private action for money damages in federal court."[42] He would have granted the Government's wish by eliminating all human rights litigation under the ATS, and would have terminated the practice of judicial incorporation of customary international law.

---

[36] 304 US 64 (1938).

[37] 124 S Ct at 2764–65. See Part II.A.

[38] Id at 2761.

[39] Id at 2769.

[40] Id at 2766 n 21.

[41] Id.

[42] Id at 2776 (Scalia concurring in part).

C.   FOREIGN SOVEREIGN IMMUNITY

One particular category of human rights litigation in recent years has involved the delayed assertion of World War II era compensation claims. Over the Government's objection, the Supreme Court lifted one barrier to such litigation in *Republic of Austria v Altmann*, holding that the expropriation exception of the Foreign Sovereign Immunities Act (FSIA) applied retrospectively to claims arising from conduct that preceded its enactment.[43] Indeed, the Court held that the exception denied the defense of foreign sovereign immunity for conduct occurring in the 1940s, before the United States adopted the "restrictive" approach to sovereign immunity in 1952.

The *Altmann* case involved disputed ownership of several Klimt paintings held by the Austrian Gallery, an instrumentality of the Austrian government. The U.S. heir of the original owners alleged that the paintings had been seized by the Nazis and subsequently expropriated by Austria after the war. Altmann sued the Gallery in federal court in California, and Austria raised the defense of foreign sovereign immunity. It argued that when the challenged acts occurred in 1948, Austria was protected from suit in the United States by absolute immunity, and that the FSIA, enacted in 1976, did not withdraw that immunity retroactively.

Understanding the retroactivity argument requires attention to both substantive and procedural aspects of foreign sovereign immunity (also known internationally as "foreign state immunity"). Over the course of the twentieth century, international law witnessed a trend from adherence to a doctrine that states were absolutely immune from suit in the courts of other states to adoption of a "restrictive" theory that denied immunity in litigation arising from the commercial activity of states and their instrumentalities (acts *jure gestionis*, as opposed to *jure imperii*). The United States joined that trend in 1952, when the State Department issued the "Tate Letter" advising that it would no longer support immunity for commercial activities of foreign sovereigns.[44] The Tate Letter was so significant because during the mid-twentieth century the Supreme Court followed a practice of total deference to Executive

---

[43] 124 S Ct 2240 (2004).

[44] Letter from Jack B. Tate, Acting Legal Adviser, U.S. Dept. of State, to Acting U.S. Attorney General Philip B. Perlman (May 19, 1952), reprinted in *Alfred Dunhill of London, Inc. v Republic of Cuba*, 425 US 682, 711 (1976).

suggestions of immunity.[45] Despite the Tate Letter, the State Department remained under pressure from foreign governments to file suggestions of immunity in dubious cases. One of Congress's main purposes in enacting the Foreign Sovereign Immunities Act was to depoliticize the field by codifying legal standards that courts could apply impartially.

The question in *Altmann* was whether the standards codified in 1976, and in particular the novel exception for suits based on expropriation where the expropriated property is owned by an instrumentality that engages in commercial activity in the United States, applied to a lawsuit brought after 1976 on the basis of earlier conduct. The Ninth Circuit held that the exception did permit Altmann's action, creating a conflict with other circuits.[46] Once the Supreme Court granted certiorari, the Solicitor General filed an amicus brief in support of Austria, arguing that the inappropriate retroactive denial of sovereign immunity "may have serious consequences for the United States' conduct of its foreign relations, including reciprocal treatment of the United States in foreign courts."[47] The Solicitor General agreed with Austria that the temporal application of the FSIA should be subject to the usual *Landgraf* analysis,[48] that exceptions to foreign sovereign immunity were substantive in nature, and that the acts of expropriation would have been shielded by sovereign immunity under U.S. practice both before 1952 and between 1952 and 1976. The Solicitor General emphasized that "the United States' longstanding policy and practice is to prevent courts from becoming entangled in the conduct of foreign relations and to resolve war-related claims through diplomatic or political, rather than judicial, means."[49]

The Supreme Court nonetheless ruled that the FSIA expropriation exception governed the dispute.[50] Justice Stevens, writing for a majority of six, began by offering an account of the history

---

[45] The Court announced this practice in *The Navemar*, 303 US 68, 74 (1938), and employed it in *Ex parte Peru*, 318 US 578 (1943), and *Mexico v Hoffman*, 324 US 30 (1947).

[46] *Altmann v Republic of Austria*, 317 F3d 954 (9th Cir 2002), revd, 124 S Ct 2240 (2004).

[47] Brief of the United States as Amicus Curiae Supporting Petitioners, *Republic of Austria v Altmann*, No 03-13, *29 (filed Nov 2003).

[48] See *Landgraf v USI Film Products*, 511 US 244 (1994).

[49] Brief of the United States (cited in note 47) at *22.

[50] The Court did not decide, however, whether the facts came within the expropriation exception, or whether the act of state doctrine barred adjudication. 124 S Ct at 2254.

of foreign sovereign immunity in the United States that emphasized the role of Executive suggestion before 1976, and that characterized immunity as a "matter of grace and comity."[51] He maintained that the usual *Landgraf* retroactivity analysis should not
apply because foreign sovereign immunity straddled the standard
categories on which it relied. The immunity was both jurisdictional and substantive; prior to 1976 foreign states had expectations of comity but "no 'right' to such immunity;"[52] and the recognition of immunity "reflects current political realities and
relationships" rather than reliance interests in shaping conduct.[53]
Accordingly, the Court would not employ the *Landgraf* interpretive framework, but found it better to defer to the most recent
decision of the political branches, "namely, the FSIA—[rather]
than to presume that decision inapplicable merely because it postdates the conduct in question."[54]

From that starting point, the Court found sufficient indications
in the FSIA that it should govern the present action. The preamble
to the FSIA directs that foreign sovereign immunity claims "should
henceforth be decided by courts . . . in conformity with the principles set forth in this chapter."[55] Other, procedural provisions of
the FSIA concededly applied to all cases. And Congress's purposes
included "clarifying the rules that judges should apply . . . and
eliminating political participation in the resolution of such
claims."[56] The Ninth Circuit's specific counterfactual analysis of
how the Executive would have responded to a request for immunity by Austria in 1948 represented "precisely the kind of detailed historical inquiry that the FSIA's clear guidelines were intended to obviate."[57]

The Court emphasized the narrowness of its holding. It had
not determined whether the facts brought the case within the
expropriation exception, but only that the exception applied to
preenactment conduct. Other defenses, like the act of state doc

---

[51] Id at 2247–49. Two concurring opinions, differing mostly in emphasis, were filed by
Justice Scalia and by Justice Breyer, joined by Justice Souter.

[52] Id at 2251.

[53] Id at 2252.

[54] Id.

[55] 28 USC § 1602.

[56] 124 S Ct at 2251.

[57] Id at 2254.

trine, might still apply. The Court's ruling concerned a pure issue of statutory construction on which the Executive's views "merit no special deference."[58] If, however, adjudication of a *particular* case raised sensitive foreign policy concerns, the Executive remained free to file a statement of interest, and it left open the question of what deference that type of submission would deserve.

The latter point sparked a sharp debate with Justice Kennedy's dissent. He argued that the Court had just reinvited the kind of political interference that the FSIA was intended to eliminate from litigation against foreign states. Moreover, allowing the Executive to displace the statutory scheme would raise separation of powers concerns, as between the President and Congress and also with regard to judicial independence.[59] Instead, he would have applied the *Landgraf* analysis and found the FSIA provision inapplicable if it created jurisdiction where none had existed before. That question should be decided based on pre-FSIA legal principles embodied in the Tate Letter, not by speculation about political factors that might have controlled a particular case. The dissent largely agreed with the Solicitor General's position, but would have remanded for "more specific briefing, arguments, and consideration of the international law sources bearing upon the scope of immunity the Tate Letter announced."[60]

D.   ANTITRUST EXTRATERRITORIALITY

The fourth decision was unanimous, and can be treated more briefly. In *F. Hoffman-LaRoche Ltd. v Empagran, S.A.*, the Court construed a provision of the Foreign Trade Antitrust Improvements Act (FTAIA) as limiting the extraterritorial reach of antitrust liability.[61] The litigation arose from the global price-fixing conspiracy among vitamin manufacturers, and the plaintiffs were foreign companies that had purchased vitamins at elevated prices abroad. The D.C. Circuit had held that the FTAIA permitted Sherman Act liability for foreign anticompetitive conduct that had "direct, substantial, and reasonably foreseeable effect" on domestic commerce, even if the injury to the foreign plaintiff arose outside

---

[58] Id at 2255.

[59] Id at 2274 (Kennedy, joined by Rehnquist and Thomas, dissenting).

[60] Id at 2270.

[61] 124 S Ct 2359 (2004).

the United States and was independent of the effect on U.S. commerce.[62] The Supreme Court reversed, holding that the FTAIA should be read as barring Sherman Act liability for independently caused foreign injury. The Court agreed with the interpretation favored by the United States as amicus curiae, although its analysis differed in nuance.

Justice Breyer wrote for the Court, and Justice Scalia filed a terse concurrence in the judgment.[63] The majority explained that independent foreign injury from the price-fixing conspiracy should not be actionable "for two main reasons."[64] The first reason began as follows:

> *First*, this Court ordinarily construes ambiguous statutes to avoid unreasonable interference with the sovereign authority of other nations. This rule of construction reflects principles of customary international law—law that (we must assume) Congress ordinarily seeks to follow.

> This rule of statutory construction cautions courts to assume that legislators take account of the legitimate sovereign interests of other nations when they write American laws. It thereby helps the potentially conflicting laws of different nations work together in harmony—a harmony particularly needed in today's highly interdependent commercial world.[65]

Under this principle of "prescriptive comity," the Court found it unreasonable to impose U.S. antitrust liability for the independent foreign injury. "[I]f America's antitrust policies could not win their own way in the international marketplace for such ideas, Congress, we must assume, would not have tried to impose them, in an act of legal imperialism, through legislative fiat."[66] Even where policies converge regarding forbidden anticompetitive conduct,

---

[62] *Empagran S.A. v F. Hoffman-LaRoche, Ltd.*, 315 F3d 338, 357 (DC Cir 2003), revd, 124 S Ct 2359 (2004). The language of the provision, 15 USC § 6a, is convoluted and too long to be worth quoting here.

[63] 124 S Ct at 2373 (Scalia, joined by Thomas, concurring in the judgment). The separate concurrence undoubtedly reflected his standing objection to use of legislative history, but may also have had other bases. Justice O'Connor did not participate in the decision.

[64] Id at 2366.

[65] Id (citations omitted). The omitted citations include a quotation of the *Charming Betsy* principle: "[A]n act of Congress ought never to be construed to violate the law of nations if any other possible construction remains." *Murray v Schooner Charming Betsy*, 6 US (2 Cranch) 64, 118 (1804).

[66] 124 S Ct at 2369.

nations may "disagree dramatically about appropriate remedies."[67] Justice Breyer took note of amicus briefs filed by foreign governments, objecting that U.S. treble damage suits bypassed local remedial policies, and undercut the incentive of firms to seek prosecutorial amnesties. The United States had also argued that the D.C. Circuit's interpretation impaired U.S. amnesty policy, and that it would "be likely to result in tension with our trading partners" and harm cooperative enforcement efforts that "depend on mutual good will and reciprocity."[68]

Justice Breyer's second reason addressed the language and history of the FTAIA. He concluded that Congress did not intend the provision to expand private antitrust liability, and that prior case law would not have led Congress to believe that independently caused foreign injury was actionable. The Court left open on remand whether the plaintiffs could prove that their injury flowed from the domestic effects of the price-fixing conspiracy.

E. HOW THE EXECUTIVE SOMETIMES LOSES IN FOREIGN AFFAIRS

Harold Koh has persuasively shown how, despite the Constitution's distribution of relevant powers among the three branches of government, the twentieth century produced a regime in which "the President (Almost) Always Wins in Foreign Affairs."[69] Executive initiative, congressional passivity, and judicial tolerance combine to produce unilateral Executive action and to defeat legislative efforts to limit Executive authority.[70] Judicial tolerance includes both deference on the merits and barriers to justiciability, which reinforce Executive dominance.[71]

The Government's failure to persuade the Supreme Court to adopt its position on three important issues of foreign relations law within a month is therefore striking.[72] The three rejected po-

---

[67] Id at 2368.

[68] Brief for the United States as Amicus Curiae Supporting Petitioners, *F. Hoffmann-La Roche Ltd. v Empagran, S.A.*, No 03-724, *20–22 (filed Feb 2004).

[69] Harold Hongju Koh, *The National Security Constitution: Sharing Power after the Iran-Contra Affair* 117 (Yale, 1990).

[70] He refers to congressional "acquiescence," id, but the term "passivity" better summarizes his findings of inaction and ineffectual activity for present purposes.

[71] Id at 134.

[72] It is even more striking when coupled with Justice O'Connor's rebuke to the Government's vision of separation of powers in *Hamdi v Rumsfeld*, 124 S Ct 2633, 2650 (2004) (plurality opinion). That case is discussed in Sunstein, *Minimalism at War* at 63 (cited in note 1), and lies outside the agreed scope of this article.

sitions might be said to share a common feature: each would remove an unduly broad range of cases from judicial cognizance. In
Rasul, the Government sought to place an entire enclave outside
the rule of law; in *Sosa*, the Government sought to eliminate a
category of litigation to avoid even the possibility of embarrassment; and in *Altmann*, more modestly, the Government sought to
exclude older cases from a superseding congressional code of immunity law. Even in *Empagran*, where the Government's position
prevailed, Justice Breyer subtly gave the Government more law
than it wanted, by invoking the *Charming Betsy* canon.

Put another way, the Government asked for sweeping victories
from a Court that often prefers to decide narrowly. That was
particularly true in *Sosa*, where the Government and other amici
proposed radical revisionism at a time when a majority of the
Court apparently saw a need for stability. In *Rasul*, the Government's claims of unchecked power were radical, but more archaic
than novel. In *Altmann*, however, the retroactivity argument was
conventional, and rule of law considerations lay on both sides of
the dispute.

Moreover, the Government did not fully lose any of these cases,
not yet. In *Rasul*, the Government lost the jurisdictional battle,
but the merits remained open on remand. In *Altmann*, the Government acted only as amicus, and Justice Breyer identified several
alternative doctrines that might prevent recovery. In *Sosa*, the Government's friend won on the merits, and the Government prevailed
fully on its own Federal Tort Claims Act defense. Supreme Court
litigation often isolates a specific legal issue, and losing the principle does not necessarily prevent the government from pursuing
its chosen course of action. In that specific sense, these decisions
may confirm Dean Koh's account of why the Executive (almost)
always wins. There are many stages at which deference strengthens
his hand.

Still, the reasons matter. They shape future controversies,
prompt or discourage dialogue among the branches and with constituencies, and change the cost of winning. It is therefore worthwhile to examine the extent and implications of the Court's defense
of the place of law within foreign relations.

II. The Law in Foreign Relations Law

The Supreme Court's decisions in June 2004 confirmed

the authority of all three branches of the federal government to contribute to the successful conduct of the nation's foreign relations. Against the Solicitor General's drumbeat that all forms of constraint may have collateral consequences that impair the prosecution of the war against terrorism,[73] the Court kept in view both the violent and pacific forms of globalization. As Justice Breyer explained in *Empagran*, "today's highly interdependent commercial world" required harmony among varying legal systems.[74] Customary international law helps maintain that harmony, and courts facilitate it by taking those system needs into account in statutory interpretation. The Government's own briefs in that case stressed regulatory cooperation, not the siege mentality of an embattled superpower.

The tripartite collaboration extends beyond transnational economic relations to transnational public relations, which are in fact inseparable from them. The President's "vast share of responsibility for the conduct of our foreign relations"[75] does not absorb all the functions of the courts and Congress in that field.

In this section, I will discuss first the Court's reaffirmation in *Sosa* of the authority of the courts to facilitate cooperation with the international system by implementing customary international law norms through the federal common law. Next, I will turn to the Court's emphasis in both *Sosa* and *Altmann* on the power of Congress to define the domestic legal framework for international cooperation. Finally, I will examine the Court's refusal in *Rasul*, a case directly involving the war against terrorism, to facilitate national security functions by defining Guantanamo as beyond the reach of the rule of law.

---

[73] The phrase "war against terrorism" deserves some comment. There is no war against terrorism as such, but (in my view) there does exist an armed conflict between the United States and al Qaeda. I will use the phrase here on the understanding that it is a conventional, possibly misleading, shorthand for an aspect of current U.S. foreign and military policy. See Joan Fitzpatrick, *Jurisdiction of Military Commissions and the Ambiguous War on Terrorism*, 96 Am J Intl L 345, 346–47 (2002) (explaining what a war on terrorism as such would mean). The Supreme Court did not endorse the concept of a general war against terrorism in its June 2004 decisions; the plurality in *Hamdi v Rumsfeld*, 124 S Ct 2633 (2004), relied upon the congressional authorization for the use of military force "against 'nations, organizations, or persons' associated with the September 11, 2001, terrorist attacks." Id at 2640 (plurality).

[74] 124 S Ct at 2363.

[75] *Altmann*, 124 S Ct at 2255 (quoting *American Insurance Association v Garamendi*, 539 US 396, 414 (2003)).

A.   SOSA AND THE JUDICIAL POWER

The *Sosa* decision raises broad and important themes concerning the role of the federal judiciary in foreign relations law, and the relationship between international law and the U.S. legal system. In the end, it provided clear answers only to narrow questions, leaving further implications to be worked out by future decisions or by legislation.

Critics of international human rights litigation have focused in recent years on two formal legal strategies that would give positive force to their substantive objections. The first, derived from Judge Robert Bork's individual opinion in *Tel-Oren v Libyan Arab Republic*,[76] contends that the Alien Tort Statute neither supplies a cause of action nor authorizes the courts to imply one. The second, broader argument—not made by Judge Bork[77]—maintains that the incorporation of customary international law into the U.S. legal system, a tradition dating back to and beyond the founding, did not weather the transition to the post-*Erie* conception of federal common law. On this view, the notion that "international law is part of our law"[78] fell away with the general common law of *Swift v Tyson*, and survives only in those states that choose to continue it as part of their own state common law. The Government made the first of these arguments vigorously, and employed elements of the second more hesitantly,[79] while amicus briefs of private parties urged it at full volume.[80]

---

[76] 726 F2d 774, 801 (DC Cir 1984) (Bork concurring).

[77] See id at 810–11, 804 nn 10 & 11 (accepting incorporated customary international law as federal common law and noting exclusive federal power over foreign relations).

[78] *The Paquete Habana*, 175 US 677 (1900).

[79] See Brief for the United States as Respondent Supporting Petitioner, *Sosa v Alvarez-Machain*, No 03-339, *29–31, 34–36 & nn 11 & 12 (filed Jan 2004) (US Sosa Merits Brief) (attempting to avoid resolution of the post-*Erie* status of customary international law by relying on arguments against implication of private rights of action). One of the Government's likely reasons for failing to align itself completely with the revisionist literature may be glimpsed in its recent brief in the Ninth Circuit's *Unocal* case, where it argued that permitting enforcement of customary international law as *state common law* would be "inconsistent with the constitutional grant of responsibility over foreign affairs to the Federal Government, to the exclusion of the states." Brief for the United States of America, as *Amicus Curiae*, *Doe v Unocal Corporation*, 9th Cir, Nos 00-56603, 00-56628, *23 n 12 (filed May 2003).

[80] For example, see Brief of Washington Legal Foundation, National Fraternal Order of Police and Allied Educational Foundation as Amici Curiae in Support of Petitioner, *Sosa v Alvarez-Machain*, No 03-339 (filed Jan 23, 2004); Brief Amicus Curiae of Pacific Legal Foundation in Support of Petitioner, *Sosa v Alvarez-Machain*, No 03-339 (filed Jan 23, 2004).

The Court held in *Sosa* that the ATS does not itself create a cause of action, but that it contemplates judicial recognition of causes of action for certain violations of international law (including, but not limited to, certain human rights violations). Although the Court spoke of "judicial recognition,"[81] it emphasized that this is not a passive act of perception, but an active deed of creation, an exercise in the making of federal common law, "adapting the law of nations to private rights."[82] The *Sosa* decision thus deals importantly with the second strategy, which questioned the role of federal common law in relation to international law.

Most of Justice Souter's opinion, however, addresses this question narrowly, in two respects. First, he repeatedly phrased the key issue as involving federal common law authority to create a private right of action to enforce an international norm. As he observed, the arguments against such authority include the Court's specific retreat in recent years from the creation of private rights of action to enforce other categories of federal law. And, indeed, international law itself does not usually specify the required remedy for violations, and certainly does not require states to provide damage remedies for violations committed by other states. Second, the existence of the ATS and the history of congressional activity and inactivity in relation to the growth of ATS litigation provided at least some legislative countenance to the federal common law role.[83]

Nonetheless, the majority also spoke more broadly to the question of federal common law, in response to Justice Scalia's advocacy of the revisionist position. Recognition and enforcement of international law as a matter of federal common law without specific legislative authorization does not overstep the proper judicial role. *Erie* did not abolish the common law activity of federal courts, but rather narrowed it to particular enclaves. One of those enclaves concerned foreign relations law, and it provided the appropriate rubric for continuity in the reception of international law. "For two centuries we have affirmed that the domestic law of the United States recognizes the law of nations."[84] The majority recalled the standard modern narrative by which the Court's opinion in the

---

[81] 124 S Ct at 2765.

[82] Id at 2764.

[83] Id at 2765.

[84] Id at 2764 (citing cases, including the emblematic *Paquete Habana*, 175 US 677 (1900)).

Sabbatino case had "endorsed the reasoning of a noted commentator who had argued that *Erie* should not preclude the continued application of international law in federal courts."[85] He was referring to Philip Jessup's editorial comment, published shortly after *Erie*, calling attention to the need for federal control of the interpretation of international law, and the inapplicability of the federalism concerns in *Erie* to issues of international law, which fall clearly within federal power. Justice Souter, in his understated way, added that "It would take some explaining to say now that federal courts must avert their gaze entirely from any international law intended to protect individuals."[86]

One might elaborate that observation as follows: the unbroken tradition of judicial recognition of international law traces back to the founding. The practice is unquestionably not impeachable on *originalist* grounds, and the revisionists do not seek to revive the Framers' understanding of international law and its relationship to domestic law. The practice of defeasible judicial incorporation of international law rules into federal law in accordance with common law methods has evolved as institutions have evolved. To claim that it violates the separation of powers contradicts the very history that informs separation of powers reasoning. It should be added that the earlier practice of incorporation was not based on the Alien Tort Statute, and so did not rely on any implicit authorization from Congress contained in that provision.

In one sense, however, Justice Scalia is correct, and the majority did not disagree. Customary international law does not *automatically* become federal law, and does not *automatically* give rise to a private right of action for money damages. It enters federal law by the agency of some branch of government, including the courts. The majority emphasized that the power to create federal common law should be exercised with restraint (at least with regard to fashioning private rights of action to enforce international law, and possibly more generally). The Court accepted some of the

---

[85] Id at 2764 & n 18 (citing *Banco Nacional de Cuba v Sabbatino*, 376 US 398, 425 (1964), and Philip C. Jessup, *The Doctrine of Erie Railroad v. Tompkins Applied to International Law*, 33 Am J Intl L 740 (1939)). See Restatement (Third) of the Foreign Relations Law of the United States § 111, Reporters' Note 3 (1987) (Restatement (Third)); Gerald L. Neuman, *Sense and Nonsense about Customary International Law: A Response to Professors Bradley and Goldsmith*, 66 Fordham L Rev 371, 374–76 (1997).

[86] 124 S Ct at 2764–65.

Government's policy concerns as reasons for caution, not for abandonment of the *Filartiga* jurisprudence. The placement of enforcement initiative in the hands of injured private parties, the identification of rules of customary international law, and the resolution of claims that foreign governments have violated the rights of their own citizens, all had foreign policy implications.[87] These counseled care in defining the scope of the private right of action, and possibly also case-by-case consideration of Executive objections to adjudicating particular disputes.[88]

Moreover, the majority observed that the federal courts "have no congressional mandate to seek out and define new and debatable violations of the law of nations."[89] In part, this observation states the obvious: U.S. courts should apply, not invent, international law, and they should scrutinize advocates' accounts of that law with care. But it also appears to state a contingent conclusion. Within the current legal framework, federal courts should be followers, not leaders, in the development of customary international law. As a result, "we are persuaded that federal courts should not recognize private claims under federal common law for violations of an international law norm with less definite content and acceptance among civilized nations than the historical paradigms familiar when § 1350 was enacted."[90] Deliberately, the Court accepts the possibility that not every customary norm will be implemented by a private right of action.[91]

These exercises in restraint in the crafting of the ATS cause of action are exercises of judicial power. *Sosa* underlines the continuing importance of the affirmative role of the judiciary in facilitating international cooperation through the application of international law. The existence and content of rules of customary international law binding on the United States should be deter-

---

[87] Id at 2763.

[88] Id at 2766 n 21.

[89] Id at 2763.

[90] Id at 2765.

[91] That restriction entails a significant guideline for the phrasing of legal conclusions in ATS cases denying liability. Because national court decisions applying international law are important data in the demonstration of international custom, federal courts rejecting ATS claims should be careful not to deny the existence of a customary international norm merely because the plaintiff has failed to prove that it possesses sufficient specificity to justify a private right of action under *Sosa*. Rather, the proper conclusion is, as the majority itself stated, the absence of a "norm of customary international law so well defined as to support the creation of a federal remedy." 124 S Ct at 2769.

mined as a matter of federal law. Where Congress has not provided explicit direction, courts ease the interaction between the domestic and international legal systems by recognizing and incorporating international norms, to the extent that they can be harmonized with other federal law. The reasoning of the majority preserves federal common law as the means by which the "old" customary international law of purely state-to-state obligations has been received into domestic law, for those instances in which it has not yet been codified by treaty or statute. That traditional function had been potentially threatened as a by-product of the attack on the "new" customary international law of human rights obligations owed also by states to their citizens. In that connection, Justice Scalia's separate concurrence had expressed a casual disregard for the continuing need for judicial recognition of "old" customary norms.[92]

The *Sosa* decision leaves room, however, for future disputes over the enforcement of customary international law as federal common law. The origins and recent history of the ATS contributed to the majority's willingness to create private rights of action, even cautiously. In a somewhat ambiguously worded footnote, Justice Souter noted that the ATS (28 USC § 1350) provided a more appropriate basis for deriving common law claims from international law than the federal question jurisdiction statute, 28 USC § 1331.[93] The Court did not address other postures in which international law norms might be applicable, and the proper amount of judicial

---

[92] See id at 2775–76 (Scalia concurring in the judgment) ("Those accepted practices have *for the most part, if not in their entirety*, been enacted into United States statutory law, so that insofar as they are concerned the demise of the general common law is inconsequential.") (emphasis added).

[93] Id at 2765 n 19 (majority). The majority disclaimed the notion, which it understood Justice Scalia as attributing to it, that every grant of federal jurisdiction carries with it a corresponding opportunity to develop federal common law, implicitly drawing on the *Lincoln Mills* model, see *Textile Workers v Lincoln Mills of Alabama*, 353 US 448 (1957) (deducing authority to create federal common law of collective bargaining agreements from a specific jurisdictional grant). In the case of Section 1331, that would authorize common law making across a vast range of federal questions, swallowing the post-*Erie* enclaves. (The footnote's cross-reference to an earlier passage describing the proper scope of federal common law making is more clearly indicated in the slip opinion, where the pages are shorter, than in the longer pages of the West Supreme Court Reporter.) This footnote should not be understood as casting doubt on whether the ATS causes of action, once recognized, arise under federal law within the meaning of Section 1331, or more generally whether customary international law rules adopted (or adapted) as federal common law rules are federal for jurisdictional purposes. Compare *Illinois v Milwaukee*, 406 US 91 (1972) (holding that actions based on federal common law claims arise under the laws of the United States within the meaning of § 1331).

initiative in those contexts. Customary international law norms might, for example, become relevant in challenges to the conduct of agency officials under the Administrative Procedure Act,[94] or as controlling secondary issues in commercial litigation, or as providing immunities or defenses. Indeed, one important reason for incorporating international norms into federal common law is that otherwise courts would sometimes be powerless to prevent *themselves* from violating international law.

The law of consular immunity provides a simple but instructive example. Under customary international law, foreign consuls enjoy an immunity from criminal and civil liability for the exercise of their official functions. The Vienna Convention on Consular Relations codifies that immunity, but only as between states parties to the Convention. Immunity for consuls from other states is governed either by bilateral consular treaties or by customary international law.[95] It is understandable that Congress, having once devoted Senate attention to the multilateral Consular Convention, would not take time to enact an express post-*Erie* statutory immunity for nonsignatories. That inertia should not enable private parties to induce federal courts to violate the immunity of consuls from the remaining states.

Both the majority and Justice Breyer's concurrence understood the judicial task as requiring reconciliation of multiple considerations of international law and foreign relations, which might pull in different directions. Justice Breyer warned that the federal courts should exercise their common law authority so as "to ensure that ATS litigation does not undermine the very harmony that it was intended to promote."[96] In particular, he argued that the same principles of comity that he had employed in *Empagran* should inform the exercise of ATS jurisdiction in cases arising in foreign

----

[94] See 5 USC § 706(2)(A) (authorizing courts to set aside agency action that is "not in accordance with law"). Under the traditional view of the role of customary international law in U.S. domestic law, it is understood that the President can perform a "controlling executive act" that supersedes its application, but that low-level officers—like the naval officer in *The Paquete Habana*, 175 US 677 (1900)—cannot. The line between the two, possibly drawn at the rank of Cabinet officers, is unsettled. See Neuman, 66 Fordham L Rev at 381–82 (cited in note 85).

[95] See Restatement (Third) at 457 (cited in note 85). Moreover, the Consular Convention itself affirms "that the rules of customary international law continue to govern matters not expressly regulated by the provisions of the present Convention." Vienna Convention on Consular Relations, preamble, TIAS 6820, 21 UST 77, 79 (1969).

[96] 124 S Ct at 2782 (Breyer concurring).

territory. Those comity principles did not counsel against U.S. regulation of the conduct of its own nationals, but did affect imposition of liability on the conduct of foreign nationals abroad. Unlike in *Empagran*, the norm of conduct allegedly violated would be international—and thus expecting compliance would not be an "act of legal imperialism [or] legislative fiat"[97]—but in practice, "different courts in different nations will not necessarily apply even similar substantive laws similarly."[98] Accordingly, in ATS cases challenging foreign conduct of foreign nationals, U.S. courts should look not only for a universal norm of conduct but for an international "procedural consensus" permitting enforcement of the norm by unrelated courts.[99] Such a consensus could be found at least with regard to violations subject to universal criminal jurisdiction, such as torture, genocide, crimes against humanity, and war crimes.

The merit of this proposed limitation could be discussed further, but the point that requires emphasis here is that Justice Breyer made particularly clear the multidirectional character of the federal courts' role in cooperating with the international legal system. Human rights norms are not the only international factor to be considered, and they receive consideration *as international law norms*, not as a judicially privileged higher category of U.S. foreign policy. In one sense, this is obvious—the human rights litigation is predicated on a statute addressing torts "in violation of the law of nations." But the Court's evenhanded approach differs from the perspective of many human rights advocates, who would assign human rights claims a quasiconstitutional position in a normative hierarchy.[100] The Court's neutrality here is consistent with its at-

---

[97] *Empagran*, 124 S Ct at 2369.

[98] *Sosa*, 124 S Ct at 2782 (Breyer concurring).

[99] Id at 2783.

[100] Such a hierarchy does exist within international law, where some customary norms protecting human rights, such as those addressing genocide and torture, may be *jus cogens*, that is, so compelling that treaty provisions contradicting them would be invalid. See Vienna Convention on the Law of Treaties, Art 53, 1155 UNTS 331; Restatement (Third) (cited in note 85) § 102 comment k (defining *jus cogens*); id § 702 comment n (describing particular human rights norms as *jus cogens*). Nonetheless, even human rights tribunals have recognized that the methods for implementing those norms must be reconciled with other norms of international law lacking *jus cogens* status, such as foreign state immunity. See *Al-Adsani v United Kingdom*, 2001-XI ECHR 79 (Grand Chamber) (holding, by nine to eight vote, that the United Kingdom did not violate the right to court access under the European human rights convention by affording foreign state immunity to Kuwait in a case involving torture).

titude in *Saudi Arabia v Nelson*, declining to stretch an exception to foreign sovereign immunity to cover the torture of a U.S. citizen employee.[101] The Court showed similar detachment in *Crosby v National Foreign Trade Council*, concluding that the federal Burma sanctions statute occupied the field and preempted the states from using their procurement policies to distance themselves from companies doing business with a deeply repressive regime.[102] The Court emphasized that the federal legislation gave the President discretion to compromise human rights goals and national security interests, that "Congress manifestly intended to limit economic pressure against the Burmese Government to a specific range," and that "[s]anctions are drawn not only to bar what they prohibit but to allow what they permit."[103]

Thus, the Court understands the creative judicial role as designed to foster coherence between other norms of federal law and the international system, not to give international law in general or international human rights law in particular priority over federal law. It performs this function provisionally, as federal common law does, subject to legislative redirection.

B.   LEGISLATIVE FRAMING AND EXECUTIVE POINTING

In both the *Sosa* and *Altmann* decisions, the Court rejected broad rules proposed by the Government that would deny jurisdiction in order to prevent even the possibility of negative impacts on foreign relations. Instead, the Court privileged the role of legislation in setting the framework for transnational litigation, while simultaneously preserving the opportunity for the Government to argue against the exercise of jurisdiction on a case-by-case basis. Courts will need to proceed cautiously in the further refinement of this complex set of interactions among the three branches.

In *Sosa*, consistent with the federal common law characterization of its inquiry, the majority repeatedly emphasized the ability of Congress to modify the framework of ATS litigation or particular subclasses. Justice Souter wrote:

[While] we would welcome any congressional guidance in ex-

---

[101] 507 US 349 (1993).

[102] 530 US 363 (2000).

[103] Id at 375, 377, 380.

ercising jurisdiction with such obvious potential to affect foreign relations, nothing Congress has done is a reason for us
to shut the door to the law of nations entirely. It is enough
to say that Congress may do that at any time (explicitly, or
implicitly by treaties or statutes that occupy the field) just as
it may modify or cancel any judicial decision so far as it rests
on recognizing an international norm as such.[104]

This language puts the point dramatically, but fundamentally it
restates the traditional qualification asserted in *The Paquete Habana*, that the Court would apply customary international law only
"where there is no treaty, and no controlling executive or legislative act."[105] After *Erie*, that qualification remains true: federal
common law is made within the framework of existing federal
statutes, and not in contradiction to it.

The majority's desire for legislative guidance was not so strong
as to impede it from careful analysis of the proffered texts. It did
not find that any existing human rights treaty, such as the International Covenant on Civil and Political Rights (ICCPR), occupied the field. Indeed, human rights treaties are intended to supplement, not to reduce, other forms of protection for individual
rights, and often include savings clauses saying so.[106] The majority
observed that the reservations, understandings, and declarations
accompanying U.S. ratification of the ICCPR, and some other
human rights treaties, included a declaration that they would not
be self-executing for the United States.[107] It interpreted these declarations as indicating that Congress was not affirmatively en-

---

[104] 124 S Ct at 2765. Presumably by "cancel any judicial decision," the Court means
that Congress has the power to block future enforcement of the same norm, not to overturn
a final judgment. Compare *Plaut v Spendthrift Farm, Inc.*, 514 US 211 (1995).

[105] 175 US 677, 700 (1900).

[106] The principal savings clause of the ICCPR provides: "There shall be no restriction
upon or derogation from any of the fundamental human rights recognized or existing in
any State Party to the present Covenant pursuant to law, conventions, regulations or
custom on the pretext that the present Covenant does not recognize such rights or that
it recognizes them to a lesser extent." International Covenant on Civil and Political Rights,
Article 5(2), 999 UNTS 171.

[107] 124 S Ct at 2763. The Court's decision apparently confirms that a declaration of
non-self-executing character is legally effective within U.S. law, a proposition that some
commentators have doubted, but that lower courts generally have not. It should be noted
that these declarations are not reservations, that is, they do not purport to modify the
international obligations of the United States under the treaties. See Restatement (Third)
(cited in note 85) § 313, comments a & g (explaining the difference between reservations
and declarations). Human rights treaties do not require self-execution, only compliance.

couraging "greater judicial creativity,"[108] but it resisted the facile conclusion that they demonstrated a congressional policy against judicial recognition of human rights norms that had achieved binding force as customary international law.

Specifically with regard to the ICCPR, the majority concluded that the declaration precluded it from viewing the prohibition of arbitrary detention in ICCPR Article 9(1) as being itself a sufficient source for a rule of international law enforceable by private right of action under the ATS.[109] But the majority rightly did not read sweeping preemptive significance into this declaration. The ICCPR contains twenty-two articles including over sixty paragraphs guaranteeing both negative and positive rights ranging from the prohibition of slavery to the right of families to protection by the state, and from the right to form trade unions to the right of ethnic minorities to enjoy their own culture.[110] The Senate's decision not to delegate the implementation of this broad charter to the courts does not preclude judicial recognition of a separate, and perhaps narrower, customary international law norm against arbitrary detention. The majority properly looked to other sources for proof of such a norm, but it failed to find sufficient evidence of a specific norm that covered Alvarez's detention.

The Court did not follow, or even mention, the Government's contention that a declaration of non-self-executing character should be regarded as a "controlling executive or legislative act" preventing recourse to customary international law.[111] The Court would be more likely, however, to find such a "controlling act" in a substantive reservation clearly designed to avoid the creation of

---

[108] 124 S Ct at 2763. The pattern of declarations is uneven, and the Court avoided the sloppy claim that the Senate consistently attaches such declarations to human rights treaties.

[109] Id at 2767. The majority described the ICCPR as having "little utility" to demonstrating a customary international norm of sufficient specificity to be actionable under the ATS. Id. Precisely what this statement means is unclear. If, however, there were more persuasive evidence of the existence of a specific customary norm, the declaration that the ICCPR would not be self-executing for the United States should not prevent the Court from regarding the treaty as additional corroborative evidence of *other civilized nations'* acceptance of the norm, which is a necessary but not sufficient condition for customary status. Treaties to which the United States is not, or indeed could not be, a party may also be relevant corroborative evidence for that purpose, taken in combination with evidence that the norm is binding independent of treaties.

[110] ICCPR articles 8(1), 23(1), 22(1), 27.

[111] See US Sosa Merits Brief (cited in note 79) at 35 ("A ratified treaty accompanied by an express declaration that it is not self-executing is plainly such a controlling act.").

an international obligation, at least so long as it remained consistent with other expressions of federal policy.[112]

The Court's preference for legislative guidance played a stronger, perhaps determinative role in *Altmann*. Indeed, the majority opinion focused so strongly on the Foreign Sovereign Immunities Act that it appeared to have lost sight of the international law lying behind it. The problem to be resolved in that decision was whether the comprehensive codification of foreign sovereign immunity in the FSIA should be applied regardless of the time frame of the events giving rise to the litigation. The Court recognized that the statute did not provide an unambiguous answer to that question, but it preferred to follow codified legislative standards that would clarify and depoliticize the immunity determination.

The majority rejected both the Ninth Circuit's and the Government's approaches based on its characterization of the jurisdictional immunity of foreign states and the Executive behavior implementing it before 1976. Reiterating and intensifying a historical account that the Court has employed in its FSIA cases, the majority described foreign sovereign immunity as purely "a matter of grace and comity"[113] that the United States has afforded on foreign policy grounds. It stated that "[t]hroughout history, courts have resolved questions of foreign sovereign immunity by deferring to the 'decisions of the political branches . . . on whether to

---

[112] The most prominent example in the literature is the U.S. reservation to the ICCPR rejecting adherence to the prohibition in Article 6(5) on capital punishment for crimes committed before the age of eighteen. The purpose of that reservation is reinforced by other U.S. actions denying international limits on the discretion of the federal government, and especially the states, to impose the juvenile death penalty. See Curtis A. Bradley, *The Juvenile Death Penalty and International Law*, 52 Duke L J 485, 525–35 (2002) (giving one account of these activities). The constitutionality of the juvenile death penalty is before the Court again in the October 2004 Term. See *Roper v Simmons*, 124 S Ct 1171 (2004) (granting certiorari). To the extent that such executions do not violate the Eighth Amendment, even if it were concluded that a norm of customary international law binding on the United States prohibits the juvenile death penalty, the reservation should currently be understood as precluding enforcement of that norm as a matter of federal common law.

[113] 124 S Ct at 2248. The notion that foreign sovereign immunity is *merely* a "matter of grace and comity," and *therefore* defeasible for human rights violators, is familiar from the human rights advocacy literature and from Judge Patricia Wald's dissent in *Princz v Federal Republic of Germany*, 26 F3d 1166, 1181 (DC Cir 1994) (Wald dissenting). Judge Wald would have applied the FSIA retroactively to the claims of a concentration camp survivor, and would have attributed an "implied waiver" of immunity to states that violate *jus cogens* norms of international law. The panel majority rejected this waiver theory as too strained an interpretation of the FSIA.

take jurisdiction.'"[114] On this basis, the majority treated past Executive suggestions of immunity as matters of ad hoc foreign policy
that could not generate justifiable expectations or rule-like patterns that would raise retroactivity concerns.[115]

The Court has described the FSIA as "a comprehensive framework for determining whether a court in this country, state or
federal, may exercise jurisdiction over a foreign state."[116] As such,
the statute often avoids the necessity for careful judicial examination of its historical and international law background. *Altmann*
may illustrate the consequences of this convenience. The Court
has become accustomed to collapse the century and a half pre-
ceding the Tate Letter into a single period, eliding well-docu-
mented changes.[117] Justice Stevens's majority opinion cites no foreign or international law sources. His short quotation from the
preamble to the FSIA omits its reference to international law,[118]
and one could read the entire opinion without intuiting that the
immunity of foreign states was a subject addressed by international
law.

To emphasize this point is not to say that closer attention to
international law would necessarily have changed the outcome.
Justice Breyer's concurrence did examine foreign and international
sources, and reached the same conclusion as the majority.[119] Austria

---

[114] 124 S Ct at 2252 (quoting *Verlinden B.V. v Central Bank of Nigeria*, 461 US 480, 486 (1983)).

[115] The Court's disparagement of prior State Department practice reflects criticisms by Congress, commentators, and the Executive Branch itself. The State Department received diplomatic pressure to grant immunity in cases not clearly within the purportedly gov-erning standards of the Tate Letter, and sometimes succumbed. Congress enacted the FSIA in part to relieve the State Department of the unwanted pressure. Nonetheless, that general proposition does not refute the Government's argument that it would never have withheld a suggestion of immunity for an expropriation claim, and that the FSIA exception therefore made new law for the United States.

[116] *Republic of Argentina v Weltover, Inc.*, 504 US 607, 610 (1992).

[117] See Louis Henkin, *Foreign Affairs and the U.S. Constitution* 54–56 (Clarendon, 2d ed 1996); G. Edward White, *The Transformation of the Constitutional Regime of Foreign Relations*, 85 Va L Rev 1, 134–45 (1999).

[118] 124 S Ct at 2252. The full section is quoted in Justice Kennedy's dissent, including the sentence, "Under international law, states are not immune from the jurisdiction of foreign courts insofar as their commercial activities are concerned . . . ." Id at 2265 (quoting 28 USC § 1602). See also HR Rep No 1487, 94th Cong, 2d Sess 8 (1976) (accompanying the bill that became the FSIA) ("Sovereign immunity is a doctrine of international law under which domestic courts, in appropriate cases, relinquish jurisdiction over a foreign state.").

[119] 124 S Ct at 2259–61 (Breyer concurring). He too described foreign sovereign im-munity as "a matter, not of legal right, but of 'grace and comity.'" Id at 22 (quoting

did not argue that asserting jurisdiction in *Altmann* would *violate* customary international law. The expropriation exception might be applied in a manner consistent with the restrictive theory of immunity as currently understood in the international community. Austria's argument rested on a retroactive change in the U.S. approach, not the U.S. adoption of an impermissible standard. The dissent similarly based its argument on "the internal integrity of American statutes."[120] The *Charming Betsy* principle, that statutes should be interpreted if possible to avoid violation of international law, did not offer guidance in *Altmann*.

Justice Stevens emphasized that the retroactivity—or, more generally, the "reach"—of the FSIA was a "'pure question of statutory construction . . . well within the province of the Judiciary,'"[121] citing his own opinion in *INS v Cardoza-Fonseca*.[122] On such questions, the Government's views held "considerable interest" but deserved "no special deference."[123] However, he added, the State Department's articulated opinion on the foreign policy consequences of a particular exercise of jurisdiction over a foreign state (or its instrumentality) might be entitled to deference.[124] He left open the extent to which the FSIA permitted a court to decline jurisdiction on foreign policy grounds, or to defer to the Executive in doing so. That form of intervention might create an additional means for accommodating the dissent's concerns about reopening

---

Verlinden, 461 US at 486). Given the Justice's consciousness of the international background, that is more surprising. In *Verlinden* itself, the Court had asserted only that foreign sovereign immunity was "a matter of grace and comity on the part of the United States, and not a restriction imposed by the Constitution." There is a large middle ground for nonconstitutional legal rules motivated by comity. Where the FSIA affords immunity, it *is* a legal entitlement, though it may be based in comity. Similarly, international law norms requiring immunity may be based in comity, but may still be rules. It is true that U.S. law can afford foreign sovereign immunity out of comity in instances where international law does not require it, and might have done so if Austria had prevailed; but neither the majority nor the concurrence appeared to be limiting their characterization to such instances.

[120] 124 S Ct at 2272 (Kennedy dissenting).

[121] Id at 2255.

[122] 480 US 421, 446, 448 (1987). *Cardoza-Fonseca* was an immigration case, involving U.S. legislation implementing a treaty for the protection of refugees. The Court rejected *Chevron* deference to the immigration officials' interpretation of the statute, relying instead on "traditional tools of statutory construction." Id at 446. Whether or which immigration cases should be regarded as coming within the field of foreign relations law is a nice question. Probably they provide an early illustration of the instability of the distinction between foreign and domestic affairs.

[123] 124 S Ct at 2255.

[124] Id.

postwar disputes that had appeared settled. Similarly, in *Sosa* the majority raised the possibility (citing *Altmann*) that courts should sometimes decline to adjudicate ATS cases because of their specific foreign policy impact, and should give "serious weight" to the Executive's assessment of the impact.[125]

These proposed approaches appear to contemplate not only deference to Executive concerns in deciding whether the public interest favors relegating the dispute to another forum,[126] but independent bases for dismissing suits that could be brought nowhere else. The lower courts have assumed that foreign policy consequences could justify dismissing ATS claims under the political question doctrine.[127] The Court in *Sosa* and *Altmann* did not specify whether it saw the problem in justiciability terms.[128] Arguably the Justices had in mind the application of a federal common law rule of foreign relations, comparable to the act of state doctrine, that would permit dismissal of an action to avoid embarrassing the Executive's conduct of foreign relations. After Justice Kennedy warned that allowing the Executive to "supersede" the FSIA standards would raise grave separation of powers questions, as well as threaten judicial independence,[129] the majority emphasized that it was considering giving the Executive's views of foreign policy impact serious weight, not controlling effect.

Both *Altmann* and *Sosa* thus emphasize the importance of general laws (legislation in the former, legislation and treaties in the latter) in creating the framework for the resolution of disputes implicating foreign relations, while inviting the Executive to point

---

[125] *Sosa*, 124 S Ct at 2766 n 21. Justice Breyer agreed, id at 2782 (Breyer concurring), and presumably it is covered by Justice Scalia's statement that he "agree[d] with much in Part IV," id at 2769 (Scalia concurring in part).

[126] Compare *Aguinda v Texaco, Inc.*, 303 F3d 470 (2d Cir 2002) (upholding *forum non conveniens* dismissal of an ATS action after concluding that the balance of private and public interests favored resolution in the courts of Ecuador).

[127] See *Kadic v Karadzic*, 70 F3d 232, 249–50 (2d Cir 1996) (considering foreign policy objections under the political question rubric, and describing Executive views as "entitled to respectful consideration," while noting that the Executive disclaimed concern); *Sarei v Rio Tinto plc*, 221 F Supp 2d 1116, 1196–99 (CD Cal 2002) (dismissing action on political question grounds after the State Department expressed concern for its impact on the ongoing peace process in Papua New Guinea).

[128] Indeed, the awkward debate between majority and dissent in *Altmann* concerning the separation of powers implications of this proposal implies that it did not. Otherwise the issues noted by the dissent ought to have included whether Congress could direct the courts to decide a nonjusticiable case.

[129] 124 S Ct at 2274 (Kennedy dissenting).

the court to the case-specific foreign policy consequences. Both decisions indicate that the courts will retain final responsibility for interpreting the legal framework and for deciding whether the foreign policy consequences are of a kind that justifies withholding adjudication. In both decisions the Court declined to interpret the framework in the manner that the Government had urged for the purpose of establishing a prophylactic barrier against adverse foreign policy consequences that might arise in a subset of cases.

Rejecting the prophylactic rule, but offering deference to statements of interest, requires the Executive to act openly to block particular adjudications. That exposes the Executive to lobbying from both foreign governments and domestic constituencies. Affording judicial deference, rather than unquestioning judicial obedience, goes further, putting pressure on the Executive to articulate reasons why the litigation would undermine legitimate foreign policy. Increasing transparency in foreign affairs can have both benefits and costs: while it contributes to political accountability, it may sometimes impair desirable diplomatic flexibility. But inducing the Executive to articulate reasons would also inhibit interventions motivated by cronyism toward corporate actors or by disagreement with the governing legal framework.[130] Courts would not be empowered to withhold deference merely because they preferred a different foreign policy.

As Justice Kennedy observed in *Altmann*, the invitation to the Executive raised serious questions about the legacy of the institution of Executive suggestion of immunity after the FSIA.[131] Louis Henkin, in his magisterial treatise on foreign affairs and the Constitution, has characterized the mid-twentieth-century practice as a possible instance of "Presidential 'Lawmaking,'" and expressed unease about the scope of such authority, especially about

---

[130] For example, given the existence of the Torture Victim Protection Act, a court should not be guided by a State Department assertion that all private damage actions against foreign torturers are per se inconsistent with its current human rights policy. I realize that this proposition depends on the assumption that congressional power would prevail in a conflict with Executive power over this aspect of foreign affairs.

[131] For clarity, I should emphasize that the institution of conclusive Executive suggestion still survives in the lower courts, some of which regard the immunity of foreign heads of state as lying outside the scope of the FSIA, and subject to the regime of suggestion. See Henkin, *Foreign Affairs* (cited in note 117) at 56 n *; *Tachiona v Mugabe*, 169 F Supp 2d 259, 268–97 (SDNY 2001) (discussing the issue at length before concluding that a suggestion of immunity was binding).

the power of the President to create law unilaterally and direct the courts to follow it.[132]

The Supreme Court itself has shown discomfort about Executive dictation to the courts, even if authorized by Congress, in a case with an arguable foreign relations dimension. *Gutierrez de Martinez v Lamagno* involved a tort action by Colombian nationals injured in an automobile accident by a Drug Enforcement Administration agent in Colombia.[133] When they attempted to sue him in the United States, the U.S. Attorney submitted a certification that he had been acting within the scope of his employment, which would have the effect of dismissing the agent as defendant and substituting the United States, which would in turn be immune from suit under the Federal Tort Claims Act because the accident occurred in a foreign country. The Supreme Court held that the federal statute authorizing the certification and substitution should be construed as permitting judicial review of the scope of employment determination. It rejected an interpretation of the statute that would "place courts in [an] untenable position" by instructing them "automatically to enter a judgment pursuant to a decision the court has no authority to evaluate."[134]

Certifying the immunity of a federal employee for an overseas tort is, of course, not quite the same as certifying the immunity of a foreign state or its agent for a similar tort in the United States. But if distinctions should be drawn in investigating the proper scope of the Executive power that the precedent of suggestions of immunity supports, then it is important to have an accurate depiction of the history and contours of the former doctrine.

The blurring of the history of foreign sovereign immunity doctrine in *Altmann* could hinder that inquiry. Overlooking the fact that conclusive suggestions of immunity represented a mid-twentieth-century innovation may create the mistaken appearance of a

---

[132] Henkin, *Foreign Affairs* (cited in note 117) at 54–61. For other assertions of the need to define the limits of the power of binding Executive suggestions, see Thomas M. Franck, *The Courts, the State Department and National Policy: A Criterion for Judicial Abdication*, 44 Minn L Rev 1101, 1133 (1960); Jack L. Goldsmith, *Federal Courts, Foreign Affairs, and Federalism*, 83 Va L Rev 1617, 1708–10 (1997).

[133] 515 US 417 (1995) (construing the "Westfall Act," 28 USC § 2679).

[134] Id at 430; see also id at 427 (criticizing an interpretation that would "cast Article III judges in the role of petty functionaries, persons required to enter as a court judgment an executive officer's decision, but stripped of capacity to evaluate independently whether the executive's decision is correct.").

deeply embedded presidential prerogative. Overlooking the fact that foreign state immunity was a customary international law norm undergoing transition may create the impression that the State Department can freely invent policies and oblige courts to implement them. Paradoxically, although *Altmann* clearly emphasizes the congressional lawmaking role in foreign affairs, the route by which it reaches its conclusion may add further obscurity to the balance of power in that field.

C. EMPIRE BEYOND "SOVEREIGNTY"

In one sense, the *Rasul* decision also relies on legislative framing, construing the federal habeas corpus statute as subjecting Executive detention at Guantanamo Bay Naval Base to judicial scrutiny. The statutory construction, however, took place against a series of background assumptions and prior judicial interpretations. It was essentially the Supreme Court, not Congress, that rejected the Executive's effort to maintain a liminal tract of territory within its exclusive governance where it could perform military and other foreign affairs functions beyond the reach of the domestic rule of law.

Although the Government argued that the status of Guantanamo raised a political question to be decided by the political branches and not by the courts,[135] the Court rightly sidestepped that claim by relying on the extent of governing power there rather than technical sovereignty.[136] The Court cannot tell the political branches what powers to acquire in overseas locales, but it can analyze the legal consequences of the powers they do acquire.

Yet the majority opinion is overdetermined—it rejected the Government's arguments on so many grounds that it is difficult to identify which were controlling. As often, that may indicate the strains of an overlapping coalition, or it may reveal the desire to leave future directions open. The implications, both as to jurisdiction and the eventual merit, deserve closer examination.

One source of uncertainty involves the relationship between factors of status and factors of location as justifications for rec-

---

[135] Brief for the Respondents, *Rasul v Bush* and *Al Odah v United States*, Nos 03-334 and 03-343, *21–23 (filed March 3, 2004).

[136] *Rasul v Bush*, 124 S Ct 2686, 2696–97 (2004). The majority fortified its domestic legal analysis with familial comparative input from the British law of empire.

ognition or denial of habeas corpus jurisdiction.[137] As previously mentioned, the majority distinguished *Johnson v Eisentrager* on several grounds. One difference was that *Eisentrager*, despite some loose dicta about aliens generally, involved aliens of enemy nationality in wartime, whereas the petitioners in *Rasul* were all allied nationals. Justice Stevens wrote, "They are not nationals of countries at war with the United States, and they deny that they have engaged in or plotted acts of aggression against the United States."[138] The question of allied nationality could have made enormous difference, given the long history of legal disabilities on enemy nationals, recognized in both international and domestic law and emphasized in *Eisentrager*.[139] It is difficult, however, to sort out the implications of that tradition for the unconventional armed conflict between the United States and al Qaeda, a non-state entity of transnational character with uncertain membership. After being mentioned once, the distinction between "friendly" and enemy *nationality* played no explicit role in Justice Stevens's analysis.[140] To the extent that his reasoning rested on analogizing Guantanamo to a U.S. territory, status considerations might have been irrelevant; in an earlier passage he had recalled the Court's prior exercise of habeas jurisdiction with regard to "admitted enemy aliens convicted of war crimes" and held within the United States and its insular possessions.[141] By the end of the opinion, however, Justice Stevens described the Court as examining "only whether the federal courts have jurisdiction to determine the legality of the Executive's potentially indefinite detention of individuals who claim to be wholly innocent of wrongdoing."[142] With-

---

[137] Justice Kennedy's concurrence more clearly relied on both status and location to distinguish *Eisentrager*, which he accepted as a valid, but limited precedent. He emphasized that *Eisentrager* had involved actual, proven enemies, not merely persons of enemy nationality. In contrast, the Guantanamo detainees had been given no opportunity to have their status determined in a legal proceeding, thus allowing both "friends and foes to remain in detention." Id at 2700 (Kennedy concurring in the judgment). Nonetheless, his opinion seems to leave open whether the location factor would have been sufficient.

For the dissenters, enemy nationality was irrelevant, and *Eisentrager* should be read as precluding habeas jurisdiction for any foreign national outside U.S. territory, in time of war or peace. Id at 2701 (Scalia dissenting).

[138] 124 S Ct at 2693.

[139] See *Eisentrager*, 339 US at 772–77.

[140] See 124 S Ct at 2693.

[141] Id (citing *Ex parte Quirin*, 317 US 1 (1942), and *In re Yamashita*, 327 US 1 (1946)).

[142] Id at 2699.

out lengthy discussion, the majority may have treated the forensically complex issue of actual enemy conduct as a substitute for the simpler formal criterion of enemy national status. If so, the implications of *Rasul* with regard to the "privilege of litigation" for detainees who are not innocent—that is, after a valid and persuasive determination of enemy conduct—are unclear. The majority observed that "nothing in *Eisentrager* or in any of our other cases categorically excludes aliens detained in military custody outside the United States from the '"privilege of litigation"' in U.S. courts," and described military custody as "immaterial to the question of the District Court's jurisdiction over their nonhabeas statutory claims."[143] The Court rightly insisted that "[t]he courts of the United States have traditionally been open to nonresident aliens,"[144] and refuted the dissent's invocation of inaccurate dicta from *Eisentrager* claiming that presence in the United States was a prerequisite to judicial protection.[145] But the absence of a categorical bar does not fully settle the scope of court access rights for proven actual enemies held at Guantanamo.[146]

Another crucial area of doubt concerns the geographical reach of the Court's reasoning. As previously mentioned, the majority's justification of habeas jurisdiction in *Rasul* includes arguments specific to Guantanamo and other arguments independent of location.[147] Similar ambiguity resides in the important footnote of

---

[143] Id at 2698–99.

[144] Id at 2698 (citing *Disconto Gesellschaft v Umbreit*, 208 US 570 (1908)). The *Disconto* decision involved a German bank defrauded by a German businessman, Gerhard Terlinden, who had fled to the United States. The bank sought to garnish the funds he brought with him, but the Wisconsin courts gave priority to the claim of the U.S. lawyer who represented Terlinden in his unsuccessful effort to resist extradition back to Germany. See *Terlinden v Ames*, 184 US 270 (1902) (upholding the extradition). The U.S. Supreme Court held that the state courts did not deprive the bank of property without due process of law by giving priority in limited funds to local creditors. *Disconto*, 208 US at 580. The case is also noteworthy for its assumption that the Due Process Clause of the Fourteenth Amendment protected a foreign bank whose only contact with the United States was its pursuit of a fugitive tortfeasor.

[145] See 124 S Ct at 2710 n 6 (quoting *Eisentrager*, 339 US at 777–78).

[146] The open questions primarily concern nonhabeas litigation. Habeas corpus looks to release, not to conditions of confinement, see *Muhammad v Close*, 124 S Ct 1303 (2004) (per curiam), and detention of prisoners of war is unquestionably legitimate for the duration of hostilities. As a result, it may be difficult to distinguish status-based denial of habeas jurisdiction from failure to state a claim in the case of prisoners of war. Compare R. J. Sharpe, *The Law of Habeas Corpus* 112–14 (Clarendon, 1976) (arguing that English cases denying prisoners of war standing to seek the writ are best understood as denying them the remedy on the merits).

[147] See text at notes 14–19.

dictum where the majority addressed the merits. Amplifying his assertion that the petitioners had alleged unlawful federal custody, Justice Stevens wrote:

> Petitioners' allegations—that, although they have engaged neither in combat nor in acts of terrorism against the United States, they have been held in Executive detention for more than two years in territory subject to the long-term, exclusive jurisdiction and control of the United States, without access to counsel and without being charged with any wrongdoing—unquestionably describe "custody in violation of the Constitution or laws or treaties of the United States." 28 U.S.C. § 2241(c)(3). Cf. *United States* v. *Verdugo-Urquidez*, 494 U.S. 259, 277–278 (1990) (KENNEDY, J., concurring), and cases cited therein.[148]

That footnote deserves some unpacking. The quoted phrase "custody in violation of the Constitution or laws or treaties of the United States" defines, as the following citation confirms, one of the bases of habeas corpus jurisdiction under Section 2241. But the citation to Justice Kennedy's concurrence in *Verdugo* can refer only to one species of unlawfulness—violation of constitutional rights. The actual thrust of this footnote is to confirm that innocent alien detainees at Guantanamo have constitutional rights. One may conjecture that some Justices wished to make this point and others were reluctant to state it more clearly.

If foreign detainees at Guantanamo have constitutional rights, then the question remains, why do they have constitutional rights—because they are detainees, or because they are at Guantanamo? The footnote raises both possibilities, and indicates two compatible but distinct trajectories for doctrinal development.

On one account, the character of Guantanamo is the key, a "territory subject to the long-term, exclusive jurisdiction and control of the United States." Justice Kennedy's concurrence spells out the reasoning more clearly: "Guantanamo Bay is in every practical respect a United States territory, and it is one far removed from hostilities;" it is "a place that belongs to the United States, extending the 'implied protection' of the United States" to aliens

---

[148] 124 S Ct at 2698 n 15 (majority).

there.[149] In that case, fundamental constitutional rights should apply at Guantanamo roughly as they do in Puerto Rico and other "unincorporated territories" under the century-old doctrine of the Insular Cases.[150] Or, put differently, the Bill of Rights should apply at Guantanamo the way the lower courts applied it to other non-sovereign territory subject to U.S. governance, like the Panama Canal Zone and the Trust Territory of the Pacific Islands.[151] That was also the basis on which the Second Circuit once approved the application of the Due Process Clause to Haitian refugees interned at Guantanamo.[152] Recognizing that fairly thick set of constitutional protections would benefit not only prisoners erroneously swept up in the war against terrorism, but also the hundreds of foreign workers employed at Guantanamo, and interdicted migrants, whom the government has continued to bring quietly to Guantanamo during the current controversy.[153] Neither the majority nor the concurrence in *Rasul* cited the lower court case law, however.[154] That may reflect the Court's usual concentration on

---

[149] Id at 2700 (Kennedy concurring in the judgment) (quoting *Eisentrager*, 339 US at 777–78). Justice Kennedy's reference to the distance from hostilities might be read as emphasizing that U.S. possession of the territory was secure, and that there were no circumstances comparable to invasion justifying extraordinary Executive power there. Justice Kennedy's concurrence was concerned with striking a balance between presidential power in the conduct of military affairs and judicial responsibility to protect the liberty of persons. Id at 2700.

[150] As every law student should learn, but most do not, the term "Insular Cases" refers to the series of cases from *De Lima v Bidwell*, 182 US 1 (1901), to *Balzac v Porto Rico*, 258 US 298 (1922), that established the framework of constitutional analysis for "unincorporated" overseas territories. Under the doctrine first articulated in Justice Edward White's concurring opinion in *Downes v Bidwell*, 182 US 244 (1901), and still in force today, the Constitution as a whole applies to all action of the U.S. government in any location, but certain clauses may not, and only genuinely "fundamental" constitutional rights apply to both citizens and aliens in the "unincorporated" territories. See Gerald L. Neuman, *Strangers to the Constitution: Immigrants, Borders, and Fundamental Law* 83–89 (Princeton, 1996); Sarah Cleveland, *Powers Inherent in Sovereignty: Indians, Aliens, Territories, and the Nineteenth Century Origins of Plenary Power over Foreign Affairs*, 81 Tex L Rev 1, 207–39 (2002). *Downes v Bidwell* was the occasion for Mr. Dooley's famous quip that, regardless of whether the Constitution follows the flag, the Supreme Court follows the election returns.

[151] See Gerald L. Neuman, *Closing the Guantanamo Loophole*, 50 Loyola L Rev 1, 15–32 (2004) (describing the historical application of fundamental constitutional rights in territories where the United States possessed full governing authority but not sovereignty).

[152] See *Haitian Centers Council, Inc. v McNary*, 969 F2d 1326 (2d Cir 1992), vacated as moot as *Sale v Haitian Centers Council, Inc.*, 509 US 918 (1993).

[153] See Neuman, 50 Loyola L Rev at 42–43 (cited in note 151).

[154] Only the dissent referred to the Panama Canal Zone, in order to illustrate that Congress knew how to extend habeas jurisdiction over nonsovereign territory when it chose. 124 S Ct at 2711 n 7 (Scalia dissenting).

its own precedents, or it may suggest that constitutional protection of the detainees rested on some other basis.

The other likely alternative would be that the subjection of the detainees to long-term U.S. power, not the subjection of Guantanamo, justifies application of constitutional rights. The majority's invocation of Justice Kennedy's concurrence in *Verdugo* underlines this possibility, because the issue in *Verdugo* was the fully extraterritorial application of constitutional rights to nonresident aliens. The nominal Opinion of the Court in *Verdugo* had cited *Eisentrager* for the proposition that nonresident aliens in foreign countries had no constitutional rights, in the course of holding that the Fourth Amendment did not extend to their property there, but only four Justices accepted this dictum.[155] Justice Kennedy, who provided the pivotal fifth vote, explained his concurrence on different grounds, applying a contextual due process approach to the extraterritorial rights of aliens adapted from Justice Harlan's concurring opinion *Reid v Covert*.[156] The landmark decision in *Reid v Covert* had overthrown the nineteenth-century approach of strictly limiting the reach of the Bill of Rights to U.S. territory, at least for citizens, responding to the vast extraterritorial presence of the U.S. military and the increased extraterritorial reach of U.S. legislation. While a plurality of four, led by Justice Black, had argued for literal application of the full Bill of Rights to U.S. citizens abroad, Justices Harlan and Frankfurter advocated a contextual approach, parallel to their contextual approach to Fourteenth Amendment due process, that could be labeled "global due process."[157] For Harlan, the proper inquiry was "which guarantees

---

[155] *United States v Verdugo-Urquidez*, 494 US 259 (1990); see Neuman, *Strangers to the Constitution* (cited in note 150) at 105–07. The degree of support that the Chief Justice's opinion received in *Verdugo* became an explicit issue in the oral argument in *Rasul*:

> MR. GIBBONS: . . . In Verdugo, speaking for four members of the Court at least, Mr. Chief Justice, you said that Eisentrager stood for the proposition that —
> QUESTION: I think I was speaking for five. I think Justice Kennedy joined the opinion.
> MR. GIBBONS: Well, he did. But he wrote separately, I think, and at least cast some doubt on whether or not he agreed with your position that there is no Fifth Amendment right for an alien outside the United States.

Transcript of Oral Argument, *Rasul v Bush*, 2004 US TRANS LEXIS 37, *20–21.

[156] 494 US at 277–78 (Kennedy concurring) (citing *Reid v Covert*, 354 US 1, 74 (1957)) (Harlan concurring in the result).

[157] See Neuman, *Strangers to the Constitution* (cited in note 150), at 92–93, 102–03 (explaining (and criticizing) the "global due process" approach).

of the Constitution should apply in view of the particular circumstances, the practical necessities, and the possible alternatives," and whether conditions would "make adherence to a specific guarantee altogether impracticable and anomalous."[158]

Since the *Verdugo* decision, lower courts have divided on its implications. Some recognized the limited nature of its Fourth Amendment holding, while others embraced its dicta as excluding any constitutional protection for nonresident aliens outside U.S. territory. The D.C. Circuit demonstrated what is ultimately at stake in that proposition by holding that foreign nationals have no constitutional right not to be tortured by U.S. agents abroad; that holding arose from an internal conflict in Guatemala and not a war against the United States.[159] Its consequences threaten detainees who are not even ostensibly related to U.S. counterterrorism efforts, such as economic migrants and bona fide refugees captured on the high seas in U.S. interdiction operations.

The *Rasul* majority's narrow reading of *Eisentrager* should lead to a wider recognition that the broad dicta contained in *Eisentrager* and in Chief Justice Rehnquist's opinion in *Verdugo* do not provide an acceptable account of the constitutional duties of the United States toward foreign nationals, especially outside the military context. In U.S. constitutionalism, rights serve as necessary correlatives that moderate and justify the exercise of legitimate governing power over human beings. The notion in *Eisentrager* that an alien's presence in the United States was an indispensible prerequisite for constitutional protection was never accurate,[160] and its logic was destroyed when the Court subsequently overthrew the regime

---

[158] 354 US at 74–75 (Harlan concurring in the result).

[159] See *Harbury v Deutch*, 233 F3d 596, 604 (DC Cir 2000), revd on other grounds as *Christopher v Harbury*, 536 US 403 (2002).

[160] See Neuman, 50 Loyola L Rev at 49–50 (cited in note 151). That overstatement ignores the protection of property within the United States owned by nonresidents, as well as the modern due process minimum contacts doctrine, which makes absence of contact with the United States a source of due process entitlement not to be sued here. See *Asahi Metal Industries Co. v Superior Court*, 480 US 102 (1987) (applying minimum contacts doctrine); *Russian Volunteer Fleet v United States*, 282 US 481 (1931) (recognizing protection by the Takings Clause). (The Russian Volunteer Fleet was a corporation owned by the Imperial Russian government at the time when the U.S. government requisitioned its property for use in World War I. See id at 487; Amos S. Hershey, *Some Questions of International Law Arising from the Russo-Japanese War, Part VI*, 16 Green Bag 659, 664 & n 3 (1904) (describing the character of the Fleet). The ownership of the corporation was later disputed between the Soviet government and emigrés, and its takings claim was eventually settled in the Litvinov Assignment. See *United States v Pink*, 315 US 203, 212–13 (1942).)

of strict territoriality of constitutional rights for citizens. The Chief Justice's suggestion in *Verdugo* that constitutional rights must arise from prior "significant voluntary connection" to the United States also overlooks relevant precedent.[161] But more fundamentally, it cannot be that involuntary captives of the United States never acquire constitutional rights in extraterritorial long-term detention. As Justice O'Connor observed with regard to extraterritorial detention of citizens in *Hamdi v Rumsfeld*, such a rule would create perverse incentives.[162] It would also revive the logic of slavery.

If the extraterritorial application of constitutional rights to foreign nationals will be governed by the Kennedy-Harlan "global due process" approach, then factors that would make adherence to a constitutional requirement "impracticable and anomalous"[163] must be taken into consideration. Justice Kennedy's characterization of Guantanamo as "far removed from hostilities"[164] may be particularly important, in qualitative rather than quantitative terms. The Constitution contemplates the suspension of the privilege of the writ of habeas corpus by Congress even within the United States when necessitated by invasion or rebellion.[165] It cannot be expected that the Court would insert constitutional standards for treatment of foreign nationals into the disorder of an active war zone overseas.[166]

For the present, however, it is likely that further developments on remand in *Rasul* will emphasize factors specific to Guantanamo, even though that should entail a thicker set of rights than might apply independent of location. If so, the evaporation of the legal black hole at Guantanamo will restore the Base to the mainstream of territorial jurisprudence. Other occasions may be required to raise the question of whether U.S. constitutionalism tolerates a

---

[161] Compare *Verdugo*, 494 US at 271, with *Plyler v Doe*, 457 US 202, 219–20 (1982), and *Mathews v Diaz*, 426 US 67, 77 (1976).

[162] *Hamdi v Rumsfeld*, 124 S Ct 2633, 2643 (2004) (plurality).

[163] *Verdugo*, 494 US at 278 (Kennedy concurring).

[164] *Rasul*, 124 S Ct at 2700 (Kennedy concurring in the judgment).

[165] See US Constitution, Art I, § 9, cl 2; *Hamdi v Rumsfeld*, 124 S Ct 2633, 2650 (2004) (plurality) (emphasizing that only Congress can suspend the writ); id at 2665 (Scalia dissenting) (same).

[166] Compare Neuman, *Strangers to the Constitution* (cited in note 150) at 110–11, 188 (agreeing that the Constitution does not impose a requirement of "due process of war"). That is not to say that armed conflict should be unrestrained, but only that the Constitution does not provide the restraints.

deterritorialized system of rightless incarceration of foreign nationals.

CONCLUSION

Justice Scalia's dissent in *Sosa*, the last of the four decisions, issued on the last day of the Term, accused the Court of being "incapable of saying that some matters—*any* matters—are none of its business."[167] Different observers might think that different cases of the past several years would best support that claim. In the foreign relations cases of June 2004, the Court's clearly stated preference for legislative guidance, and its openness to consideration of Executive dissuasion from the exercise of jurisdiction, indicate that the Court has no intention of usurping a leading role. These decisions do demonstrate, however, that the Supreme Court at the start of the twenty-first century will not shrink from participating in the project of working out the legal consequences of globalization.

---

[167] *Sosa*, 124 S Ct at 2776 (Scalia dissenting).

JULIAN KU AND JOHN YOO

BEYOND FORMALISM IN FOREIGN AFFAIRS: A FUNCTIONAL APPROACH TO THE ALIEN TORT STATUTE

For almost a quarter century, courts and judges, government offi-cials and law professors have argued over the place of international law within the American legal system. Today, the "modern position" accepted by several courts of appeals and many leading international and foreign relations law scholars maintains that the federal courts can interpret and enforce customary international law (CIL) as fed-eral common law. Incorporation of CIL as federal law formally occurs through the Alien Tort Statute (ATS), a previously obscure and largely ignored subsection of the Judiciary Act of 1789, whose text allows aliens to seek damages for torts in violation of the law of nations in federal court.[1] According to its supporters, the ATS allows the United States to play an important role in the devel-opment and enforcement of CIL generally, and human rights law specifically.[2]

Julian Ku is Associate Professor of Law, Hofstra University School of Law. John Yoo is Professor of Law, University of California at Berkeley School of Law (Boalt Hall), and Visiting Scholar, American Enterprise Institute.

AUTHORS' NOTE: We would like to thank Brad Clark, Jesse Choper, Bill Dodge, Dan Farber, Phil Frickey, John Manning, Paul Mishkin, Jide Nzelibe, Peter Spiro, and Michael Ramsey for their comments on the manuscript. Katherine Graf provided excellent research assistance. The article benefited from comments received at a conference on international law at Boalt Hall.

[1] 28 USC § 1350.

[2] Two of the ATS's most prominent academic supporters along these lines are Deans

Critics, however, respond that standard approaches to the federal common law as well as the Constitution's formal allocation of the foreign affairs power deprive the courts of any authority to assimilate substantive CIL as federal law.[3] Rather, the ATS vested the federal courts with jurisdiction to hear cases between aliens and, presumably, American defendants—provided that Congress has also created a specific cause of action. Thus was launched one of the sharpest and most bitter debates in recent international legal scholarship, featuring an outpouring of articles even though ATS suits reaching the courts of appeals have numbered no more than two dozen. It is fair to say that neither side has convinced the other.

In last Term's *Sosa v Alvarez Machain*, the Supreme Court waded into this debate for the first time.[4] The decision reflected the stalemate in formalist arguments over the interpretation of the ATS. Drawing upon the textual and structural insights provided by the modern position's critics, the Court concluded that the ATS is merely a jurisdictional statute. Nonetheless, with little explanation, the Court also refused to stop the lower courts from allowing aliens to seek damages in federal court for CIL violations. Why? We believe that the Court was reluctant to end federal judicial participation in the development and enforcement of CIL for unstated functional, policy, or pragmatic reasons, which have also been unexplored in the academic debate.

We use the Court's under-theorized conclusion as an opportunity to take a different approach. Rather than reexamine the ATS's text, structure, and history, we conduct a comparative institutional analysis of the role of the courts in foreign affairs. This approach takes two steps. First, it seeks to define the purpose or social goal of the ATS. Without a definition of the statute's purpose, we cannot de-

---

Harold Koh and Anne-Marie Slaughter (formerly Burley). See, for example, Harold Hongju Koh, *Transnational Public Law Litigation*, 100 Yale L J 2347 (1991); Anne-Marie Burley, *The Alien Tort Statute and the Judiciary Act of 1789: A Badge of Honor*, 83 Am J Intl L 461 (1989).

[3] The most prominent of the critics have been Professors Curtis Bradley and Jack Goldsmith. See, for example, Curtis A. Bradley and Jack L. Goldsmith, *Customary International Law as Federal Common Law: A Critique of the Modern Position*, 110 Harv L Rev 815 (1997).

[4] 124 S Ct 2739 (2004). A number of authors have already discussed the *Sosa* case. See, for example, Eugene Kontorovich, *Implementing Sosa v. Alvarez-Machain: What Piracy Reveals About the Alien Tort Statute*, 80 Notre Dame L Rev 111 (2004); Mark K. Moller, *Old Puzzles, Puzzling Answers: The Alien Tort Statute and Federal Common Law in Sosa v. Alvarez-Machain*, 2004 Cato Sup Ct Rev 209 (2004); Edward T. Swaine, *The Constitutionality of International Delegations*, 104 Colum L Rev 1492 (2004); J. Harvie Wilkinson III, *Our Structural Constitution*, 104 Colum L Rev 1687 (2004).

termine whether judicial participation is the most effective institutional tool. Second, we compare the institutional capabilities of
the judiciary and the executive in implementing foreign policy in
general, and in applying CIL in particular. Both a macro- and micro-
assessment of the federal courts reveals significant institutional
weaknesses in the implementation of foreign policy and CIL. We
conclude that the executive branch can more effectively achieve the
purpose behind the ATS.

Defenders of the modern position have argued that a jurisdictional approach to the ATS would disrupt American foreign relations by allowing the states, rather than a single federal judiciary,
to make and enforce CIL. Recent changes, recognized by the Supreme Court, in the relationship between the executive branch and
the states in foreign relations address this concern. The Court has
recognized the functional superiority of the President in managing
foreign affairs by permitting presidential declarations of international policy to preempt state law. Thus, CIL could continue as
part of the common law of the states—enforceable in state court
or through diversity jurisdiction in federal court—subject to federal
preemption by the President. Under this system, courts would continue to adjudicate CIL cases, while at the same time allowing a
functionally superior executive branch to oversee and unify the interpretation of CIL when necessary.

Part I discusses the development and widespread embrace of the
modern position on the question of CIL's status as federal law. It
then describes the formalist challenge, which generated several responses built on arguments of statutory and constitutional text and
history. Part II describes *Sosa*'s conflicted nature: its adoption of
the recent critique of the modern position, but also its preservation
of a federal court role in developing and enforcing CIL through
the ATS. This outcome represents an unspoken recognition of the
power of the policy goals behind the modern position.

Part III offers a functional assessment of the statutory purpose
of the ATS and of the institutions best positioned to carry it out.
We define the ATS's policy as one designed to promote the development and enforcement of CIL generally, and human rights
more specifically. We argue that the *Sosa* Court's reading of the
ATS assumes that Congress has delegated authority in this area to
the courts. Part III concludes that the federal courts have few institutional advantages, and many disadvantages, in the interpretation

and application of CIL. We contend that the executive branch is institutionally superior to the courts in achieving national policy goals in this area.

Conflict between the executive and courts, or disruption in national control over the implementation of CIL, will not occur under the proposal unveiled in Part IV. We argue that the interpretation and enforcement of CIL has long been treated as common law independently interpreted and applied by the state courts. State control of CIL does not create harmful decentralization of foreign policy because of federal preemption by the President. Strong functional reasons support a state-led system of CIL development, supervised by the executive branch, over the system endorsed in *Sosa*.

I

More than two decades of vigorous debate over the ATS among international and foreign relations law scholars preceded *Sosa*. After the Second Circuit's 1980 decision in *Filartiga v Pena-Irala*,[5] scholars widely hailed the ATS as a vehicle for the incorporation of international law into U.S. domestic law and as an important mechanism for the development of international law generally. In the last decade, however, critics have raised serious questions about *Filartiga*'s consistency with the statute's history, its original meaning, and the Constitution's structure. Because of the ATS's brevity and the paucity of historical evidence, the academic literature has reached a stalemate.

A.   FILARTIGA AND THE ACADEMY

Filartiga was the first modern decision to enforce CIL in federal court through the ATS. It held that the ATS granted federal courts jurisdiction over lawsuits brought by aliens seeking damages for violations of international human rights law. The Second Circuit endorsed two principles that would become the subject of substantial academic discussion. First, *Filartiga* held that the exercise of jurisdiction over a lawsuit alleging violations of CIL was consistent with Article III's limitations on federal subject matter jurisdiction.[6] Even though the suit, between two aliens, did not fall

---

[5] 630 F2d 876 (2d Cir 1980).

[6] Id at 885.

under diversity jurisdiction, *Filartiga* held that subject matter jurisdiction existed because the case involved "the law of nations, which has always been part of the federal common law."[7] Second, *Filartiga* held that the Constitution did not require Congress to incorporate the law of nations by statute, despite Congress's power to "Define and Punish Offences against the Law of Nations."[8] "This extravagant claim," *Filartiga* observed, "is amply refuted by the numerous decisions applying rules of international law uncodified in any act of Congress."[9] Although conceding that federal courts could not "make" new causes of action, *Filartiga* nonetheless concluded that the federal courts were authorized to enforce rights widely recognized and accepted as CIL, even where Congress had not specifically defined such CIL. Such lawsuits could even be brought against alien defendants for acts that occurred abroad.

Prior to *Filartiga*, some leading international legal scholars had advocated the use of domestic courts to incorporate international law into domestic U.S. law.[10] But *Filartiga* gave the idea new life. Rather than focusing on state practice and international relations, scholars could point to a growing number of new judicial decisions that demonstrated both the reality and efficacy of international law.[11] Professor Henkin's article from 1984 was representative:

> As a result, there is now general agreement that international law, as incorporated into domestic law in the United States, is federal, not state law; that cases arising under international law are "cases arising under . . . the Laws of the United States" and therefore are within the judicial power to the United States under article III of the Constitution; that principles of international law as incorporated in the law of the United States are "Laws of the United States" and supreme under article VI; that international law, therefore, is to be determined independently by the federal courts, and ultimately by the United

---

[7] Id.

[8] US Const, Art I, § 8.

[9] *Filartiga*, 630 F2d at 886.

[10] See, for example, Richard Lillich, *The Proper Role of Domestic Courts in the International Legal Order*, 11 Va J Intl L 9 (1970); Richard Falk, *The Role of Domestic Courts in the International Legal Order* (Syracuse, 1964).

[11] The status of international law as law has been a long-standing preoccupation of international legal scholars. For a discussion of the international law academy's struggle with critics of the "lawness" of international law, see Anne-Marie Slaughter Burley, *International Law and International Relations: A Dual Agenda*, 87 Am J Intl L 205, 207–20 (1992).

States Supreme Court, with its determination binding on the state courts; and that a determination of international law by a state court is a federal question subject to review by the Supreme Court.[12]

On the doctrinal front, *Filartiga* also achieved wide acceptance. The American Law Institute's 1986 *Restatement (Third) of U.S. Foreign Relations Law,* which reflected the views of the leading international law scholars of the day, departed from past views and endorsed *Filartiga.* It held that "[c]ustomary international law is considered to be like common law in the United States, but it is federal law. A determination of international law by the Supreme Court is binding on the States and on State courts."[13] The *Restatement (Third)* followed *Filartiga*'s analysis of the judicial enforceability of CIL in federal courts. It commented that "there is no reason to treat claims arising under international law any differently from those arising under other federal law."[14] More explicitly, the *Restatement (Third)* endorsed *Filartiga*'s grant to individuals of a cause of action in federal courts for violations of international human rights law.[15]

As Professor Stephan has observed, these doctrinal shifts wrought a "revolution in U.S. foreign relations law. . . ."[16] The adoption of the *Restatement* meant that,

> [t]he construct called customary international law existed not as a locus of scholarly debate and speculation, but as an independent source of judicial power to pronounce norms and punish wrongdoers. Any person injured by a violation of customary international law could seek redress against any subject of international law, foreign or domestic, state or private. Labeling a desired outcome customary international law provided federal court jurisdiction and ousted prior rules based on common law or statute.[17]

---

[12] Louis Henkin, *International Law as Law in the United States,* 82 Mich L Rev 1555, 1559–60 (1984) (footnotes omitted).

[13] Restatement (Third) of the Foreign Relations Law of the United States § 111 (1986).

[14] Id at § 111 n 4.

[15] Id at § 703 n 7.

[16] Paul B. Stephan, *Courts, the Constitution, and Customary International Law: The Intellectual Origins of the Restatement (Third) of the Foreign Relations Law of the United States,* 44 Va J Intl L 33, 47 (2003).

[17] Id.

B. FILARTIGA'S FORMALIST CRITICS

Filartiga was not accepted without dissent. In 1986, Professor Philip Trimble wrote an early critique of the idea that CIL constituted federal law,[18] and two years later Professor Arthur Weisburd expanded the challenge to the domestic legal status of international law.[19] Academic discussion, however, did not flare up into a full-fledged controversy until the 1997 publication in the *Harvard Law Review* of an article by Professors Curtis Bradley and Jack Goldsmith criticizing what they called the "modern position" that CIL enjoyed the status of federal common law.[20] These critics offered a two-pronged formalist critique challenging *Filartiga*'s interpretation of the text and purpose of the ATS.

They argued that Congress must specifically enact a cause of action to incorporate specific international norms. This argument drew upon Judge Robert Bork's concurrence in a 1984 case, *Tel-Oren v Libyan Arab Republic*, in which the D.C. Circuit refused to permit an ATS suit seeking damages for a terrorist attack.[21] According to Judge Bork, the *Filartiga* approach "would authorize tort suits for the vindication of any international legal right."[22] This "result would be inconsistent with the severe limitations on individually initiated enforcement inherent in international law itself, and would run counter to constitutional limits on the role of federal courts."[23]

Scholars expanded upon Judge Bork's critique by turning to the ATS's history.[24] In the most detailed of these investigations, Professor Bradley concluded that the ATS's drafting history largely (although not entirely) supported Judge Bork's reading. According to Professor Bradley, there was no evidence that Congress intended the ATS to create a federal statutory cause of action for

---

[18] Phillip R. Trimble, *A Revisionist View of Customary International Law*, 33 UCLA L Rev 665, 669–70 (1986).

[19] See Arthur Weisburd, *The Executive Branch and International Law*, 41 Vand L Rev 1205, 1239–40 (1988); see also Arthur M. Weisburd, *State Courts, Federal Courts, and International Cases*, 20 Yale J Intl L 1, 38–44 (1995).

[20] Bradley and Goldsmith, 110 Harv L Rev 815 (cited in note 3).

[21] *Tel-Oren v Libyan Arab Republic*, 726 F2d 774 (DC Cir 1984).

[22] Id at 812.

[23] Id.

[24] See, for example, Curtis A. Bradley, *The Alien Tort Statute and Article III*, 42 Va J Intl L 587 (2002); Joseph M. Sweeney, *A Tort Only in Violation of the Law of Nations*, 18 Hastings Intl & Comp L Rev 445 (1995).

violations of CIL.[25] Nonetheless, there was evidence that Congress expected that alien plaintiffs could bring lawsuits under the ATS because federal courts were authorized to apply CIL as part of the general common law.[26] But in order to satisfy Article III's restrictions on federal court jurisdiction, Professor Bradley argued that the ATS required any such lawsuits to be brought against a U.S. citizen defendant.[27] *Filartiga*-style lawsuits involving two alien parties would not be permitted, although more modern lawsuits against U.S. corporate defendants or U.S. government actors themselves would be—whether or not modern CIL forms part of the federal common law.

This last question, however, has proved the most controversial. According to the critics, giving CIL the status of federal common law is unjustified as a matter of historical practice and doctrine.[28] Prior to *Erie v Tompkins*,[29] CIL had constituted part of the general common law, which was independently interpreted by federal and state courts. It never enjoyed the status of the "Laws of the United States" under Articles III and VI of the Constitution which were supreme over inconsistent state law. Since *Erie* famously divested federal courts of their general common lawmaking powers, the federal courts also lost their power to apply CIL as general common law.[30] If *Erie* rejected general federal common law, then it also rejected most *Filartiga*-style lawsuits because they usually involve alien-versus-alien lawsuits.[31] Such suits, lacking diversity, would not satisfy any of the requirements of Article III federal subject matter jurisdiction.[32] Suits between aliens and U.S. defendants would, after *Erie*, simply become diversity lawsuits that apply state common law.[33]

---

[25] See Bradley, 42 Va J Intl L at 592–97 (cited in note 24).

[26] Id at 619–37.

[27] Id.

[28] See, for example, Bradley and Goldsmith, 110 Harv L Rev 815 (cited in note 3).

[29] 304 US 64 (1938).

[30] Bradley and Goldsmith, 110 Harv L Rev at 817 (cited in note 3).

[31] Curtis A. Bradley and Jack L. Goldsmith, *The Current Illegitimacy of International Human Rights Litigation*, 66 Fordham L Rev 319, 311 (1997).

[32] Id at 357–63.

[33] Bradley and Goldsmith, 110 Harv L Rev at 817 (cited in note 3). Of course this would depend on whether the state in question has recognized CIL as part of its common law.

C. THE FORMALIST DEFENSE

This critique provoked an energetic response from *Filartiga*'s defenders in the legal academy. Much of it has taken the form of formalist rebuttals plumbing the historical origins, text, and statutory purpose of the ATS and the historical status of CIL in domestic law. First, scholars argued that the requirement that Congress create an explicit cause of action is ahistorical, because the first Congress presumed that CIL lawsuits could be brought under the general common law.[34] Thus, the first Congress fully expected that the ATS would be used by aliens to bring lawsuits in federal courts without any separate statutory authorization from Congress. Such a reading is bolstered by historical materials, later cited by the Court in *Sosa*, suggesting that Congress enacted the ATS in response to violence against foreign ambassadors stationed in the United States.[35] Second, *Filartiga*'s defenders cited various Founding-era materials suggesting that CIL was understood to have been incorporated as federal law by the Constitution's use of the phrase "Laws of the United States" in Article III.[36] As a matter of the original meaning, and as a matter of subsequent judicial practice, CIL was always understood to be a question of federal law controlled by federal courts.

Third, *Filartiga*'s defenders argued that whatever the original meaning of the ATS, the federal legislative and executive branches had both ratified *Filartiga*'s reading of the ATS.[37] For instance, when enacting the Torture Victim Protection Act (TVPA)[38] amending the ATS, Congress had the opportunity to register its disapproval of *Filartiga*. Instead, Congress added a cause of action for torture explicitly designed to reject Judge Bork's concurrence in *Tel-Oren*. Moreover, the TVPA's legislative history suggested that Congress agreed with *Filartiga*'s conception of the status of

---

[34] See, for example, William S. Dodge, *The Historical Origins of the Alien Tort Statute: A Response to the Originalists*, 19 Hastings Intl L & Comp L Rev 221 (1996).

[35] See text accompanying notes 66–69.

[36] See, for example, Beth Stephens, *The Law of Our Land: Customary International Law as Federal Law After Erie*, 66 Fordham L Rev 393 (1997); Gerald L. Neuman, *Sense and Nonsense About Customary International Law: A Response to Professors Bradley and Goldsmith*, 66 Fordham L Rev 371 (1997).

[37] See Ryan Goodman and Derek Jinks, *Filartiga's Firm Footing: International Human Rights and Federal Law*, 66 Fordham L Rev 463 (1997).

[38] PL 102-256, 106 Stat 73 (March 12, 1992).

CIL as federal law.[39] And the State Department had approvingly cited the post-*Filartiga* ATS litigation in the context of reports to international institutions on compliance with U.S. obligations under international law.[40]

D. THE FORMALIST STALEMATE

At the very least, this debate within the legal academy established that the *Restatement (Third)* had prematurely embraced *Filartiga*. As even *Filartiga*'s formalist defenders have admitted, the text of the ATS does not, by itself, establish a cause of action. *Filartiga*'s defenders and critics appear to agree on this point.[41] Despite exhaustive investigations, however, neither side has been able to fill in the textual gaps left by the ATS, nor have they produced direct evidence on the intent of the ATS's drafters. For instance, *Filartiga*'s defenders routinely cite general statements by the Founders about the problems of state violations of the law of nations.[42] But none of these statements was made in the context of the ATS's enactment, and it remains impossible to link those statements directly to the intentions of the its drafters.[43] Critics have fared somewhat better by examining letters from members of the first Congress discussing the ATS.[44] But even this evidence, while more persuasive than the general statements cited by *Filartiga*'s defenders, has not proven conclusive.[45]

Neither side has been able to provide a concrete textual or historical resolution of the question of CIL's status as federal or

---

[39] See Torture Victim Protection Act of 1991, S Rep 102-249, 102d Cong (Nov 19, 1991).

[40] See, for example, *Consideration of Reports Submitted by States Parties Under Article 19 of the Convention: Report of the United States of America*, UN Comm Against Torture, Addendum, P277, UN Doc CAT/C/28/Add.5 (2000) (emphasis in original).

[41] See, for example, Bradley, 42 Va J Intl L at 592–97 (cited in note 24); Dodge, 19 Hastings Intl L & Comp L Rev at 238–40 (cited in note 34).

[42] See, for example, Dodge, 19 Hastings Intl L & Comp L Rev at 226–30 (cited in note 34).

[43] Id. Dodge describes the 1781 Continental Congress Resolution seeking state action to punish violations of the law of nations, the Marbois affair involving a 1784 attack on the French ambassador, and an essay from the Federalist Papers by John Jay about the Constitution. None of these materials discuss the actual ATS nor do they even specifically propose a statute like the ATS.

[44] See Bradley, 42 Va J Intl L at 620–21 (cited in note 24).

[45] See, for example, Dodge, *The Constitutionality of the Alien Tort Statute*, 42 Va J Intl L 687, 697–98 (2002) (pointing out that ATS drafters' correspondence did not describe any limits on the scope of ATS).

state common law. The constitutional text mentions international law only once, in allocating the power to "define and punish offences" against the law of nations to Congress.[46] *Filartiga* and the *Restatement* hold that CIL forms part of the "Law of the United States" in Articles III and VI and, therefore, exists as federal law.[47] Critics have pointed out that although there are some general statements on the importance of maintaining national control over CIL, there are also many general statements relegating CIL to nonfederal status.[48] Thus, while both sides can point to some historical evidence that supports their view, the evidence is again inconclusive (though the critics have again provided more persuasive evidence).[49]

Despite the *Filartiga* critics' more persuasive arguments, it is not possible to conclude with confidence that they are correct. More importantly, even in areas where the critics and defenders agree, formalist analysis provides little guidance on how to treat the ATS after *Erie*'s abolition of "general common law." Formalist arguments have proven unable to establish a consensus on the proper reading of the ATS. They also have little to say about the ATS in a post-*Erie* era where CIL now includes international human rights law.[50]

Stalemate between formalist supporters and critics of *Filartiga* should shift the focus to functional arguments. *Filartiga*'s defenders have celebrated *Filartiga*'s policy benefits as the development of CIL in U.S. domestic law *and* international law. Dean Koh, for example, has called *Filartiga* "the *Brown v Board of Education* of" the movement to bring international and foreign law into the

---

[46] US Const, Art I, § 8.

[47] 630 F2d at 886–87; Restatement (Third) at § 111 comment d; § 111(2) and comment e; § 112(2) and comment a; § 326 comment d.

[48] See, for example, Bradley and Goldsmith, 110 Harv L Rev at 824–27 (cited in note 3).

[49] Compare Bradley, 42 Va J Intl L at 597–619 (cited in note 24); Dodge, 42 Va J Intl L at 702–11 (cited in note 45).

[50] Professor Michael Ramsey, for instance, has argued that the text of the Constitution supports treating CIL as "non-preemptive" federal law. Professor Ernest Young reaches a similar conclusion. Professor Aleinikoff has recently advocated congressional action to codify CIL along these lines. See Michael D. Ramsey, *International Law as Part of Our Law: A Constitutional Perspective*, 29 Pepperdine L Rev 187 (2001); Ernest A. Young, *Sorting Out the Debate Over Customary International Law*, 42 Va J Intl L 365 (2002); T. Alexander Aleinikoff, *International Law, Sovereignty, and American Constitutionalism: Reflections on the Customary International Law Debate*, 98 Am J Intl L 91 (2003).

domestic U.S. system.[51] As he noted, *Filartiga* opened the door for a wave of litigation in U.S. federal courts by plaintiffs seeking to vindicate rights under CIL, especially international human rights law. Such litigation did not merely vindicate the rights of victims of human rights abuses; it served a larger systemic role in the development of CIL. In Dean Koh's conception, ATS litigation allows individuals to use the "transnational public law litigation process" to initiate, develop, and solidify norms of CIL.[52] Dean Slaughter (formerly Burley) argues that modern ATS lawsuits represent a "badge of honor" for the United States.[53] The "badge" demonstrates a deep commitment to the enforcement and development of international human rights law. Dean Slaughter explicitly argues in favor of the modern use of the ATS even while conceding that "definitive proof of the intended purpose and scope of the [ATS] is impossible."[54]

Koh and Slaughter's arguments lead to the conclusion that whether or not the ATS was actually intended to permit *Filartiga*-style lawsuits as a formal matter, its present benefits for U.S. foreign policy in generating respect and compliance with international law should prevail. In contrast, critics such as Professors Bradley and Goldsmith have challenged *Filartiga*'s interpretation of the ATS as "illegitimate" after *Erie*,[55] but have not offered a functional assessment of ATS litigation. As we explain in the next part, the lack of analysis of the ATS's functional implications likely influenced the *Sosa* Court's decision to preserve the doctrine, if not the rationale, behind *Filartiga*.

II

This part analyzes the Supreme Court's first and only effort to come to grips with the ATS's meaning in last Term's *Sosa v Alvarez-Machain*. It criticizes the grounds on which the Court chose to preserve the holding of *Filartiga* despite recognizing that decision's serious problems under conventional federal common law and statutory interpretation doctrines. Once stripped of its

---

[51] Koh, 100 Yale L J at 2366 (cited in note 2).

[52] Id.

[53] See, for example, Burley, 83 Am J Intl L 461 (cited in note 2).

[54] Id at 463.

[55] See, generally, Bradley and Goldsmith, 66 Fordham L Rev 319 (cited in note 31).

fairly unpersuasive formalist arguments, *Sosa* instead shows that the Court was reluctant to withdraw the federal judiciary from the making and enforcement of CIL or to impose any meaningful limitations on federal court lawmaking for unstated policy reasons. Part III will then assess these policy reasons on institutional grounds by comparing the costs and benefits of federal judicial participation in the making and enforcement of CIL.

A. SOSA

Advocates for the modern position could not have chosen a less propitious case for the Court to review than *Sosa*. *Sosa* marked Dr. Alvarez-Machain's second trip to the Supreme Court; his first was notably unsuccessful.[56] In 1985, members of a Mexican drug cartel allegedly kidnapped an agent of the Drug Enforcement Agency, Enrique Camarena-Salazar, and tortured him to death. From 1984 to 1985, Agent Camarena-Salazar had proven extremely successful in frustrating the operations of the cartel, with one raid alone seizing billions of dollars worth of marijuana.[57] Dr. Alvarez-Machain allegedly prolonged Agent Camarena-Salazar's life to extend the torture and interrogation.[58] Five years later, a United States grand jury indicted Dr. Alvarez-Machain and a warrant was issued for his arrest. After efforts to persuade the Mexican government to hand over Dr. Alvarez-Machain failed, the DEA hired Mexican bounty hunters—including the ultimate defendant in the case, Jose Francisco Sosa—who abducted him and then transferred him for arrest by American officials.[59]

Alvarez-Machain's first trip to the Supreme Court challenged his abduction as a violation of the United States–Mexico extradition treaty. Writing for a 6–3 majority, Chief Justice Rehnquist held that the agreement did not explicitly forbid abductions that occurred outside the extradition process. Instead, the Court applied the *Ker-Frisbie* doctrine, which holds that a federal court can exercise jurisdiction over a criminal defendant brought before it through a forcible abduction, and that due process is satisfied so

---

[56] *United States v Alvarez-Machain*, 504 US 655 (1992).

[57] These additional facts can be found in *United States v Zuno-Arce*, 44 F3d 1420 (9th Cir 1995).

[58] *Sosa*, 124 S Ct at 2746.

[59] Id.

long as the defendant receives a fair trial on the substantive charges.[60] The Court reversed the Ninth Circuit's holding that the treaty applied to Alvarez-Machain's abduction and permitted his prosecution to proceed.[61]

Upon remand, the district court tried Alvarez-Machain and ultimately granted a motion for acquittal. Alvarez-Machain then brought a suit under the ATS against Sosa for arbitrary arrest, which he claimed constituted a violation of the law of nations.[62] The district court granted summary judgment in favor of the plaintiff and awarded him $25,000. He found a sympathetic hearing before a panel of the Ninth Circuit and a subsequent en banc court, which agreed that Alvarez-Machain's arbitrary arrest violated CIL and created an ATS cause of action.[63] Reversing, the Court ruled that the ATS did not provide a cause of action for Alvarez-Machain's claim, with Justice Souter adding to his growing roster of majority opinions in foreign affairs cases.[64]

In winning the battle, however, opponents of the ATS may well have lost the war. First, the Court rejected the argument that the ATS merely granted jurisdiction to the federal courts. This was a surprising outcome, because Justice Souter at times declared that the ATS was, indeed, jurisdictional in nature and did not *sua sponte* create any new causes of action. "All Members of the Court agree that § 1350 is only jurisdictional," Justice Souter remarked at one point.[65] But the ATS must do more because of the Framers' concerns about the national government's inability to enforce inter-

---

[60] 504 US at 661–63. The doctrine takes its name from *Ker v Illinois*, 119 US 436 (1886), and *Frisbie v Collins*, 342 US 519, rehearing denied, 343 US 937 (1952).

[61] *Alvarez-Machain* was decided the same Term as the better-known *United States v Verdugo-Urquidez*, which involved similar facts. 494 US 259 (1990). Verdugo-Urquidez was a co-conspirator in the death of Camarena-Salazar; while DEA officials succeeded in obtaining his transfer by Mexican police, they also searched his properties without a search warrant. Verdugo-Urquidez challenged his prosecution on the ground that the searches violated the Fourth Amendment. The Court held that the Fourth Amendment does not apply to aliens who have no significant link to the United States when they are the subject of government action outside the United States.

[62] He also brought a claim for a tort under the Federal Tort Claims Act against the United States, which the Court dismissed and we do not discuss here. *Alvarez-Machain*, 124 S Ct at 2747–54.

[63] 255 F3d 1045 (2001), aff'd by 331 F3d 604, 641 (9th Cir 2003) (en banc).

[64] See, for example, *American Insurance Association v Garamendi*, 539 US 396 (2003); *Crosby v National Foreign Trade Council*, 530 US 363 (2000).

[65] 124 S Ct at 2764.

national law within the United States.[66] As several historical studies have shown, one of the problems that beset the Articles of Confederation was that the Continental Congress possessed no domestic legislative or funding powers to implement treaties.[67] In particular, the Court referred to the Continental Congress's 1781 appeal that states punish violations of international law, and a well-known 1784 incident in which no federal remedy was available for an attacked French diplomat.[68] This history led Justice Souter to conclude that "there is every reason to suppose that the First Congress did not pass the ATS as a jurisdictional convenience to be placed on the shelf for use by a future Congress or state legislature that might, some day, authorize the creation of causes of action or itself decide to make some element of the law of nations actionable for the benefit of foreigners."[69] The Court, however, could not provide any direct historical evidence to support this point, as conventional legislative history from this period is almost nonexistent. Rather, Justice Souter relied on what he called "[t]he anxieties of the preconstitutional period" in rejecting the idea "that the statute was not meant to have a practical effect."[70]

Second, the Court reached back to historical sources to give substantive content to its jurisdictional-but-not-jurisdictional interpretation of the ATS. Justice Souter argued that the law of nations, as it existed in the late eighteenth century, regulated private individual conduct by guaranteeing safe conducts, prohibiting attacks on ambassadors, and outlawing piracy.[71] According to the Court, Congress would have intended the ATS to provide jurisdiction for this limited set of violations.[72] But how does this work with the Court's observation that the ATS does nothing more than simply create jurisdiction for torts in violation of the law of nations? According to Justice Souter, the ATS created jurisdiction for a limited set of torts under international law, and those torts

---

[66] Id at 2757.

[67] For one such review of the history of this period, see John Yoo, *Globalism and the Constitution: Treaties, Legislative Power, and the Original Understanding*, 99 Colum L Rev 1955 (1999).

[68] 124 S Ct at 2756–57.

[69] Id at 2758.

[70] Id.

[71] Id at 2756 (citing 4 Blackstone, *Commentaries* *68).

[72] Id.

would be supplied by the common law. "In sum, although the ATS is a jurisdictional statute creating no new causes of action, the reasonable inference from the historical materials is that the statute was intended to have practical effect the moment it became law. The jurisdictional grant is best read as having been enacted on the understanding that the common law would provide a cause of action for the modest number of international law violations with a potential for personal liability at the time."[73]

Despite opening the door (to borrow the Court's metaphor) to a reading of the ATS as enforcing substantive norms itself, the Court appeared determined to limit the possible causes of action. As Justice Souter wrote, "there are good reasons for a restrained conception of the discretion a federal court should exercise in considering a new cause of action of this kind. Accordingly, we think courts should require any claim based on the present-day law of nations to rest on a norm of international character accepted by the civilized world and defined with a specificity comparable to the features of the 18th-century paradigms we have recognized."[74] But what are those "good reasons"? They are the ones, it seems, that have been put forward by the ATS's formalist critics. First, the Court acknowledged that the nature of the common law has changed between 1789 and today—it is no longer transcendental law "discovered" by the state and federal courts. Second, the foundational *Erie Railroad Company v Tompkins*[75] in 1938 changed the role of federal courts by denying the existence of a general federal common law and permitting only interstitial federal common lawmaking. As the Court observed, "the general practice has been to look for legislative guidance before exercising innovative authority over substantive law. It would be remarkable to take a more aggressive role in exercising a jurisdiction that remained largely in shadow for much of the prior two centuries."[76] Third, the Court in recent years has made clear that it will not infer a private cause of action for violations of a domestic statute unless Congress clearly so intended.[77]

---

[73] Id at 2761.

[74] Id at 2761–62.

[75] 304 US 64 (1938).

[76] 124 S Ct at 2762.

[77] Id at 2762–63 (citing *Correctional Services Corp. v Malesko*, 534 US 61, 68 (2001); *Alexander v Sandoval*, 532 US 275, 286–87 (2001)).

These concerns reflect the federal courts' general reluctance in the wake of *Erie* to engage in lawmaking. They are certainly familiar to the scholars who have explored the scope and processes of federal common law over the last decades, several of whom have come to doubt the modern case for the place of CIL as federal law.[78] The Court, however, added two more reasons, specific to the foreign affairs context. First, because of changes in international law, ATS suits now can call upon federal courts to declare that foreign governments have violated the rights of their own citizens. This, according to Justice Souter, risks "impinging on the discretion of the Legislative and Executive Branches in managing foreign affairs."[79] Second, to the extent that the political branches have addressed the issue, they have generally refused to make human rights treaties self-executing or to create new statutory causes of action to enforce international law.[80]

Despite these concerns, the Court refused to "close the door" on the notion that the ATS gives rise to some causes of action, or that new substantive standards could emerge as international law evolved. Justice Scalia, joined by Chief Justice Rehnquist and Justice Thomas, argued in concurrence that the ATS was *only* jurisdictional and could not even permit claims based on the substantive norms recognized in the late eighteenth century. Justice Souter responded that federal common lawmaking could continue, albeit cautiously and reluctantly. "[W]e are persuaded that federal courts should not recognize private claims under federal common law for violations of any international law norm with less definite content and acceptance among civilized nations than the historical paradigms familiar when § 1350 was enacted."[81] In applying this test, the Court found that Alvarez-Machain's claim of arbitrary detention did not rise to the level of universal recognition, binding obligation, and specificity that characterize only the highest norms of CIL. In part, the Court clearly was troubled by the practical implications of recognizing such a cause of action, which would

---

[78] See, for example, Young, 42 Va J Intl L 365 (cited in note 50); Daniel J. Meltzer, *Customary International Law, Foreign Affairs, and Federal Common Law*, 42 Va J Intl L 513 (2002).

[79] 124 S Ct at 2763.

[80] With one notable exception, the Torture Victim Protection Act of 1991, Pub L No 102-256, 106 Stat 73.

[81] 124 S Ct at 2765.

require the federal courts to review "any arrest, anywhere in the world, unauthorized by the law of the jurisdiction in which it took place."[82] In part, the Court considered Alvarez-Machain's purported norm to be aspirational in nature, to lack a specific definition, and to be lacking in the universal acceptance by civilized nations sufficient to qualify as a binding rule of customary law.

Although Alvarez-Machain lost his case, supporters of the modern position could gain a great deal of succor from the decision. Justice Souter's opinion essentially left intact much of existing ATS case law, as developed primarily by the Second and Ninth Circuit Courts of Appeals. Alvarez-Machain's fault was not that he sought a remedy through the ATS, but that he failed to show that a right against arbitrary detention had truly become a rule of CIL.

B.   SOSA'S INTERNAL FAULTS

The debate between the *Sosa* majority and minority took place on fairly straightforward formalist grounds. No one doubted that if Congress, under its Article I, Section 8 power to define offenses under the law of nations, had decided to incorporate international law through a statute, it could have. The only question was whether the ATS ought to be interpreted as doing so. The Court could not bring itself to shut the door completely on any federal judicial role in the enforcement of CIL. The Court's reasons, however, were anything but convincing. Justice Souter relied on three pieces of historical evidence, but those historical materials fail to show that the members of the first Congress understood the ATS to create substantive causes of action.

First, Justice Souter believed it significant that Oliver Ellsworth had drafted the ATS, because Ellsworth had also been both a member of the Continental Congress in 1781 when it requested that states enact laws punishing attacks on ambassadors and violations of safe passage and a member of the Connecticut legislature when it complied with that request. Second, the first Congress had enacted criminal statutes prohibiting violation of safe conducts, piracy, and attacks on ambassadors,[83] which Justice Souter believed showed that Congress would not have enacted a civil

---

[82] Id at 2768.

[83] An Act for the Punishment of Certain Crimes Against the United States, § 8, 1 Stat 113–14; id § 28 at 118.

statute that waited upon further action to become effective.[84] Third, international law authorities at the time, most notably Vattel, declared that states should not only criminally punish those who attack ambassadors but provide for compensation as well.[85]

To put it charitably, these pieces of historical evidence are weak. Ellsworth's membership in the Continental Congress and the Connecticut legislature tells us virtually nothing about the intentions of the first Congress in enacting the ATS. The Court provides no statements from Ellsworth or any of his contemporaries about the ATS, nor does it show any consistent train of thought on Ellsworth's part on the question of enforcement of CIL. This stands in sharp contrast, for example, to the clear public positions that leading Framers, such as James Madison and Alexander Hamilton, took on the question of the enforcement of another species of international law, treaties, both before and after the ratification.[86]

Justice Souter's second piece of evidence undermines his own conclusion. If Congress were capable of enacting specific criminal statutes addressing the problem, why would it then turn around and enact a civil statute that most everyone concedes is ambiguous and unclear to address the very same conduct? A third odd historical inference is made in regard to Vattel's comments. While Vattel does believe that states should compensate victims of attacks that violate international law, he does not address whether such compensation should come about as a matter of civil suits.

In response to Justice Scalia's concurrence, the Court sought further support in two precedents, *Banco Nacionale de Cuba v Sabbatino*,[87] and *The Paquete Habana*.[88] In the former, Justice Souter observed, the Court had commented that "it is, of course, true that United States courts apply international law as a part of our own in appropriate circumstances,"[89] while in the latter the Court declared: "International law is part of our law, and must be ascertained and administered by the courts of justice of appropriate jurisdiction, as often as questions of right depending upon it are

---

[84] 124 S Ct at 2758–59.

[85] Id at 2761 (citing Vattel, at 463–64).

[86] Yoo, 99 Colum L Rev at 2010–21, 2078–82 (cited in note 67).

[87] 376 US 398 (1964).

[88] 175 US 677 (1900).

[89] 376 US at 423.

duly presented for their determination."[90] From these cases, Justice Souter drew the conclusion that "the domestic law of the United States recognizes the law of nations," and has done so for 200 years, and issued the rejoinder that "[i]t would take some explaining to say now that federal courts must avert their gaze entirely from any international norm intended to protect individuals."[91]

Neither of these cases, however, has anything to do with the ATS; if anything, they undermine the idea that the federal courts have power to enforce CIL as federal law. *Sabbatino*, for example, applied the act of state doctrine in an action arising out of the nationalization of foreign assets by the Cuban government. An American middleman purchased sugar that had been owned by a Cuban firm, C.A.V., whose assets had been expropriated; after it took possession of the goods, the American company paid the proceeds to C.A.V. rather than the Cuban government.[92] Invoking diversity jurisdiction, Banco Nacional sued under state law in federal district court for the money, and claimed that the legality of the expropriation could not be reviewed because of the act of state doctrine.

In applying the act of state doctrine, the Court rejected the notion that its use was compelled by international law. Instead, as Justice Harlan wrote for the Court, the act of state doctrine "arises out of the basic relationships between branches of government in a system of separation of powers. It concerns the competency of dissimilar institutions to make and implement particular kinds of decisions in the area of international relations."[93] While the Court observed that *Erie Railroad* did not apply to the act of state doctrine, it emphasized that the rule was necessary to promote judicial restraint, or "a basic choice regarding the competence and function of the Judiciary and the National Executive in ordering our relationships with other members of the international community."[94] Thus, to the extent *Sabbatino* enshrined the act of state doctrine

---

[90] 175 US at 700. The Court also cited *The Nereide*, 13 US (9 Cranch) 388, 423 (1815) (Marshall, CJ) ("[T]he Court is bound by the law of nations which is a part of the law of the land"); and *Texas Industries, Inc. v Radcliff Materials, Inc.*, 451 US 630, 641 (1981) (recognizing that "international disputes implicating . . . our relations with foreign nations" are one of the "narrow areas" in which "federal common law" continues to exist).

[91] 124 S Ct at 2764–65.

[92] 376 US at 401.

[93] Id at 423.

[94] Id at 425.

as federal common law, this was not because federal courts had a mandate to incorporate international law norms as federal law. Not only does *Sabbatino* ignore the ATS, but, if anything, its separation of powers core militates against Justice Souter's reading and toward judicial abstention.

The Paquete Habana voyages even farther from the ATS. During the Spanish-American war, American warships captured two coastal fishing vessels off Cuba.[95] After a federal district court condemned the ships as prizes, their crew appealed to the Supreme Court on the ground that the American navy had captured the ships in violation of CIL. They claimed, and the Court agreed after a lengthy historical analysis of state practice from the 1400s, that CIL prohibited the seizure of such civilian vessels during wartime. Several factors distinguish *The Paquete Habana* from *Sosa*. First, the rule of the case is not simply the oft-quoted "[i]nternational law is part of our law." Rather, the Court continues, courts should consult "the customs and usages of civilized nations" when "there is no treaty, and no controlling executive or legislative act or juridical decision."[96] Thus, an executive order standing alone could override the application of CIL, which could not happen with judicial interpretation of a federal statute such as the ATS. Second, the case arose in prize jurisdiction, where, like the admiralty jurisdiction, the courts had developed and applied federal common law rules. There was no "tort" as the phrase is used in the ATS; rather, the cause of action arose under the laws of war. Third, in *The Paquete Habana* itself, the President had ordered the military to carry out its blockade in Cuba in accordance with the international laws of war—just the "controlling executive" action required.[97] There was no conflict between executive policy and international law, and thus no occasion for the judiciary to examine whether CIL independently applied.[98]

---

[95] 175 US 677.

[96] Id at 700.

[97] Id at 712; see also Bradley and Goldsmith, 66 Fordham L Rev at 353 n 191 (cited in note 31); Michael J. Glennon, *May the President Violate Customary International Law? Can the President Do No Wrong?* 80 Am J Intl L 923, 923 n 6 (1986).

[98] Despite this, *The Paquete Habana* and *Sabbatino* are routinely cited for the more tenuous proposition that federal courts have the power to incorporate CIL as federal law directly, without the intervention of a statute (or executive policy). See, for example, Goodman and Jinks, 66 Fordham L Rev at 481 (cited in note 37). The reasoning must run, we suppose, that if federal courts can directly incorporate international law as federal law, much in the way that the judiciary creates rules to govern interstate disputes and federal

Lastly, the Court relied on a series of questionable assumptions about congressional approval of previous ATS decisions. According to the Court, Congress's silence must signify some level of implicit agreement with the lower courts' expanded application of the ATS over the last two decades. Put aside for the moment that, even accepting the Court's argument at face value, legislative silence today could only inform us about the current Congress's preferences, not the intentions of the first Congress that enacted the ATS in 1789. Also put to one side that the Supreme Court does not employ a strong form of stare decisis in statutory interpretation cases.[99] Justice Souter assumes that ATS cases are sufficiently important to outweigh other important items on Congress's limited agenda (a doubtful proposition these days), that silence reflects the wishes of a majority (rather than, perhaps, the opposition of filibustering minority or a President and one-third of the Senate), and that Congress regularly overrides judicial interpretations with which it disagrees. The accuracy of these assumptions depends on facts for which no conclusive empirical data exist,[100] and there are certainly plausible arguments that run in the other direction.

It is possible that the Court had a more subtle reason in mind for applying what is essentially a strong form of statutory stare decisis. Some have argued that refusing to reverse erroneous precedents has the effect of promoting democracy by forcing the legislature to make its preferences known.[101] Again, this depends on speculative assumptions about the operations of Congress. Professor Vermeule, however, has put forward the more nuanced argument that, in the presence of empirical uncertainty, adopting a

---

instrumentalities, then doing so pursuant to the ATS is a far smaller step. This certainly seems to have been the reasoning of the lower courts, most prominently the Second Circuit in *Filartiga*. *Filartiga v Pena-Irala*, 630 F2d 876, 887 (2d Cir 1980).

[99] See, for example, *Hubbard v United States*, 514 US 695, 715 (1995); William N. Eskridge, Jr., *The Case of the Amorous Defendant: Criticizing Absolute Stare Decisis for Statutory Cases*, 88 Mich L Rev 2450, 2462 (1990).

[100] In the leading empirical study on this question, William Eskridge concluded that Congress does monitor judicial decisions involving statutory interpretation and will override "textualist" decisions more often than those that rely on legislative history or congressional purpose. William N. Eskridge, Jr., *Overriding Supreme Court Statutory Interpretation Decisions*, 101 Yale L J 331 (1991). Adrian Vermeule, however, has raised significant doubts about whether Eskridge's data actually support that conclusion. See Adrian Vermeule, *Interpretive Choice*, 75 NYU L Rev 74, 104–06 (2000).

[101] See, for example, Larry Marshall, *Let Congress Do It: The Case for an Absolute Rule of Stare Decisis*, 88 Mich L Rev 177, 208–15 (1989).

rule of absolute stare decisis in statutory interpretation cases will at least produce a reduction in decision costs—litigants will no longer seek the overrule of statutory precedents, judges will not have to expend resources reevaluating them, and the legal system will gain in stability.[102]

It is doubtful, however, whether those benefits apply in the ATS context. *Sosa* brought no stability gains because the Supreme Court had not yet addressed the validity of the ATS's modern interpretation; one could also just as easily argue that it was the Second Circuit's decision in *Filartiga*, followed most vigorously by the Ninth Circuit in the cases leading up to *Sosa*, that had introduced instability to the legal system. In the context of decision costs, courts will probably face few to zero efforts seeking to reverse the Court's reading of the ATS. But it is unclear at best whether a contrary result would have had any disruptive effect on the overall stability of statutory precedents.[103] Permitting ATS suits to continue, however, may well increase decision costs. ATS cases are difficult. They require the acquisition of costly information: legal rules are derived from unfamiliar materials, namely, signs of state practice and foreign and international legal materials, and facts come from events that occurred outside the territorial United States. *Sosa* provided a far from simple test for distinguishing between enforceable and nonenforceable CIL norms. Additionally, ATS cases often involve multipolar disputes in which multiple potential parties raise legal claims, and chains of events are complex and multifaceted. They frequently involve delicate matters of international relations that are the focus of policies managed by the political branches. In the past, cases went undefended as foreign leaders accused of violations of human rights refused to appear in U.S. courts. As cases have begun to involve corporations and elements of the federal government, however, more vigorous defenses have begun.

Sosa purported to settle the ATS question using standard formalist tools of text, history, structure, and precedent. None of these arguments proved convincing. Indeed, as Justice Scalia's con-

---

[102] Vermeule, 75 NYU L Rev at 143–45 (cited in note 100).

[103] In other words, if the Court applies only a soft canon of statutory decisis to all statutory precedents, a decision to apply the precedent with regard to a single statute will likely make no difference in the overall number of challenges brought to precedents in other statutory areas.

currence pointed out, the formalist arguments, if anything, should have led the Court to the opposite holding. The academic stalemate may have contributed to the odd nature of the Court's decision in *Sosa*, which seems to acknowledge both sides of the debate, but could not really choose between them. While the Court seems to admit the compelling nature of the formalist arguments against federal common lawmaking in general and incorporation of CIL in particular, it would not adopt their conclusion. At the same time, the Court could not develop any convincing reasons of its own, based in the text, structure, or history of the ATS, to allow judicial development of substantive causes of action under the ATS. It settled upon a muddled, tentative decision that kept the door open for federal court recognition of certain CIL causes of action, but failed to explain how far open that door should remain or why that door should be open in the first place.

III

The Court did not consider the ATS from a functional perspective, even though it might well have done so given its unsatisfactory formalist rationales. A functional analysis seeks to determine whether, from a normative perspective, judicial implementation of international law through the ATS is the more effective method to achieve the government's desired policies. This approach asks two questions. First, what are the goals or purposes of the ATS? In other words, what end is the government seeking to achieve? Second, does a comparative analysis show that the courts or the executive would more effectively achieve those goals or purposes in this area?[104] This analysis seeks to move beyond the formalist stalemate over whether the ATS authorizes federal courts to enforce and develop CIL to the second-order question whether other institutions, in particular the executive branch, are better suited to carrying out the purpose that the *Sosa* Court assigns to federal courts.

---

[104] Scholars such as Neil Komesar, Cass Sunstein, and Adrian Vermeule have undertaken a similar approach to questions ranging from statutory interpretation to regulatory decision making. See, for example, Neil K. Komesar, *Imperfect Alternatives: Choosing Institutions in Law, Economics, and Public Policy* (Chicago, 1994); Cass Sunstein and Adrian Vermeule, *Interpretation and Institutions*, 101 Mich L Rev 885 (2003).

A. STATUTORY PURPOSE

The starting point for evaluating the Court's approach to the ATS is to define its purpose. We do not mean "purpose" in the sense used in the legislative history debate, in which "purposivism" suggests an approach that gives courts greater discretion to interpret statutory language to achieve the "purpose" of a statute.[105] Rather, before we can address the effectiveness of the *Sosa* Court's interpretation of the ATS, we first must identify the national policy sought. We would conduct a similar inquiry to determine whether any institutional mechanism can be regarded as better or worse in comparison with another. We cannot judge, for example, whether the independent counsel statute was superior to the pre- and post-Act system of appointment of special counsels by the Attorney General, unless we first have defined the problem that Congress sought to address.[106] This will give us the necessary context within which to judge whether courts are the best institutional option to achieve national policy.

1. *Sosa and statutory purpose*. *Sosa* proved a disappointment in identifying the purpose of the ATS. Justice Souter began his inquiry with an examination of the ATS's historical context. The first Congress's silence has left scholars in the position of arguing over levels of generality. Critics of the modern position have argued for a fairly low level of generality, and so have looked to the specific placement of the ATS within the overall structure of the Judiciary Act of 1789.[107] As the Judiciary Act of 1789 generally created the basics of the federal court system and established federal subject matter jurisdiction, it would be odd to read the ATS as pursuing a different purpose. Section 1350 only sought to recognize the basis for a type of party-based jurisdiction—suits by aliens—that Congress subsequently could use in enacting specific causes of action. ATS defenders have described the purpose of the ATS at a fairly high level of generality. According to them, the United States wanted to take its place among the nations of the

---

[105] See, for example, John F. Manning, *Textualism and the Equity of the Statute*, 101 Colum L Rev 1, 3, 7 (2001) (criticizing purpose-based approach to statutory interpretation); William N. Eskridge, Jr. and Philip P. Frickey, *Statutory Interpretation as Practical Reasoning*, 42 Stan L Rev 321 (1990) (arguing that courts should make policy judgments in implementing statutory purpose).

[106] Compare *Morrison v Olson*, 487 US 654 (1988) (discussing benefits of independent counsel statute).

[107] Bradley, 42 Va J Intl L at 593 (cited in note 24).

world, and the Framers believed that this required the United States to enforce and obey the law of nations.[108] In fact, one can understand the academic debate over the ATS as a failure to come to agreement on the appropriate level of generality to use in interpreting the statute.

The Court, however, followed neither of these approaches. While it looked to the diplomatic problem that had beset the national government under the Articles of Confederation, it rejected the idea that the ATS should be so limited. Justice Souter also looked to the opinion of Framing-era legal authorities that such attacks required a damages remedy, but then rejected that purpose as too narrow. Given that Congress has enacted statutory crimes to address these violations, such a reading would render the ATS effectively meaningless.

Sosa concludes that the ATS's purpose is to provide a remedy for CIL violations that have achieved universal consensus.[109] Unlike its earlier discussion of the framing-era context, however, *Sosa* fails to explain what purpose this broader reading serves. It is easy to understand, for example, why the ATS's statutory purpose might extend beyond providing jurisdiction for subsequent statutory causes of action. Attacks on foreign diplomats had disrupted American foreign relations, national law provided no remedy, so Congress sought to fill the gap by creating a damages action. But *Sosa* reads the ATS to go beyond Blackstone's trio of offenses that were aimed chiefly at prohibiting CIL violations by American private parties. Moreover, Congress has already fulfilled this goal by enacting federal statutes implementing the very international law obligations—prohibitions on torture, genocide, and war crimes—that *Sosa* identified as cognizable ATS claims.[110]

Sosa's broader reading of the ATS, therefore, encompasses fundamentally different CIL norms and contemplates more than simply preventing U.S. citizens from violating international law. As the *Sosa* Court noted, the most significant uses of the statute have included actions by aliens against officials of their own governments, as with the *Filartiga* case against a Paraguayan officer for

---

[108] See, for example, Burley, 83 Am J Intl L 461 (cited in note 2).

[109] The Court did not address the ATS's additional language permitting torts for violations of treaties.

[110] See, for example, Torture Statute, 18 USC § 2340 (2000); War Crimes Act, 18 USC § 2441 (2000); Genocide Convention Implementation Act, 18 USC § 1091 (2000).

torture, the *Trajano* suit in the Ninth Circuit against former Filipino dictator Ferdinand Marcos, or the *Karadzic* litigation against a Serb warlord.[111] These cases did not involve the failure of the United States to enforce international law against its own citizens; they did not involve American citizens as defendants; nor did the events at issue have any significant nexus with the United States at the time of their commission. Rather than preventing Americans from causing offense to foreign nations, *Sosa* allows aliens to sue other aliens, corporations, foreign governments, and perhaps even the United States government for violations of international law. The ATS's purpose has been transformed from keeping the United States out of diplomatic incidents to keeping other nations to their international obligations.

In fact, the ATS may play only a marginal role in achieving what the *Sosa* Court believed to be its original purpose: to ensure the United States and its citizens comply with international law. So far, the United States government has enjoyed sovereign immunity to ATS suits, as it would to other causes of action unless specifically overridden.[112] Criminal laws already exist to prosecute Americans who commit serious violations of international law of the kind that concerned Blackstone.[113] The *Sosa* Court's refusal to limit enforceable CIL norms to those supporting the statute's original purpose embraces a broader statutory purpose—enforcing international law against foreign nations on behalf of that nation's citizens. But *Sosa* nowhere explains (*a*) what problem Congress (of 1789 or of today) seeks to address, or (*b*) why or how the ATS might be a means to solve the problem. This is a serious defect in the Court's opinion.

2. *Possible statutory purposes.* Academic supporters of the ATS have suggested a number of possible statutory purposes. None of them, however, are linked in any significant way to traditional signs of congressional purpose, such as other parts of the U.S. Code or legislative history:

- the ATS could be designed to allow the United States to speak

---

[111] *Filartiga v Pena-Irala*, 630 F2d 876 (2d Cir 1980); *In re Estate of Ferdinand Marcos*, 25 F3d 1467 (9th Cir 1994); *Kadic v Karadzic*, 70 F3d 232 (2d Cir 1995).

[112] See, for example, *Sosa*, 124 S Ct at 2747–48; *Al Odah v United States*, 321 F3d 1134, 1149–50 (DC Cir 2003) (Randolph, J, concurring), reversed on other grounds; *Rasul v Bush*, 124 S Ct 2686 (2004).

[113] See sources cited note 83.

with one voice in foreign affairs by centralizing control over international law in the federal courts;[114]
- the ATS could have as its purpose to prevent American states, corporations, and individuals from violating international law;[115]
- or the ATS could be intended to promote the development and enforcement of international law itself.

The first two purposes seem especially unlikely. There does not seem to be any firm evidence that these are systematic problems. Even if they were, Congress has ample tools at its disposal that are less blunt than incorporating CIL wholesale. Congress, for example, has enacted criminal laws prohibiting the commission of torture, genocide, and war crimes, the three most significant norms recognized as jus cogens.[116] It has also specified particular conditions under which plaintiffs can bring civil suits alleging torture or injuries from terrorist acts into federal courts.[117]

That leaves the third purpose. Such a broad, open-ended goal evokes the liberal internationalism of a Woodrow Wilson or Jimmy Carter, and may explain why the *Sosa* Court shied away from stating it clearly. We do not seek to criticize this purpose. Congress has sufficient authority under Article I, Section 8 to enact a statute that created a cause of action to achieve it. We also do not dispute that international human rights recently has played an important role in recent American foreign policy, from President Reagan's criticism of the "evil empire" of the Soviet Union to President Clinton's decision to wage war in Kosovo. We need only consider whether this is indeed the ATS's purpose, or at least that the *Sosa* Court believes this to be its purpose, to discuss whether the ATS actually makes sense as a tool to achieving its goals.

Although the *Sosa* Court did not explicitly embrace this view, its endorsement of lower federal court decisions expanding the scope of the ATS supports this broader purpose. As *Sosa* itself more or less admits, the lower federal courts clearly have expanded the ATS beyond its original purpose. What is important, however,

---

[114] Harold H. Koh, *Is International Law Really State Law?* 111 Harv L Rev 1824, 1832 (1998).

[115] Id at 1840, 1850.

[116] Torture Statute, 18 USC § 2340 (2000); War Crimes Act, 18 USC § 2441 (2000); Genocide Convention Implementation Act, 18 USC § 1091 (2000).

[117] Torture Victim Protection Act, 28 USC § 1350; 18 USC § 2333.

is not whether this is consistent with the intentions of the first Congress, on which little historical evidence exists, but whether that purpose is in line with the preferences of current Congresses. While it is unlikely that the Congress at the time of *Sosa*'s decision would have delegated such authority, it is possible that it would have met with congressional approval at the time of *Filartiga*. Those decisions cannot be overturned by Congress today, even if the President and the median member of Congress disagree, unless they can put together enough votes to override a filibuster in the Senate. So today we can say, after *Sosa*, that the ATS promotes a national policy in favor of the development and enforcement of international law. It remains unusual, however, in foreign affairs because it is delegated to the federal courts, rather than the political branches.

B.   INSTITUTIONAL COMPETENCE: A COMPARATIVE ANALYSIS

Now that we have determined the statutory purpose most consistent with the *Sosa* decision, we can analyze whether the delegation of power to the federal courts is the most effective means of policy implementation. This section argues that the design and operation of the judiciary give it a comparatively weak institutional vantage point from which to achieve foreign affairs goals of the sort envisioned by the ATS. This is not to say that federal courts cannot play a role in the development and enforcement of CIL. Instead, we are making the more modest second-order argument that as a matter of institutional competence, the federal judiciary suffers significant disadvantages in such a role compared to the executive branch. We necessarily base our institutional assessment on certain generalizations and assumptions about how these institutions work because it is difficult to imagine a sufficiently rigorous empirical test of these functional claims. Even conceding these limitations to our approach, in light of the formalist stalemate over the proper interpretation of the ATS, identifying these institutional disadvantages tips the scale against the *Sosa* Court's reading of the ATS.

1. *Judicial competence.* It is important to distinguish between both micro- and macro-level characteristics of the judiciary. Several characteristics of the federal courts at the micro level—the operation of individual judges in individual lawsuits—limit the information that flows to courts and the options available to them.

At a macro level, certain system-wide features of the Article III judiciary may poorly equip it to carry out national policy on a global scale.

a) Micro-institutional factors. Defining features of the Article III courts make them superior to other branches in performing certain functions, but also make them comparatively less well suited to playing a leading foreign relations role. Federal courts are designed to be independent from politics, to passively allow parties to drive litigation, and to receive information in highly formal ways. These characteristics may make courts more neutral in their decision making and fairer in their attitude toward parties. But they also may render them less effective tools in achieving national goals in international relations. Comparison of courts with other institutions may make these points more salient.

An initial difference between courts and other institutions is access. Compared with other institutions, courts have high barriers to access.[118] Congress has somewhat moderately difficult barriers—it is generally thought that interest groups must provide campaign contributions or political support in order to obtain access to political leaders.[119] The executive branch has lower barriers than Congress; it is probably easier for individuals and groups to provide information to, and make requests of, agencies, although perhaps with no greater chances of success.

By contrast, courts have numerous doctrines that limit access. Under standing doctrine, for example, plaintiffs must have suffered an actual injury in fact which is traceable to conduct on the part of a defendant who can remedy the harm.[120] The timing of the case must be just right, neither too early and therefore unripe nor too late and therefore moot.[121] It cannot raise political questions whose determination is constitutionally vested in another branch.[122] The plaintiff must actually be able to claim to benefit from a cause of action created under federal law. Litigation itself

---

[118] Komesar, *Imperfect Alternatives* at 125 (cited in note 104).

[119] See Robert Cooter, *The Strategic Constitution* 51–74 (Princeton, 1999) (discussing interest group theory of politics). Other studies, however, show that members of Congress are responsive to public pressure as reflected through the media and constituents.

[120] See, for example, *Lujan v Defenders of Wildlife*, 504 US 555 (1992).

[121] See, for example, *DeFunis v Odegaard*, 416 US 312 (1974) (mootness); *United Public Workers v Mitchell*, 330 US 75 (1947) (ripeness).

[122] *Nixon v United States*, 506 US 224 (1993).

demands significant resources, at least in comparison with means of accessing the executive or legislative branches.

There are also significant differences in the way courts acquire and process information. Courts gather knowledge through a painstaking and expensive process of discovery, conducted by the contending parties. That information must satisfy the federal rules of evidence—it must survive tests for relevance, credibility, and reliability—and the parties must present it to the court in accordance with formal courtroom procedures. By contrast, the executive branch collects information through agency experts, a national and global network of officials and agents, and links with outside groups and foreign governments. Congress can acquire information from the executive branch or outside groups via relatively inexpensive hearings. Also, a court generally cannot update its information except in the context of a new case. Thus, if a court has made a decision based on information available to it at time 1, it generally will not continue to gather information thereafter—even if it would lead it to change its decision—until another case raising the same issue appears.[123]

Article III creates significant limitations on the ability of federal courts to dynamically integrate its actions with national foreign policy. Once the President and Congress have enacted a statute or the President and the Senate have approved a treaty, the judiciary's constitutional responsibility is to execute those goals in the context of Article III cases or controversies. Federal judges cannot alter or refuse to execute those policies, even if the original circumstances that gave rise to the statute or treaty have changed.[124] If a federal court, for example, finds that a defendant has violated the Helms-Burton Act by "trafficking" in property confiscated by the Cuban government, it must render judgment for an American plaintiff who once owned that property.[125] Article III requires a federal court to reach that decision even if the effects of the judgment in that particular case would actually harm the national interest or conflict with other countries' view of CIL.

---

[123] See, for example, Thomas R. Lee, *Stare Decisis in Economic Perspective: An Economic Analysis of the Supreme Court's Doctrine of Precedent*, 78 NC L Rev 643 (2000).

[124] For a contrary view, see Guido Calabresi, *A Common Law for the Age of Statutes* (Harvard, 1985).

[125] See John Yoo, *Federal Courts as Weapons of Foreign Policy: The Case of the Helms-Burton Act*, 20 Hastings Intl & Comp L Rev 747 (1997).

A last micro difficulty arises from the substantive challenge presented by CIL. CIL is a very different subject than that usually encountered by federal courts. Many observers admit that the very concept of CIL—law that "results from a general and consistent practice of states followed by them from a sense of legal obligation" rather than through positive enactment[126]—is fraught with difficulty.[127] It is unclear whether CIL should prevail because of actual state consent to a rule, or because state practice reflects international consensus on a rule.[128] It is unclear how widespread state practice must be, how long it must continue, and how consistent it must be to qualify as CIL.[129] It is not even clear what counts as state practice, whether it should be limited to actions or declarations, and whose practice—that of the great powers, that of the leading nations of each region in the world, that of every nation in the world—matters.[130] It is not clear when state practice can be said to arise out of a sense of legal obligation rather than through coincidence or expedient coordination.[131] It is also controversial whether the views of other actors, such as law professors and judges, should have weight in determining international law.[132]

Even if the very nature of CIL were not so uncertain and ambiguous, it is likely that the federal courts either would experience a high error rate or high decision costs in determining its content. CIL involves sources that are not often encountered by federal judges or American lawyers. The very source of CIL—state practice—is not easily discovered. State practice may not even be reflected in publicly available documents, but may more often lie in the archives of the State Department and foreign ministries, or

---

[126] Restatement (Third) at § 102(2) (cited in note 13).

[127] Compare Anthony A. D'Amato, *The Concept of Custom in International Law* at 4 (Cornell, 1971), with Ian Brownlie, *Principles of Public International Law* at 5–6 (Oxford, 4 ed 1990).

[128] Compare Prosper Weil, *Toward Relative Normativity in International Law?* 77 Am J Intl L 413, 433 (1983).

[129] These well-known problems with CIL are discussed in D'Amato, *The Concept of Custom* 6–10 (cited in note 127).

[130] See Patrick Kelly, *The Twilight of Customary International Law*, 40 Va J Intl L 449, 500–501 (2000) (describing lack of agreement on sources of state practice for purposes of determining CIL).

[131] Jack Goldsmith and Eric Posner, *A Theory of Customary International Law*, 66 U Chi L Rev 1113, 1176–77 (1999).

[132] This practice has been criticized by Bradley and Goldsmith, 110 Harv L Rev at 872–76 (cited in note 3).

may rest in the preserve of unwritten custom. American-trained judges—almost all of them generalists—would have to survey the actions of governments over the course of dozens if not hundreds of years, and make fine-grained judgments not just about what states have done, but why they did it. Take the most prominent example of a federal court attempting to divine CIL: the *Paquete Habana* case itself. Justice Gray surveyed centuries of policies, declarations, and naval actions to determine the legal status of coastal fishing vessels. It appears that he may have gotten the record of state practice wrong—states did not consistently refrain from seizing small fishing vessels during wartime.[133] Even if Justice Gray had accurately described practice, he failed to show that the protection of coastal fishing vessels had arisen out of a sense of legal obligation, rather than out of an interest by states in coordinating their activities or because of a fear of retaliation.[134]

A useful analogy can be made here to the arguments about the use of legislative history. Whether courts should consult legislative history has become one of the focal points for broader debates about the nature of legislation, judicial competencies, and the purpose of interpretation. To summarize briefly, many who believe that courts should seek out Congress's "intent" or broader "purpose" find reliance on legislative history, along with other policy considerations, generally acceptable.[135] A minority argue that legislative history ought not be used, either because there is no such thing as a collective intent or because consulting legislative history evades the formal separation of powers.[136] Professor Vermeule makes a similar argument to the one made here: even if courts should seek legislative intent, their "limited interpretive competence" suggests that they "might do better, even on intentionalist grounds, by eschewing legislative history than by consulting it."[137]

---

[133] Goldsmith and Posner, 66 U Chi L Rev at 1148 n 101 (cited in note 131).

[134] Id.

[135] See, for example, William N. Eskridge, Jr., *Textualism, the Unknown Ideal?* 96 Mich L Rev 1509 (1998) (reviewing Antonin Scalia, *A Matter of Interpretation: Federal Courts and the Law* (Princeton, 1997)); Daniel A. Farber and Philip P. Frickey, *Legislative Intent and Public Choice*, 74 Va L Rev 423 (1988); Eskridge and Frickey, 42 Stan L Rev (cited in note 105).

[136] See, for example, John F. Manning, *Textualism as a Nondelegation Doctrine*, 97 Colum L Rev 673 (1997); Frank H. Easterbrook, *Text, History, and Structure in Statutory Interpretation*, 17 Harv J L & Pub Pol 61, 68 (1994).

[137] See Adrian Vermeule, *Legislative History and the Limits of Judicial Competence: The Untold Story of Holy Trinity Church*, 50 Stan L Rev 1833 (1998).

Judges may have limited abilities to understand and properly use legislative history, leading to high decision costs in conducting extensive reviews of legislative history without any corresponding reduction (and perhaps even an increase) in error costs.

If this is true with legislative history, these costs will only be compounded with CIL. The sources of legislative history at least rest within the general bounds of American public law, and so will be familiar to most judges. While expensive to gather and analyze in relation to other forms of American legal research,[138] legislative history may well be cheap to use in comparison to sources of CIL, which comes in different languages, involves not just texts but practices, and is recorded in sources that are often not publicly available. Even the use of more conventional public sources, such as multilateral treaties and the resolutions of the United Nations General Assembly, has serious interpretive problems. It is highly questionable, for example, that nations that refuse to sign treaties, for example, should be held to the same norms because they have "ripened" into custom, or that CIL should be read to go beyond the standards set by a widely joined treaty. Decisions by organs of the United Nations, particularly of the General Assembly, have no formal authority to declare CIL, if by definition that law represents the practice of *states*, not the opinions of international organizations.[139] The most pertinent evidence of state practice will be the most expensive to come by, and there is no empirical showing yet that federal courts will perform better in their use than any other institution.

b) Macro-institutional factors. The organization of the federal judiciary as an institution perhaps has even more significant effects on the comparative ability of the courts to achieve foreign policy goals. First, the federal judiciary is a generalist institution composed of generalist judges. Members of the judiciary are not usually chosen because of any expertise in any particular subject, unlike, say, the way in which scientists may be hired for work at the

---

[138] See, for example, Kenneth W. Starr, *Observations About the Use of Legislative History*, 1987 Duke L J 371, 377; Eskridge, 96 Mich L Rev at 1541 (cited in note 135); Vermeule, 50 Stan L Rev at 1868–69 (cited in note 137).

[139] The legitimacy of this "new" CIL is debated by Prosper Weil, 77 Am J Intl L 413 (cited in note 128), and Alain Pellet, *The Normative Dilemma: Will and Consent in International Lawmaking*, 12 Australian YB Intl L 22 (1992), and is summarized in Antonio Cassese and Joseph H. H. Weiler, eds, *Change and Stability in International Lawmaking* (De Gruyter, 1988).

Department of Energy, the Environmental Protection Agency, or the Food and Drug Administration. This is even more so the case in foreign affairs. Judges are not chosen because of any background in specific regions or areas, nor are they selected because they have experience in national security issues. As an institution, the judiciary is unlikely to have great facility with international legal, political, or economic theories or materials, and its members are more likely to be chosen because of their prominence as litigators or as public officials. It is difficult to recall more than a handful of judges who had significant foreign affairs experience before their appointment to the federal bench.

Second, of the three branches of government, the judiciary is the most decentralized. The front line of the judiciary is composed of 94 district courts, which are staffed by more than 667 judges.[140] Until appellate courts have ruled on a legal issue, the judges in these district courts can hold 667 different interpretations of the law. There are 13 federal courts of appeals, with 179 judges.[141] The Supreme Court currently hears between 70 and 85 cases per year, while about 60,000 cases a year are filed in the Courts of Appeals and about 325,000 cases are filed a year in the district courts.[142] Given the other demands on the Supreme Court's caseload, it is doubtful that the Court could devote a significant portion of its docket to correcting erroneous interpretation of international law, mistaken interference with foreign policy, or misapplications of the ATS. Unless this happens, the geographic organization of the federal courts may well produce disharmony on questions of foreign policy and a diversity of possible applications of international law.

In some areas, this level of decentralization might not pose such a problem. Geographically organized courts may better tailor national policies to local conditions, allow for diversity and experimentation in federal policies, and provide a more effective voice for local communities in federal decision making. These are not positive values, however, in foreign affairs. The Constitution

---

[140] History of Federal Judgeships, US District Courts, at http://www.uscourts.gov/history/tableh.pdf.

[141] History of Federal Judgeships, US Courts of Appeals, at http://www.uscourts.gov/history/tablec.pdf.

[142] Judicial Caseload Indicators 2003, at http://www.uscourts.gov/caseload2003/front/Mar03Txt.pdf.

sought to centralize authority over foreign affairs to provide the nation with a single voice in its international relations, so as to prevent other nations from taking advantage of the disarray that had characterized the Articles of Confederation.[143] Indeed, in cases such as *Crosby* and *Garamendi*, the Court recently has preempted state efforts to influence foreign nations precisely because of the need for a uniform foreign policy set by the Congress or President.[144] This rationale, however, offered to justify national preeminence over the 50 states, applies with force to a federal judiciary of 94 district courts and 13 appellate courts. Judicial implementation of foreign policy promises disharmony where uniformity is supremely important.

Third, institutional structure suggests that judicial activity in foreign policy may be slow, in terms of both implementation and self-correction. Lawsuits can often take years to complete. Even when cases are expedited, they require many months from time of filing to final judgment and appeal. To use *Sosa* as an example, eleven years passed between the filing of his ATS claim in federal district court and the Supreme Court's decision last Term. While they did not reach extensive discovery or trial proceedings, recent Supreme Court cases on Massachusetts's efforts to sanction Burma and California's efforts to provide remedies for Holocaust victims still took several years to adjudicate.[145]

Delay also affects not just initial decisions, but also monitoring and feedback. Slowness obviously impedes the swift and effective execution of foreign policy. Delay infects the judiciary's institutional systems for communicating between its different units and for correcting errors. While the federal courts have an appeals court system for detecting and correcting errors, it can take months if not years to run its course. Even if a district or circuit judge acts in defiance of established circuit or Supreme Court precedent, litigation is needed to correct the error. Standards of review concerning fact-finding may even render some decisions immune from appellate review despite contrary or conflicting re-

---

[143] See, generally, Frederick Marks, *Independence on Trial: Foreign Affairs and the Making of the Constitution* (LSU, 1973).

[144] *Garamendi*, 539 US 396 (2003) (cited in note 64); *Crosby v National Foreign Trade Council*, 530 US 363 (2000).

[145] The lawsuit in *Garamendi* began in 1999 and was not finally decided by the Supreme Court until 2003. 539 US at 512. *Crosby* began in 1998 and was not decided by the Supreme Court until 2000. 530 US at 371.

sults reached by different trial courts in similar cases. Transmission of information identifying and correcting errors may become garbled within the system, which helps explain the repeated cycles of repeal and remand that can occur in the context of a single case.[146] Judicial errors or deviations from policy may take years to reverse or may even go entirely uncorrected.

The judiciary's institutional characteristics render it superior to other institutions for certain kinds of decisions. It can address issues more fairly, with less interference from the political branches, and it can implement federal policy over a wide number of cases throughout the country. It can help solve political commitment problems between interest groups or between branches of government due to its high level of insulation from outside control. Its virtues, however, also create its problems as an institutional actor in foreign affairs. Its evenhandedness and passivity create problems in effectively gathering and processing information and in coordinating its policies with other national actors. Its procedural fairness and geographic decentralization prevent it from acting swiftly in a unified fashion, and it lacks effective tools for the rapid assimilation of feedback and the correction of errors.

Even if the statutory purpose of the ATS is the development and enforcement of international law generally, and human rights more specifically, the courts are by no means the most effective institutional mechanism. ATS suits require courts to acquire information about events that usually have occurred abroad and that involve parties outside their jurisdiction. They demand that courts interpret and apply norms whose sources can be difficult to discover and discern. They often involve sensitive judgments that may impact broader, ongoing relations with other nations. This is not to say that courts could not perform this function if need be; courts have interpreted open-ended clauses of the Constitution and have attempted to manage institutions ranging from schools to prisons.[147] Rather, the central question is, from a comparative institutional perspective, whether there is reason to think that courts would be *equal or superior* to other branches of government in achieving national policy on international law or human rights.

2. *Executive branch competence and comparative institutional ad-*

---

[146] Martin Shapiro, *Toward a Theory of Stare Decisis*, 1 J Legal Stud 125, 125–34 (1972).

[147] See John Yoo, *Who Measures the Chancellor's Foot? The Inherent Remedial Power of the Federal Courts*, 84 Cal L Rev 1121 (1996).

vantage. To complete our study, we must conduct a comparative analysis. As Professors Sunstein, Vermeule, and Komesar have argued with regard to allocating decisions among courts, agencies, and markets, simply deciding on a social goal is not enough.[148] We must also make comparative judgments on the ability of different institutions to achieve those goals. Such comparative institutional judgments have been applied in both constitutional and statutory interpretation.[149] Even if the judiciary would perform poorly at enforcing national policy in the human rights area, it still may be the best institutional mechanism available. A comprehensive analysis of the effectiveness of the ATS at promoting international law and human rights requires a judgment of the relative ability of the judiciary and the institution most likely to replace it: the executive.

a) Deference and foreign affairs. Evaluation of the comparative advantages and disadvantages of the judiciary versus the executive in implementing foreign affairs goals parallels arguments surrounding the review of agency interpretations of law.[150] In *Chevron U.S.A. Inc. v Natural Resources Defense Council, Inc.,*[151] the Court established a well-known two-part test for reviewing executive branch interpretation of ambiguous statutes. First, the courts ask whether Congress has clearly addressed the interpretive question at hand. If not, then judges are to defer to the agency interpretation if it is based on a reasonable or permissible reading of the statute.[152]

We are not so much interested in whether *Chevron* establishes the correct rule as we are in the comparative institutional considerations that motivated the Court's thinking. *Chevron* itself iden-

---

[148] Sunstein and Vermeule, 101 Mich L Rev at 917–19 (cited in note 104); Komesar, *Imperfect Alternatives* (cited in note 104).

[149] Constitutional scholars such as John Hart Ely and Jesse Choper, for instance, have applied such comparative institutional analysis to defend their theory of constitutional interpretations. Choper's defense of political safeguards for federalism relied heavily on his assessment of the comparative institutional advantages of judicial versus political branch enforcement of federalism. Jesse Choper, *Judicial Review and the National Political Process: A Functional Reconsideration of the Role of the Supreme Court* (Chicago, 1981).

[150] Curtis Bradley has also sought to draw upon *Chevron* in the foreign affairs context. His inquiry concerned whether *Chevron* principles support judicial deference to executive branch interpretation of different forms of international law. Curtis A. Bradley, *Chevron Deference and Foreign Affairs*, 86 Va L Rev 649 (2000). Our approach is different: we seek to learn from *Chevron*'s observations on the relationship between agencies and courts to reach judgments about the institutional abilities of each branch.

[151] 467 US 837 (1984).

[152] Id at 842–43.

tified two reasons of judicial policy that supported this approach. First, judicial deference to reasonable agency interpretations assumes that agencies usually possess expertise in administering regulatory statutes superior to that of the judiciary. Second, deference recognizes that the executive branch can claim greater political accountability than the judiciary, implying that interpretation ought to pursue present policy goals and that the electorate ultimately could change unwanted interpretations.[153]

Scholars have debated in great detail the relative virtues and defects of the *Chevron* regime, and the Court recently has demarcated the limits of deference to agency interpretation at rule making and formal adjudication.[154] Agency expertise and accountability, however, continue to remain central justifications for judicial deference, and it is useful to understand them through an institutional lens. *Chevron* locates interpretation in the institution that has the superior level of technical competence. Unlike federal judges, agency personnel are experts at their subject, who often have received their training and devoted their careers to policymaking in a discrete specialty, and have access to technical experience and information accumulated by a wide bureaucracy.

To be sure, agency decision making does not depend solely on technical decisions, but rather requires officials to reach decisions involving a mixture of factual determinations and value judgments.[155] And agencies are not just run by civil servants, but are managed by a thin crust of political appointees chosen by the President. But executive branch officials are more politically accountable than federal judges, and mistakes of agency interpretation are more likely to be corrected. Congress also has any number of formal and informal tools for placing political pressure on agencies to reverse unwanted actions. Congress can hold hearings, refuse to confirm nominees to the agency, and reduce agency budgets for enforcement. Congress can use interest groups and the media to generate public opposition to executive policy.

By contrast, the federal judiciary is designed to be outside the

---

[153] On this point, see Laurence H. Silberman, *Chevron—The Intersection of Law and Policy*, 58 Geo Wash L Rev 821 (1990).

[154] *United States v Mead Corp.*, 533 US 218 (2001).

[155] There is a wide literature, for example, on whether cost-benefit analysis should be used by agencies and whether they are capable of following it properly. See, for example, Matthew D. Adler and Eric A. Posner, *Rethinking Cost-Benefit Analysis*, 109 Yale L J 165 (1999); Lisa Heinzerling, *Regulatory Costs of Mythic Proportions*, 107 Yale L J 1981 (1998).

reach of normal politics. Federal judges have life tenure and a permanent salary, and for the most part have reached the end of their official careers so they are not beholden to political groups for their advancement. Because of its internal system of precedent, the federal courts generally do not reverse a decision simply because of political opposition or pressure. In order to change a judicial decision, Congress generally can resort only to the single formal process set out in Article I, Section 7 for the enactment of legislation. Because of the hurdles of bicameralism and presentment, this makes it far more difficult for Congress to correct mistakes in policy by the federal courts.[156]

In terms of comparative institutional advantage, it may be useful to express these values in terms of error and decision costs. We can make the reasonable assumption that deference to agencies is likely to lead to lower error costs in decision making. Their technical competence in specialized areas is less likely to produce incorrect decisions because agencies may be more familiar with the meaning of Congress's instructions in the context of a heavily regulated, factually complex field. Their expertise and knowledge also make it more likely that they will set the appropriate technical standard within the parameters set by Congress. At the same time, however, agencies may well incur higher decision costs than courts. They reach their judgments after gathering broader amounts of information than judges, although they do not do so within the context of litigation. Their decisions follow the pure standard of acting reasonably under the totality of the circumstances, rather than following clear ex ante rules. Error correction by the political branches, however, seems superior to that of courts. Holding oversight hearings and threatening budget cuts present a far less difficult method to change incorrect agency interpretations than does the enactment of specific override legislation.

A third justification for judicial deference did not appear in *Chevron*, but implicates core questions of institutional design. A President provides a single policy vision that sets a uniform regulatory policy throughout the nation. Federal courts, by contrast, are organized into thirteen different circuit courts of appeals organized by geography. Because of the Supreme Court's limited docket, the decisions of the circuit courts represent the final word

---

[156] See, for example, Cooter, *The Strategic Constitution* (cited in note 119).

of the Article III judiciary in 99 percent of all cases. *Chevron*, in essence, promotes national uniformity in administrative law by ensuring that statutes will not be interpreted differently in different regions.[157] If federal courts could review agency interpretations de novo or under a less deferential regime, it is likely that administrative rules would be applied differently in different circuits.

b) The executive branch's institutional advantages. These institutional considerations bear significantly on the choice between courts and executives in foreign affairs. First, consider the factor of institutional structure. Putting aside for the moment the formal question of where the President's foreign affairs power comes from, the executive branch seems much better structured for the conduct of foreign relations than the courts. As Alexander Hamilton argued in *Federalist No. 70*, the executive is structured for speed and decisiveness in its actions, and is better able to maintain secrecy in its information gathering and its deliberations. "Decision, activity, secrecy, dispatch will generally characterize the proceedings of one man, in a much more eminent degree, than the proceedings of any greater number; and in proportion as the number is increased, these qualities will be diminished."[158] In the years leading up to World War II, the Supreme Court made a similar observation. *United States v Curtiss-Wright Export Corporation* famously observed: "In this vast external realm, with its important, complicated, delicate and manifold problems, the President alone has the power to speak or listen as a representative of the nation." Quoting from a Senate report, the Court further explained that "[t]he nature of transactions with foreign nations . . . requires caution and unity of design, and their success frequently depends on secrecy and dispatch."[159] As Dean Koh describes it, "[h]is decision-making processes can take on degrees of speed, secrecy, flexibility, and efficiency that no other governmental institution can match."[160] If anything, national security and

---

[157] Peter Strauss, *One Hundred Fifty Cases per Year: Some Implications of the Supreme Court's Limited Resources for Judicial Review of Agency Action*, 87 Colum L Rev 1093 (1987).

[158] Federalist 70 (Hamilton) in Merrill Jensen, John P. Kaminski, and Gaspare J. Saladino, eds, 16 *The Documentary History of the Ratification of the Constitution* 397 (State Historical Society of Wisconsin, 1986).

[159] 299 US 304, 319 (1936).

[160] Harold Koh, *National Security Constitution* 119 (Yale, 1990).

foreign policy demands since World War II have led to even more concentration of authority in the executive branch. The history of American foreign relations has been the story of the expansion of the presidency thanks to its structural abilities to wield power quickly, effectively, and in a unitary manner—a fact bemoaned by critics of the "imperial presidency."[161]

Institutional design leads to advantages in specialized competence. The United States operates large bureaucracies designed to develop and implement foreign policy. For fiscal year 2005, for example, the Bush administration's budget request for the State Department and other foreign affairs agencies totaled $31.5 billion.[162] The State Department employed 32,997 officials and civil servants.[163] That does not include the budget and personnel figures for the Defense Department, the Central Intelligence Agency, the Treasury Department, the Justice Department, and the White House staff, all of which have significant roles in developing foreign policy. These agencies employ experts in specific subjects, such as arms control or human rights, or certain nations and regions, such as State's Asia or Africa desks. Many of the staff who work on these issues have developed their areas of expertise by spending their careers immersing themselves in local cultures, learning languages, or gaining experience in the international politics of a region. The federal judiciary, by contrast, operates on a budget of roughly $5.42 billion with 34,399 employees, who must devote their efforts to the adjudication of disputes involving federal law.

Executive branch agencies have access to broader forms of information about foreign affairs than those available to a court. In regard to classes of information, the executive branch has access to certain types of information, such as that produced by clandestine agents or electronic eavesdropping, which cannot be publicly disclosed. Even though such information cannot be produced in an open court, it can provide invaluable data on the plans and intentions of other governments and the possible effects of American foreign policy. In terms of receiving and processing that information, the executive branch is not restricted by the structures

---

[161] Id at 118–23; see generally Arthur M. Schlesinger, Jr., *The Imperial Presidency* (Houghton Mifflin, 1973).

[162] Fact Sheet, at http://www.state.gov/r/pa/prs/ps/2004/28709.htm.

[163] Table, at http://www.opm.gov/feddata/html/2004/march/table2.asp.

that limit the information that a court may consider.

By contrast, the very nature of courts as decision-making institutions may impede their ability to perform a role in foreign affairs. As work on structural injunctions has shown,[164] courts are relatively poor at gathering information, especially when a case extends beyond the pure historical facts behind a single transaction or accident to broader political, economic, and social events and trends. Courts experience difficulty in weighing policy alternatives and in calculating costs and benefits. Courts have been shown to be unable to gather and to absorb the sort of sufficient, objective data required to make considered decisions when more than just historical fact and causation are involved.

In addition to gathering and processing information, the executive branch has broader tools at its disposal to achieve foreign policy goals. In the field of foreign affairs, the discretion and authorities available to the President generally go beyond those enjoyed by agencies in domestic affairs. The President is the sole organ of the nation in its diplomatic relations, commander-in-chief of the military, and director of the clandestine services. These inherent authorities could be used in a variety of ways to achieve foreign policy goals such as the promotion of international human rights. In the diplomatic realm, they range from negotiating and drafting international agreements to pressuring other nations to follow human rights norms to seeking to isolate states with poor human rights records. Intelligence agencies could take covert action to destabilize nations that abuse human rights or even capture war criminals. As commander-in-chief, the President could issue orders to the military to restore order in states where central authority has collapsed, as in Somalia or Haiti, or ultimately to use force to end human rights abuse by states, as in Kosovo, or to produce regime change, as in Iraq.

The executive branch can also make significant progress toward foreign policy goals without having to rely on inherent constitutional authority.[165] Under the International Economic Emergency Powers Act (IEEPA), the President can impose sanctions

---

[164] Peter Schuck, *Suing Government: Citizen Remedies for Official Wrongs* 394–404 (Yale, 1983); Donald L. Horowitz, *The Courts and Social Policy* 156–61 (Brookings, 1977).

[165] For an overview of the statutory law in the area of economics and national security, see Harold Koh and John Yoo, *Dollar Diplomacy/Dollar Defense: The Fabric of Economics and National Security Law*, 26 Intl Law 715 (1992).

against entities ranging from individuals to nations.[166] If these nations pose a threat to U.S. national security and foreign policy, the President may declare a national emergency that then triggers the authority to freeze foreign assets in the United States and to restrict all commercial contacts with a foreign nation.[167] Under the Export Administration Act, the President can place restrictions on exports to a nation that poses a threat to American national security or foreign policy.[168] The President can deploy these powers as a scalpel or as a hammer. They can be used in a fine-grained manner when aimed at a particular individual, such as apprehending Slobodan Milosevic. They can be used more broadly to try to coerce a nation to change its treatment of its own citizens, as with South Africa in the 1980s or with the former Yugoslavia and Iraq in the 1990s.

In comparison, courts have few effective tools to enforce compliance with their decisions, and those tools use sanctions or the punishment of individuals to leverage broader policy or institutional changes. Again drawing from the structural injunction context, courts possess imperfect tools for communicating their decrees, and they must rely upon other institutions and personnel to disseminate and implement their orders. Courts have few resources to compel compliance on the part of defendants or to create positive incentives to encourage adherence to judicial orders. Aside from a contempt order, judges generally rely upon the moral persuasiveness and the institutional legitimacy of their decisions to encourage compliance. These problems are only compounded with regard to foreign affairs. Parties will often be outside the United States and outside the reach of a federal district court or federal marshals. In most ATS suits, for example, plaintiffs have failed to collect any of the money they have been awarded by ATS judgments.

Third, executive policy in foreign affairs is subject to greater political accountability. One advantage of the courts, in certain situations, is their relative insulation from political control. Delegation to courts may help preserve a legislative majority's vic-

---

[166] 50 USC § 1701 et seq.

[167] Id at § 1702.

[168] Id at § 2401 et seq.

tories by making them more difficult to reverse in the future,[169] or provide a means to overcome a commitment problem.[170] Cost, however, is the flip side of the benefit of locking in policies or making a credible commitment. In order to achieve these ends, Congress must accept a loss of flexibility in policy implementation, a reduction in institutional expertise, and less ability to reflect changing legislative wishes. Many of these arguments have been brought to bear on the study of delegation of authority to agencies; the primary insight is that bureaucracies can be "inefficient by design" because of the desire of groups in the legislature to insulate agencies that share their views from being overturned or influenced by later winning coalitions in the legislature.[171]

As a matter of comparative institutional analysis, it would seem that delegation to the courts would experience these costs and benefits more intensely than delegation to executive branch agencies. Delegation of international law and human rights decisions to courts would lock in policies such that only overriding legislation could change national goals. Compared to the executive branch, courts are relatively impervious to oversight hearings, budget controls, and other informal political controls. They are also less subject to the formal political control of elections. Except for the long-term use of the appointment power of federal judges, only a statute would allow the President and Congress to force a change of direction in policy. While this gives courts greater political insulation, it also deprives them of the flexibility to adjust policy in light of changes in preferences, new circumstances, or new information and expertise.

Delegation to the executive branch, rather than the courts, in the area of CIL and human rights also may make more sense because of the President's enhanced constitutional role in foreign affairs. As the sole representative of the nation in its international relations, the President develops foreign policy, communicates with other nations, and reaches international agreements. By custom, presidents also make a variety of informal commitments with other nations. As commander-in-chief, the President can use force

---

[169] See, for example, Rui J. P. de Figueiredo, Jr., *Electoral Competition, Political Uncertainty, and Policy Insulation*, 96 Am Pol Sci Rev 321 (2002).

[170] Vesting a foreign affairs decision in the courts can provide the political branches with a costly signal that they intend to abide by an international agreement.

[171] Id at 322–23 (discussing sources).

to achieve foreign policy, but he can also make use of less violent forms of persuasion or coercion as well. Human rights, of course, have constituted an important element in American foreign policy. Presidents have used human rights to undermine antagonistic regimes, as President Reagan did with the Soviet Union, or have pursued them as a goal in themselves, as did President Carter.

Effectiveness would arguably be enhanced if the same institution exercised control over international law and human rights as well as broader foreign policy. Otherwise, the United States might send conflicting signals to other nations about its policies. To take an extreme case, suppose the United States sought to wage a war to promote humanitarian goals, such as the end of a genocidal conflict. Such a war would arguably violate the prohibition on the use of force contained in the U.N. Charter.[172] Indeed, the International Court of Justice has held that this rule is not just a positive rule of the Charter, but a rule of CIL.[173] Suppose an alien harmed by American military action in the war brought an ATS suit against the U.S. government and its officials alleging the war violated CIL. A judicial decision to promote CIL through the ATS could conflict with the decision of the executive branch to use force in the same case, to the point of even frustrating the substantive improvement of human rights conditions in the area of conflict.

In light of these considerations, it seems that the executive branch is superior to the courts for achieving the ATS's statutory purpose. The executive branch has better means for developing information on foreign affairs, has far more tools to bring to bear against violators of human rights or international law, and can display more flexibility in responding to changing international conditions while remaining more accountable politically. Congress, however, might still delegate authority in these areas to the courts rather than agencies depending on the propensity of the executive branch to violate CIL itself. If the executive branch were to prove more likely to violate CIL than the courts, then Congress might choose to vest the authority for its enforcement in the latter.

Two considerations make it unlikely that this is the case. First, the ATS currently does not operate to prevent the United States

---

[172] For a discussion of the international legal rules governing the use of force, see John Yoo, *Using Force*, 71 U Chi L Rev 729 (2004).

[173] *Case Concerning Military and Paramilitary Activities in and Against Nicaragua (Nicaragua v. United States)*, 1986 ICJ 14, 146.

from violating CIL because it does not override sovereign immunity. Second, even if Congress had chosen the ATS to provide a means for the courts to control executive branch violations of CIL, the courts' own doctrines permit the President to violate CIL. *The Paquete Habana* itself recognizes that CIL may be overridden by a "controlling executive" action.[174] This makes sense, because in order to change CIL the President may need to violate CIL—one of the ways to change a rule of CIL is to engage in state practice that establishes a different rule.[175] Presidents also may need to violate CIL in order to vindicate other foreign policy goals, such as using force to protect human rights (as in Kosovo) or to prevent the proliferation of weapons of mass destruction. It does not appear that Congress intends to limit the President's flexibility in protecting national security or promoting foreign policy goals by imposing CIL standards on his actions through the ATS.

IV

Even if one agrees with our functional critique of the *Sosa* Court's reading of the ATS, we would still have to offer an alternative reading of the statute that is consistent with both the statutory text and with existing doctrine but which also incorporates our conclusions about the functional superiority of the executive branch over the federal courts in the development of CIL. Our functional analysis supports reading the ATS as a jurisdictional statute that does not authorize federal courts to engage in the development and enforcement of any kind of CIL as part of their common lawmaking powers. As a doctrinal matter, however, we recognize that many courts, including the *Sosa* Court, follow *The Paquete Habana*'s declaration that "international law is part of our law" and must exist in some part of the domestic legal system cognizable by courts even when Congress has not acted to implement such norms by statute.

For this reason, in addition to reading the ATS as a pure jurisdictional statute providing a basis for subsequent congressional

---

[174] *The Paquete Habana*, 175 US at 712.

[175] See, for example, *Authority of the Federal Bureau of Investigation to Override Customary or Other International Law in the Course of Extraterritorial Law Enforcement Activities*, 13 Op Office Legal Counsel 163, 170–71 (1989) (discussing whether Congress and the executive can override CIL).

implementation of CIL, our functional analysis suggests that modern CIL should be treated like the rest of the pre-*Erie* general common law: as part of the common law of the states. As we explain, unlike the federal common law approach adopted by the *Sosa* Court, treating uncodified CIL as state common law will result in active participation by the institution best positioned to assess and enforce CIL: the federal executive.

A.   THE JURISDICTIONAL READING OF THE ATS

Our jurisdictional reading is at least as consistent with the text, structure, and history of the ATS as the *Sosa* Court's quasi-jurisdictional reading, if not more so. Indeed, the *Sosa* Court admitted as much when it also concluded that the ATS's text and structure did not create a statutory cause of action. But the *Sosa* Court nonetheless decided to keep the door "ajar" for federal court development and enforcement of certain universally accepted norms of CIL. Neither the *Sosa* Court, nor its academic supporters, have offered a functional justification for giving federal courts a central role in the development and enforcement of CIL. This is perhaps not surprising because a functional analysis of the institutional consequences of the *Sosa* Court's reading of the ATS leads us to conclude that federal courts are not the best positioned institution to develop and enforce CIL. Rather, a functional analysis supports a jurisdictional reading of the ATS that leaves CIL enforcement either to Congress or to the common law of the several states.

Ironically, the perceived functional implausibility of the jurisdictional reading of the ATS has been one of the chief arguments for maintaining the federal status of CIL endorsed by *Sosa*. As Dean Koh has argued, treating CIL as state law could result in fifty different state interpretations of CIL and would be inconsistent with the traditional "one voice" conception of U.S. foreign relations law.[176] Moreover, treating CIL as state common law appears on its face to resemble the *Sosa* Court's reading in preserving a role for functionally inferior courts in the development and enforcement of CIL.

We agree that these are serious objections to the reading of the ATS we propose here. Indeed, they are the only objections that have any force. These objections, however, can both be answered

---

[176] See Koh, 111 Harv L Rev at 1824, 1841 (cited in note 114).

by recognizing the power of the President to supervise and independently preempt divergent interpretations of CIL. Thus, reading the ATS as a jurisdictional statute only and removing CIL from the federal courts' common lawmaking powers does not leave CIL to the whims of fifty different state court systems that might be even less functionally competent than the federal judiciary. Rather, our jurisdictional reading of the ATS places CIL in the state and federal courts under the direct supervision of the federal executive.

Although the *Sosa* Court also contemplates a role for the executive branch, its suggestion that "in appropriate cases" the executive branch's views be given "strong deference" still assumes that federal courts, rather than the executive branch, will hold the final determination on how and whether to apply a CIL norm.[177] Indeed, as we explain below, under the *Sosa* Court's implicit recognition of CIL as federal law, giving the executive the final word would threaten federal judicial independence. This problem does not, however, arise if CIL is treated as a type of state common law.

Thus, unlike the *Sosa* Court's reading of the ATS, the institution most responsible for the development and enforcement of CIL under our reading of the ATS will be the federal executive. As we have explained, the executive has substantial institutional advantages over courts in the development and enforcement of CIL. In the next two sections, we demonstrate that, in addition to the functional advantages of relying on executive supervision of CIL that we identified in Part II, treating CIL as state common law with active presidential supervision is also well grounded as a matter of historical practice and strengthened by the Court's recent decision in *American Insurance Association v Garamendi*.[178]

B.   STATE COURTS AND CIL

As the *Sosa* Court pointed out, the Supreme Court has long "affirmed that the domestic law of the United States recognizes the law of nations."[179] But the *Sosa* Court failed to acknowledge that, prior to *Filartiga*, this affirmation of CIL has been as much

---

[177] *Sosa*, 124 S Ct at n 21.

[178] 123 S Ct 2374 (2003).

[179] Id at 2764.

the task of state courts operating independently and without the supervision of the federal courts.

1. *CIL as general common law*. Prior to the seminal case of *Erie*, most scholars agree that CIL formed part of the general common law.[180] In contrast to the post-*Erie* system, federal courts were not bound by state court interpretations of general common law and state courts were not bound by federal court interpretations of general common law. Thus, when cases involving the application of CIL fell within the jurisdiction of state courts, those courts applied CIL independently without the possibility of appeal to the federal courts or the Supreme Court. Similarly, federal courts applied CIL without being bound by state court interpretations. Each system, therefore, applied CIL independently of the other.[181]

The Supreme Court consistently confirmed this understanding of the pre-*Erie* status of CIL, holding that CIL "is one of those questions of general jurisprudence" or general common law.[182] On a number of occasions, the Court also confirmed that it had no appellate jurisdiction over state court interpretations and applications of CIL. Thus, in 1875, the Court refused to accept appellate jurisdiction over a state court decision applying the "general laws of war, as recognized by the law of nations" because such a case did not involve the "Constitution, laws, treaties, or executive proclamations of the United States" under the contemporary version of today's federal question jurisdiction statute.[183]

Less than a decade later, the Court similarly refused to review a state court decision affirming the legality of an abduction of a criminal defendant overseas in violation of CIL because "the decision of that question is as much within the province of the state court as a question of common law, or of the law of nations . . . ."[184] Although some commentators have simply rejected these and other decisions reach-

[180] See, for example, Restatement (Third), pt I, ch 2, introductory note at 41; Young, 42 Va J Intl L at 365, 374 (cited in note 50); Neuman, 66 Fordham L Rev at 373 (cited in note 36); Stephens, 66 Fordham L Rev at 400 and n 34 (cited in note 36); see also *Sosa*, 124 S Ct at 2770.

[181] For the leading account of the operation of the general common law system, and its difference from the modern, positivistic understanding of federal and state common law, see William A. Fletcher, *The General Common Law and Section 34 of the Judiciary Act of 1789: The Example of Marine Insurance*, 97 Harv L Rev 1513 (1984).

[182] *Huntington v Atrill*, 146 US 657, 683 (1892).

[183] See *New York Life Insurance v Hendren*, 92 US 286 (1875).

[184] *Ker*, 119 US at 444 (cited in note 60).

ing the same result as wrongly decided,[185] the fact remains that no Supreme Court decision in the pre-*Erie* regime ever held that the state court interpretations of CIL could be reviewed by federal courts.[186]

After *Erie*, some courts followed the logic of *Erie*'s holding and treated CIL as a form of state common law. In 1948, Judge Learned Hand interpreted CIL to grant diplomatic immunity from civil suit to a French diplomat accredited as a minister to Bolivia. Applying *Erie*, Hand held that the suit was governed by the law of New York, "and although the courts of that state look to international law as a source of New York law, their interpretation of international law is controlling upon us, and we are to follow them so far as they have declared themselves."[187] Judge Hand then surveyed both New York state court cases and general international law authorities to resolve the case in favor of the foreign diplomat.

2. *Case study in CIL development: foreign sovereign immunity*. A review of one particular doctrine of CIL, foreign sovereign immunity, illustrates two important practical aspects of the CIL-as-general-common-law system relevant to our jurisdictional reading of the ATS. First, state courts, both before and after *Erie*, interpreted the CIL of foreign sovereign immunity independently of federal courts, even in matters directly implicating foreign relations, by adjudicating sensitive litigations against foreign sovereigns. Second, the executive branch, rather than federal courts, served as the chief mechanism for deciding how to deal with the sensitive foreign policy implications of such cases.[188]

Although the doctrine of foreign sovereign immunity for foreign governments was first announced in the United States by Chief Justice Marshall in 1812,[189] this doctrine of CIL was independently

---

[185] See Neuman, 66 Fordham L Rev at 374 n 14 (cited in note 36); Restatement (Third) § 111 n 4.

[186] Indeed, one of the interesting aspects of the scholarly debate is that while there is virtually no judicial precedent prior to *Filartiga* supporting federal court control over the interpretation and application of CIL, leading scholars managed to achieve wide acceptance for this view. See, for example, Restatement (Third) § 111. This consensus was achieved despite the fact that the only federal court to directly consider the question of CIL after *Erie* prior to *Filartiga*, Judge Learned Hand in the Second Circuit, essentially followed *Erie* and past practice and treated CIL as part of New York's common law. See *Bergman v De Sieyes*, 170 F2d 360 (2d Cir 1948).

[187] *Bergman*, 170 F2d at 361 (cited in note 186).

[188] For a longer and more detailed review of the pre-*Erie* system's treatment of CIL, see Julian G. Ku, *Customary International Law in State Courts*, 42 Va J Intl L 265 (2001).

[189] *Schooner Exchange v McFaddon*, 11 US 116 (1812).

developed by both state and federal courts. As early as 1857, the Supreme Court of New York began modifying the absolute theory of immunity outlined by Marshall by refusing to dismiss the government of Nicaragua from being joined to lawsuit on the grounds that "joinder" was not "necessarily derogatory to the character or independence of a state. . . ."[190] Much later, a New Jersey court expanded this modification of strict absolute immunity by outlining a restrictive theory of foreign sovereign immunity limited to those "acts done under color of the authority conferred upon it," and not "in excess of that authority and without legal justification."[191]

One interesting example of how states and federal courts operated independently in the development of this CIL doctrine may be seen in judicial development of the foreign sovereign immunity waiver doctrine. In 1922, a complicated litigation involving a state-owned Portuguese company proceeded simultaneously in New York state and federal courts. Curiously, while the New York state court found that the company, which claimed sovereign immunity, had not waived this immunity by answering the U.S. plaintiffs' complaints on the merits, the Second Circuit reached the exact opposite conclusion twelve days later in the federal side of the action.[192] Plaintiffs then returned to the New York state court seeking reversal, but the New York state court simply refused to follow the Second Circuit's interpretation of CIL.[193] The New York state court thus rejected the Second Circuit's interpretation of CIL as applied to the exact same set of facts.

The possibility that federal and state courts could reach inconsistent results, even in cases involving the same facts, highlights the major flaw in the pre-*Erie* system of CIL. Because CIL was part of the general common law, there was no basis for seeking federal or Supreme Court action to unify the interpretation or application of CIL, even doctrines such as foreign sovereign immunity that directly implicated foreign sovereign interests. Unlike the modern position endorsed by the *Sosa* Court's reading of the ATS, the Supreme Court could not overrule state court interpretations of CIL.

On the other hand, the pre-*Erie* system did have a mechanism

---

[190] *Manning v Nicaragua & Accessory Transit Co.*, 14 How Pr 517 (New York, 1857).

[191] *Pliger v United States Steel Corp.*, 130 A 523 (NJ 1925).

[192] *De Simone v Transportes Maritimos De Estado*, 191 NYS 864, 867 (App Div 1922); *The Sao Vicente*, 281 F 111, 114 (2d Cir 1922).

[193] *De Simone v Transportes Maritimos de Estado*, 192 NYS 815, 181–19 (App Div 1922).

for handling the sensitive foreign policy consequences of cases that involved foreign sovereigns: the federal executive branch. For instance, the executive, through an appearance amicus curiae by a United States Attorney, convinced a New York state court to grant Mexico sovereign immunity in a lawsuit seeking remedies for an alleged default of its sovereign bonds.[194] This practice continued two decades later in a subsequent litigation over a later Mexico default of a different set of sovereign bonds. A U.S. attorney appeared in New York state court on behalf of Mexico to advocate giving Mexican assets immunity from seizure by bondholders.[195] While some courts hesitated to require absolute deferral to the President, the Supreme Court eventually recognized the executive's final authority on determinations of sovereign immunity in 1945.[196] Thus, "if the Executive announced a national policy in regard to immunity generally, or for the particular case, that policy was law for the courts and binding upon them, regardless of what international law might say about it."[197]

As a result, the executive, rather than federal courts, served as the institution responsible for assessing the effect of a court's application of the CIL of foreign sovereign immunity on U.S. foreign policy and, perhaps, the content of CIL itself. During this period, the executive branch would receive petitions from foreign governments, hold administrative hearings, and then issue letters to courts stating the position of the U.S. government on a foreign government's sovereign immunity request.[198] While some have argued that the President cannot determine CIL for the courts and can only order courts to disregard CIL,[199] for our purposes this is a distinction without a difference. Under either view, the executive, and not

---

[194] *Hassard v Mexico*, 61 NY 939 (1899).

[195] *Gallopin v Winsor*, 251 NY 48 (1931).

[196] *Mexico v Hoffman*, 324 US 30 (1945). Curiously, despite the holding in this case requiring courts to defer to the executive branch's views, the State Department continued to claim that "a shift in policy by the executive cannot control the courts . . . ." See Letter from Acting Legal Adviser, Jack B. Tate, to Department of Justice, May 19, 1952, 26 Dept State Bull 984 (1952).

[197] See, for example, Louis Henkin, *Foreign Affairs and the U.S. Constitution* 56 (Oxford, 1996).

[198] For a description of this quasi-administrative process, see Frederic Alan Weber, *The Foreign Sovereign Immunities Act of 1976: Its Origin, Meaning and Effect*, 3 Yale Stud World Pub Order 1, 12–13 (1976).

[199] See id at 56 n 68.

the federal courts, has the final word on how to resolve an issue of CIL for purposes of U.S. domestic law.

Interestingly, this practice of executive control over the application of foreign sovereign immunity was applied to both state and federal courts even after *Erie* supposedly unified (at least in the view of the *Sosa* Court) federal court control over CIL. Thus, in 1940, a New York court refused to give immunity to a Polish state-owned bank after noting the executive branch's refusal to appear in court.[200] In 1941, Maine's highest court granted such immunity solely on the basis of the executive's appearance in its court.[201] As the Pennsylvania Supreme Court noted in 1945:

> When the Department of State makes known its determination with respect to political matters growing out of or incidental to our Government's relations with a friendly foreign state, it is the duty of the courts to abide by the status so indicated or created and to refrain from making independent inquiries into the merit of the State Department's determination or from taking any steps that might prove embarrassing to the Government in the handling of its foreign relations.[202]

This executive lawmaking regime continued until 1975, when Congress intervened to codify the law of foreign sovereign immunity as federal statutory law.[203]

Congress's intervention changed the role of the executive branch in the oversight of the CIL of foreign sovereign immunity but it did not eliminate it. Questions of sovereign immunity for heads of state and former heads of state remained uncodified and continued to be tightly supervised by the executive.[204] As for the areas of foreign sovereign immunity that Congress did codify, Congress did not act due to any doubts about the executive's authority to engage in this kind of lawmaking. Instead, it acted, among other reasons, "in order to free the Government from the case-by-case diplomatic pressures."[205] For our purposes, it is worth noting that when the

---

[200] *Ulen & Co. v Bank Gospodarstwa Krajowegao*, 24 NYS2d 201 (App Div 1940).

[201] *Miller v Gerrocarrill Del Pacificio de Nicaragua*, 18 A2d 688, 690 (Me 1941).

[202] *FW Stone v Petroleous Mexicanos*, 42 A2d 57, 59–60 (Pa 1945).

[203] Foreign Sovereign Immunities Act, 28 USC §§ 1330, 1602–11.

[204] See, for example, *United States v Noriega*, 117 F3d 126 (11th Cir 1997) (rejecting sovereign immunity for Panamanian leader on grounds that executive branch "has manifested its clear sentiment that Noriega should be denied head-of-state immunity.").

[205] *Verlinden BV v Central Bank of Nigeria*, 461 US 480, 488 (1983).

executive administration of the CIL of foreign sovereign immunity proved imperfect, Congress did not simply return such determinations to the common law powers of the courts, which it might well have done if the federal courts had the kind of central role in the administration of CIL contemplated by the *Filartiga* and *Sosa* courts. Rather, it created "a comprehensive set of legal standards governing claims of immunity in every civil action against a foreign state or its political subdivisions, agencies, or instrumentalities"[206] that placed the federal courts under strict statutory limitations. Indeed, subsequent courts later understood Congress' action to require courts to adhere to Congress' legal standards, even if such standards differed or came into conflict with changing notions of the CIL of foreign sovereign immunity.[207]

C.   EXECUTIVE SUPERVISION OF CIL: THE GARAMENDI OPTION

While the pre-*Erie* regime of CIL as general common law persisted for a substantial period of time, in some cases the system resulted in inconsistent interpretations or applications of CIL. Such inconsistencies have fueled critics of Judge Hand's suggestion that CIL has become part of the common law of the several states after *Erie*. After all, adopting Judge Hand's view would result in fifty different interpretations of CIL doctrines such as foreign sovereign immunity with chaotic implications for the ability of the United States to maintain a unified voice on foreign affairs.[208]

As the practice of state courts with respect to foreign sovereign immunity recounted above suggests, however, there is no reason to believe that granting federal courts broad authority over CIL development, as the Court did in *Sosa*, will result in a superior system. Indeed, as we have pointed out, federal courts suffer from many disabilities that make them less than ideal arbiters of CIL, especially in matters implicating sensitive issues of foreign relations. Rather, we believe both the historical record and functional considerations support reading the ATS as merely jurisdictional, thus leaving to the executive branch, rather than the federal courts, the power to supervise CIL development as a matter of domestic

---

[206] Id.

[207] *Argentine Republic v Amerada Hess Shipping Corp.*, 488 US 428 (1989) (holding that Congress did not authorize federal courts to interpret Foreign Sovereign Immunities Act to exempt any violations of international law that Congress did not specifically identify).

[208] Koh, 111 Harv L Rev at 1841 (cited in note 114).

law. The Supreme Court's recent decision in *American Insurance Association v Garamendi*[209] confirms and strengthens this belief.

1. *Garamendi.* In *Garamendi*, the Supreme Court considered the constitutionality of the Holocaust Victim Insurance Relief Act (HVIRA), a California statute requiring insurance companies to disclose information about World War II–era insurance policies held by Holocaust victims.[210] An association of insurance companies, including foreign insurance companies who bore the brunt of the disclosure requirements, challenged HVIRA on the grounds that the state law impermissibly intruded into the federal government's exclusive authority over foreign affairs. The United States government, as well as the German government, filed briefs in support of the insurance companies. By a 5–4 majority, the Court agreed that the state law was preempted.[211]

What makes *Garamendi* important for our purposes is not that the Court decided to preempt a state law, but the basis for the supposed preemption. A trial court had invalidated HVIRA on the grounds that it interfered with the federal government's exclusive control over foreign affairs.[212] The trial court had relied on the Supreme Court's decision in *Zschernig v Miller*,[213] which authorized federal courts to preempt state laws that intruded into foreign affairs even without a direct conflict with a federal statute, treaty, or executive agreement.[214] *Zschernig*'s conception of a "dormant foreign affairs preemption" power for federal courts had been sharply criticized by commentators and sparingly applied by courts.[215]

The *Garamendi* Court did not reject *Zschernig*. On the other hand, it also did not extend *Zschernig*'s endorsement of an independent federal court power to supervise foreign relations. Instead,

---

[209] 539 US 396 (2003) (cited in note 64).

[210] See Cal Ins Code §§ 13800–07.

[211] 539 US 396.

[212] See, for example, *Gerling Global Reinsurance Corp. of Am. v Quackenbush*, 2000 US Dist LEXIS 8815 (June 9, 2000).

[213] 389 US 429 (1968).

[214] *Gerling Global*, 2000 US Dist LEXIS 8815, *19.

[215] See, for example, *Gerling Global v Low*, 240 F3d 739 (9th Cir 2001) (noting that *Zschernig* has been applied sparingly). For critical commentary, see Jack L. Goldsmith, *Federal Courts, Foreign Affairs, and Federalism*, 83 Va L Rev 1617, 1643–58 (1997); Michael D. Ramsey, *The Power of the States in Foreign Affairs: The Original Understanding of Foreign Policy Federalism*, 75 Notre Dame L Rev 341 (1999).

the Court found the California law preempted because the law created a clear conflict with a "consistent Presidential foreign policy."[216] Importantly, the Court did not rely on a treaty, statute, or executive agreement to find preemption. Rather, it gleaned this "consistent Presidential foreign policy" by reviewing statements made by U.S. officials responsible for negotiating settlement agreements with foreign governments and insurers.[217] Because these statements by executive branch officials indicated a national policy to encourage voluntary repayment of insurance policies rather than mandatory disclosures, "state law must give way where, as here, there is evidence of clear conflict between the policies adopted" by the "federal executive authority" and the states.[218]

Thus, the *Garamendi* Court neatly sidestepped the main criticism of *Zschernig*, which attacked *Zschernig*'s empowerment of federal courts to preempt independently state laws in the complete absence of any input from (or indeed in opposition to) the wishes of the President or Congress. By relying on executive "statements" of national policy, the *Garamendi* Court avoided the problem of unchecked federal courts by empowering the executive branch to settle future disputes over state interference with foreign affairs by issuing statements of national policy.

As Justice Ginsburg argued in her dissent, the Court's reliance on statements by individual members of the executive branch "places the considerable power of foreign affairs preemption in the hands of individual sub-Cabinet members of the Executive Branch."[219] Even if the officials faithfully represented the executive's policy, the dissent argued that the decision might result in giving such officials "the power to invalidate a state law simply by conveying the Executive's views on matters of federal policy."[220]

2. *Garamendi and CIL.* Although the decision did not involve state court interpretations of CIL, *Garamendi* matters because the power of the federal courts to independently oversee state activities in foreign affairs is deeply intertwined with federal courts' powers over the development of CIL. As suggested above, supporters of the *Sosa* Court's reading of the ATS have argued that control over

---

[216] *Garamendi*, 539 US 396, 399–400.

[217] Id.

[218] Id.

[219] Id at 442.

[220] Id.

CIL must remain under the authority of the federal courts because only federal courts can unify disparate and inconsistent interpretations of CIL.[221] In this view, CIL is simply one part of the larger foreign relations law controlled and developed by federal courts. Just as states cannot intrude on matters involving foreign relations by enacting laws like HVIRA, states cannot be allowed to intrude on foreign relations by developing and interpreting CIL independently.

Although *Garamendi* might be understood as a defeat for "foreign relations federalism" and state participation in matters relating to foreign affairs,[222] it is hardly an unqualified endorsement of *Zschernig*'s reliance on *federal courts* to police state activities. Rather, *Garamendi*'s reliance on the statements and actions of executive branch officials to discern a "consistent Presidential foreign policy" in conflict with the state law affirms that the federal *executive*, rather than the federal *courts*, holds the primary responsibility for determining which state laws and policies unduly interfere with national policies.

This reliance on the executive to oversee the states on matters implicating foreign affairs is hardly radical. Nor is this authority limited to executive supervision of state activities that offend foreign governments such as HVIRA. If anything, the tradition of executive supervision of states is stronger and deeper in the context of the development of CIL. As explained above, the federal executive has long exercised the right to intervene in lower state and federal court decisions implicating the CIL of foreign sovereign immunity.

Thus, while federal and state courts differed on the application of the CIL of foreign sovereign immunity, the federal executive's statements were treated as authoritative. Nor was this executive power limited to the question of recognizing governments. Thus, for example, the executive's independent decision to recognize a restrictive theory of foreign sovereign immunity in the famous State Department Tate Letter[223] was followed by courts, including

---

[221] See, for example, Koh, 111 Harv L Rev 1824, 1841 (cited in note 114).

[222] For the most prominent academic defenders, see Goldsmith, 83 Va L Rev at 1643–58 (cited in note 215); Ramsey, 75 Notre Dame L Rev 341 (cited in note 215); Peter J. Spiro, *Foreign Relations Federalism*, 70 U Colo L Rev 1223 (1999).

[223] Letter from Jack B. Tate, Acting Legal Adviser for the State Department, 26 Dept State Bull 984 (1952).

the Supreme Court, even though this interpretation of CIL did not directly implicate the recognition of any particular foreign government.[224] Moreover, despite Justice Ginsburg's criticism of the *Garamendi* Court's reliance on "statements by sub-Cabinet officers,"[225] the CIL of foreign sovereign immunity has long been controlled by actions (such as the Tate Letter) of sub-Cabinet officers in the State Department's Legal Advisor's office or the Department of Justice.[226]

For this reason, *Garamendi* only serves to strengthen the executive's already well-established role in the supervision of CIL. *Garamendi*'s preference for using statements by sub-Cabinet officials to determine whether a state law conflicts with national policy reaffirms the ability of such officials to control the development of CIL in lower courts as well. *Garamendi* reminds us that the federal court–centered system endorsed by *Sosa* is not the only system capable of providing a coherent national approach to the development of CIL. Indeed, given our functional analysis of federal courts, the system endorsed by *Sosa* is not even the best system for achieving uniformity in the development of CIL.

Under this understanding of *Garamendi* and consistent with past practice, the President controls CIL in three different ways.

- The President has the authority to declare, on behalf of the United States, adherence, rejection, or interpretations of CIL on the international plane. Most CIL requires state consent and most scholars agree that the President holds the primary authority to issue or withhold such consent for the United States. One of the more uncontroversial examples of this practice is President Truman's 1945 proclamation declaring that the United States would subject the underwater continental shelf abutting the coasts of the U.S. as part of U.S. territory.[227] A more controversial example of this practice is President

---

[224] See, for example, *Isbrandtsen Tankers v President of India*, 446 F2d 1198 (2d Cir 1971) (following Tate Letter).

[225] *Garamendi*, 539 US at 442 (cited in note 64).

[226] The executive's practice with regard to foreign sovereign immunity was somewhat controversial in the academy but it persisted without much controversy in the courts until Congress's codification in 1975. See, for example, Philip C. Jessup, *Has the Supreme Court Abdicated One of Its Functions?* 40 Am J Intl L 168 (1946).

[227] Policy of the United States with Respect to the Natural Resources of the Subsoil and Sea Bed of the Continental Shelf, Presidential Proclamation 2667, Sept 28, 1945, 10 Fed Reg 12303 (1945).

Bush's 2001 determination that al Qaeda and Taliban detainees captured in Afghanistan are not subject to the full protections of the customary laws of war.[228]

- The President may declare a national policy to adhere, reject or interpret a principle of CIL that preempts the entire field of CIL from state common law development. For example, in the aforementioned laws-of-war example, any presidential determination on the limited rights of unlawful combatants under the laws of war would likely completely preempt any independent state adjudication of CIL of those rights, including lawsuits by such individuals seeking to challenge the President's interpretation. Thus, if an unlawful combatant (say from Guantanamo Bay) sues for violations of the law of war, the whole field would be controlled by presidential determinations of the applicability of the CIL of war to such combatants.[229]

- The President may declare a national policy to accept, reject, or interpret a principle of CIL that comes into conflict with a specific interpretation of CIL under a state's common law. If a state adopts an interpretation of CIL, for instance, that foreign sovereign immunity protects a particular head of state, the President can override that particular interpretation while still leaving the state the authority to interpret other related forms of CIL such as whether head-of-state immunity applies to former heads of state.[230]

Both the majority and the dissent in *Garamendi* accepted an independent role for the executive in the preemption of state activity. Instead, the dispute centered on the exact form of executive intervention, with the dissent demanding a "formal" authoritative act by the President himself while the majority was content to rely upon statements made by sub-Cabinet officers as long as those statements accurately expressed the conflict between state and national policy.[231] For our purposes, we believe the President and his subordinates are authorized to use a variety of legal mecha-

---

[228] See, for example, John Yoo and James Ho, *The Status of Terrorists*, 44 Va J Intl L 207 (2003).

[229] This would not prevent such an individual from bringing a suit on other grounds, however, including violations of constitutional or other domestic law rights.

[230] Compare *Republic of Austria v Altmann*, 124 S Ct 2240, 2254 (2004).

[231] *Garamendi*, 539 US at 442 (Ginsburg, J, dissenting) (cited in note 64).

nisms to express national policy ranging from presidential declarations to Tate-Letter-like statements by sub-Cabinet officials to statements of interests filed in the context of particular litigations. As long as there is no dispute within the executive branch as to what the national policy requires with respect to CIL, we believe any of the above mechanisms will suffice.

Of course, the President's authority to issue such declarations or interpretations is not exclusive. Rather, it is subject to congressional override for matters falling within the shared powers of Congress and the President. In the absence of congressional intervention, however, the President's interpretation of CIL would be the final word.[232]

Our proposal results in a substantially different role for the executive than the *Sosa* Court envisions. While the *Sosa* Court noted that "there is a strong argument to give serious weight"[233] to executive branch views of the impact of an ATS suit on foreign policy, it did not issue the same kind of absolute rule of deference to executive determinations that it required in the context of foreign sovereign immunity. Indeed, despite paying lip service to the importance of leaving much control over CIL to the political branches, the *Sosa* Court showed surprisingly little regard for the opinions of either the President or the Senate in its resolution of the *Sosa* case itself.

For instance, while conceding that the political branches of the U.S. government had, through its non-self-execution declarations, refused to give judicial effect to treaty norms prohibiting arbitrary detention, it nonetheless conducted its own independent analysis of the CIL issues raised by *Sosa*. It not only failed to give any deference to the executive branch's views on the subject, but it did not consider the Senate's decision to make such norms non-self-executing as a limitation on its ability to revive such a norm through the common lawmaking process.[234]

Under the reading of the ATS we have suggested, the question of whether Alvarez-Machain's abduction violated CIL would be a

---

[232] We limit our argument to the President's ability to interpret CIL in absence of congressional action and do not address the related, but distinct question of the President's authority to interpret treaties. For a detailed discussion of this issue, see John C. Yoo, *Treaty Interpretation and the False Sirens of Delegation*, 90 Cal L Rev 1305 (2002), and Michael P. Van Alstine, *The Judicial Power and Treaty Delegation*, 90 Cal L Rev 1263 (2002).

[233] *Sosa*, 124 S Ct at 2767.

[234] See, for example, id at 2768–69.

matter of state common law. If the executive intervened in the same or similar manner that it did in Alvarez-Machain, the court hearing the case would give absolute deference to the executive's determination as a matter of national policy, assuming of course that Congress (or the treaty makers) have not codified this particular CIL norm by treaty or federal statute.

D. POSSIBLE OBJECTIONS

While *Garamendi* provides doctrinal support for our proposal for state court control over CIL (supervised by the federal executive), critics are likely to offer a number of objections. We consider each in turn.

1. *The inadequacy of state courts.* Perhaps the most counterintuitive component of our jurisdictional reading of the ATS is the idea that CIL will form part of the common law of the states rather than federal law. As proponents of the modern position have argued, CIL seems to logically fall within the purview of the federal government because foreign affairs is clearly a national rather than a state matter. Moreover, as we have pointed out in our functional analysis of the ATS, CIL needs to be unified.

The first response, of course, is that under our proposal CIL would form part of the common law of the states but it will be the President that is responsible for unifying the treatment of CIL for the United States as a whole. As we have explained in Part III, the executive branch has many more resources at its disposal for assessing and interpreting CIL. Unlike federal courts, which rely on private litigants to remove cases to its jurisdiction and private litigants to properly brief the issue before it, the executive branch can intervene wherever and whenever it chooses to by the simple expediency of issuing a document similar to the Tate Letter. If diplomatic or administrative pressures prove too burdensome, the executive can seek congressional codification of the substantive CIL standards it has adopted as it did in the case of foreign sovereign immunity.

Moreover, even if one accepted the idea that state governments have no role in the administration and interpretation of CIL, an idea one of us has disputed at length elsewhere,[235] our proposal

---

[235] Julian G. Ku, *The State of New York Does Exist: How the States Control Compliance with International Law*, 82 NC L Rev 457 (2004).

will almost certainly result in most CIL litigation returning to federal courts. The difference will be that such litigation must satisfy federal diversity jurisdiction requirements and will be governed by the common law of the state where the federal court resides. Thus, even if state courts and institutions were deemed somehow inferior, as a functional matter, to federal courts, our proposal does not preclude plaintiffs from going to federal courts anyway (assuming they can satisfy diversity requirements).

Additionally, treating CIL as state common law helps to avoid conflicts between courts and the executive over control of the interpretation of federal law. Under the current system, if the executive seeks to stop a court from adhering to a principle of CIL, a court empowered by the *Sosa* decision to interpret CIL might reject the President's views on a question of CIL on the grounds that the court's power to independently interpret federal law is being threatened. For instance, some courts have resisted analogous efforts by the executive to require courts to defer to the executive's interpretation of a treaty, suggesting that if "[t]he Government equates deference to submission," then it "would conflate" giving the executive's views deference "with surrendered judicial independence."[236] Presumably, courts might raise similar concerns in the context of executive views on CIL if such views were absolutely binding on federal courts.

Such concerns may be misguided, especially in the context of treaty interpretation.[237] Even so, this continuing tension between judicial independence and executive competence could be largely avoided if state (or federal courts sitting in diversity) are merely applying CIL as a doctrine of state common law. Absolute deference by state or federal courts to executive statements of CIL would not threaten the separation of powers since courts still retain their judicial power over federal law. Moreover, the Court's own precedents consistently permit greater presidential leeway over state law as opposed to the other branches of the federal government. As *Garamendi* illustrates, the Court has determined that the President, who holds the "vast share of responsibility for foreign affairs," already has the unilateral ability to preempt state law based on his determination of a "clear conflict" with a "consistent na-

---

[236] *Tachiona v Mugabe*, 186 F Supp 2d 383 (SDNY 2002).

[237] See Yoo, 90 Cal L Rev 1305 (cited in note 232).

tional policy."[238] And as we have explained above, this doctrinal result has sound functional benefits given the President's numerous institutional advantages over federal courts in the determination of national policy toward CIL and international human rights law. Just as importantly, it also helps to preserve the role of federal courts as fair institutions relatively independent of political manipulation.

2. *The dangers of presidential authority over CIL.* The second main objection to our jurisdictional reading of the ATS is that it would confer too much power on the President with respect to the interpretation and application of CIL. It is true that our proposal gives the President the discretion to interpret, apply, and even violate CIL. But we do not find this objection problematic for the following reasons.

First, it is well settled that the United States, as a sovereign, has the authority to violate CIL. U.S. courts, for instance, have long recognized that Congress has the power to violate treaties and CIL for purposes of domestic law. Hence, courts will enforce statutes passed later in time even if they conflict with treaties, and courts will also enforce statutes that violate CIL (although they will try to interpret both to avoid conflict).[239] Similarly, the Supreme Court has recognized that even though international law is "part of our law," it is subject to preemption by a "controlling executive act."[240]

Second, the President is the best-positioned institution to determine whether and how the United States as a whole should adhere to a particular rule or interpretation of CIL. As we have explained, much of CIL is determined by state practice and, under the U.S. system, the President is the chief interlocutor with foreign nations and international institutions. As such, the President is well positioned to assess various possible interpretations of CIL and harmonize those interpretations with the foreign policy goals of the United States. The President can also assess the continuing validity of a previously accepted CIL rule given changed foreign

---

[238] *Garamendi*, 539 US at 399–400.

[239] *Whitney v Robertson*, 124 US 190 (1888); *Murray v The Schooner Charming Betsy*, 6 US 64 (1804). For a discussion of the issues raised by conflicts between treaties and federal statutes, see Julian G. Ku, *Treaties as Laws: A Defense of the Last in Time Rule for Treaties and Federal Statutes*, 80 Ind L J (forthcoming Winter 2005).

[240] *The Paquete Habana*, 175 US at 712.

policy circumstances or changes in state practice. Moreover, the question from a functional perspective is not whether the President is likely to incorrectly interpret or violate CIL. The proper question is whether the President is better positioned than federal courts in determining how and whether to apply a rule of CIL. As we have argued, federal courts have few if any institutional advantages in the interpretation and enforcement of CIL, especially in the harmonization of CIL rules with the broader foreign policy goals which they have no ability to assess. Notably, neither the *Sosa* Court nor other defenders of the modern position have offered a defense of federal court control over CIL on anything other than formal grounds.

Third, under our view, Congress has the authority to override most presidential interpretations of CIL as well as presidential decisions to violate CIL. After all, Congress has the power to "define and punish offences against the Law of Nations."[241] Moreover, it has been delegated a number of specific powers to regulate foreign commerce and the military.[242] While there are some matters allocated by the Constitution to the President exclusively, many CIL questions do not fall within that category and can be regulated by Congress if it chooses. Additionally, as we explained above, Congress exercises substantially more influence over the executive branch than it does over the courts because it does not have to rely solely on its legislative power to override a decision. It can hold oversight hearings, change budget allocations, and block the appointment of executive officers, to name just a few of these nonlegislative mechanisms that would enable it to oversee executive interpretations of CIL. If Congress chooses not to act, either formally or informally, we believe the President rather than the federal courts should retain the authority to determine U.S. policy toward CIL.

3. *The end of foreign relations federalism?* Finally, our proposal will likely be criticized, in the same way that *Garamendi* has already been attacked, for transferring excessive authority to the President at the expense of the states.[243] Professors Denning and Ramsey have recently argued, for instance, that principles of federalism

---

[241] US Const, Art I, § 8.

[242] Id.

[243] Brannon P. Denning and Michael D. Ramsey, *American Insurance Association v. Garamendi and Executive Preemption in Foreign Affairs*, 46 Wm & Mary L Rev 325 (2005).

and separation of powers require formal preemption by the statute or treaty over state activities implicating foreign affairs.[244] Indeed, the expansive nature of modern CIL encompassing traditionally state law areas such as family and criminal law might allow a President to wield CIL aggressively to unilaterally override state policies.[245] While we are more sympathetic to these objections than the others we have addressed, we nonetheless find them unconvincing.

It is true that states have historically interpreted CIL as part of their common law, but such interpretations or applications of CIL have never been considered strong candidates for protection under principles of federalism. For instance, state interpretation of the CIL respecting foreign sovereign immunity may implicate some traditional state interests, but very weak ones, if at all. This is probably why states welcomed executive interventions in this area of CIL. Their interest in maintaining an independent interpretation of the CIL of human rights is probably just as weak given that they have legislative authority to guarantee many of the same substantive results without relying on CIL. Thus, allowing the President to override state judicial interpretations of CIL or state statutes purporting to implement CIL will be unlikely to threaten basic state autonomy since the states could simply accomplish the same goals through other means. It is also worth pointing out that under our view, Congress will have the power to repeal the President's actions against the states because presidential determinations of the effect of CIL on state law fall squarely within Congress's traditional powers to define CIL.

The most difficult case occurs when existing non-CIL state law comes into conflict with CIL. For instance, the juvenile death penalty as administered by the states may violate CIL.[246] Under our view, however, the President cannot exercise his CIL interpretive power over the states unless the state is explicitly interpreting CIL. In other words, unless the state adopts an interpretation of CIL that permits such executions, there is no basis for the President to intervene. Even if a criminal defendant raises an argument based upon CIL in order to challenge his sentence, the

---

[244] Id.

[245] Id.

[246] See, for example, William A. Schabas, *Is the United States Death Penalty System Inconsistent with International Human Rights Law?* 67 Fordham L Rev 2793 (1999).

President could not necessarily exercise the *Garamendi* power to preempt the state's death sentence. If the state is merely applying its non-CIL statutory or common law on a matter within its traditional legislative competence, a presidential intervention might not satisfy *Garamendi*'s requirement of balancing among the national policy interest, the strength of the state's interest, and the clarity of the conflict.

To be sure, the *Garamendi* framework counsels deference to the executive branch and undoubtedly strengthens the President's ability to wield CIL against the states. Even so, the proper question for supporters of federalism is whether the President is *more* likely than a federal court to preempt of state laws on the basis of CIL. While the President is not constrained by the same political process constraints that scholars have relied upon to enforce principles of federalism, the President is still politically accountable, at least when compared to federal courts. Moreover, a review of historical practice demonstrates that the President is often hesitant to undermine state autonomy in order to ensure compliance with international law, even where his constitutional authority seems undisputed.[247] Not only have past presidents relied on state governments to independently ensure compliance with international law, but recently, presidents have even permitted state governments to openly defy international law obligations out of deference to state autonomy and federalism (and perhaps political calculation).[248] For this reason, we doubt that injudicious executive use of the power to preempt state laws by declarations of national policy will occur very frequently or more frequently than it might occur with federal courts holding this power.

CONCLUSION

Sosa represents the culmination of nearly 25 years of debate over the status of CIL in U.S. courts. As we have explained, it can be fairly read to endorse the majority view of international legal scholars of the importance of preserving an independent federal court role in the interpretation and enforcement of CIL. Though *Sosa* recognized the force of the formalist critique, the

---

[247] See Ku, 82 NC L Rev at 495–97 (cited in note 235) (discussing executive's reluctance to intervene into state activities that injure alien residents).

[248] See id at 510–21 (discussing executive's reluctance to intervene in state criminal punishment on the basis of international court judgments).

Court was ultimately persuaded that the ATS litigation was necessarily a job for the federal courts. It refused to accept that "federal courts must avert their gaze from CIL" and that it was required by the formalist critique to remove "independent judicial determination" of CIL.[249]

While we disagree with the Court's reading of the ATS, especially its unpersuasive attempt to marshal historical sources for its conclusion, we believe that the real flaw in its decision lies in a failure to seriously consider the functional difficulties of maintaining the existing system of ATS litigation. While scholars and judges have widely celebrated the ATS as a mechanism for developing and enforcing international law and human rights, they have not examined whether the federal courts are the most appropriate institution for achieving those goals.

Our main goal here has been to provide the functional analysis that has generally been missing from the ATS debates. We conclude that the modern position's view of the ATS cannot be justified either as a reflection of congressional intent in the enactment of the ATS or as a matter of superior institutional competence on the part of federal courts. Federal courts suffer from many institutional shortcomings, especially when compared to the executive branch, in achieving national goals in foreign relations.

We also believe that the *Sosa* Court may not have fully understood that there is a doctrinally sound and functionally superior alternative system to the modern position. If federal courts are divested of their jurisdiction over ATS litigation, CIL litigation may still be entertained as part of the common law of the states. We believe this system is superior to the existing one because unlike current ATS litigation, the President has the independent authority to preempt state law interpretations of CIL. Thus, the executive branch would replace federal courts as the domestic institution responsible for developing, unifying, and interpreting U.S. obligations under CIL. We hope that our discussion can shift the terms of the ATS debate away from its largely inconclusive battles over the historical origins of the statute to a more broad-based analysis of the consequences of the modern position and to a deeper consideration of the possible alternatives.

---

[249] *Sosa*, 124 S Ct at 2764–65.

KATE STITH

CRIME AND PUNISHMENT UNDER THE
CONSTITUTION

Everyone is suddenly in an uproar over sentencing. Ironically, the
essential holdings of *Apprendi v New Jersey*[1] and *Blakely v Washington*[2]
seem constitutionally obvious—even as their full implications remain decidedly unclear.[3] All these decisions hold is that when a
legislature decides that certain conduct warrants an increase in criminal punishment, such conduct is part of the "crime" that must be
charged and proven in accordance with the requirements of the
Fifth, Sixth, and Fourteenth Amendments of the Constitution. The
decisions mean that legislatures cannot accomplish an end run
around the rights that the Constitution guarantees "[i]n all criminal
prosecutions"[4] by moving part of the "prosecution" from the trial
phase to the sentencing phase. Yet these two cases, and especially
Blakely, have caused consternation and provoked cries of impending
doom.[5] There are four reasons for the alarm bells.

Kate Stith is Lafayette S. Foster Professor of Law, Yale Law School.

[1] 530 US 466 (2000).

[2] 124 S Ct 2531 (2004).

[3] See note 194 for a catalogue of some of the ambiguities of the *Blakely* holding.

[4] US Const, Amend VI.

[5] See *Blakely*, 124 US at 2550 ("What I have feared most has now come to pass: Over
20 years of sentencing reform are all but lost . . . .") (O'Connor dissenting); *United States
v Booker*, 375 F3d 508, 515 (7th Cir 2004) (Easterbrook dissenting), cert granted, 125 S
Ct 11 (Aug 2, 2004); Frank Bowman, *Train Wreck? Or Can the Federal Sentencing System
Be Saved?* 41 Am Crim L Rev 217 (2004); Douglas Berman, *Supreme Court Cleanup in
Aisle 4*, SLATE, July 16, 2004, online at http://slate.msn.com/id/2104014 ("Blakely is the
biggest criminal justice decision not just of this past term, not just of this decade, not just
of the Rehnquist Court, but perhaps in the history of the Supreme Court").

First, even though the *Blakely* majority notes in a footnote that "we express no opinion" on the Federal Sentencing Guidelines (FSG),[6] the opinion goes out of its way to imply that the elaborate new system constructed in the 1980s to govern federal sentencing[7] is unconstitutional as now implemented. The rule announced four years ago in *Apprendi* required that any fact increasing the "statutory maximum" sentence must be tried to a jury and proven beyond a reasonable doubt, while the *Blakely* rule requires that any fact that increases the maximum *lawful sentence* must be thus tried and proven.[8] Inasmuch as the FSG are rules that prescribe the lawful sentences in federal courts, *Blakely* would appear to apply to them.[9]

Law professors and journalists—not to mention the Department of Justice, Congress, and the Supreme Court—are federocentric. Because the FSG are part of the federal criminal justice system, and because of the radical changes they imposed on that system, they have been an object of widespread interest and controversy since their inception.[10] The very idea that this major congressional initiative might be unconstitutional is "disastrous"[11] to its supporters[12]

---

[6] *Blakely*, 124 S Ct at 2538 n 9. The full footnote is quoted in note 202.

[7] The FSG were promulgated by the United States Sentencing Commission (USSC) pursuant to the Sentencing Reform Act of 1984, Pub L No 98-473, tit II, 98 Stat 2017 (1984), codified at 28 USC § 991(a) et seq and 18 USC § 3551 et seq (2000 & Supp 2004). The first set of Guidelines became effective on November 1, 1987, see USSC, *Federal Sentencing Guideline Manual* (1987).

[8] Compare *Apprendi*, 530 US at 490, with *Blakely*, 124 S Ct at 2540.

[9] The decisions in *Apprendi* and *Blakely* are analyzed in depth in Section II.B and Section III.

[10] See Michael Tonry, *Sentencing Matters* 72 (Oxford, 1996) (the FSG "are the most controversial and disliked sentencing reform initiative in U.S. history"); Kate Stith and José A. Cabranes, *Fear of Judging: Sentencing Guidelines in the Federal Courts* 11, 195–96 (Chicago, 1998).

[11] *Blakely*, 124 S Ct at 2544 (O'Connor dissenting).

[12] Less than two weeks after *Blakely* was decided, the Deputy Attorney General sent a memorandum to all federal prosecutors directing them to argue that the FSG were still valid but also directing them to take measures to protect convictions in the event that the FSG are held unconstitutional. *Memorandum from James Comey, Deputy Attorney General, to All Federal Prosecutors* ("Departmental Legal Positions and Policies in Light of *Blakely v. Washington*") (July 2, 2004), reprinted at 16 Fed Sent Rptr 357 (2004). Eleven days later the Senate Judiciary Committee held a hearing on the "crisis" the case had caused. *Blakely v Washington* and the Future of the Federal Sentencing Guidelines: Hearing before the Senate Committee on the Judiciary, 108th Cong, 2d Sess (July 13, 2004). See also S Con Res 130, 108th Cong, 2d Sess (July 21, 2004) (urging Supreme Court "to resolve the current confusion and inconsistency in the Federal criminal justice system by promptly considering and ruling on the constitutionality of the Federal Sentencing Guidelines").

and a hope on the near horizon to its critics.[13] There is, moreover, heated disagreement over how the FSG might be remedied by either the Supreme Court or Congress if *Blakely* is extended to them.[14] *Blakely* was decided on June 24, 2004, at the end of the Court's October 2003 Term. Over the summer, the Court granted certiorari in two cases, *United States v Booker*[15] and *United States v Fanfan*,[16] in which it will address whether and how *Blakely* affects the FSG, and it heard argument on those cases the first day of its October Term, 2004. These cases are *sub judice* as this essay is written.

Second, the rules in *Blakely* and *Apprendi* raise constitutional doubts about aspects of the sentencing systems of many states that have adopted mechanisms similar to (though not as radical as) the FSG. Despite our chronic federocentrism, states, of course, account for the lion's share of criminal prosecutions and convictions nationwide. Because of their diverse sentencing systems and procedures, it could take states years and many resentencings to decipher and comply with the implications of the Court's recent decisions.[17]

---

[13] See, for example, Albert W. Alschuler, *To Sever or Not to Sever? Why Blakely Requires Action by Congress*, 17 Fed Sent Rptr 11 (2004).

[14] If the Court holds that the FSG are unconstitutional, the Court could, inter alia, allow them to continue to function as "law" but with a requirement of jury fact finding for aggravating facts that increase the lawful sentence. Alternatively, the Court or Congress could avoid the constitutional issue identified in *Apprendi* and *Blakely* by changing the FSG to nonbinding, true guidelines. The question of remedy was the second question on which the Court granted certiorari in the *Booker* and *Fanfan* cases. The present essay does not address this issue.

[15] 375 F3d 508 (7th Cir 2004) (holding that under *Blakely* judge may not make factual finding that increases sentencing range), cert granted, 125 S Ct 11 (Aug 2, 2004).

[16] Certiorari in the *Fanfan* case was directly from the United States District Court for the District of Maine, *United States v Fanfan*, 04-47-P-H (D Me) (June 28, 2004) (holding that under *Blakely* the court could impose sentence only within range authorized by jury verdict); the sentencing is unreported. See 125 S Ct 11 (Aug 2, 2004) (granting cert).

[17] *Blakely* has consequences not just for states with comprehensive sentencing reform guidelines—such as Minnesota, North Carolina, Oregon, Tennessee, and, of course, Washington—but also for every state that provides for aggravated sentences upon judicial fact finding, including Alaska, Arizona, California, Colorado, Indiana, New Jersey, New Mexico, and Ohio. See Jon Wool and Don Stemen, *Aggravated Sentencing: Blakely v. Washington—Practical Implications for State Sentencing Systems*, Pol & Prac Rev (Vera, State Sentencing and Corrections Program) (Aug 2004), online at http://www.vera.org/section8/section8_3.asp. For a discussion of the impact of *Blakely* in California, see J. Bradley O'Connell, *Amazing Stories: Blakely v. Washington and California Determinate Sentences*, 16 Fed Sent Rptr 348 (2004). The online website written and maintained by Professor Douglas Berman has comprehensively reported on *Blakely*-related cases in many states. See http://sentencing.typepad.com.

Third, *Blakely*'s reaffirmation and enlargement of the rule in *Apprendi* raises the specter that thousands, perhaps hundreds of thousands, of *past* criminal sentences in both state and federal criminal justice systems will be challenged, perhaps resulting in significantly lower sentences in some cases.[18]

The fourth reason that *Apprendi* and *Blakely* have provoked such an uproar is simply that everyone thought the Supreme Court had definitively resolved the constitutionality of the new determinate sentencing systems and already certified the constitutionality of both the FSG and the United States Sentencing Commission.[19] Indeed, the Court *had* done so, and now appears to have changed its mind.

In this essay I focus on the last issue, which in turn has two parts. First, why was it so widely assumed by legislatures, commentators, and the Supreme Court itself that the new sentencing systems were constitutional? Second, how is it that a majority of the Supreme Court came to upset that widely shared understanding? These questions undoubtedly have many different answers, depending on the perspective from which they are addressed. Over the last fifty years, critical variables have undergone substantial change: political trends within society, the personnel and politics of the Court, and the relationship between Congress and the Court. One significant change may be a growing awareness by Supreme Court Justices of the consequences the FSG have had on criminal practice in the federal courts, including a remarkable

---

[18] Justice O'Connor stressed this concern in her *Blakely* dissent, noting that between the day after *Apprendi* was decided (June 27, 2000) and March 31, 2004, there were over 270,000 defendants sentenced in federal court alone. See 124 S Ct at 2549 n 2 (O'Connor dissenting). While discussion of retroactivity is beyond the scope of this article, it seems unlikely that either *Blakely* or *Booker* and *Fanfan* would be held retroactive to the date of the decision in *Apprendi*, as Justice O'Connor seemed to suggest. For an excellent discussion of the applicability of *Blakely* on both direct appeal and collateral review, see Nancy J. King and Susan R. Klein, *Beyond Blakely*, 16 Fed Sent Rptr 316, 321 (2004).

[19] If the Court's decisions in *Booker* and *Fanfan* do strike down the FSG as we know them, another fundamental question arises: Is the United States Sentencing Commission, which was created and chartered by Congress to write the FSG, itself unconstitutional because it is an executive branch agency that has been delegated broad-scale authority to write federal criminal laws? The constitutionality of the Sentencing Commission is discussed in text accompanying notes 110–17. The cases now under review do not directly raise this issue, which in any event could be mooted if the Court or Congress were to make the FSG advisory rather than binding, or if Congress were to enact the FSG into federal statutory law.

reduction in the incidence of trial,[20] and the irrepressible phenomenon of "fact-bargaining."[21]

These considerations may help explain why the Supreme Court has altered its understanding of the applicability of constitutional norms to criminal sentencing. But this essay is written primarily from the perspective of constitutional interpretation and doctrine, the manner in which the Supreme Court itself addresses these issues. The traditional understanding of criminal sentencing was established in the era of "discretionary" sentencing, before the reform movement of the 1980s sought to reduce sentencing disparity by codifying aggravating and mitigating sentencing factors. The most important case reflecting the traditional understanding, *Williams v New York*,[22] was decided more than a half-century ago. *Williams* rejected a challenge under the Due Process Clause of the Fourteenth Amendment to sentencing systems in which the judge could impose any sentence within the broad limits specified by the legislature in the statute defining the crime of conviction. The judge was not required to make any factual findings or to justify his sentence; indeed, he could impose sentence "giving no reason at all."[23]

The main reason *Apprendi* and *Blakely* caught so many people (including the dissenters on the Court) off guard is that *Williams* seemed capable of deflecting any constitutional challenge to the recent sentencing reform efforts. After all, if it was constitutional for judges to sentence on the basis of half-facts or no facts at all, as *Williams* held, then surely it must be constitutional for legislatures

---

[20] The percentage of convictions in federal court obtained by plea of guilty, rather than trial, has grown from approximately 85 percent in 1990 to 97 percent in 2002. Compare Administrative Office of the U.S. Courts, *Federal Offenders in the United States Courts, 1986 through 1990* 50 (1990) (table showing that of 46,725 defendants convicted in 1990 in federal court, 40,452 entered pleas of guilty or nolo contendere), with United States Sentencing Commission, *Sourcebook of Federal Sentencing Statistics* 21 (2003) (table showing that of 63,996 defendants convicted in 2002 federal court, 62,145 entered pleas of guilty or nolo contendere).

[21] The Department of Justice has sought by national directives to limit this aspect of plea bargaining under the FSG since their inception. See Stith and Cabranes, *Fear of Judging* at 136–40 (cited in note 10); *Memorandum from Attorney General John Ashcroft to All Federal Prosecutors* 6–7 (Sept 22, 2003) (policy concerning charging criminal offenses, disposition of charges, and sentencing), online at http://www.fpdpaw.org/pdf/doj-plea-memo.pdf. But these directives appear to be "honored most often in the breach." King and Klein, 16 Fed Sent Rptr at 321 (cited in note 18). See also note 247 and accompanying text.

[22] 337 US 241 (1949). Justice Black's opinion in *Williams* is explored at some length in text accompanying notes 46–59.

[23] Id at 252. See Section I.B.

to codify the factors relevant to sentencing and require judicial fact finding, to a preponderance of the evidence, before imposing a sentence. It would seem logically inconsistent to permit discretionary sentencing with essentially no "process," while subjecting codified sentencing to constitutional requirements relating to accusation and proof of crimes. We may call this puzzle the "*Williams* paradox."[24]

Over the past six years, a majority of the Supreme Court has come to appreciate that the previous doctrinal treatment of judicial sentencing discretion does not insulate the new systems of sentencing from constitutional scrutiny. Binding sentencing guidelines essentially replace "discretion" with "law." The rule of *Blakely* is simple: Once the *law itself* identifies which facts warrant greater punishment, these facts are functionally "elements" of the crime, requiring the usual constitutional protections of jury trial and proof beyond a reasonable doubt. Notably, *Apprendi* and *Blakely* do not seek to resolve the *Williams* paradox; instead they reject the premise that *Williams* has any applicability to the new regimes of codified sentencing factors. While they leave the paradox unresolved (and *Blakely* even quotes *Williams* without disapproval),[25] the recent decisions may well be on a collision course with that case from an earlier era. The Court may continue simply to tolerate the logical disjunction between its approach to discretionary sentencing and its approach to rule-bound sentencing. It is at least arguable, however, that if the Court really means what it is now saying, it will revisit *Williams*'s rejection of any due process limitation on the exercise of judicial sentencing discretion.

I. Constitutional Basics

A. DEFINING AND PROVING CRIMES

It is a truism that few provisions of the Constitution place limits on the legislature's power to criminalize particular conduct.[26] The democratic process itself may be the most important constitutional

---

[24] This "paradox" is discussed in text accompanying notes 118–27 and in Section III.

[25] See 124 S Ct at 2538, discussed in text accompanying notes 219–21 and n 230.

[26] The government's police power is broad, limited primarily by the substantive requirements of the First Amendment, the Equal Protection Clause of the Fourteenth Amendment, constitutional privacy values, and the Eighth Amendment's ban on cruel and unusual punishments. But see also Section IV.

restraint on legislative overreaching.[27] At the same time, the accused has an array of constitutional protections, which we usually think of as "procedural" rights, that limit the government's ability to impose punishment for crime. The most powerful procedural protection is the requirement that the government prove the defendant's guilt beyond a reasonable doubt, a right long recognized but not "constitutionalized" (as a matter of due process) until the *Winship* case in 1970.[28] Without referring to the idea of "elements" of a crime, *Winship* held that the heightened standard of proof applies to "every fact necessary to constitute the crime with which [the defendant] is charged."[29]

Five years after *Winship*, the Court in *Mullaney v Wilbur*[30] unanimously held that the label the legislature affixes to a fact that must be proved at trial does not necessarily determine the burden of proof required by the Constitution. If *Winship* were "limited to those facts that constitute a crime as defined by state law," a legislature could undermine the requirement of proof beyond a reasonable doubt by "redefin[ing] the elements that constitute different crimes, characterizing them as factors that bear solely on the extent of punishment."[31] This decision, which struck down Maine's law placing the burden on the defendant to prove the "heat of passion" partial defense to murder,[32] could be read to suggest that all statutory "affirmative" defenses are unconstitutional.[33] *Mullaney* thus raised the daunting prospect that the Constitution not only requires proof beyond a reasonable doubt of

---

[27] See John Hart Ely, *Democracy and Distrust: A Theory of Judicial Review* (Harvard, 1980).

[28] 397 US 358 (1970) (Brennan). Justice Harlan wrote a concurring opinion, id at 368 (Harlan concurring). Three Justices dissented, id at 375 (Burger dissenting, joined by Stewart); id at 377 (Black dissenting).

[29] Id at 364 (majority).

[30] 421 US 684 (1975).

[31] Id at 698.

[32] The jury in *Mullaney* was instructed that "malice aforethought is an essential . . . element of the crime of murder," but that the jury should presume malice if the homicide was intentional *unless* the defendant established by a preponderance of the evidence that he acted in the "heat of passion." Id at 686. This use of a presumption would appear to violate the later case of *Sandstrom v Montana*, 442 US 510 (1979) (holding that both conclusive and burden-shifting presumptions are unconstitutional).

[33] The Model Penal Code had taken such an approach, generally requiring the government to prove beyond a reasonable doubt the absence of a defense once evidence of that defense is put forth by the defendant. See American Law Institute, Model Penal Code, § 1.12 (Proposed Official Draft, 1962). In the ensuing years, many states adopted this approach. See *Patterson v New York*, 432 US 197, 208 n 10, 209 n 11 (1977).

every fact that constitutes a crime, but also requires federal courts to police how the states define crimes.

Two years later, a divided Court narrowed *Mullaney*'s reach. In *Patterson v New York*,[34] the Court upheld a New York statute that required defendants to prove a similar, but broader, partial defense to murder.[35] *Patterson* did not entirely back away from *Mullaney*'s insistence that a state could not avoid *Winship* by merely recharacterizing "elements" as "factors" bearing "solely on the extent of punishment." But while *Patterson* warned that there are some, unstated, "constitutional limits beyond which the States may not go,"[36] it declined to adopt as a constitutional rule the idea

> that a State must prove beyond a reasonable doubt every fact, the existence or nonexistence of which it is willing to recognize as an exculpatory or mitigating circumstance affecting the degree of culpability or the severity of the punishment.[37]

Patterson thus clearly rejected a broad reading of *Mullaney*—that all factors identified by the legislature as relevant to the degree of a crime, or to its punishment, must be treated as "elements" of the crime for constitutional purposes and thus be proven by the government beyond a reasonable doubt.

The decision affirmed the long-held belief that in our constitutional system, legislatures have broad authority to decide what conduct should be criminalized. At the same time, *Patterson* reaffirmed *Winship*'s procedural guarantee that the state must "prove beyond a reasonable doubt 'every fact necessary to constitute the crime with which [the defendant is] charged.'"[38] *Patterson* also made clear that the legislature has authority to decide what conduct is relevant by way of mitigation or defense, and affirmed that

---

[34] 432 US 197 (1977) (White). Three Justices dissented, id at 216 (Powell dissenting, joined by Brennan and Marshall).

[35] New York criminalized as "second-degree murder" all intentional takings of a life except those where the defendant more likely than not acted with extreme emotional disturbance (in which case the crime was "manslaughter"). See id at 198 (majority).

[36] Id at 210.

[37] Id at 207. See also id at 210 (expressly declining "to adopt as a constitutional imperative, operative countrywide, that a State must disprove beyond a reasonable doubt every fact constituting any and all affirmative defenses related to the culpability of an accused").

[38] Id at 206, quoting *Winship*, 397 US at 364.

such facts are *not* subject to the constitutional standard of proof.[39]

The *Patterson* dissenters rightly noted that the protections offered to defendants by the majority's approach are "formalities."[40] This is because the protection offered by *Winship*—proof beyond a reasonable doubt—is itself a formality in the sense that it concerns the *procedure* that must attend prosecution of the crime, rather than the content of the criminal prohibition itself.[41] Putting aside the still-unclear "constitutional limits beyond which the State may not go,"[42] *Patterson* signaled that the Court would defer to the legislature's judgment concerning the content of the law,[43] while holding true to *Winship*'s demand that the Constitution's "formalities" be observed in the enforcement of the law.[44]

The debate in *Patterson* thirty years ago presaged, to some extent, the recent debate in *Apprendi* and *Blakely*.[45] Each of these cases raises the question of which legislatively identified "facts" the Constitution requires the government to prove beyond a reasonable doubt. For present purposes, the important point is that under all these cases—*Patterson*, *Blakely*, and *Apprendi*—the answer is at least those "facts" that the legislature has decided are part of the crime.

---

[39] Id at 209 ("To recognize at all a mitigating circumstance does not require the State to prove its nonexistence . . . .").

[40] Id at 224 (Powell dissenting). See also id at 224, 225 (referring to majority as "formalistic").

[41] The theory enunciated in *Patterson* would, for instance, allow a state to define as "murder" any intentional taking of a life, treating all defenses, even self-defense, as mitigating factors with the burden of persuasion on the defendant. Indeed, the Supreme Court in 1987 upheld precisely such a criminal statute, in *Martin v Ohio*, 480 US 228 (1987).

[42] See text accompanying note 36.

[43] Perhaps due to the insistence of the *Patterson* dissenters that the decision "drains . . . *Winship* . . . of much of its vitality," see id at 216 (Powell dissenting), *Patterson* was understood by some commentators and even a majority of the Court to stand for a broader proposition: that the courts will almost always defer to whatever *label* a legislature attaches to a "fact" in statutes defining crimes, in the sense that the statutory label determines the constitutional burden of proof required. See *McMillan v Pennsylvania*, 477 US 79, 85–86 (1986). To be sure, in *Patterson* itself the majority had no constitutional complaint about either the label or the burden of proof attached to the label, but the label was not central to the Court's decision. *Patterson* is discussed further in text accompanying notes 124, 129–31, 232–33.

[44] 432 US at 210.

[45] This point has been noted by several commentators, and is pursued in thoughtful detail in Joseph L. Hoffmann, *Apprendi v. New Jersey: Back to the Future?*, 38 Am Crim L Rev 255 (2001).

B. SENTENCING

While the Constitution has been interpreted by the Supreme Court to impose many formal protections at the adjudicatory stage of the criminal process, it was assumed before *Apprendi* that the Constitution affords few protections at sentencing. The Sixth Amendment's protections "[i]n all criminal prosecutions" seemed to be only about trials—the adjudicatory stage of the criminal process that precedes sentencing.

As noted in the introduction to this essay, *Williams v New York*,[46] decided in 1949, is the landmark decision that has been understood to stand for the proposition that defendants have virtually no rights in the determination and pronouncement of sentence. In that case, a New York jury convicted the defendant of felony murder, committed during a burglary, and recommended life imprisonment instead of the death penalty. The sentencing judge rejected that recommendation. In explaining his decision, he recounted the brutal facts of the case and referred to information that he had learned from a presentence report, prepared by the probation department as required by New York law,[47] and to information he had received from various individuals, apparently including the probation officers who prepared the presentence report.[48] Although the defendant had no prior convictions, the sentencing judge credited the conclusion of the presentence report that the defendant had committed thirty additional burglaries in the two months prior to his arrest.[49] The judge also concluded that the defendant had "a morbid sexuality" and was a "menace to society."[50] In light of all

---

[46] 337 US 241.

[47] See id at 243, which quotes § 482 of the New York Criminal Code as providing:

. . . Before rendering judgment or pronouncing sentence the court shall cause the defendant's previous criminal record to be submitted to it, including any reports that may have been made as a result of a mental, phychiatric [*sic*] or physical examination of such person, and may seek any information that will aid the court in determining the proper treatment of such defendant.

[48] 337 US at 242. A short but excellent account of the *Williams* case based on the actual sentencing record as well as on the Supreme Court's opinion can be found in Kevin R. Reitz, *Sentencing Facts: Travesties of Real-Offense Sentencing*, 45 Stan L Rev 523, 528–31 (1993).

[49] 337 US at 244. The probation officer apparently received this information from the police; the presentence report recounts police investigation that had connected the defendant with at least some of the 30 additional burglaries. See Reitz, 45 Stan L Rev at 529 n 34 (cited in note 48) (summarizing presentence report).

[50] 337 US at 244.

the information he had considered, the judge said he could "find no basis whatsoever on which I can extend to [the defendant], in good conscience, the consideration which the jury has recommended."[51]

Before both the New York Court of Appeals and the Supreme Court, Willliams argued that his death sentence was imposed pursuant to procedures that violated due process, for he had not been given "reasonable notice of the charges against him" or "an opportunity to examine adverse witnesses."[52] Justice Black's opinion for the Court rejected these claims, over Justice Murphy's dissent.[53] With only one additional reference to the particular facts of the case before it, the Court in *Williams* addressed in all-embracing terms the constitutionality of two features of the New York sentencing regime (and most likely in every jurisdiction in the nation at that time): broad judicial discretion, and the use of "out-of-court information to assist [the judge] in the exercise" of this discretion.[54] The Court referred to this country's history of judicial discretion in determining criminal sanctions, asserted that "out-of-court affidavits" have been used "frequently," and said that sentencing judges "naturally have in mind their knowledge of the defendant's personality and background."[55] This social history was

---

[51] Reitz, 45 Stan L Rev at 530 n 39 (cited in note 48) (quoting the transcript of the sentencing of Williams). Although the Supreme Court in *Williams* did not quote this statement of the sentencing judge, its narrative of the facts did explain that the judge rejected the jury's recommendation on the basis of the presentence report and other information from the presentence investigation. See 337 US at 242–44.

[52] 337 US at 245, quoting *Oliver*, 333 US 257, 273 (1948) (holding that secret trial for contempt of court violated Due Process Clause of Fourteenth Amendment), which apparently was the basis for the defendant's claims. Justice Black's opinion initially intimated that the defendant failed to raise his due process claims in the sentencing proceeding, noting that "[t]he accuracy of the statements made by the judge as to appellant's background and past practices were not challenged by appellant or his counsel, nor was the judge asked to disregard any of them or to afford appellant a chance to refute or discredit any of them by cross-examination or otherwise," 337 US at 244. Yet Justice Black did not rely on any notion of forfeiture or default—probably for good reason, because apparently neither the defendant nor his counsel had the opportunity to read the presentence report, see id at 253 (Murphy dissenting). It would have been difficult for counsel, upon hearing these allegations for the first time at the sentencing hearing, to have known whether or how to refute them. Indeed, it appears that neither the defendant nor his counsel even had an opportunity to deny or rebut the allegations, even had there been an opportunity to do so, see note 61.

[53] 337 US at 252–53 (concluding that due process was violated because the death sentence was imposed in reliance on "evidence that would have been inadmissible at the trial . . . . [and none of which] was subject to scrutiny by the defendant.") (Murphy dissenting).

[54] Id at 252 (majority)

[55] Id at 246.

entirely appropriate, in the Court's view; sentencing should not be "hedged in" by the rules that encumber adjudication, because the functions of trial and sentencing are completely different. Whereas "[i]n a trial before verdict the issue is whether a defendant is guilty of having engaged in certain criminal conduct of which he has been specifically accused," the task of the sentencing judge is to determine "within fixed statutory or constitutional limits . . . the type and extent of punishment after guilt has been determined." Noting that the recently adopted Federal Rules of Criminal Procedure provided for presentence reports,[56] the Court explained that obtaining "the fullest information possible concerning the defendant's life and characteristics" is "[h]ighly relevant—if not essential" to the selection of sentence.[57]

It was "[a]lmost as an afterthought," as one commentator has noted,[58] that Justice Black added, "no federal constitutional objection would have been possible if the judge here had sentenced appellant to death because appellant's trial manner impressed the judge that appellant was a bad risk for society, or if the judge had sentenced him to death giving no reason at all."[59]

This is a remarkable opinion. The defendant in *Williams* had not been allowed to review the presentence report on which the New York trial judge based his determinations about the defendant's past conduct and his conclusions about the defendant's likely future if not given the death penalty.[60] The defendant was apparently not told until the sentencing hearing itself that the report accused him of committing thirty additional burglaries. He was never told of the evidence supporting these charges, or who made the allegations. Nor was he advised on what basis the judge

---

[56] Id at 246. While the Federal Probation Act of 1925 provided that probation officers would obtain information relevant to sentencing to assist judges, it did not require written reports. Just three years before *Williams*, the Supreme Court had approved the Federal Rules of Criminal Procedure, including Rule 32 (governing sentencing), which provided for written presentence reports. It surely is not irrelevant that as submitted to the Supreme Court under the Rules Enabling Act, the proposed Rule 32 provided that the defendant's counsel "and other interested parties" could examine the presentence report, but this provision was removed by the Supreme Court before it sent the Rules on to Congress. See Note, *Right of Criminal Offenders to Challenge Reports Used in Determining Sentence*, 49 Colum L Rev 567, 568 n 16 (1949).

[57] 337 US at 247.

[58] See Elizabeth T. Lear, *Is Conviction Irrelevant?* 40 UCLA L Rev 1179, 1209 (1993).

[59] 337 US at 252.

[60] See id at 253 (Murphy dissenting) ("the report . . . was not subject to examination by the defendant").

determined that his interest in sex was "morbid."[61] There is no suggestion in *Williams* that the judge considered or knew of any mitigating evidence regarding the defendant. And it appears that the judge need not have given any reason for the sentence he imposed.[62]

While the Court's policy arguments about the benefits of sentencing without trial-like procedures may have been persuasive (ironically foreshadowing Justice Breyer's arguments to the same effect in *Apprendi* and *Blakely*),[63] the opinion engaged in essentially no analysis of the defendant's claims that the Constitution guaranteed him the right to confront those who provided information forming the basis for the judge's decision to impose the death penalty. For Justice Black, the answer to these constitutional claims was not to be found in the Constitution, but in the nature of the sentencing proceeding. Reading between the lines of his opinion, Justice Black's position was as follows: First, the constitutional requirement that a defendant be informed of the accusations against him is not relevant because at sentencing the defendant is not "accused" of anything. Second, the constitutional right of confrontation does not apply because there is nothing—no "witnesses," no *evidence*—to "confront." Sentencing as understood in *Williams* did not involve accusation, proof, guilt, or, for that matter, law. Rather, the judge was making a decision—a discretionary judgment—involving the particular defendant's character and likely future conduct in light of the purposes of punishment to be served in the particular case. At its core, Justice Black's argument was that more information yields better decisions.

Justice Black did not elaborate an understanding of the non-adjudicatory nature of sentencing, but we can readily imagine some of the considerations that informed his views. Perhaps, for instance, the judge's decision at sentencing is comparable not to what juries or other fact finders do at trial, but to what an employer

---

[61] Indeed, a student law review note on the *Williams* decision in the New York Court of Appeals in the case flatly concluded, "There is no indication that the defendant was afforded any opportunity to *controvert* these prejudicial accusations [in the presentence report]." Note, 49 Colum L Rev at 567 (cited in note 56) (emphasis added). Curiously, Justice Black generally cited to this law review note at one point in his own opinion, but appears not to have found any particulars in it worth mentioning. See 337 US at 252 n 7 (majority).

[62] See text accompanying note 59.

[63] See *Apprendi*, 530 US at 555–59 (2000) (Breyer dissenting); *Blakely*, 124 S Ct at 2551 (Breyer dissenting). See also text accompanying notes 209, 215.

does in deciding whom to hire for a sensitive position, what a counselor does in giving career advice, or what a doctor does in diagnosing a condition and prescribing treatment. In 1949, it would have been difficult to imagine that any purpose would be served by arbitrarily limiting the information available to these types of decision makers, or by trying to shape their decision-making process into a "system" involving discrete "facts" to be "proved" to a particular degree of certainty. So too, perhaps, with judging in criminal sentencing.

Williams, it has been noted,[64] was written in the heyday of the rehabilitative ideal of sentencing and punishment. The opinion discussed at length the goals of "[r]eformation and rehabilitation of offenders," insisting that these "[m]odern changes in the treatment of offenders make it more necessary now than a century ago for observance of the distinctions in the evidential procedure in the trial and sentencing processes."[65] As Professor Kevin Reitz has observed, "This has led some to argue that *Williams* has lost precedential force in the contemporary era of guidelines and retributive justice."[66]

This argument has weight, but it misses the essential point of *Williams*—sentencing was, as Marvin E. Frankel famously complained more than two decades later, "lawless"[67] except for statutory limitations on the type and duration of sentence.[68] Justice Black did not limit either the holding or the reasoning of *Williams* to sentencing regimes in which rehabilitation is the stated statutory purpose of criminal punishment. He was, after all, writing for the

---

[64] See, for example, Stith and Cabranes, *Fear of Judging* at 28–29 (cited in note 10); Reitz, 45 Stan L Rev at 531, 542–43 (cited in note 48); Lear, 40 UCLA L Rev at 1209–10 (cited in note 58); Susan N. Herman, *The Tail That Wagged the Dog: Bifurcated Fact-Finding Under the Federal Sentencing Guidelines and the Limits of Due Process*, 66 S Cal L Rev 289, 316–20 (1992).

[65] 337 US at 248–49. See generally Francis A. Allen, *The Decline of the Rehabilitative Ideal* 5–8 (Yale, 1981).

[66] Reitz, 45 Stan L Rev at 543 (cited in note 48), citing Herman, 66 S Cal L Rev at 318–19 (cited in note 64). See also Stith and Cabranes, *Fear of Judging* at 150–52 (cited in note 10), concluding: "The old and new regimes of 'real-offense' sentencing thus differ both in theory (rehabilitative versus punitive) and in practice (discretionary versus mandatory)." This revisionist view of *Williams* would permit introduction of constitutional protections in the new systems without overruling *Williams* outright.

[67] Marvin E. Frankel, *Criminal Sentences: Law Without Order* x (Hill and Wang, 1973).

[68] See Stith and Cabranes, *Fear of Judging* at 9 (cited in note 10) ("From the beginning of the Republic, federal judges were entrusted with wide sentencing discretion . . . , permitting the sentencing judge to impose any term of imprisonment and any fine up to the statutory maximum").

ages. He wrote in the broadest of terms, not *justifying* so much as *explaining* the traditional understanding of sentencing as a stage wholly unlike, and unrelated to, the previous stages of accusation and proof. *Williams* does not seek to justify the lawlessness of sentencing; its basic assumption and point of departure is the proposition that sentencing is, by its very nature, not subject to law.

Williams has been understood to endure as a ringing endorsement of the constitutionality of discretionary sentencing without limitation on the nature of information obtained by the sentencing judge or the fact-finding process employed. As described below, during the remainder of the discretionary sentencing era, the Supreme Court declined to apply evidentiary rules, burdens of proof, jury trial rights, the prohibition on double jeopardy, or most other constitutional protections to the sentencing phase. Meanwhile, in 1970, Congress enacted a statute that relied in part on *Williams*. Still on the books, the statute provides that there should be:

> no limitation . . . placed on the information concerning the background, character, and conduct of a person convicted of an offense which a court of the United States may receive and consider for the purpose of imposing an appropriate sentence.[69]

It bears repeating that in upholding the broad authority of judges to exercise discretion in sentencing, *Williams* reaffirmed an important limitation on that authority—that "the punishment to be imposed" must be "within limits fixed by law."[70] That is, the Court in *Williams* would not have upheld the death sentence imposed in that case had it not been a lawful sentence under New

---

[69] Pub L No 91-452, Title X, § 1001(a), 84 Stat 951 (1970), codified at 18 USC § 3661 (2000). The provision was enacted as part of the Organized Crime Control Act of 1970, which provided for enhanced sentences for "dangerous special offender[s]," requiring proof of that status only to on a preponderance of the "information" at sentencing. The "no limitation on information" provision, however, was general, applying to all criminal defendants, not just those alleged to be dangerous special offenders. The House Report explaining this provision cited *Williams* as authority. HR Rep No 91-1549, 91st Cong, 2d Sess 63 (1970).

[70] *Williams*, 337 US at 246. The entire sentence, which Justice Stevens repeats in *Apprendi*, 530 US at 481, reads: "[B]oth before and since the American colonies became a nation, courts in this country and in England practiced a policy under which a sentencing judge could exercise a wide discretion in the sources and types of evidence used to assist him in determining the kind and extent of punishment to be imposed within limits fixed by law." See also *Williams*, 337 US at 247 (referring to sentencing "within fixed statutory or constitutional limits").

York law for the crime of which the jury had found the defendant guilty. Moreover, since 1798 it had been clear that the ex post facto clauses of Article I prohibit imposition of a higher punishment than the law provided at the time the crime was committed.[71]

Together, *Patterson*[72] and *Williams* map nearly, but not entirely, boundless territory in which a legislature may define and punish crimes. *Patterson* imposed virtually no substantive constraints on the conduct that may be punished, and *Williams* imposed virtually no constraint on the process by which the judge metes out punishment. The only significant limitations that the state had to accommodate were (1) the requirement of *Winship*[73] that whatever conduct the state seeks to punish must be proved beyond a reasonable doubt, and (2) the requirement, reaffirmed by *Williams*, that the punishment imposed be within the limits previously fixed by law.

It is a curiosity that *Williams* has been continually cited as good law throughout more than five decades of extraordinary change in sentencing law. Even in the three decades following *Williams*, during the remainder of the discretionary era, there were important changes in both sentencing procedures and the constitutional underpinnings of the criminal justice system more generally. Most importantly, the "criminal procedure revolution" of the 1960s transformed the constitutional understanding of the previous, adjudicatory, stage of the criminal justice process. *Gideon*,[74] *Mapp*,[75] *Duncan*,[76] and *Winship*[77] hold, respectively, that the states, as well as the federal government, have to provide counsel in felony cases, may not introduce evidence in criminal trials that was obtained in violation of the Fourth Amendment, must provide for jury trials in serious cases, and must prove every element of a crime beyond a reasonable doubt.

Capital sentencing was also constitutionally reconstructed, with the Supreme Court holding that both mandatory death sentences[78]

---

[71] US Const, Art I, § 9, cl 3 (federal), § 10, cl 1 (state); *Calder v Bull*, 3 US 386, 390 (1798).

[72] 432 US 197, discussed in Section I.A.

[73] 397 US 358, discussed in Section I.A.

[74] *Gideon v Wainwright*, 372 US 335, 343–44 (1963).

[75] *Mapp v Ohio*, 367 US 643, 650–60 (1961).

[76] *Duncan v Louisiana*, 391 US 145, 161–62 (1968).

[77] 397 US at 361.

[78] *Roberts v Louisiana*, 431 US 633, 635–37 (1977) (under Eighth and Fourteenth Amendments); *Sumner v Shuman*, 483 US 66, 78 (1987) (same).

and fully discretionary death sentences[79] are unconstitutional, and overruling the holding of *Williams* in the narrow context of the death penalty.[80] The Court also has held that capital sentencing juries may not be limited in their consideration of mitigating factors,[81] and must find at least one aggravating factor before determining that a death sentence should be imposed.[82] Even outside of the death penalty context, the Court held that "a sentence founded at least in part upon misinformation of constitutional magnitude" is invalid.[83]

Moreover, barely mentioning *Williams*, the Court held that the right to counsel applies at sentencing.[84] In 1975, defendants in federal court gained the right to review presentence reports,[85] and to present information disputing the assertions in the report.[86] Some federal courts went further in trying to bring due process protections into the sentencing phase. The United States Court of Appeals for the Fifth Circuit asserted in 1973 that the "discretion [of the

---

[79] *Furman v Georgia*, 408 US 238, 239–40 (1972) (under Eighth and Fourteenth Amendments).

[80] *Gardner v Florida*, 430 US 349, 358–62 (1977) (due process is violated if death penalty is imposed on basis of information not disclosed to defendant or his counsel).

[81] See *Lockett v Ohio*, 438 US 586, 604–05 (1978).

[82] See *Gregg v Georgia*, 428 US 153, 206 (1976).

[83] *United States v Tucker*, 404 US 443, 447 (1972). *Tucker* was foreshadowed by *Townsend v Burke*, 334 US 736 (1948), decided the year before *Williams*. In *Townsend*, the Court held that due process was violated when the sentencing judge relied extensively on false allegations of past convictions and the defendant did not have counsel; at the same time the Court noted "that mere error in resolving a question of fact on a plea of guilty by an uncounseled defendant in a noncapital case would [not] necessarily indicate a want of due process of law." Id at 741 (Jackson).

[84] *Mempa v Rhay*, 389 US 128 (1967), is the case usually cited for the proposition that the right to counsel attaches at sentencing. The Syllabus of the Court's opinion, id at 129, actually states this holding more clearly than the opinion itself. The case concerned a proceeding which was simultaneously a revocation of parole and a sentencing; the Court said that "[a]ll we decide here is that a lawyer must be afforded at this proceeding, whether it be labeled a revocation of probation or a deferred sentencing." Id at 136. *Mempa* contained no discussion of *Williams*. Ten years later, in *Gardner v Florida*, 430 US at 358, the Court confirmed that the rule in *Mempa* required counsel at sentencing, in both capital and noncapital cases. The Court noted, however, that "[t]he fact that due process applied [to sentencing] does not, of course, implicate the entire panoply of criminal trial procedural rights," id at 258 n 9, and appeared to overrule *Williams* only in the context of a capital case, id at 257 ("In 1949, when the *Williams* case was decided, no significant constitutional difference between the death penalty and lesser punishments for crime had been expressly recognized by this Court.").

[85] FRCrP 32(c)(3)(A) was amended to provide for defense access to most parts of the presentence report. See Pub L No 94-64, § 3, 89 Stat 370, 376 (1975). The provision regarding disclosure to the defendant and his attorney is now in Rule 32(e)(2).

[86] See, for example, *United States v Berrios*, 869 F2d 25 (2d Cir 1989).

sentencing judge] is not, and never has been absolute" and that "it is our duty to insure that rudimentary notions of fairness are observed in the process at which sentence is determined."[87] The United States Court of Appeals for the Second Circuit was more specific in imposing some due process limitations on fact finding at sentencing. In *United States v Fatico*,[88] it held that where sentencing hearings involve disputed factual allegations which the judge determines are relevant to his exercise of sentencing discretion, it is appropriate to hold an evidentiary hearing, with testimony and opportunity for cross-examination. The Second Circuit did not clearly establish a single burden of proof for these "*Fatico* hearings," though it did reject the argument that proof beyond a reasonable doubt is necessary.[89]

The criminal procedure revolution made a few other inroads with respect to the sanctioning process, including the right to confront and cross-examine adverse witnesses in parole revocation[90] and probation revocation hearings.[91] The parole release decision itself also underwent significant change in many jurisdictions. For instance, federal parole authorities began to use guidelines in the early 1970s, and in 1976 Congress enacted a parole reform statute that required the United States Parole Commission to issue rules that would govern the parole release decision.[92]

Yet none of these developments caused the Supreme Court to reconsider the central message for which *Williams* had come to stand: that the decision as to type and duration of sentence is not subject to procedural constraints. Thus, in the 1959 case of *Williams v Oklahoma*,[93] the Court relied on *Williams* (*v New York*) to hold that the sentencing "court's consideration of the [murder of which the defendant had previously been convicted] . . . as a circumstance

---

[87] *United States v Espinoza*, 481 F2d 553, 558 (5th Cir 1973). See also *United States v Clements*, 634 F2d 183, 186 (5th Cir 1981) (while appellate court "will not review the severity of a sentence imposed within statutory limits," it "will carefully scrutinize the judicial process" of the sentencing).

[88] 603 F2d 1053 (2d Cir 1979), affg 458 F Supp 388 (EDNY 1978) (Weinstein).

[89] 603 F2d at 1057 n 9.

[90] *Morrissey v Brewer*, 408 US 471, 487–89 (1972) (but allowing exception to confrontation requirement for good cause).

[91] *Gagnon v Scarpelli*, 422 US 778, 786 (1973) (confrontation requirement subject to exception for good cause).

[92] Pub L No 94-233, § 2, 90 Stat 220 (1976), previously codified at 18 USC § 4203(a)(1), repealed by Sentencing Reform Act of 1984, 98 Stat 2017 (see note 7).

[93] 358 US 576 (1959).

involved in the kidnaping crime cannot be said to have resulted in punishing [the defendant] a second time for the same offense."[94] In 1972, the Court approved the Federal Rules of Evidence, which expressly provided they would not apply at sentencing hearings.[95]

Six years later, the Court relied on *Williams* to reject a broad constitutional attack on the lack of procedural requirements at sentencing. In *United States v Grayson*,[96] the defendant claimed that the judge's discretionary decision to increase his sentence because of his alleged perjury at trial constituted potential double jeopardy, punishment without charge, and conviction without jury trial rights.[97] Chief Justice Burger's opinion in *Grayson* did intimate that such an increase in sentence is "permissible" only because it is relevant for the purposes of rehabilitation, whereas it would be "improper" to increase the period of incarceration "for the purpose of saving the Government the burden of bringing a separate and subsequent perjury prosecution."[98] Yet the Court ultimately dismissed this concern, concluding that as a practical matter it would be impossible to police or prove such improper judicial motivation.[99]

II. CONSTITUTIONAL RIGHTS IN CODIFIED SENTENCING REGIMES

A. THE PREVIOUS UNDERSTANDING

For Judge Frankel, the "father of sentencing reform,"[100] it was remarkable that the constitutionality of a "lawless" discretionary sentencing regime was never questioned,[101]—even as, we might add, legislatures and lower courts sought to make parole a less

---

[94] Id at 586. The majority opinion contained very little reasoning beyond reliance on *Williams v New York*. Only Justice Douglas registered a dissent, see id at 587 ("JUSTICE DOUGLAS, being of the view that petitioner was in substance tried for murder twice in violation of the guarantee against double jeopardy, dissents.").

[95] FRE 1101(d)(3), enacted as part of Pub L No 93-595, § 3, 88 Stat 1926, 1947 (1975). The Advisory Committee noted that this rule "is not intended as a expression as to when due process or other constitutional provisions may require an evidentiary hearing." 56 FRD 183, 351 (1972).

[96] 438 US 41 (1978).

[97] Id at 45. The defendant also claimed that considering alleged trial perjury unconstitutionally burdened his right to testify, id at 55. The three dissenting Justices agreed with this claim. Id at 55 (Stewart dissenting).

[98] Id at 53 (majority)

[99] Id at 53–54.

[100] See 128 Cong Rec S 26503 (Sept 30, 1982) (Sen Kennedy).

[101] See note 67.

discretionary and more uniform system and to make judicial sentencing more of an adversary, fact-finding proceeding.[102] What may be even more remarkable is that when "law" was brought into the sentencing stage, as Judge Frankel sought, *Williams* remained the basis for the nearly universal understanding[103] that the due process and other constitutional protections governing "all criminal prosecutions" (in the words of the Sixth Amendment) still do not apply.

As recounted at length elsewhere,[104] reform efforts directed at parole were ultimately overtaken by another, more significant campaign to transform the way criminal sanctions are determined—the movement to codify a law of sentencing (often accompanied by the abolition of most aspects of parole). To summarize the long, complicated story: As faith in the rehabilitative model waned, and as concern grew about disparities and asserted inequalities in sentences, sentencing reformers and their legislative allies sought both to reduce judicial discretion in sentencing and to minimize or abolish parole.[105] The major juridical innovation of modern sentencing reformers has been the "sentencing factor."[106]

---

[102] See Section I.B.

[103] But see Lear, 40 UCLA L Rev at 1218–38 (cited in note 58) (arguing in 1993 that Fifth and Sixth Amendment rights should attach to finding of aggravating factors under the FSG, and questioning applicability of *Williams* and its progeny). Many other scholars and judges argued before *Apprendi* that the FSG's requirement that the defendant be punished for "relevant conduct" and other nonconviction facts violates fairness and constitutional due process values.

[104] See Stith and Cabranes, *Fear of Judging* at 29–48 (cited in note 10); Tonry, *Sentencing Matters* at 27–31 (cited in note 10); Kate Stith and Steve Y. Koh, *The Politics of Sentencing Reform: The Legislative History of the Federal Sentencing Guidelines*, 28 Wake Forest L Rev 223, 230–81 (1993).

[105] The loss of faith in the rehabilitative model of sanctioning was the primary reason for the elimination of *parole* (and the indeterminate sentencing that went with it). The even more significant impetus for restrictions on *judicial discretion* was the desire to reduce interjudge disparity in sentencing. At the time the federal Sentencing Reform Act was enacted, it was generally recognized that federal parole policies had the effect of reducing disparity, but parole would no longer be needed to perform that function once judges' discretion was significantly limited. See Stith and Koh, 28 Wake Forest L Rev at 229 (cited in note 104).

[106] The term "sentencing factor" did not appear in United States Reports until 1986, in *McMillan v Pennsylvania*, 477 US 79, 86 (1986), as Justice Stevens noted in *Apprendi*, 530 US at 485. But, not surprisingly, the concept's origins can be traced back farther. For several decades prior to the 1980s, state penal codes (following the Model Penal Code) had listed a variety of general considerations that sentencing judges should or could take into account; these were advisory in nature and were often stated at a high level of generalization, such as "protection of society" or the amenability of the defendant to rehabilitation. See Model Penal Code, § 210.6(3) (Aggravating circumstances), § 210.6(4) (Mitigating circumstances) (ALI, Proposed Official Draft, 1962). Independently, as capital

The explicit purpose of sentencing factors, which may be aggravating or mitigating, is to reduce the discretionary authority of the sentencing judge. In general, the presence of a mitigating factor allows a judge to impose a lower sentence or a less severe form of punishment altogether, while the presence of an aggravating factor allows a judge to impose a higher sentence. In sentencing systems (such as the FSG) that require a judge to choose a particular sentence within a specified range, mitigating factors generally lower both ends of the range—the maximum and the minimum—while aggravating factors generally increase both the maximum and the minimum. There are several other variants. For instance, some statutory schemes provide for aggravating factors that only trigger or raise the mandatory minimum sentence; in other schemes, aggravating factors only raise the maximum sentence.

The statutory placement of sentencing factors also varies among jurisdictions. Sentencing factors may be stated in the statutory definition of the crime itself. Occasionally, they are newly specified in stand-alone sentencing enhancement statutes (most commonly for "hate crimes," crimes where a weapon is used, and crimes committed by prior felons). Finally, sentencing factors may be specified in binding "guidelines," which themselves may be codified in a statute (as in the state of Washington, for example) or promulgated as administrative regulations duly issued by an agency that has been delegated such rule-making authority (as with the FSG and in some state systems).[107]

The constitutional basics explored above leave little doubt that a legislature, with its broad power to define crimes and punishments, may define an array of sentencing factors as a way of reducing judicial discretion in sentencing. *Patterson* affirms that there are few if any limitations on the power of the legislature to define crimes and to provide for *mitigating* factors (such as the partial defense at issue in that case) that lessen the degree of the crime

---

punishment jurisprudence developed in the late 1970s, the concept of "aggravating" and "mitigating" circumstances took on greater significance. In particular, finding at least one aggravating circumstance became a prerequisite for imposing a capital sentence. See *Gregg v Georgia*, 428 US 153, 193–95 (1976). Most of the sentencing reform efforts of the 1980s and 1990s refined the definitions of sentencing factors and applied them in noncapital cases.

[107] For a recent discussion of the variety of state sentencing systems, see Anne Skove, Nat'l Center for State Courts, *Blakely v. Washington: Implications for State Courts* (July 16, 2004).

or the severity of punishment.[108] Moreover, the long history of parole, as well as the Supreme Court's decisions addressing parole, suggest that there are few if any constraints on the power of a legislature to delegate to an administrative agency the authority to mitigate punishment, either within a fully discretionary system or through a system of rules or guidelines.[109]

However, the legislative specification of *aggravating* sentencing factors that increase punishment raises two fundamental constitutional questions. The first is whether an administrative agency may, consistent with separation of powers principles, exercise broad authority to formulate aggravating sentencing factors and specify their impact on the type and severity of sentence that may be lawfully imposed. Soon after the FSG became effective in the late 1980s, *Mistretta v United States*[110] answered this question in the affirmative, but only by adopting two bald fictions: (1) that the United States Sentencing Commission is "an independent commission in the judicial branch,"[111] and (2) that the Commission's rules "do not bind or regulate the primary conduct of the public or vest in the Judicial Branch the legislative responsibility for establishing minimum and maximum penalties for every crime."[112] Armed with these fictions, the Court could claim that the Commission is not engaged in "the legislative business of

---

[108] See 432 US 197, discussed in Section I.A.

[109] See *Miller v Florida*, 482 US 423, 434–35 (1987) (discussing in *dicta* reasons that ex post facto prohibition does not apply to parole); *United States v Addonizio*, 442 US 178, 179 (1979) (sentencing court may not grant collateral relief to defendant when change in parole policies increases actual duration of sentence).

[110] 488 US 361 (1989).

[111] Id at 368, citing 28 USC § 991(a). This statutory characterization of the Sentencing Commission was in the first bill introduced by Senator Kennedy in 1977, a bill that provided for a sentencing commission whose members would be appointed by the United States Judicial Conference. The characterization remained even when the proposed legislation was altered to provide for presidential appointment and Senate confirmation. See Stith and Koh, 28 Wake Forest L Rev at 254 (cited in note 104). See also id at 280 ("[*Mistretta*] accepted at face value this statutory figleaf, obfuscating the obvious functional placement of the Commission under the control of the elected branches of government.").

In 2003, Congress amended the Sentencing Reform Act to provide that "no more than" (rather than "at least") three of the seven Commissioners may be judges, see PROTECT Act of 2003, Pub L No 108-21, § 401(n)(1), 117 Stat 667, 676 (2003), amending 28 USC § 991(a) (Supp 2004). This change in the lawful makeup of the Commission makes even more ridiculous the pretense that the Commission is in the "judicial branch" and challenges the fictional account of *Mistretta* even on its own terms. See also Steven L. Chanenson, *Hoist with Their Own Petard?* 17 Fed Sent Rptr 20 (2004).

[112] 488 US at 396.

determining what conduct should be criminalized,"[113] and that the FSG "do no more than fetter the discretion of sentencing judges to do what they have done for generations—impose sentences within the broad limits established by Congress."[114] Of course, what "sentencing judges . . . have done for generations" is a reference to the exercise of sentencing discretion, as upheld by *Williams*.[115]

Even if we assume for the sake of argument that the Court's account of the actual operation of the FSG is accurate, the Court's position in *Mistretta* boils down to the proposition that if it is constitutional for individual judges to exercise sentencing discretion within the limits set by statutes defining crimes (and *Williams* says it is), then it is also constitutional for the "judicial branch," acting in some more collective or centralized manner, to set down sentencing rules that inhabit that same "discretionary" space. In both situations, the end result is a criminal sentence within statutory limits, and the sentence has been determined by the judicial branch. Any "law" that is being pronounced in the FSG binds only sentencing judges, and this law is made by the judicial branch itself. In sum, *Mistretta* is premised on *Williams*, in combination with the two fictional characterizations of the FSG. Only Justice Scalia dissented in *Mistretta*, insisting that the FSG are "significant, legally binding prescriptions governing application of governmental power against provide individuals"[116] and that such broad delegation of lawmaking power—the creation of a "junior-varsity Congress"—violates the Constitution.[117]

The second constitutional question raised by the use of aggravating sentencing factors is whether it is constitutional to bring "law" to sentencing without subjecting this law to the limitations and procedures found in the Fifth and Sixth Amendments and elsewhere in the Constitution. This question is even more fundamental and applies to states as well as the federal government. A few years before *Mistretta*, in a case involving a newly enacted state law that employed an aggravating sentencing factor, the Court also answered the question in the affirmative, though by

[113] Id at 407.

[114] Id at 396.

[115] See Section I.B.

[116] 488 US at 413 (Scalia dissenting).

[117] Id at 427 (Scalia dissenting).

only a 5–4 majority. *McMillan v Pennsylvania*,[118] decided in 1986, explicitly made the "greater includes lesser" argument that also underlies *Mistretta*. That is, given *Williams*'s holding that the Due Process Clause permits judges to exercise unfettered discretion in determining the extent of punishment, it must also satisfy due process for the state to replace this discretionary space with rules that provide *more* "process," by specifying which facts warrant a greater or lesser punishment. Indeed, it would be paradoxical to hold that *some* law, here taking the form of codified sentencing factors and fact finding by judges under a preponderance of the evidence standard, is worse than virtually *no* law at all, as was the case under fully discretionary regime.

The sentencing factor at issue in *McMillan* was legislatively codified in the form of a 1982 "Mandatory Sentencing Law" that required at least a specified minimum sentence if the sentencing judge concluded, by a preponderance of the evidence, that the defendant had "visibly possessed a firearm" during the crime of conviction.[119] The majority opinion by Justice Rehnquist stated that this provision "gives no impression of having been tailored to permit the visible possession finding to be a tail which wags the dog of the substantive offense"[120] or to "evade" the rule of *Winship*.[121] The majority understood the lesson of *Patterson* to be that, barring such wag-the-dog circumstances,[122] *Winship*'s requirement of a heightened standard of proof "for every fact necessary to constitute the offense charged"[123] does not apply "to facts not formally identified as elements of the offense charged."[124] The aggravating factor at issue in *McMillan* neither altered the crime of which the defendant had been convicted nor increased the range of punishment to which he was exposed. Rather, it "operate[d] solely to limit the sentencing court's discretion in selecting a penalty within the range already available to it without the special

---

[118] 477 US 79 (1986).

[119] Id at 81.

[120] Id at 88.

[121] Id at 89, discussing *Winship*, 397 US 258 (1970).

[122] The Court noted that it had "never attempted to define precisely" what constitute such exceptional circumstances. See 477 US at 86.

[123] 397 US at 364.

[124] 477 US at 86.

finding of visible possession of a firearm."[125] Citing *Williams* for the proposition that "[s]entencing courts have traditionally heard evidence and found facts without any prescribed burden of proof at all,"[126] the opinion professed "some difficulty fathoming why the due process calculus would change simply because the legislature has seen fit to provide sentencing courts with additional guidance."[127] Thus, as law was introduced to the formerly discretionary system of sentencing, the Court relied on the "*Williams* paradox" to reject application of due process guarantees.

Justice Stevens's dissent in *McMillan* urged that the statutory aggravating factor functionally operated as an element of the crime "[b]ecause [it] . . . describes conduct that the Pennsylvania Legislature obviously intended to prohibit, and because it mandates lengthy incarceration for the same," and hence under *Winship* had to be proved beyond a reasonable doubt to a jury.[128] Averring to the argument in the *Patterson* dissent,[129] Justice Stevens recognized that his "distinction between aggravating and mitigating factors" had been criticized as "formalistic."[130] Justice Stevens, having joined the majority opinion in *Patterson*, responded to this complaint by suggesting that "the continued functioning of the democratic process" would constrain legislatures from such transparent rewriting of the criminal code.[131]

No one on the Court seemed to notice any inconsistency between *McMillan* and a case decided unanimously the next year, *Miller v Florida*, which applied the ex post facto prohibition to changes in a state's statutory sentencing guidelines. *Miller* characterized the guidelines at issue there as "law . . . [not] simply

---

[125] Id at 88.

[126] Id at 91.

[127] Id at 92.

[128] Id at 96 (Stevens dissenting). In Justice Stevens's view, "*Winship* and *Patterson* teach that a State may not advance the objectives of its criminal laws at the expense of the accurate fact finding owed to the criminally accused." Id at 102 (Stevens dissenting).

[129] 432 US 197 at 224 n 8 (Powell dissenting). See discussion in text accompanying note 40.

[130] 477 US at 100–01 (Stevens dissenting).

[131] Id (Stevens dissenting). Two of the other three dissenters had dissented in *Patterson*, see 432 US at 216 (Powell dissenting, joined by Brennan and Marshall). Joined by Justice Blackmun in *McMillan*, they agreed with Justice Stevens that the aggravating sentencing factor should be treated as an "element" of the crime for purposes of the *Winship* rule, but also argued, in an echo of *Mullaney*, 421 US at 698, that the Court should leave open whether the absence of a mitigating factor might also be an "element" for constitutional purposes. See id at 93–94 (Marshall dissenting).

flexible 'guideposts' for use in the exercise of discretion."[132] *Miller*, unlike *McMillan*, seemed to recognize that once "law" is introduced to sentencing, constitutional constraints on law's implementation become applicable.

For more than a decade after *McMillan*, it seemed that *Williams* would provide constitutional protection not only to judicially determined sentencing facts that trigger a mandatory minimum sentence, as in *McMillan*, but also to those that raise maximum permissible sentences. Thus, in 1990, the Court, by a 5–4 vote, upheld a capital sentencing system in which the death penalty could be imposed only if the sentencing judge found at least one aggravating circumstance.[133]

Between 1993 and 1998, the Court heard four cases that raised various due process challenges to the FSG. In the first two cases, the Court explicitly relied on *Williams* and its progeny to conclude that the due process protections of trial are not applicable in the context of sentencing under the FSG. In upholding the Guideline requiring an upward adjustment of the sentencing range upon a finding of obstruction of justice,[134] a unanimous Court held that the case was controlled by *United States v Grayson*,[135] the pre-FSG case that held sentencing judges could take perjury at trial into account. It was irrelevant, in the Court's estimation, whether the increase in punishment "stems from a congressional mandate [or] from a court's discretionary judgment."[136] Two years later, in *Witte v United States*,[137] a majority of six Justices followed *Williams v Oklahoma*[138] in holding that the constitutional prohibition of double jeopardy was not violated when a defendant's sentence was mandatorily enhanced under the FSG on the basis of an uncharged drug transaction, and the defendant was then separately prosecuted, convicted, and punished for the same transaction.[139]

---

[132] 482 US 423, 435 (1987) (O'Connor).

[133] *Walton v Arizona*, 497 US 639 (1990).

[134] *United States v Dunnigan*, 507 US 87 (1993).

[135] 438 US 41, cited in 507 US at 97–98. *Grayson* is discussed in text accompanying notes 96–99.

[136] *Dunnigan*, 507 US at 98.

[137] 515 US 389 (1995).

[138] 358 US 576, cited in 515 US at 398–400. *Williams v Oklahoma* is discussed in text accompanying notes 93–94.

[139] In *Witte*, Justices Scalia and Thomas concurred in the judgment on the ground that the Double Jeopardy Clause prohibits "successive prosecution, not successive punishment."

The remaining two challenges to the FSG were handled in ways that may be charitably characterized as unfortunate. In 1998, in *Edwards v United States*,[140] the defendant sought to raise, inter alia, a Sixth Amendment objection to judicial fact finding under the FSG. Curiously, the Court was able unanimously to reject the claim without ever actually discussing the applicability of the Constitution's right to jury trial to aggravating factors that increase a sentence under the FSG. Instead, Justice Breyer's opinion just assumed that there is no constitutional infirmity in the FSG's requirement that sentencing courts increase the sentencing range on the basis of "relevant conduct" not tried to the jury.[141] Perhaps *Edwards* seemed to be an easy case because just a year earlier the Court in *United States v Watts*[142] had rejected an even more direct challenge to the FSG. In *Watts*, the Court issued a per curiam opinion, without full briefing or argument, relying upon *Williams* and *McMillan* to uphold the provision of the FSG that conduct for which the jury *acquitted* the defendant nonetheless must form the basis for sentence enhancement if found by the judge using a preponderance standard.[143]

Only Justice Stevens dissented on the merits in *Watts*.[144] He reprised the now decade-old argument of his *McMillan* dissent[145]— that codified aggravating sentencing factors function as "elements"

---

515 US at 407 (Scalia concurring). Only Justice Stevens, who had written the major dissent in *McMillan*, dissented in *Witte*, arguing that by increasing punishment for unconvicted conduct, the FSG put a defendant once "in jeopardy," and that a subsequent conviction for the same conduct constituted double jeopardy, see 515 US at 411–12 (Stevens concurring in part and dissenting in part). Justice Stevens also bemoaned "the Court's failure to recognize the change in sentencing practices caused by the Guidelines." Id at 412 (Stevens concurring in part and dissenting in part).

[140] 523 US 511 (1998).

[141] See id at 514, citing United States Sentencing Guidelines (USSG) § 1B1.3 (requiring that relevant conduct be taken into account at sentencing). The jury had been instructed to convict the defendant if he distributed either powder cocaine or crack cocaine (or both), and made no special findings as to what kind of cocaine had been distributed. The judge found that both forms of cocaine had been involved, resulting in a higher sentence than could have been imposed under the FSG had only powder cocaine been distributed. Justice Breyer concluded that no Sixth Amendment issue need be addressed, because the sentence imposed was lower than the statutory maximum provided for distribution of powder cocaine. See 523 US at 515.

[142] 519 US 148 (1997) (per curiam).

[143] Id at 151–52 (citing *Williams*); id at 156 & n 2 (citing *McMillan* and noting that *Watts* is not a case in which there is "a tail which wags the dog").

[144] Id at 159 (Stevens dissenting). Justice Kennedy dissented on the ground that full briefing and argument should be set in the case, id at 170–71 (Kennedy dissenting).

[145] See text accompanying notes 128–31.

for constitutional purposes and hence must be proved to a jury beyond a reasonable doubt.[146] In *Watts*, however, Justice Stevens went even further, arguing for the first time that the reasoning of *Williams* was not applicable to the new codified sentencing regimes because such regimes are not based on the rehabilitative ideal that figured so prominently in *Williams*.[147] For the Court, though, *Williams* had determined once and for all that no "process" was due at sentencing, whether sentencing is discretionary or rule-bound. *Williams* was always the answer—*Williams* and the apparent paradox that would be created were the Court ever to require more in the way of "process" than *Williams* had blessed.

B.   THE NEW UNDERSTANDING

In *Watts*, Justice Stevens was alone. That would soon change. In retrospect, the pivotal cases were *Almendarez-Torres v United States*,[148] decided a few months after *Edwards* in 1998, and *Jones v United States*,[149] decided the next year. By only a 5–4 majority, the first case upheld a federal statute under which a felony recidivist was subject to an enhanced sentence, even though the fact of a previous conviction, found and relied upon by the sentencing judge, was neither alleged in the indictment nor part of the underlying immigration offense to which the defendant pleaded guilty.[150]

The critical dissenting opinion, in which four Justices expressed constitutional doubt about judicial fact finding of sentencing factors, was written by Justice Scalia, joined not only by Justice Stevens but also by Justices Souter and Ginsburg.[151] The dissent's language clearly foreshadows *Apprendi*, *Blakely*, and the challenges to the FSG now before the Supreme Court. The four dissenting Justices believed that the fact of a previous conviction should have been "treated as an element of [the] crime—to be charged in the

---

[146] See 519 US at 166 (Stevens dissenting).

[147] Id at 165 (Stevens dissenting).

[148] 523 US 224 (1998).

[149] 526 US 227 (1999).

[150] See *Almendarez-Torres*, 523 US at 247 (Breyer joined by Rehnquist, O'Connor, Kennedy, and Thomas).

[151] Id at 248 (Scalia dissenting).

indictment, and found beyond a reasonable doubt by a jury,"[152] because they were "genuinely doubtful" that

> the Constitution permits a judge (rather than a jury) to determine by a mere preponderance of the evidence (rather than beyond a reasonable doubt) a fact that increases the maximum penalty to which a criminal defendant is subject . . . .[153]

The following year, in *Jones*, Justice Thomas joined with the four dissenters to form a new majority—what would become the *Apprendi* and *Blakely* majorities. This new five Justice majority determined that an apparent aggravating factor in the federal carjacking statute should be interpreted as a statutory element of the crime, because reading the statute to allow an enhanced sentence upon judicial finding of the factor would raise "grave and doubtful constitutional questions."[154] Here a footnote significantly alluded to the constitutional rights to proof beyond a reasonable doubt and to jury trial.[155] The Court sought to distinguish *Almendarez-Torres* because of the special nature of the factual finding in that case.[156]

When the *Jones* issue arose in the context of a state statute, the *Jones* majority could not construe the statute to avoid the constitutional issue.[157] It had to face the Constitution itself, and did so the next year, in *Apprendi*.[158] Apprendi had pleaded guilty to firearms offenses. As required by New Jersey's "hate crime" law, the judge imposed an enhanced sentence because he found, by a preponderance of the evidence, that the crime had been motivated by racial animus. Had the "hate crime" allegation not been triggered by the motion of the prosecutor at the sentencing stage, or

---

[152] Id (Scalia dissenting).

[153] Id at 251 (Scalia dissenting).

[154] *Jones*, 526 US at 239, quoting *Attorney General v Delaware & Hudson Co.*, 213 US 366, 408 (1909). Justice Souter wrote the majority opinion, which was joined by Justices Stevens, Scalia, Thomas, and Ginsburg.

[155] See 526 US at 251 n 11.

[156] See id at 248–49 (referring to "tradition of regarding treating recidivism as a sentencing factor," and to the "distinctive significance of recidivism").

[157] The doctrine of constitutional doubt, see *Delaware & Hudson Co.*, 213 US at 408 ("where a statute is susceptible of two constructions," one of which is constitutionally doubtful, the Court should avoid the constitutional question by adopting the other construction), only applies in cases involving the construction of a federal statute.

[158] 530 US 466.

had the judge not found racial bias on this more-likely-than-not standard, the statutory range within which the judge could fix sentence was five to ten years; application of the hate crime enhancement led to a higher statutory range, and the judge imposed a sentence of twelve years. For the reasons it had suggested in *Jones*, the Court held that judicial application of the hate crimes enhancement violated the Constitution.[159]

Apprendi was surely a triumph for its author, Justice Stevens, who reiterated some of his earlier dissent in *Watts*. He stressed that *Williams* only upheld the constitutionality of allowing a judge to determine sentence "within the limits fixed by law."[160] New Jersey's hate crime law altered those limits—by providing for a higher sentencing range for racially motivated crimes. Thus, the *Apprendi* Court reasoned, hate is the "functional equivalent of an element of a greater offense than the one covered by the jury's guilty verdict."[161] *Apprendi* self-consciously described its own holding in a way that avoided disturbing *Almendarez-Torres*: "*Other than the fact of a prior conviction*, any fact that increases the penalty for a crime beyond the prescribed statutory maximum must be submitted to a jury, and proved beyond a reasonable doubt."[162]

But the most far-reaching opinion in *Apprendi* was that of Justice Thomas, in which he explained the reason for the shift in his vote between *Almendarez-Torres* in 1998, and *Jones* and *Apprendi* in the course of the next two years.[163] In *Almendarez-Torres*, he candidly observed, he had "succumbed" to a logical "error"—assuming that the "traditional" sentencing regime, in which judges had discretion to take nonconviction facts into account, could be equated with a codified sentencing regime in which the legislature specifies relevant facts for sentencing.[164] He explained:

> [T]his approach just defines away the real issue. What matters is *the way* by which a fact enters into the sentence. If a fact is by law the basis for imposing or increasing punishment—for

---

[159] See id at 476, citing *Jones*, 526 US 227.

[160] 530 US at 481, quoting *Williams*, 337 US at 246.

[161] 530 US at 494 n 19.

[162] Id at 490 (emphasis in original). Whether *Almendarez-Torres* will survive recent developments is uncertain. See note 191.

[163] See id at 499 (Thomas concurring).

[164] See id at 520 (Thomas concurring).

establishing or increasing the prosecution's entitlement—it is an element.[165]

In other words, it does not matter whether the aggravating "fact" specified by the legislature is the kind of fact that judges might "traditionally" take into account in exercising discretion. Once the fact is specified "by law [as] the basis for imposing or increasing punishment," a new element for at least some constitutional purposes has been added to the crime itself.

Justice Thomas went even further than Justice Scalia had gone in his *Almendarez-Torres* dissent and further than Justice Stevens had gone in the *Apprendi* majority, concluding that aggravating facts that raise the minimum penalty (as in *McMillan*)[166] are likewise the constitutional equivalent of an "element"—because whether a sentencing factor has the effect of raising the maximum or the minimum (or both, as under the FSG), it increases the authorized punishment.[167] Two years later, in *Harris v United States*,[168] three others in the *Apprendi* majority (Justices Stevens, Souter, and Ginsburg) joined with Justice Thomas in urging that *McMillan* be overruled.[169] Justice Scalia, however, joined the four *Apprendi* dissenters to uphold judicial fact finding of an aggravating factor that raises the minimum but not the maximum lawful sentence.[170] For reasons he has not explained and that are not immediately apparent, Justice Scalia remained of the view that the only facts requiring jury trial are those that increase the maximum penalty.[171]

---

[165] Id at 521 (Thomas concurring) (emphasis in original).

[166] 477 US 79. *McMillan* is discussed in Section II.A.

[167] See id at 522 (Thomas concurring).

[168] 536 US 545 (2002).

[169] See id at 572 (Thomas dissenting).

[170] See 536 US at 556–57 (concluding that *Apprendi* does not require overruling *McMillan*) (Kennedy joined by Rehnquist, Scalia, and O'Connor). The fifth vote for upholding *McMillan* was provided by Justice Breyer. See id at 569 (concluding that *Apprendi* and *McMillan* cannot "easily" be distinguished, but expressing the view that *Apprendi* was wrong and that he "cannot yet accept its rule") (Breyer concurring).

[171] Justice Scalia had joined the majority opinion in *McMillan* in 1986. See 477 US 79. Yet the tension, even discontinuity, between *McMillan* and *Harris*, on the one hand, and *Apprendi* on the other, seems obvious enough. Informed accusation, jury trial, and proof beyond a reasonable doubt would appear critical whenever the legislature specifies a fact that enhances punishment, whether that enhancement raises the punishment floor or ceiling. If *Harris* and *McMillan* are not overruled, legislatures would be unconstrained by constitutional requirements of accusation and proof in specifying aggravating factors triggering mandatory minimum sentences; in addition to statutory minimum sentences, guide-

Harris appeared to retreat from *Apprendi*. Yet on the same day in June 2002 that *Harris* was handed down, the Court actually extended *Apprendi* in a case where the aggravating fact only permissively, rather than mandatorily, increased the defendant's maximum sentence. In *Ring v Arizona*,[172] the Court applied *Apprendi* to a capital sentencing system in which the death penalty could only be imposed if the judge found, beyond a reasonable doubt, legislatively specified aggravating circumstances. The five Justices in the *Apprendi* majority (now joined by Justice Kennedy, and with Justice Breyer concurring on other grounds) held this system unconstitutional. *Ring* explicitly overruled the Court's 1990 decision which had relied on *Willliams* to uphold judicial fact finding as a prerequisite to imposition of the death penalty.[173] We may note that in *Ring*, the legislature's specification of a sentencing factor had the effect of increasing judicial discretion by authorizing the judge to impose a higher sentence but not requiring her to do so. The Supreme Court held that the system was unconstitutional for the same reason that application of New Jersey's "hate crime" law in *Apprendi* was unconstitutional—facts increasing the maximum sentence must be found by a jury, not a judge.[174]

Absent a change of heart by one of the Justices in the *Apprendi* majority, the result in *Blakely*[175] was foreordained by *Apprendi* and *Ring*. The rule expressed in *Apprendi* is broad: ". . . [A]ny fact that increases the penalty for a crime beyond the prescribed statutory maximum must be submitted to a jury, and proved beyond a reasonable doubt."[176] The application of this rule to the facts before the Court in *Blakely* is straightforward. In assessing the constitutionality of Washington's sentencing laws, the United States Supreme Court was, of course, bound by the authoritative

---

lines systems could be altered to provide that aggravating sentencing factors raise only the minimum of the sentencing range, with the maximum in all cases being that allowed for the statutory offense of conviction.

Blakely does not address *Harris*, thereby leaving it intact for the time being. Whether *Harris* will fall, especially if *Booker* and *Fanfan* follow *Blakely*, is one of the many present uncertainties in the aftermath of *Blakely*, discussion of which is beyond the scope of this essay.

[172] 536 US 584 (2002).

[173] See id at 609, overruling *Walton v Arizona*, 497 US 639 (1990). *Walton* is discussed in text accompanying note 133.

[174] See 530 US at 609.

[175] 124 S Ct 2531.

[176] 530 US at 490.

construction of those laws by the Washington Supreme Court. As thus construed, the Washington system increased the statutorily prescribed maximum sentence if the judge found one or more aggravating facts beyond the facts of conviction.[177] The rule of *Apprendi* fit like a glove.

There was, to be sure, a nontraditional sentencing system at issue in *Blakely*. In Washington, sentencing factors and their effects on sentences were codified in a "Sentencing Reform Act,"[178] which was enacted into law by the state's legislature—rather than specified in discrete criminal statutes defining crimes (as in *Jones*) or in stand-alone sentencing enhancement statutes (as in *Apprendi*). Like most comprehensive sentencing reforms, Washington's Sentencing Reform Act (which was drafted by the Washington State Sentencing Commission) was an overlay on the state's traditional criminal code. Under the Act, the defendant's calculated sentencing range depended both on the crime of which he was convicted and on the presence of nonconviction aggravating and mitigating factors.[179] In the case before the Court, Blakely had pleaded guilty to second-degree kidnapping, which under the criminal code was a "class B felony" with a maximum penalty of ten years in prison. Washington's Sentencing Reform Law provided a relatively low "standard" sentencing range (thirteen to seventeen months) for this crime, but also specified several aggravating facts that would raise the standard range.[180] Interestingly, in 1983, long before *Apprendi* (and, to be sure, before the Court's 1986 decision in *McMillan*), the Washington legislature had decided to treat aggravating facts raising the "standard" range as equivalent to elements of the crime, requiring that they be charged in the information or indictment and proved to a jury.[181] When Blakely pleaded guilty, he had stipulated to one such aggravator (use of a firearm), which

---

[177] See *Blakely*, 124 S Ct at 2535, citing relevant Washington criminal statutes and *State v Gore*, 143 Wash2d 288, 21 P3d 262, 277 (2001).

[178] See 124 S Ct at 2534.

[179] The operation of Washington's statutory guidelines system, which was enacted into law in 1983, is described in Washington Sentencing Guidelines Commission, *Adult Sentencing Guidelines Manual 2003* I-22 (2003).

[180] See 124 S Ct at 2535.

[181] See Wash Rev Code § 9.94A.125 (2000), now codified as § 9.94A.602 (2004) (requiring sentence enhancement for deadly weapon; requiring jury trial and special verdict; originally enacted in 1983); *Petition of Gunter*, 102 Wash2d 769, 689 P2d 1074 (1984) (jury must find fact beyond a reasonable doubt).

raised his standard sentencing range to 49 to 53 months.[182] There was no *Apprendi* problem in the calculation of this standard range, for there was no judicial fact finding involved.

Washington's Sentencing Reform Act also provided, however, for an "exceptional" sentence, allowing (but not requiring) the judge to go above or below the standard range if she found "substantial and compelling reasons justifying an exceptional sentence."[183] If that were all the Washington Sentencing Reform Act provided, then it would be possible to argue that *Williams*, not *Apprendi*, controlled. *Williams*, after all, had upheld discretionary sentencing. If Washington simply allowed judges to exercise their judgment that a sentence higher (or lower) than the standard sentence is "justified," it would be barely distinguishable from *Williams*.

But Washington did more than that; it provided for judicial fact finding as a prerequisite to imposition of the exceptional sentence and required the judge to state his reasons on the record,[184] just as Arizona had required in *Ring*.[185] Any doubt that Washington required judicial fact finding for the imposition of an exceptional sentence had been removed by the Washington Supreme Court in an earlier case, holding that appellate review would be under a "clearly erroneous" standard, the standard usually applied to fact finding by a lower court.[186] And any ambiguity as to whether the judge could impose an exceptional sentence only on the basis of the crime of conviction itself was removed when the Washington Supreme Court further clarified that the stated reasons justifying an exceptional sentence must "take[] into account factors other than those which are used in computing" the standard sentencing range.[187]

In Blakely's case, the prosecutor had not sought an exceptional sentence. But the sentencing judge on his own initiative believed

---

[182] See 124 S Ct at 2535.

[183] See id, citing Wash Rev Code Ann § 9.94A.120(2) (West, 2000), now codified as § 9.94A.535 (2004).

[184] See 124 S Ct at 2535, citing Wash Rev Code Ann § 9.94A.120(3) (West, 2000).

[185] See *Ring*, 536 US at 592–93 (citing provisions of Arizona law).

[186] See 124 S Ct at 2535, citing *State v Gore*, 21 P3d at 277 (2001).

[187] See 124 S Ct at 2535, citing *State v Gore*, 21 P3d at 277.

that a statutory aggravating factor ("deliberate cruelty")[188] might be present. After a three-day bench hearing that included testimony from mental health experts,[189] the judge made a finding that this aggravating factor was present. The judge further decided that the presence of this factor warranted an exceptional sentence higher than the 53 months at the top of the standard sentencing range (but still below the 10-year maximum for a "class B felony"). He sentenced Blakely to 90 months in prison.[190]

All the Court had to do to decide *Blakely* was to apply the rule exactly as *Apprendi* had stated it: "Other than the fact of a prior conviction,[191] any fact that increases the penalty for a crime beyond the prescribed statutory maximum must be submitted to a jury and proved beyond a reasonable doubt."[192] Blakely's sentence violated *Apprendi* because a "fact that increase[d] the penalty for [his] crime beyond the prescribed statutory maximum" was found by a judge, instead of a jury, and was found to a preponderance of the evidence, instead of beyond a reasonable doubt. *Blakely* presented an opportunity to clarify that the term "statutory maximum" refers to any applicable sentencing statute, whether a traditional criminal statute (as in *Jones*), a special enhancement statute (as in *Apprendi*), or a general sentencing code (as in *Blakely*).

Instead, Justice Scalia's opinion for the majority in *Blakely* em-

---

[188] See 124 S Ct at 2535, citing Wash Rev Code Ann § 9.94A.390(a)(h)(iii) (West, 2000), now codified as § 9.94A.535(2)(h) (2004). The provision includes "domestic violence with deliberate cruelty" in a nonexhaustive list of aggravating factors justifying an exceptional sentence.

[189] See 124 S Ct at 2535 (referring to three-day bench hearing with testimony from, inter alia, "medical experts"); *State v Blakely*, 111 Wash App 851, 860, 47 P3d 149, 154 (2002) (noting that testimony was from "mental health experts"), rev den, 148 Wash2d 1010, 62 P3d 889 (2003).

[190] 124 S Ct at 2535–36.

[191] In quoting *Apprendi*'s holding, see 124 S Ct at 2536, *Blakely* included this preliminary phrase effectively safeguarding *Almendarez-Torres*, see discussion at text accompanying notes 148–53. Yet the majority opinion in *Blakely* never mentions the case by name nor otherwise adverts to the issue it raised. Inasmuch as Justice Thomas has said his vote in that case is was in error, see text at note 164, all five Justices in the *Apprendi* and *Blakely* majority have expressed disagreement with *Almendarez-Torres*. No historical reason has been suggested for treating the fact of a prior conviction differently from other facts triggering higher punishment. See *Almendarez-Torres*, 523 US at 258–62 (Scalia dissenting), and *Apprendi*, 530 US at 501–18 (Thomas concurring). Nor is it clear how much "protection" the *Almendarez-Torres* exception really provides from the *Blakely* rule, since many sentencing enhancement factors relating to recidivism require more complex fact finding than the relatively simple question of whether the defendant had a prior conviction. See O'Connell, 16 Fed Sent Rptr at 351–52 (cited in note 17).

[192] 530 US at 490. *Apprendi* is discussed in text accompanying notes 158–67.

barked on a more ambitious journey, holding that the "'statutory maximum' for *Apprendi* purposes" is not the maximum sentence authorized by statute for the crime of conviction, but

> the maximum sentence a judge may impose *solely on the basis of the facts reflected in the jury verdict or admitted by the defendant.* In other words, the relevant "statutory maximum" is not the maximum sentence a judge may impose after finding additional facts, but the maximum he may impose *without* any additional findings.[193]

It seems clear that these words were chosen by Justice Scalia with the FSG in mind.[194] The language *Blakely* self-consciously uses to restate the *Apprendi* rule makes irrelevant the major distinction between the system in the state of Washington and the system headquartered in Washington, D.C.—that the FSG are not embodied in a statute, but rather, in administrative regulations. *Blakely* would have come out the same way if the Court had just said that the "'statutory maximum' for *Apprendi* purposes" is the maximum sentence provided for *in* a statute. Instead, in *Blakely* the word "statutory" is transmuted to mean "lawful" or "authorized by law." At several points the Court dispenses with the word "statutory" entirely, using the word "law" instead. For instance:

> When a judge inflicts punishment that the jury's verdict alone does not allow, the jury has not found all the facts "which the law makes essential to the punishment," and the judge exceeds his proper authority.[195]

---

[193] 124 S Ct at 2536–37 (emphasis in original) (citations omitted).

[194] While it would appear clearly to encompass systems like the FSG, the *Blakely* rule is ambiguous or incomplete in other important respects. Questions remaining include: (1) Does a "fact" include issues such as whether the defendant is "amenable to rehabilitation," or whether "general deterrence is of overriding significance" in the particular case? (2) May facts other than those specifically alleged in the indictment or information be "reflected in the jury verdict"? (3) When a defendant pleads guilty, does he only "admit" the facts formally alleged (or stipulated at the plea hearing), or may statements at the hearing (or silence in the face of statements) constitute further "admissions"? (4) Does a defendant "admit" any facts in an *Alford* plea (in which the defendant denies his guilt even while pleading guilty)? Justice Scalia also noted that defendants could "waive" their *Apprendi* and *Blakely* rights in plea agreements, including consenting to judicial fact finding, see 124 S Ct at 2541. It is unlikely, however, that a defendant may constitutionally waive the standard of proof beyond a reasonable doubt; this has been the assumption in both state and federal practice since *Winship*, 397 US 359 (1970). Perhaps most significantly, it is unclear how double jeopardy principles apply to the rules in both *Apprendi* and *Blakely*, or whether the rules place any limitation on imposition of consecutive sentences.

[195] 124 S Ct at 2537, quoting J. Bishop, 1 *Criminal Procedure* § 87 at 55 (2d ed, 1872).

At another point *Blakely* states that the jury must find "the facts essential to lawful imposition of the penalty."[196] These statements of the rule of *Blakely* encompass any fact which, if found, increases the *maximum lawful* sentence that a judge may impose.

A lawful maximum sentence may, of course, be determined solely by reference to statutes—as in *Jones*, *Apprendi*, *Ring*, and *Blakely*. But it may also be determined pursuant to statutes that do not themselves specify sentence durations, but instead delegate some or all of that authority to a rule-making agency, as in the federal sentencing system. The Sentencing Reform Act that Congress enacted in 1984 is itself a *law* that requires judges to determine criminal sentences (including both calculation of the sentencing range, and any departure from that range) in accordance with the rules promulgated by the Sentencing Commission, the FSG.[197] The FSG do not themselves become law until they are laid before Congress for 180 days.[198] And the Supreme Court has held that the Sentencing Commission's "Policy Statements" and "Commentary," as well as those rules it formally denominates "Guidelines," have the full force and effect of law, equivalent to statutory limitations on sentencing authority.[199]

Accordingly, under the Sentencing Reform Act of 1984, the FSG do exactly what *Blakely* forbids. The regime created by Congress and the Sentencing Commission requires judges to find aggravating as well as mitigating facts, and the finding of aggravating facts increases the sentence that the judge may (in most cases, must) lawfully impose. As I have elsewhere noted:

> In effect, the Commission has invented numerous new "Guidelines crimes," each a variant of one or another statutory crime and each with its own mandated range of punishment. . . .

---

[196] 124 S Ct at 2540. See also id at 2539 (*"Apprendi . . .* ensure[s] that the judge's *authority* to sentence derives wholly from the jury's verdict.") (emphasis in original).

[197] See 18 USC § 3553(b) (2000), providing that except where departure is permitted, judge "shall impose a sentence of the kind, and within the range," set by the FSG. Moreover, departures may be imposed only as expressly permitted by the FSG or where a judge finds a fact "of a kind . . . not adequately taken into consideration" by the FSG. Id. Judicial fact finding, both in calculating the Guidelines range and in any departure decision, is subject to appellate review. See 18 USC § 3742(e) (2000).

[198] During this period, Congress may amend or disapprove of the Guidelines laid before it. 28 USC § 994(p) (2000).

[199] See *Williams v United States*, 503 US 193, 201 (1992) (Guidelines and Policy Statements are binding on federal courts); *Stinson v United States*, 508 US 36, 42–43 (1993) (Commentary also binding).

> [T]he defendant is sentenced for [this] criminal conduct without recourse to a grand jury or to a petit jury, and without the basic procedural protections of a trial, most important the requirement that the fact-finder be convinced beyond a reasonable doubt . . . .[200]

All three dissenting opinions in *Blakely* (by Justices O'Connor, Kennedy, and Breyer) recognized with varying degrees of directness that under the rule of *Blakely*, the FSG are unconstitutional as presently implemented under the Sentencing Reform Act of 1984.[201] Justice Scalia's response, in a footnote, that "we express no opinion on [the FSG]"[202] is itself pregnant with meaning for what it does *not* say. In making a similar point, the *Apprendi* majority had stated in a footnote that the Court was expressing "no view" on the FSG "beyond what this Court has already held," and had specifically cited the 1998 *Edwards* case, in which a Sixth Amendment attack on the FSG had been rejected, or at least deflected.[203] By contrast, the footnote in *Blakely* does not mention *Edwards* or any other case upholding the constitutionality of the Guidelines—including *Mistretta*.

One or more of the Justices in the *Blakely* majority may yet draw back from the clear implications of the text of *Blakely*, joining with the four dissenters to distinguish and uphold the FSG in the cases now under review. It seems unlikely that any Justice would do that, having but a few months earlier joined in a holding that speaks directly to arrangements of the sort embodied in the FSG and to the constitutional error of providing for increases in the maximum lawful sentence on the basis of judicial fact finding.

---

[200] Stith and Cabranes, *Fear of Judging* at 148, 150 (cited in note 10).

[201] See 124 S Ct at 2543, 2549–50 (presenting arguments that majority's rule invalidates FSG) (O'Connor dissenting); id at 2550–51 (expressing regret that majority imposes changes in state and federal sentencing systems without awaiting "constructive discourse" with Congress and state legislatures) (Kennedy dissenting); id at 2551–58 (discussing options of state and federal legislatures and federal prosecutors under majority's rule) (Breyer dissenting).

[202] Id at 2538 n 9 (majority). The full footnote reads:

> The United States, as *amicus curie*, urges us to affirm. It notes differences between Washington's sentencing regime and the [FSG] but questions whether those differences are constitutionally significant. See Brief for United States as *Amicus Curiae* 25–30. The Federal Guidelines are not before us, and we express no opinion on them.

[203] *Apprendi*, 530 US at 497 n 21, citing "Edwards v United States, 523 US at 515 (Breyer for a unanimous court) . . . ." *Edwards* is discussed in text accompanying notes 140–41.

III. THE PARADOX OF SENTENCING?

The majority and dissenting opinions in both *Apprendi* and *Blakely* are like the proverbial two ships passing in the night. For the majority, led by Justices Stevens and Scalia, the starting proposition is the Constitution—in particular, its requirement in criminal cases of proof beyond a reasonable doubt (under *Winship*),[204] and of jury trial (under the Sixth Amendment).[205]

The dissenters embark from a notably different point. For Justices Breyer and O'Connor in particular, the starting point is *Williams*[206] and the understanding that it is permissible under the Constitution for judges to exercise sentencing discretion. Thus, the dissents begin not with the role of the jury or with proof beyond a reasonable doubt, but with the role of the sentencing judge. As Justice Breyer notes in *Apprendi*, "In modern times, the law has left it to the sentencing judge to find those facts which (within broad sentencing limits set by the legislature) determine the sentence of a convicted offender,"[207] and *Williams* upheld the constitutionality of this system.[208]

The dissenters' principal concern is whether the legislature should be permitted to devise a new system—a better system, in their view—in order to control the sentencing disparity and arbitrariness that are inevitable consequences of the exercise of judicial discretion. For the dissenters, the issue of sentencing factors is the same as the issue of defenses in *Patterson*,[209] decided in 1977,

---

[204] See *Apprendi*, 530 US at 476–77, where Justice Stevens pronounces, "At stake in this case are constitutional protections of surpassing importance," and then quotes the Due Process Clause of the Fourteenth Amendment, the Sixth Amendment's jury clauses, and the holdings of cases enunciating the right to proof beyond a reasonable doubt, *Winship*, 397 US 358, 364 (1970), *United States v Gaudin*, 515 US 506, 508 (1995), and *Sullivan v Louisiana*, 508 US 275, 278 (1995).

[205] See *Blakely*, 124 S Ct at 2538, where Justice Scalia pronounces, "Our commitment to *Apprendi* . . . reflects not just respect for longstanding precedent, but the need to give intelligible content to the right of jury trial."

[206] 337 US 241 (1949). *Williams* is discussed in Section I.B and in text accompanying notes 84, 94, 96, 115–17, 126–27, 143–47, 208, 230.

[207] See *Apprendi*, 530 US at 555 (Breyer dissenting). See also *Blakely*, 124 S Ct at 2543 (O'Connor dissenting).

[208] *Apprendi*, 530 US at 557, noting that *Williams* upheld sentencings "without benefit of trial-type evidentiary rules" (Breyer dissenting). It is not clear that Justice Black would have agreed that in exercising discretion, judges are "find[ing]" "facts" or hearing "evidence," see text at notes 52–64.

[209] 432 US 197. *Patterson* is discussed in Section I.A and in text accompanying notes 72–73, 108–109, 129.

before the advent of sentencing reform and codified sentencing factors. They understand *Patterson* to have upheld the legislature's power to distinguish between the "elements" of a crime (which must be proven by the government beyond a reasonable doubt) and the "defenses" to the crime (which the defendant may be required to prove), while at the same time vaguely warning of "constitutional limits" beyond which a legislature could not tread.[210]

Similarly, the dissenting Justices in *Apprendi* and *Blakely* recognize that there may be constitutional limitations on the legislature's power to devise a system of criminal sentencing,[211] but would allow the legislature broad leeway to draw the line between the "crime" phase and the "punishment" phase of the criminal justice process. In charging and proving the "crime," the government must abide by the constitutional requirements of jury trial and proof beyond a reasonable doubt. But once the legislatively defined line is crossed into the subsequent realm of punishment, those requirements do not apply—whether the domain of punishment is one characterized by broad judicial discretion (as in *Williams*), or by sentencing rules that judges must apply (as in *Apprendi* and *Blakely*). In the dissenters' view, it is for the legislature to decide how punishment will be determined.

Justice O'Connor objects that the rule of *Blakely* will put a straitjacket on legislatures, leaving them the "constitutional choice between submitting every fact that increases a sentence to the jury or vesting the sentencing judge with broad discretionary authority."[212] While Justice O'Connor is correct that the framers of the Constitution never envisaged such a choice, she is mistaken in suggesting that these are the only two choices *Blakely* leaves open[213] and that therefore "[t]he legacy of today's opinion, whether

---

[210] See *Apprendi*, 530 US at 529–32, discussing *Patterson* (O'Connor dissenting).

[211] See id at 552–53, citing the warning in *McMillan*, 477 US at 89, that state cannot enact a statute that "evade[s]" *Winship*'s requirements (O'Connor dissenting). See also 530 US at 563, noting *McMillan*'s "tail which wags the dog" caveat, 477 US at 88, about legislative power, 477 US at 88 (Breyer dissenting).

[212] 124 S Ct at 2548 (O'Connor dissenting).

[213] Justice O'Connor also is mistaken in her statement that "broad judicial sentencing discretion was foreign to the Framers." Id at 2548 (O'Connor dissenting). A similar statement is made by Justice Stevens for the *Apprendi* majority, see 530 US at 481 (asserting that there was a nineteenth-century shift to "statutes providing fixed-term sentences"). In fact, the First Congress enacted criminal statutes that reposed significant discretion to federal sentencing judges. See, for example, 1 Stat 29, 46–47 (1789); 1 Stat 112, § 2 (1789). See generally Stith and Cabranes, *Fear of Judging* at 9–10, 197–98 (cited in note 10).

intended or not, will be the consolidation of sentencing power in the State and Federal Judiciaries."[214] As Justice Breyer recognizes, the rule in *Blakely* allows the legislature to leave as much or as little sentencing discretion with judges as they choose. Justice Breyer's analysis is both more elaborate and more pragmatic than that of Justice O'Connor. He argues that neither of the two choices Justice O'Connor poses (fully discretionary sentencing, or a requirement of constitutional proof of every sentencing factor) *nor any combination of the two* is practical in the modern era.[215]

Rather, the dissenters see a much better option (what might be called a "third way") for the punishment phase. This option is the approach that the Court struck down in *Apprendi* and *Blakely*—allowing judges to make the findings of fact necessary to apply legislatively devised sentencing rules.[216] The dissenters see this "third way" as a variant of the old discretionary approach upheld in *Williams*—in which the punishment phase is free of the constitutional requirements regarding accusation and proof. For the dissenters, it is logically inconsistent—creating what I have called the "paradox" of *Williams*[217]—to require that codified sentencing factors be charged and proved in conformity with the Fifth and Sixth Amendments, when no such requirements are imposed on judges exercising unregulated and unreviewable sentencing discretion. If the Constitution is not offended by a single judge implicitly finding facts when imposing a sentence, as the Court held in *Williams*, how can it possibly be offended by the judge applying sentencing rules codified in advance?

The majority in *Blakely* answers this question by rejecting its premise—that judicial fact finding of codified sentencing factors

---

[214] 124 S Ct at 2543 (O'Connor dissenting).

[215] See id at 2552–59 (Breyer dissenting). Justice Breyer asserts, in addition, that none of the options left open by *Blakely* bodes well for defendants. See id at 2556, citing Stephanos Bibas, *Judicial Fact-Finding and Sentence Enhancements in a World of Guilty Pleas*, 110 Yale L J 1097 (2001) (Breyer dissenting). This argument is persuasively disposed of by Justice Scalia. See 124 S Ct at 2541–43, citing Nancy J. King and Susan R. Klein, *Apprendi and Plea Bargaining*, 54 Stan L Rev 295 (2001). Professor Bibas is correct that there may be situations in which particular defendants may prefer the right to argue facts before a sentencing judge rather than to a jury, due primarily to discontinuities in the plea-bargaining "market." But, ceteris paribus, defendants are advantaged by being granted the right to insist on jury trial for all accusations, a right which is valuable in part because it can be waived in return for prosecutorial concessions.

[216] See *Blakely*, 124 S Ct at 2544–45 (discussing sentencing reforms) (O'Connor dissenting); *Apprendi*, 530 US at 555–56 (same) (Breyer dissenting)

[217] See text accompanying notes 124, 126–27.

is a "lesser-included" version[218] of the system upheld in *Williams*. *Blakely* cites *Williams* and its validation of judicial sentencing discretion,[219] and thus appears to accept the notion of a constitutional divide between (1) proof of "crime," on the one hand, and (2) discretionary determination of "punishment," on the other. From the perspective of the majority, however, the codification of sentencing factors actually *moves the location* of the constitutional divide. *Williams* upheld a system in which the legislature chose to repose sentencing discretion (including implicit fact finding) in judges. When legislatures moved toward more codified sentencing structures in the 1980s—whether in the form of sentence-enhancing statutes such as New Jersey's "hate crime" law and California's various weapon statutes, or in the form of binding guidelines—they created a new system. This new system consisted of sentencing rules, including rules specifying which bad acts deserve more punishment. In thus *supplanting* discretion with law, legislatures themselves decided to place on the "crime" side of the constitutional divide some of the decision making that formerly was on the discretionary, "punishment" side of that line.[220] Just as "the Constitution follows the flag,"[221] *Winship, Apprendi,* and *Blakely* hold that the protections of the Fifth and Sixth Amendments (and presumably the ex post facto prohibition as well) follow a

---

[218] See text accompanying notes 115–17.

[219] See 124 S Ct at 2538, note 230.

[220] There is one notable difference between the sentencing factor at issue in *Blakely* and the elements of a crime as traditionally understood. Criminal juries are instructed that if they do find the requisite facts (beyond a reasonable doubt), they are bound by law to find the defendant guilty of the crime charged, not some lesser crime. In the FSG, most aggravating sentencing factors—whether labeled "relevant conduct," enhancements, or adjustments—likewise apply in a mandatory fashion. If the judge finds the requisite facts, he must increase the sentencing range as specified in the FSG, see notes 106–07, 249. See also *Apprendi*, 530 US at 471 (under New Jersey hate crime statute, finding of bias required sentencing enhancement).

In *Blakely*, however, even though the judge found "deliberate cruelty," he was not required to impose an exceptional sentence, see text at notes 183–90. The FSG operate similarly with respect to "departures" from the calculated sentencing range, see 18 USC § 3553(b)(2000). See also *Ring v Arizona*, 435 US 584, 595 (sentencing judge to determine, after finding aggravating factor, whether mitigating factors nonetheless "call for leniency"). For the majority in *Blakely*, it makes no difference "[w]ether the judicially determined facts *require* a sentence enhancement or merely *allow* it," 124 S Ct 2538 n 8 (emphasis in original). In either event, "the verdict alone does not authorize the sentence," id.

[221] Whether in fact "the Constitution follows the flag" was a major controversy in the aftermath of our nation's acquisition of territories during and after the Spanish-American war, and in the *Insular Cases*, including *Downes v Bidwell*, 182 US 244 (1901). The issue continues to arise, see, for example, *Rasul v Bush*, 124 S Ct 2686 (2004).

legislature's action to subject particular conduct to punishment. For the Justices in the majority in these two cases, the *Williams* paradox is not nearly as important as the paradox that would be created if the legislature were required to meet constitutional standards of proof for facts it labels "elements" but not for those facts it chooses to label "aggravating sentencing factors."

If one believes that legislatures or commissions are better suited than judges to determine the moral significance of different types of facts, the codified sentencing approach will be preferred to one that leaves these decisions to judges. It is possible (though by no means obvious) that legislative rules are less likely to be arbitrary, and more likely to accord with the values of the polity along many dimensions, including severity. And enlightenment sensibilities tend to be offended by reposing authority in an individual whose only qualification is her appointment to office.[222] This is why we prefer, and on the federal level the Constitution requires,[223] that crimes be specified by legislatures, rather than by common-law courts. Reformers sought codification of sentencing because they were skeptical of the individual judge as decision maker, wanted to ensure that the same factors are considered in all cases, and trusted in democratic decision making.[224] But these very reasons lead inexorably to the conclusion, as *Blakely* suggests (and Justice Scalia concluded in dissent in *Mistretta*),[225] that whoever promulgates sentencing rules is engaged in lawmaking.[226]

There is a lesson here for proponents of sentencing reform: If we criticize discretionary sentencing regimes as "lawless" and favor the infusion of "law" into the process of sentencing, we should not be surprised to find the new law-based process subjected to constitutional strictures. All that *Apprendi* and *Blakely* hold is that the usual constitutional requirements apply to execution of the law.

Still, the *Williams* paradox remains. One way to resolve it would

---

[222] These concerns are critically analyzed in Stith and Cabranes, *Fear of Judging* at 51–62, 112–18 (cited in note 10).

[223] See *United States v Hudson & Goodwin*, 11 US 32 (1812).

[224] See generally Stith and Koh, 28 Wake Forest L Rev 223 (cited in note 104).

[225] See *Mistretta*, 488 US at 427 (Scalia dissenting). *Mistretta* is discussed in text accompanying notes 110–17.

[226] See also Stith and Cabranes, *Fear of Judging* at 77 ("The Commission's Guidelines supplement congressionally enacted laws as the effective federal criminal code.") (cited in note 10).

be to carry *Blakely* to its logical conclusion: Whenever judges are authorized to exercise sentencing discretion (wide-open discretion as in *Williams* or guided discretion as under advisory guidelines), they could consider *only* the facts admitted by the defendant or found by a jury beyond a reasonable doubt, as well as mitigating facts of the sort that may come to their attention in a presentence report. This approach would resolve the lack of congruence between discretionary fact finding and rule-bound fact finding, though it might be hard to implement as a practical matter.[227] The Court might well prefer to abide some logical inconsistency than to hold that the Constitution imposes such strict and difficult-to-enforce constraints on legislatures and sentencing judges.

There is another constitutional avenue open to the Court. Even if the specific requirements of the Sixth Amendment and of *Winship* (and perhaps those of the Double Jeopardy and Ex Post Facto Clauses) do not apply to the exercise of discretion in criminal sentencing, the requirement in the Fifth and Fourteenth Amendments of "due process of law" may place some limitations on implicit fact finding, and for that matter implicit lawmaking, by sentencing judges. The requirement of due process might be satisfied if the judge's discretionary sentencing decision is subject to review for abuse of discretion. And there might be no due process concern if the absolute quantum of unreviewable discretion is small, as is true under the FSG. In the balance required by the idea of due process, some weight must be given, after all, to the value of individualizing sentences[228] and to the reality that a code cannot specify every relevant factor. On the other hand, in the unlikely event of a return to a broad discretionary system without even appellate review for abuse of discretion, *Blakely* might bring us full circle, forcing reconsideration of the due process challenges that *Williams* and its progeny rejected out of hand.[229] Can it be said today that due process of law is satisfied when a state actor is given authority to impose (or not impose) severe limitations on

---

[227] The Second Circuit tried something similar with its *"Fatico"* requirement, see text accompanying notes 88–89. Too often, it seems, judges may convince themselves that they have not relied on disputed facts. See also *Grayson v United States*, 438 US 41, 53–54 (1978) (discussing but not adopting limitation on judicial sentencing discretion), which is discussed in text accompanying notes 87–88.

[228] Compare *Roberts v Louisiana*, 431 US 633 (1977) (requiring individualization of sentencing decision in capital cases); *Woodson v North Carolina*, 428 US 280 (1976) (same).

[229] See Sections I.B and II.A.

an individual's liberty without "giving [any] reason at all"—as proclaimed in 1949 in *Williams* and quoted again in *Blakely*?[230]

IV. The Importance of Procedure

For now, the constitutional status of *Williams*-style discretionary sentencing is not in question. To have raised doubts in *Apprendi* or *Blakely* about the extent to which *Williams* remains good law would have upset not only the new sentencing order, but the traditional order as well. Discretionary sentencing is still common in many states[231] and, as noted above, is incorporated in smaller ways even in the new systems. At the same time, it is important to understand that the ostensible affirmation of such a system in *Apprendi* and *Blakely* is not necessary to the rules these cases set forth.

In the last analysis, these decisions are not about the judicial role in sentencing (as the dissenters urged) nor about the jury's role in fact finding (as Justice Scalia in *Blakely* urged). They are about the power of the legislature to criminalize conduct. That power is limited most importantly not by "substantive" constitutional constraints on the content of the criminal law (of which there are few), but by the Constitution's requirements that certain procedures be followed in allegation and proof of the conduct the legislature has chosen to punish. Simply put, unless the legislature provides for the system of criminal adjudication required by the Constitution (including formal accusation, confrontation, findings of fact beyond a reasonable doubt, and application of law), it cannot punish the conduct.

From this perspective, the significance of *Patterson*[232] is not its hollow warning that there are "constitutional limits" on legislative definition of crime but rather its primary, "formalist" holding that crimes *defined by law* must be proven beyond a reasonable doubt.[233] Justice Scalia asserts that *Blakely* presents a question about the role

---

[230] 124 S Ct at 2538, noting that *Williams* involved an indeterminate-sentencing system in which the judge could have "sentenced [the defendant] to death giving no reason at all" (quoting 337 US at 252).

[231] See Skove, *Implications for State Courts* at App E ("Sentencing Practices and Other Relevant Policies in the States") (cited in note 107).

[232] 432 US 197.

[233] *Patterson* is discussed in Section I.A and text accompanying notes 72–73, 108–09, 129, 209–10.

of juries ("the very reason the Framers put a jury-trial guarantee in the Constitution is that they were unwilling to trust government to mark out the role of the jury"),[234] asserting that the holding of *Blakely* will interpose the jury as "circuitbreaker in the State's machinery of justice."[235] Yet Justice Scalia's focus on juries seems exaggerated. Juries are not told the sentencing consequences of their fact finding, and continue after *Apprendi* and *Blakely* to have no role in the finding of mitigating facts. *Blakely* is not so much a lesson about the role of the jury as it is a command to the legislature: The legislature cannot transfer from the trial phase (with all its protections, including the right to jury trial) over to the sentencing phase the "inquisition into the facts of the crime the State *actually* seeks to punish."[236]

It is true, as Professor Stuntz has explored at length,[237] that the Constitution's protections relating to criminal prosecutions are only "procedural," and their practical consequences may be undone by the legislature through changes in the substantive criminal law. In response to the *Apprendi* line of cases, these changes might include increases in permissible sentences, or a schedule of minimum sentences if *Harris* remains good law.[238] It is beyond the scope of the present essay to predict how states with systems like Washington's may respond to *Blakely* or how Congress may respond to *Booker* and *Fanfan* if those cases hold, as seems likely, that the *Blakely* rule dooms the FSG as now implemented. There is already widespread speculation that invalidation of the present system of federal sentencing would ultimately make things worse for defendants than do the FSG, because Congress may respond by making federal punishments even harsher and by reducing judicial discretion even more.[239] We should note, however, that such speculation is not addressed to the issue before the Court—which is how the Constitution should be interpreted, not how harshly

---

[234] 124 S Ct at 2540.

[235] Id at 2539.

[236] Id (emphasis in original).

[237] See William J. Stuntz, *Substance, Process, and the Civil-Criminal Line*, 7 J Contemp Legal Issues 1 (1996).

[238] See note 171.

[239] See, for example, Stephanos Bibas, *Blakey's Federal Aftermath*, 16 Fed Sent Rptr 331, 337 (2004).

defendants should be punished.[240] As Justice Stevens recognized in his dissent in *McMillan*, the Court's essential role is to "identify genuine constitutional threats," leaving other issues to the "continued functioning of the democratic process."[241]

Moreover, as it happens, there is no evidence that state legislatures or Congress responded to *Apprendi* by restructuring statutory aggravating and mitigating factors[242]—just as there was little change in the statutory structure of "elements" and "defenses" in response to *Patterson*.[243] Indeed, Kansas, which had a statutory guideline system remarkably close to that at issue in *Blakely*, amended its statutes after *Apprendi* to provide for jury trial and proof beyond a reasonable doubt of aggravating sentencing factors.[244] If Congress does respond to *Booker* and *Fanfan* with a transparent restructuring of federal sentencing law to avoid the rule of those cases (and the rules of *Winship* and the Sixth Amendment), there will be opportunity for the Court to decide whether at last a legislature has exceeded the "constitutional limits beyond which [it] may not go."[245]

Possibly the most, but surely the least, we can expect from our courts is that they block legislative end-runs around the Constitution's formal requirements (as the majority in *Patterson* understood). In requiring that aggravating facts be charged and proved pursuant to constitutional standards, *Apprendi* and *Blakely* deny legislatures the power to impose punishment for bad acts of which the defendant has not been convicted, however efficient and uni-

---

[240] One might as readily complain, with respect to application of most Bill of Rights guarantees to the states, that defendants are now punished more severely than they were before the Court got serious about constitutional rights.

[241] 477 US at 100 (Stevens dissenting). Justice Stevens cited Ely, *Democracy and Distrust* (cited in note 27).

[242] See Nancy J. King and Susan R. Klein, *Essential Elements*, 54 Vand L Rev 1467, 1547–54 (2001) (listing hundreds of state or federal statutes subject to *Apprendi*; none yet amended).

[243] See id at 1546, which presents a summary table showing that a total of nine states amended their homicide statutes as allowed by *Patterson v New York*, 432 US 197 (1977), and that no state amended their homicide statutes as allowed by *Martin v Ohio*, 480 US 228 (1987), see note 41. *Patterson* itself predicted as much, see 432 US at 211 (noting that "long accepted rule" allowing state to place burden of proving defenses on defendant had "not led to such widespread redefinition of crime and reduction of the prosecution's burden that a new constitutional rule was required").

[244] See Kan Stat Ann § 21–4718 (Supp 2003). The Kansas Supreme Court had issued a decision similar to the Supreme Court's subsequent decision in *Blakely*, see *State v Gould*, 271 Kan 394, 23 P3d 1801 (2001).

[245] *Patterson*, 432 US at 210.

formly administered the system devised by the legislature. The immediate and salutary effect of these decisions is to ensure that before a defendant pleads guilty, he will know the complete crime of which he is accused[246]—the crime which, if he goes to trial, will have to be proved beyond a reasonable doubt. The demise of systems that leave to the sentencing phase the finding of facts that by law warrant additional punishment will reduce the current practice of under-the-table "fact bargaining" regarding "sentencing factors" devised by statute or by administrative agencies.[247] What is now "fact bargaining" will become above-the-table charge bargaining, and defendants will know all the charges against them before they bargain. Surely this is an improvement worthy of widespread support.

Apprendi and *Blakely* also presage the end of the pretense that a judge is empowered under our Constitution to convict and punish a defendant for conduct that is criminalized, but that a prosecutor has not charged. Consider the peculiarity of that three-day sentencing hearing in *Blakely*, where the prosecutor had to call witnesses to prove an accusation, spelled out in the criminal code, that he had never charged.[248] The FSG contemplate similar "adjudications"—dare we call them trials?—in federal court.[249] A holding that the federal system must comport with *Blakely* would deny this power of conviction to federal judges. Whatever one's view of judicial discretion at sentencing, such proceedings (per-

---

[246] As described supra, codified sentencing factors are not part of the indictment or other formal charge. In the federal system, the defendant need not be informed before she pleads guilty, or decides to go to trial, of the aggravating sentencing factors that the government intends to prove at sentencing. See FRCrP 11 (no requirement that defendant be advised of relevant sentencing factors or likely sentence under FSG). Nonetheless, for over a decade, pursuant to *United States v Pimentel*, 932 F2d 1029, 1034 (2d Cir 1991), federal prosecutors in the six districts of the Second Circuit have provided pre-plea letters that set forth the government's position on application of the FSG. See, for example, *United States v Huerta-Moran*, 352 F3d 766 (2d Cir 2003).

[247] For a discussion of "fact bargaining," see Stith and Cabranes, *Fear of Judging* at 132–40 (cited in note 10). See also Tony Garoppolo, *Fact Bargaining: What the Sentencing Commission Hath Wrought*, 10 Crim Prac Man (BNA) 405 (1996); FRCrP 11(c)(1) (allowing plea agreements concerning which sentencing factors of the FSG apply in case-at-hand).

[248] See notes 188–89 and accompanying text.

[249] The Sentencing Reform Act requires judges to apply all relevant sentencing factors, whether or not either party so requests, see 18 USC § 3553(b). See also USSG § 6A1.3 (Resolution of Disputed Factors); § 6B1.2 (plea agreement that includes dismissal of charge does not preclude court from considering charge as sentencing factor requiring higher sentencing range); § 6B1.4(d) ("The court is not bound by the [plea-agreement] stipulation, but may with the aid of the presentence report, determine the facts relevant to sentencing").

mitted by Washington State's system and required by the FSG) offend fundamental constitutional values. Given where we are today, *Blakely* is an easy case—and so are *Booker* and *Fanfan*.

PHILIP HAMBURGER

THE NEW CENSORSHIP:
INSTITUTIONAL REVIEW BOARDS

Do federal regulations on Institutional Review Boards violate the First Amendment? Do these regulations establish a new sort of censorship? And what does this reveal about the role of the Supreme Court?

Institutional Review Boards (so-called "IRBs") license research in accord with federal policy. The federal government seeks to minimize the risk that research performed on human subjects will cause them harm, and the government therefore has adopted regulations that induce universities and other research institutions to establish IRBs.[1] In accordance with these regulations, a research institution typically creates at least one IRB and requires students, teachers, and other personnel to get the IRB's permission before they conduct research on human subjects. Thus, a professor who wants to study human subjects must first submit a proposal to the IRB, which will review the proposal and evaluate its risk and on this basis will grant or deny him permission to do his research.[2] The professor must

Philip Hamburger is John P. Wilson Professor of Law, University of Chicago Law School.

AUTHOR'S NOTE: This article benefited substantially from a faculty workshop at Columbia Law School and from the thoughtful, learned comments of Elmer Abbo, Eric Claeys, Fredric Coe, Harold Edgar, James Lindgren, William Marshall, Henry Monaghan, Robert Perlman, David Rabban, Margaret Schilt, Richard Shweder, Geoffrey Stone, and my research assistant, Alix Weisfeld. Obviously, it should not be assumed that any errors or opinions are theirs. For the sake of confidentiality, most of the researchers and some others who shared their insights cannot be mentioned here, but I am deeply grateful to them.

[1] See, for example, 45 CFR Part 46. All citations here to CFR refer to the 2004 version.

[2] See, for example, 45 CFR Part 46.

get this prior permission not only if he wants to conduct a dangerous physiological experiment but also if he merely wants to ask individuals about their political opinions. The primary question here is whether the federal regulations establishing this system of licensing violate the First Amendment. The initial constitutional problem points to a second, more general concern, that government has developed a new kind of censorship. This, in turn, reveals a third, even more expansive danger, that the Supreme Court's doctrines on federal spending and on the First Amendment have undermined this Amendment's guarantee against licensing and have thereby weakened the capacity of the people to preserve their freedom from censorship.

The federal government adopted regulations on IRBs because research on human subjects can be dangerous. Much research on human subjects causes little or no harm, but there are grim examples of research that has gone awry, causing serious injury and even death. Although the risks of a research project cannot always be measured, they can often be anticipated and minimized, and to this end, it has long seemed essential that there be legal mechanisms to limit the risks to human subjects. The federal government began to use review boards for its own scientists in the 1950s, and the World Health Organization endorsed such committees in its *Declaration of Helsinki* in 1964.[3] The demands for IRBs gathered support after Henry K. Beecher published his prominent critique of medical studies in which researchers put subjects at risk without adequately seeking informed consent, and especially after the *New York Times* published an expose of the Tuskegee syphilis study.[4] In response to the anxieties about harm from research, the federal government could have relied upon approaches that did not involve licensing

---

[3] World Health Organization, *Declaration of Helsinki*, 2 British Med J 177 (July 18, 1964). For the early history of IRBs in the federal government, see William J. Curran, *Governmental Regulation of the Use of Human Subjects in Medical Research: The Approach of Two Federal Agencies*, 98 Daedalus 542, 574–77 (1969); Robert J. Levine, *Ethics and Regulation of Clinical Research* 322–25 (1986).

[4] Henry K. Beecher, *Ethics and Clinical Research*, 274 New Eng J Med 1354 (1966). The Tuskegee study began in the early 1930s and aimed to examine the course of untreated syphilis in black men in Macon County, Alabama. Particularly after the 1972 *New York Times* article, the study came under severe criticism for misinforming the men that research was free medical treatment, for failing to seek informed consent, and for not informing the men about penicillin or giving it to them when this remedy became generally available for civilians after World War II. For this history and brief summaries of some of the more prominent research projects that came under criticism, see Levine, *Ethics and Regulation* at 69–72 (cited in note 3).

and that were more proportionate to the dangers of research. Instead, it began to adopt policies in the 1960s, and regulations in the 1970s, that systematically persuaded private and state institutions to adopt IRBs.[5] In some specialized contexts, the government directly required IRBs, but more generally it made IRB licensing a condition of its support for research, and this general use of IRBs to protect human subjects is the focus of this inquiry.[6]

The primary constitutional problem is the First Amendment's prohibition against licensing.[7] This Amendment generally forbids licensing of the press and, presumably, of speech.[8] In this regard, it responds to dangers that became evident in seventeenth-century England, where the Star Chamber issued regulations requiring persons to get permission from a licensor before they printed or caused to be printed any book or pamphlet. This licensing has come to be known as "censorship," and the First Amendment prohibits it. Of course, government frequently licenses conduct and products, as when the FDA licenses drugs, but the government cannot, consistently with the First Amendment, institute licensing of speech or of the press. Accordingly, it seems necessary to consider the constitutionality of the federal regulations on IRBs. These regulations establish mechanisms under which students, teachers, and others must get permission to conduct their research, and the regulations

---

[5] In 1966, for example, the Surgeon General issued a policy statement "extending the requirements of 'prior review of research involving human beings' to all PHS grants," and he introduced the system of institutional assurances. Curran, 98 Daedalus at 577 (cited in note 3). For the introduction of the regulations in the early 1970s, see Thomas A. Huff, *The IRB as Deputy Sheriff: Proposed FDA Regulation of the Institutional Review Board*, 27 Clinical Research 103 (1979). For an overview of the history from the 1940s to the present, see National Research Council, *Protecting Participants and Facilitating Social and Behavioral Sciences Research*, ch 3 (2003).

[6] The government directly requires IRBs in two specialized regulatory regimes, which lie beyond the scope of the more general inquiry here. First, some statutes and regulations enforced by the Food and Drug Administration ("FDA") require the use of IRBs, and, second, the Privacy Rule under the Health Insurance Portability and Accountability Act of 1996 ("HIPAA") requires the use of either Privacy Boards or IRBs. Whereas the federal government uses conditions on its support for research as its general means of securing IRB protection for human subjects, the laws associated with the FDA more narrowly require the use of IRBs to protect human subjects in exempted investigations, and the HIPAA Privacy Rule requires the use of IRBs or Privacy Boards to protect the privacy of medical information. They thus use IRBs in ways that extend beyond the government's standard regime for protecting human subjects, and because they therefore require slightly different analysis, they are left for separate consideration.

[7] Incidentally, it will be seen below that licensing by IRBs is not the only means of preventing injuries to human subjects. See text at notes 160–63.

[8] US Const, First Amendment (1791); Leonard Levy, *The Emergence of a Free Press* (1985).

thereby seem to be in tension with the First Amendment's prohibition against licensing. As it happens, there are other important constitutional questions about the regulations—questions about the enumeration of powers; about vagueness and overbreadth; about different types of speech; even about a possible right of research or inquiry. The most basic issue, however, is the licensing of speech or the press.[9]

Curiously, the First Amendment problems with IRBs are both familiar and largely unexamined. Over the past several decades, professors and students have frequently complained that IRBs abridge their liberty—both their freedom from censorship and their more general academic freedom.[10] Their complaints, however, have elicited little serious attention, and it is difficult to find systematic, scholarly studies that question the constitutionality of the federal regulations.[11] Indeed, among government regulators and members

[9] The licensing of speech, or of the press, is examined here largely without elaboration of the other constitutional issues. Similarly, this inquiry focuses on only the most prominent federal IRB regulation—the so-called Common Rule—and on its enforcement through conditions on government spending. See text at note 6. This essay thus leaves the other constitutional issues, other modes of securing compliance, other federal regulations, let alone the state IRB laws, to be explored elsewhere.

[10] Many academics, especially in the humanities and social sciences, have made such complaints, and although most do so in a rather diffuse manner, some are more effective. For example, an ethnographer, Jack Katz, writes: "It is a growing dilemma for the ethnographer whether to take a stand against IRBs' unannounced, presumably unintended, and increasing infringements of constitutionally protected inquiry and expression. IRBs act in the classic posture of censorship boards when they require prior approval of inquiries that would be the right of any U.S. resident to make. Prior[] restraints, as opposed to processes of review and sanctioning after the fact, impose especially troublesome chilling effects." Incidentally, he also notes: "We should remember that the Bill of Rights speaks not of 'journalism' but of freedoms of assembly (association), speech (making inquiries through questioning and observing practices that are routine in everyday social life) and press (publication)." Jack Katz, *To Participants in the UCLA, May 2002, Fieldwork Conference* (May 8, 2002), at http://leroyneiman.sscnet.ucla.edu/katz5_8.htm.

[11] There have been only a few systematic, academic legal inquiries into the lawfulness of the federal regulations under the First Amendment. John Robertson defends the constitutionality of the laws on IRBs on both spending and First Amendment grounds. John Robertson, *The Law of Institutional Review Boards*, 26 UCLA L Rev 484 (1979); John Robertson, *The Scientist's Right to Research: A Constitutional Analysis*, 51 S Cal L Rev 1203, 1277 (1977). In another piece, he "show[s] that governmental regulation of social research through the IRB system . . . is constitutionally legitimate." John A. Robertson, *The Social Scientist's Right to Research and the IRB System*, in Tom L. Beauchamp et al, eds, *Ethical Issues in Social Science Research* 357 (1982).

In the law reviews, apparently only a student note argues that the current regulations are unconstitutional, and, revealingly, it does so only by suggesting that research is expressive conduct, which must be evaluated under *United States v O'Brien*, 391 US 367 (1968). Michael D. Davidson, Note, *First Amendment Protection for Biomedical Research*, 19 Ariz L Rev 893, 917–18 (1977). In a recent unpublished draft, however, Matthew Finkin argues against IRBs as prior restraints. "Pre-Approval of Social Science Research and the Erosion of Academic Freedom" (unpublished draft, cited with author's permission).

of IRBs, the constitutional issues raised by researchers tend to get almost casually dismissed.[12]

---

[12] One researcher states that there is an "absence in IRB culture of any recognition of First Amendment issues." Jack Katz, *To Participants in the UCLA, May 2002, Fieldwork Conference* (May 8, 2002), at http://leroyneiman.sscnet.ucla.edu/katz5_8.htm. In fact, the constitutional complaints about IRBs are well known, but they tend to get casually brushed aside with relatively little analysis, and even the formal defenses of the constitutionality of IRBs sometimes have a peculiarly dismissive tone.

The tone of the regulators may be observed in the recollection of the head of the office that would become the Office for Human Research Protections: "The charges were led by . . . [Ithiel de Sola] Pool . . . , who insisted that . . . our four pages of fine print in the *Federal Register* were about to lay waste to the First Amendment of the Constitution." C. R. McCarthy, "Introduction: The IRB and Social and Behavioral Research," in J. E. Sieber, ed, *NIH Readings on the Protection of Human Subjects in Behavioral and Social Science Research* 8–9 (1984), as quoted in National Research Council, *Protecting Participants* at 71 (cited in note 5).

Some defenders of IRBs dismiss the First Amendment concerns as rhetoric. For example, Robertson (who takes the constitutional issues more seriously than most commentators) is reported to have suggested that "scientists are fond of using the 'rhetoric of rights' to support the freedom of inquiry." He apparently stated that research is protected by the First Amendment but that First Amendment rights are "negative rights" and that they therefore offer only limited protection against conditions on funding. Vivien B. Shelanski, *"Government Control of Science,"* Opening Session of the Second National Symposium on Genetics and the Law, Boston, May 21–23, 1979, 4 Science, Technology, & Human Values 46, 47 (1979). Levine writes: "Opponents of federally mandated IRB review and approval of research involving human subjects commonly refer to this activity as 'prior restraint.' This rhetorical device seems to support their claim that it is unconstitutional, a violation of the First Amendment. Actually, according to Tribe . . . the First Amendment is not an absolute bar to prior restraint, . . ." After acknowledging some countervailing arguments, he quickly concludes: "I have no wish to enter this debate. I do, however, wish that all concerned would cease to call IRB review prior restraint unless they intend the proper meaning of this term." Levine, *Ethics and Regulation* at 359 (cited in note 3).

A prominent example of how the First Amendment problems get dismissed appears in a report published by the Association of American University Professors ("AAUP"), which ordinarily is devoted to protecting the freedom of academics. In opposition to arguments about "prior review," the report states: "This position rests on the mistaken premise . . . that scholars have the right to be provided with federal funds to support their research without providing assurances that they will protect their human subjects." In support of this position, it quotes: "If no right is violated by the imposition of a particular condition on federal research funds, then plainly no academic freedom is violated by the imposition of that condition on federal research funds. No one complains if a federal agency aims at ensuring that its available research funds be expended on scientifically valuable research; and no one complains if it establishes a fair system of peer review (a form of 'prior review') for assuring itself of the scientific value of a research proposal. HHS may certainly require assurance of the scientific value of a research project before funding it; we think HHS may also require assurance that the risks imposed by the research are reasonable before funding it." AAUP, *Protecting Human Beings: Institutional Review Boards and Social Science Research*, Academe: Bulletin of the AAUP 55, 58–59 (May–June 2001). It should not have been difficult to discern that the government's review of research proposals for purposes of determining its own action (whether in funding outside researchers or directing the work of internal researchers) reveals little about the constitutionality of laws setting up a system of licensing for human subjects research by students, faculty, and other personnel in universities and other research institutions across the country. As will be seen below, moreover, the suggestion that the government requires IRBs merely to avoid funding dangerous research is mistaken.

As for the "prior review" of research that is not federally funded, the report states: "The

IRBs have not elicited much constitutional concern in part because the federal regulations on IRBs adopt mild methods and appeal to popular moral sentiments, and this suggests the second problem here, that the regulations establish a new, soft kind of censorship. Instead of harshly imposing the force of law on individuals, this censorship seeks only the cooperation of institutions; instead of attempting to repress popular opinion, it appeals to the moral sensibilities of a majority. Indeed, rather than aim at political or religious ends, this censorship aspires to be bureaucratic, and rather than threaten civil liberties, it attempts to protect them. This is disarmingly unlike the censorship of the Star Chamber, and it is almost enough to make censorship attractive.[13]

With this mild and moral tenor, the new censorship seems to slip past both political and constitutional barriers. At the very least, this censorship escapes popular opposition. In addition, it appears to avoid constitutional obstacles—preeminently, those of the First Amendment. To be sure, the federal regulations on IRBs are unambiguously within the purview of the First Amendment, for although they concern research, they directly target and even specify speech and the press—for example, by defining "research" in terms of speech and the press.[14] In other ways, however, the federal regulations seem to escape the First Amendment. Under the Court's doctrine on spending, Congress enjoys an expansive power to spend and place conditions on its spending, without clear limitations, and the federal regulations on IRBs take advantage of this uncertainty to introduce licensing not by force of law, but rather by means of

---

absence of a direct financial connection between the government and the individual scholar . . . does not relieve the researcher of the professional obligation not to harm human subjects. Accordingly, a university's effort to ensure that all researchers comply with its human-subject regulations does not offend academic freedom. . . ." Id at 59. Leaving aside the attribution of professional obligations to researchers (for which, see note 161), a researcher's moral duty to avoid harm sheds scarcely any light on the question of what method of enforcing his duties (whether moral or legal) the government can ask a university to impose.

[13] Of course, even the old censorship contained elements of the new. Especially in a free society, a government cannot easily license speech or the press without the cooperation of other institutions, and therefore already in the sixteenth and seventeenth centuries, the English government sought to enlist the assistance of organizations and individuals. For example, it delegated some licensing functions, as seen, to prelates, judges, and university officials, it relied on the Stationers Company (or printers' association) for some enforcement, and it encouraged the English to support the licensing as part of a moral endeavor to prevent "abuses" in the press. The new censorship, however, takes the cooperation (including the moral emphasis and the delegation to other institutions) even further.

[14] See Part III below.

conditions on federal support for research—an approach that may seem, initially, to sidestep the First Amendment's limit on the constraints of law. Similarly, under the Court's First Amendment decisions, there is reason to think that this Amendment's guarantee of speech and the press no longer establishes any absolute prohibition, and the federal regulations on IRBs make use of this opening to introduce licensing as necessary to protect human subjects—a moral end that may appear to outweigh the constitutional presumption against the means. In fact, as will be seen, the federal regulations on IRBs fail to satisfy the First Amendment, but they allow a casual observer to believe that they might get by, and this has been enough to make the new censorship legally plausible.[15]

Yet the new censorship escapes the First Amendment only because of a third problem: that the Court has undermined the First Amendment freedom of speech, or of the press, in ways that diminish the confidence of Americans that they have a right to be free from the new censorship. Shortly before proposing the Bill of Rights, James Madison wrote to Thomas Jefferson that in a nation in which the people control the government, a bill of rights would be valuable primarily because "[t]he political truths declared in that solemn manner acquire by degrees the character of fundamental maxims of free Government, and as they become incorporated with the national sentiment, counteract the impulses of interest and passion."[16] In modern terms, the people would "internalize" the truths enumerated in the Bill of Rights, and even if a majority would not immediately restrain itself, it would, perhaps, when a minority appealed to the fundamental maxims of the Bill of Rights, to which Americans as a whole, including the majority, had become attached.

The Supreme Court, however, has developed and legitimized a Congressional spending power that seems to allow Congress to impose licensing through conditions on its spending, and having internalized this conception of a federal spending power only slightly limited by notions of unconstitutional conditions, observers often assume that if the government uses conditions on its spending to obtain IRBs, there is no clear or substantial First Amendment

---

[15] Incidentally, the regulatory regimes associated with the FDA and HIPAA directly impose a requirement that one get permission without provoking opposition because, unlike the more general implementation of IRBs through federal support for research, they place their burdens on relatively narrow categories of institutions and individuals.

[16] James Madison, Letter to Thomas Jefferson (Oct 17, 1788), in Robert Rutland et al, eds, 11 *Papers of James Madison* 297 (1977).

objection.[17] The Court, moreover, in expanding the First Amendment freedom of speech, or of the press, has suggested that this freedom is never absolute—that even the Amendment's prohibition on licensing is always subject to overriding government interests—and many commentators have therefore assumed that the moral purposes of IRBs can outweigh the constitutional objections.[18] In such ways, while the Court has expanded federal power and individual liberty, it has compromised one of the "fundamental maxims of free Government" in the enumeration of rights. It thus has weakened an essential mechanism by which a majority and the government might refrain from imposing the new censorship and by which minorities and individuals might resist it.[19] As it happens, the federal

---

[17] See, for example, the quotations from the AAUP report in note 12. In the late 1970s, John Robertson wrote: "Constitutional rights are rights against government interference or restriction, not entitlements to a particular share of public resources," and even as to IRB review of research not funded by the federal government, he stated that "[i]t is unlikely . . . that review of non-funded research as a condition of federal funding would be held to be an unconstitutional condition." Roberston, 26 UCLA L Rev at 507, 509 484 (cited in note 11). In the early 1980s, he concluded that "Social scientists thus are treated no differently from journalists. Both are subject to employer constraints . . . . both are subject to restrictions attached to grants of public funds. If the government gave grants to newspapers to foster investigative reporting, it could, as it does with human subject research funds, condition them on reporters having a publisher's ethics committee approve their investigative techniques." Robertson, in Beauchamp, *Ethical Issues in Social Science Research* at 363 (cited in note 11).

[18] See, for example, quotations from the AAUP Report in note 12. In 1979, Ithiel de Sola Pool wrote a short but prominent article pointing out that the proposed regulations on IRBs were a prior restraint on speech and the press and were therefore unconstitutional "censorship." Ithiel de Sola Pool, *Protecting Human Subjects of Research: An Analysis on Proposed Amendments to HEW Policy*, 12 PS 452 (1979). The brief response published in the same journal summarily pointed out that the courts had abandoned any absolute conception of First Amendment rights: "The . . . important question . . . is whether the First Amendment provides an absolute right that takes precedence over other constitutional rights. (This seems to be Pool's position, and it is one denied by the courts.)" Later, this response suggested that what was needed was "a complex balancing act." Harvey Boulay, Richard Goldstein, and Betty Zisk, *Protecting Human Subjects of Research: Proposed Amendments to HEW Policy* 13 PS 452 (1980).

What appears to be the sole law review piece arguing against the constitutionality of IRBs similarly does not treat licensing as strictly forbidden, and after examining research as expressive conduct, it concludes that "because the Supreme Court's approach to first amendment issues seems to vary from case to case, it is impossible to draw absolute conclusions pertaining to the proper standard of review for legislation which allegedly abridges researcher's [sic] rights. The problem is compounded by the need to apply a variable standard to the different types of research depending on the extent to which they entail nonexpressive actions." Its strongest conclusion is therefore that "the government bears the burden of proving regulatory necessity" and that "the government demonstrate a compelling interest in support of the regulation." Davidson, 19 Ariz L Rev at 895, 917–18 (cited in note 11).

[19] For an illustration of how even a group that advocates freedom of speech in universities has succumbed, see the report of the AAUP quoted in note 12. See also text at note 189.

regulations on IRBs are probably unconstitutional even under the Court's spending and licensing doctrines. Yet through these doctrines, the Court has left the people with little sense that the new censorship is unconstitutional, and it has thereby diminished their capacity to preserve their liberty.

Lest this third point, about the role of the Court, seem insufficiently concrete, imagine that the Court had not created a spending power until it had developed a fully functional doctrine of unconstitutional conditions. Imagine, moreover, that the Court had not suggested that government interests could outweigh the First Amendment's core prohibition against laws licensing verbal speech or the press.[20] Then, Congress and the executive branch probably would not have imposed IRBs in the first place. The advocates of regulating research might not have even sought a system of licensing. At the very least, those who were censored would have been confident that their constitutional rights had been infringed and would have long ago defended themselves—initially in Congress, and then in court. Under the Supreme Court's doctrines, however, Americans have lost any clear sense that they have a right to be free of the new censorship.

The Court could have avoided lending legitimacy to the new censorship by taking greater care in developing its doctrines on spending and licensing. For example, if the Court had been more systematic in developing its doctrine of unconstitutional conditions, the spending power would not have created an end run around the First Amendment. In the context of the federal government, the doctrine of unconstitutional conditions is primarily a judicial response to the dangers arising from the judicial development of a Congressional spending power, and this attempt to contain the spending power may therefore be inherently unstable and even less susceptible of precision than most judicially developed constitutional law. Yet as IRBs illustrate, if the judges remain attached to a federal spending power, they must somehow bring strength and clarity to the limitations on this power, for otherwise Americans will be unable adequately to protect their liberty. Fortunately, as will be seen, the doctrine of unconstitutional conditions renders the federal regulations on IRBs unconstitutional, but this was not

---

[20] By "verbal speech or the press," this article means the use of words, numbers, or other language of the sort traditionally associated with speech or printing presses. More generally, see text at notes 39–42.

clear enough to restrain the government from adopting the regulations, and the spending power as limited by the current, somewhat feeble doctrine of unconstitutional conditions has left those who might have resisted the censorship without a clear sense that they have a constitutional right against it.

The other doctrine in which the Court has unnecessarily created space for the new censorship concerns licensing. The Court sometimes lumps licensing together with other mechanisms—primarily judicial injunctions—under the rubric of "previous restraints." Anxious to explain First Amendment limits on judicial injunctions, the Court suggests that injunctions are similar to licensing in that both mechanisms can impose pre-publication review on speech or the press.[21] The Court thus defends a freedom from some injunctions, but at the cost of obscuring the distinctiveness of licensing and depriving it of its central place in First Amendment doctrine. Indeed, by associating licensing with the other restraints, which are not absolutely prohibited, the Court can scarcely avoid the conclusion that licensing, like the other restraints, is only presumptively prohibited and that it can be justified by sufficiently substantial government interests.[22] Yet, as will be seen, the licensing of speech or of the press—at least licensing of the verbal core of speech or the press—is very different from other pre-publication restraints and is absolutely prohibited. Other pre-publication restraints, notably judicial injunctions, impose prior review, but they do not generally require persons to get permission before speaking, writing, printing, or publishing. In contrast, licensing makes it necessary for persons to get permission, and it thus is dangerous in different ways than other constraints on the press.[23] The First Amendment centrally and unequivocally forbids laws requiring that one get permission for verbal speech or the press, and even while the Court was developing broader, nonabsolute freedoms (for injunctions, post-publication restraints, and nonverbal speech and the press), it could have done more to preserve the unqualified character of this core freedom from licensing. The Court needs to restore the cen-

---

[21] See text at note 31. Vincent Blasi observes that "[t]he Court no longer asks whether a challenge procedure amounts to the equivalent of a licensing system," but instead inquires about "[p]rior restraint." Vincent Blasi, *Toward a Theory of Prior Restraint: The Central Linkage*, 66 Minn L Rev 11, 12 (1981).

[22] See text at notes 36–38.

[23] For the dangers of licensing, see Thomas Emerson, *The Doctrine of Prior Restraint*, 20 Law & Contemp Probs 648 (1955).

trality of licensing in the First Amendment. It usually understands that licensing is distinctively prohibited, but it denies that there is any unequivocal freedom from licensing, and it thereby diminishes the capacity of Americans to preserve this freedom.

In sum, the federal regulations on IRBs would appear to violate the First Amendment. This will become apparent from six observations: (I) at least for verbal speech and the press, the First Amendment absolutely bars laws requiring licensing; (II) the federal regulations on IRBs set up a system of licensing; (III) these regulations target and even specify speech and the press as the object of their licensing, including verbal speech and the press; (IV) the federal government imposes this licensing by means of unconstitutional regulatory conditions on federal spending and by means of state tort law; (V) the injury arising from research on human subjects does not justify the licensing; (VI) the licensing causes serious injuries to researchers and their use of speech and the press. These observations reveal that the federal regulations on IRBs are constitutionally vulnerable. They further suggest that the regulations establish a new censorship, which dispels opposition through its mild and moral tenor, but which remains as unconstitutional as the old. Most broadly, they hint at the danger of Supreme Court doctrines that undermine enumerated rights—doctrines that allow those in power to believe they need not worry about abridging such rights and that leave those whose rights are abridged without confidence that they have constitutional grounds on which to protest.

I. THE FIRST AMENDMENT

The First Amendment states that "Congress shall make no law . . . abridging the freedom of speech, or of the press," and from its inception, it has been understood to bar the federal government from adopting licensing laws.[24] During the past century, the Amendment has more generally been interpreted to prohibit both pre- and post-publication restraints, and as a result of these expansive modern conceptions, the freedom of speech, or of the press, often seems contingent on government interests.[25] Nonethe-

---

[24] US Const, First Amend (1791); *Lovell v Griffin*, 303 US 444, 451 (1938); Levy, *The Emergence of a Free Press* (cited in note 8); Philip Hamburger, *The Law of Seditious Libel and the Control of the Press*, 37 Stan L Rev 661 (1985).

[25] For the dynamic by which the expansion of a right can lead to diminished access, see Philip Hamburger, *More Is Less*, 90 Va L Rev 835 (2004).

less, the Amendment's traditional, core prohibition against licensing of verbal speech or the press remains absolute.

Licensing was the method of regulating the press that prevailed in sixteenth- and seventeenth-century England, where the Star Chamber attempted on behalf of the government to prevent "abuses" of the press by establishing a system of licensing printing.[26] The Star Chamber delegated to various specialized licensors—such as the judges, the Earl Marshall, the prelates, and university officials—the task of licensing manuscripts within their areas of specialization. The university officials, for example, shared with the prelates a jurisdiction over all books but especially those "of Divinity, Phisicke, Philosophie, [and] Poetry."[27] Although they could deny a license to a manuscript, they more often gave licenses, even if sometimes only after making deletions or other modifications.

The First Amendment has been understood from the time of its adoption to forbid the government from imposing this licensing of printing. In opposition to censorship, John Milton and others in seventeenth-century England argued for "the Liberty of unlicens'd Printing," and this liberty to use a printing press without prior permission became known as the freedom of the press.[28] In 1695, when John Locke joined the protests against licensing, the English government abandoned its licensing statute, and in the eighteenth century, both Englishmen and Americans claimed primarily this

---

[26] *A Decree of Starre-Chamber, Concerning Printing*, sig A4[r] (1637). For the legal mechanisms used in seventeenth-century England to control the press, see Hamburger, 37 Stan L Rev 661 (cited in note 24).

[27] *A Decree of Starre-Chamber*, sig B3[r–v], § III (cited in note 26).

[28] John Milton, *Areopagitica: A Speech of Mr. John Milton for the Liberty of Unlicens'd Printing* 1 (1644). Like the licensors, Milton concerned himself with the licensing of printing rather than publication. Although publication or the sharing of a writing with another person was an element of the crime of seditious libel, unlicensed printing was what violated the licensing laws. Being in part a rejection of licensing, the First Amendment specifies the freedom of the *press*. Thus, the Amendment at its core protects the mere saying and printing of words, even if they are not shared with others; it most essentially concerns the words themselves, and cannot be confined to a freedom of publication or communication. This matters here because IRBs license a range of handwritten notes, printed surveys, tabulations of data, e-mails, and other informal materials. These are not publications in the lay sense. If prepared by a researcher for his own benefit, they may not be considered publications as a matter of law. Perhaps, moreover, they will not even be considered communications in a narrow or immediate sense. IRBs thus illustrate the importance of recalling that First Amendment doctrine has its foundations not merely in a freedom of publication or communication, but, more fundamentally, in a freedom of speech, or of the press.

freedom from licensing as their freedom of the press.[29] Similarly, although they were not as clear about their conception of freedom of speech, they evidently assumed that speech was also to be free from laws requiring that one get prior permission. Of course, many Americans were not unaware of the danger from injunctions and post-publication penalties, but when they discussed such matters, they usually assumed that the laws would employ these mechanisms against the injurious use of speech or the press, and they therefore tended to emphasize that the First Amendment protected against licensing. Thus, the licensing condemned by Milton and Locke was what the First Amendment's guarantee of speech and the press most clearly forbade.[30]

Today, however, this First Amendment freedom from licensing has expanded, first, into a freedom from prior restraints. According to the Supreme Court, the freedom from licensing should be understood more broadly to include, in addition, a freedom from some types of judicial injunctions. It thus seems to be not merely a freedom from licensing, but more generally a freedom from pre-publication restraints.[31]

Second, since its adoption, the First Amendment has come to prohibit a wide range of post-publication restraints on speech and the press—most notably, if these restraints discriminate on the basis of content or if they suffer from excessive vagueness or overbreadth. Content discrimination occurs with greatest clarity when a law penalizes a particular point of view, although also frequently when a law penalizes a subject matter or class of speaker.[32] Even if a law

---

[29] John Locke, Common's Resolutions on the Licensing Bill (1695), Carl Stephenson and Frederick George Marcham, eds, *Sources of English Constitutional History* 619 (1937). As the Supreme Court has explained: "The struggle for the freedom of the press was primarily directed against the power of the licensor. It was against that power that John Milton directed his assault by his 'Appeal for the Liberty of Unlicensed Printing.' And the liberty of the press became initially a right to publish 'without a license what formerly could be published only with one.'" *Lovell v Griffin*, 303 US 444, 452 (1938) (note omitted). See also Levy, *The Emergence of a Free Press* (cited in note 8); Hamburger, 37 Stan L Rev at 661 (cited in note 24).

[30] US Const, First Amend (1791); Levy, *The Emergence of a Free Press* (cited in note 8).

[31] *Near v Minnesota*, 283 US 697 (1931). The conception of licensing as a pre-publication restraint drew upon the words of Blackstone in William Blackstone, *Commentaries*, *151–52. Even in *Near*, however, the Court clearly understood that it had to depict the injunction in the case as analogous to licensing. See note 45.

[32] *Burson v Freeman*, 504 US 191 (1992); *Simon & Schuster, Inc. v Members of the New York State Crime Victims Board*, 502 US 105 (1991); *Boos v Barry*, 485 US 312 (1988); *Carey v Brown*, 447 US 455 (1980); *Police Dept v Mosley*, 408 US 92 (1972). Laws can violate the First Amendment either by discriminating among different speakers, types of speech,

regulates conduct that would not ordinarily be considered speech or the press, content discrimination can reveal that, in fact, the law does abridge speech or the press.[33] For example, although a law prohibiting the burning of cloth does not abridge this freedom, a law prohibiting the burning of the flag does.[34] In contrast to laws that penalize on the basis of content, the laws regulating speech or the press that are unduly vague or overbroad do not so directly abridge the freedom of speech or that of the press, but according to the Supreme Court, they can impermissibly discourage or "chill" expression.[35]

---

and points of view or by ecumenically suppressing speech or the press without regard to such differences. The suppression could be viewed as discrimination against speech and the press as a whole, just as the discrimination could be viewed as suppression. For purposes of content discrimination, the Court often seems to treat obscenity, deceit, and incitement as distinctions of conduct rather than content.

[33] The Court examines the interests of the government in order to determine whether a regulation of conduct is, in reality, a regulation of speech or the press that discriminates on the basis of conduct or that otherwise abridges the freedom of speech or the press. According to the Court in *O'Brien*, "a government regulation is sufficiently justified if it is within the constitutional power of the Government; if it furthers an important or substantial governmental interest; if the governmental interest is unrelated to the suppression of free expression; and if the incidental restriction of alleged First Amendment freedoms is no greater than is essential to the furtherance of that interest." *United States v O'Brien*, 391 US 367, 377 (1968). Such a law must be narrowly tailored, but it does not have to be the least burdensome "imaginable." *Ward v Rock Against Racism*, 491 US 781 (1989). Under this *O'Brien* test, even a statute for which "the governmental interest is unrelated to the suppression of free expression" can be held unconstitutional under a balancing test. (Incidentally, subsequent cases have suggested that the prohibited activity must be expressive in a manner more like burning a draft card than nudity. *Barnes v Glen Theatre, Inc.*, 501 US 560 (1991); *Arcara v Cloud Books, Inc.*, 478 US 697 (1986).)

More to the point here, if the governmental interest in a statute is related to the suppression of free expression, it is "outside of *O'Brien*'s test, and we must ask whether this interest justifies" the application of the statute "under a more demanding standard"—in effect, strict scrutiny and its more severe weighing of government interests. *Texas v Johnson*, 491 US 397, 403 (1989). This emphasis, however, on finding a government interest in suppression of free exercise fails to capture the degree to which the Court also, perhaps, more directly examines legislation to see if it engages in content discrimination. A suggestion of this became apparent in *Eichman*, when the Court said that the statute contained "no explicit content-based limitation," but it was "nevertheless clear that the Government's asserted interest is 'related "to the suppression of free expression"' . . . and concerned with the content of such expression." *United States v Eichman*, 496 US 310, 315 (1990). See also John Hart Ely, *Flag Desecration: A Case Study in the Roles of Categorization and Balancing in First Amendment Analysis*, 88 Harv L Rev 1482 (1975).

[34] *United States v Eichman*, 496 US 310 (1990).

[35] A law constraining speech or the press is unconstitutionally vague if persons of "common intelligence must necessarily guess as its meaning and differ as to its application." *Connally v General Construction Co.*, 269 US 385 (1926); *Coates v City of Cincinnati*, 402 US 611 (1971).

The Court has stated the overbreadth doctrine in terms of "substantial overbreadth," *Broadrick v Oklahoma*, 413 US 601, 615 (1973), but the precise degree of overbreadth that matters remains elusive. *Virginia v Hicks*, 539 US 113 (2003); *Virginia v Black*, 538 US 343 (2003); *Watchtower Bible and Tract Society of New York, Inc. v Village of Stratton*, 536 US 127 (2002); *Ashcroft v Free Speech Coalition*, 535 US 564 (2002); *Brockett v Spokane*

These expansive conceptions of freedom from pre- and post-publication constraints have required the use of various balancing tests to protect government interests. The freedom from pre-publication restraint is so broad that it seems necessarily contingent on the countervailing interests of government, and the more expansive freedom from post-publication restraints seems all the more contingent. Accordingly, when the Supreme Court first treated the Amendment's prohibition on licensing as a barrier to pre-publication restraints, such as judicial injunctions, it stipulated various exceptions.[36] Similarly, when the Court began to treat the First Amendment as a bar against post-publication restraints, it qualified the constitutional right by weighing it against the government's concerns—an approach that today can involve either a general balancing test or a strict scrutiny search for a compelling government interest.[37] In these ways, all First Amendment claims

---

Arcades, Inc., 472 US 491 (1985); *Members of the City Council of the City of Los Angeles v Taxpayers for Vincent*, 466 US 789 (1984); *New York v Ferber*, 458 US 747 (1982); *Dombrowski v Pfister*, 380 US 479 (1965). In *Hicks*, the Court explained that "[r]arely, if ever, will an overbreadth challenge succeed against a law or regulation that is not specifically addressed to speech or to conduct necessarily associated with speech (such as picketing or demonstrating)." *Virginia v Hicks*, 539 US 113, 124 (2003). It will be seen that the federal regulations on IRBs focus on conduct necessarily associated with speech and, in addition, specify and otherwise target speech and the press.

Obviously, the vagueness doctrine has due process overtones, and overbreadth is ostensibly a standing doctrine. They are, however, largely substantive doctrines. For the substantive character of the overbreadth doctrine, see Henry Monaghan, *Overbreadth*, Supreme Court Review 1 (1981).

[36] *Near v Minnesota*, 283 US 697 (1931). For the way in which broadened definitions of rights often invite qualifications on access, see Hamburger, 90 Va L Rev 835 (cited in note 25).

Thomas Emerson observed the weakness of the Court's prior restraint doctrine in the late 1960s, when IRBs were coming into vogue: "[I]t is hard to say how much vitality the doctrine of prior restraint retains at the present time. . . . it has been applied loosely to areas beyond its original scope and limited drastically in some areas central to its original purpose . . . . When employed in this way the concept becomes so broad as to be worthless as a legal rule. . . . The result . . . is that, to a substantial extent, a 'prior restraint' now merely signifies a type of restriction that the courts will scrutinize with special care." Thomas I. Emerson, *The System of Freedom of Expression* 511 (1970). Emerson did not recognize that the danger arose from the Court's tendency to generalize about prior restraint without retaining the distinctive category of licensing of verbal speech or the press, but his characterization of the result is suggestive.

[37] *Schenck v United States*, 249 US 47 (1919). For later cases, such as *United States v O'Brien*, 391 US 367 (1968), which elaborate the current doctrine, see note 33. As the Court explained in *R.A.V.*, "[e]ven the prohibition against content discrimination . . . is not absolute." *R.A.V. v City of St. Paul, Minnesota*, 505 US 377, 387 (1992). Before the Court began to justify constitutional limits on injunctions and pre-publication restraints by blurring the distinction between them and licensing, it spoke about the freedom from licensing in sweeping terms. For example, Holmes wrote for the Court that "the main purpose of such constitutional provisions is 'to prevent all such previous restraints upon publications as had been practised by other governments,' and they do not prevent the

for freedom of speech, or of the press, have come to seem contingent on government interests, and even the freedom from licensing has become only a presumption, which can be outweighed by government interests. Yet the First Amendment's traditional bar against licensing was more clear-cut—indeed, it was absolute—and surely it should remain uncompromised.[38]

A third expansion of the freedoms of speech and the press has taken these freedoms beyond the verbal nucleus of "speech" and "the press" to all sorts of expressive conduct and uses of government property.[39] This expanded protection is necessarily somewhat contingent, and in recognition of this, the Court weighs government interests and even permits limited types of licensing. In particular, the Court allows government interests to justify laws licensing expressive conduct (such as nudity) or licensing access to what is understood to be common or public property (such as the airwaves or municipal pavements)—property to which the public has strong claims but for which government needs an orderly manner of division.[40] Sometimes, the Court even allows licensing of conduct that

---

subsequent punishment of such as may be deemed contrary to the public welfare. The preliminary freedom extends as well to the false as to the true; the subsequent punishment may extend as well to the true as to the false." *Patterson v Colorado*, 205 US 454, 462 (1907) (citations omitted). This passage is often taken to be significant for its permissive approach to subsequent punishment. More to the point here, however, it suggests the strength of the "preliminary freedom." Indeed, although Holmes acknowledged much room for subsequent punishments, his words about "the main purpose" left at least some space for constitutional limits on such punishments.

[38] It is difficult to find eighteenth-century discussions of the freedom of the press from licensing that suggest it can be overcome by the weight of government interests. Indeed, the very concept of a freedom from licensing was based on the assumption that government could protect the interests of society and government after publication. In the mid-twentieth century, a well-known debate centered on the claim that the freedom of speech, or of the press, is absolute, but that debate focused on broader conceptions of the freedom of the press than the freedom under consideration here—the freedom from any law licensing verbal speech or the press. For a summary of part of the debate, see Alexander Meiklejohn, *The First Amendment Is an Absolute*, Supreme Court Review 245 (1961).

It has sometimes been noted that the Securities Act of 1933 establishes a system of licensing. The Act, on its face, forbids the sale or transportation of securities before a registration statement is in effect, but it uses the prohibition on the sale or transportation of securities to obtain licensing of registration statements. Securities Act of 1934, § 5(a). Obviously, if such licensing is constitutional, this would not necessarily imply the constitutionality of the licensing of research.

[39] For the conception of "verbal speech or the press" in this article, see note 20.

[40] In these ways, such property is very different from government funds. For the licensing of conduct in ways that indirectly burden speech or the press, see *FW/PBS v City of Dallas*, 493 US 215 (1990), concerning licensing of sexually oriented businesses. For examples of the licensing of access to common or public property, see *Cox v New Hampshire*, 312 US 569 (1941); *National Broadcasting Co. v United States*, 319 US 190 (1943); *Thomas v Chicago Park District*, 534 US 316 (2002).

lies just beyond the verbal core of speech and the press. For example, in *Freedman v Maryland*, the Court gave First Amendment protection to movies, but mindful of government interests in treating movies differently from more purely verbal speech or the press, it stated that the licensing of movies would be constitutional—at least "if it takes place under procedural safeguards designed to obviate the dangers of a censorship system."[41] Such concessions to government interests may be necessary for the expansion of the freedom of speech, or of the press, beyond its traditional verbal nucleus, but these concessions do not diminish the First Amendment's absolute protection for its core freedom from licensing of verbal speech or the press. Although contingent when expanded to protect against licensing of nonverbal speech and the press, the Amendment remains at its core an absolute bar against licensing of verbal speech or the press.[42]

Admittedly, the First Amendment's unyielding prohibition on licensing of speech and the press has largely been left on the sidelines

---

[41] *Freedman v Maryland*, 380 US 51 (1965). For recent decisions that apply modified versions of *Freedman*'s procedural requirements to the licensing of sexually oriented or adult businesses, see *City of Littleton, Colorado v Z.J. Gifts D-$, L.L.C.*, 124 S Ct 2219 (2004); *FW/PBS, Inc. v Dallas*, 493 US 215 (1990).

Incidentally, although the Court did not differentiate the sound track and the projected images, these two elements invite slightly different analysis. Imagine that the sound track of the movie were reduced to an audiotape, without any visual images: This sound track seems to fall unambiguously within the category of speech, and presumably, the government could not legislate that producers or theaters must get licenses for the words of sound tracks, even if it requires the licensors to use the highest possible procedural safeguards. (Of course, it could license emissions of noise above safe decibel levels, as long as it imposed this requirement generally rather than just on speech or the press.) In contrast to the words of the sound track, the images are less fully protected. Although the Supreme Court has come to understand visual displays as part of speech and the press, it has not given them the same degree of protection as merely verbal speech and thus has been willing to allow the government to license them. In this sense, the Court treats them more like conduct.

When defending expanded conceptions of rights, lawyers and judges are almost inevitably tempted to blur the distinction between the core freedom and the newer freedoms to which the core has been extended. Hamburger, 90 Va L Rev at 835 (cited in note 25). For example, in justifying its expanded conceptions of the freedom of speech and of the press, the Court blurs the distinction between speech and expressive conduct, and in lumping them together, it often seems to conclude that licensing is presumptively unconstitutional, but not absolutely so. This, however, should not be understood to mean that the core freedom from the licensing of verbal speech or the press is really as contingent as the freedom from the licensing of less narrowly verbal conduct, such as movies.

[42] The exceptions listed by the Supreme Court in *Near v Minnesota* in connection with judicial injunctions do not clearly apply to licensing, for although the government could enact a rule against publication of, for example, certain troop movements, and could obtain an injunction against an attempt to publish such information, this is not to say that it could enact a general rule requiring one to get permission before publishing information about troop movements. *Near v Minnesota*, 283 US 697, 716 (1931). See text at note 147.

of First Amendment theory. Although licensing or censorship of the press was a serious danger in the sixteenth and seventeenth centuries, the threats to freedom of speech, or of the press, in the past century have appeared to come mostly from other pre-publication restraints (mainly judicial injunctions) and from various post-publication restraints (such as laws penalizing political dissent). Licensing has therefore tended to seem a relatively narrow and even antiquated concept, which has been largely displaced by the broader and more up-to-date concepts of pre-publication and post-publication restraints. Yet as already suggested, beneath the surface formed by the concepts of pre- and post-publication restraints, the Supreme Court has continued to preserve at least some elements of a distinctively strong prohibition on licensing, and this poses the central constitutional problem for federal regulations on IRBs.[43]

Licensing is more severely prohibited than other First Amendment problems primarily because it undermines the ideal that one does not need permission to speak or print. It has sometimes been argued that licensing is forbidden because it restrains speech before publication, and on this assumption, it has not been clear whether pre-publication restraints are really more dangerous than post-publication restraints.[44] More fundamentally, however, licensing is

---

[43] It is generally recognized that there is a particularly strong prohibition against prior restraints, but because of the injunction cases, neither courts nor commentators ordinarily concede that there is an even stronger prohibition against licensing. For example, in *Southeastern Promotions*, the Supreme Court wrote: "The presumption against prior restraints is heavier—and the degree of protection broader—than that against limits on expression imposed by criminal penalties. Behind the distinction is a theory deeply etched in our law: a free society prefers to punish the few who abuse rights of speech *after* they break the law than to throttle them and all others beforehand. . . . the line between legitimate and illegitimate speech is often so finely drawn that the risks of freewheeling censorship are formidable." *Southeastern Promotions, Ltd. v Conrad*, 420 US 538, 559–60 (1975).

In *Posadas de Puerto Rico Assoc. v Tourism Co.*, the Court upheld Puerto Rican regulations requiring licensing of gambling advertisements, but as the Court noted, the "prior restraint" argument "was not raised by appellant either below or in this Court," and the Court therefore "express[ed] no view" on this question. *Posadas de Puerto Rico Assoc. v Tourism Co.*, 478 US 328, 348 n 11 (1986). Even in its analysis of the regulations as commercial speech, the case has been much criticized. *44 Liquormart, Inc. v Rhode Island*, 517 US 484 (1996); *Greater New Orleans Broadcasting Ass'n v United States*, 527 US 173 (1999).

[44] See, for example, Justice Frankfurter's opinion for the Court in *Kingsley Books, Inc. v Brown*, 354 US 436 (1957). Earlier, Paul Freund argued that "it will hardly do to place 'prior restraint' in a special category for condemnation. What is needed is a pragmatic assessment of its operation in the particular circumstances." Paul Freund, *The Supreme Court and Civil Liberties*, 4 Vand L Rev 533, 539 (1951). In contrast, Thomas Emerson argues that prior restraint is more dangerous. Emerson, 20 Law & Contemp Probs at 648 (cited in note 23).

More generally, the notion of prior restraint has come into dispute. Martin H. Redish,

a system by which government requires permission for speech or the press, and in this respect, it differs even from other pre-publication restraints, such as judicial injunctions, which interfere prior to publication but without establishing a general expectation that one must get permission.[45]

By requiring that one get permission, licensing laws reverse the ordinary presumption of liberty. Whereas a person is usually free to do as he pleases, as long as he does not violate a known rule of law, licensing laws leave him unfree, until the government or its surrogates give him permission. In matters of speech or the press, licensing encourages Americans to believe that they need permission to speak, print, or otherwise use language, and any such sense of dependence on a licensor's permission seems incompatible with the vigorous speech and press that are essential for protecting liberty. Government depends upon the authority of the people, but if government can make the people feel dependent on it for permission to use speech or the press, they can hardly be expected to assert their authority in limiting government and holding it to account.[46] In this way, the licensing of speech and the press not only reverses the ordinary presumption of liberty but also begins to invert the very relationship of the people to their government.

This central feature of licensing—that one needs permission—has not received much attention. Certainly, the need to get per-

---

The Proper Role of the Prior Restraint Doctrine in First Amendment Theory, 70 Va L Rev 53 (1984); John Jeffries, *Rethinking Prior Restraint*, 92 Yale L J 409 (1982); Blasi, 66 Minn L Rev at 14 (cited in note 21); Owen M. Fiss, *The Civil Rights Injunction* 68–74 (1978); Stephen Barnett, *The Puzzle of Prior Restraint*, 29 Stan L Rev 539 (1977).

[45] This was almost recognized even in *Near v Minnesota*, in which the Court treated an injunction as analogous to licensing. Chief Justice Hughes argued for the Court that if the statute authorizing the injunction were constitutional, "it would be but a step to a complete system of censorship," and "[t]he recognition of authority to impose previous restraint upon publication in order to protect the community . . . necessarily would carry with it the admission of the authority of the censor against which the constitutional barrier was erected." *Near v Minnesota*, 283 US 697, 721 (1931). For more on the relationship between the freedom of speech, or of the press, and the authority of the people in relation to government, see Alexander Meiklejohn, "The First Amendment Is an Absolute," Supreme Court Review 245, 254, 258, 265 (1961).

[46] For the relationship between the First Amendment and the character desirable in citizens, see Vincent Blasi, *Free Speech and Good Character: From Milton to Brandeis to the Present*, in Lee C. Bollinger and Geoffrey R. Stone, eds, *Eternally Vigilant: Free Speech in the Modern Era* 61 (2002)—although the argument here concerns a narrower portion of the First Amendment liberty and a narrower degree of individual independence than discussed by Blasi. In defending the extension of the prohibition against licensing to a prohibition of injunctions, Blasi focuses on the indignity of licensing rather than the central issues of permission, but he recognizes the implications of licensing for the relation between citizens and their government. Blasi, 66 Minn L Rev at 71 (cited in note 21).

mission for the use of speech or the press (in contrast to conduct or the use of government property) is more closely associated with the seventeenth century than the twenty-first. As revealed by IRBs, however, the danger that Americans need to get permission before speaking, reading, writing, printing, or publishing is far from obsolete.

II. Federal IRB Regulations

An understanding of how the federal government runs up against the First Amendment's prohibition on licensing must be based on the details of the government's IRB regulations and policies. Put simply, the regulations establish a system under which persons hoping to conduct research on human subjects at almost all universities and other research institutions must first submit a research proposal to an IRB. The IRB then reviews the research and decides whether the inquiry can proceed. In particular, the IRB will forbid the research, approve it, or, most frequently, offer approval if aspects of it are abandoned or modified.[47] Thus, researchers must get permission, and the IRB can suppress the proposed research—either entire projects or portions of them. The regulations are also vague and overbroad—problems often associated with li-

---

[47] This tripartite division developed already in the 1960s, when one observer wrote: "[A]s a practical matter, many committees probably operate in such a way that few applications are clearly and unequivocally turned down. The research protocol is probably returned for further explanation and revision until the problems are ironed out to the satisfaction of the investigator and the review committee. . . . If an impasse should result, the investigator might well be allowed to withdraw the application rather than have it stamped 'disapproved.'" Curran, 98 Daedalus at 586 (cited in note 3). Levine makes similar assumptions but notes four different categories of decision—approved, approved contingent upon specific revisions, tabled, and disapproved. Levine, *Ethics and Regulation* at 332–34 (cited in note 3). He also emphasizes that the IRB "nearly never" labels a project "disapproved" but instead gives the researcher a chance to withdraw it. Id at 333. On account of both the conditional approvals and the withdrawals, the small number of formal decisions to disapprove cannot be taken at face value. In its Terms for Federalwide Assurances, OHRP spells out the three types of decision and states the power of modification with unusual bluntness: "The IRB(s) will have authority to approve, require modifications in, or disapprove the covered human subject research." OHRP, *Federalwide Assurance of Protection for Human Subjects*, Terms of the Federalwide Assurance for Institutions Within the United States, Part A.5, at http://www.hhs.gov/ohrp/humansubjects/assurance/filasurt.htm.

The power to modify can come in the form of either a contingent approval—that is, an approval subject to conditions—or a deferral with recommendations for changes. A large but uncertain number of the modifications focus on informed consent, which, as will be seen, can become a significant barrier to research.

censing.[48] It is, however, the licensing itself—the requirement that researchers get permission—that is the focus of this inquiry.

A. THE COMMON RULE

The basic regulatory scheme is known as the "Common Rule" because it has been adopted by seventeen federal departments and agencies—most prominently, the Department of Health and Human Services ("HHS"). Supplementary regulations establish specialized rules for research on vulnerable subjects, such as (in the HHS regulations) pregnant mothers, fetuses, neonates, children, and prisoners.[49] The Common Rule as adopted by HHS has particularly wide application, and therefore this essay concentrates on HHS's version, but it does so to illustrate all the federal regulations that adopt or supplement the Common Rule. In these regulations, which are casually referred to here as the "federal regulations on IRBs," the central requirement is that an IRB must review and decide whether to approve any "research" involving "human subjects."[50]

A human subject is defined by the Common Rule as "a living individual" about whom an investigator conducting research obtains "data through intervention or interaction with the individual" or "identifiable private information."[51] The rule thus relies upon privity and the character of the information to determine if research has a human subject. The notion of "identifiable private

---

[48] For example, the regulations are vague in allowing IRBs to make decisions without rules and even on the basis of "prevailing community standards and subjective determinations," and they are overbroad in requiring IRBs to evaluate the mere risk of harm and thus requiring them to prevent much speech and the press that will not turn out to be injurious.

The overbreadth doctrine has been applied to permit facial challenges to licensing laws. In *City of Lakewood v Plain Dealer Publishing Co.*, a city ordinance gave the mayor discretion to grant or deny permits for newspaper vending machines on city sidewalks. Although he had not misused his powers, the Court held the ordinance unconstitutionally overbroad on the ground that "a facial challenge lies whenever a licensing law gives a government official or agency substantial power to discriminate based on the content or viewpoint of speech by suppressing disfavored speech or disliked speakers." *City of Lakewood v Plain Dealer Publishing Co.*, 486 US 750 (1988). See also *Forsyth County, Ga. v Nationalist Movement*, 505 US 123 (1992), in which a county permit ordinance allowing the county administrator to adjust fees up to $1,000 a day was held unconstitutionally overbroad.

[49] 66 Fed Reg 56775; 43 id 53655; 48 id 9818; 56 id 28032.

[50] 45 CFR Part 46. For the current statutory authorization for the HHS regulations, see 42 USC § 289 (2004). For descriptions of some early IRBs, see Levine, *Ethics and Regulation* at 328–41 (cited in note 3), and the sources cited at id 327.

[51] 45 CFR § 46.102(f).

information" is particularly expansive and unclear, for it is understood to go beyond confidential medical records and other information acquired within a fiduciary duty to include other, more loosely private information, but how far it goes in this direction is not specified. For example, it may, perhaps, include information in a manuscript autobiography that an author shares with a scholar of literature, and it may include what a person says publicly in front of a limited audience, such as in a classroom.[52]

Research is defined as a "systematic investigation" that is designed to develop or contribute to "generalizable knowledge."[53] The regulations thereby adopt the scientific model of research, in which a researcher systematically and self-consciously tests a hypothesis or at least seeks evidence that may eventually lead to the formulation of a general statement. Most academic inquiry, however, is systematic in one way or another by the standards of the researcher's discipline, and almost all serious research can be understood to test or contribute to knowledge that is generalizable at one level or another. To be sure, in the humanities and social sciences, the investigation may not be obviously systematic, and the generalizable conclusions may be so understated as to be evident only to initiates. Nonetheless, as defined by the Common Rule, research can reasonably be understood to include more than just the inquiry that openly adopts the scientific model. For example, in medicine, HHS's Office for Human Research Protections ("OHRP") has stated that quality improvement studies can be subject to IRBs, and in the humanities and social sciences, IRBs enjoy jurisdiction over history and other largely nonscientific inquiry.[54]

---

[52] The latter interpretation has been taken by IRBs at, for example, Reed College and the University of Illinois. Reed College Human Subjects Research Committee (IRB), *Summary of Review Categories and Procedures*, p 4 (2003–04); David Wright, *Creative Nonfiction and the Academy: A Cautionary Tale*, 10 Qualitative Inquiry 202, 204–05 (2004).

[53] 45 CFR § 46.102(d).

[54] For the quality improvement studies, see J. Lynn, *When Does Quality Improvement Count as Research? Human Subject Protection and Theories of Knowledge*, 13 Quality and Safety in Health Care 67 (2004); Kristina C. Borror, Compliance Oversight Coordinator, HHS, Letter to Dennis Swanson and Associate Vice Chancellor Dr. Juhl, University of Pittsburgh (April 4, 2002). For more on quality improvement studies, see text at notes 183–84. The reach of IRBs over the humanities and social sciences can be illustrated by an IRB at Florida State University that claimed jurisdiction over all of the humanities, including literature, religion, and music. Christopher Shea, *Don't Talk to the Humans: The Crackdown on Social Science Research*, 10 Lingua Franca 26, 29 (2000). See also the view of the National Bioethics Advisory Commission, discussed in AAUP, *Protecting Human Beings*, Academe: Bulletin of the AAUP at 58 (cited in note 12).

With a broad sense of its general jurisdiction over human subjects "research," at least one IRB has even attempted to license a literary essay. This occurred at the University of Illinois, where a professor of creative literature asked his students to tell stories about themselves in ways that adopted the techniques of creative writing. The approach is known as "creative nonfiction" because it self-consciously explores the subjective character of attempts to depict the truth. The professor subsequently wrote an essay about this teaching experience, in which he himself used the methods of creative nonfiction, and in which he used fictional names when referring to the students. After the piece was accepted by the *Kenyon Review*, the IRB charged him with "bad research practices" for failing to get the permission of the students before making allusions to them and their descriptions of their experiences.[55] Of particular concern to the Executive Secretary of the IRB was that the professor's "article discussed the moral dilemmas" he faced "when a student in a creative writing class submitted an essay suggesting the student had taken part in a gang-related murder some years earlier." On this account, "the IRB chair threatened to prevent publication of the article" if the professor "didn't withdraw it from [the] Kenyon Review." After the professor's colleagues came to his defense and persuaded the IRB to back down, he got his work published, but these events suggest how the expansive definition of "research" leaves some IRBs with a sense that even in the humanities they have a power to examine merely verbal "research" before it is undertaken, let alone published.[56]

When considering whether to approve research projects, IRBs must weigh risks and benefits. In particular, they must determine that "[r]isks to subjects are reasonable in relation to anticipated benefits, if any, to subjects, and the importance of the knowledge that may reasonably be expected to result."[57] The Common Rule

---

[55] Wright, 10 Qualitative Inquiry 202, 204–05 (cited in note 52).

[56] E-mail message from Professor Dennis Baron (Oct 20, 2004) (who at the time of the incident was head of the English Department). Part of this account is confirmed by other e-mails. In particular, only minutes after the Executive Secretary finally called Wright to explain that the IRB would end its investigation, Wright wrote an e-mail to various colleagues in which he explained that the Executive Secretary had "called to let me know that the IRB 'considers action unnecessary' in this case. it 'doesn't fit the category' and is 'not worth pursuing from an IRB standpoint.' he added that, likewise, the IRB 'won't pursue the Kenyon Review' to have them remove the essay from their publication. (hurrah.)" E-mail message from David Wright to five colleagues (May 10, 2002).

[57] 45 CFR § 46.111(a)(2).

thus gives IRBs some principles with which to evaluate research, but it does not give them a rule or even a loose standard with which to determine what combination of risk and benefit is permissible.[58] An IRB must therefore rely on its own judgment. Indeed, the Common Rule offers its principles only as the minimum, and an IRB may in addition apply its own institution's moral standards.[59] Moreover, at least one member of each IRB must be unaffiliated with the institution that established the IRB, and this member is expected to represent the "perspective" of the "local community."[60] Overall, as explained by OHRP, an IRB must make "a judgment that often depends upon prevailing community standards and subjective determinations of risk and benefit. Consequently, different IRBs may arrive at different assessments of a particular risk/benefit ratio."[61]

In order to weigh the risks and benefits of research, IRBs need to review the details of a researcher's procedures. For example, when a research project (in medicine or the social sciences) involves a survey or interview, IRBs tend to ask the researcher to submit his questions ahead of time in writing so that the IRB can review the risks they may create. After reviewing and sometimes modifying the questions, IRBs require the researcher to adhere to these written questions. A researcher therefore cannot shift his line of questioning, follow up on points raised by the subjects, or engage in normal conversations.

The federal government encourages IRBs to calculate the risks of marginal harms. When the federal government asks universities and other institutions to give assurances that they have IRBs, it suggests that they establish IRBs on the principles of the *Belmont Report*—issued in 1979 by the National Commission for the Pro-

---

[58] The "risk" to be considered in the approval of research is undefined, for as the OHRP *Guidebook* acknowledges, "[f]ederal regulations define only 'minimal risk'"—the standard for expedited review. OHRP, *Institutional Review Board Guidebook*, ch III, Part A.

[59] 45 CFR § 46.102(h). See also Levine, *Ethics and Regulation* at 342 (cited in note 3).

[60] OHRP, *Institutional Review Board Guidebook*, ch I, Part B. For the membership requirement, see 45 CFR § 46.107(d).

[61] OHRP, *Institutional Review Board Guidebook*, ch III, Part A. Much research has established the variability of IRB determinations. See, for example, Mary Terrell White and Jennifer Gamm, *Informed Consent for Research on Stored Blood and Tissue Samples: A Survey of Institutional Review Board Practices*, 9 Accountability in Research 1 (2002); Jon Mark Hirshon, Scott D. Krugman, et al, *Variability in Institutional Review Board Assessment of Minimal-Risk Research*, 9 Academic Emergency Med 1417 (2002); Thomas O. Stair, Caitlin R. Reed, et al, *Variation in Institutional Review Board Responses to a Standard Protocol for a Multicenter Clinical Trial*, 8 Academic Emergency Med 636 (2001).

tection of Human Subjects of Biomedical and Behavioral Research.[62] According to this report, IRBs need to anticipate a broad range of harms, including legal, economic, social, psychological, and "other possible kinds" as yet undefined.[63] In explaining to IRBs how they should evaluate such harms, the National Science Foundation advises that risks of "legal harm," "financial harm," "moral harm," social "stigma," mental "upset," or "worry" can be sufficient reasons to deny permission to do research.[64] Furthermore, the government reminds IRBs to be careful about the injuries arising from the study of "sensitive" topics. For example, the *Institutional Review Board Guidebook*—published by OHRP—suggests that IRBs need to consider the emotional harms arising from research and explains: "Stress and feelings of guilt or embarrassment may arise simply from thinking or talking about one's own behavior or attitudes on sensitive topics such as drug use, sexual preferences, selfishness, and violence."[65] In this way, the govern-

---

[62] HHS, *Federal Wide Assurance (FWA) for the Protection of Human Subjects for Domestic (U.S.) Institutions*, p 1 (version date 03/20/2002). Alternatively, institutions can negotiate for some other statement of principles.

[63] National Commission for the Protection of Human Subjects of Biomedical and Behavioral Research, *Belmont Report*, Part C.2 (1979). Increasingly, some institutions now expand upon the "respect for persons" discussed by the *Belmont Report* (in Part B.1) and insist that IRBs should attend to *"Dignitary harm,"* which "can result when individuals are treated as means to an end and not as people deserving respect for their own values and preferences." National Research Council, *Protecting Participants* at 28 (cited in note 5). In this spirit, Columbia University, for example, informs its faculty that the "primary responsibility" of its IRB "is to protect the rights, privacy and dignity of human research participants." E-mail from Provost Alan Brinkley and Executive Vice President for Research to Faculty, Administrators, and Students at the Morningside Campus (Oct 15, 2004).

[64] National Science Foundation, Division of Institution and Award Support, *Frequently Asked Questions and Vignettes*, at http://www.nsf.gov/bfa/dias/policy/hsfaqs.htm. In contrast, the Kalven Report states: "The mission of the university is the discovery, improvement, and dissemination of knowledge. Its domain of inquiry and scrutiny includes all aspects and all values of society. A university faithful to its mission will provide enduring challenges to social values, policies, practices, institutions. By design and by effect, it is the institution which creates discontent with the existing social arrangements and proposes new ones. In brief, a good university, like Socrates, will be upsetting." Kalven Committee, *Report on the University's Role in Political and Social Action* (1967), at http://www.uchicago.edu/docs/policies/provostoffice/kalverpt.pdf.

[65] OHRP, *Institutional Review Board Guidebook*, ch III, Part A. Bradford Gray notes the early history of the sensitivity requirement: "The 1974 regulations made no reference to the sensitivity of the questions asked in research. Some IRBs, however, apparently have made the sensitivity of the questions asked in social or psychological research a factor in their risk-benefit judgments. The 1981 regulations may encourage this practice by making the collection of 'sensitive aspects of an individual's behavior such as illegal conduct, drug use, sexual behavior, or use of alcohol' a factor in determining whether certain social and behavioral research will [be] exempt from the regulations." He adds: "The possibility is troublesome for First Amendment reasons . . ."; Bradford H. Gray, *The Regulatory Context*

ment leaves IRBs in no doubt that research on "sensitive" topics (including research involving nothing more than asking questions) should get a particularly thorough examination.

The federal regulations even require that IRB members be chosen for their sensitivity to "community" attitudes. Each IRB, according to the Common Rule, must "be sufficiently qualified through the experience and expertise of its members, and the diversity of the members, including considerations of race, gender, and cultural backgrounds and sensitivity to such issues as community attitudes, to promote respect for its advice and counsel in safeguarding the rights and welfare of human subjects."[66] It is a mere curiosity that the decisions of an IRB are called its "advice and counsel" and that diversity is valued so that it can "promote respect" for such advice and counsel. More pertinent for constitutional analysis is the requirement of "sensitivity" to "community attitudes" (and other "such issues," whatever they may be).[67]

---

of Social and Behavioral Research, in Beauchamp, *Ethical Issues in Social Science Research* at 348–49 (cited in note 11).

[66] 45 CFR § 46.107(a).

[67] Incidentally, the regulations also require IRBs to ensure that the researcher's selection of subjects is "equitable," thus subjecting to censorship his decision about whom he will study. The regulations explain: "In order to approve research covered by this policy the IRB shall determine that . . . . Selection of subjects is equitable. In making this assessment the IRB should take into account the purposes of the research and the setting in which the research will be conducted and should be particularly cognizant of the special problems of research involving vulnerable populations, such as children, prisoners, pregnant women, mentally disabled persons, or economically or educationally disadvantaged persons." 45 CFR § 46.111(a)(3).
There is a long history of academics studying the impoverished, the weak, and the oppressed—both to draw attention to their needs and to explore the intellectual questions that can be understood only by examining such groups. The *Belmont Report*, however, examines the selection of subjects as a matter of "justice" and asks: "Who ought to receive the benefits of research and bear its burdens? This is a question of justice, in the sense of 'fairness in distribution.'" After alluding briefly to the Tuskegee syphilis study, it concludes that "against this historical background, . . . conceptions of justice are relevant to research involving human subjects," and it elaborates that "the selection of research subjects needs to be scrutinized in order to determine whether some classes (e.g., welfare patients, particular racial and ethnic minorities, or persons confined to institutions) are being systematically selected simply because of their easy availability, their compromised position, or their manipulability, rather than for reasons directly related to the problem being studied." National Commission for the Protection of Human Subjects of Biomedical and Behavioral Research, *Belmont Report*, Part B.3 (1979). These concerns are reasonable, but they are only a few of many reasonable considerations relevant to the selection of research subjects. None of this, moreover, explains why the selection of subjects is a matter of general government regulation, for although the government can chose to fund only such studies as examine subjects who meet its criteria, its legislative interests in preserving equal rights surely do not extend to controlling the selection of evidence in intellectual inquiries. Most essentially, however, even the strongest claims about justice would not warrant the requirement that researchers must get prior permission from licensors.

B. INFORMED CONSENT

The federal regulations require researchers to obtain informed consent, which means that researchers must get permission not only from the IRB but also from the persons they study. The regulations state that, in general, "no investigator may involve a human being as a subject in research covered by this policy unless the investigator has obtained the legally effective informed consent of the subject," and the regulations require this consent to be "documented by the use of a written consent form approved by the IRB and signed by the subject."[68]

The regulations borrow these informed consent requirements from medicine. Doctors have a Hippocratic duty and a duty to avoid negligent injury, and in any case, they need to avoid committing a battery against their patients, and thus on grounds of both morals and prudence, they typically have reason to keep their patients informed and to get their consent. The federal regulations, however, more broadly require that informed consent be obtained by researchers, most of whom are not doctors.

Like journalists, researchers who are not doctors usually do not owe a specially high standard of care to their subjects. Indeed, researchers sometimes, quite legitimately, have an almost adversarial relationship to their subjects. Nonetheless, under the regulations, even researchers who merely inquire about political opinion or observe public behavior must often preface their interviews or observations with warnings about the dangers of talking to them or of allowing them to observe, and they must obtain signed documents evidencing the consent of the subjects. By requiring researchers to begin their colloquies not with a question, but with a printed warning and a request for a signature, the regulations discourage persons from talking to researchers and often probably skew the results.

Informed consent thus has the very opposite effect among researchers as among doctors. For doctors in their relationship to their patients, and for others (including researchers) who engage in physical contact that might be considered a battery, consent—together with the information necessary for it—is, at the very least, a prudent precaution, and the need for this consent stimulates the

---

[68] 45 CFR § 46.116; 45 CFR § 46.117(a).

flow of information.[69] In contrast, when informed consent is generally required of researchers in their relationship to the rest of society (regardless of whether they would otherwise be committing a battery), the requirement of informed consent is a barrier to the transmission of information and even the asking of ordinary questions. Nor should this be a surprise: It is one thing to choose to get permission to do what would otherwise be an intentional physical tort; it is another to be required to get permission to engage in inquiry. As imposed on research, informed consent thus becomes a democratized licensing system, whereby intellectuals must get permission from individuals before talking with them, before observing them, and even before reading about them.

IRBs compound the problem of informed consent by requiring researchers to get prior IRB approval for their informed consent forms and by rewriting these forms to make them more onerous. When IRBs expect that the research will cause stress to the subjects or will be controversial, they increase their scrutiny of informed consent and tend to ask the researchers to give their subjects extra strong warnings about the risks of participation.[70] The largest single class of modifications to research probably involve changes in informed consent, and although the changes are often small, they almost always impede consent.

Incidentally, both the informed consent requirement and the need for IRB approval apply not only to research requiring intervention or interaction with human subjects but also research that reexamines data collected in earlier research, if it contains

---

[69] Obviously, however, this is not to say that (in the absence of IRB regulations) the same amount of information must be provided by doctors conducting research on their patients and persons conducting research outside of a doctor-patient relationship.

[70] Most IRBs have the good sense not to advertise their approach to controversial research, but at Florida State University, the IRB candidly states that "full committee review is required when . . . research is of a controversial nature." Florida State University, Office of Research, *Human Subjects Committee*, at http://www.research.fsu.edu/humansubjects/applications/full.html. The IRB even asks researchers questions such as: "Is the research area controversial and is there a possibility your project will generate public concern? If so, please explain?" Florida State University, *Human Subjects Application to the Institutional Review Board for Research Involving Human Subjects*, at http://www.research.fsu.edu/humansubjects/applications/documents/irbapp1299.txt, quoted by Christopher Shea, *Don't Talk to the Humans: The Crackdown on Social Science Research*, 10 Lingua Franca 26, 29 (2000).

IRBs can in some instances waive the requirement of informed consent or at least that concerning documentation of informed consent, but they are notoriously hesitant to grant a waiver and frequently do so only if the researcher agrees not to collect information about the identity of the subjects or about sensitive matters. Yet if the researcher uses informed consent of the stringent sort required by many IRBs or if he accepts the demand that he obtain signed documentation of the consent, he is less likely to collect useful information.

"identifiable private information." As already noted, private information is understood to include much information that is not proprietary, subject to a fiduciary duty, otherwise confidential, or even very personal.[71] Scholars who wish to examine such data after a research project is complete must typically secure further informed consent for the new use of the data and must get additional approval from an IRB.

C. EXCEPTIONS AND EXEMPTIONS

To make the indeterminate breadth of the licensing more manageable, the regulations carve out various exceptions and exemptions, but these do not spare researchers from having to get permission. One of the exceptions is "[e]xpedited review." The Common Rule makes expedited review available for a project if it does not go beyond various commonplace procedures listed by HHS, such as the use of surveys or the collection of blood samples by venipuncture. Yet even this research is eligible for expedited review only if the IRB determines that it involves "no more than minimal risk."[72]

The exemptions are broader. For example, there are exemptions for reading publicly available documents and for surveys, interviews, or observations of public officials. The exemption of research on public officials apparently rests on the assumption that this would be political speech, but it is oddly narrow, for it refers to "elected or appointed public officials"—the latter being usually understood to include only appointees who are public figures. Of course, it is also strangely narrow because research on persons

---

[71] 45 CFR § 102(f)(2). For example, "*[p]rivate information* includes information about behavior that occurs in a context in which an individual can reasonably expect that no observation or recording is taking place." Id. To recognize the breadth of this concept of private information, consider its application to the research that might be done in a restaurant: Private information would include ethnographic observations and linguistic observations about the language used by waiters and waitresses. Accordingly, if the researcher would learn the identity of the persons (which would be very likely in a small town), and if he aimed to develop or contribute to generalizable knowledge (which would be very likely if he were an academic), his research would be subject to approval by an IRB, which would seek to protect the subjects from the usual array of legal, economic, social, and mental harms.

[72] 45 CFR § 46.110(b)(1). In addition, some "minor changes in previously approved research" can receive expedited review. 45 CFR § 46.110(b)(2). The Common Rule defines minimal risk to be when "the probability and magnitude of harm or discomfort anticipated in the research are not greater in and of themselves than those ordinarily encountered in daily life or during the performance of routine physical or psychological examinations or tests." 45 CFR § 46.102(i).

who are not officials (including the poor, ill, and oppressed) can be equally political. The regulations further exempt research consisting of a researcher's "survey procedures," "interview procedures," and "observation of public behavior," but not if the identity of the subject will be identifiable from the researcher's records and the disclosure of the information could harm the subject—for example, in his employability or reputation.[73] Accordingly, this research is not exempt if it will elicit controversial opinions. As the National Science Foundation explains, such research is exempt only if the "information would not cause harm to the individual if it were known"—"[f]or example, recording observations of everyday public behavior, or interviewing people about noncontroversial opinions or preferences."[74]

These exemptions, however, do not really allow researchers to escape the licensing, because the government expects the IRBs to determine whether a research project falls within the exemptions, thus even making exempt research subject to the prior judgment of the IRB. In the words of OHRP, it "recommends that institutions adopt clear procedures under which the IRB (or an authority other than the investigator) determines whether proposed research is exempt from the human subjects regulations."[75] The government ex-

---

[73] 45 CFR § 46.101(b)(2). Compared to the rest of the regulations, the harm element is stated narrowly here, but it remains very broad: "Research involving the use of educational tests (cognitive, diagnostic, aptitude, achievement), survey procedures, interview procedures or observation of public behavior, unless: (i) information obtained is recorded in such a manner that human subjects can be identified, directly or through identifiers linked to the subjects; and (ii) any disclosure of the human subjects' responses outside the research could reasonably place the subjects at risk of criminal or civil liability or be damaging to the subjects' financial standing, employability, or reputation." Id.

[74] National Science Foundation, Division of Institution and Award Support, *Frequently Asked Questions and Vignettes*, at http://www.nsf.gov/bfa/dias/policy/hsfaqs.htm.

[75] OHRP, *Guidance on Written IRB Procedures*, Additional OHRP Guidance, Part D(1) (July 11, 2002), at http://www.hhs.gov/ohrp/humansubjects/guidance/irbgd702.htm. Indeed, this is sometimes required in an institution's assurance—as when the University of Chicago assures the government: "All human subject research which is exempt under Section 101(b)(1–6) or 101(i) will be conducted in accord with . . . this Institution's administrative procedures to ensure valid claims of exemption." University of Chicago, *Multiple Project Assurance of Compliance with DHHS Regulations for Protection of Human Research Subjects* 3, Part III.B. The ethnographer Jack Katz complains that "the requirement to apply to receive a certification as exempt guts the protections" of "the exemption criteria." Jack Katz, *To Participants in the UCLA, May 2002, Fieldwork Conference* (May 8, 2002), at http://leroyneiman.sscnet.ucla.edu/katz5_8.htm.

Incidentally, to avoid unnecessary delays, IRBs can publish general determinations that some types of information (for example, publicly available data sets) are exempt, but even when researchers confine their work to such information, IRBs feel obliged under the regulations to require the researchers to "register" their research projects with the IRB. For example, the University of Chicago's Social and Behavioral Sciences IRB emphasizes

pects researchers to get an IRB's permission even for exempt research because the extent of the exemptions is not always clear and the government does not trust researchers to exercise good judgment. For example, the exemption for observations or surveys of elected or appointed public officials does not clearly extend to any but the highest-level appointees, and therefore an IRB needs to pre-examine all research on public officials to ensure that research extending beyond the narrow exemption will undergo the IRB's full process of approval, modification, or denial.[76]

D. CONSEQUENCES

The IRBs do not formally impose "penalties" on students, faculty, or other researchers for failing to conform to the regulations. They certainly, however, impose consequences.

IRBs frequently approve research only after requesting modifications, and IRBs thereby, in effect, suppress the modified aspects of the research.[77] For example, if the questions in a survey or interview are likely to elicit what an IRB considers confidential, sensitive, or private information, it will sometimes require researchers to omit or alter their questions. More frequently, IRBs give approval on the condition that the researcher not collect names or other identifying information about the subjects. In a similar spirit, IRBs sometimes require researchers to assure the IRB that they will not disclose and thus not publish the infor-

---

that such "researchers do need to register their research" with the IRB. University of Chicago, Social and Behavioral Sciences IRB, *Policy on Public Use Data Sets*, at http://humansubjects.uchicago.edu/sbsirb/publicpolicy.html. For example, the University of Chicago lists as exempt the data published on the website of the U.S. Bureau of the Census, but even under this dispensation, a researcher working from the public census data must register his research by submitting information about it to the IRB.

[76] Another reason that the regulations require researchers get permission even for exempt research is that the government encourages IRBs to apply not only the federal regulations but also the ethical principles of its institution, and IRBs can do this only if they review exempt research as well as that which requires approval. From this perspective, the National Science Foundation advises IRBs: "When the subjects are public officials or candidates for public office, the research is exempt even when identifiers are included or disclosure might be harmful. However, all research should be bound by professional ethics and respect for respondents to guard their privacy whether or not the research is exempt (unless the participants understand that their information may be made public and permission is granted)." National Science Foundation, Division of Institution and Award Support, *Frequently Asked Questions and Vignettes*, at http://www.nsf.gov/bfa/dias/policy/hsfaqs.htm.

[77] For example, an IRB will write to a researcher that specified "problems were identified and need to be addressed in an amendment resubmission in order for the project to proceed." Letter from IRB to investigator.

mation, and IRBs frequently use informed consent forms to get researchers to make such statements.[78] Indeed, by requiring excessively somber warnings in informed consent forms—even those for social science research—IRBs can ensure low participation, and in this way can force a halt to research they find objectionable, without formally denying approval.

IRBs also routinely require researchers to destroy data or information after they have used it. IRBs often ask researchers to strip identifying information from data and even sometimes ask that they eventually destroy the codes that link the identifying information to the rest of the data. IRBs occasionally even require researchers to dispose of all their data, and they regularly instruct researchers to destroy video and audio tapes.[79] In the words of the federal regulations, an IRB must determine that "[w]hen appropriate, the research plan makes adequate provision for monitoring the data collected to ensure the safety of subjects."[80]

If research needs approval and does not get it, the IRB can stop the research, and if the research departs from a condition imposed by an IRB, the IRB can "terminate approval."[81] From the IRB's

---

[78] IRBs also sometimes require researchers to obtain certificates of confidentiality—that is, federal certificates that purportedly allow researchers "to refuse to disclose identifying information on research participants in any civil, criminal, administrative, legislative, or other proceeding, whether at the federal, state, or local level." NIH has made clear that it "would like to encourage" the use of these certificates. NIH, Office of Extramural Research, *Certificates of Confidentiality Kiosk*, at http://grants1.nih.gov/grants/policy/coc/.

[79] This destroys the possibility of later verifying transcriptions or other information drawn from the recordings.

[80] 45 CFR § 46.111(a)(6). At some universities, IRBs allow researchers to place the identifying information in the hands of third parties so that replication remains possible, but if the information is kept in two places, it is unlikely that researchers will be able to locate both parts after one or two decades have passed. The National Science Foundation goes so far as to state that even without a request from an IRB, a professor has an obligation to destroy data—for example, if a student becomes a research subject and reveals "some sanctioned behavior," such as "plagiarism on the part of the student," then "[t]o protect the student, the record should be erased immediately." National Science Foundation, Division of Institution and Award Support, *Frequently Asked Questions and Vignettes*, at http://www.nsf.gov/bfa/dias/policy/hsfaqs.htm.

IRBs also license the reuse of data, and thus researchers who seek data already collected and available at an institution need to get IRB approval, even though this is really just a question of sharing information or publication. For example, an IRB at one institution recently wrote to some investigators: "Upon receipt of a security protocol, the . . . IRB will authorize the release of data. If data is to be linked with identifiers, a document attesting that the appropriate security procedures are in place must be submitted along with the names, titles, and affiliations of the individuals who will have access to the linked data. Each person with access to the linked data must provide certification of having taken human subject protections training and must sign a statement [that] names of any research subjects will be protected." Letter from IRB to investigators.

[81] 45 CFR § 46.113.

perspective, it takes these actions to prevent harm to human subjects rather than to penalize researchers, but the implications extend further than the research.[82] According to OHRP, "[w]hen unapproved research is discovered, the IRB and the institution should" not only "act promptly to halt the research" but should also "address the question of the investigator's fitness to conduct human subject research."[83] If the IRB finds him unfit (even if merely for failing to ask for prior permission to study), it can prevent him from doing other research on human subjects.[84] More typically, the IRB will simply take into account a researcher's prior "'virtue'" or "track record" of cooperation with the IRB when making decisions about his proposals.[85]

IRBs often discourage publication in ways that go beyond their mechanisms for securing nondisclosure of information. Some university IRBs have intervened even after research or other inquiry has been completed, and thus have directly interfered with publication (such as at George Washington, Illinois, and Pittsburgh). Most IRBs, however, leave control of publication to others.[86] Many

---

[82] Of course, there is also evidence that IRBs act to avoid federal consequences for their institution. See Yvonna S. Lincoln and William G. Tierney, *Qualitative Research and Institutional Review Boards*, 10 Qualitative Inquiry 219, 225 (2004).

[83] OHRP, *Institutional Review Board Guidebook*, ch I, Part D. Strikingly, it adds: "Beyond the obvious need to protect the rights and welfare of research subjects, the credibility of the IRB is clearly at stake." Id.

[84] Indeed, the oldest independent IRB in the country declares: "IRBs have the authority to approve, require modifications to, or disapprove the proposed study protocols and consent forms for research which will involve human subjects. In addition, IRBs must review and approve or disapprove the investigator for the research." Western Institutional Review Board, *About Us*, at http://www.wirb.com/.

[85] As Robert Levine states, "many IRBs take the investigator's 'virtue' into account in making decisions about protocols. For example, Shannon and Ockene report on their IRB's disapproval of a low risk protocol based, in part, on the fact that the investigator had a poor relationship with the IRB . . . . In the same paper, they report their IRB's approval of a high risk protocol; one important factor was that the investigator had 'an excellent track record in terms of trustworthiness, exemplified by his willingness to report immediately any problem in research by notifying the appropriate people.' Moreover, 'within the medical center . . . he was perceived to be skilled and trustworthy.'" Levine, *Ethics and Regulation* at 27 (cited in note 3).

[86] For Illinois, see David Wright, *Creative Nonfiction and the Academy: A Cautionary Tale*, 10 Qualitative Inquiry 202, 204–05 (2004), discussed at notes 55–56. At George Washington, after researchers obtained approval for experiments related to human cloning, the IRB later discovered that they had already done the research when they got approval, and as Harold Edgar and David Rothman explain: "When it learned of this breach, the IRB penalized the investigators, compelling them to withdraw an abstract of their findings." Harold Edgar and David J. Rothman, *The Institutional Review Board and Beyond: Future Challenges to the Ethics of Human Experimentation*, 73 Milbank Quarterly 489, 499 (1995). At the University of Pittsburgh, the Senior Vice Chancellor for the Health Sciences

journals have so deeply absorbed the ethos of licensing that they will not publish work unless it has been licensed by an IRB, and in some fields, a scholar who does not have IRB permission may have difficulty finding a reputable journal to publish his research.[87] Taking advantage of this, IRBs often warn students and professors that they need IRB permission for their research if they hope to get it published.[88] Under pressure from OHRP to prevent violations of IRB regulations, some IRBs match their approvals against publications by the faculty to check that their faculty have obtained IRB approval for their research, and some scholars therefore hesitate to publish or draw attention to licensed research even after it is written. They understand that if the IRB learns they did not get prior approval, they might in the future have difficulty getting permission for a project. Increasing the disincentive for publishing unapproved work, universities sometimes warn of "serious consequences" for those who do not follow the IRB rules.[89]

---

required personnel in his division to submit their manuscripts to him. Upon getting a piece accepted in a peer-reviewed journal, a researcher was required to send him a copy of the manuscript so that an individual in his office could review it for compliance with IRB and related licensing rules, and, at least in theory, the Vice Chancellor would have a manuscript pulled if it did not conform. Not surprisingly, after a number of years of such review, manuscripts tended to comply with the licensing rules, and the Chancellor ended this experiment.

[87] In this connection, the International Committee of Medical Journal Editors includes in its *Uniform Requirements for Manuscripts Submitted to Biomedical Journals* a requirement that: "When reporting experiments on human subjects, authors should indicate whether the procedures followed were in accordance with the ethical standards of the responsible committee on human experimentation . . ." . International Committee of Medical Journal Editors, *Uniform Requirements for Manuscripts Submitted to Biomedical Journals*, Part II.F, at http://www.icmje.org/#protect. For a brief account of the history of this sort of policy among journals, see Levine, *Ethics and Regulation* at 27–31 (cited in note 3).

[88] Although these warnings usually occur in private communications between IRBs and individual researchers, they can also appear in print. After posing the question, "What's the worst that can happen if I don't request IRB approval?" one IRB explains: "Articles may not be published: Many professional journals require evidence of IRB approval when considering articles for publication." University of Alaska Fairbanks, Institutional Review Board, *Ensuring the Rights and Welfare of Human Participants in Research* 11, at http://www.auf.edu/irb/faqs.html.

[89] University of Chicago, Social and Behavioral Sciences Institutional Review Board, *Frequently Asked Questions* 2, at http://humansubjects.uchicago.edu/sbsirb/faq.html (dated 2/13/2003). See also, for example, e-mail message from Provost Alan Brinkley and Executive Vice President for Research to Faculty, Administrators, and Students at the Morningside Campus (Oct 15, 2004). At a recent meeting held by the Northwestern University IRB, when a representative of the IRB referred to such consequences, a law professor "asked what would happen if I went ahead without approval, and I was told that there would be disciplinary action at the highest levels; I could be subject to severe sanctions." He also said that nonconforming "students could have their diplomas withheld; faculty might even be dismissed." Conversation with Professor Cynthia Bowman, Northwestern University Law School (Dec 10, 2004).

More generally, researchers recognize that IRB licensing is conducted under authority or color of federal law, and they therefore fear that they would be violating federal policy if they published without IRB approval.

The practical implications of IRBs can be illustrated by a hypothetical history student who wants to study the participation of women in the 1964 campaign for equal voting rights. If she hopes to write to some of the women to get their accounts of their experiences, she must first consult an IRB for "approval" of the project, including the specific questions she plans to ask the women. If the student wants only to read about the women in books available in the university library, she need not consult the IRB, but if she obtains from one of the women letters she received from another woman describing their activities in 1964, the student cannot read the correspondence for her research unless she first gets the IRB's approval.[90] If the IRB is concerned that either of the women may be "upset" or may suffer any social "stigma" from the student's writing or publishing of her paper, it can ask the student to warn the women of the dangers and can require her to get their permission before she reads the letters. It can also ask the student not to identify the women in her paper or her publication. It can additionally ask the student, after she has finished her project, to destroy any portions of her notes that mention their identity.

Incidentally, the student herself cannot ask for IRB approval because students might not be sufficiently responsive to IRB requests. Thus, at most universities, the "principal investigator" must be a faculty member. The professor is therefore required to claim a role that he in fact does not have, and the student must, in effect, get the permission of both a teacher and the IRB. So stringent is the licensing requirement that if the student needs "approval" for her research and proceeds without it, she cannot get approval retroactively, even if her research clearly created no more than minimal risk. At best, she can get a statement from the IRB that her research would have been approved if submitted before its inception (a statement that can ameliorate some of the difficulties of getting journals to accept unapproved work). If she

---

[90] Of course, she could read the letters if not doing research on the women, which raises an initial question as to whether the licensing concerns private information or intellectual inquiry.

avoids these problems by getting prior approval, she must act on it promptly, lest it expire, at which point the IRB will peremptorily instruct her that (in the words of one university IRB) "no research related activities . . . can take place until the IRB has approved the continuation of research."[91]

In these ways, the federal regulations on IRBs set up a system of licensing. The next step is to consider whether the regulations interfere with speech or the press, and after that, to inquire whether they amount to the sort of federal action that violates the First Amendment.

III. Licensing of Speech and the Press

The regulations require IRB licensing of "research," and it may therefore be thought that they license conduct rather than speech or the press.[92] Certainly, many laws regulate conduct in ways that indirectly burden speech or the press, without violating the First Amendment.[93] As it happens, however, although the IRB regulations appear to focus on conduct, they discriminate on the basis of content and thus target speech and the press. At key points, moreover, they candidly require IRBs to license the verbal core of speech and the press. Thus, in one way or another, the regulations take aim at speech and the press, as can be observed in six illustrations.[94]

---

[91] Communication from a Midwestern IRB to an investigator (2004), given by the investigator to the author.

[92] It is possible that the Amendment protects not merely the freedoms of speech and the press but also a freedom of research or inquiry. The licensing of research is more intrusive and, perhaps, more dangerous than the licensing of speech or press, for it bars not merely the reduction of ideas to speech or print, but even the development of ideas. Here, however, there is no need to pursue this line of reasoning, for the federal regulations target and even specify speech and the press.

[93] See note 33.

[94] Doctrinally, even to the extent the IRB regulations concern conduct, they engage in content discrimination and thus amount to the licensing of speech and the press under *O'Brien*. Of course, the *O'Brien* test is a measure of whether a post-publication restraint violates the First Amendment rather than whether a law licensing conduct really licenses speech or the press, but to the extent the *O'Brien* test establishes a method of discerning content discrimination, it is relevant. Under this test, it is an open question whether the regulation of research "is within the constitutional power of the Government," and of particular significance, it is dubious whether the IRB regulations further a governmental interest "unrelated to the suppression of free expression." *United States v O'Brien*, 391 US 367, 377 (1968). See also note 33. Indeed, the regulation of research, as such, necessarily suppresses expression—whether in the research or in the publication of its results.

Incidentally, *O'Brien*'s focus on the government's interest and the relation of this interest to suppression may not always be adequate to the task of discerning whether licensing of

First, the IRB regulations impose licensing on research at research institutions, and they thereby discriminate against inquiry
and publication. Research is conduct that involves inquiry or the
pursuit of curiosity, and when done at a research institution
(whether a private firm or a university), it almost always leads to
some publication or at least internal communication about it. This
in itself does not necessarily protect the research, but in imposing
licensing on research at research institutions, the government licenses, not the proximate causes of harm, but rather the inquiry
and publication inherent in institutional research. In this way, the
regulations concerning IRBs differ from those regarding FDA
drug licensing. The FDA licenses the sale of new drugs against
the background of a general federal prohibition on the marketing
of new drugs. In contrast, the government imposes IRB licensing
on research at institutions, while simultaneously leaving the same
conduct unconstrained if done not as part of such research. It thus
imposes licensing not on any particularly dangerous substance or
activity, but on the pursuit of curiosity and publication that takes
place at universities and other research institutions.

Imagine if Congress were to prohibit journalists from investigating and asking questions, unless they first obtained permission
from a Newspaper Review Board. In particular, imagine that they
had to get permission from a board of journalists and community
members, who were to ensure that each journalist would disclose
his identity, warn persons of the dangers of talking to him, get a
signed consent form, engage in no deceit, intrude on no one's

---

conduct is really a licensing of speech or the press. A government interest related to
suppression was clear enough in seventeenth-century England, but it may not always be
apparent under a popularly elected government seeking popular ends. For example, the
new censorship attempts to satisfy popular moral anxieties about the risks of research,
and, in this context, the government's interest is not likely to seem related to the suppression of free expression. More generally, in its deference to government interests, the
O'Brien test is necessarily incomplete. As Madison explained in *Federalist* No. 44, the
enumeration of powers was an enumeration of the "objects" of government or what *O'Brien*
calls a "governmental interest." Federalist 44, in Jacob E. Cooke, ed, *The Federalist* 304
(1961). In contrast, the enumeration of rights defines exceptions to the powers, and therefore an examination of the legitimacy of the government's object or interest will not always
be an adequate measure of the abridgement of the right.

A further, curious twist is that content discrimination in the regulation's treatment of
conduct may amount to an express regulation of speech and the press. It will be seen
below that the IRB regulations expressly define "research" in terms of speech and the
press, and within this context, the regulatory distinctions concerning the conduct involved
in research are merely further refinements of the express licensing of the speech and press
involved in "research."

privacy, and otherwise cause no harm.[95] Imagine further that that Congress asked Newspaper Review Boards to prevent journalists from causing "upset," "worry," social "stigma," "moral harm," or any legal or economic loss.[96] Even to the extent these harms are within the constitutional reach of law, the government cannot impose its regulation of such harms only on journalists, and especially not by requiring them to get approval before they do their investigation. So, too, for research and researchers.

Second, in establishing IRB licensing, federal regulations single out for constraint the pursuit of a particular conception of knowledge, and this similarly reveals that the regulations license speech and the press. In requiring the licensing of "research," and in defining research as a "systematic investigation" designed to produce "generalizable knowledge," the regulations specify modern, empirical, scientific method and constrain it in its most important application, human beings. The modern, empirical, scientific conception of knowledge, especially as applied to human beings, created much of the modern world by dismantling medieval scholasticism. Even today, it continues to be contested when it challenges traditional religious notions of truth—for example, in debates about evolution and the verity of scripture, and in controversies about abortion and about conception as the beginning of human life. More broadly, even among scientists, the empirical, scientific conception of knowledge stimulates anxieties about its consequences for human beings, whether in health, morals, politics, social relations, or the environment. Yet this does not mean that government can constitutionally discriminate against those who pursue the modern, empirical conception of knowledge. In particular, when government regulations specify or otherwise target this conception of knowledge for licensing, they discriminate on the basis of content. The government could just as well impose licensing on scholars who engage in elenctic dialogue about the nature of man on the ground that this puts interlocutors at risk of social stigma and mental upset. If this targeting of Platonists and their method would violate the First Amendment, so does the

---

[95] This is not beyond the imagination of the defenders of IRBs. See, for example, Roberston's comments on the subject in note 17.

[96] National Science Foundation, Division of Institution and Award Support, *Frequently Asked Questions and Vignettes*, at http://www.nsf.gov/bfa/dias/policy/hsfaqs.htm.

targeting of researchers who explore knowledge about human beings by means of direct empirical study.

Monkeys illustrate the danger. The government can license the
handling of monkeys, without violating the First Amendment.
Similarly, it can license the application of drugs to monkeys. Yet
it cannot license the handling of monkeys only in modern scientific
research, any more than it could license the handling of these
primates only in biblically oriented research.[97] Whether with regard to monkeys or men, the law cannot single out one conception
of knowledge for constraint—least of all, for licensing.

Third, the regulations require IRBs to evaluate the risks and benefits of research and thus require IRBs to weigh the value of the
particular scientific methods proposed by researchers. The regulations even require IRBs to weigh the methodology of projects that
rely exclusively upon observation, reading, speaking, writing, and
printing. One of the government's purposes in creating IRBs was to
"improve the quality of a research protocol," and its regulations expressly require IRBs to ensure that "[r]isks to subjects are minimized"
by the use of "procedures which are consistent with sound research
design." Moreover, the regulations require IRBs to weigh the risks
of research against the benefits, and IRBs therefore cannot escape
the obligation to consider the quality of the research and its methodology.[98] As OHRP explains: "Specification of quality standards in
the conduct of research is an important function of the institutional
leadership. Insistence upon well-conceived and -conducted research
should be evident both in written policies and in actions of institutional officials. . . . Approval procedures should be devised such that
the institution supports only well-designed and properly executed
research." To ensure that IRBs appreciate their methodological obligation, OHRP cautions: "Research that is conducted so poorly as
to be invalid exposes subjects and the institution to unnecessary
risk."[99] The regulations thus require IRBs to become arbiters of the
value of different research methods, including merely verbal methods,
and the regulations thereby subject methodology to a process that

---

[97] In fact, there are Institutional Animal Care and Use Committees, but they can be
left for another day.

[98] For the government's purposes, see HEW, FDA, Standards for Institutional Review
Boards for Clinical Investigations, 43 Fed Reg 35188 (Aug 8, 1978) (re NIH's requirements
for IRBs). For the regulations, see 45 CFR § 46.111(1) & (2).

[99] OHRP, *Institutional Review Board Guidebook*, ch I, Part B.

inevitably discriminates against unconventional or unpopular approaches.[100] Few matters are more contested in academia than methodology, but IRBs enjoy power over methods, and they often return
proposals to researchers with requests for methodological changes—
in effect, suppressing the method that the researchers initially proposed.

In each of these three examples, the regulations focus on what
could be considered conduct, but they do so in ways that discriminate on the basis of content, and they thus target speech and the
press. The regulations, however, go even further, for in the remainder of the six illustrations given here, it will be seen that the
regulations candidly target verbal speech and the press as the objects
of the licensing.

Fourth, the IRB regulations define the licensed conduct so
broadly as to impose licensing on substantial amounts of conduct
that consists solely of noninjurious reading, observing, analyzing,
speaking, writing, or printing. Many research projects consist of
little more than these activities. For example, much research (in
fields including medicine, politics, and increasingly law) consists of
making otherwise lawful observations, printing and distributing surveys, tabulating the results, and analyzing them. Indeed, many research projects only involve reading and analyzing preexisting data.
Although the fact that injurious conduct consists exclusively of various forms of speech or of the press does not automatically give it
constitutional protection from post-publication penalties, the IRB
licensing is not a post-publication restraint, and in any case, research
is not itself an injury. Of course, IRB licensing is an attempt to
prevent harm from research, but rather than punish actual injury,
it restricts proposed research because of the mere risk or possibility
that it may eventually produce injury. By lumping all research together, the regulations require IRBs to interfere with much entirely

---

[100] Some commentators complain of the "monitoring, censuring, and outright disapproval of projects that use qualitative research, phenomenological approaches, and other
alternative frameworks for knowing and knowledge." Lincoln and Tierney, 10 Qualitative
Inquiry at 220 (cited in note 82). "The issues—frequently cited as bases for rejection—
seem to be nonquantitative or experimental research methods (i.e., qualitative methods),
new paradigms for inquiry (e.g., phenomenological, feminist, post-modern, Foucauldian,
and/or constructivist), and lack of fit with traditional rigor criteria (e.g., generalizability,
replicability, objectivity)." Id. See also id at 230.

Of course, the government and any board upon which it relies are free to consider
methodology when making decisions about research by the government's own employees,
about giving money to outside researchers, or about giving researchers access to its facilities
or to persons whom it has in its custody.

harmless reading, observing, analyzing, speaking, writing, and print-ing—even though these things have not yet caused any injury and in most instances will probably not do so. This "overbreadth" re-veals that the regulations impose licensing directly on speech and the press—including much purely verbal speech and the press.[101]

Fifth, the government requires IRBs, in evaluating the risks and benefits of research, to weigh the risks and benefits of publication. Although the licensing of publication is not the goal of the federal government, the failure of a researcher to obtain a license to do research has profound consequences for her ability to publish—a connection that the government clearly understands and that aca-demic institutions and their IRBs sometimes exploit by warning faculty and students that if they do not first get approval, they may have difficulty publishing their work.[102] More directly, the govern-ment's own regulations reveal the role of IRBs in licensing publi-cation, for in evaluating the risks of a research project, an IRB must consider whether "[r]isks to subjects are reasonable in relation to anticipated benefits, if any, to subjects, and the importance of the knowledge that may reasonably be expected to result."[103] Thus, on the one hand, an IRB must take into account the risk arising from publication of the research (including the risks of worry, upset, moral harm, and other injuries not ordinarily cognizable at law or under the First Amendment). On the other hand, the IRB must consider "the importance of the knowledge" that the researcher hopes to obtain and publish—as if IRBs were the arbiters of what is important enough to be studied and published.[104] This judgment about the potential "risks and benefits" of doing research, including the possible "risks and benefits" of publication, makes the IRBs licensors or censors of the press in its most traditional verbal form. Although IRBs license research, they do so by considering the dan-ger and value of publication.[105]

---

[101] The overbreadth may be of constitutional interest on its own, but it is of significance here because it reveals the direct licensing of speech and the press. For the substantial overbreadth test, see note 35.

[102] See notes 87–88.

[103] 45 CFR § 46.111(a)(2).

[104] Id.

[105] The regulations apparently recognize that this inclusion of the risks and benefits of publication in IRB evaluations runs up against the First Amendment, for the regulations promptly add: "The IRB should not consider possible long-range effects of applying knowl-edge gained in the research (for example, the possible effects of the research on public

Sixth, and most fundamentally, the regulations define "research" in terms of speech and the press, and thus when requiring IRBs to license research, the regulations directly make speech and the press the object of the licensing. The regulations define research as "systematic investigation . . . designed to develop or contribute to generalizable knowledge," and as a result, they apply only to the inquiry that is designed to advance "generalizable" knowledge. Although knowledge can perhaps be generalizable without being yet reduced to a statement, generalizable knowledge is the knowledge that has at least the potential to be reduced to a statement. The definition of research in terms of "generalizable knowledge" makes sense if research is understood in terms of modern scientific method, which seeks to develop knowledge in the form of statements that are sufficiently general that they can be applied or tested elsewhere. Yet by adopting this definition, the regulations select for licensing not injury, nor mere inquiry or the pursuit of curiosity, but rather such inquiry as is designed to make possible a statement with wider application or significance. The regulations thus candidly constrain verbal speech and the press—indeed, precisely the sort that is apt to be important.

Finally, it must be emphasized that nothing in the First Amendment stands in the way of the government's adopting laws prohibiting physical injury or even licensing dangerous activities. But this is precisely what the government has not done. By using licensing, it regulates the risk of injury from research rather than the injury itself, and because the risk will usually not become a reality, the regulation of this mere possibility is highly overinclusive. This overinclusive regulation of the mere risk of injury is all the more distant from a lawful prohibition on injury because it includes the risk of harms—such as "upset," social "stigma," and "moral harm"—that are the ordinary consequence of free discussion and publication. If legally cognizable harms were its sole concern, the government could rely upon the general rules against negligence or could adopt rules against specific, substantive types of injury. The government

---

policy) as among those research risks that fall within the purview of its authority." 45 CFR § 46.111(a)(2). The First Amendment, however, forbids the licensing of speech and the press, not just the long-term application of speech and press for public policy.

The degree to which doctors view IRBs as licensors of publications is evident from the growing tendency of doctors who do innovative medical procedures to seek IRB approval, in case they afterward wish to publish an account of their work. The innovative character of the procedures does not make them "research," but the doctors assume that it is prudent to get IRB approval if publication is likely.

could even (within its enumerated powers) license dangerous activities, as it does with the distribution and development of pharmaceuticals. It cannot, however, establish licensing for "research" that it defines in its regulations to include a vast amount of harmless speech and the press. Nor can it adopt licensing regulations that target the curiosity of researchers, the consequences of their publications, their scientific empiricism, their methodologies, or their attempts to reach generally stated conclusions, as if these were particularly dangerous circumstances. Although the government regulations require the licensing of "research" to prevent researchers from doing harm, they neither penalize any actual injury nor license a genuinely dangerous activity, but instead single out speech and the press for licensing.[106]

IV. FEDERAL ACTION

The government's regulations on IRBs run afoul of the First Amendment only to the extent that they impose licensing of speech or the press by force of law, and it is not immediately clear whether they do this. Rather than bluntly require the use of IRBs, the government seems ordinarily to adopt milder approaches: For research receiving its support, the government requires institutions to use IRBs as a condition of government support, and for other research, which is not federally funded, the government simply invites institutions to use IRBs voluntarily.[107] On closer examination, however, the government does not make the regulations merely conditional and optional. In particular, there is reason to worry that the government imposes unconstitutional conditions and co-opts the force of state law.

In analyzing these two issues, it is useful to keep in mind that what matters for the First Amendment is whether the government has legislated beyond its constitutional limits rather than the degree

---

[106] For the safety of research in general, see Levine, *Ethics and Regulation* at 39–40 (cited in note 3). See also text at notes 152–57.

[107] For the conditions, see 45 CFR § 46.101(a). The regulations refer to human subjects research "supported" by the government so as to include even research that gets only the most minimal support, such as the loan of a book, but this essay refers interchangeably to "support," "funds," and "grants" because this has been the practical application of the regulations thus far. Nonetheless, the regulations' emphasis on support is significant. See note 130.

For the optional adoption of IRBs, see HHS, *Federalwide Assurance (FWA) for the Protection of Human Subjects for Domestic (U.S.) Institutions* 2 (version date 03/20/2002). For the required uses of IRBs in connection with the FDA and HIPAA, see note 6.

of government coercion or the existence of institutional or individual consent. When contracting or otherwise dealing with the government, a person can waive a particular exercise of a constitutional right, including the right of speech, or the press. Such consent, however, cannot authorize the federal government to legislate or adopt policies beyond its constitutional powers. The First Amendment is particularly explicit about this, for in focusing on legislation, it specifies that Congress shall make no law abridging the freedom of speech, or of the press. Accordingly, as illustrated by notions of overbreadth, the mere making of such a law is unconstitutional.[108] It does not matter whether the law specifies a harsh or mild penalty or whether a person's exercise of his speech or press rights has yet been subjected to any penalty. Nor does it matter whether an affected individual has consented. The government's simple act of making the law is enough to violate the Constitution, and accordingly, in evaluating the constitutionality of the federal regulations on IRBs, coercion and consent are not necessarily relevant considerations.

A. UNCONSTITUTIONAL CONDITIONS

The first way in which the federal regulations on IRBs conflict with the First Amendment is through the government's use of unconstitutional conditions. Formally, the regulations impose conditions on government support for research. In reality, however, the government goes further, for it uses these conditions to exercise regulatory power over speech and the press. In this way—through the regulatory use of conditions—the government appears to have made a law that violates the First Amendment.[109]

If understood primarily as a response to the structural problem arising from the judicial development of a federal spending power,

---

[108] To be precise, the point is evident in the assumption about Congressional power that can be discerned in ideas about overbreadth. Obviously, this is not to say that anyone will necessarily have standing, for this is a different question. For more expansive implications of the assumption about Congressional power, see Michael C. Dorf, *Facial Challenges to State and Federal Statutes*, 46 Stan L Rev 235 (1994).

[109] The literature on unconstitutional conditions is substantial. Some salient articles are Seth F. Kreimer, *Allocational Sanctions: The Problem of Negative Rights in a Positive State*, 132 U Pa L Rev 1293 (1984); Richard Epstein, *Unconstitutional Conditions, State Power, and the Limits of Consent*, 102 Harv L Rev 4 (1988); Kathleen Sullivan, *Unconstitutional Conditions*, 102 Harv L Rev 413 (1989); Lynn Baker, *The Prices of Rights: Toward a Positive Theory of Unconstitutional Conditions*, 75 Cornell L Rev 1184 (1990); Lynn Baker, *Constitutional Federal Spending After Lopez*, 95 Colum L Rev 1911 (1995).

the doctrine of unconstitutional conditions must focus on the distinction between purchases and regulation. Of course, the doctrine could be understood more broadly as a solution to the full range of injustices arising from government benefits or privileges—for example, it could be understood to apply to state spending and to include equal protection issues—but on the more modest and manageable assumption that the distinct and central problem of federal spending requires a distinct doctrinal response, the doctrine will be more narrowly understood here mostly as a solution to this federal problem. Perhaps state spending also requires a doctrine of unconstitutional conditions, but as will be seen, the doctrine as applied to federal spending is particularly necessary because of the structural problems created by the judges.[110] The basic frame-

---

[110] Conditions on state spending need not be treated in the same way as conditions on federal spending. With respect to a federal spending power, the judicially created doctrine of unconstitutional conditions is necessary as a means of limiting the structural dangers that the judiciary itself stimulated through its development of a federal spending power. In contrast, with respect to state spending, the need for a doctrine of unconstitutional conditions is less clear, and any such doctrine perhaps need not be as strong, for the states have always had a general power to spend, and therefore the states' imposition of conditions on their spending does not so clearly create a structural problem. In short, the traditional power of a state to spend does not raise the same structural dangers as the federal power to spend, and because the judiciary created the federal problem, they have a particular responsibility to cure it. Other issues can also be distinguished from those on federal spending—particularly equal protection questions and related public forum issues. If the Equal Protection Clause of the Fourteenth Amendment provides for equal privileges as well as equal protection of natural rights, then there is no reason to think of the equal protection cases in terms of a doctrine of unconstitutional conditions. For example, in *Southeastern Promotions*, the Court held that a municipal board's denial of permission to use a municipal auditorium for the musical *Hair* violated the First Amendment. *Southeastern Promotions, Ltd. v Conrad*, 420 US 538, 559–60 (1975). Of course, whether the use of a municipal auditorium is really equivalent to the use of a public park is rather doubtful. One need only imagine an application by the Ku Klux Klan to use a city auditorium for a musical called *Robes*. What matters here, however, is simply that this problem is more easily understood in terms of equal protection than in terms of unconstitutional conditions. If, nonetheless, it is treated as an unconstitutional conditions problem, it is not clear that it should be understood in terms of the same doctrine as is applied to federal spending.

Even as applied to federal spending, the so-called doctrine of unconstitutional conditions should probably be viewed as two separate doctrines. On the one hand, when Congress spends (whether under its enumerated powers or under a spending power), it surely cannot purchase rights the Constitution allocates elsewhere—this being a limit arising from the assumption that Congress has only such powers as granted to it in the Constitution. On the other hand, in response to its expansion of federal power, especially its creation of a federal spending power, the Court should recognize that Congress sometimes uses spending that is more clearly authorized by the Court than the Constitution to regulate in ways that evade the enumerated limitations on federal power, and the Court should therefore conceive of this regulatory spending as subject to these limitations—at least, that is, those enumerated in the Bill of Rights. See note 115. To avoid unnecessary complexity, however, this essay treats these two doctrines together as the doctrine of unconstitutional conditions applicable to federal spending.

work of the doctrine was laid out two decades ago by Seth Kreimer, who distinguishes between threats and offers—threats being subject to the regular constitutional limitations, and offers not being subject to constitutional limitation, unless they deprive individuals of inalienable rights.[111] The general outline of this analysis captures the structural problem raised by federal spending, but as will be seen, each component of the analysis could, perhaps, be understood in terms that more closely match this problem—that is, in terms of regulation and purchases, regulation being subject to the usual constitutional limitations on federal constraints, and purchases not being subject to such limitations, unless they are purchases of rights that the Constitution allocates elsewhere.

The doctrine of unconstitutional conditions limits the government's ability to use its spending in ways that evade the Constitution's limitations. The Bill of Rights typically places limitations on constraints rather than privileges—that is, on the force of law rather than on the government's distribution of money and other benefits. Although the Establishment Clause of the First Amendment directly limits the government's distribution of privileges, most guarantees in the Bill of Rights, including the guarantee of speech and the press, merely limit the government's constraints. Congress has accordingly sometimes evaded the constitutional limitations on its imposition of constraints by placing conditions on its distribution of privileges. In particular, when Congress acts by means of its spending, it can achieve the effect of a constraint without formally resorting to the constraining force of law, and it can thus avoid compliance with the constitutional limits on constraints of law in both the enumeration of Congressional powers and the Bill of Rights.

The Court acknowledges this reality in its doctrine of unconstitutional conditions. As a distinct constitutional requirement, the doctrine of unconstitutional conditions is rather tenuous, for it lacks its own foundation in the text and is at best ill-defined and amorphous. Nonetheless, as an acknowledgment of the reality of government spending and how it is used, the doctrine is valuable. It recognizes that even though government spending does not formally violate the Constitution's limits on the government's imposition of constraints, such spending may still, in reality, con-

---

[111] Kreimer, 132 U Pa L Rev at 1301 (cited in note 109).

stitute a means of constraint and thus a means of accomplishing what the Constitution forbids.

This inquiry into the realities of the matter is necessary because the spending power itself is a judicial creation. Ordinarily, there would be little reason to go beyond the formal prohibitions of the Constitution, and where the First Amendment prohibits only government restraints, there is usually no need to consider whether government spending is, in reality, a restraint. Yet when Congress and the Supreme Court took a Hamiltonian approach to the taxing power and carved out a spending power, they developed Congress's power in a way that was not clearly limited—not even by most of the Bill of Rights. In fact, the so-called Spending Clause was written as a limitation on the taxing power and was carefully drafted so that it would not imply a general power to spend—thus leaving Congress to spend only as permitted under its other powers.[112] The Supreme Court, however, long ago held that Congress has a general spending power as part of its power to tax, and the Court therefore found itself in the awkward situation of having

---

[112] For the history of the Spending or General Welfare Clause, see Jeffrey T. Renz, *What Spending Clause? (Or the President's Paramour): An Examination of the Views of Hamilton, Madison, and Story on Article I, Section 8, Clause 1 of the United States Constitution*, 33 John Marshall L Rev 81 (1999). The crucial evidence, which Renz only notes in passing, is that there was a surreptitious attempt to create a separate spending power by adding a semicolon in the middle of the first paragraph of Section 8 of Article I of the Constitution. Id at 105. On September 4, 1787, the Committee of Eleven reported to the Convention a draft of what became Section 8 that read: "The Legislature shall have power to lay and collect taxes, duties, imposts, and excises, to pay the debts and provide for the common defense and general welfare of the United States." Journal (Sept 4, 1787), Max Farrand, 2 *Records of the Federal Convention* 493 (1937). On September 12, the Committee on Style reported a version of this paragraph, and on the next day, it distributed a printed version of its report. John Quincy Adams's Memoirs (Jan 11, 1823), Farrand, 3 *Records* 457 Appendix CCXLIV. In this printed report, however, there was not a comma, but a semicolon after the word "excises"—so that "to pay the debts and provide for the common defence and general welfare of the United States" became an additional power, conjoined to the power to tax, rather than merely a limitation on it. Id at 594 (Report, Sept 12, 1787). The Convention, however, recognized this alteration and rejected it. At stake was simply the addition and removal of a single dot above a comma. Rarely has so much rested on so small a point.

Its importance was recognized already in early debates about the Constitution. For example, in 1798, Albert Gallitin told the House of Representatives, "he was well informed that those words had originally been inserted in the Constitution as a limitation to the power of laying taxes. After the limitation had been agreed to, and the Constitution was completed, a member of the Convention, (he was one of the members who represented the State of Pennsylvania [i.e., Gouverneur Morris]) being one of a committee of revisal and arrangement, attempted to throw these words into a distinct paragraph, so as to create not a limitation, but a distinct power. The trick, however, was discovered by a member from Connecticut, now deceased, and the words restored as they now stand." Albert Gallatin in the House of Representatives (June 19, 1798), 3 *Records* 378 Appendix CCLXXXI.

conceded to Congress a power that is not clearly limited, whether by the enumeration of Congressional powers or most of the enumeration of rights.[113] For example, Congress has no power to impose constraints on speech or the press, let alone research, and the First Amendment bars constraints that abridge the freedom of speech, or of the press, but if Congress has a general power to spend subject to conditions, it can use conditions on its spending to regulate speech and the press without limitation by either the enumerated powers or the enumerated rights. This is an enormous structural problem. Having legitimated this escape from the Constitution's formal limitations, the judges can surely place some limits on Congress's use of it. Among other things, they should inquire whether, in reality, the conditions on spending are being used to constrain in a manner analogous to the force of law, and if so, whether they are being used to impose constraints of a sort forbidden by the Constitution.

This understanding that a condition can serve as a constraint is essential for preventing the judicially developed spending power from becoming an end run around the guarantee of speech and press in the First Amendment. The Bill of Rights created, as Madison explained, "particular exceptions to the grant of power," and thus the First Amendment unequivocally limits any Congressional power to spend.[114] Although in developing a spending power, the Court allowed Congress to escape the limitations specified in the enumeration of Congress's powers, it apparently is not willing to let Congress use the spending power as a path around the First Amendment.[115]

---

[113] The attempts of the Justices to resolve this conundrum are evident in *United States v Butler*, 297 US 1, 66 (1936), and *South Dakota v Dole*, 483 US 203 (1987).

[114] Madison's speech of June 8, 1789 (as reported in *Congressional Register*), in Helen E. Veit, Kenneth R. Bowling, et al, eds, *Creating the Bill of Rights* 83 (1991).

[115] In *South Dakota v Dole*, the Court stated that "we have noted that other constitutional provisions may provide an independent bar to the conditional grant of federal funds." *South Dakota v Dole*, 483 US 203, 208 (1987). In *League of Women Voters*, it held a federal condition unconstitutional under the First Amendment. *FCC v League of Women Voters*, 468 US 364 (1984). In *Rust*, the Court acknowledged that there were circumstances in which the First Amendment limited conditions on federal spending. *Rust v Sullivan*, 500 US 173, 194 (1991).

Although for purposes of this inquiry, it is only necessary to focus on the Constitution's enumerated rights, the reasons for the doctrine of unconstitutional conditions suggests that any spending power should also be limited by the enumerated powers. Certainly, the legislative and judicial creation of a spending power permits an end run around the enumerated powers as much as around the enumerated rights. As the Court candidly admitted in *Dole*, "objectives not thought to be within Article I's 'enumerated legislative fields' . . .

To understand when Congressional spending violates the First Amendment's guarantee of freedom of speech, or of the press, it is first necessary to distinguish (as suggested by Lynn Baker) between purchases and regulation.[116] If the doctrine of unconstitutional conditions is understood broadly as a cure for the unjust distribution of government privileges, then this distinction may be inadequate, but if the doctrine is understood more narrowly as an attempt to contain the structural damage done by judicial acceptance of a spending power, then the most basic question is whether the government has merely made an expenditure for a benefit defined by a condition or has, in reality, used the condition to create a substitute for the constraining force of law. In less abstract terms, the issue is whether the government's conditional spending amounts to a purchase or a regulation.

Conditions on mere purchases are generally constitutional, unless they are attempts to purchase rights that the Constitution allocates to others. Whether Congress acts under its enumerated powers or under a spending power, it is free to place conditions on its purchases, such as its contracts for goods and services, including speech or the press.[117] Nonetheless, such purchases are

---

may nevertheless be attained through the use of the spending power and the conditional grant of federal funds." *South Dakota v Dole*, 483 US 203, 207 (1987). With this in mind, Lynn Baker, not unlike James Madison, argues that any regulatory use of the spending power should be limited not only by the enumeration of rights but also by the enumeration of Congressional powers. Baker, *Conditional Federal Spending*, 95 Colum L Rev at 1935 (cited in note 109).

Yet the use of enumerated Congressional powers to limit the spending power is questionable, for if there is a spending power, it is not evident why it would be limited by the other, more clearly enumerated powers. For example, there is no reason to think that the Commerce Clause is limited by any other enumerated power in Article I, Section 8 of the Constitution. (Of course, each grant of power must be interpreted in accord with the whole of the Constitution, including other grants of power, but the other grants thereby reveal the scope of the commerce power; they do not limit it.) In these circumstances, even if the doctrine of unconstitutional conditions brings the Bill of Rights to bear against the federal spending power, it cannot easily apply the enumeration of powers to limit this power. It would seem, therefore, that the Court's latter-day creation of a "spending power" threatens to unravel the limited character of American government, and the doctrine of unconstitutional conditions probably cannot adequately repair the damage. This point, however, need not be pursued here.

[116] Lynn Baker draws a distinction between regulatory and reimbursement spending. Id at 1954.

[117] *National Endowment for the Arts v Finley*, 524 US 566 (1998); *United States v American Library Association, Inc.*, 539 US 194 (2003). In *Rust*, the Court noted that it was "not the case of a general law singling out a disfavored group on the basis of speech content, but a case of the Government refusing to fund activities, including speech, which are specifically excluded from the scope of the project funded." *Rust v Sullivan*, 500 US 173, 194–95 (1991). The government in *Rust* "used private speakers to transmit specific information pertaining to its own program." *Rosenberger v Rector and Visitors of University of Virginia*,

limited by the Constitution if Congress attempts to purchase what the Constitution elsewhere carves out from Congressional power.[118] This minimal limitation on purchases is not merely a response to the creation of a spending power; rather, it arises from the fact that the Constitution gives Congress limited powers, and presumably Congress cannot purchase a power over rights that the Constitution gives to others. Congress thus can reach an agreement with a person for him to waive a particular exercise of one of his rights, but it cannot purchase the right in general or even a significant part of it.[119] To take two clear-cut examples, although

---

515 US 819, 833 (1995).

Incidentally, in *Finley*, the Court stated that "when the Government is acting as patron rather than as sovereign, the consequences of imprecision are not constitutionally severe." *National Endowment for the Arts v Finley*, 524 US 566, 589 (1998). As will be seen, however, when the government uses conditions on spending as a means of regulation, it is acting as a sovereign.

[118] Kathleen Sullivan takes such a view, although she takes it much more broadly than it is understood here, and she combines it with a theory of strict scrutiny. Her central point, however, is very apt even for this article's limited version of the doctrine of unconstitutional conditions—that "[t]he doctrine of unconstitutional conditions holds that government may not grant a benefit on the condition that the beneficiary surrender a constitutional right, even if the government may withhold that benefit altogether." Sullivan, 102 Harv L Rev at 413 (cited in note 109).

[119] The two categories can be illustrated by some of the cases. For example, *Rust* involved the waiver of a particular exercise of the right of freedom of speech rather than a purchase of the right in general, as the Court seemed to appreciate when it pointed out that the regulation placed the condition on the program rather than the grantee. The Court explained that the regulations "do not force the Title X grantee to give up abortion-related speech; they merely require that the grantee keep such activities separate and distinct from Title X activities. Title X expressly distinguishes between a Title X *grantee* and a Title X *project*. . . . The Title X *grantee* can continue to perform abortions, provide abortion-related services, and engage in abortion advocacy; it simply is required to conduct these activities through programs that are separate and independent from the project that receives Title X funds." *Rust v Sullivan*, 500 US 173, 197 (1991). (The Court then added: "In contrast, our 'unconstitutional conditions' cases involve situations in which the government has placed a condition on the *recipient* of the subsidy rather tha[n] on a particular program or service, thus effectively prohibiting the recipient from engaging in the protected conduct outside the scope of the federally-funded program." Id.) For other examples of nonregulatory conditions involving only a waiver of a particular exercise of a right, see *Regan v Taxation with Representation or Washington*, 461 US 540 (1983); *Snepp v United States*, 440 US 507 (1980).

League of Women Voters is an example of the purchase of a right in general or at least a substantial portion of it. In this case, the Court overturned a condition that required noncommercial educational stations to avoid editorializing, which amounted to a large part of their First Amendment right of speech and press. *FCC v League of Women Voters*, 468 US 364 (1984). At the very least, this condition amounted to a purchase of a right that the Constitution denies to the federal government. In addition, as will be seen in note 130, it could be viewed as a regulation, but this point can wait.

A more complex case is *Legal Services Corporation v Velazquez*, 531 US 533 (2001). The Court held unconstitutional the government's condition on its funding of the Legal Services Corporation that the corporation not engage in representation involving an effort to amend or otherwise challenge the validity of existing welfare law. Even if this was not

Congress can purchase a federal employee's waiver of his freedom of speech as to information acquired in his employment relationship, it cannot purchase a general sacrifice of his freedom of speech as to all matters in all of his relationships. This bar against Congress's purchase of a right the Constitution allocates to others is not a severe limit, and otherwise, Congress is free to place conditions on its purchases.

In contrast, Congress sometimes uses a condition on its spending to create what is really a means of regulation, and in these instances, it faces more substantial limitations. The spending power is not an excuse for regulating in a manner forbidden by the Constitution, and therefore if, in reality, Congress is regulating, it cannot do so in a way that violates the Bill of Rights. As the Supreme Court stated in *South Dakota v Dole*, the government can use conditions to define what it is purchasing, and it can also use conditions to regulate, but "other constitutional provisions may provide an independent bar to the conditional grant of federal funds"—not least, it may be presumed, when the federal government uses conditions to regulate in a manner inconsistent with the First Amendment.[120]

B.   UNCONSTITUTIONAL CONDITIONS AND IRBS

The application of the unconstitutional conditions doctrine to the federal IRB regulations must follow their structure. The regulations most basically create an "ethical principles" condition. On

---

a large part of the corporation's right of speech, or that of their clients, the condition limited the ability of the judges to hear arguments from the corporation's lawyers questioning the constitutionality of welfare laws. In this way, according to the Court, it "threatens severe impairment of the judicial function." Id at 546. Thus, the condition was, perhaps, an attempt to purchase a right allocated by the Constitution to the judiciary itself. Alternatively, however, the condition could be viewed as being, in reality, a regulation—indeed, one that abridged the freedom of speech of the poor.

Another unusual case is *United Public Workers v Mitchell*, 330 US 75 (1947). The Hatch Act made it unlawful for most federal executive branch employees to take any active part in political management or in political campaigns, and in *Mitchell*, the Court upheld this. Yet although the statute had the effect of placing a condition on federal employment, it was, more fundamentally, a direct regulation.

As observed in note 110, the cases on federal spending as a means of regulation should probably be understood as distinct from the cases on state spending or on equal protection. The cases on state spending respond to issues somewhat different from the structural problem of a judicially created federal spending power and therefore should not be viewed as involving the same doctrine of unconstitutional conditions. Moreover, cases based on equal protection doctrine are perhaps most concretely understood in terms of equal protection rather than unconstitutional conditions.

[120] *South Dakota v Dole*, 483 US 203, 208 (1987).

this foundation, they then add an IRB licensing condition.

The "ethical principles" condition derives from the statement in the IRB regulations that an institution can receive federal support for human subjects research only if it gives the government "[a] statement of principles governing the institution in the discharge of its responsibilities for protecting the rights and welfare of human subjects of research conducted at or sponsored by the institution, regardless of whether the research is subject to Federal regulation." The regulations add that "[t]his may include an appropriate existing code, declaration, or statement of ethical principles, or a statement formulated by the institution itself."[121] Accordingly, before giving support for research at an institution, the government asks the institution to assure the government "that all of its activities related to human subject research, regardless of funding source, will be guided by . . . ethical principles." In particular, it requires the institution to choose between the ethical principles in either the *Belmont Report* (which sets out ethical principles and guidelines for protecting human subjects, and which assumes the existence of IRBs) or ethical principles elaborated in another document, as negotiated between the institution and the government.[122] The government in this way uses its funding of some research to get "ethical principles" for other research.

By leveraging its conditions on federally supported human subjects research to control the "ethical principles" of all human subjects research, the government reveals that it is not simply specifying the sort of research it is willing to fund, but is attempting generally to regulate the ethics of human subjects research. If as suggested in Part III, the federal regulations on IRBs define "research" in terms of speech and the press, then this regulatory use of a condition to impose "ethical principles" on research is troubling. The problem is partly that Congress is using its spending to regulate speech and the press, over which Congress does not have regulatory power.[123] Even more pointedly, Congress appears

---

[121] 45 CFR § 46.103(b)(1).

[122] HHS, *Federalwide Assurance (FWA) for the Protection of Human Subjects for Domestic (U.S.) Institutions*, p 1 (version date 03/20/2002). Apparently, relatively few American research institutions have negotiated an alternative statement of ethical principles.

[123] For the limits on Congressional power, see *United States v Lopez*, 515 US 549 (1995). For Congress's lack of power over speech or the press, see Philip Hamburger, *Natural Rights and Positive Law: A Comment on Professor McAffee's Paper*, 16 SIU L J, 307, 310–11 (1992).

to be using conditions to regulate speech and the press in a manner incompatible with the First Amendment.

In particular, the requirement of "ethical principles" in "research" is a form of content discrimination. In many areas of research, ethical principles are continually contested, and in some fields, such as the humanities and social sciences, supposedly unethical modes of inquiry (such as not disclosing one's identity, taking a person unawares, and causing offense or disgust) are often crucial means of expressing challenges to conventional assumptions, including ethical principles.[124] The content discrimination is all the more problematic when the "ethical principles" condition is applied to purely verbal research—whether in the hard sciences, the soft ones, or the humanities—for in verbal research, a provocative and apparently unethical form of inquiry (including aggressive questioning about sensitive and embarrassing issues, deceit of the sort that does not clearly give rise to legal liability, and the exposure of "private" information and the identity of the human subject) is the very essence of the research. One need only imagine, for example, how a professor could usefully study members of the Ku Klux Klan or high-ranking corporate officials if he had to get their informed consent, if he could not engage in ruses to gain their trust, or if he could not later publish private information that caused emotional and even financial and legal harm.[125]

---

[124] Incidentally, Justice Frankfurter wrote: "No field of education is so thoroughly comprehended by man that new discoveries cannot yet be made. Particularly is that true in the social sciences, where few, if any, principles are accepted as absolutes." *Sweezy v New Hampshire*, 354 US 234, 250 (1957).

[125] The example of a Klansman is used by Linda Shopes, *Institutional Review Boards Have a Chilling Effect on Oral History*, Perspectives 62 (Sept 2000); Cary Nelson, *Can E.T. Phone Home?* 89 Academe 30 (2003). Incidentally, note that there are distinctions among proprietary information, information as to which one has a fiduciary duty, and information that is private merely in the sense that it was shared in a meeting rather than on prime time television.

The stifling implications of the "ethical principles" condition are also evident from its application to research on human subjects who are public officials. Research on these human subjects is at least "exempt" from needing IRB approval. Yet even leaving aside that the exemption must nonetheless be confirmed by the IRB, the "ethical principles" condition remains in place and thus limits aggressive questioning of public officials. As the National Science Foundation advises IRBs: "When the subjects are public officials or candidates for public office, the research is exempt even when identifiers are included or disclosure might be harmful. However, all research should be bound by professional ethics and respect for respondents to guard their privacy whether or not the research is exempt (unless the participants understand that their information may be made public and permission is granted)." National Science Foundation, Division of Institution and Award Support, *Frequently Asked Questions and Vignettes*, at http://www.nsf.gov/bfa/dias/policy/hsfaqs.htm.

Thus, in using its funding for some research to secure "ethical principles" for all research at an institution, the government employs its spending to regulate—indeed, to regulate in a manner that apparently violates the First Amendment.

In addition, the government imposes an IRB condition: It requires institutions receiving its support for human subjects research to establish IRBs—at least for the supported research—and this condition is, in reality, a means of regulation. As noted above, whereas a condition that is not regulatory can violate a person's freedom of speech, or of the press, only if the condition is a purchase of a substantial portion of this right, a condition that amounts, in reality, to a regulation can violate the First Amendment in the same way as any other regulation.

Although the IRB condition applies only to federally funded research, its breadth suggests that it is regulatory. The government makes IRBs a condition of all types of research on human subjects that it supports, even though much of the research is not at all dangerous. If the government merely wanted to avoid supporting dangerous research, it could easily distinguish dangerous physiological research from largely harmless inquiries, such as social science surveys and historical research, which do not ordinarily cause legally cognizable injuries. At the very least, it could leave all purely verbal research beyond the jurisdiction of the IRBs. Instead, it makes IRBs a condition of all human subjects research that it supports. The breadth of this condition suggests that it cannot be understood as a narrow attempt by the government to protect its legitimate interests in preserving proprietary information, supporting a particular point of view, or not funding dangerous activities. It looks like a regulation rather than a purchase.[126]

The regulatory character of the condition requiring IRBs for federally supported research becomes further evident from the fact that it is part of a wider scheme to pressure research institutions to employ IRBs for all research, regardless of the source of fund-

---

[126] For similar reasons, the current authorizing statute (like the original National Research Act of 1974) is also probably unconstitutional. The current act states, in part: "The Secretary shall by regulation require that each entity which applies for a grant, . . . for any project or program which involves the conduct of biomedical or behavioral research involving human subjects submit . . . assurances . . . that it has established (in accordance with regulations . . .) a board (to be known as an 'Institutional Review Board') to review biomedical and behavioral research involving human subjects conducted at or supported by such entity in order to protect the rights of the human subjects of such research." 42 USC § 289.

ing. The history of the IRB movement makes this clear, for the goal and effect was to adopt licensing as a means of protecting human subjects in all research rather than simply to ensure that the federal government did not support dangerous research.[127] As might be expected, therefore, the proposed draft of the federal regulations published in 1979 by the Department of Health, Education, and Welfare ("HEW") would have "require[d] IRB review and approval of research involving human subjects, even if it is not supported by Department funds."[128] When faced with protests against this federal condition—one of the few half-successful attempts of academics to limit such censorship—the government adopted the predecessors of the current regulations, which simply employed less direct mechanisms to achieve the same end.[129] For

---

[127] The necessity of pursuing the goal of general regulation though the limited jurisdiction of Congress and its relevant committee was frequently made explicit. For example, in 1974, the Committee Report on the National Research Act, Pub L 93-348, stated: "It is the Committee's belief that the establishment of such a commission [the National Commission for the Protection of Human Subjects] is essential to the development of a system where human subjects of biomedical and behavioral research are adequately protected. The Committee agrees with those witnesses who testified that the scope of the inquiry, findings, and procedure of such a national commission should cover all biomedical and behavioral research involving human subjects. But the Committee also recognizes that its jurisdiction is limited to those programs and activities defined in the Public Health Service Act, the Community Mental Health Centers Act and the Developmental Disabilities Act, and that further expansion would be a complicated matter . . ." 2 *United States Congressional and Administrative News*, 93d Cong, 2d Session 1974, 3653. See also National Research Act, Pub L 93-48 (July 12, 1974). In 1978, the National Commission for the Protection of Human Subjects recommended that federal law should be enacted or amended to allow HEW "to promulgate regulations governing ethical review of all research involving human subjects that is subject to federal regulation." National Commission for the Protection of Human Subjects of Biomedical and Behavioral Research, *Report and Recommendations: Institutional Review Boards* 3 (DHEW Publication No 78-0008) (1978).

Today, the National Science Foundation answers the question "What are the overall goals of the federal policy (the Common Rule)?" by stating generally: "The major goal is to limit harms to participants in research. That means no one should suffer harm just because they became involved as subjects or respondents in a research project. Institutions engaged in research should foster a culture of ethical research." National Science Foundation, Division of Institution and Award Support, *Frequently Asked Questions and Vignettes*, at http://www.nsf.gov/bfa/dias/policy/hsfaqs.htm.

[128] Proposed Regulations Amending Basic HEW Policy for Protection of Human Research Subjects, 44 Fed Reg 47688 (Aug 14, 1979).

[129] The head of the organization that drafted the regulations and that later became OHRP has explained that the government responded to the First Amendment objections raised by Pool and others simply by adopting less direct means of achieving the same regulatory ends: "Friendly champions of social and behavioral sciences showed us how to back away from our unpopular positions while continuing to offer what we felt were reasonable protections for the dignity and rights of subjects involved in social and behavioral research—to say nothing of saving the face and the jobs of OPRR staff." C. R. McCarthy, *Introduction: The IRB and Social and Behavioral Research*, in J. E. Sieber, ed, *NIH*

example, the regulations apply the "ethical principles" condition to *all* research at an institution and thus commit the institution to the ethical foundations for IRBs, regardless of the source of support for the research. Moreover, as will be seen shortly, federal administrators have often refused to accept assurances that do not impose IRBs on all research, regardless of funding, and the federal regulations co-opt the force of state law to pressure institutions to adopt IRB licensing for all research, even it is if not federally funded. In these circumstances, the condition that institutions must use IRBs for federally supported research is, in reality, just part of a broader scheme of regulation. As noted in Part III, the federal regulations directly target and even specify speech and the press, and because they regulate speech and the press by means of licensing, they appear to violate the First Amendment.[130]

Readings on the Protection of Human Subjects in Behavioral and Social Science Research 8–9 (1984), as quoted in National Research Council, *Protecting Participants* 71 (cited in note 5).

[130] Of course, there are other possible indicia that a condition on spending is, in reality, a regulation—for example, the reach of the spending, the degree of coercion, the nexus of the condition to the spending or whether it is germane, and the disproportionality between the condition and the spending. See, for example, *FCC v League of Women Voters*, 468 US 364, 399–401 (1984), for the Court's assumption that the disparity between the support and the condition was significant. It is not clear, however, that any of these considerations should alone be dispositive.

Some of the indicia mentioned in this footnote are slightly relevant to IRB regulations but not as much as those mentioned in the text. If the federal government funded most of the human subjects research in a broad field of inquiry, such as medicine or biology, this would, perhaps, be an indication that the condition is regulatory. Moreover, the IRB condition seems disproportionate because the federal regulations place the condition not on funding, but on any support, however minor. 45 CFR § 46.101(a).

As for the degree of coercion, the coercive effect of conditions is not necessarily an indication that they are regulatory, but coercion is certainly very much evident in the federal government's relationship to universities. This power is partly a matter of funding. It is also, however, created by the cross-conditioning of grants through "assurances" from institutions rather than researchers. OHRP reminds institutions of this cross-conditioning through its site visits and the implicit threat of a shutdown. OHRP can suspend an institution's assurance of its compliance even if only one researcher covered by the assurance is found to be out of compliance. If the institution elects to assure the government that it follows the regulations for research not supported by the government, then OHRP can even suspend the assurance for a compliance failure by a researcher working without any federal funding. As many social science researchers—for example, historians—cannot reasonably do their research without departing from IRB requirements, OHRP can easily find violations, and therefore its site visits are viewed with trepidation. Most violations are nothing more than failures to follow the licensing procedures. Even when a noncomplying researcher does cause serious harm, the government ordinarily has little reason to assume that other, unrelated research at the institution is causing any injury, and the additional problems it finds are usually only procedural. Accordingly, when OHRP responds to serious injuries in a research project by threatening to shut down all federally funded research at the institution, it makes an utterly disproportionate in terrorem threat. In the late 1990s, the predecessor of OHRP briefly shut down research at about a half dozen institutions, and since then its site visits have carried an implicit and sometimes explicit threat of a shutdown. In the words of a former head of this office, "[t]he suspensions

Thus far, it has been assumed here that a condition will be unconstitutional if the government uses it to regulate in a way that
violates the First Amendment, but the constitutional test for regulatory conditions may, perhaps, be more sensitive than this. In particular, it has been questioned whether the government can use a
condition to require licensing in even a single grant for university
researchers, if the condition is likely to invite a more general imposition of such conditions.[131] In 1991, in *Stanford v Sullivan*, NIH
had awarded a grant to researchers at Stanford University on the
condition that they "obtain government approval before publishing
or otherwise publicly discussing preliminary research results." When
the university challenged this condition, a U.S. District Court held
the condition unconstitutional under the First Amendment, explaining that otherwise, "the result would be an invitation to censorship
wherever government funds flow, and . . . thus . . . an enormous
threat to the First Amendment rights of American citizens and to a
free society."[132] Apparently, therefore, the IRB condition is vulnerable
as an unconstitutional regulation and even, perhaps, as an invitation
to unconstitutional regulation.

C. CO-OPTING STATE LAW

The second sort of federal action evident in the federal regulations on IRBs is that they co-opt the force of state law. Although

created a crisis of confidence and a climate of fear." Greg Koski, *Beyond Compliance . . .
Is It Too Much to Ask?* 25 Ethics & Human Research 5 (2003).

  Incidentally, one effect of this climate of fear is to give force to the guidance, advice,
and recommendations of OHRP. Although couched in mild terms, these attempts to counsel institutions seem more like commands. Indeed, OHRP uses its site visits and the threat
of shutdowns to get institutions, including universities, to impose education requirements
on their teachers, students, and other personnel who study human subjects. These required
classes include indoctrination on the importance of IRBs and the need to cooperate with
them. The reach of the education requirements can be illustrated by an e-mail sent by
Columbia University to all of the faculty, students, and administrators at its main campus,
in which the Provost admonished: "All personnel involved in the conduct of human research must take and pass the appropriate human subject research training course before
embarking on such research." Indeed, "[c]onducting human subjects research without
appropriate training and review could have serious consequences." E-mail from Provost
Alan Brinkley and Executive Vice President for Research to Faculty, Administrators, and
Students at the Morningside Campus (Oct 15, 2004).

  [131] A condition on a single grant would also probably be unconstitutional, even if it did
not attempt to regulate beyond the limits on federal power, if it generally deprived an
individual of a right—for example, if it required a person to give up his right to a jury
trial not merely in a particular case but in all cases in which he might one day be a party.
This, however, is not clearly the problem here.

  [132] *Stanford v Sullivan*, 773 F Supp 472, 473, 478 (1991).

the federal regulations do not directly require IRBs, they take advantage of state law to achieve the same end—even for research that is not federally supported.

The commitment of institutions to adhere to the federal regulations on IRBs is said to be "[o]ptional" for research not funded by the federal government.[133] When the government asks an institution to provide an assurance that all of its federally supported research will comply with the government's "Terms of Assurance" and thus with its IRB regulations, the government also asks the institution to indicate whether it "elects" to apply the federal regulations on IRBs "to all of its human subject research regardless of source of support."[134] Thus, whereas for government-supported research, the use of IRBs is a condition, for other research, the government merely suggests that institutions voluntarily commit to using them. Although the government makes this suggestion under the heading of "[o]ptional," it clearly assumes that IRBs are the conventional method by which institutions should ensure their adherence to "ethical principles" and that its regulations are the appropriate standard for IRBs, even for research not supported by the government.[135] Moreover, it hopes institutions will elect to adhere to the federal regulations for such research, because this makes an institution subject to enforcement by OHRP for any breach of the assurance, regardless of the funding. With these aspirations in mind, the government has not always viewed the election as optional. For example, in the 1970s, HEW regulations threatened to deny funding to institutions that did not follow this department's IRB policies for all human subjects research, regardless of the source of funding.[136] For a while in the 1990s,

---

[133] See, for example, HHS, *Federalwide Assurance (FWA) for the Protection of Human Subjects for Domestic (U.S.) Institutions*, p 2 (version date 03/20/2002).

[134] See, for example, id. Under the HHS regulations, institutions can choose to assure the government that they will adhere to Subpart A—the Common Rule—or Subparts A, B, C, and D. Id.

[135] For the heading, see, for example, id.

[136] Robertson wrote in 1979: "DHEW requires institutions to commit themselves to review all research, regardless of funding, in the sense that failure to conform to the DHEW policy in nonfunded research may be taken into account 'in evaluating applications or proposals for support of activities covered by this part.' 45 CFR § 46.121(b) (1977). Strictly speaking, such review is not a requirement for a general assurance, though failure to include it could mean as a practical matter no funding." Robertson, 26 UCLA L Rev at 499 (cited in note 11). Incidentally, early in the 1970s, before the adoption of the regulations, HEW employed a more general approach, which did not focus as closely on the assurance. For example, in the 1971 "Yellow Book," HEW stated: "If, in the judgment

moreover, the predecessor of OHRP apparently declined to accept assurances in which institutions failed to make the election. As dryly put by one observer, if you declined, "you were urged strongly" to reconsider.[137] This was an additional unconstitutional condition, and partly as a result, in the late 1990s, almost all American colleges and universities that had a so-called Multiple Project Assurance made the election. Since 2000, however, the election has become more optional, and OHRP now more clearly accepts assurances that decline to apply the regulations to research unsupported by the federal government.[138]

In fact, strong arm tactics are no longer necessary, because once the government had elevated IRBs as the standard method of avoiding research injuries, it could rely on state tort law to induce research institutions to use IRBs. By establishing IRB licensing as the standard method of preventing research injuries, the government made IRB licensing an attractive means for institutions to limit state tort liability, and the government has thereby created

of the Secretary, an institution fails to discharge its responsibilities for the protection of the rights and welfare of the individuals in its care, whether or not DHEW funds are involved, he may question whether the institution and the individuals concerned should remain eligible to receive future DHEW funds for activities involving human subjects." *The Institutional Guide to DHEW Policy on Protection of Human Subjects* 17 (DHEW Pub No (NIH) 72-102) (1971).

[137] Conversation with former head of a university IRB. Prior to December 2000, the standard form of assurance for an institution at which many persons conducted research was the so-called Multiple Project Assurance, and of the just under five hundred institutions that had given such an assurance, only about a half dozen (by one account only five) had not elected to apply the Common Rule to all of their human subjects research, regardless of the source of funding. Indeed, the government's sample Multiple Project Assurance stated: "MPA institutions generally elect to comply with all Subparts of 45 CFR 46 for any research conducted under their auspices (i.e., regardless of the source of support). . . . This has been taken into account in working the sample text"—that is, the form did not even leave space to opt out of the election. Division of Human Subjects Protections, Office for Protection from Research Risks, NIH, DHHS, *Sample Language for a DHHS Multiple Project Assurance . . . in Accordance with the Federal Policy (Effective August 19, 1991)* (June 1999 version), at http://www.hhs.gov/ohrp/humansubjects/assurance/mpa.htm. Today, approximately 75 percent of major domestic research institutions are said to commit themselves to adhere to the Common Rule, and some observers speculate that more than 90 percent and perhaps almost all of American colleges and universities make this election, although this is unclear, because the numbers are not currently available from OHRP.

[138] Even today, however, it is not clear whether a major institution can make such an election without some bargaining. The election still matters as a mechanism for allowing OHRP to enforce the regulations as to research the government does not support. The government, however, does not care as much as it used to whether institutions make the election, because institutions now have another reason to use IRBs, under at least equivalent standards, for research on human subjects, regardless of the election, and regardless of the source of funding. Accordingly, many institutions now consider the election little more than a technicality about OHRP's jurisdiction—that is about reporting requirements and enforcement.

powerful pressures on institutions to adopt IRB licensing for all human subjects research conducted under their auspices. Institutions have good reason to worry about the legal risks of failing to adopt IRBs for all of their human subjects research. Of course, an institution need not accept federal grants. Moreover, even if it does accept federal support, it can choose its own methods of enforcing "ethical principles" in its non-federally-funded research—for example, by instituting IRBs less severe than those stipulated in the federal regulations, or by establishing clear rules and subsequent penalties. Yet IRB licensing—particularly IRB licensing of the severity specified in the federal regulations—clearly has the government's approval as the appropriate method of ensuring ethical research, and this licensing therefore offers institutions, if not an entirely safe harbor, at least a safer harbor than not using such IRBs. To be precise, if an institution does not use IRBs, or if it uses an IRB less intrusive than those required by the federal regulations, the institution must worry that it will be accused by a litigant of adopting a less careful and thus less reasonable means of ensuring adherence to "ethical principles" or otherwise preventing harm. Accordingly, against the background of state tort law, institutions fear they will be held liable for their failure to use licensing—whether for federally funded research or other research.[139] Indeed, they must be vigilant not only in estab-

---

[139] The AAUP Report explains: "Consider the following: a privately funded research project is carried out at a university, one of the human subjects claims to have been harmed by the research, and the subject sues the university. Consider further that the university's IRB does not review research that is not funded by the government. The litigant will almost certainly argue that the university's failure to review privately funded research while it reviews government-funded research is proof that it acted unreasonably. Conversely, if the university's IRB has approved the research, the university will cite that fact as evidence of its reasonableness in permitting the research to go forward. Whatever the merits of these arguments, the university's legally prudent course of action, so the lawyers will advise, is for its policy to apply to all research on human subjects, irrespective of the source of funding. An aversion to legal risks may also help explain the actual decision of IRBs, to the extent that they seek to protect the institution (and perhaps themselves as well) from lawsuits that allege mistreatment of human research subjects." The Report adds that "no university is likely to want to explain to either the government or the public why its commitment to avoid harming the human subjects of research is limited by the source of funding for the research. This prospect is even less attractive as IRBs expand their authority in response to concerns that the government must do more to protect human research subjects." AAUP, *Protecting Human Beings*, Academe: Bulletin of the AAUP at 60 (cited in note 12).

Indeed, it has been argued that "research institutions must increasingly take a conservative approach to granting licenses for social research because IRB approval is one criterion for determining whether the university is culpable, with the researcher for harm to subjects." Lauren H. Seiler and James M. Murtha, *Federal Regulation of Social Research: Is "Prior Review" Posing a Threat to Academic Freedom?* 53 Freedom at Issue 26, 29.

lishing licensing but also in doing it thoroughly. As OHRP explains when reminding IRBs to evaluate methodologies, "[r]esearch that is conducted so poorly as to be invalid exposes subjects and the institution to unnecessary risk."[140] No institution's legal counsel, risk management officer, or insurer can ignore this legal risk. As a result, the government's choice has become that of private and state institutions.[141]

This would not be of so much concern if the federal government had merely published safety standards and encouraged institutions to adopt them. Certainly, the First Amendment does not prevent government from using its powers of persuasion and even its spending and regulatory powers to encourage institutions to adopt what it considers reasonable means of avoiding harm. Here, however, the government has advocated a mechanism that it is constitutionally forbidden from imposing, it has employed unconstitutional conditions to ensure wide use and acceptance of this mechanism, and it has relied upon this wide use and acceptance to trigger liability under state tort law for institutions that do not adopt the mechanism for all of their research. In sum, rather than use the force of federal law to require the licensing, the federal government has substituted, first, the regulatory force of the conditions on its spending and, second, the force of state law.

---

[140] OHRP, *Institutional Review Board Guidebook*, ch I, Part B. The government has long understood that if it could use federal funding to make IRB review "widespread," it could establish this as the standard of care for all research on human subjects. In 1978, when discussing the tort liability of researchers, the National Commission for Protection of Human Subjects revealed its understanding of the effect of the federal regulations on the law of negligence: "In negligence per se jurisdictions, violation of IRB rules could be taken as evidence of negligence. In other jurisdictions, the widespread use of IRBs in the research community may create a standard of care for the conduct of all research." National Commission for the Protection of Human Subjects of Biomedical and Behavioral Research, *Report and Recommendations* 86 (cited in note 127).

[141] A small number of universities, including the University of Chicago, have declined to assure the federal government that they will apply the Common Rule or the other IRB regulations to research not supported by the government. Yet this does not mean that such universities can afford to abandon the licensing system—just that they can avoid reporting to OHRP and can avoid its oversight with respect to research not funded by the federal government. Indeed, the University of Chicago answers the question "Why is my research subject to review?" by explaining that it has negotiated an assurance with OHRP and that, "[i]n addition, federal laws require this protection. In order for the University to fulfill its responsibility, all human subjects research conducted under its auspices must receive appropriate review and approval." University of Chicago, Social and Behavioral Sciences IRB, *Frequently Asked Questions*, at http://humansubjects.uchicago.edu/sbsirb/faq.html.

D. THE GOVERNMENT'S USE OF SURROGATES

This discussion of unconstitutional federal action must close by noting that the federal government's delegation of licensing to other institutions does not insulate it from its responsibility under the First Amendment. On the contrary, the delegation to surrogates confirms that the government is using its conditions and other pressures to regulate, in this instance by the forbidden method of licensing.[142]

In some parts of the world, governments regularly pay or coerce private groups to carry out policies the government cannot openly pursue. These governments have liberal constitutions that protect the freedoms of speech and of the press, and technically, in accord with their constitutions, these governments respect such rights. In practice, however, these governments reward and pressure private groups to do what the government cannot. Somewhat similarly, the federal government has not imposed IRB licensing, but instead has pressured private and state institutions do so. It has thereby established licensing that it itself cannot constitutionally adopt by pressing the institutions to act as its surrogates.

The regulatory and unconstitutional character of this use of surrogates is evident from *Rust v Sullivan*, in which the Supreme Court noted the devolution of regulation that might occur through the government's conditions on its grants.[143] Congress had funded family planning services on the condition that the projects receiving the funding not counsel or otherwise encourage abortion as a method of family planning. This condition limited both the entities that provided the services and the doctors who worked for them, and in *Rust*, the Court upheld the condition. This result was not altogether surprising, for the government funded the services on which it placed the condition, and the doctors did not clearly have more than an ordinary contractual or employment relation to the providers of the services. Accordingly, the Court could treat the problem as a conventional instance of a condition on purchased services and could bypass the more serious problem of the government's use of surrogates to limit freedom.

This issue about surrogates, however, is inescapable for IRBs,

---

[142] Among the recent discussions of the danger that the delegation of governmental power can become a means of evading constitutional limitations, see Gillian Metzger, *Privatization as Delegation*, 103 Colum L Rev 1367, 1432, 1462 (2003).

[143] *Rust v Sullivan*, 500 US 173, 176 (1991).

because the government uses conditions and more forceful legal pressure to establish IRBs as a means of regulation, and it does so in institutions that otherwise leave much freedom of speech and press to their personnel. Students, teachers, and even many commercial researchers necessarily enjoy an intellectual freedom that prevents them from being simply identified with their institutions. Anticipating this sort of problem, the Court in *Rust* explained that "the university is a traditional sphere of free expression so fundamental to the functioning of our society that the Government's ability to control speech within that sphere by means of conditions attached to the expenditure of Government funds is restricted by the vagueness and overbreadth doctrines of the First Amendment."[144] Thus, the intellectual independence of researchers in relation to their employers may transform ordinary conditions on grants into unconstitutional conditions by clarifying that the government is using its grants to obtain regulation through surrogates. Far from insulating the government, its devolution of licensing to universities confirms that in pressuring them with conditions and legal liability, it is making them instruments for imposing regulation—indeed, an unconstitutional kind of regulation: the licensing of speech and the press.

V. Injury Is Not a Justification

It may be thought that even if the IRB regulations would ordinarily be unconstitutional, they are justified by the distinctive magnitude and frequency of the injuries caused by research on human subjects. For decades, the danger to human subjects has seemed to make IRBs a moral necessity, and certainly research injuries can be very serious. Yet they do not justify unconstitutional licensing. Even if the First Amendment is not understood to create an absolute guarantee against the licensing of speech or the press, the licensing established by the federal regulations on IRBs is a

---

[144] Id. See also *Sweezy v New Hampshire*, 354 US 234, 250 (1957). The Court recently echoed this sort of claim about the distinctive freedom enjoyed in universities when it decided *Grutter v Bollinger*, 539 US 1, 17 (2003). Yet it is difficult to understand why some Americans enjoy greater First Amendment freedoms than others simply because they are fortunate enough to attend or work at institutions of higher learning. Instead, what seems to underlie the Court's concerns is the danger that the government is purchasing not merely products or services but also the use of institutions to regulate others.

disproportionate response to the danger of research on human subjects.[145]

The amount of injury that could, perhaps, justify a law licensing verbal speech and the press is not clear, because the precedents tend to involve injunctions.[146] To be sure, there are cases on laws licensing common space or expressive conduct—even conduct (such as showing a movie) that comes close to the verbal core of speech and the press. Yet the Supreme Court cases on laws concerning prior review of verbal speech or the press typically involve injunctions rather than licensing. In 1931, when discussing judicial injunctions in *Near v Minnesota*, Chief Justice Hughes wrote that prior restraints could be constitutional if used against the dangers of national security, obscenity, and violence or insurrection. Yet he apparently was speaking of judicial injunctions rather than licensing, as suggested by his illustration that "a government might prevent actual obstruction to its recruiting service or the publication of the sailing dates of transports or the number and location of troops."[147] His reference to preventing "actual" obstruction suggests that he was thinking of injunctions rather than a system of licensing, which would ordinarily have the more general effect of limiting the risk of obstruction. Similarly, in 1979, when the government obtained an injunction against the *Progressive Magazine* to prevent it from publishing information about how to construct a thermonuclear weapon, the question was not licensing, but merely an injunction, and the constitutionality even of this injunction has been questioned.[148] The Supreme Court, however, has shied away from upholding the constitutionality of licensing under laws that target, not expressive conduct, nor access to common property, but the verbal core of speech or the press.[149] Ac-

---

[145] In terms of the Court's doctrines, the government's interests in preventing research harms do not overcome the presumption against licensing, and the IRB regulations are not narrowly tailored to this objective.

[146] See discussion of *Freedman v Maryland*, 380 US 51 (1965), at note 41.

[147] *Near v Minnesota*, 283 US 697, 716 (1931).

[148] *United States v The Progressive, Inc.*, 467 F Supp 990 (WD Wis 1979); L. A. Powe, *The H-Bomb Injunction*, 61 U Colo L Rev 55, 61 (1990).

[149] As noted earlier, the cases that seem to uphold such licensing turn out to involve licensing of conduct or of access to common or public property. See text at note 40. Although *Posadas* involved a regulation that required licensing of verbal speech and the press, the Court explained that the question of prior review did not come before it. See note 43. Another distinction concerns nonregulatory conditions involving only a waiver of a particular exercise of a right, as in *Snepp*. See note 119.

cordingly, in considering regulations that specify verbal speech and the press as the object of licensing, it is not evident what danger would be so great as to warrant putting aside the First Amendment's central prohibition on such laws.

Many commentators defend IRBs by suggesting that they are necessary to prevent a repetition of the violations of rights associated with Nuremberg and Tuskegee. The Nuremberg Code was a list of ten requirements for ethical research on human beings that the Military Tribunal at Nuremberg adopted in 1947 in its trial of the doctors who experimented on the inmates of Nazi concentration camps. In the context of these experiments, IRBs seem to enjoy the overwhelming moral legitimacy that comes with opposing the Nazi experiments. Yet because of the character of these experiments, their goals, and their context, they reveal little about the dangers of research in a free society. In contrast, the Tuskegee syphilis study is at least a relevant exemplar of what can go wrong in American research. Even allusions to Tuskegee, however, cannot transform censorship into a necessary, moral, or constitutional solution. It is one thing to protect "vulnerable populations."[150] It is another to protect them by violating one of the most significant guarantees of liberty in the Bill of Rights. The use of IRBs is particularly regrettable because, as will be seen, there are other, entirely constitutional means of limiting the harms from research.[151]

In general, licensing of speech and the press is disproportionate to the injuries arising from human subjects research. Leaving aside, for a moment, the relative risks of research, the total amount of injury seems too mundane to overcome the presumption of unconstitutionality. Although the injuries done by research can be serious, the total amount of such injury (whether before or after the wide-scale adoption of IRBs in the 1970s and 1980s) has been far less than the harm arising from many entirely ordinary activ-

---

[150] 45 CFR § 46.111(a)(2).

[151] See text at notes 160–63. If an academic attempted today to expose another Tuskegee study, it is not clear whether he could get approval from an IRB. Even if he could get approval, the IRB would be so concerned about the risk to the reputations of the patients and the doctors that it would probably create severe obstacles by requiring informed consent for any interviews and by protecting the identities of the patients and doctors. Were the academic to collect any useful information under these conditions, he might therefore end up exposing an unspeakable study by unnamed persons concerning an unmentionable disease in an undisclosed location. If the location were not disclosed, however, most IRBs would probably allow the researcher to name the disease.

ities, such as roller-blading or simply walking. For example, deaths and lasting disabilities from experimentation have never been common in America, even without IRBs, but deaths and permanent disabilities from walking (whether from collisions or less dramatic accidents) are numerous. The almost negligible overall harm from research on human subjects reveals little about the relative risk of the research, but it does raise a question as to why the research requires licensing.[152] Adding to this disproportionality is the very method of licensing. Whatever the frequency of serious injuries from research, the harms are hypothetical at the time of licensing.[153] Therefore, to the extent the government relies upon licensing to prevent injury, it inevitably deters and prevents many interactions, communications, and other instances of research that would not have been injurious.

As for the relative risk of research, it does not appear to be unusually high. Even in 1966, when IRBs were still novel and therefore could not have been the explanation for an absence of harm, the Surgeon General acknowledged that "there is a large range of social and behavioral research in which no personal risk

---

[152] A 1979 survey showed that "fewer than 2% of sociology or IRB chairs evidenced firsthand or indirect knowledge of harmful items," but that 25 percent of IRB chairs "found it necessary to deny permission to a survey research project because of the sensitive nature of items in a questionnaire or interview schedule." Seiler and Murtha, 53 Freedom at Issue at 30 (cited in note 139), also quoted by Ithiel de Sola Pool, *Response*, 13 PS 203, 204 (1980).

There are very limited useful data about research risks in the 1950s and 1960s. Moreover, such evidence as exists is not very helpful for understanding the degree to which special regulation, let alone the use of IRBs, is necessary, for the context of research has changed dramatically. Today, for example, researchers are much more self-conscious about informed consent and about the danger of legal liability. What would reveal the effect of IRBs would be a large-scale controlled experiment involving similar research, some with IRBs, and some without. In the absence of such a study, it is difficult to know whether IRBs substantially diminish research harms. The advocates of IRBs, however, had little interest in such an experiment in the 1960s, and now that IRBs are required, the experiment can no longer be done.

Revealingly, some of the most notorious instances of unethical research in the mid-twentieth century were reviewed by ethics committees. For example, according to a report of the National Research Council, "[t]he Willowbrook study had been reviewed by an ethics committee, and the Tuskegee study apparently had also had such a review, but neither study was stopped until the media reports and subsequent public reactions." National Research Council, *Protecting Participants* at 63 (cited in note 5). Evidently, IRBs can be only as effective as the substantive principles of their time and community, and what was needed to avoid or at least end the problems at Tuskegee and Willowbrook was not IRB licensing, but better principles.

[153] Although the risk to a group of human subjects in a particular research project is not necessarily hypothetical, the actual harm to any particular subject is almost always hypothetical.

to the subject is involved."[154] Moreover, in examining a wider range of research (including medical studies), a distinguished defender of IRBs, Robert Levine, raises serious doubts. He observes that although "[m]uch of the literature on the ethics of research . . . reflects the widely held and, until recently, unexamined assumption that playing the role of research subject is a highly perilous business," and although this assumption was "clearly evident in the legislative history" of the 1970s, "some empirical data have become available that indicate that, in general, it is not particularly hazardous to be a research subject."[155]

Writing in 1981, on the basis of risk studies done when the IRB regime was significantly less intrusive than it became over the following decades, Levine found that the risk from being a research subject was not especially hazardous. Some evidence suggested that even in the relatively risky category of "'therapeutic research' . . . the risk of either disability (temporary or permanent) or of fatality was substantially less than the risk of similar unfortunate outcomes in other medical settings involving no research." He concluded that "the role of research subject is not particularly hazardous in general," and "arguments for policies designed to restrict research

---

[154] As quoted by Gray, *Ethical Issues in Social Science Research* at 331 (cited in note 65). Astonishingly, the Surgeon General made this statement about the absence of risk in much social and behavioral research when issuing a "clarification" that "the requirement of institutional review 'applies to all investigations that involve human subjects, including investigations in the behavioral and social sciences.'" Id. Although IRBs often concern themselves with the stress that may be caused by questions, a 1979 study of the harm to survey respondents from the stressful content of questions revealed little such harm. The study asked sociology and IRB chairs if they knew of "harmful items from: 1) their own research, 2) professional literature, 3) word of mouth, or even a rumor. . . . Among 270 responding sociology and IRB chairs, five each reported knowledge of one case of an interview which led to results they considered of substance. None of these cases involved physical injury. All were judged harmful on the basis of emotional reactions during the course of an interview or subsequent to it." This was less than 2 percent of such chairs. Seiler and Murtha, 53 Freedom at Issue at 29–30 (cited in note 139).

[155] Levine, *Ethics and Regulation* at 39 (cited in note 3).
When defenders of IRBs speak of "risk," they often refer to a few, isolated instances of severe harm or to widespread but much less serious types of physical discomfort or mental distress. Levine notes the curiosity that "[b]iomedical researchers have contributed importantly to this incorrect belief [that research is distinctively hazardous]." He explains: "To many members of the public and to many commentators on research involving human subjects who are not themselves researchers, the word 'risk' seems to carry the implication that there is a possibility of some dreadful consequence; this is made to seem even more terrifying when it is acknowledged that, in some cases, the very nature of this dreadful consequence cannot be anticipated. And yet, it is so much more common that, when biomedical researchers discuss risk, they mean a possibility that there might be something like a bruise after a venipuncture." Id.

generally because it is hazardous are without warrant."[156] Of course, some particular research projects are relatively hazardous, and Levine had to work from studies done after the introduction of IRBs, but overall, the risk from research on human subjects appears to be quite mundane, and therefore the remedy of licensing is disproportionate.[157]

There have been, furthermore, many complaints that IRBs are not very effective in preventing injury. Even many proponents of IRBs worry about this problem, though their response is to seek improvements in the IRB system. For example, after studying IRBs, HHS's Office of Inspector General questions "the effectiveness of the IRB system" and therefore proposes that it be made more rigorous. In one study of clinical trials, the office "discovered inadequacies related to IRB oversight in each case."[158] There is, in fact, reason to believe that IRBs have not been the primary obstacle to research harms and that, instead, "the most important reason that the record is so good and that there have been so few

---

[156] Robert J. Levine, *Ethics and Regulation of Clinical Research* 25–26 (1981). He adds: "Equally unsupportable are arguments that, because research is generally safe, there is no need for any restriction." Id. Similarly, see Levine, *Ethics and Regulation* at 39–40 (cited in note 3). At issue, however, is not whether there should be "any restriction," but rather whether the restriction should consist of unconstitutional licensing.

E. L. Pattullo also notes that the regulation of harms to human subjects "cannot be accounted for by the record of injury to subjects. Of 2384 research projects surveyed in 1974–1974, 3 per cent were reported to have caused harmful effects to a total of 158 subjects, with most of the harm characterized as 'trivial or only temporarily disabling.' Given the size of the research enterprise ($8 billion of heath-related research in 1980) and the number of subjects involved annually, the incidence of injury appears extremely small." E. L. Pattullo, *Institutional Review Boards and the Freedom to Take Risks*, New Eng J Med 1156 (Oct 28, 1982). He also writes that "there was not much of a problem to begin with. Despite the handful of horror stories, the record of the professions in protecting their human subjects is remarkably good." E. L. Pattullo, *Institutional Review Boards and Social Research: A Disruptive, Subjective Perspective, Retrospective and Prospective*, in Joan E. Sieber, *NIH Readings on the Protection of Human Subjects in Behavioral and Social Science Research* 10, 13–14 (1984).

[157] Unfortunately, in the 1960s, as already noted, there was little interest in systematically collecting empirical evidence about the relative safety of research with and without IRBs, and now that IRBs are pervasive, it is difficult to obtain such information. See note 152.

[158] HHS, OIG, *Institutional Review Boards: A Time for Reform* vi, 1 (1998). See also HHS, OIG, *Institutional Review Boards: Their Role in Reviewing Approved Research* (1998). Nonetheless, many officials and others have recently suggested that the government should require IRBs for all research on human subjects. For example, a recent commission led by a former president of Princeton, Harold Shapiro, states: "No one should participate in research unless independent review concludes that the risks are reasonable in relation to the potential benefits." National Bioethics Advisory Commission, *Ethical and Policy Issues in Research Involving Human Participants*, Summary 2 (2001).

injuries is that most researchers are keenly aware of the potential for injury and take great care to avoid it."[159]

IRB licensing is all the more disproportionate as a response to research injuries because there are other, more clearly constitutional mechanisms for preventing harms from research. The federal government can weigh the risks of research when authorizing its own researchers to pursue their investigations, when granting funds to outside researchers, and when controlling access to persons in the government's custody and to government facilities (such as military bases and prisons).[160] In addition, the federal

---

[159] Levine, *Ethics and Regulation* at 40 (cited in note 3).

A recent study of the risks of Phase 1 clinical trials of anticancer drugs reveals that death rates have decreased, and, on this basis, it purports to provide evidence that IRBs reduce risks. Examining reports of trials conducted during periods at the beginning and the end of the 1990s (1991–94 and 1999–2002), the study observes that the odds of a patient dying from experimental treatment become less than one-tenth of what the odds had been earlier. Thomas G. Roberts et al, *Trends in the Risks and Benefits to Patients with Cancer Participating in Phase 1 Clinical Trials*, 292 JAMA 2130 (Nov 3, 2004). In speculating about the causes of the decline, the authors note that the drugs administered in the trials have become considerably less toxic. Secondarily, they point to "better supportive care," increased "oversight by IRBs," and publication bias (as their samples came from published studies). Id at 2138. They conclude that the increased supervision of IRBs may have contributed to the decline in deaths.

This study, however, reveals little about the need for IRBs. First, even if, perhaps, IRBs may have been a contributing factor in the decreased death rate, the study does not measure the efficacy of IRBs. Far better for this purpose would be a controlled experiment. See notes 152 and 157. Second, from the report of the study, it would appear that the data are just as consistent with changes in the toxicity of the drugs used in cancer trials, let alone other changes that occurred in medicine during the 1990s. As the authors suggest, changes in drugs were almost surely the primary cause of the decrease. Third, even if the evidence showed that IRBs significantly reduce risks in Phase 1 cancer trials, this evidence would be of little significance in evaluating the merits of IRBs without information as to whether or not IRBs impede the development of cancer treatments and thus create risks— perhaps risks for the very same patients they seek to protect. Fourth, although it is quite possible that evidence will one day show that IRBs reduce risks in research as obviously dangerous as Phase 1 cancer trials, this is of little help in determining whether IRBs reduce risks in other, less dangerous research, including much medical research. Fifth, the government can make laws requiring licensing for the use of dangerous drugs, without licensing research or otherwise legislating on speech or the press.

More generally, although "phase 1 cancer trials are considered among the most risky in all of medicine," it is curious that the benefits of using IRBs even for this sort of study remain a matter of speculation. Id at 2139. Modern medicine is based on evidence and scientific methods of proof, and IRBs bar or modify research that does not adequately meet these standards. The value of IRBs themselves, however, has never been examined in a manner that satisfies such criteria. It is curious that so many persons who uphold the demanding standards of modern scientific method assume the value of IRBs as a matter of faith.

[160] Curran observed in 1969 that "the NIH staff and study sections have always given attention to ethical issues in project applications, both before and after adoption of the 1966 guidelines. . . . Often the issue would be inextricably woven into the general issue of the merits of the application." Curran, 98 Daedalus at 587 (cited in note 3).

government can perhaps license some particularly injurious types of physical conduct (at least within the extent of its powers), as long as it does not target researchers or otherwise aim its licensing at speech or the press. More broadly, the law can impose after the fact liability for harm and can do so even for harm caused by speech or the press—again, as long as the law remains within the parameters of the First Amendment. Even without special regulation, researchers can generally be held liable for negligently harming others. Under this standard, researchers would ordinarily find themselves in a position similar to that of journalists, but some—most clearly, physicians studying their own patients— would find themselves under a higher duty of care.[161] Although such an approach will not prevent all injury, it discourages harm in a way that does not violate the First Amendment.[162] Of course,

---

[161] It is difficult and constitutionally problematic to argue that researchers in general owe a duty to their subjects analogous to that of doctors to their patients. Versions of such an argument can be found in the *Belmont Report* and elsewhere. National Commission for the Protection of Human Subjects of Biomedical and Behavioral Research, *Belmont Report*, Part B.2 (1979); *Grimes v Kennedy Krieger Inst., Inc.*, 782 A2d 807, 858 (Md 2001). Others suggest the possibility of a more general fiduciary duty. Angela R. Holder, *Do Researchers and Subjects Have a Fiduciary Relationship?* 4 IRB: Ethics and Human Research 6–7 (1982); Richard Delgado and Helen Leskovac, *Informed Consent in Human Experimentation: Bridging the Gap Between Ethical Thought and Current Practice*, 34 UCLA L Rev 67, 107–12 (1986); Roger L. Jansson, *Researcher Liability for Negligence in Human Subject Research: Informed Consent and Researcher Malpractice Actions*, 78 Wash L Rev 229 (2003). Yet in many instances, this approach to researchers is not unlike attributing to journalists a professional duty to treat the subjects of their investigations in a manner that does no harm and that even helps them—as if journalists had a professional duty to show respect and to avoid causing distress, upset, or moral, economic, legal, or reputational harm. Such notions about a researcher's professional duty, enforced by federal law, are simply incompatible with the First Amendment.

Incidentally, at least for research by doctors, some commentators may consider a negligence standard too harsh. Certainly, many doctors seem to think it too severe in actions for medical malpractice.

[162] The shadow of the censorship will linger even if the regulations are held unconstitutional. The government has spent several decades and much money pressing universities to impose IRBs and requiring academics to undergo "education" or indoctrination about the importance of IRB licensing. Moreover, the government has elevated IRBs as the standard means of reducing the risk of research injuries. Accordingly, with or without federal regulations, research institutions will continue to cling to IRBs as a means of limiting their tort liability for the negligence of their researchers.

This damage to the traditions of independence among academics will not easily be repaired. Ideally, after the government expended so much effort and money to get IRBs, it might now spend an equal amount to persuade institutions to get rid of them. More practicably, because of the role of tort law in inducing institutions to adopt IRBs, it is worth noting some possible limits on negligence.

First, institutions do not and should not all have equal control over their personnel, and they therefore should not, perhaps, be equally vulnerable for the negligence of their personnel. Although the law holds a business corporation responsible for the negligence of its servants or agents within the scope of their employment, it is not clear that the law

this is not to say that the mere application of negligence doctrine is a perfect solution. The point is simply that a plausible and lawful response to research injuries already exists in the legal system, and this makes it difficult to conclude that a fear of research injuries can justify the extraordinary response of imposing licensing.[163]

In calculating the value of IRBs, one could take into account their prevention of the harms of offense, embarrassment, or other mental discomfort arising from research. Yet from a legal perspective, these are so trivial, immeasurable, or subjective as to be not typically cognizable at common law. For example, the negligent infliction of mental distress does not ordinarily create liability, unless it is in-

---

should equally hold academic institutions responsible for the negligence of all of their personnel in all facets of their academic conduct. For example, students are not servants or agents of their university, and perhaps teachers are not ordinarily servants or agents in all aspects of their teaching, research, or public service. It may seem odd to consider them independent contractors in the business sense, but they have long enjoyed an equivalent independence in an intellectual sense. With this in mind, the Supreme Court has repeatedly observed the independence enjoyed by teachers, students, and other academic personnel in academic institutions. See, for example, *Sweezy v New Hampshire*, 354 US 234, 250 (1957); *Rust v Sullivan*, 500 US 173, 176 (1991); *Grutter v Bollinger*, 539 US 1, 17 (2003). To be sure, there is no academic freedom clause in the Constitution, but in light of the fact and tradition of academic independence, a court could, perhaps, recognize a common law presumption that neither the government nor an academic institution has a power to control academic personnel in their realm of academic freedom, including their research, unless an institution or the government clearly undertakes to control such matters, and that therefore the law does not attribute to the institutions the negligence of their personnel in this sphere of independence. For example, universities reward professors for their public service, but if a professor serves on the board of a charitable organization and breaches his fiduciary duties, he will be held liable, and the university will not be vulnerable on his account. The same should be true of his teaching and research. A professor doing research or teaching as part of a distinctively institutional project (such as an alumni fund-raising event) might be a servant and agent for these purposes, but he is not so clearly a servant or agent for his other research or teaching. In particular, he might be a servant and an agent for purposes of teaching or conducting research in accord with his contractual duties, but not as to his choices in teaching and doing research within the sphere of his independence. In these decisions, he should be understood to stand on his own.

Second, it may be doubted whether state law can give any advantageous legal significance to an academic institution's licensing of speech or the press. If state law treats institutional licensing of speech or the press as a stronger defense against claims of negligence than other precautions, it creates legal incentives for institutions to require such licensing, and it thus in effect penalizes institutions that do not adopt licensing. If the states thereby pressure institutions to become surrogates for imposing censorship, this may violate the Fourteenth Amendment to the extent this Amendment applies First Amendment freedoms to the states. *Gitlow v New York*, 268 US 652 (1925). At the very least, it probably violates state constitutional guarantees of freedom of speech or of the press.

[163] Obviously, the mechanism for discouraging harm need not be the same as the mechanism for compensating injuries. As it happens, most institutions are sufficiently concerned about their reputation that they usually are eager to compensate for injuries, and this may be the reason there have been so few legal actions.

cidental to a physical injury or occurs in unusually personal circumstances. Not only much of the mental harm but also many of the moral, social, legal, and economic harms that IRBs aim to prevent are little more than the unavoidable costs of the freedom of speech or of the press, and to this extent, the government cannot penalize or prevent them. Such injury is ordinarily beyond government intervention even after the injury has occurred, and it can therefore hardly justify interference beforehand, when its occurrence is merely speculative.[164]

Lest it be thought that research on human subjects poses a special risk that requires licensing, it should be recalled that journalism and medical treatment can create at least equal risks for human subjects without needing prior permission. A journalist who investigates a corrupt corporate officer or a corrupt judge may hope to cause his discomfort, ignominy, and punishment but would have little hope of attaining this desirable end if she had to conform to an IRB's consideration of every question she planned to ask the officer or judge. Similarly, doctors often develop new treatments and use drugs and medical devices for "off label" purposes, and they need this freedom to help their patients. Far from being considered threats to society that require a board's advance permission, the novel treatments given by these doctors are merely the most interesting of the innumerable, little experiments by which doctors every day figure out a diagnosis, prescribe a course of treatment,

---

[164] In *Cohen v California*, 403 US 15 (1971), the Court overturned a conviction for the "offensive conduct" of wearing a jacket displaying the words "Fuck the Draft" and explained that the words were not directed to an individual and thus, however offensive in general, were not fighting words. More recently in *Texas v Johnson*, 491 US 397 (1989), the Court explained that "a primary 'function of free speech under our system of government is to invite dispute,'" id at 408 (quoting *Terminiello*), and that '[i]f there is a bedrock principle underlying the First Amendment, it is that the Government may not prohibit the expression of an idea simply because society finds the idea itself offensive or disagreeable." Id at 414. See also, for example, *R.A.V. v City of St. Paul, Minnesota*, 505 US 377 (1992); *Boos v Barry*, 485 US 312 (1988); *Terminiello v Chicago*, 337 US 1 (1949); *Chaplinsky v New Hampshire*, 315 US 568 (1942).

Recognizing that the actual harm done by research may not warrant licensing, some commentators add that IRBs are necessary to give potential research subjects the confidence to participate in research, and that this matters both for promoting research and for ensuring that racial minorities participate and thus get the benefits of research. Such arguments, however, raise many questions. For example, it is by no means clear that licensing is the best way to encourage confidence among potential human subjects. Even if it were, the government's alleged interest in raising the reputation of research among human subjects seems a rather dubious basis for justifying the licensing forbidden by the First Amendment. If the research itself does not do the extraordinary harm that might justify licensing, the mere reputation of the research for doing harm cannot justify it.

observe the results, and then adjust their treatment and, sometimes, their diagnosis. Surgeons often engage in innovative procedures that are risky for their patients, and although they make decisions leading to numerous injuries and deaths each year, they are free to reach their own judgments as to whether they should consult with other specialists or whether they should proceed on their own.[165] Journalists and doctors thus sometimes cause harm, and if it is of a sort cognizable by law, they must face the consequences—but only *after* there is an injury. In both journalism and medicine, harms similar to those arising from research are not thought to require licensing, and it is therefore difficult to justify licensing for research.[166]

VI. The Injuries Caused by IRBs

Laws that abridge the freedom of speech, or of the press, are unconstitutional without proof of particular injury, but it is not necessary to insist on this point, for IRB licensing does much harm. The licensing injures researchers, their use of speech and the press, and their pursuit of knowledge.

IRBs delay research. The delays are inevitable for many reasons—for example, because IRBs usually meet only monthly or quarterly, because IRBs frequently will not approve a proposal at the first meeting at which it comes up (and sometimes will not even get to the proposal), and because IRBs often will have questions for the researcher or requests for modification. Sometimes, repeated exchanges with the researcher are necessary. Accordingly, for social science research at most institutions, a several-month wait is typical.[167]

Although delay may not seem a particularly serious injury, researchers usually have reason to think otherwise. If a social science

---

[165] Surgeons tend to get IRB approval for their work only when they expect they will want to publish about it.

[166] Of course, doctors are licensed, but the relevant point here is that their treatments are not.

[167] Conversation with Tom W. Smith, Director of the General Social Survey at the National Opinion Research Center (Dec 10, 2004). Four to six weeks is considered rapid at most institutions. Id. According to one estimate, "institutional review times can vary from 3 weeks to 18 months." Secretary's Advisory Committee on Human Research Protections, July 26–27, 2004 Meeting, Washington, D.C., *Summary Minutes* 38 (2004) (Dr. Weiner).

researcher wants to ask Americans what they think about a recent political scandal or how they plan to vote, he often must wait for approval of his questions and methods, by which time the scandal may be long forgotten and the election may be over.[168] If a literature or history professor needs to interview an elderly author, musician, or former politician, the professor must in some instances worry that the "human subject" will die before the research is approved.[169] If a researcher gets a sabbatical or grant to do research, and the IRB delays her work, it can waste her year off and her grant money.[170] More generally, IRBs often require researchers to devote precious time and energy to a long and arduous review process. As put by a medical researcher, "[c]ompletion of a study can be delayed or thwarted if [one's] personal energies are not sufficient to create the amount of detailed writing [needed]

---

[168] For dangers of delays through licensing, see *City of Littleton, Colorado v Z.J. Gifts D-$, L.L.C.*, 124 S Ct 2219 (2004); *FW/PBS, Inc. v Dallas*, 493 US 215 (1990); *Freedman v Maryland*, 380 US 51 (1965). According to the Court, prior restraints "are the most serious and the least tolerable infringement on First Amendment rights," because they cause "an immediate and irreversible sanction" and "damage can be particularly great when the prior restraint falls upon the communication of news and commentary on current events" in which "the element of time is not unimportant." *Nebraska Press Association v Stuart*, 427 US 539 (1976) (invalidating a temporary state court order against publication of confessions and other matters that strongly implicated the accused). See also the concurrence of Black, J, joined by Douglas, J, in *New York Times Co. v United States & United States v Washington Post Co.*, 403 US 713 (1971) (affirming a decision against a restraining order in one case and reversing such an order in the other).

[169] After attempting to record the memories of a woman who in 1944 fought in the Warsaw uprising, a professor states: "This woman is now 81 years old and her life is not unlimited. She has a story to tell, and she wants to tell it. . . . I was waiting, waiting, and waiting, and hoping that my source was not going to die before I received permission." She eventually received approval after five months. Conversation with Professor Cynthia Bowman, Northwestern University Law School (Dec 10, 2004).

[170] For an example, see AAUP, *Protecting Human Beings*, in Academe: Bulletin of the AAUP at 63–64 (cited in note 12).
Whether or not teachers have failed to get tenure because of delays in getting permission to do their research is unclear, but students certainly suffer from the tardiness of IRBs. Lincoln and Tierney, 10 Qualitative Inquiry at 222 (cited in note 82). To avoid such difficulties, many graduate students in the social sciences avoid doing their own empirical work and thus graduate without any independent practical experience in their field of research. Jack Katz writes to his fellow ethnographers that "we see the chilling effects on less secure students and junior colleagues who, feeling overwhelmed at the problems of fitting their research ideas into the regulatory system, are abandoning important lines of investigation before they begin." Jack Katz, *To Participants in the UCLA, May 2002, Fieldwork Conference* (May 8, 2002), at http://leroyneiman.sscnet.ucla.edu/katz5_8.htm. Incidentally, it will be recalled that students not only must get approval from an IRB but also must get a faculty member to serve as a principal investigator, and at least in one instance, in Boston University's dentistry program, when a faculty advisor did not bother to get IRB approval for a student's research, the student could not complete his work and was expelled for his slow progress. *Missert v Trustees of Boston University*, 73 F Supp 2d 68 (1999).

. . . to convince the IRB . . . of the merit of the project."[171]

Even worse, IRBs directly suppress speech and the press. In the seventeenth century, licensors sometimes crossed out offending passages in manuscripts prior to publication, and today IRBs similarly request modifications in research. IRBs apparently request modifications in most research proposals that require approval (according to one report, in more than 80 percent), which means that every year they impose changes on at least tens of thousands of proposals and probably more than a hundred thousand.[172] Although some changes are minor, others are not.[173] For example, in reviewing proposals to interview individuals, IRBs frequently require researchers to submit their questions to the IRB in writing, and then demand that the researchers drop or alter their questions—as when, for example, in reviewing a survey on religion or sex, an IRB rephrases a question that it considers too intrusive. Of course, many researchers are reluctant to prepare written questions, for this stifles conversation and prevents the researchers from spontaneously following paths of inquiry that open up during an interview. Nonetheless, IRBs tend to insist on seeing written questions, and they expect researchers to adhere to the script. When IRBs worry that research will collect confidential or otherwise sensitive information, they often require researchers to ensure that after they collect and use the data, they will strip it of "identifiers" or will otherwise destroy it—a practice that limits the

---

[171] James Reilly, *Innovative Tools, Regulatory Bodies, and the Creative Surgeon,* 129 Archives of Otolaryngology—Head & Neck Surgery 678 (2003). He also notes that "[a]s intelligent humans, we must constantly observe, test, and verify. We must never stifle our inquiring minds . . . . The FDA and IRBs are not repositories of new ideas." Id.

[172] For the percentage, see AAUP, *Protecting Human Beings,* Academe: Bulletin of the AAUP at 56 (cited in note 12). A 1998 study commissioned by NIH states: "Overall, in 73 percent of IRBs, one-quarter or fewer protocols were approved as submitted," and "[i]n fact, 34 percent of IRBs did not approve any (zero) protocols as submitted in 1995; 10 percent approved one-quarter to one-half; and 6 percent more than one-half of protocols." James Bell, John Whiton, and Sharon Conelly, *Final Report: Evaluation of NIH Implementation of Section 491 of the Public Health Service Act, Mandating a Program of Protection for Research Subjects* 61 (June 15, 1998). One observer with extensive experience believes that IRBs currently seek modification of 90–95 percent of proposals requiring approval. For a summary of some research on the average number of reviews conducted by IRBs, see National Research Council, *Protecting Participants* at 36 (cited in note 5).

[173] Many modifications concern informed consent, but these modifications are often very significant, for the way in which a researcher approaches a research subject can be determinative of the response rates and even the substantive results. Understanding this, IRBs not infrequently respond to research they consider too sensitive by using informed consent modifications to render it impracticable. They thus quash the research without having to deny permission.

opportunity for future researchers to replicate the study or to use the data for other research.[174]

IRBs frequently interfere with methodology, and although they claim that they thereby improve research, they in fact may have the opposite effect. According to a study based on 1995 data, 55 percent of IRB members believed that their decisions improved the scientific quality of research done on human subjects—but only 37 percent of the researchers agreed.[175] IRBs sometimes merely make flawed but trivial changes in methodology—as when an IRB at a Midwestern university recently objected to an informed consent document because it enumerated the risks in a column of text with bullets in front of each risk rather than in paragraphs.[176] Other methodological interference is not so comic—as when IRBs do not appreciate the benefits of what they consider unorthodox methods and therefore decide that the benefits are outweighed by the risks.[177] Of course, whether or not the IRBs improve methodology is not the issue, for in matters of speech and the press, it is not a licensor's judgment that matters. If IRBs license speech and the press, an IRB that imposes its methodology abridges a researcher's First Amendment freedom.

A related problem is that researchers cannot do their work anonymously. Some research is sufficiently controversial or is based on sufficiently unconventional methods that researchers may hesitate to inform anyone that they are doing it until they are confident that they will get valuable results or results they will feel comfortable publishing. Accordingly, by requiring researchers to share their research plans with colleagues on IRBs, the licensing system leaves researchers in doubt as to whether they can explore projects anonymously, and it thereby sometimes discourages them from experi-

---

[174] The particular practices of IRBs vary considerably. Some IRBs allow the preservation of identifiers in a separate location with codes that allow the identifiers to be linked back to the rest of the data; many others allow the separate preservation of identifiers but only for a limited time; others require a broader destruction of data, either immediately or after several years. Even when IRBs do not require the eventual destruction of the identifiers, they separate them from the rest of the data and thus make it highly improbable that future generations will be able to go back and make full use of the information.

[175] Bell, Whiton, and Conelly, *Final Report* at 61 (cited in note 172). The researchers were presumably all principal investigators, and both the board members and these investigators were randomly selected by the chairs of the boards.

[176] Communication from researcher.

[177] Lincoln and Tierney, 10 Qualitative Inquiry at 220, 230 (cited in note 82), quoted in note 100.

menting with new methods and examining controversial topics.[178]

The practical consequences of IRBs are predictable. Some researchers avoid innovative research and novel techniques that might provoke an IRB to request changes in a proposal.[179] Others abandon their work when they find that the time and paperwork required for approval are unduly burdensome. Some scholars begin research but then give up along the way, when the IRB delays them, or when they find that their project as rewritten by the IRB is not worth pursuing. Lacking the imprimatur of an IRB, much important research never even gets started. Even if unapproved research gets done and gets written up as an article, it sometimes does not get published. It is one thing for a researcher to write an article; it is another for him to publish it and thereby reveal that his research violated what appears to be federal policy. Although his research

---

[178] For the First Amendment's protection of anonymity in speech and the press, see *Buckley v Am. Constl Law Foundation, Inc.*, 525 US 182 (1999); *McIntyre v Ohio Elections Commission*, 514 US 334 (1995); *Talley v California*, 362 US 60 (1960). In *Buckley v Valeo*, 424 US 1 (1976), the Court upheld a federal law requiring political candidates and political committees to keep records of contributions, but the Court distinguished this regulation of gifts for the sake of preventing corruption from other regulation of speech or the press.

[179] "A variety of strategies have been devised by researchers to overcome persistent rejection by IRBs, including several that actually undermine the work but that have the effect of permitting graduate students to complete their doctorates." Lincoln and Tierney, 10 Qualitative Inquiry at 222 (cited in note 82).

After describing the IRB evaluation of the importance of research, the AAUP comments on the chilling effect of this evaluation: "The mere existence of the requirement that IRBs evaluate the risks of the research in relationship to its importance can have an inhibiting effect on the work of scholars. Inhibitions on research can have numerous causes, and academic researchers take for granted the pressures that derive from having their work reviewed by colleagues. But the pressures of IRB reviews are different, for behind them is the weight of the government and the specter of the official control of opinion. This is not to say that control of opinion is the purpose of IRB reviews; manifestly it is not. But an IRB review that seeks to evaluate the importance of research can lean in that direction if only because judgments about the importance of research are highly speculative. From the perspective of the scholar with so much at stake in obtaining IRB approval, the uncertainty about whether any particular research project will be considered important in relation to its risks, and the vagueness of such an inquiry, may dampen enthusiasm for challenging traditional habits of thinking, testing new theories, or criticizing social and political institutions. Why chance an IRB's displeasure when a more cautious approach is likely, so the scholar might plausibly reason, to secure uncontroversial approval?" The Report adds: "Evidence that IRB reviews may have had such repressive effects is anecdotal, gleaned from the surveys of several professional organizations described earlier in this report. But a description of the challenges of applying IRB reviews to social science research would be seriously incomplete if it ignored the danger to freedom of research—if only through self-censorship—implicit in the requirement that IRBs evaluate the importance of research." AAUP, *Protecting Human Beings*, Academe: Bulletin of the AAUP at 61–62 (cited in note 12). Although not inaccurate, this account of the chilling effect does not acknowledge that IRBs actually prevent research and modify it, thus directly suppressing the affected portions.

may be of a sort that the IRB would have approved, he must worry that if he publishes it, the IRB will view him as uncooperative and therefore be unreceptive to his future research proposals. It might even investigate him and expose him to what his university warns are "serious consequences" for unlicensed research.[180] In all of these ways, an incalculable amount of knowledge is lost.

An example of the damage can be observed at the journalism department of Duke University. In this department, one professor says that because of IRBs "he now limits his class projects to 'bland topics and archived records.'" Another, Margaret Blanshard, writes that "I am . . . leaving the contemporary period behind. It is far safer in the nineteenth century. . . . [Y]ou do not have to worry about the IRB when you work in the nineteenth century."[181] Blanshard adds: "I have seen students alter research projects to avoid IRB contact. I have seen some give up projects because of the red tape involved. I have heard words such as 'thought control' used far too often . . . ." She concludes: "A better formula for stultifying research is beyond contemplation."[182]

---

[180] University of Chicago, Social and Behavioral Sciences Institutional Review Board, *Frequently Asked Questions* 2, at http://humansubjects.uchicago.edu/sbsirb/faq.html. See also e-mail message from Provost Alan Brinkley and Executive Vice President for Research to Faculty, Administrators, and Students at the Morningside Campus (Oct 15, 2004).

Of course, there are other incentives for cooperation. For example, "a single, and especially an unfunded, researcher lacks the resources to contest an unreasonable and intransigent IRB. . . . Further, IRBs are required to be composed of persons of high reputation. To challenge an IRB on campus or in court could retard a career." Seiler and Murtha, 53 Freedom at Issue at 30 (cited in note 139). A professor from UCLA points out that "higher status people get more leverage" with IRBs, and this suggests that those who are apt to have the most difficulties with IRBs are not those who are in the best position to resist them. Conversation with Professor Jack Katz, UCLA (Dec 13, 2004).

[181] Indeed, in saying this Blanshard explained that she was following the example and reasoning of yet another scholar—"a fellow media historian" who had told Blanshard of her decision to retreat from contemporary matters. Margaret A. Blanshard, *For the Record*, 88 Academe (May–June 2002), at http://www.aaup.org/publications/Academe/2002/02mj/02mjftr.htm.

[182] Id. At the School of Journalism at University of North Carolina at Chapel Hill, "[n]ews stories that use social science research methods such as public opinion polls and field experiments are subject to IRB review." AAUP, *Protecting Human Beings*, Academe: Bulletin of the AAUP 55, 59 (cited in note 12).

At Northwestern University Law School, where professors used to encourage students to do original empirical research, several professors now actively discourage their students from collecting data because, as put by one of these teachers, "[t]he delays in approval and the interference with research design usually make it impossible to go though the IRB process, conduct the research, and write it up in one term, or even two. The IRB process diminishes our ability to train our students to do research." E-mail message from James Lindgren (Dec 10, 2004). Faculty also trim their own work. One explains: "I try to avoid doing the sort of research that will require me to go before an IRB. I think about ways to answer a question that allow me to avoid going before an IRB, and if I cannot,

The loss of knowledge is particularly poignant in quality improvement projects—the inquiries made by doctors about how to
improve the treatment of patients. If quality improvement projects
are subject to IRBs, doctors have reason not to do these investigations, for these projects involve a process of tinkering with treatments, and they therefore are difficult to get through an IRB's
approval process. In particular, these studies cannot always be reduced to the rigid, formal protocols of scientific research assumed
by IRBs, which can insist upon giving approval to each little
change.[183] To avoid these problems, doctors sometimes do not
bother to get prior permission from an IRB, but then they have
reason to avoid publishing their results, lest the IRB detect their
noncompliance. This happened at the University of Pittsburgh,
where an IRB subjected doctors to an investigation for their failure
to get prior approval of a published quality improvement study.[184]
Doctors thus face impediments to inquiring and publishing about
the care they give their patients, and obviously it is not the doctors
who thereby suffer the most.

The full extent of the damage remains unknown because licensing
does not publicly punish speech or the press, but, instead, suppresses
it. The amount of the harassment, intimidation, and abandoned
research is largely a matter of anecdote, for it is difficult to calculate
the effect of licensing on scholars who abandon or alter their projects (whether in anticipation of IRB demands or in response to
them), let alone the effect on those who never even begin. IRBs,
moreover, usually operate in secret, and because researchers are

I try to find another subject." Conversation with Professor Cynthia Bowman, Northwestern
University Law School (Dec 10, 2004).

[183] This is also a problem with oral history and especially ethnographic research, in
which "research practice" is often "indistinguishable from the researcher's social life as
conducted outside the framework of research." Jack Katz, *To Participants in the UCLA,
May 2002, Fieldwork Conference* (May 8, 2002), at http://leroyneiman.sscnet.ucla.edu/
katz5_8.htm.

[184] Lynn, 13 Quality and Safety in Health Care at 67 (cited in note 54). Apparently,
IRBs held back for years from treating quality improvement studies as research for fear
that if they had to review and approve such studies, they would discourage these inquiries
about improving medical care. This was particularly a matter of concern because the
doctors who were most likely to be discouraged were academic doctors, who need to
publish. Nonetheless, in responding to the events at Pittsburgh, OHRP issued a letter
stating that quality improvement studies could qualify as research under federal regulations,
and therefore the problem is now unavoidable. See note 54.

Similar problems could, perhaps, arise in medical case studies, but fortunately OHRP
and most IRBs have thus far refrained from viewing these as systematic investigations
designed to develop or contribute to generalizable knowledge. 45 CFR § 46.102(d).

afraid of antagonizing IRBs, or of being condemned for violating federal policy, the researchers tend to speak about their troubles—about the damage to their work and their struggles to evade IRBs—only on condition of anonymity.[185] If, however, the licensing thus tends to escape public scrutiny, perhaps the Constitution's prohibition against licensing deserves all the more attention.

VII. Conclusion

Research on human subjects can cause harm, and to protect against the dangers of such research, the federal government pressures universities and other research institutions to establish IRBs. Under this system, academics and others must get the permission of an IRB before doing research on human subjects. This is licensing, and it raises serious constitutional questions.

The primary problem is that the federal regulations conflict with the First Amendment. This Amendment prohibits licensing of speech or the press, and it is particularly clear-cut in forbidding the licensing of verbal speech or the press. Nonetheless, the regulations define "research" in terms of speech and the press and then require that the research be licensed. Although the regulations ostensibly encourage this licensing by means of government spending, they actually go much further, for they rely on the force of unconstitutional regulatory conditions and state tort law. The government thus requires licensing of speech and the press, and even if the First Amendment creates only a presumption rather than a prohibition against such licensing, the government's interest in preventing the relatively modest overall danger of human subjects research cannot overcome this constitutional barrier.

The unconstitutionality of IRBs can be illustrated, once again, by the supposition about Newspaper Review Boards or NRBs. Suppose the federal government were to fund investigative journalism at newspapers on the condition that the funded journalists get NRB permission before beginning their inquiries. Suppose, moreover, the NRBs were required to ensure that the journalists did not ask questions or otherwise investigate in a way that might cause the investigated person to lose his job or even to feel stress or upset on

---

[185] Other commentators on IRBs have noticed this. For example, in his essay on IRBs, Cary Nelson reports that with one exception, everyone he interviewed, including board members, "requested anonymity." Nelson, 89 Academe at 30 (cited in note 125).

account of the "sensitive" character of the inquiry. This condition on funding might seem justified, for investigative journalists sometimes obtain their stories by deceit, trespass, and receipt of unlawfully obtained property; they regularly disclose private, confidential, or otherwise sensitive information; they investigate at the risk of causing harm, including personal and financial ruin, suicide, divorce, imprisonment, and even political violence. Nonetheless, the conditions requiring NRBs would be unconstitutional—even if the newspapers consented to the NRBs, and even if the government sought NRBs only for federally funded investigations. If conditions requiring NRBs are unconstitutional, so are those requiring IRBs.

A second, more general concern is that the government has established a new type of censorship. If the government had directly required licensing, or if it had used the licensing to suppress popular opinion, it probably could not have succeeded. Yet by avoiding the direct force of federal law and by appealing to widespread moral sensibilities, it has largely bypassed political barriers and has given the appearance of getting around the constitutional obstacles. The government thereby has maintained censorship in America for over three decades. As seen, however, the licensing cannot really escape the constitutional problems. The new censorship therefore is no less unconstitutional than the old.

Third, and most broadly, the success of the new censorship suggests much about the role of the Supreme Court. Never before in the history of the United States has the federal government imposed an elaborate system of licensing on academic and other empirical inquiry. Such censorship, however, seems constitutionally plausible to many Americans, largely because of doctrines on spending and licensing adopted by the Supreme Court. It therefore is necessary to consider the danger of judicial doctrines that undermine enumerated rights—doctrines that signal to those in power that they are not constrained by these rights and that suggest to those whose rights are abridged that they have no constitutional basis on which to protest.

For example, the Supreme Court's doctrines on spending and licensing emboldened the federal government in establishing censorship. In the 1970s, when the federal government developed what became the current regulations on IRBs, it examined the Court's doctrines and, on this basis, contemplated its licensing scheme not with a sense that it had to restrain itself, but with a sense of constitutional opportunity. Most prominently, in the 1978 report to Congress by the National Commission for the Protection of Human Subjects, the Commission relied upon the Court's doctrines to put aside objections that "the requirement of prior review and approval by an IRB" might "violate constitutional rights of academic freedom and free inquiry." The Commission examined the Court's speech and press doctrines and concluded that the government may "regulate. . . the methods used in . . . research, in order to protect interests in health, order and safety."[186] Moreover, it observed that the Court's spending doctrine gave Congress even greater freedom, for "[w]here the IRB system is imposed on researchers as a condition of . . . receipt of research funds, the same constitutional limitation will not apply."[187] In such ways, the federal government recognized that the Court's doctrines regarding licensing and spending created a constitutional opening for the new censorship, and Congress and the executive therefore felt free to impose IRBs without regard to the First Amendment.

At the same time, the Supreme Court's doctrines have undermined the ability of researchers to assert their First Amendment rights. For example, in 2003, in the most recent agitation against IRBs, oral historians in the American Historical Association and the Oral History Association sought to relax the grip of IRBs on oral history—history done through taped interviews. They had no confidence, however, that they could prevail in a constitutional challenge to the regulations, and therefore rather than pursue the constitutional issues, they merely attempted (unsuccessfully) to show that the regulations did not apply to oral history—an approach that has not proved very successful.[188]

---

[186] National Commission for the Protection of Human Subjects of Biomedical and Behavioral Research, *Report and Recommendations* 78–79 (1978).

[187] Id. It continued: "Neither the government nor a university has a legal obligation to support research of any particular kind, nor hire researchers in a particular area. . . . Thus, an institution may empower the IRB to apply both content and manner restrictions to research that it funds, whether or not such a system would be constitutional if directly imposed by the state on nonfunded research." Id at 79–80. Even as to research the federal government did not fund, the Commission observed that the matter "has not yet been definitively settled," and that the courts would probably "permit regulation of nonfunded activities when reasonably related to the purpose of the federal spending." Id at 77.

For other examples of how the Court's doctrines left the impression that the government could constitutionally establish its system of IRBs, see notes 12, 17, 18.

[188] The historians attempted to avoid the jurisdiction of IRBs by de-emphasizing the broader significance of their work: They argued that "oral history interviews, in general, are not designed to contribute to 'generalizable knowledge'" and claimed that as a result,

Researchers who oppose IRBs face many difficulties, but none more debilitating than the doctrines of the Supreme Court, for these doctrines give the impression that researchers are without a plausible constitutional claim. Recognizing the implications of the Court's doctrines, the proponents of IRBs have inculcated a sense of submission by popularizing the catchphrase, "Research is a privilege, not a right." Even major universities sententiously recite this statement to their professors and students.[189] In this atmosphere, researchers have difficulty defending their freedom. They cannot find an unequivocal right against the licensing in the Court's doctrines, and when they ask lawyers, they are confirmed in their un-

---

"oral history interviewing, in general," is beyond the definition of "research" in the regulations. This is plausible only on the improbable assumption that most oral history is not designed to contribute to generalizable knowledge. All of this, however, has turned out to be of limited significance, because IRBs tend to recognize that much oral history contributes to generalizable knowledge. American Historical Association and Oral History Association, *Oral History Excluded from IRB Review*, at http://omega.dickinson.edu/organizations/oha/org_irb.html. See also *Exclusion of Oral History from IRB Reviews: An Update*, at http://www.historians.org/Perspectives/Issues/2004/0403/0403new1.cfm.

For an illustration of how even a group that advocates freedom of speech in universities has succumbed on the questions of spending and licensing, see the report of the AAUP quoted in note 12.

[189] See, for example, *An Industry on Trial*, 11 Research Information Bulletin (Oct 1997), quoting Curt Meinert, director of the Center for Clinical Trials at Johns Hopkins School of Hygiene and Public Health, at http://www.wfubmc.edu/or/pursuit/pursuit/_oct97/page6.html. One variant is that "human subject research is a privilege, not a right." University of North Carolina at Chapel Hill, *Institutional Review Standard Operating Procedures* 14 (Dec 12, 2003). Similarly, see Stuart Plattner, *Human Subjects Protection and Cultural Anthropology* 76 Anthropological Q (Spring 2003). (Plattner is a Human Subjects Research Officer at the National Science Foundation.) Another variant, from Rutgers University, states: "Congress has declared that conducting research is a privilege, not a right." Memo to Members of the University Community, re Announcement of the Human Subjects Assessment Initiative, from Michael B. Breton, Associate Vice President Research and Sponsored Programs, and Karen M. Janes, Associate Director Research Integrity and Compliance at Rutgers University (May 3, 2004), at http://orsp.rutgers.edu/Humans/assessment.asp.

At least a small number of researchers have protested. Complaining about this "mantra," some observe that "having one's research funded is a privilege, but research per se is just a form of learning, a feature of human existence not requiring the permission of anyone else." John Mueller, John Furedy, and Clive Seligman, Letter, *Re: "IRBs for Dummies,"* 16 Observer [American Psychological Society] (Feb 2003), at http://mueller.educ.ucalgary.ca/ObserverFeb2003-Dummies.html. Others write: "Somehow the 'agenda of inquiry' must be restored to its preeminent status over the 'agenda of control.' It has become chic in some quarters to try to deflect criticism of the ethics industry with an observation such as 'Research is a privilege, not a right.' This fatuous thinking simply conceals an effort to maintain control at all costs. Research is a job requirement for faculty, and research is a degree requirement for students. Freedom of inquiry is widely accepted and respected in everyday life, it is a truly just part of the natural order of human existence. *That that inquiry is so much more constrained on campus than in the everyday world, without good cause, is something we should all decry.*" John Mueller and Steve Lupker, SAFS *Letter on Research Ethics*, at http://www.safs.ca/issuescases/ethics.html.

derstanding that the First Amendment protects almost nothing absolutely and that Congress can spend largely as it pleases.[190] Convinced by the Court's doctrines that they cannot rely on the First Amendment, researchers moderate their protests, plead for relief, or just acquiesce.[191]

---

[190] Conversations with researchers about lawyers. In 1982, Roberston commented on the government's use of conditions to obtain IRBs: "Neither scientists nor institutions have challenged in court the power of Congress to impose such conditions, perhaps because the Supreme Court, if ever faced with the question, is likely to construe Congress's conditional spending power broadly and to approve such conditions." Robertson, in *Ethical Issues in Social Science Research* 361 (cited in note 11).

[191] Revealingly, when the American Historical Association and Oral History Association attempt to hold off the IRBs, they did not really protest but instead negotiated their statement with OHRP and then used its concurrence as a sort of imprimatur: "The Office for Human Research Protections concurs with this policy statement, and it is essential that such an interpretation be made available to the many IRBs currently grappling with issues of human subject research." American Historical Association and Oral History Association, *Oral History Excluded from IRB Review*, at http://omega.dickinson.edu/organizations/oha/org_irb.html.

When they become convinced that there is little point in pursuing a First Amendment claim, academics have tended to fall back on more amorphous ideals, such as academic freedom or a right to research, but with limited legal foundation for these claims, the researchers do not get very far.

EMILY BUSS

CONSTITUTIONAL FIDELITY
THROUGH CHILDREN'S RIGHTS

In 1967, the Supreme Court decided the landmark case of *In re Gault*, which famously declared that "neither the Fourteenth Amendment nor the Bill of Rights is for adults alone."[1] This important step forward in the recognition of children's constitutional rights, however, was immediately followed by a serious misstep: In defining children's due process rights, the Court limited its universe of options to those specific rights already afforded to adults. The Court asked "Which adult procedural rights should we extend to children?" rather than asking, more basically, how to achieve the due process value of "fundamental fairness" for children.

As the Court turned its attention to other claims of children's constitutional rights, it repeated *Gault*'s mistake again and again: Whether considering speech rights, privacy rights, or rights of protection, the Court has routinely started with the specifics of adult rights and whittled down to children's. This "adult-minus" orientation has prevented the Court from accounting for children's differences in a manner that maintains fidelity to the principles animating constitutional rights. The result is a range of distortions in analysis and outcome that disserves children and rights alike.

Emily Buss is Professor of Law, The University of Chicago.

AUTHOR'S NOTE: Thanks to Mary Anne Case, Martin Guggenheim, David Meyer, and Elizabeth Scott for their helpful comments on previous drafts, and to Sheila Beail, Sarah Meltzer, and Brian Rubens for their excellent research assistance.

[1] 387 US 1 (1967).

This distortion comes from focusing on the adult cases at the level of application rather than principle. Where the details of the adult cases drive the Court's analysis of children's rights, they predictably cast the circumstances of childhood as a counterweight to the rights. Sometimes the counterweight is sufficient (children are different enough) to justify denying children some or all of what adults get. Sometimes (more rarely) the counterweight is insufficient, and children get the same rights as adults. But whether the Court affords or denies children rights, it has failed, under this approach, to take account of childhood in a manner that maintains the rights' coherence. To achieve coherence, the Court should begin by assuming an identity of principle animating the constitutional rights afforded children and adults. Where children's rights do not match those of adults, it should be because the special circumstances of childhood change how these constitutional principles are best achieved, whether that means greater, lesser, or simply different rights for children.

This article has two aims: The first is to demonstrate the many different ways in which the Court's adult-minus reasoning has impaired its rights analysis. The second is to suggest how the Court's analysis of children's constitutional rights might look different, if it accounted for the experience of childhood in a deeper, more integrated manner. In some cases, I will suggest that the Court should have reached different outcomes; in others, only that it should have altered its analysis. I do not attempt to prescribe a full set of rights for children or to present an exhaustive list of the Court's mistakes. Rather, I seek to reveal a handicap that the Court has imposed on its own analysis, in the hope of improving that analysis in the future.

Before turning to this discussion, it is worth noting how this project differs from other comprehensive discussions of children's rights, particularly those that prescribe a scheme of rights that diverges from current doctrine. These discussions typically start with the child and articulate the set of rights most suited to serving children's interests. Many of these accounts consider how the Constitution should be interpreted to serve these interests, but this constitutional analysis is secondary to the articulation of an ideal rights vision for children.[2] I come at the question from the other

---

[2] See, for example, Barbara Bennett Woodhouse, *Children's Rights*, in *Handbook of Youth and Justice* (Plenum, 2001); Michael Wald, *Children's Rights: A Framework for Analysis*, 12 UC Davis L Rev 255 (1979).

direction. I take the Court's articulation of constitutional principles as a given, and consider how those principles can be more coherently applied to children. I accept the Constitution "as is," and focus on the corruption of established constitutional principles that occurs when the Court considers the constitutional claims of children.

To say that the analysis of children's constitutional rights should be true to the principles that motivate these rights for adults is hardly to make the rights inquiry simple: For some rights, the motivating principles are highly contested, and for all rights, application of these general principles to specific facts can support multiple results. Greater fidelity to constitutional principles will not make the Court's analysis of children's rights any easier, but it should make it better.

I. How Children Are Different

In analyzing children's constitutional claims, the Court routinely declares, first, that children have constitutional rights, and, second, that these rights need not be coextensive with those of adults. These conclusions are relatively uncontroversial. Most people consider personhood sufficient to put children under the constitutional umbrella, and the significant differences between children and adults a justification for adjusting constitutional application, rather than rethinking the Constitution's applicability altogether. But in implementing this sensible framework, the Court has fallen short both in articulating the relevant differences and in construing the significance of those differences. I begin with a brief consideration of the first failure, before turning to the second.

Although the Court repeatedly points to children's differences to justify affording children diminished rights, it rarely articulates those differences, let alone explains why they dictate the particular rights reductions it has imposed. The Court's most thorough account of these differences is set out in *Bellotti v Baird (Bellotti II)*,[3] where the Court explained that "the peculiar vulnerability of children; their inability to make critical decisions in an informed, mature manner; and the importance of the parental role in child rearing," were the three reasons why "the constitutional rights of children cannot be equated with those of adults."[4] This list, while

---

[3] 443 US 622 (1979).

[4] Id at 634.

it offers a fine start, is thin and incomplete. My primary objection, however, is not with the list, itself, but with the use to which the Court has put it. Before moving on to those issues of application, I will offer my own list of children's differences which both amplifies and organizes the list offered by the Court.

What is most distinct about childhood is that it is a period of rapid change. Adolescents have little in common with infants, and neither is much like 7-year-olds, but they are all engaged in the same process of development that leads them from infancy to adulthood. Change, of course, occurs throughout life, but an important distinction between adulthood and childhood is that the pace of change slows dramatically. This is in part due to physiological forces, and in part due to environment. Precisely when we "come to rest" in adulthood is affected by societal expectations about when that transition will occur.

We can further break down the change that occurs in childhood into two categories, one universal and one individualistic. The first, universal, form of development moves a child through a predictable progression that ultimately produces an individual with adult-level capacities for cognitive and social functioning. The second, individualistic, form of development moves a child through a process of shaping that produces a specific adult with distinct views, skills, and style. While these two forms of development clearly interrelate, distinguishing between them helps illuminate their respective relevance for rights analysis. I will consider children's development of capacities and identity in turn, before introducing children's third salient difference, their custodial status.

A. CHILDREN'S EMERGING CAPACITIES

Over the course of childhood, adult capacities gradually emerge. The capacity whose relevance to children's exercise of rights is most commonly noted is the capacity for logical thinking. Children gradually acquire the capacity for abstract reasoning, and, until they do, they are significantly impaired in their ability to weigh various options in making choices for themselves.[5] The capacity for logical thinking has most relevance for the exercise

---

[5] For a good summary of children's cognitive development, see Wallace J. Mlyniec, *A Judge's Ethical Dilemma: Assessing a Child's Capacity to Choose*, 64 Ford Rev 1873, 1875–83 (1996).

of autonomy rights, which reflect our faith in individuals' competence to assess their own interests. Thus, impairments in reasoning capacity might justify modifying choice rights, particularly when the choices children make will have serious consequences for themselves or others.

Many of the Court's children's rights cases, however, do not consider children's right to make choices. Rather, they consider children's right to be treated a certain way by adjudicators, for example, or protected from a certain sort of intrusion into their body or property. In these contexts, the capacity for logical reasoning plays a less significant role. Even among autonomy rights, other capacities will matter as well.

Also relevant to rights analysis is the capacity for moral reasoning. Before children acquire the ability to understand right and wrong in more abstract and principled terms, their moral perceptions are tied to the views of adults in a position to reward and punish their behavior.[6] This capacity, too, bears on children's qualification to make autonomous choices and it has special relevance to assessments of culpability for choices made. A younger child's conception of why and whether some act is wrong might not match that of an adult, and this, in turn, might justify an alteration in rights analysis in contexts when culpability matters.

Related to children's moral development is their understanding of rights, themselves. As with moral development, children's understanding of rights evolves from the concrete and person-focused, to the abstract and absolute. Before mid-adolescence, many children will not understand that they have rights that exist independent of a police or school official's preference to the contrary.[7] Children's emerging understanding of rights is of particular importance when the choices protected by the rights are distinct from those with which they have everyday experience. Thus, trial rights, such as the right to counsel or the privilege against self-incrimination, are particularly likely to befuddle a child, on whom these rights have been imposed by the misfortune of an arrest.

As important for children's exercise of rights are two aspects of

---

[6] Lawrence Kohlberg, *The Development of Children's Orientations Toward a Moral Order: Sequence in the Development of Moral Thought*, in William Damon, ed, *Social and Personality Development, Essays on the Growth of the Child* 388 (W.W. Norton, 1983).

[7] For a discussion of this issue, see Emily Buss, *The Role of Lawyers in Promoting Juveniles' Competence as Defendants*, in Thomas Grisso and Robert G. Schwartz, eds, *Youth on Trial* (Chicago, 2000).

development that have received inadequate attention from lawyers and courts, namely, sociocognitive and identity development.[8] Sociocognitive development encompasses the child's emerging understanding of roles and the self's relationship with others in those roles. Identity development encompasses the child's emerging understanding of self as a distinct individual with a unique set of attributes and beliefs. The fact that children's understanding of self, other, and the relationship between the two emerges gradually has significant implications for children's rights. Sociocognitive development matters for any right in which the relationship between a child and others is implicated, whether directly (as with the right to counsel) or indirectly (as with the right to make choices that will affect others). Identity development is implicated whenever it matters that the child can perceive herself as an exerciser of rights or an actor in a process.

While children's impaired capacities might serve as a justification for altering their rights, these impairments have largely disappeared by mid-adolescence. To the extent deficits remain, it is not in raw capacity, but in context-specific performance.[9] Adolescents show considerable variation in their ability to achieve their capacities, depending on the context in which the capacities are tested. As a general matter, the more comfortable the context—the more familiar the setting, the issues, the individuals involved, and the process—the higher (meaning more mature) will be the child's level of performance.[10] This suggests that concerns about children's capacities should not necessarily lead to a reduction in rights. Rather, they might call for an adjustment of the context in which, or the process by which, rights are exercised, in order to enhance children's comfort, understanding, and, hence, performance as rights exercisers.

---

[8] For a general discussions of these aspects of development, see William Damon and Daniel Hart, *Self-Understanding in Childhood and Adolescence* (Cambridge, 1988), and Robert L. Selman, *The Growth of Interpersonal Understanding* (Academic, 1980).

[9] See Elizabeth S. Scott, *Criminal Responsibility in Adolescence: Lessons from Developmental Psychology*, in Grisso and Schwartz, *Youth on Trial* 291, 302–03 (2000) (arguing that, while some studies suggest that the reasoning capacities of children in mid-adolescence match those of adults, many factors compromise adolescents' ability to exercise those capacities as effectively as adults).

[10] See Laura A. Berk, *Child Development* 22 (Allyn & Bacon, 6th ed 2003) (noting studies that suggest that "the maturity of children's thinking may depend on their familiarity with the task and the kind of knowledge sampled.").

B. CHILDREN'S EMERGING IDENTITIES

While children share some generic progressions, their development is also highly individualized, producing adults with vastly diverse abilities, interests, and beliefs. One important implication of this identity development for rights analysis is that it renders children particularly subject to influence. What and how they learn, with whom they associate, and who serves as their role models will all have a profound effect on who they grow up to be.[11]

How the relative malleability of children's identities should affect their rights is complicated. On the one hand, society's interest in ensuring children's exposure to positive influences (whether good values, productive education, or cultural connections) and preventing their exposure to negative influences (including labor, exploitation, antisocial influences, or unproductive distractions) is offered as a standard justification for curtailing the rights of children. On the other hand, society's interest in shaping children into proficient rights exercisers may argue for giving children exposure to, and the opportunity to experiment with, the exercise of rights.[12] Here, again, there is likely to be a link between context and performance. Unless rights are afforded in a manner that is comprehensible to children, courts should be slow to assume that children will derive any educational benefit from the granting of rights. Conversely, a denial of rights, in terms that are poorly understood by children, runs the risk of inadvertently misleading children about the nature of their rights.

Schools figure centrally in this balance between controlled influence and opportunities for rights exercise. Schools serve as one of the primary sites for positive influence, for the development of basic intellectual skills, the acquisition of knowledge, and the cultivation of prosocial behavior. To accomplish all this, schools need a level of control that may justify a diminution of rights. But schools are also one of the best testing grounds for the exercise of rights, offering students a society of peers with whom to interact and a governmental authority structure against which to push. Any

---

[11] For a general discussion of children's development of a unique identity, see Gerald R. Adams, Thomas P. Gullotta, and Raymond Montemayor, eds, *Adolescent Identity Formation* (Sage, 1992); Damon and Hart, *Self-Understanding* (cited in note 8).

[12] See Frank Zimring, *The Changing Legal World of Adolescence* (Collier Macmillan, 1982).

analysis that takes only one of these two mechanisms of influence into account is developmentally incomplete.

Children's emerging understanding of themselves as unique individuals identified by their views, aptitudes, and tastes also increases their qualification to make long-term judgments for themselves. The more fixed their identities become, the more their current assessments of costs and benefits to their interests are likely to equate with those assessments several years hence. The fact that this fixing of identity generally occurs between adolescence and young adulthood adds support to capacity-based arguments for diminishing or delaying children's autonomy rights. But, as noted, many of the constitutional claims asserted by children do not involve classic autonomy rights. In the many cases where the Court addresses children's right to procedures, privacy (in its passive usage), and protection, differences in capacity and the fluidity of identity do not attenuate children's qualification to achieve the constitutional principles at stake, though they will alter the means by which these principles are achieved.

C. CHILDREN'S CUSTODIAL STATUS

Children's ongoing development, both universal and individualistic, has served to justify children's confinement to the custodial control of others, primarily parents and secondarily schools. We confine children to others' custody, both to protect them from the bad outcomes that would be produced if they were left to their own devices and to allow these custodians to exert a positive influence over the ongoing process of development. Of course, this confinement reflects a serious, child-specific diminution in constitutional rights of its own, for it deprives children of the liberty safeguarded by the Due Process Clause for all adults. For my purposes here, I am willing to concede the basic validity of the state's imposition of parental authority and compulsory education on children. What remains of children's rights, after making this considerable rights-impairing concession, is the more interesting and difficult question.

Children's unique custodial status can be viewed as an additional difference between children and adults that must be taken into account in applying constitutional principles. The double layering of the issues of "pure" minority and minority-specific context is, in fact, typical in children's rights cases: The Court considers what

First Amendment or Fourth Amendment rights a child has *at school*, or what right to control mental health treatment or abortion decisions a child has *within a family*. In many of these cases, the Court points to the special context as its own justification for a curtailment of rights, without acknowledging that the context already reflects a serious rights curtailment. While these special custodial contexts may, in some circumstances, demand additional rights curtailments to be effective, the analysis may also cut the other way. It is easier to justify a regime that deprives children of substantial freedom (the child-specific contexts) if it is done in a manner that serves the constitutional principles at stake.

In sum, we can describe children's differences in three rough categories: The first are differences in capacity. Relevant capacities include not only the decision-making capacity identified in *Bellotti*, but also the capacities for moral reasoning, social interaction, and self-understanding. While the difference between the capacities of young children and adults is profound, the difference between the capacities of older children and adults is relatively superficial. The second difference between adults and children is in the fluidity of their identities. Children's ongoing process of identity development renders them more open to both positive and negative influences than adults. It also raises questions about a child's qualification to act on behalf of her future self. The third difference is inspired by the other two: Children function within custodial relationships that dramatically alter their experiences, status, and opportunities.

The list set out by the Court in *Bellotti* captures a good portion of these differences, if only in the sketchiest form. But in analyzing children's rights in specific cases, the Court has failed to put the list to good use. In case after case, the Court does little more than mention some item on the list to justify some curtailment in the rights of children. Instead, the Court should consider how child-specific differences might alter the way in which constitutional principles are achieved.

II. The Court's Adult-Minus Approach

The Court's error plays out in different ways. In some cases, it skews outcomes; in others, it distorts the constitutional analysis. What is common to all is that children, at best, get adult rights. They never get more, and the possibility of enhancing their rights is never seriously considered. They never get something entirely different, even if a different scheme might serve constitutional principles far better for children. And they often get less, a crude less, best accounted for by starting from the detail of the adult right and cutting back. The assumption pervading the Court's analysis is that children are entitled to "adult-minus" constitutional rights.

In each context in which I criticize the Court's analysis, my argument will follow the same basic structure. First, I will frame the constitutional inquiry by describing, in simple terms, the principles said to animate the right. Second, I will describe the adult detail that has been developed to serve the constitutional principles identified. Third, I will demonstrate that the Court's analysis of children's rights consists of an unprincipled application of the adult detail, sloppily discounted to account for their minority. Finally, I will suggest how the Court's analysis could be improved by focusing on the constitutional principles at stake and the child-specific adaptations required to ensure that those principles are achieved. My aim is not to prescribe the detail of children's constitutional rights, but to suggest the general direction that a more principled analysis would take.

I begin with the cases addressing children's due process rights in the juvenile justice context, both because the adult list of required procedures is so clearly defined, and because the principles said to animate these rights so clearly call for a different set of procedures for children. I then consider a range of rights claims in the school context, to illustrate how the adult-minus orientation has prevented the Court from giving proper consideration to children's school experience. I next turn to children's rights claims in the context of the parent-controlled family. Here, again, I conclude that the Court has disserved constitutional principles by failing to account for the parent-child relationship in a meaningful way. I close with a brief discussion of the abortion and death penalty cases, which, however flawed in other respects, reflect a greater fidelity to constitutional principles in their analysis of children's rights.

A. PROCEDURAL DUE PROCESS RIGHTS

1. *Due process principles.* The Due Process Clause is often said to guarantee "fundamental fairness" in the state's dealings with

individuals.[13] Two primary fairness values—the values of accuracy in decision making and participation by the individual affected—animate the Court's due process analysis.[14] But what constitutes accuracy, and how best to accomplish meaningful participation, varies with context and with participant.[15]

The Court has considered how the Due Process Clause applies to children in a range of contexts including the juvenile justice system, schools, and mental health facilities. In all these contexts, the Court's analysis fits the adult-minus pattern: First, the Court declares that the Due Process Clause applies to children. Second, it assumes that the maximum protection afforded children would be that afforded to adults. And, third, it concludes that children's unique legal and developmental status justifies affording children something less than the full scope of the adult right. In most cases, whether the Court ultimately recognizes or denies the disputed due process protection, the Court's analysis disserves the values the clause is said to protect. By limiting its selection to those procedures established for adults, the court either applies ill-fitting procedures that alienate, rather than include, children in the process, or rejects such procedures as ill-fitting, leaving children with no fairness protection at all.

a) Adult criminal process and its misapplication to children. The Court has most extensively developed children's due process rights in juvenile justice proceedings. In this context, the Court's adult-focused approach is particularly obvious. In case after case beginning with *Gault*, the Court has worked its way through the menu of adult criminal procedure rights, asking which items should apply to children, and which should not. Over time, the Court has concluded that children get some rights (the rights to notice, to counsel, and to proof of guilt beyond a reasonable doubt, the right against self-incrimination, and the right of confrontation),[16] but

---

[13] See, for example, *Daniels v United States*, 532 US 374, 386 (2001) (Scalia, concurring in part) (noting the "precepts of fundamental fairness inherent in 'due process'").

[14] See Martin H. Redish and Lawrence C. Marshall, *Adjudicatory Independence and the Values of Procedural Due Process*, 95 Yale L J 455, 487–88 (1986) (noting the "inseparable connection between participation and result efficacy").

[15] See *Cafeteria Workers v McElroy*, 367 US 886, 895 (1961) ("the very nature of due process negates any concept of inflexible procedures universally applicable to every imaginable situation").

[16] *In re Gault*, 387 US 1 (1967); *In the Matter of Winship*, 397 US 358 (1970).

not others (the rights to a jury trial and to bail).[17] The result is an adult-minus juvenile justice system that is not "fundamentally fair" for children.

Two distinct legal trends converged in *Gault*. The first was the development of criminal due process rights for adults, and the second was the development of a separate juvenile justice system. Prior to *Gault*, the Court had developed its application of the Due Process Clause to the state criminal prosecutions of adults in considerable detail. "Fundamental fairness," in that context, was increasingly construed to encompass the procedural protections set out in the Bill of Rights. Under the theory of incorporation, the Fifth Amendment right against self-incrimination and the Sixth Amendment trial rights, including the right to counsel, compulsory process, and confrontation, were made applicable to state criminal defendants through the Fourteenth Amendment's Due Process Clause.[18] These rights, enshrined by the Framers, were deemed to secure meaningful participation and accuracy in decision making for adults.

Meanwhile, the juvenile court, conceived of as a civil court, evolved without any procedural protections. Although the informality of juvenile justice proceedings was designed to bring the accused and decision maker closer together, the lack of procedural protections, joined with insufficient resources, prevented the system from giving the accused any meaningful consideration at all.[19] Gerald Gault's case provided the Court with a particularly alarming example of this procedural neglect: Accused of making a single obscene phone call that was never proved in court, Gerald was sent to a juvenile detention facility for up to six years. Convinced of the unfairness of this processless system, the Court turned to its well-developed adult model for a constitutional solution.

The Court was right to conclude that Gerald Gault's due process rights had been violated. But it was wrong to limit its search for solutions to the set of rights prescribed for adults, which are

---

[17] *McKeiver v Pennsylvania*, 403 US 528 (1971); *Schall v Martin*, 467 US 253 (1984).

[18] For an account of this evolution of the conception of "fundamental fairness" toward the incorporation approach, see Tracey Meares, *What's Wrong with Gideon?* 70 U Chi L Rev 215 (2003).

[19] See President's Commission on Law Enforcement and Administration of Justice, *Task Force Report: Juvenile Delinquency and Youth Crime* 7 (GPO, 1967).

poorly designed to achieve accuracy of results and meaningful participation for children. This is in part because children's ongoing development greatly affects their ability to comprehend and take part in formal judicial proceedings and in part because the special substantive aims of the juvenile court (themselves driven by children's developmental differences) complicate the concepts of accuracy and participation.

i) Children's impaired capacity to participate in formal proceedings. A highly formalized proceeding controlled by unfamiliar adults and invisible rules is not well designed to ensure children's comprehension or participation. Limits in abstract reasoning and social experience impair most children's ability to grasp the "us" of the law that bestows rights and imposes consequences. Moreover, children's sociocognitive immaturity prevents them from understanding the role of the lawyers through whom they are expected to exercise their rights and otherwise participate in the process.

As noted earlier, limitations in abstract reasoning prevent many children from understanding rights as absolutes. Rather, they perceive rights as privileges bestowed by authority figures, perhaps their lawyers, but more likely the police and prosecutors who stand against them. This confusion compromises their understanding of the process and limits their ability to participate effectively.[20]

Compounding the problem is children's difficulty understanding their lawyers' role, and their relationship with those lawyers. Understanding that an unknown, professional adult is required to take direction from a child client further taxes the child's powers of abstract reasoning, requiring him to grasp the lawyer's commitment to professional principles over personal preferences. The lawyer's obligation to defer to the views of a child client is inconsistent with a child's entire world of experience. Adults in charge of professional situations do not take direction from children, especially children accused of wrongdoing.

Children who are confused and, perhaps, distrustful of the system and their relationship with their lawyers are unlikely to track the process, share sensitive information, or exercise control over the lawyers' involvement in the process. As a result, their lawyers will be hampered in their ability to act as their agents, either in pressing for accuracy of findings or in securing children's input

---

[20] See Thomas Grisso, *Juvenile Competency to Stand Trial*, 12 Crim Just 5 (1997).

in the process. Even to the extent the lawyer succeeds, the client may not perceive the success. Meanwhile, because the formal structure of lawyer-led witness interrogation precludes other opportunities for input, it keeps the accused child at an alienating distance from victim and decision maker.

Finally, formality and the involvement of lawyers and other court professionals slow the process, attenuating the child's memory of relevant events and obscuring the connection between the offense and the court-imposed consequences. This, too, undermines a child's experience of participation, both by diminishing his ability to play an effective role in his own defense and by increasing his alienation from the proceeding.

Of course, children's differences in sociocognitive capacity diminish with age, and by mid- to late adolescence most children demonstrate adult-like social understanding, at least in familiar domains. The unfamiliarity and stressful nature of the criminal process may, however, cause children to perform at the lower end of their developmental range.[21] Moreover, there is some evidence to suggest that adolescent offenders are likely to be slower to develop the relevant capacities than their nonoffending peers. All that being said, there is no reason to think that 18 years of age best captures the time at which most individuals are prepared to understand a formal adjudicatory process and participate effectively. Indeed, if adult functioning is the benchmark, the empirical evidence suggests that 16 years of age might be a more accurate age at which to draw a purely capacity-based line.[22] The thrust of my analysis is not to establish a precise age below which adult procedural protections are inadequate (such developmental precision is unrealistic), but rather to demonstrate that, with decreasing age, those protections become decreasingly effective at securing the protections the Constitution guarantees.

Children's inability to participate meaningfully in criminal proceedings has served as one of the primary arguments against ex-

---

[21] Berk, *Child Development* at 248 (cited in note 10) (noting that people are most likely to engage in the highest-level, abstract reasoning in contexts in which they have had extensive experience).

[22] See Thomas Grisso, Laurence Steinberg, et al, *Juveniles' Competence to Stand Trial: A Comparison of Adolescents' and Adults' Capacities as Trial Defendants*, 27 L & Human Beh 333 (2003) (reporting findings of a comprehensive study that suggested that youth 15 years old and younger were more likely to manifest impairments suggesting incompetence to stand trial than older youths or adults, and tended more often than older individuals to make choices that reflected compliance with authority and psychosocial immaturity).

tending adult criminal court jurisdiction to them.[23] But in one sense, the case against the adult-style process is even stronger for children tried in the juvenile justice system, with its distinct substantive aims. In this system, the procedures developed to secure meaningful participation and accurate decision making for adults in criminal court offer a particularly poor constitutional fit.

ii) The special meaning of accuracy and participation in the juvenile system. As originally envisioned, the juvenile process focused heavily on rehabilitation, eschewing the assignment of blame and imposition of punishment associated with the adult system.[24] While states have expanded the purposes of their juvenile justice systems to encompass punitive ends, they have maintained a commitment to rehabilitation, despite a widespread rejection of this aim in the adult system.[25] This commitment to rehabilitation in the juvenile system can be attributed to the recognition that children's identity development continues through adolescence. A child not yet fixed in his behaviors and attitudes is more likely to respond to influences pointing him in a positive direction.

The juvenile justice system aims to rehabilitate its subjects through two primary mechanisms, one procedural and one substantive, and adult-style process interferes with both. As a matter of procedure, the system intends for the court to communicate to children its concern for their well-being and ambitions for their improvement, in the hope that this will help inspire children to turn things around. This message of concern is unlikely to get through, however, to a child who is alienated from the process. Thus, a failure to secure meaningful participation in the juvenile justice context imposes an extra cost on children, who are denied the intended benefit of the special relationship between system actors and themselves.[26]

---

[23] Id.

[24] See Elizabeth Scott, *Criminal Responsibility in Adolescence*, in Grisso and Schwartz, *Youth on Trial* at 294 (cited in note 7) ("The new juvenile court was grounded in a commitment to the rehabilitation of young offenders and a rejection of retribution as a legitimate purpose of state intervention").

[25] See, for example, Albert W. Alschuler, *The Changing Purposes of Criminal Punishment*, 70 U Chi L Rev 1, 9 (2003) (summarizing the rejection of rehabilitation as a primary goal of criminal sentencing for adults in recent decades).

[26] The Court claimed to accommodate the distinct rehabilitative aims of the juvenile court by eliminating certain items, particularly the right to jury trial, from the adult due process list. But nowhere in the cases did the Court offer a systematic account, explaining why some adult details are consistent with the rehabilitative aim, and others are not.

As a matter of substance, the juvenile justice system aims to tailor the consequences imposed on juvenile offenders to meet their treatment needs. While it has taken many decades to identify programs that actually help, recent studies have identified certain programs that have demonstrated considerable success in reducing recidivism rates, even among serious juvenile offenders.[27] The empirical literature also reveals another significant fact about the identity development of offenders: Left to their own devices, a large percentage of juveniles will simply outgrow their offending behavior.[28]

To achieve the rehabilitative aims of the juvenile justice system, the process must not only distinguish offenders from nonoffenders, but also offenders in need of treatment from offenders better left alone. And for those in need of treatment, the system must accurately assess each offender's needs and prescribe a program well designed to meet those needs. Thus "accuracy" means considerably more in this setting than in the adult criminal proceeding.

Moreover, the expanded scope of the accuracy demanded in juvenile justice proceedings carries with it a heightened need for participation. Accuracy in treatment planning, even more than adjudicative accuracy, requires the accused's meaningful participation. A decision maker will be seriously compromised in his ability to assess an individual's therapeutic and social support needs if it fails to hear the individual's own views on the subject. Moreover, the prescribed treatment is unlikely to succeed if the individual on whom the treatment is imposed does not perceive the value of that treatment.[29]

b) Fidelity to due process principles in the juvenile justice system.

---

[27] See Mark W. Lipsey, *Can Rehabilitative Programs Reduce the Recidivism of Juvenile Offenders? An Inquiry into the Effectiveness of Practical Programs*, 6 Va J Soc Pol & L 611 (1999) (employing meta-analysis to demonstrate program success with juveniles, particularly older juveniles charged with relatively serious offenses).

[28] See Terrie E. Moffitt, *Adolescence-Limited and Life-Course-Persistent Antisocial Behavior: A Developmental Taxonomy*, 100 Psychological Rev 674 (1993) (concluding that, for most juvenile offenders, the offending reflects ongoing development, which they will outgrow when they take on adult roles).

[29] It should be noted that the Supreme Court has never applied the Due Process Clause to the dispositional phase of a juvenile proceeding. In the shadow of *Gault*, however, state courts and legislatures have extended adult-style rights to these proceedings as well. See, for example, Samuel M. Davis, *The Role of the Attorney in Child Advocacy*, 32 J Family L 817 (1994). A due process challenge to these sorts of dispositional proceedings could bring the constitutional issue back before the Court.

Instead of looking to the adult list of procedural details to determine which among them should apply to children, the Court should return to the principles inspiring those details and ask how those principles can best be achieved for children. To achieve the due process principles of accuracy and participation in the juvenile justice system, the process must be coherent and accessible to children. This requires, most centrally, a familiar means of interaction among the participants. Children are most familiar with direct conversation in ordinary language. This is what they have experienced in their families, with their friends, and in their schools. They also know that to speak directly to an individual, or in a group, is to participate. A proceeding that builds on that experience has a far greater chance of securing meaningful participation—actual involvement and an understanding of the significance of that involvement—than a proceeding that imposes layers of people and rules between the child's thoughts and the ideas communicated.

A juvenile justice system that affords due process to children might provide for children's direct and informal conversation with witnesses (including the victim) and with the decision maker. This direct interaction, conducted in plain language with realistic opportunities for questions from the child, could enhance the child's understanding of the state's proof and his "own" defense. He might also better understand the nature and extent of the harm associated with the offense and the reasons why various consequences are imposed on him, if he is adjudicated delinquent. But, most centrally, the child would likely experience himself as a participant in the decision-making process, an experience children are unlikely to have if their lawyers stand in for them, and allow them to talk only if and when they take the stand.

This approach would not require the abandonment of lawyers for children, but it might alter their role. Lawyers could still advise children of their rights and assist them in uncovering relevant information. But they would not displace children as participants in the proceeding, nor would they lead the case against them. An abandonment of formal witness-lawyer colloquies might, in turn, lessen the need to rely on judges as decision makers. Instead, decision makers might be those whose professions prepare them to speak comfortably with children, to assess the credibility of conflicting claims, and to select a program of response well designed to help those offenders who need the state's assistance.

Finally, such proceedings might be required to be convened and completed quickly. A swifter response could help children to connect past acts with current proceedings and current proceedings with future consequences. Children's greater memory of, and connection with, relevant events at the time they are addressed will likely improve their ability to participate both as witnesses and strategists.

One objection to this approach is that it requires judges interpreting the Constitution to become child development experts. There is something to this concern, but much to be said to counter it as well. First, and most important, is the inevitability of this role. Unless we abandon all distinctions between the rights afforded to children and adults, we necessarily ask courts to determine when, and to what extent, such distinctions are appropriate, and the answers are necessarily developmentally based. What distinguishes my approach is less its recognition of the importance of development than its insistence that the developmental inquiry be tied to constitutional principles rather than to irrelevant details.

Second, my approach gives the legislative process greater control over the content of children's rights than the adult-minus approach, under which the Court defers to its own prior conclusions about adult rights, and decides which among them should apply to children as well. Of course, the way to give the legislative process full authority over developmental assessments is to defer absolutely to its judgments when children are involved. But once we've determined that the Constitution imposes some limits on legislative actions affecting children, then a process that gives legislatures the first opportunity to develop child-specific law mindful of these principles can be more deferential than the adult-minus alternative. Indeed, the Court in *Gault* would have done better to simply reject the Arizona procedures afforded to Gerald as constitutionally inadequate, and leave the further development of those procedures, in the first instance, to the legislative process.[30]

---

[30] This was one aspect of Justice Harlan's criticism of the majority opinion. In his separate opinion, he faulted the Court for deciding more than it had to, and advocated that the Court approach its due process analysis as follows: "[f]irst, no more restrictions should be imposed than are imperative to assure the proceedings' fundamental fairness; second, the restrictions which are imposed should be those which preserve, so far as possible, the essential elements of the State's purpose; and finally, restrictions should be chosen which will later permit the orderly selection of any additional protections which

c) Adult civil process and its misapplication to children in schools. The Court has taken the same adult-minus approach to children's due process rights in other contexts such as the schools. As in the juvenile justice setting, this has produced ill-fitting procedural protections that disserve due process principles.

The basic principles animating the Court's due process analysis in the adult civil context are the same as in the criminal process (accuracy and participation), and the full list of adult rights in the civil setting resembles the criminal list (a formal hearing with counsel, witness examination, and cross-examination, presided over by a neutral decision maker). The Court shrinks the adult list in certain civil contexts, not because it concludes that the list disserves the due process principles in those contexts, but because it determines that the costs of the process are high enough and the stakes for the individual low enough to justify some diminutions in accuracy and participation.[31]

In considering the due process rights of schoolchildren, the Court began with the assumption that the full list of adult procedures would maximize the process values for children. Nonetheless, the Court has sharply curtailed the procedural list in the school setting out of concern for the effect these procedures would have on school functioning. Thus, the adult detail provided the process ideal, and the school interests justified the departure from the ideal. The Constitution, the Court concluded, entitled children to adult-minus due process rights in school.

Both steps in the Court's analysis are flawed. Perhaps even more than in the juvenile justice context, the full adult set of procedural details is unlikely to secure a child's meaningful participation in school-related decision making. And although affording procedural protections may impose special costs in the school setting, it will also provide special benefits, for a child's interest in participation takes on special value in the educational setting.

The Court has considered due process challenges to school discipline policies in two cases: *Goss v Lopez*[32] and *Ingraham v Wright*.[33] In *Goss*, students challenged an Ohio statute permitting

---

may ultimately prove necessary." 387 US at 72 (Harlan concurring in part and dissenting in part).

[31] I will discuss this balancing test, set out in *Mathews v Eldridge*, 424 US 319 (1976), in Part IIIC below.

[32] 419 US 565 (1975).

[33] 430 US 651 (1977).

school suspensions of up to ten days without a hearing; in *Ingraham*, students challenged a Florida statute that authorized corporal punishment without a hearing. In *Goss*, the Court held that students were entitled to some notice and opportunity to be heard, and that this notice and hearing should occur prior to the suspension, whenever feasible. In *Ingraham*, the Court concluded that no pre-paddling notice or hearing was required. Read together, these decisions reflect an adult-focused view of strong and weak procedural protections that disserves the goals of accuracy and, especially, meaningful participation for children.

In *Goss*, the Court held that the Due Process Clause entitled children to notice and a hearing before they were deprived of their property and liberty interests in a public education through a suspension. The Court concluded that fairness could be achieved by providing prompt and informal notice and a chance for the student's input, quickly followed by a decision on the suspension. The Court might have conceived of the swiftness and informality of the process as procedural assets for children, serving their participation and possibly accuracy interests better than slower, more formal procedures. But, instead, it viewed these features only in negative terms. Children got some procedural protection, but considerably less than that commonly afforded adults, because the state interest in limiting procedures weighed heavily on the other side. The rights to counsel, to confrontation, and the like were rejected, not because such procedural rights would disserve a child's participatory interests (as they likely would), but because they would be financially and pedagogically costly for the school.[34]

---

[34] The *Goss* Court explained:

> We stop short of construing the Due Process Clause to require, countrywide, that hearings in connection with short suspensions must afford the student the opportunity to secure counsel, to confront and cross-examine witnesses supporting the charge, or to call his own witnesses to verify his version of the incident. Brief disciplinary suspensions are almost countless. To impose in each such case even truncated trial-type procedures might well overwhelm administrative facilities in many places and, by diverting resources, cost more than it would save in educational effectiveness.

419 US at 583. The Court's interpretation of *Goss* in subsequent cases emphasizes this negative message. See, for example, *New Jersey v TLO*, 469 US 325 at 349 (Powell concurring) ("The *only* process found to be 'due' [in *Goss*] was notice and a hearing described as 'rudimentary'; it amounted to *no more than* 'the disciplinarian . . . informally discuss[ing] the alleged misconduct with the student minutes after it has occurred.'"); *Vernonia School Dist. 47J v Acton*, 515 US 646, 656 ([*Goss*] "requires *only* that the teacher 'informally discuss the alleged misconduct with the student minutes after it has occurred'") (emphases added).

Children in school were placed at the low end of the adult scale as a concession to the interests of the state.

Although the suggestion that children are entitled to, rather than relegated to, informality and speed may have an Orwellian "less rights are more" feel, the difference between the positive and negative conception of these attributes has real consequences for children. Conceiving of informality and speed as positive aspects of a child's procedural right to a comfortable and comprehensible involvement in decision making can help guard against the state's inclination to slip from "informal" procedures to token or non-existent procedures, as occurred in the juvenile justice context prior to *Gault*. Moreover, if a child's right to informality and speed is conceived in positive terms, the right can serve as a constitutional counterweight to the conflicting procedural rights of adults when children and adults are involved in litigation together. If children's procedural rights are conceived as lesser versions of adults', then their involvement in litigation with adults will be seen as having a simple rights-expanding effect. But if their procedural rights are conceived as different from those of adults, the courts will then have to weigh these competing claims against one another.[35]

The thin procedural protections afforded children in *Goss* gave way entirely in *Ingraham*. The Court acknowledged that corporal punishment implicated liberty interests, but nevertheless dismissed the students' due process argument, concluding that the school was not required to afford children *any* pre-paddling opportunity to present their account or otherwise question the school's determination to strike them. The Court suggested that the school's potential civil or criminal liability for the wrongful use of corporal

---

[35] This sort of direct procedural conflict is most likely to arise in the family law context, where parents battle one another for custody, or the state seeks an involuntary termination of a parent's parental rights. In these contexts, the values of accuracy and meaningful participation are likely to be achieved for adults and children in very different ways. For adults, the accuracy that matters is classic fact-finding accuracy, achieved through witness examination and cross-examination, and meaningful participation best achieved through the representation of able counsel. For children, however, "true" family is as much secured through swiftness and finality as it is through the thoroughness of the fact-finding process, and meaningful participation likely undermined by the intimidating context of full formal procedures. In my experience as a lawyer for children, children's interests in swift and comprehensible decision making were routinely sacrificed to adult procedural interests, with their accompanying delays. Unless the child's fairness values are viewed as distinct and independently protected, we cannot expect them to stand up against the fairness claims of co-litigating adults.

punishment rendered any procedural protections unnecessary.[36] Comparing this liability scheme to *Goss*'s procedural requirements, the Court concluded that "[t]he subsequent civil and criminal proceedings available in this case may be viewed as affording substantially greater protection to the child than the informal conference mandated by *Goss*."[37]

This reliance on the possibility of ex post liability is an odd means of securing due process. While the threat of liability will have some effect on the "accuracy" of a school's decisions, it will have no effect on the subject's participation in decision making. The Court's analysis is particularly jarring when applied to children, who would have no knowledge of this liability scheme, or their ability to use it. The Court's complete disregard for the participatory value is in part a product of its adult-minus approach and its negative ("only this") conception of children's procedural rights. Having pushed children to the low end of the adult scale in *Goss*, it then conceived of the *Goss* hearing as a trivial event whose loss was insignificant.[38]

d) Fidelity to due process principles in schools. When potential school disciplinary action is sufficiently severe to implicate due process protections, those protections should be designed to secure the meaningful participation of the accused child prior to the disciplinary action. What this means will vary with the issues (what does the school claim the child did and what consequences does it seek to impose). As in the adult context, the seriousness of the

---

[36] 430 US at 678–79.

[37] Id at 678 n 46.

[38] Other language in *Ingraham* suggests that the adult model forced an *over*-assessment of potential procedural protections, which, in turn, led to the complete denial of prehearing rights. In justifying the denial of any pre-paddling process to children, the Court explained that "[h]earings—even informal hearings—require time, personnel, and a diversion of attention from normal school pursuits. . . ." 430 US at 680. In a subsequent footnote, the Court noted the "inevitable attendant publicity within the school" that would accompany any prior hearing. Id at 681 n 50. These assumptions about the nature and scope of the child's pre-paddling opportunity for input, and even the choice of the word "hearing" to describe that potential process, also reflect how encumbered the Court's analysis was by the adult detail.

The space between affording a "hearing" with attendant contributions of "personnel" and consequential "publicity," and paddling children for disciplinary infractions without hearing from them first, is big enough to afford meaningful process (serving both accuracy and participation values) to children. Again, the particulars of that process might take a number of forms, but the basic protection—ensuring children an opportunity to speak, and be listened to, before being paddled—need be neither too cumbersome for school functioning, nor too trivial to be of value to the child.

accusation and the potential consequences should affect the level of procedural protections afforded, but this child-specific variation should not simply slide up and down the adult procedural scale. Rather, the procedural scale for children should take account of child-specific differences along its entire length. What matters is that the student understand the school's position and have some opportunity to influence it.

This means that, even for the most serious liberty- or property-depriving actions of the school, the child is entitled to a process that looks very different from the adult process. As in the juvenile justice system, a highly formalized process dominated by lawyers and controlled by arcane evidentiary rulings will not secure a student's meaningful participation, even in secondary school.[39] And for those students facing disciplinary action at a particularly young age, the confusion and discomfort generated by standard adult-style procedures will be greater still.

Fidelity to due process principles also means that, for less serious deprivations of a child's liberty, whatever lesser process is afforded should be guided by the same participatory aim. Even the simplest notice and opportunity to be heard must be understood by the student, and when circumstances suggest that the student is confused about the school's actions or unaware of his opportunity to participate, the school cannot hide behind the fact that it has satisfied some *Goss*-inspired steps in its procedure manual.[40]

The obligation to secure children's meaningful participation derives from the due process guarantee of contemporary fairness. But the benefits of children's participation will extend to their exercise of due process rights as adults. Students' experience, as participants, will improve their participation skills and teach them that their participation is valued. Thus, a rights system that adapts

---

[39] Students' due process challenges to school disciplinary proceedings frequently focus on the omission of some formal procedural detail at the expense of this larger and more principled argument. See, for example, *Snyder ex Rel Snyder v Farnsworth*, 896 F Supp 96 (ND NY 1995); *Carey v Maine School Administration District #17*, 754 F Supp 906 (1990).

[40] For this reason, the school procedures at issue in *S.G. v Sayerville Board of Education*, 2003 US App LEXIS 12315 (3d Cir 2003), while technically in compliance with the letter of *Goss*, were constitutionally insufficient. In that case, a kindergartner, who had been absent the day the school's policy prohibiting all threatening talk related to guns was announced to students and parents, was suspended after he made a statement about shooting his friends during a game of cops and robbers on the playground. Relying on the specific requirements set out in *Goss*, the court improperly rejected his contention that his rights were violated because he did not understand what was said to him at the meeting, and because his parents were not present to support his participation.

to children's current level of development is likely to enhance their development as rights holders over time. These educational benefits might be conceived as a sort of bonus, distinct from what due process requires, but a positive effect of proper rights recognition. In other rights contexts, however, such as the Fourth Amendment context discussed below, the central childhood project of learning must be taken into account in the rights analysis if that analysis is to remain faithful to the constitutional principles at stake.[41]

B.   OTHER SCHOOL-BASED RIGHTS

The distortions introduced by the adults-minus approach vary with right, context, and case, but one theme from *Goss* and *Ingraham* runs throughout the school-based rights claims: the interests of schools are perceived simplistically as counterweights to the rights claims. This use of school interests as a blunt, rights-reducing instrument is problematic for at least two reasons: First, compulsory schooling is itself rights limiting. It therefore must be independently justified, and that justification bears on the appropriateness of any further rights constriction. Second, schools bear considerable responsibility in preparing children for adult citizenship. For this reason, their policies, however justified by a child's current developmental status, should also be assessed for their developmental effects. To explore these two issues, I consider the Court's treatment of students' First and Fourth Amendment claims. While both issues are implicated in both sets of cases, I focus on the rights-limiting effect of schools in the First Amendment context and their rights-informing effect in the Fourth Amendment context.

1. *Children's speech rights in school.* The Court's school speech cases follow the familiar adult-minus pattern: Starting with *Tinker*

---

[41] The Court has occasionally recognized the teaching value associated with affording children rights, but here, too, the analysis is superficial and adult-focused. In cases as early as *West Virginia v Barnette*, the Court argued that denying children rights would "strangle the free mind at its source and teach youth to discount important principles of our government as mere platitudes." 319 US 624, 637 (1943). While the Court is right to recognize the connection between children's treatment and their development as rights holders, it has failed to take the analysis beyond the simplest connection: The fact that children learn about rights by being given rights, the Court reasons, sometimes argues for treating adults and children the same. For a more sophisticated consideration of how adolescents' experience as rights holders might enhance their competence to exercise rights as adults, see Zimring, *The Changing Legal World of Adolescence* at 89–117 (cited in note 12).

v Des Moines School District[42] (decided two years after *Gault*), the Court has consistently declared that schoolchildren's speech is protected by the First Amendment. Noting the special demands of the school context, however, the Court has approved content-based censorship of both spoken[43] and printed speech[44] that goes far beyond what has been permitted for adults. More to the point, the Court's analysis has failed to take account of the special characteristics of compulsory schooling that might justify an expanded view of rights in this context. Put simply, the Court has put adult speech rights on one side of the balance and school needs on the other to justify reduced protection of children in schools. Instead, it should analyze how the school context, and especially the centrality of that context for children's speech, might alter the weight of the expressive claim before balancing that claim against the competing interest in censorship.

a) First Amendment principles. As in the due process context, an analysis of children's First Amendment rights should begin with the principles animating the right. Three principles have commonly been identified to justify the protection of speech under the First Amendment. First, free speech facilitates the search for truth, and allows ideas to be tested in Holmes's "marketplace of ideas." Second, free speech facilitates self-governance through the sharing of information and viewpoints among potential voters. Third, free speech facilitates self-fulfillment through autonomous expression.[45] While these three justifications do not dictate the same result in every case, they are closely intertwined. Together, they capture the central principles that have motivated the Court's analysis of adults' speech rights under the Constitution.[46]

---

[42] 393 US 503 (1969).

[43] *Bethel School Dist. v Fraser*, 478 US 675 (1986).

[44] *Hazelwood School Dist. v Kuhlmeier*, 484 US 260 (1988).

[45] See, for example, Geoffrey R. Stone, Louis M. Seidman, Cass R. Sunstein, and Mark V. Tushnet, *Constitutional Law* 998–1002 (Aspen, 4th ed 2001) (describing truth seeking, self-governance, and self-fulfillment as the three primary justifications for speech protections); John E. Nowak and Ronald D. Rotunda, *Constitutional Law* 1061 (West, 6th ed 2000) (listing identified justifications as including truth seeking, self-fulfillment, policing of government abuse, and providing a "safety valve" for the maintenance of public order).

[46] See Edward J. Bloustein, *The Origin, Validity and Interrelationships of the Political Values Served by Freedom of Expression*, 33 Rutgers L Rev 372 (1981) (noting that the "attainment of knowledge . . . consensual participation in government . . . and the dignity of self-expression" are "so interdependent that they really represent three aspects [of] a single value").

All three of these principles can be applied to children's speech. The connection between speech and the pursuit of truth is particularly powerful in its application to children. At no time in life are humans more actively devoted to the pursuit of truth than in the period of rapid development and education associated with childhood. Children devote a substantial portion of their day, and a substantial fraction of their attention, to the acquisition of knowledge and the development of beliefs. Speech among children and between children and adults plays an important role in shaping these emerging understandings and beliefs.[47] Developmentally primed for this influence, children, and particularly adolescents, are more open to the marketplace of ideas than most adults, whose views may be better articulated, but also more fixed.

The self-governance rationale for protecting speech might seem ill-fitted to children, who do not vote. But the justification is generally conceived more broadly, extending to speech that serves the ends of self-government indirectly, as well as to speech designed directly to affect the democratic process.[48] Compared to adult artistic speech, for example, political speech by adolescents is likely to have a more direct effect on voting. Moreover, children's speech experience may critically affect their future speech habits and expectations as democratic participants.

The self-fulfillment rationale raises interesting questions in its application to children. While our willingness to constrain children's autonomy in other contexts might suggest similar constraints on speech, the argument is at least as strong the other way. As noted earlier, the best justifications for qualifying children's autonomy rights are their lesser capacities and the fluidity of their identities. These differences matter the most where the stakes involved in their choices are particularly grave and long-

---

[47] See Ritch C. Savin-Williams and Thomas J. Berndt, *Friendship and Peer Relations*, in S. Shirley Feldman and Glen R. Elliot, eds, *At the Threshold: The Developing Adolescent* 277, 279 (Harvard, 1990) ("[B]y allowing oneself to become vulnerable around a coequal, adolescent friends share with one another their most personal thoughts and feelings, become sensitive to the needs and desires of others and in the process acquire a deep understanding of the other and the self"); Michael D. Berzonsky, *A Process Perspective on Identity and Stress Management*, in Adams, Gullotta, and Montemayor, *Adolescent Identity Formation* at 198 (cited in note 11) (finding that adolescents actively engaged in the process of sorting out their identities look to others for ideas about the alternatives to consider).

[48] Compare Alexander Meikeljohn, *The First Amendment Is an Absolute*, 1961 Supreme Court Review 245, 255 ("self-government can exist only insofar as the voters acquire the intelligence, integrity, sensitivity, and generous devotion to the general welfare that, in theory, casting a ballot is assumed to express").

lasting. Speech offers children a chance to pursue their self-ful-fillment in a manner that minimizes the risks associated with that pursuit and, in the process, facilitates the development of the very capacities and stability of identity on which full autonomy in adult-hood depends.[49]

    b) Adult First Amendment detail and its misapplication to children. The Court has drawn upon the principles of truth-seeking, self-governance, and self-fulfillment to develop a vast body of adult First Amendment detail. And, as in other constitutional contexts, the Court has attempted to apply that adult detail to children's rights claims, without regard for the quality of the fit. I will focus on one aspect of that detail—the public forum doctrine—to dem-onstrate how poorly it serves the underlying constitutional prin-ciples when applied to children.

    The public forum doctrine calibrates the degree of protection afforded to speech based on the purpose and nature of the forum in question. In those forums traditionally used for purposes of "assembly, communicating thoughts between citizens, and dis-cussing public questions," the state's authority to regulate speech is very limited.[50] But in forums reserved for some other purpose, regulation is permitted, so long as it is "reasonable."[51]

    The Court's willingness to permit greater speech restrictions in "non-public forums" rests, in part, on the assumption that indi-viduals have access to less restricted speech elsewhere.[52] Moreover, even in the nonpublic forum context, the Court considers whether other avenues of expression are open to the speaker, in assessing the reasonableness of a challenged regulation.[53] And in almost all

---

[49] For a consideration of how discussion among peers facilitates the development of self-reflection and independent thinking, see Emily Buss, *The Adolescent's Stake in the Allocation of Education Control Between Parent and State*, 67 U Chi L Rev 1233, 1270–75 (2000).

[50] *Hague v CIO*, 307 US 496 (1939).

[51] See, e.g., *International Society for Krishna Consciousness v Lee*, 505 US 672 (1992).

[52] If these traditional public forums cease to provide this opportunity, the Court's con-tinued insistence on giving them special First Amendment protection (and other govern-ment spaces lesser protection) becomes problematic. See *International Society for Krishna Consciousness v Lee*, 505 US 672, 698 ("In a country where most citizens travel by auto-mobile, and parks all too often become locales for crime rather than social intercourse, our failure to recognize the possibility that new types of government property may be appropriate forums for speech will lead to a serious curtailment of our expressive activity") (Kennedy, concurring in the judgment).

[53] See id at 685 (reasonableness of Port Authority's prohibition of solicitation within the airports was established, in part, by its allowance of solicitation on airport sidewalks, frequented by all but 3 percent of the airport users); *Jones v North Carolina Prisoners' Labor*

adult contexts where considerable regulation of adult speech is permitted, such as government workplaces, the military, and prisons, some voluntary action, avoided by most adults, was necessary to subject them to these regulations.[54] Thus, the public forum doctrine ensures the availability of speakers and listeners in the abundance required to make the marketplace (and, relatedly, informed self-governance) work for adults.[55] But the assumption about the availability of alternative forums for speech does not hold for children. In applying the public forum construct to schoolchildren, the Court has failed to account for the pervasive restrictions on children's access to traditional public spaces and other venues of public discourse imposed by the state.

In *Hazelwood School District v Kuhlmeier*,[56] the Court concluded that a high school principal's decision to pull two pages out of a school newspaper because he objected to their content did not violate journalism students' First Amendment rights. Rejecting the students' claim that the school newspaper was a public forum, the Court determined that the principal's actions satisfied the "reasonableness" standard applicable to nonpublic forums. But in neither step of its analysis did the Court consider the students' relevant speech alternatives. In adult-minus fashion, the Court considered the students' speech rights against a backdrop of adult speech opportunities, rather than taking account of the significant difference in speech opportunities imposed in large part by schools themselves.

Compulsory education represents an enormous limitation on the liberty of students, a limitation justified by the state's compelling interest in producing a participating, self-sufficient citi-

---

Union, Inc., 433 US 119, 131 (finding that the regulation of bulk mail distribution in prison was not unreasonable, in part because "other avenues of outside information flow by the [speaker] remain available.").

[54] An important exception to this generalization is the military draft. Although the draft imposes speech restrictions on adults who have in no sense volunteered, it shares with other adult contexts a limited reach. Only a small fraction of all adults are subject to the draft at any time, whereas all children are required to attend school. All this is not to suggest that the limitation of the speech rights of drafted adults is not significant (indeed, these adults will likely have a heightened interest in influencing the government's actions), but only to recognize that the speech restriction imposed by schools covers a far greater proportion of potential child speech.

[55] Cass Sunstein, *republic.com* (Princeton, 2001) at 30–32 (listing, among the achievements of the public forum doctrine, its insurance that "speakers can have access to a wide array of people. . . . and people generally will be exposed to a wide variety of people and views").

[56] 484 US 260 (1988).

zenry in adulthood.[57] However justified this restriction on freedom, it clearly imposes considerable constraints on children's speech opportunities. School takes the bulk of the child's day and controls the availability of her audience of peers. In this way, schools produce "captive speakers" as well as the more obvious "captive audience," and even the audience's captivity has a speech-denying as well as a speech-compelling effect. If children are to have a meaningful opportunity for the sort of abundant speech needed to achieve the truth-seeking and self-governance values, they need to have that opportunity in school.[58]

In taking account of the alternative avenues of speech available to adults challenging speech restrictions, the Court recognizes that these First Amendment aims cannot be achieved unless opportunities to exchange ideas exist in fact, and not just in theory. But by imposing the adult set of forum-based restrictions on school speech, the Court makes these First Amendment aims nearly impossible to achieve for children. This loss is of particular concern because of children's special qualification to achieve some of these aims through their speech.

c) Fidelity to First Amendment principles in schools. Children's lack of effective speech alternatives justifies a school-based enhancement of children's speech rights. The centrality of the school for children might qualify the school as a child-only public forum (thereby entitling student speech to heightened protection), or it might at least cast doubt on the reasonableness of speech regulations. But trying to tinker with the detail of the adult doctrine to make it fit with children's experience may be more trouble than it's worth. What is important is ensuring that the underlying principles of the First Amendment are preserved for children. If children and society are to achieve the benefits that flow from free speech, then child speakers should have opportunities to speak, and child listeners to hear, in a context that serves those ends.

This expansive view of children's speech rights in school would

---

[57] See, e.g., *Wisconsin v Yoder*, 406 US 205 (recognizing state's interest in ensuring that all children get the education necessary "to prepare citizens to participate effectively and intelligently in our open political system . . . and [to] prepare individuals to be self-reliant and self-sufficient participants in society").

[58] Some children's opportunity to engage in the robust exchange of ideas will be further limited by parental control, who can prevent them from attending public schools, as well as other potential venues for this exchange. This fact only enhances the value of market access for those whose parents will tolerate it.

not preclude all regulation of speech in that context. Rather, it calls for a more careful weighing—a weighing that accounts for the special value of school speech for children as well as any special interests in regulation the school setting creates. Some speech may so disrupt basic school functioning that its regulation would be justified, despite the high stakes for children's speech.[59] But a general interest in maintaining curricular control, such as that asserted in *Hazelwood*, would not be sufficient. Indeed, it is precisely this sort of curricular control that threatens to preempt the field for children's speech. Unless children's speech is protected within the curriculum, the state can exercise near-absolute control over children's access to the marketplace of ideas.

What it means to protect student speech within the curriculum is somewhat puzzling, for the general design of the curriculum (whether, for example, a journalism course is offered at all) is clearly in the hands of the state. Can we really call exercising control over the content of a school newspaper "censorship" when the school was not under any obligation to produce a newspaper at all? This tension between what is being given and what is being taken by the state can be found in many speech contexts (the state chooses whether to create and maintain a public park) and has been most pointedly pressed in the government-funding context. But the tension is starkest for children, because their baseline "free" state has been so thoroughly eclipsed by the state's assignment of their control to schools and parents. The special custodial control exercised over children might argue against affording them any rights at all. But if such rights are recognized, they will inevitably be exercised within contexts controlled by others. This suggests that the usual categories of state deprivation and state subsidization are particularly unhelpful as applied to children. If the First Amendment protects free speech in school, it necessarily limits the domain of curricular control.

To justify censorship of children's speech in school, the state should have to point to some interest that is more specific and compelling than its general interest in controlling how and what children learn. One such interest, already mentioned, is an interest

---

[59] This approach is consistent with the standard set out in *Tinker v Des Moines School Dist.*, 393 US 503, 509 (holding that students' school speech could not be regulated where it did not "'materially and substantially interfere with the requirement of appropriate discipline in the operation of the school,'") (quoting *Burnside v Byars*, 363 F2d 744, 749 (5th Cir 1966)).

in avoiding serious disruption of the learning environment. Such an exception could include not only the obvious forms of disruption—the student who shouts things out in the middle of class—but also more controversial grounds for censorship, such as a student's use of hate speech, if that speech could be shown seriously to disrupt the learning process. First Amendment claimants could require a school system to prove the connection between speech and disruption, though courts should afford the school systems some deference in the assessment of that proof. That deference cannot, however, inspire the Court to drift from serious disruption to curricular interference or student discomfort, if it is to preserve any meaningful First Amendment right for students.

Another possible justification for censorship might be the protection of other children, for school speech involves young listeners and readers, as well as young speakers. In the adult realm, the Court has shown little sympathy for claims that censorship is required to protect an unwilling audience, reasoning that adults are free to "avert their eyes," if not to walk away. Children, in contrast, may lack these abilities, both because their liberty is so restricted in the school setting and because they lack the socio-cognitive maturity to make wise self-protective choices. The danger in recognizing this exception is that it could easily swallow the rule—whatever the school deems offensive could readily be recast as offensive to students. Thus, the exception would need to be further qualified to protect students from specific harms, such as an invasion of privacy, the creation of fear, or harassment. While these more specific exceptions all have analogs in the adult context, the school would be justified in interpreting each of these exceptions somewhat more broadly in recognition of child listeners' special vulnerabilities and less well developed coping skills. Again, First Amendment litigation could put this defense to its proof, requiring a school system to prove more than that the speech gave offense.

The fault of the Court's analysis, then, is not its recognition that some school-based concerns weigh against children's interest in free speech, but rather its assumption that the school context, in all respects, weighs against children's speech interests. In failing to recognize the relative dearth of speech options available to children, the Court has systematically undervalued children's school-based speech.

2. *Children's privacy rights in school.* We see this same simplistic treatment of schools as a counterweight to rights in the Fourth Amendment context, where students have challenged schools' authority to search their property and their persons. The Court has considered such Fourth Amendment challenges in three cases. In *New Jersey v T.L.O.,*[60] the Court allowed the search of a student's purse without probable cause.[61] In *Vernonia v Acton*[62] and *Board of Education v Earls,*[63] the Court allowed suspicionless urinalysis drug testing of athletes and all extracurricular participants, respectively. In all three decisions, the Court employed the adult-minus approach. It declared that the Fourth Amendment protected schoolchildren from unreasonable searches, applied the adult conventions in assessing children's privacy interests, and concluded that the schools' interest in educational and disciplinary control outweighed those interests.[64] As in the First Amendment context, the Court accounted for the school setting only on the rights-restricting side of the ledger. Absent once again was any consideration of how the school setting might enhance the privacy interests at stake.

In addressing the First Amendment, I argued that the restrictions imposed on child speakers by compulsory schooling called for enhanced speech protection within that setting. In the Fourth Amendment context, I will consider how a school's effect on children's developing understanding of themselves and their relationship to state authority should alter the Court's analysis. In particular, I conclude that the effects of a school's search policy on children's identity development ought to be taken into account in analyzing their privacy interests.

a) Fourth Amendment principles. The Fourth Amendment's prohibition of "unreasonable" searches has been interpreted to require a balancing of the extent of the privacy invasion against the importance of the search to the state. The Fourth Amendment recognizes the value of the individual's control over his body, information, and property, and limits the state's ability to intrude on these interests to serve its own ends.

---

[60] 469 US 325 (1985).

[61] Id.

[62] 515 US 646 (1995).

[63] 536 US 822 (2002).

[64] See, for example, *Vernonia* at 656–57, 665.

Children, too, have an interest in maintaining the privacy of their person and property which can come into conflict with the state's interest in discovering information. But these interests, and their relationship to state interests, are not identical to those of adults. This is particularly true in the school setting, where the teaching function entangles state interests with those of the children. A school search shapes children's understanding of their privacy interests, as well as their understanding of when and why those interests may be justifiably compromised. Before examining how the developmental influence of the search should affect the "reasonableness" determination, I will demonstrate how the Court's adult-minus approach has prevented it from considering this influence altogether.

b) Adult Fourth Amendment detail and its misapplication to children. In applying the Fourth Amendment to adults, the Court has developed an elaborate construct of rules and exceptions to determine, first, what constitutes a search and, second, when a search is reasonable. Here again, I will focus on only one detail of that construct and how it has been applied to children. In assessing the constitutionality of the state's action, the Court asks, first, whether it impinges upon legitimate expectations of privacy and, second, the extent of the intrusion it imposes on these expectations.

This analysis is poorly designed to capture the privacy interests of children in school. In particular, it fails to consider the significance of children's ongoing identity development to their experience and perception of privacy. An expectations standard overlooks the fact that children's expectations, particularly expectations about themselves and how they relate to others, are in a process of active development. A test based on formed expectations offers little protection to children against the interests of the state.

In the school drug testing cases, *Vernonia* and *Earls*, the poor fit of the expectations test is particularly apparent. In both cases, the Court asked whether the tested students had a legitimate expectation of privacy with regard to urine testing, and concluded that their expectations were minimal because schools have considerable authority to exercise control over their students.[65] This

---

[65] In *Vernonia*, the Court suggested the special circumstances of athletic participation further diminished athletes' expectations of privacy. In addition to the fact that the same objection can be made to this more detailed expectation assessment, note that the Court

analysis is circular. Students will expect the school to exercise the degree of control it has been permitted to exercise.

Tying rights to expectations is circular for adults as well as for children, because whatever rights are afforded will, in turn, shape those expectations in the future. But the problem is considerably greater for schoolchildren, both because their expectations are in an active state of flux, and because schools play a major role in shaping those expectations. If rights in schools are grounded on student expectations, then the extent of those rights can be controlled by the very state actors against whom the rights pertain. An expectations-based assessment of privacy interests gives the Court very little to weigh against the state interest in conducting a search.

The Court further undervalued the privacy interests of children in *Vernonia* and *Earls* when it considered the degree of intrusion imposed by drug testing. In this second step of the adult-based privacy analysis, the Court concluded that requiring students to urinate into a cup in a stall while a monitor stands outside listening for "the normal sounds of urination," and to then hand the specimen over to the monitor, constitutes a "negligible" intrusion. Negligible, perhaps, for adults, but hardly for children, for whom the listening and looking by an unfamiliar adult can readily translate a commonplace act into an excruciatingly embarrassing one.

In suggesting that urine collection constitutes a greater intrusion for children than for adults, I am not arguing that childhood embarrassment should determine which searches are lawful. The point is not to champion a child-authentic application of the adult test, but rather to ask whether the adult test makes any sense in light of the adaptations childhood demands. The Court's decision in *Earls* upholding drug testing despite the lack of evidence of any serious drug problem, particularly among those being tested, suggests that, absent adaptation, the Fourth Amendment is unlikely to afford children any significant protection in school.

c) Fidelity to Fourth Amendment principles in schools. If the Fourth Amendment is to have any meaning for children in schools, the Court must take account of children's privacy interests in very different terms. Because their understanding of themselves and of their relationship with society and the state is still in an active

---

declared that these special circumstances were not determinative when it turned its attention to *Earls*.

process of development, children do not yet possess meaningful "expectations" that can drive the rights analysis. A developmentally focused analysis of the Fourth Amendment would ask not whether a search is expected to give offense to a student's privacy sensibilities, but, rather, what message the search conveys about the nature and extent of a student's privacy interests against the state. While this question does not lend itself to easy answers, it more coherently captures the stakes of school searches for children than a test that assumes children's privacy sensibilities are (or ought to be) relatively fixed.

This approach calls on courts to make normative judgments. But, so, too, does the adult "legitimate expectations" inquiry.[66] Asking what expectations of privacy an individual *should* have is common to both tests. What distinguishes the child's test is the focus on how those expectations are shaped. Because that process should be designed to nurture the "legitimate expectations" recognized in adulthood, courts will necessarily look to the adult cases in defining the expectation-creating rights of children. Building children's rights upon adult detail in this way is appropriate, for a primary aim of the child-specific adaptation is to prepare children for their exercise of rights as adults.

As a general matter, focusing on the expectations created by the school's treatment of children might incline courts toward a more privacy protective approach, for children are unlikely to perceive the state's obligation to respect individual privacy unless the protection is strong enough to have evident effect.[67] Moreover, this focus should lead courts to be most wary of search methods deemed particularly problematic for adults, lest the childhood search experience undermine future adult expectations. On this

---

[66] The Court has suggested that the "legitimation of expectations of privacy by law must have a source outside of the Fourth Amendment [including] understandings that are recognized and permitted by society." *Rakas v Illinois*, 439 US 128, 144 n 12 (1978). But this judicial assessment of societal understandings has repeatedly, if never expressly, led courts to make their own judgments about the validity of the privacy expectations articulated in the cases before them. Christopher Slobogin and Joseph Schumacher's counterfactual proposal to base these assessments on empirical information helps to make the point. See Slobogin and Schumacher, *Reasonable Expectations of Privacy and Autonomy in Fourth Amendment Cases: An Empirical Look at "Understandings Recognized and Permitted by Society,"* 42 Duke L J 727 (1993).

[67] Schools could enhance the teaching value further by taking affirmative steps to make their students aware of privacy-invading actions school officials are prevented from taking by the Fourth Amendment, but such affirmative steps would not be constitutionally required.

dimension, urine testing should prompt greater concern than purse searches, and strip searches, tolerated on several occasions under the adult-minus approach, should prompt the greatest concern of all.[68]

A focus on the expectation-creating effects of school searches should also lead the Court to take into account students' likely awareness and understanding of the school's justifications for the search. The more a child understands the purpose and importance of the search, the less likely she is to perceive it as devaluing her privacy interests. To some extent, this consideration, too, calls for an especially strong justification for a search. But it also suggests that the process leading up to a search should bear on the search's constitutionality. On this ground, the Court might have distinguished *Vernonia* from *Earls*, despite the similarity of the intrusions. Because the drug problem and the school district's earlier unsuccessful attempts to solve it were more apparent in *Vernonia*, students likely had a better sense than in *Earls* of the weight of the interests justifying the search.[69]

How a search is conducted also takes on special significance where the focus is on the child's learning process. Most obviously, the method and context of a search should convey respect for the privacy interests of students. Less obviously, the choice of which children to search has important implications for the learning process. Adult-style, suspicion-based searches may disserve children's emerging understanding of themselves and their relationship with the state. In the circumstances of *Vernonia* and *Earls*, narrowing the search to students who raised individualized suspicion, as the dissent in *Vernonia* advocated, might have done more developmental harm than good.[70]

---

[68] See, for example, *Phaneuf v Cipriano*, 330 F Supp 2d 74 (D Conn 2004) (holding that a strip search of a student conducted in an unsuccessful search for marijuana did not violate the student's Fourth Amendment rights); *Williams v Ellington*, 936 F2d 881 (6th Cir 1991) (concluding, in the context of its qualified immunity analysis, that a strip search of a student in an unsuccessful search for drugs was reasonable).

[69] In the Vernonia School District, the drug problem was severe, and the attention to the problem considerable. Other efforts were made to address the problem, and their failure demonstrated. Before implementing the drug testing policy, the district convened a "parent input night," at which the parents present gave their unanimous approval. *Vernonia*, 515 US 646, 648–50. In the Pottawatomie County School District, in contrast, while there was some evidence of drug use, there was no evidence of a severe or widely publicized drug use problem. Moreover, the record in *Earls* does not suggest that the district engaged in a process of problem solving in the public eye.

[70] The Court in *Vernonia* took note of the likely practical problems associated with

Individualized suspicion requirements reduce the number of individuals searched, but intensify the intrusion for those searched.
This intensification is likely to be particularly severe for children,
whose treatment by school officials will rarely be kept private,
despite the best of intentions, and for whom the assignment of
suspicion is likely to have a substantial stigmatizing effect.[71] Unlike
adults, children may not have either the power or the understanding to control their behavior to avoid being singled out. Thus,
for children, whatever privacy gains come from an individualized
suspicion standard may be swamped by the privacy losses associated with this relatively public display of individual accusation.

In all the school-based cases, whether the right in question is
due process, speech, or privacy, the Court has failed to integrate
the special nature of the school context into its rights analysis.
Instead, school needs are crudely relied upon as a counterweight
to the rights claim. Children get adult-minus rights, because
schools have a strong interest in keeping rights in check. If children
are to be afforded rights in school, those rights must be adapted
to reflect the child's experience, including the aspects of experience
that argue for enhanced or altered rights. To the extent the school
setting justifies a diminution of rights, that diminution, too, should
be tailored to reflect the educational impact on children's understanding of their present and future rights.

C. CHILDREN'S RIGHTS WITHIN THE PARENT-CONTROLLED FAMILY

Like schools, parents are state-supported entities with authority
to exercise control over children for their own good. While a case
can be made for granting parents rights in lieu of granting rights
to their children,[72] a decision to grant children independent rights

---

conducting suspicion-based searches, but it portrayed these problems as justifications for
the greater privacy intrusion associated with suspicionless searches, rather than as problems
implicating privacy interests of their own that suspicionless searches might mitigate. *Vernonia*, 515 US at 663–64.

[71] Martin Belsky makes a version of this argument in *Random v. Suspicion-Based Drug
Testing in the Public Schools—A Surprising Civil Liberties Dilemma*, 27 Okla City L Rev 1
(2002), though his focus is on the harm associated with stigma, rather than the developmental effects of being stigmatized.

[72] In a nutshell, the argument is that, to the extent children require some adult to assert
rights on their behalf, we should not expect other third parties to do better than parents
at identifying children's interests. As this argument suggests, it is strongest in cases where
the child is not in a position to identify his interests on his own, whether because of his
age or because of the nature of the right in question. I have argued, elsewhere, that
developmental considerations counsel against affording children autonomy rights before

calls into question how to harmonize these rights with those of their parents. The Court, however, has demonstrated the same lack of sophistication in analyzing children's rights in this context as it has in the school context. This failure is illustrated by *Parham v J.R.*[73] and *DeShaney v Winnebago County Social Services*,[74] though it takes a different form in each.

1. *Procedural due process rights within the parent-controlled family.* In *Parham*, the Court considered what process was due before a child could be institutionalized by his parents for psychiatric care against his own wishes. As in the school context, the Court simplistically relied on that relationship to justify a diminution of children's due process rights. And here, again, the Court buried the significance of its rights conclusion in the labyrinth of ill-fitting adult detail. Had the Court been more faithful to principle, it would have been forced to confront the real trade-offs at stake in the case. If the Court's decision in *Parham* is justified, it is only because children have other, developmentally based interests that may outweigh their interest in the values the Due Process Clause protects.

a) (More) adult civil process and its misapplication to children. Between *Goss* and *Parham*, the Court decided *Mathews v Eldridge*,[75] an adult due process case that converted the developing doctrine into a three-part test. In determining what process is due in civil cases, the Court considered three factors: the nature of the private interest at stake, the relative accuracy of the challenged and proposed procedures, and the state's interests implicated by the procedural choice.[76] Of note, for adults as well as children, is *Mathews*'s exclusive focus on the process value of accuracy and its failure to consider distinct participatory values.[77] Even taken on its own terms, however, the test translates awkwardly to the parent-

---

they are in a position to make the relevant choices on their own. See Buss, *Allocating Developmental Control Among Parent, Child and the State*, 2004 U Chi Legal Forum 27, 36–40.

[73] 442 US 584 (1979).

[74] 489 US 189 (1989).

[75] 424 US 319 (1976).

[76] Id at 335.

[77] A number of scholars have criticized *Mathews*'s exclusive focus on accuracy in addressing adults' due process rights. See, for example, Martin Redish, *Electronic Discovery and the Litigation Matrix*, 51 Duke L J 561 (2001) (arguing that the fundamental fairness protected by the Due Process Clause protects dignity interests as well as the interest in accuracy identified in *Mathews*).

child context. It assumes a single individual with a single interest, rather than an individual in a relationship, whose interest in the relationship may pull against his interests as an individual. In applying the *Mathews* test to the more complex web of interests pressed in *Parham*, the Court failed to make the adjustments necessary to maintain the test's integrity.

In *Parham*, two subclasses of children, one in the custody of their parents, the other in the custody of the state (in foster care), challenged laws allowing the involuntary institutionalization of children for psychiatric treatment with custodial consent. In considering the children's due process challenge, the Court announced that "it is not disputed that a child, in common with adults, has a substantial liberty interest in not being confined unnecessarily for medical treatment."[78] But this acknowledgment was dramatically undercut by the following qualification:

> In applying [the *Mathews*] criteria, we must consider first the child's interest in not being committed. Normally, however, since this interest is inextricably linked with the parents' interest in and obligation for the welfare and health of the child, the private interest at stake is a combination of the child's and parents' concerns.[79]

This, to be clear, in the context of a case asking what process was required to determine whether, in fact, the child and parents' interests were aligned. In conventional adult-minus style, a declaration of children's rights was matched with an unreflective excuse for curtailing them.

In this aspect of its analysis, the Court might be criticized for failing to apply the adult test correctly, rather than for applying the adult test to the detriment of children's distinct interests. Under *Mathews*, the relevant interest is the liberty or property interest of the rights holder. In *Parham*, that interest is the child's interest in avoiding wrongful (meaning medically unjustified) institutionalization, an interest that is not diminished by any conflicting interest of the parent. If the parent-child relationship can be factored into the *Mathews* standard, it must be through the other two parts of the test, addressing the procedural costs and the reliability

---

[78] 442 US at 600.

[79] Id (footnote omitted).

of competing procedures. But by simply adding the parents' interests to the same side of the scales as the child's liberty interest,
the Court confused the entire *Mathews* inquiry: Why worry about
accuracy, or the procedural costs involved in resolving a dispute,
when the two sides are in fact one?

A more careful consideration of these other *Mathews* factors
calls into question the test's ability to account for the parent-child
relationship, even when properly applied. On the question of reliability, the Court suggests that a parent's devotion to her child's
interests minimizes the risk of erroneous institutionalization. But
the whole issue in these cases is whether attention to the child's
interests has broken down in the face of the severely stressful
circumstances that drive a parent to seek her child's removal from
the home. Thus, application of the accuracy prong to the parental
consent mechanism is ultimately elusive, for the real challenge is
to distinguish among parents whose motives diverge.[80]

The third *Mathews* factor concerns the costs to the state of
providing additional procedural protections. Under this factor, the
Court identifies the administrative burdens associated with formal
hearings and the diversion of state psychiatric staff from treatment
to court appearances.[81] While this test can be interpreted to encompass societal costs as well as the immediate costs of the procedures, it does not include costs to the rights holder, whose interests are assumed to weigh in favor of more process.[82] This
assumption, however, does not hold up for children, who may
have conflicting interests—a liberty interest weighing in favor of
enhanced procedures, and a dependency interest weighing against
them. Children generally have an interest in the preservation of
the parent-child relationship, even when parents make bad choices
on their behalf.

---

[80] Nor does it help, as the Court suggests, that the law requires a reviewing physician
to endorse the parents' wishes. 442 US at 606–09. Such physician screening would clearly
not survive a due process challenge if applied to involuntarily committed adults, and there
is nothing to suggest that the process would be any more accurate as applied to children.
See *Addington v Texas*, 441 US 418, 427 (1979) (holding that the Due Process Clause
requires that an adult's need for hospitalization be proved at a civil commitment hearing
by clear and convincing proof).

[81] 442 US at 604–06.

[82] The Court's subsequent summary of its *Parham* decision reinforces this limitation in
its analysis. See *Youngberg v Romeo*, 457 US 307, 321 (1982) ("In determining [in *Parham*]
that procedural due process did not mandate an adversarial hearing, we weighed the liberty
interest of the individual against the legitimate interests of the State, including the fiscal
and administrative burdens additional procedures would entail.").

Clearly, the Court intended to take account of this dependency interest in its analysis. But by cramming its analysis into the *Mathews* test, the Court obscured the real issue pressed by the case. A straightforward application of *Mathews* reveals that the constitutional stakes for children are high and that the law in question does little to assure that children's liberty will be infringed only when medically necessary. If we conclude that children can be deprived of substantial liberty through an error-prone process that affords relatively modest benefits to the state, it must be because we think children gain something of considerable value from this scheme.

Thus, the inadequacy of the adult detail in this setting is not its inability to isolate the child's process interest, but its failure to account for a factor, unique to childhood, that weighs against that interest. Sensitive to this factor, but unwilling to depart from adult detail in its analysis, the Court tried to force the child's interest in the parent-child relationship into the test, where it does not belong. The effect of this contortion was to minimize the constitutional stakes of its decision for the child.

b) Fidelity to procedural due process principles in the parent-controlled family. Had the Court distinguished more carefully between the due process principles and the countervailing values at issue in the case, it would have recognized how poorly the *Parham* process protects a child's substantial liberty interest in avoiding confinement to a mental institution and being improperly identified as seriously mentally ill.[83] A more principled analysis would not necessarily have led the Court to reject the commitment process, but it would have required it to identify and weigh the competing interests with greater clarity and care.

The only interest identified in the litigation weighty enough to justify denial of important process rights for children is their own countervailing interest in the parent-child relationship. Any judicial or quasi-judicial hearing designed to scrutinize the decisions parents make on behalf of their children, particularly when they are struggling as parents, will likely disrupt the relationship and undermine parental authority in a manner that harms the parent-child relationship. While the redesign of state decision-making

---

[83] In his opinion, Justice Brennan points to studies suggesting that a majority of children institutionalized for mental health treatment do not, in fact, require hospitalization. 442 US at 629 (Brennan concurring in part and dissenting in part).

processes I advocated earlier to improve children's comprehension and involvement might also minimize the harms imposed on the parent-child relationship, the Court might still reasonably conclude that any extrafamilial decision making on this issue would be harmful.

Requiring the Court to take greater care in distinguishing the child's constitutional interests from countervailing child-specific interests would improve the analysis in several respects. First, and most obviously, it would ensure that the Court considers whether those countervailing interests are weighty enough to justify curtailing a child's constitutional rights. Second, it would prevent any particular decision in which the Court rules against the rights claim from artificially deflating the value of the constitutional interest in subsequent cases. Finally, it would protect the adult doctrine from the risk of corruption associated with the Court's attempt to justify child-specific ends within a doctrine not designed to measure those ends.

The practical implications of this altered analysis become apparent when we consider the second subclass of plaintiffs, children in foster care, whose due process challenge was also rejected by the Court. If the Court had done a better job of distinguishing its analysis of the child's liberty interest from the risks to the parent-child relationship, it likely would have reached a different outcome for the children in foster care. For these children, the liberty interest is the same, but the accuracy assurances are weaker still (a more desperate, less emotionally committed custodian with a well-established financial arrangement with the treatment provider) and the burdens on parental functioning are nonexistent. Only by downplaying the accuracy issue and muddling the interest analysis could the Court conclude that the process sought had roughly equal constitutional value for the two classes of children.

2. Substantive due process rights within the parent-controlled family. The Court has interpreted the Due Process Clause to afford substantive rights to adults in a number of contexts, in some of which it has addressed the rights' application to children as well. I consider the Court's analysis of children's abortion rights in the next section. In this section, I consider children's right to personal security, the right asserted in *DeShaney v Winnebago County*.[84] In

---

[84] 489 US 189 (1989).

DeShaney, the Court again engaged in adult-minus reasoning to curtail the rights of children. In failing to recognize the substantial restrictions imposed on children's liberty by the state, the Court severed its analysis of children's right to personal security from the principles animating that body of constitutional law.

a) Substantive due process principles. The overarching value motivating the Court's substantive due process analysis is individual liberty. The Court has repeatedly recognized that the Constitution protects the individual's ability to control important aspects of her life, free from government interference. In most substantive due process contexts, determining what forms of liberty should receive how much protection calls for the articulation of additional constitutional values, many of which are contested. But in *DeShaney*, the liberty interest at stake was the uncontested and uncomplicated interest in personal security.[85]

b) Adult substantive due process detail and its misapplication to children. In most adult contexts, the liberty principle is served by affording individuals so-called "negative" rights. Substantive due process rights prevent the state from interfering with individual choice-making, rather than guaranteeing any state provided benefits. Despite the strength of the liberty principle, the Court has recognized certain adult contexts, such as incarceration and involuntary commitment, in which the state can impose severe restrictions on an individual's liberty. Even in these settings, however, the Constitution constrains the nature and extent of those restrictions, preserving some degree of freedom for the confined individual and minimizing the harm imposed by the state's constraints. Because liberty rights in these contexts entitle individuals to certain treatment at the hands of the state, they are sometimes described as "positive" rights, though, again, the state's affirmative obligation derives from its initial compromise of an individual's "negative" rights.

In *Youngberg v Romeo*,[86] the Court considered the substantive due process claim of a retarded adult, Nicholas Romeo, who had been repeatedly injured by fellow residents in his facility. There

---

[85] See *Youngberg v Romeo*, 457 US 307, 315–16 (1982) (noting the Court's recognition of the right to personal security as a "'historic liberty interest' protected substantively by the Due Process Clause").

[86] Id. Romeo also complained that the facility violated his substantive due process rights when it subjected him to bodily restraint and when it failed to provide him with an appropriate training program. Id at 316.

was no claim that the state caused the violence, but the Court nevertheless determined that the state could be held liable under the Due Process Clause for failing to prevent the violence. Building on earlier decisions finding that the state has an obligation to protect and care for prisoners, the Court concluded that the state's obligation to those confined because of mental disorders is at least as great.[87] Because an individual's interest in personal security survives involuntary commitment, the Court reasoned, the state could restrict Romeo's freedom only if it assured a certain level of personal safety. Thus, fidelity to the liberty principle demanded that the state take some affirmative precautions to minimize the harm caused by the commitment, even if the commitment itself was justified.

In *DeShaney*, the Court lost sight of the connection between liberties diminished and obligations owed. In that case, a child sued the state for failure to protect him from his violent father, whose repeated attacks left him severely retarded. The Court denied the claim, noting that the Constitution rarely affords individuals affirmative protection from harm. The Court acknowledged the exceptions, but denied their applicability to DeShaney, because he was neither in jail, nor in a mental health facility. By focusing on the adult-derived detail of prisons and mental institutions, the Court ensured that DeShaney's circumstances could be distinguished. Had the Court remained faithful to the principle articulated in *Youngberg*, it would have addressed the liberty infringement imposed on children by the state.

The very language the Court used to distinguish *Youngberg* belies the distinction. The Due Process Clause imposes affirmative obligations, the Court explained, only when the state

> by the affirmative exercise of its power so restricts an individual's liberty that it renders him unable to care for himself. . . . In the substantive due process analysis, it is the State's affirmative act of restraining the individual's freedom to act on his own behalf—through incarceration, institutionalization, or other similar restraint on personal liberty—which is the "deprivation of liberty" triggering the protections of the Due Process Clause.[88]

---

[87] Id at 321–22 ("Persons who have been involuntarily committed are entitled to more considerate treatment and conditions of confinement than criminals whose conditions of confinement are designed to punish.").

[88] 489 US at 200.

Thus, the relevant question is whether the state had restricted DeShaney's liberty in a manner that impaired his ability to ensure his own security.

In many respects, a child's "confinement" to his parents parallels a retarded adult's confinement to an institution. Children are no more free than institutionalized adults to leave, either on their own or with the assistance of others. Standing rules and substantive laws prevent concerned individuals from intervening on children's behalf, and in DeShaney's case, the state-entered custody decree prevented even his mother from stepping in. Moreover, the state prohibits children from working, signing contracts, or even registering themselves for school, thereby preventing even the most able-bodied (and minded) among them from "acting [freely] on their own behalf." That a child's impairment also has a basis in competence does not distinguish children from retarded adults. In both cases, the need for assistance in no way undermines the state's obligation to ensure that the custodian to whom it assigns authority is at least minimally safe.

   c) *Fidelity to substantive due process principles in the parent-controlled family.* The Court in *DeShaney* expressly reserved the question whether children in foster care have a due process right to safety, noting that some lower courts had determined, based on *Youngberg*, that they were entitled to this protection.[89] These cases help draw the conceptual connection between institutions for the retarded and private family homes like Joshua DeShaney's. In between are state-paid and -supervised foster families, charged with the care of children in a family-like setting, where the private families fail. While the Court noted the parallels between foster families and institutions, it overlooked the parallels between foster families and "private" families. Both are authorized to care for children by state law, with the expectation that they will meet certain obligations to the child.

To say that the state has some affirmative obligation to protect a child from harm in a private home is not to say how the state must meet that obligation. In *Youngberg*, the Court limited the state's

---

[89] 489 US at n 9. Since *DeShaney* was decided, several other Circuits have concluded that the Due Process Clause entitles children in foster care to some level of safety. See, for example, *Nicini v Morra*, 212 F3d 798 (3rd Cir 2000); *Lintz v Skipski*, 25 F3d 304 (6th Cir 1994); *Norfleet v Arkansas Dep't of Human Servs.*, 989 F2d 289 (8th Cir 1993); *Yvonne L. v New Mexico Dep't of Human Servs.*, 959 F2d 883 (10th Cir 1992); *K.H. v Morgan*, 914 F2d 846 (7th Cir 1990).

liability to the most egregious failings. By tying the obligation to professional standards and directing strong deference to professional judgment, the Court limited the state's constitutional liability considerably.[90] Applying similar reasoning in the foster care context, lower courts have suggested that the scope of liability might be further reduced because the agency relationship between the state and the foster parent is weaker than that between the state and institutional personnel and the opportunities for state monitoring are more attenuated.[91] Following this line of analysis to children in private homes where the state's involvement with the family is even weaker would suggest that only in the most extreme and obvious cases of maltreatment would the state be held responsible for failing to prevent the harm caused by its delegated custodian.

DeShaney might be such an extreme and obvious case, but that is a separate question. Maintaining fidelity to the liberty principle identified in *Youngberg* does not dictate the outcome, but it does require the Court to recognize that the state bears some affirmative responsibility for ensuring that some minimal level of care is provided to all children confined by the state to parental control. In failing to acknowledge the distinct burdens on liberty imposed by the legal status of childhood, the Court denies children the constitutional protections it has afforded to similarly encumbered adults.

III. STEPS IN THE RIGHT DIRECTION

On occasion, the Court has done better. I turn now to two sets of cases that show some promise in maintaining constitutional fidelity in their analysis of children's rights. The first are the abortion cases, which recognize a child's right to choose to undergo an

---

[90] 457 US at 321–23 (noting that decisions made in the institution by professionals were "presumptively valid" and directing that liability could only be imposed if a decision reflected "a substantial departure from professional judgment, practice or standards.").

[91] The court makes this argument in *Taylor v Ledbetter*, 818 F2d 791, 796 (11th Cir 1987) ("The lack of proximity in the foster home situation simply suggests that deliberate indifference is not as easily inferred or shown from a failure to act."). Note that the court applies the "deliberate indifference" standard articulated for Eighth Amendment liability in *Estelle v Gamble*, rather than the professional deference standard articulated in *Youngberg*. While it is not clear from the courts' decisions how distinct these two standards are, or which, if either, is more appropriately applied in the foster care context, it is clear that both of these standards are designed to limit state constitutional liability to the instances where state failures are most egregious. For a brief consideration of these two standards, and their application in the foster care context, see *Nicini v Morra*, 212 F3d at 811 n 9.

abortion, but modify the right in ways designed to capture children's impaired decision-making capacity and dependent relationship with their parents. The second are the death penalty cases. In both, disagreement about the animating constitutional principles complicates the analysis, but in both, the Justices' approach to children's rights is consistent with the principles espoused in their opinions.

A. ABORTION AND CHILDREN

For more than three decades, the Court has recognized the right to abortion as a substantive due process right, but the values animating the right continue to be a matter of debate. At least three distinct values—sex equality, bodily integrity, and procreative control—have been offered to justify a woman's right to choose an abortion. Each of these values has different implications for the application of the right to children.

Many argue that the primary justification for affording abortion rights is to secure women's equality.[92] Because women bear the brunt of the burden of an unwanted pregnancy, the abortion right is essential to ensuring women's equal place in society. This is especially so because conventions of sex inequality may make it difficult for women to avoid getting pregnant in the first place.[93] If the aim of securing women's equality animates the abortion right, then minors should probably have at least as great a right to an abortion as adult women. However unequal the power between adult sexual partners, that inequality is likely to be even greater in adolescence.[94] And however great the burdens imposed on women by an unwanted pregnancy, those burdens are surely greater for adolescents.

A second value often identified with the abortion right is that of bodily integrity.[95] While this value is often conflated with pro-

---

[92] See, for example, Ruth B. Ginsburg, *Some Thoughts on Autonomy and Equality in Relation to Roe v. Wade*, 63 NC L Rev 375 (1985); Catharine A. MacKinnon, *Reflections on Sex Equality under Law*, 100 Yale L J 1281, 1308–24 (1991); Cass Sunstein, *Neutrality in Constitutional Law (with Special Reference to Pornography, Abortion, and Surrogacy)*, 92 Colum L Rev 1 (1992); *Planned Parenthood v Casey*, 505 US 833, 856 ("The ability of women to participate equally in the economic and social life of the Nation has been facilitated by their ability to control their reproductive lives.").

[93] See MacKinnon, 100 Yale L J at 1312 (cited in note 92).

[94] Note that statutory rape laws are grounded on this concern.

[95] *Planned Parenthood v Casey*, 505 US at 915 (Stevens, concurring in part and dissenting in part) (contrasting the state's interest in potential life with the "woman's constitutional

creative liberty, it is useful, for purposes of child-specific analysis, to distinguish these two values. As a distinct value, "bodily integrity" focuses on choices about what is done to one's body, rather than on the implications of those choices for procreation. We traditionally afford strong protection to an individual's control of her own body. We would not tolerate, for example, a compelled organ transplant, even if it produced great benefit to others.[96] If the value of allowing every individual to control her body animates the adult abortion right, then, again, the argument for affording children full abortion rights is strong, though perhaps not as strong as under the equality principle. Although we might distrust a minor's ability to make sound, long-term decisions about her body, neither the choice to have an abortion nor the choice to continue a pregnancy to term is likely to have long-term physical effects. To the extent either carries long-term bodily risks, it is more likely to be continuing the pregnancy, particularly for a young teenage girl.[97]

The third value identified with the abortion right is procreative liberty. Here, the differences between minors and adults may well matter.[98] In deciding whether or not to give birth to a child, profound, life-long moral and emotional issues are at stake. Children, with their lesser experience and focus on the short term, might be ill-prepared to make such procreative choices.[99] If procreative freedom animates the abortion right, we might well want to impose some constraints, particularly constraints that help minors with the decision-making process.

---

interest in liberty . . . [including] a right to bodily integrity, a right to control one's person").

[96] See, for example, Judith J. Thomson, *A Defense of Abortion*, 1 Phil & Pub Aff 47 (1971) (comparing abortion prohibition to a law compelling organ donation).

[97] See Barbara Lowenthal and Richard Lowenthal, *Teenage Parenting, Challenges, Interventions, and Programs*, 74 Childhood Educ 29 (1997) (noting special health risks of pregnancy, labor, and delivery for adolescents).

[98] *Planned Parenthood v Casey*, 505 US at 851 ("Our law affords constitutional protection to personal decisions relating to marriage, procreation, contraception, family relationships, child rearing, and education"). Philip P. Heymann and Douglas E. Barzelay, *The Forest and the Trees: Roe v. Wade and Its Critics*, 53 BU L Rev 765, 772–75 (1973) (asserting that the right to abortion is among those rights of an "individual to make for himself [the] fundamental decisions that shape family life: whom to marry; whether and when to have children; and with what values to rear those children.").

[99] Note that some dispute this conclusion. See, for example, Gary B. Melton and Anita J. Pliner, *Adolescent Abortion: A Psycholegal Analysis*, in Gary Melton, ed, *Adolescent Abortion: Psychological and Legal Issues* 1, 18–19 (Nebraska, 1986) (concluding that adolescents and adults are similarly equipped to decide whether or not to terminate a pregnancy).

In *Bellotti v Baird*,[100] the plurality's endorsement of decision-making constraints explicitly aimed to serve this third principle. In describing what is uniquely important about the abortion right, Justice Powell noted the "grave and indelible" consequences associated with the decision whether or not to become a parent and its high moral and religious stakes.[101] The importance of procreative decision making, in his view, argued both for the recognition of abortion rights for minors and for a modification of the adult right to provide decision-making support. Justice Powell then described his vision of the appropriate modifications, a vision that has now been adopted by a majority of the Court.[102]

In *Bellotti* and subsequent cases, the Court has developed a "bypass" procedure whereby a minor seeking an abortion can avoid obtaining parental consent by petitioning a state adjudicator to find either that she is mature enough to make the abortion decision on her own or that the abortion is in her interest. This bypass system was designed to protect minors' decision-making authority, while channeling that decision-making process through adults (whether parents or bypass adjudicators) who could help ensure that the minor made her decision with some thought and care. Many objections have been raised to the bypass process, not the least of which is that it discourages those least prepared to take on the responsibilities of parenthood from obtaining an abortion. Moreover, states' tendency to interpret the bypass requirement as a *judicial* requirement has significantly limited the child-specific procedural opportunity created by *Bellotti*.[103] In a very basic sense, however, the *Bellotti* line reflects the Court's attempt to be true to constitutional principle while adapting the right to the special circumstances of childhood.[104]

---

[100] 443 US 622 (1979).

[101] Id at 640–42.

[102] Martin Guggenheim suggests that Justice Powell was interested, not in supporting minors' independent decision making, but rather in diversifying the set of adults with authority to control the decision. While Guggenheim convincingly argues that it is problematic to describe granting the state increased authority over a child's abortion decision as the granting of a right to children, there is little evidence that Powell was engaged in the sort of "subterfuge" that Guggenheim suggests. See Martin Guggenheim, *Minor Rights: The Adolescent Abortion Cases*, 30 Hofstra L Rev 589, 639 (2002).

[103] While the Court has not limited these bypass mechanisms to judicial proceedings, only Connecticut provides for some form of mandatory counseling outside the judicial setting for minors (there under the age of 16). See Conn Gen Stat § 19a-601(2003).

[104] Done right, a principled analysis of children's rights should also prove useful in the

B.   THE DEATH PENALTY AND CHILDREN

The Court's analysis of children's Eighth Amendment rights has been particularly faithful to constitutional principle. This is not to say that the Justices agree on the relevant principles, but rather that their principled disagreement is faithfully reflected in the cases considering the claims of children. While the Court has split between those who believe children's development is highly relevant to the Eight Amendment inquiry and those who find it irrelevant, both approaches can be traced directly to the Justices' different views about the principles that animate the right.

In *Thompson v Oklahoma*,[105] Justice Stevens wrote a plurality opinion declaring it unconstitutional to impose the death penalty on an individual convicted of a crime committed when he was 15 years old. Justice Stevens's opinion is full of developmental analysis, offered to argue that the death penalty is excessive and ineffective when applied to children.[106] Justice Scalia's dissent, in contrast, dismissed the developmental analysis as irrelevant and limited its analysis to the indicators of societal consensus captured in democratic lawmaking.[107] In *Stanford v Kentucky*,[108] the Court reached the opposite conclusion for 16- and 17-year-old offenders, and the positions of the majority and dissenters were reversed.[109]

---

ongoing development of those rights and principles in the adult context. Thus, the *Bellotti* Court's decision to single out procreative values, in its analysis of children's rights, ought to carry over to its analysis of adult cases. Conversely, a willingness to engage other values, most distinctly equality values, in analyzing the subsequent abortion rights claims of women should cast doubt on the integrity of the *Bellotti* analysis. Put positively, a proper analysis of children's rights may force the Court to clarify constitutional principles left obscure in the adult cases, in order to formulate child-specific adaptations. Put negatively, a failure to connect the principles elicited in children's rights cases to the ongoing development of rights in the adult context would signal a constitutional failure as serious as that reflected in cases that attach children's rights to no principles at all.

To the extent we think the muddle preserves a kind of stability in areas of controversy, we might reasonably fear that a principled approach to children's constitutional rights could have a destabilizing effect. Without minimizing this concern, I note that this risk of instability is always present, whenever the next case in a line of analysis is pressed. If children's rights cases do not create this risk, it is only because they are being isolated from the process of constitutional development that comes with ongoing interpretation. This is the cost, to the Constitution itself, of the adult-minus approach.

[105] 487 US 815 (1988).

[106] Id at 833–38.

[107] Id at 872–74.

[108] 493 US 361 (1989).

[109] Here I am suggesting the division was slightly more clean that it actually was, because Justice O'Connor concurred in the judgment in *Thompson*, and then joined most, but not all, of Justice Scalia's opinion in *Stanford*. While Justice O'Connor agreed with Justice

Just as this article was going to press, the Supreme Court decided *Roper v Simmons*,[110] which reversed *Stanford* and raised the
age line to 18. There is much to be said about the opinions in
Roper that will have to be said elsewhere. What is important to
note here is that the various opinions manifest the same fidelity
to principle manifested in *Thompson* and *Stanford*.

On both sides of the issue, the Justices' distinct views about the
principles animating the Eighth Amendment determined whether
(and how) they took children's ongoing development into account.
While all agreed that the Eighth Amendment required them to
consider "evolving standards of decency," they disagreed about the
source of those standards. For some (now a majority) of the
Justices, the Eighth Amendment secures justness in punishment
in an absolute sense that demands the Court's assessment of the
proportionality of punishment to crime and criminal, and of the
effectiveness of the punishment in accomplishing penal goals. For
others, the Eighth Amendment secures societal acceptance of punishment, best measured by the legislative enactments of the states
and Congress.

For those Justices making their own proportionality assessment,
social scientific evidence about child development is central to
their analysis. Adolescent impulsiveness, limited life experience,
vulnerability to peer pressure, and short-term perspective all reduce their control over their own actions and their appreciation
for the significance of those acts. These same qualities also call
into question the deterrent value of the death penalty for juveniles,
particularly when it is imposed only rarely.[111]

In all the decisions, Scalia has criticized this reliance on social
science. He rightly points out that it is irrelevant to an evaluation
of the existing national legal consensus. His argument is not that
development does not bear on culpability or the effectiveness of
punishment, but rather that the Eighth Amendment does not serve
these values directly. For Scalia, the Eighth Amendment serves
the value of consensus in punishment, albeit a consensus likely
driven by popular conceptions of culpability and effective punish-

---

Scalia that the Court should look to objective indicia of society's views, she took a somewhat
different view of what indicia should be considered, and how the various indicia should
be interpreted.

[110] No 03-633, March 1, 2005.

[111] 487 US at 833–38; 492 US 394–96 (Brennan dissenting).

ment. Under this view, an understanding of child development might properly shape the popular consensus, but has no place in the Court's assessment of what that consensus is.[112]

Some might object that this description of the two positions distorts the debate, and that the dispute is not over Eighth Amendment values, but rather over which institutions are most competent to make judgments about those values. While I would dispute the extent to which these questions can be disentangled, my argument does not depend on this point. Either way, there is a difference in basic principles at stake, and that difference tracks the different approaches to child development evidenced in the opinions.

These cases help illustrate that a commitment to child-sensitive rights analysis is not, by itself, outcome determinative. The approach embraces a range of outcomes, so long as those outcomes reflect a harmonizing of a right's underlying principles with the special features and experience of childhood. While the Justices take two different views of the relevance of child development to their Eighth Amendment analysis, they share the fidelity to principle that I am advocating here. This does not mean that I view both positions as equally good, but, rather, as equally principled.

CONCLUSION

Fidelity to principle does not make the analysis of children's rights any easier. If anything, this approach makes the task more difficult. For many rights, the animating principles are murky or contested. And even where the principles are clear, the adaptations demanded by childhood to achieve those principles may not be. The adult-minus approach avoids these difficulties by leaving the analysis of principle to other cases and by paying just enough attention to the unique characteristics of childhood to justify rights reductions.

But such passivity in constitutional interpretation is never acceptable. When decisions involving children are not faithful to the larger project of constitutional interpretation, they will inevitably have some distorting effect on constitutional rights overall. More immediately, the adult-minus approach disserves children, who are proclaimed to be constitutional rights holders, but then afforded scant constitutional attention.

---

[112] 487 US at 872–74 (Scalia dissenting); 492 US at 377–79.

What makes the child-specific modification of constitutional rights difficult is not the identification of principles, which is standard, if tricky, fare in constitutional interpretation. Rather, it is the application of those principles to children, who vary over time, and one from another. Perhaps development is too complex, idiosyncratic, and poorly understood to be incorporated into constitutional analysis.

This is a powerful objection, and an objection that can be made to any attempt to make the law more child-sensitive. But what is the alternative? Unless we refuse to recognize any constitutional rights in children, or insist on affording them the same rights we afford to adults, we are forced to find some middle ground, giving them some rights, but adjusting those rights to take account of their special, developmentally based circumstances. In the end, the most damning aspect of the adult-minus approach is not that it fails to take account of children's unique developmental circumstances, but that it does so badly.

A better accounting of children's differences in constitutional analysis would leave more of the specific developmental work to the democratic process. Just as we defer to the states to draw age lines for a broad range of obligations and privileges, so might we, for example, defer to the states to develop the detail of a decision-making process that secures children the meaningful participation guaranteed by the Due Process Clause. The adult-minus approach is unprincipled, not because it shows too much deference to the states, but because it shows too much deference to the detail of its own prior cases, developed to achieve constitutional principles for adults.

ADAM B. COX

PARTISAN GERRYMANDERING AND
DISAGGREGATED REDISTRICTING

Should federal courts police partisan gerrymandering? This question has lurked in the background of voting rights cases ever since the Supreme Court first waded into the political thicket in *Baker v Carr*.[1] For nearly two decades the Court has been explicitly divided over the answer to the question, and commentators have been similarly split. Despite these deep divides, however, both courts and commentators are united on one point—that congressional gerrymanders and state legislative gerrymanders should be treated identically by courts. Both constitutional jurisprudence and legal scholarship have uniformly assumed that these two types of gerrymanders pose the same problems and are subject to the same solutions.

This past Term the Supreme Court entrenched this assumption in constitutional doctrine when it decided *Vieth v Jubelirer*.[2] *Vieth*, a partisan gerrymandering case from Pennsylvania, represented the Court's first crack at resolving the question whether federal courts should police partisan gerrymandering since a fractured Court said "yes" eighteen years ago in *Davis v Bandemer*.[3] The Court treated

Adam B. Cox is Assistant Professor of Law, The University of Chicago Law School.

AUTHOR'S NOTE: I would like to thank Ahilan Arulanantham, Samuel Issacharoff, Elizabeth Milnikel, Richard Pildes, Adrian Vermeule, and the participants in the University of Chicago Law School faculty workshop for insightful comments. Many thanks also to Linda Boachie-Ansah for extremely valuable research assistance.

[1] 369 US 186 (1962).

[2] 124 S Ct 1769 (2004).

[3] 478 US 109 (1986).

Vieth as a referendum on *Bandemer*. And over the disagreement of four Justices, it reaffirmed *Bandemer*'s basic holding that federal constitutional challenges to partisan gerrymandering are justiciable.[4] In a strange omission, however, not one of the five opinions in *Vieth* mentioned a central distinction between *Bandemer* and *Vieth*—that the former concerned a challenge to state legislative districting, while the latter involved a challenge to congressional districts.[5] No Justice questioned whether this difference had any normative or constitutional significance. Nor has any commentator.

This article challenges the conventional view that federal congressional and state legislative political gerrymanders are functional equivalents.[6] To the contrary, these two types of gerrymanders raise quite distinct conceptual, normative, and constitutional questions. The differences make clear that the Court was wrong to treat *Vieth* as a referendum on *Bandemer*. Moreover, these differences create unique—and unrecognized—challenges for courts trying to police partisan gerrymandering in the federal congressional context.

Part I elaborates the analytic difference between state and congressional redistricting and shows that the courts and commentators have been inattentive to this basic conceptual point. When a court evaluates a gerrymandered state legislative districting plan, it can assess the districting plan that helps determine the composition of the entire state legislature. For this reason, the court can locate the harm of the partisan gerrymander at the institutional level of the state legislature itself.[7] In contrast, when a court evaluates a single state's congressional districting plan, the most that the court can conclude is that the state's *congressional delegation* has been manip-

---

[4] Justice Scalia, announcing the judgment of the Court dismissing the plaintiffs' claims, argued for a plurality that *Bandemer* should be overturned. See *Vieth*, 124 S Ct at 1792 (plurality). But five members of the Court refused to overrule *Bandemer*'s justiciability holding. See id at 1795 (Kennedy concurring); id at 1799 (Stevens dissenting); id at 1815 (Souter, joined by Ginsburg, dissenting); id at 1822 (Breyer dissenting).

[5] Compare *Bandemer*, 478 US at 113, with *Vieth*, 124 S Ct at 1773.

[6] Throughout this article, I use "congressional" to refer only to the national legislature. For that reason, I often will not explicitly note that congressional districts are "federal."

[7] This is exactly how the Supreme Court framed its inquiry in *Bandemer*; it evaluated the state legislative districting plan from a statewide perspective, rather than attempting to locate district-specific injuries. See *Davis v Bandemer*, 478 US 109, 127 (1986) (noting that the claim "made by the appellees is . . . that the apportionment discriminates against Democrats on a statewide basis," and stating that "although the statewide discrimination asserted here was allegedly accomplished through the manipulation of individual district lines, the focus of the equal protection inquiry is necessarily somewhat different from that involved in the review of individual districts").

ulated in favor of one political party or the other. In other words,
evaluating the potential political gerrymander of a single congressional districting plan in isolation prevents a court from identifying
the harms, if any, that stem from the manipulation of the composition of Congress as a whole. Instead, the harm must be located
at the institutional level of the state congressional delegation or
individual congressional districts.[8]

Part II explains that this feature of congressional redistricting
poses a problem because the conventional arguments about why
partisan gerrymanders are harmful generally describe harms that
turn on the structure of representation in Congress *as a whole*—not
on the consequences of redistricting for a small subset of seats within
Congress. For this reason, judicial review that focuses only on a
single state's redistricting plan cannot hope to identify the presence
of these injuries. Moreover, as Part III shows, alternative theories
of partisan gerrymandering's harm are unlikely to solve this problem. The alternatives also generally focus on Congress as a whole.
And while governmental purpose-based theories of injury (and perhaps other theories that are completely disconnected from the actual
electoral consequences of redistricting) could escape this nationwide
institutional perspective, such theories would cut deep against the
grain of the Court's long-standing and correct recognition of the
inevitable role that partisan advantage-seeking plays in redistricting.
In short, therefore, the way in which federal courts review congressional partisan gerrymandering claims today—examining individual states' redistricting plans in isolation—makes it impossible
for courts to identify the presence or absence of the harms commonly thought to flow from partisan gerrymanders.

Part IV asks what this shortcoming of contemporary judicial review means for the capacity of courts to curtail the ills of congressional partisan gerrymanders. With respect to *Vieth* itself, the
analytic structure of congressional gerrymanders shows that the
approaches to policing partisan gerrymandering advocated by individual Justices in the case miss the mark. If the harms of congressional partisan gerrymanders can be identified only by reference

---

[8] In *Vieth*, the plaintiffs asserted that the injury of congressional gerrymandering
stemmed from Pennsylvania's drawing districts that biased the state's congressional delegation in favor of the Republican party. Even if Democrats won a majority of the statewide
vote, the plaintiffs alleged, they would win only a minority of the state's congressional
seats. It was this delegation-level bias, they argued, that violates the Equal Protection
Clause.

to Congress as a whole, the efforts by members of the Court to identify such harms within the current delegation-centric structure of judicial review are doomed to fail. This leaves courts with three options: they can restructure judicial review so that courts can evaluate the combined consequences of every state's congressional redistricting; they can abandon any effort to directly identify the *existence* of harms caused by congressional partisan gerrymanders and instead develop prophylactic rules that reduce the *risk* that state redistricting efforts will together produce a nationwide harm; or they can give up on policing partisan gerrymanders in the context of congressional redistricting.

Various coordination problems among the states and within the judiciary make the first option implausible as a practical matter. The second option is theoretically attractive: judicial intervention at the state level can reduce the risk of Congress-wide injuries. Theoretical niceties aside, however, the practical attractiveness of this option depends on the answers to underexplored questions—such as how likely it is that the effects of individual states' redistricting plans accumulate to produce congressional-level harms. And if judicial intervention is warranted, the disaggregated nature of congressional redistricting affects how courts should structure state-level review and calls into question some popular proposals for jurisprudential reform.

I. The Disaggregated Nature of Congressional Redistricting

Congressional and state legislative gerrymanders raise quite distinct analytic, normative, and constitutional questions. But both courts and legal commentators have largely overlooked this point, typically analyzing state and congressional redistricting in the same fashion. This oversight is perhaps understandable: the process of congressional and state legislative redistricting is facially identical in most states, and this similarity makes it easy to miss a critical structural distinction between the two—that state legislative redistricting plans affect the composition of the entire legislature, while congressional redistricting plans affect the composition of only a subpart of the legislature. As the following parts will show, however, this difference has substantial implications for the theory and practice of judicial oversight of partisan redistricting.

In order to identify the important analytic difference between state legislative and congressional redistricting, it is necessary first to understand the way in which these types of redistricting are very much the same. In both instances, the state government has initial authority to draw the boundaries for all of the legislative districts in the state.[9] With respect to state legislative districts, the state's authority to draw district lines is inherent in state sovereignty and reserved in the federal Constitution. (The authority is, of course, subject to numerous federal constitutional and statutory constraints.) States obviously do not have inherent sovereign authority to fashion *federal* congressional districts,[10] but Article I, Section IV of the Constitution delegates this authority initially to states. That clause, typically referred to as the Elections Clause, provides that "[t]he Times, Places and Manner of holding Elections for Senators and Representatives, shall be prescribed in each State by the Legislature thereof; but the Congress may at any time by Law make or alter such Regulations, except as to the Places of chusing Senators."[11] The Supreme Court has consistently interpreted the clause as conferring congressional districting authority on states.[12] And while the clause gives Congress the power to supersede state regulations of congressional elections, Congress has not used this power to divest states of redistricting authority.[13]

---

[9] While the focus of this article is on districted elections, it is important to note that legislative representatives can be selected through a number of different mechanisms. These mechanisms differ in many dimensions: in whether voters cast ballots for parties or candidates, in how many votes are allotted to each voter, in how votes are aggregated to determine a winner, and so on. See Gary Cox, *Making Votes Count: Strategic Coordination in the World's Electoral System* (Cambridge, 1997). Despite the existence of myriad possibilities, the single-member district plurality voting election structure is by far the most common in the United States. Federal law requires that it be used for all congressional elections, see note 13, and nearly every state uses this election structure (or a close variant) for state legislative elections as well.

[10] Consider *United States Term Limits, Inc. v Thornton*, 514 US 779 (1995).

[11] US Const, Art I, § 4.

[12] See, for example, *Growe v Emison*, 507 US 25, 33–35 (1993). See also Adam B. Cox, *Partisan Fairness and Redistricting Politics*, 79 NYU L Rev 751, 791 & n 148 (2004). Founding-era history also supports the conclusion that the Election Clause's initial grant of authority to states includes the power to regulate redistricting. See id at 790.

[13] Congress has used this power to require that states elect their congressional representatives from single-member districts. See 2 USC § 2c ("In each State entitled in the Ninety-first Congress or in any subsequent Congress thereafter to more than one Representative under an apportionment made pursuant to the provisions of section 2a(a) of this title, there shall be established by law a number of districts equal to the number of Representatives to which such State is so entitled, and Representatives shall be elected only from districts so established, no district to elect more than one Representative . . . ."). See generally *Branch v Smith*, 538 US 252 (2003) (discussing 2 USC § 2c). Congress first enacted the single-member-district requirement in 1842. See Act of June 25, 1842, § 2, 5 Stat 491 (corresponding to 2 USC §§ 2a–2c).

Thus, the process for state legislative and federal congressional redistricting is superficially identical in many respects. In each instance the state—typically through its ordinary legislative process—carves up the state's territory into a number of districts sufficient to select the total number of representatives to be elected statewide. But this sameness of process disguises an important difference: in the state legislative context, the state is drawing district lines for the entire legislative assembly; in the congressional context, however, the state is drawing district lines for only its own congressional delegation—that is, for only a subpart of Congress as a whole. Another way to put this is that the process for redistricting each state legislature is consolidated, while the process for redistricting Congress is disaggregated.

The disaggregated nature of congressional redistricting fundamentally alters the analytic structure of judicial review of congressional partisan gerrymandering claims.[14] When a court evaluates a claim that a state legislative districting plan constitutes an impermissible partisan gerrymander, it is assessing the districting plan that helps determine the composition of the entire state legislature. For this reason, the court can locate the harm of the partisan gerrymander at the institutional level of the state legislature itself. Or, to put it slightly differently, the court can adopt a systemwide account of the harm caused by the partisan gerrymander. When a court evaluates a single state's congressional districting plan, however, the most that the court can conclude is that the state's *congressional delegation* has been manipulated for partisan ends.[15] In other words, evaluating the potential political gerrymander of a single congressional districting plan in isolation prevents a court from identifying harms that stem from the manipulation of Congress as a whole. Instead, the harm must be located at the institutional level of the state congressional delegation or some lower level.

In light of the Supreme Court's existing partisan gerrymandering

---

The requirement was later dropped and reinstated, and at one time included an additional requirement that congressional districts be equipopulous. See Cox, 79 NYU L Rev at 794 n 162 (cited in note 12).

[14] The focus in this article is exclusively on partisan gerrymandering, but the article's analysis is relevant to other types of gerrymandering claims as well.

[15] As I explain later, there are several ways in which district lines might be manipulated for partisan ends. They might be manipulated to bias the composition of the delegation in favor of one political party or the other, to reduce the competitiveness of seats held by either party, or in some other fashion.

jurisprudence, one would have expected the Court to have noticed this crucial distinction in the *Vieth* litigation. Prior to *Vieth*, the Supreme Court had adjudicated a partisan gerrymandering claim on only one occasion—in *Davis v Bandemer*.[16] *Bandemer* concerned a state legislative redistricting plan; the plaintiffs in that case alleged that Indiana's state legislative redistricting scheme constituted an unconstitutional partisan gerrymander.[17] To evaluate the claim, the plurality opinion in *Bandemer* examined the effect of the redistricting plan on the structure of representation in the entire legislature.[18] It was at the institutional level of the legislature as a whole, rather than at some lower institutional level such as individual districts, that the plurality sought to identify the injury of partisan gerrymandering. In contrast to *Bandemer*, *Vieth* concerned an alleged congressional partisan gerrymander; the *Vieth* plaintiffs alleged that the congressional districts drawn in Pennsylvania following the 2000 census were politically gerrymandered.[19] Because the case concerned an alleged congressional partisan gerrymander, the *Vieth* Court was precluded from adopting the analytic perspective that the plurality had applied in *Bandemer*—it did not have the option of identifying the harm of partisan gerrymandering at the institutional level of the legislative assembly.

Surprisingly, none of the opinions in *Vieth* mention this fact or

---

[16] 478 US 109 (1986). The Court had summarily affirmed a number of other partisan gerrymandering cases that came to the Court on direct (rather than certiorari) review, but *Bandemer* was the Court's only previous partisan gerrymandering opinion. In *Bandemer* the Court had held that partisan gerrymandering claims were justiciable under the Equal Protection Clause. Id at 127. But the Court set forth such an exceedingly stringent (or maybe even incoherent) standard for demonstrating unconstitutionality that no partisan gerrymandering claims brought since *Bandemer* had been successful. See Cox, 79 NYU L Rev at 796–98 (cited in note 12). Consider also Samuel Issacharoff, Pamela S. Karlan, and Richard H. Pildes, *The Law of Democracy* 866 (2d rev ed, 2002).

[17] *Bandemer*, 478 US at 115.

[18] See id at 127 (noting that the claim "made by the appellees is . . . that the apportionment discriminates against Democrats on a statewide basis," and stating that "although the statewide discrimination asserted here was allegedly accomplished through the manipulation of individual district lines, the focus of the equal protection inquiry is necessarily somewhat different from that involved in the review of individual districts").

[19] *Vieth*, 124 S Ct at 1773. *Vieth* arose out of Pennsylvania's congressional redistricting following the 2000 census. Republicans controlled the state's redistricting process and produced a district map that, according to Democrats' claims, ensured Republicans would capture a supermajority of the congressional seats even if the party captured only a minority of the statewide congressional votes. See Brief for Appellants, *Vieth v Jubelirer*, No 02-1580, *2 (filed Aug 29, 2003) (available on Lexis at 2002 US Briefs 1580). Democrats sued in federal court, contending that the redistricting scheme violated the Constitution. See *Vieth v Pennsylvania*, 188 F Supp 2d 532 (MD Pa 2002); *Vieth v Pennsylvania*, 241 F Supp 2d 478 (MD Pa 2003).

appear to recognize that *Vieth* might pose different questions than did *Bandemer*.[20] The Court split five ways in *Vieth*. Writing for a plurality of four, Justice Scalia concluded that *Bandemer*'s justiciability holding had been in error; claims of partisan gerrymandering, he wrote, present nonjusticiable political questions.[21] Justice Kennedy concurred in the judgment upholding the dismissal of the plaintiffs' claims, but he did not agree with the plurality that partisan gerrymandering claims should be nonjusticiable.[22] Justices Breyer, Ginsburg, Stevens, and Souter dissented in three opinions, each opinion concluding that the district court was wrong to dismiss the plaintiffs' claims—and each opinion suggesting a different test for identifying the existence of an impermissibly harmful partisan gerrymander.[23] Despite the extremely fractured nature of the Court's decision, the Justices were in agreement on one score: each saw *Vieth* as a referendum on the Court's earlier decision in *Bandemer*. None of the Justices appears to have thought that there would be any reason to treat the partisan gerrymandering claim leveled against the state legislative plan in *Bandemer* differently than the claim leveled against the congressional redistricting at issue in *Vieth*.[24]

---

[20] Nor, perhaps surprisingly, did the litigants (in particular, the defendants) bring up this potentially important distinction between the two cases.

[21] *Vieth*, 124 S Ct at 1778.

[22] Id at 1793 (Kennedy concurring in the judgment). Instead, Kennedy concluded that the plaintiffs' claims should be dismissed because he could not think of a workable standard for evaluating their partisan gerrymandering claim. See id at 1796–97. He expressed hope that such a standard would eventually be found, and it was this optimism that led him to conclude that it was too soon to hold partisan gerrymandering claims nonjusticiable. Id at 1794–96. As Justice Scalia pointed out, however, it is a bit difficult to see how Justice Kennedy's conclusion about the current absence of an administrable standard is much different than a finding of current nonjusticiability. Id at 1792 (plurality). And if they are different, it is tough to see why a plaintiff's claim should be dismissed simply because the *court* cannot decide on the appropriate standard for evaluating the plaintiff's claim.

[23] Justice Stevens drew on the *Shaw v Reno* line of racial redistricting cases to develop his proposed test. He argued that legislative purpose should be the touchstone of the partisan gerrymandering inquiry: a legislative district has been unconstitutionally politically gerrymandered, he concluded, if partisanship was the predominant motive for the design of the district. See id at 1808–13 (Stevens dissenting). Justice Souter drew on Title VII and Voting Rights Act litigation to construct his favored inquiry, arguing that the concept of vote dilution should guide courts in partisan gerrymandering cases. See id at 1817–19 (Souter dissenting). Justice Breyer argued that partisan gerrymandering jurisprudence should focus on preventing unjustified minority entrenchment. See id at 1825–27 (Breyer dissenting).

[24] See *Vieth*, 124 S Ct at 1773 (plurality) (framing the question as "whether our decision in *Bandemer* was in error," without acknowledging that *Bandemer* might be importantly different than *Vieth*); id at 6 (Kennedy concurring) (treating *Bandemer* as posing the same

Largely without discussion, the Justices in *Vieth* simply adopted either a delegation- or district-specific perspective of the harm caused by partisan gerrymanders.[25] Only Justice Kennedy hinted at the possibility of a legislature-wide perspective. Near the close of his opinion, he suggested that it may be misleading to try to identify impermissibly "excessive" partisan gerrymanders by focusing on each state delegation in isolation. As an illustration, he described the cumulative effect of several hypothetical districting plans: "In one State, Party X controls the apportionment process and draws the lines so it captures every congressional seat. In three other States, Party Y controls the apportionment process. It is not so blatant or egregious, but proceeds by a more subtle effort, capturing less than all the seats in each State. Still, the total effect of Party Y's effort is to capture more new seats than Party X captured. Party X's gerrymander was more egregious. Party Y's gerrymander was more subtle. In my view, however, each is culpable."[26] While Justice Kennedy is vague about what conclusions should follow from the possibility that partisan gerrymanders may either accumulate or cancel out across several states, his example does implicitly acknowledge the possibility that a congressional delegation-centric perspective may be inadequate to identify certain harms that flow from partisan gerrymanders.

Like the Court, the substantial commentary about *Vieth* has also been inattentive to the important analytic differences between *Vieth* and *Bandemer*.[27] Legal commentators have widely criticized the

---

justiciability question as *Vieth*). This oversight is perhaps more understandable for some Justices than others. Justice Stevens, for example, clearly adopted a district-centric purpose analysis for evaluating partisan gerrymandering claims. Because he chose to locate the injury of partisan gerrymandering at the district level, it made sense to treat congressional and state legislative districting as posing the same question. But even Justice Stevens apparently saw state-level analysis the only alternative to his district-centric perspective; he too omitted the possibility of adopting a legislature-wide perspective. See *Vieth*, 124 S Ct at 1779–80, 1805–07 (Stevens dissenting).

[25] See *Vieth*, 124 S Ct at 1828–29 (Breyer dissenting) (adopting a statewide perspective); id at 1817 (Souter dissenting) (suggesting that a statewide perspective is important but focusing first on individual districts); id at 1799, 1805 (Stevens dissenting) (adopting a district-level perspective). Justice Stevens goes so far as to suggest that the Court's racial gerrymandering jurisprudence overruled *Bandemer*'s statewide focus and required that all questions of fairness in redistricting be resolved at the district level—whether racial, political, or some other sort of fairness is at issue. Id at 1805.

[26] *Vieth*, 124 S Ct at 1798 (Kennedy concurring).

[27] Lower courts have also been inattentive to the distinction, regularly applying *Bandemer* in the congressional context without discussion. See, for example, *O'Lear v Miller*, 222 F Supp 2d 850, 853–59 (ED Mich 2002) (employing *Bandemer* to evaluate Michigan's congressional districts, and adopting a statewide, delegation-specific perspective). Moreover,

Court for continuing, or perhaps even exacerbating, the jurisprudential muddle that has existed since *Bandemer* was handed down
eighteen years ago.[28] But none has criticized the Court's decision
to treat congressional and state legislative districting as the same.
To the contrary, legal scholarship appears to have uniformly overlooked the analytic significance of the disaggregated nature of congressional redistricting.[29] The scholarship suffers from the same
blind spot that afflicts the Court in *Vieth*.

II. Partisan Gerrymandering's Harms: The Conventional Accounts

While the literature has treated partisan gerrymandering
claims in the state legislative and congressional contexts as inter-
changeable, the dominant accounts of why partisan gerrymanders
are harmful cannot be squared with this undifferentiated treatment.
The disaggregated nature of congressional redistricting makes it
impossible for a court evaluating one state's congressional redistricting scheme to identify injuries that stem from the manipulation

on at least one occasion a lower court expressly refused to treat congressional partisan
gerrymandering claims differently than state legislative ones. See, for example, *Badham v
Eu*, 694 F Supp 664, 668 (ND Cal 1988). Consider also *Anne Arundel County Republican
Central Committee v State Admin. Bd of Election Laws*, 781 F Supp 394, 399 & n 7 (D
Maryland 1991) (noting that *Bandemer* "address[ed] a challenge to the partisan redistricting
of the Indiana legislature, not to congressional redistricting," but nonetheless applying
Bandemer to evaluate the constitutionality of Maryland's congressional redistricting
scheme).

[28] See, for example, Heather Gerken, *Lost in the Political Thicket: The Court, Election Law,
and the Doctrinal Interregnum*, 153 U Pa L Rev 503 (2004); Samuel Issacharoff and Pamela
S. Karlan, *Where to Draw the Line? Judicial Review of Political Gerrymanders*, 153 U Pa L
Rev 541 (2004). When the Supreme Court noted probable jurisdiction in *Vieth*, most
observers predicted that this meant the Court would clarify partisan gerrymandering jurisprudence by either reaffirming the justiciability of partisan gerrymandering claims and
supplying a more workable standard for adjudicating such claims, or by overruling *Bandemer* and holding that partisan gerrymandering claims present nonjusticiable political
questions. Instead, the Court fractured so badly that it was not able to head down either
of these paths.

[29] See, for example, Gerken, 153 U Pa L Rev at 505–10 (cited in note 28) (arguing that
Vieth involves "structural" rather than "individual rights" claims and contending that those
claims need to be resolved at the *state* level, rather than the individual voter or district
level). In this year's *Harvard Law Review* Foreword, Richard Pildes does hint at the potential
significance of congressional redistricting's disaggregated nature. See Richard H. Pildes,
Foreword: The Constitutionalization of Democratic Politics, 118 Harv L Rev 28, 73 (2004)
("Unlike a state house or senate, in which majority control of representation translates
into majority control of governance, majority control of a congressional delegation translates into no value other than fair representation itself . . . ."). The Foreword continues
to argue, however, that "[t]he baseline for measuring whether, and to what extent, unfair
partisan gerrymandering has occurred must be statewide." Id.

of the legislative assembly as a whole. But the central contemporary accounts of partisan gerrymandering's harms—the partisan bias account and the anticompetition account—conceptualize those injuries at the legislature-wide level. They do not explain why the partisan manipulation of a small subset of seats within the legislature is harmful, independent of what happens to other seats. Consequently, a court reviewing a congressional redistricting plan for these injuries cannot determine—at least within the current structure of redistricting litigation—whether that plan does or does not cause an injury.[30]

A. THE PARTISAN BIAS ACCOUNT

One central contemporary account of the injury caused by partisan gerrymanders identifies the harm as the introduction of partisan bias. Theories of partisan bias condemn districting arrangements that make it easier for one party than the other to convert votes cast in its favor on election day into legislative seats.[31] The injury occurs, in other words, when one party can capture a greater share of seats in the legislature than the other party for a given level of electoral support. For example, if Democrats garner 53 percent of the vote and thereby capture 60 percent of the seats in the legislature, then in an unbiased system the Republicans will also capture 60 percent of the legislative seats if they garner 53 percent of the vote. If the Republicans were to capture a greater seat share in this situation—say 70 percent—the system would contain partisan bias in favor of the Republicans.[32]

Because partisan bias is a function of how votes translate into

---

[30] In describing these accounts of the harmfulness of partisan gerrymandering, I do not mean to defend the idea that partisan bias, anticompetitive effects, or both are harms that we should be trying to prevent. Rather, my claim is simply that these notions of harm, whatever their appeal as normative principles, are typically conceptualized as systemwide injuries produced by redistricting.

[31] For a detailed explanation of partisan bias, see Gary King, *Representation Through Legislative Redistricting: A Stochastic Model*, 33 Am J Pol Sci 787 (1989).

[32] Note that this account of partisan fairness requires only symmetry, not proportionality, in the translation of votes into seats. An absence of partisan bias is perfectly consistent with the presence of a systemwide "winner's bonus"—that is, with the party that garners a majority of the vote capturing a larger majority of the legislative seats. Thus, this sort of fairness does not call into question the single-member districted electoral structure used in congressional elections, even though single-member districts typically lead to a winner's bonus.

a party's share of seats in a legislative assembly,[33] partisan bias in congressional districting cannot be identified by evaluating one state's congressional redistricting plan in isolation. Whether an effort to gerrymander one state's congressional districts for political gain actually introduces partisan bias into the composition of Congress can be determined only by reference to what has happened to the congressional districts in other states as well. Congressional gerrymanders in different states may tend to accumulate in a way that introduces partisan bias in Congress—or they may cancel each other out—but there is no way to determine this by examining one congressional districting plan in isolation.

Of course, one could say that partisan bias exists whenever one party can capture more seats in a *congressional delegation* than the other party for a given level of electoral support in the state. But it is not clear why we should care about partisan symmetry in a small subset of the legislature's districts. The partisan distribution of legislative power, which is what the bias account is concerned with, is a function of how many seats each party holds (to be more precise, its seat share) in the legislative assembly as a whole.[34] The seat share of each party in Congress is obviously connected to the composition of each congressional delegation, but those delegations are, for these purposes, in some sense arbitrary subparts of the legislative institution. The bias account's concern about the distribution of party power in the legislature does not provide any reason why one would care about the existence of partisan bias in such a subpart, except to the extent that such bias influenced the level of bias in the system as a whole.

The fact that partisan bias in congressional redistricting cannot be identified at the state level means that one cannot evaluate congressional and state legislative redistricting in the same way so long as partisan bias is the injury that one is trying to identify.[35]

---

[33] For statements in the scholarship to the effect that the concept of partisan bias is defined with reference to the legislature as a whole, see, for example, Gary King, *Electoral Responsiveness and Partisan Bias in Multiparty Democracies*, 15 Legis Stud Q 159, 160 (1990); Sam Hirsch, *The United States House of Unrepresentatives: What Went Wrong in the Latest Round of Congressional Districting*, 2 Election L J 179, 190 (2003).

[34] See, for example, Andrew Gelman and Gary King, *Enhancing Democracy Through Legislative Redistricting*, 88 Am Pol Sci Rev 541, 543–46 (1994).

[35] This does not mean, of course, that it is impossible to intervene at the state level to police national partisan bias. It means only that a court cannot determine whether Congress contains partisan bias by examining a single state's congressional redistricting plan in isolation. I discuss in Part IV the possibility that courts might be able to intervene at the

Nonetheless, case law and legal scholarship sometimes apply the concept of partisan bias to congressional redistricting plans that affect the composition of only individual congressional delegations—without appearing to recognize that the theory underlying the concept does not explain why partisan bias in a state's congressional delegation is undesirable.[36]

Justice Breyer appears to make just this error in *Vieth*. He argued in that case that the Court should police the congressional redistricting process in order to prevent "unjustified entrenchment."[37] Breyer defined entrenchment as "a situation in which a party that enjoys only minority support among the populace has nonetheless continued to take, and hold, legislative power."[38] The central feature of this entrenchment injury—the idea that the harm occurs when a party that receives a minority of the vote can capture a majority of the seats—is a close variant of the bias injury. As with partisan bias, the concern is that one party can translate its votes into legislative seats more efficiently than the other party: on Breyer's definition one party can capture a majority of the seats with a minority of the votes, but the other party would by definition capture less than a majority of the seats were it to receive a minority of the vote.[39] Breyer identified the democratic harm of unjustified entrenchment as flowing from the principle of majority control of legislative bodies: "[I]t would seem reasonable that a majority of the people of a State could elect a majority of that State's legislators. To conclude differently, and to sanction minority control of state legislative bodies, [would violate the principle that legislatures] should be bodies which are collectively re

---

state level to control national partisan bias even if they cannot directly identify its presence or absence.

[36] See Cox, 79 NYU L Rev at 767 n 60 (cited in note 12) (noting that the jurisprudence and legal literature commonly focus on partisan bias at the congressional delegation level).

[37] *Vieth v Jubelirer*, 124 S Ct 1769, 1825 (2004) (Breyer dissenting).

[38] Id.

[39] In fact, this demonstrates that the point about partisan bias can be generalized to any theory under which partisan gerrymandering's injury is a function of how votes translate into a seat share of legislative power. Consider, for example, the position that partisan fairness in districting should be defined by reference to proportional representation. This idea of partisan fairness is quite different from a prohibition on partisan bias, and it requires that one commit to a different concept of representation. But proportional representation is like partisan bias in one important respect. Both are a function of the relationship between votes and seat share in the legislature. As a result, neither can be identified by examining the votes-to-seats relationship for a small subset of the legislative assembly.

sponsible to the popular will."[40] This principle of majoritarianism, he concluded, condemns "entrenchment where the House of Representatives or similar state legislative body is at issue."[41] But while Breyer grounded his theory of harm in the principle of majority control of legislative bodies, he applied the concept to the congressional redistricting plan at issue in *Vieth*—despite the fact that it would be impossible to tell by examining that plan whether there was unjustified minority entrenchment in the House of Representatives.[42]

B.   THE ANTICOMPETITION ACCOUNT

A second central account of the injury caused by partisan gerrymandering identifies the harm as the reduction of electoral competition. This account of gerrymandering's harm is grounded on the legal theory of political competition that Samuel Issacharoff and Richard Pildes have elaborated in recent years.[43] Their work draws on existing competition-based accounts of democracy in the political science literature,[44] along with an analogy to antitrust doctrine, to suggest that courts should use constitutional law to invalidate legal rules that are designed to reduce the competitiveness of political markets.[45] In a recent piece in *Harvard Law Review*,

---

[40] Id at 1825 (internal quotation marks omitted).

[41] Id.

[42] The plaintiffs in *Vieth* appear to make a similar mistake. They argue that Pennsylvania's redistricting plan causes a constitutionally cognizable harm because it enables a Republican minority to capture a majority of the state's congressional delegation. See Brief for Appellants, *Vieth v Jubelirer*, No 02-1580, *3 (filed Aug 29, 2003) (available on Lexis at 2002 US Briefs 1580) (arguing for judicial intervention where partisan manipulation of district lines "reaches the point where one political party guarantees itself a solid majority of seats, even if [that party] wins only a minority of the votes"). But they argue that this consequence of the districting plan constitutes a cognizable harm because it violates principles of *legislative* majoritarianism. See id at *22 ("[A] biased map designed to transform a voting minority into a *legislative* majority is . . . a clear violation of the principle of electoral equality . . . .") (emphasis added). See also id (quoting *Reynolds v Sims* for the proposition that a majority of voters should be able to control the composition of the majority in the *legislature*).

[43] See, for example, Samuel Issacharoff and Richard H. Pildes, *Politics as Markets: Partisan Lockups of the Democratic Process*, 50 Stan L Rev 643 (1997); Richard H. Pildes, *A Theory of Political Competition*, 85 Va L Rev 1605 (1999).

[44] See, for example, Joseph A. Schumpeter, *Capitalism, Socialism, and Democracy* (Harper, 1942); Richard A. Posner, *Law, Pragmatism, and Democracy* (Harvard, 2003). See also Richard H. Pildes, *Competitive, Deliberative, and Rights-Oriented Democracy*, 3 Election L Q 685 (2004) (reviewing *Law, Pragmatism, and Democracy*).

[45] I say somewhat elliptically that the theory is concerned with regulations of the political process that are "designed" to reduce competition because the theory is a bit vague about

Issacharoff applied this theory and its antitrust analogy to the redistricting process.[46] He argued that partisan gerrymandering is harmful where it leads to a "constriction of the competitive processes by which voters can express choice," and he contended that courts should intervene to prevent this harm.[47]

Whether the anticompetition account of the harm of partisan gerrymandering embodies a legislature-wide institutional perspective turns on how the account answers the question: competition for what? Must every seat be competitive? Every congressional delegation? Or is the account concerned with the legislature as a whole? Perhaps surprisingly, it turns out that this question gets largely ignored when the anticompetition account is employed against partisan gerrymandering.[48] Unlike the partisan

---

whether it is concerned with (1) legal rules that depress competition, regardless of the reasons for those legal rules (although the reasons might in some cases be evidence of the actual effect of the rules); (2) legal rules that are adopted for the reason of depressing competition, regardless of the actual effect of the rules on competition; or (3) legal rules that are both adopted for the reason of depressing competition and have the effect of doing so. Different theories of political philosophy and constitutional law could underwrite any one of these variants, and it is difficult to read Pildes's and Issacharoff's political markets approach as clearly endorsing one of these possibilities to the exclusion of the others. That said, I will treat the anticompetition account as ultimately concerned with the actual anticompetitive consequences of particular electoral rules. (I discuss in Part III the implications of injury theories that are completely disconnected from electoral consequences.) This is the conventional understanding of the account in both the legal and political theory literature, and Issacharoff appears to focus on actual electoral consequences when he applies the anticompetition idea to political gerrymandering. See, for example, Samuel Issacharoff, *Gerrymandering and Political Cartels*, 116 Harv L Rev 593, 622 (2002) (focusing on "whether the parties are forced to compete for the votes of the electorate . . . and are in a deep sense accountable to changes in the preferences of the electorate . . . . on this view, the competitiveness of elections emerges as a central guarantee of the integrity of democratic governance"); id at 600 (describing partisan gerrymandering's injury as the "constriction of the competitive processes by which voters can express choice"); id at 615 (arguing for focus on ensuring the existence of an "appropriately competitive electoral process"). Consider also Samuel Issacharoff, *Private Parties with Public Purposes: Political Parties, Associational Freedoms, and Partisan Competition*, 101 Colum L Rev 274, 280–81, 299, 308–09 (2001) (describing the "functional" anticompetitive account as concerned with ensuring the "proper level of competitiveness in the political marketplace," suggesting that the theory's application to a particular regulatory practice should turn on the existence or absence of empirical evidence that the practice actually disables competition). To the extent Issacharoff focuses on the reasons (or purposes) underlying redistricting legislation, it seems to be because he sees these reasons as proxies for (or evidence of) the actual anticompetitive effects of redistricting plans. See Issacharoff, 116 Harv L Rev at 626 (cited above).

[46] Issacharoff, 116 Harv L Rev 593 (cited in note 45).

[47] Id at 600.

[48] This ambiguity itself has gone unnoticed in the literature. The most common criticism of Pildes and Issacharoff's theory is that it does not answer the question, "How much competition?"—that is, that the theory leaves unspecified (in a way that the bias account does not) the baseline from which a court would measure distortions in the system. See,

bias account, which expressly adopts a legislature-wide institutional perspective, descriptions of the anticompetition account have been inattentive to the question of institutional perspective.[49]

Given the seeming ambiguity of the anticompetition account, one might think that the account is perfectly consistent with any of the available institutional perspectives. If that were true, then in the context of congressional gerrymandering the account could be read as concerned with protecting electoral competition in individual districts, in state congressional delegations, or in Congress as a whole. And if the injury could be identified by reference to congressional delegations or individual districts, congressional partisan gerrymanders would not necessarily pose different challenges for courts than state legislative gerrymanders. Nonetheless, while anticompetition effects could be identified from any of the institutional perspectives described above, the theory driving the account is actually quite difficult to square with anything other than the legislature-wide perspective. Like the bias account, the anticompetition account's underlying theory of harm does not justify concern for the consequences of redistricting for individual congressional delegations in isolation.[50]

Certain features of districted elections make it very difficult to reconcile the anticompetition account with an institutional focus on individual districts or congressional delegations. As I noted above, the anticompetition account is grounded in the idea that

---

for example, Richard L. Hasen, *The "Political Market" Metaphor and Election Law: A Comment on Issacharoff and Pildes*, 50 Stan L Rev 719, 724–28 (1998); Bruce E. Cain, *Garrett's Temptation*, 85 Va L Rev 1589, 1600–03 (1999). But see Pildes, *A Theory of Political Competition*, 85 Va L Rev 1605 (cited in note 43) (responding to this criticism). This objection is, in my view, overblown and in any case is not relevant to my point here.

[49] Issacharoff never explicitly specifies the object of competition when he argues that congressional partisan gerrymanders should be policed to protect competition. In some places, he does suggest a legislature-wide institutional perspective. For example, his emphasis on the responsiveness of the legislative assembly as a whole to shifts in electoral preferences suggests such a perspective. Issacharoff, 116 Harv L Rev at 615 (cited in note 45). Moreover, Issacharoff relies extensively on evidence about the current nationwide competitiveness of congressional races to support his claim that political gerrymanders have produced detrimental anticompetitive effects. Id at 623–24. He highlights the large fraction of congressional seats that are uncompetitive, and suggests that it is the size of this fraction, and not the fact that any individual congressional seat is uncompetitive, that gives rise to the harm. But elsewhere he relies on evidence that is more consistent with a focus on congressional delegations rather than Congress. Id at 623, 625.

[50] As with partisan bias, this conclusion does not mean that it is impossible to intervene state-by-state to police national anticompetitive effects. See note 35. See also Part IV (discussing the possibility of state-by-state intervention). It does mean, however, that courts cannot identify the existence of the anticompetitive harms by examining any individual state's redistricting plan in isolation.

competitive pressure is necessary to make a legislative institution *as a whole* responsive to the will of the electorate. It is true that one way to ensure the responsiveness of the legislative assembly would be to guarantee that every individual legislator is responsive by requiring high levels of interparty competition for every seat. But single-member districted elections are largely incompatible with a rule that requires competitive elections in every district. First, as a practical matter, it will often be difficult or impossible to draw all districts to be competitive. Where a state leans heavily in favor of one party, for example, it is impossible for the general elections in every congressional district to be competitive. Likewise, in places where there are large, geographically compact, politically homogenous groups of voters, there may be no reasonable redistricting arrangement that is capable of carving up these pockets of partisan voters into seats that produce competitive general elections.[51]

Even where districts could be drawn that would make elections in every district competitive—perhaps in some states that are closely divided between the parties, for example—democratic theorists generally agree that it would be a very bad idea to draw districts that produced only close races. If every district were highly competitive, the electoral system would have two features that these theorists often argue are undesirable: first, the system of representation would be extremely volatile; second, it would begin to approach a pure winner-take-all system, where the party that captured a slim majority of the statewide vote could easily capture nearly all of the state's seats.[52] While such a result is not *necessarily* a bad thing, there is no suggestion in the literature that partisan gerrymandering's injury is that it does not create a sufficiently winner-take-all system of representation, and Issacharoff expressly disclaims the idea that this is the anticompetition injury

---

[51] I say "reasonable" because it is technically possible to divide any bloc of partisan voters, so long as one is willing to ignore entirely any interest in drawing districts that are contiguous, compact, etc.—that is, so long as one is willing to abandon any connection between districted elections and physical geography.

[52] In the limiting case where each party captures the same vote share in every district that it captures systemwide (the districts-as-microcosms condition), the electoral structure creates a pure winner-take-all system. The party that captures a majority of the systemwide vote will capture every legislative seat. Drawing lines to produce competition in every district increases the probability of this result.

that concerns him.[53] Accordingly, he acknowledges that the anticompetition account does not operate at the district level; it is perfectly consistent with the account, he concludes, for some individual districts to be noncompetitive.[54]

The fact that it is difficult to make sense of the anticompetition harm at the level of individual districts makes it hard to understand at the congressional delegation level as well. As Issacharoff notes, "[t]he normal distribution of populations across 435 congressional districts will yield a range of districts, from those that are highly competitive and will likely elect centrist candidates or swing from election to election between the two major parties, to those that are more politically homogenous and will gravitate toward the poles of the political spectrum."[55] Once we agree that a perfectly healthy system of congressional representation can contain a number of noncompetitive seats, however, one would need—in order to defend a delegation-specific perspective for the anticompetition harm—an independent justification of why it is undesirable to lump a number of those noncompetitive seats in one congressional delegation. The existing literature contains no account of why it might be undesirable for noncompetitive seats to be clustered closely together as a matter of geography. (And, in fact, there is some empirical evidence that such clustering is a natural tendency for districting in the United States.) Moreover, even if one had a theory about why such geographic clustering was a problem, one would still need to explain why it would make sense to privilege, for purposes of identifying such clustering, the subparts of the legislative institution constituted by each state's congressional districts over subparts of the legislative institution defined in some other fashion. Needless to say, an explanation of this is also absent from the existing literature.

In short, therefore, the anticompetition account of the injury caused by partisan gerrymandering is most sympathetically understood as concerned with the systemwide effect on legislative responsiveness of anticompetitive districting practices. As such,

---

[53] See Issacharoff and Karlan, 153 U Pa L Rev at 574 (cited in note 28). Consider also Issacharoff, 116 Harv L Rev at 628 (cited in note 45) ("No districting scheme could (or should) aspire to recreate the exact partisan balance of the state or jurisdiction as a whole [because] [t]he resulting legislature would replicate the winner-take-all feature of at-large elections . . . .").

[54] See Issacharoff and Karlan, 153 U Pa L Rev at 574 (cited in note 28).

[55] Id.

the injury can only be identified by understanding the electoral consequences of redistricting for congressional representation as a whole. The injury cannot be identified by examining one state's congressional redistricting scheme in isolation.

III. The Possibility of Delegation-Specific Harms

Perhaps an alternative account of the harmfulness of partisan gerrymandering can salvage the delegation-specific focus of congressional gerrymandering cases. In this part, I will discuss a few possibilities. The first is what I will call the polarization account. While this injury theory might seem initially appealing, it turns out to have the same structure as the bias and competition accounts discussed above: the injury is typically conceptualized at the level of the legislative assembly and it is difficult to explain why polarization within a single congressional delegation would be cause for concern. Thus, this alternative account of the harm that flows from partisan gerrymanders does not underwrite the courts' identical treatment of congressional and state legislative political gerrymanders. Second, I will discuss the possibility of rehabilitating the congressional-delegation-specific focus by shifting away from the first-order electoral consequences of redistricting and toward the reasons underlying redistricting legislation. Such a shift in perspective can save the focus on individual congressional redistricting plans, but it can do so only by ignoring the inevitable role partisanship plays in the redistricting process and by abandoning the focus on the actual electoral consequences of redistricting legislation. Last, I will explore the possibility of saving the delegation-specific focus by conceptually disaggregating the major political parties into separate state groups. Disaggregating the parties, however, does nothing to shift the focus of the conventional injury accounts away from the legislature as a whole.

A. THE POLARIZATION ACCOUNT

One possible alternative account is that we might be concerned that partisan gerrymanders will lead to more polarized congressional delegations—that is, that such gerrymanders would systematically eliminate centrist legislators, both Democrat and Republican, even if they did not introduce bias or decrease competition.[56] Despite the superficial appeal of this account, it suffers from two shortcomings. First, the link between partisan gerrymandering and increased polarization is not as clear as is frequently suggested. More important, to the extent such gerrymanders produce polarization, it is polarization of the structure of representation in the legislature as a whole that is a concern, not polarization in any individual district or small subset of the legislative assembly. In other words, this theory of democratic injury shares the same structure as the partisan bias and anticompetition injuries.

Whether partisan gerrymanders lead to the selection of more ideologically extreme legislators is difficult to determine both theoretically and empirically. In part, it depends on the type of partisan gerrymander that a state undertakes. Political gerrymanders are often divided into two types: partisan and bipartisan.[57] Partisan gerrymanders are those in which one political party draws district lines that favor it and harm the other party. In contrast, bipartisan gerrymanders are those in which both parties agree to draw district lines that make each party more secure, without necessarily favoring one party over the other.[58] While the distinction between these two types of gerrymanders is somewhat crude, it can be made

---

[56] Sam Issacharoff and Pam Karlan have recently suggested that polarization represents one of the harms caused by partisan gerrymandering. See Issacharoff and Karlan, 153 U Pa L Rev at 574 (cited in note 28) ("The perverse consequence of the incumbent gerrymander is that it skews the distribution politically by driving the center out of elected office at the legislative level."). Consider also Samuel Issacharoff, *Collateral Damage: The Engendered Center in American Politics*, 46 Wm & Mary L Rev 415, 427–28 (2004) (arguing that partisan gerrymandering eliminates the mechanisms that "pull partisan impulses back toward the electoral center"); Issacharoff, 116 Harv L Rev at 628–29 (cited in note 45) ("If each district can potentially be gerrymandered to render it uncompetitive, the result is to create strong incentives toward polarization as the parties become more susceptible to partisan homogeneity . . . ."). To be clear, however, Issacharoff and Karlan appear to be suggesting a slightly different argument than the one I describe above. They hint (and Issacharoff states more directly in another recent article) that the degree of polarization may be correlated with a lack of accountability to changes in the electorate's political preferences. See Issacharoff and Karlan, 153 U Pa L Rev at 574 (cited in note 28); Issacharoff, 46 Wm & Mary L Rev at 425 (cited in note 56) ("As a result [of polarization], the elected representatives are increasingly removed from the population's preferences and unaccountable to changes in the desires or views of the electorate."). In other words, they link the polarization idea with the anticompetition idea. At least in theory, however, these concepts need not be linked: Congress can become more polarized without becoming less responsive to shifts in electoral preferences.

[57] See, for example, David Butler and Bruce Cain, *Congressional Redistricting: Comparative and Theoretical Perspectives* 9–11 (Macmillan, 1992).

[58] See Gary W. Cox and Jonathan N. Katz, *Elbridge Gerry's Salamander: The Electoral Consequences of the Reapportionment Revolution* 31 (Cambridge, 2001).

more precise by treating partisan gerrymanders as those that introduce *bias* into the system and bipartisan gerrymanders as those that reduce the *competitiveness* (or responsiveness) of the system.[59] In practice, political gerrymanders are often a hybrid of these two types.[60] Nonetheless, distinguishing between bias effects and competition effects is crucial to assessing the claim that partisan gerrymanders lead to a more polarized legislative body.

There is little reason to think that partisan gerrymanders—that is, gerrymanders that introduce bias in favor of one party—will have a systematically polarizing effect on the composition of a state's congressional delegation. In order to introduce bias into a districting arrangement, redistricting authorities take advantage of the fact that voters of different partisanship are not distributed evenly around the state.[61] This uneven distribution makes it possible to draw district lines that affect the expected partisan composition of different districts. To bias a districting plan in favor of Republicans, for example, redistricting authorities "pack" and "crack" voters that tend to support Democrats. Packing Democratic voters into a small number of districts where they constitute large supermajorities ensures Democratic victories in those districts but reduces the total number of seats Democrats capture by increasing the number of wasted Democratic votes—that is, votes cast for Democrats that are either unnecessary or insufficient to win a seat. Cracking, the complement of packing, similarly wastes Democratic votes by splitting blocks of Democratic voters into a number of districts where Republican voters will predominate. By maximizing the number of wasted votes for the other party and minimizing the number of wasted votes for itself, a party in control of redistricting distributes its votes more efficiently, and thereby biases a districting plan in its favor.

While introducing bias into a congressional delegation in this fashion will change the expected partisan composition of each district, it will not necessarily increase the extent to which the

---

[59] Of course, this typology is itself somewhat crude. Under certain conditions, a party in control of the redistricting process might seek to maximize its seat share by increasing responsiveness. See Cox and Katz, *Elbridge Gerry's Salamander* at 33 (cited in note 58).

[60] For a formal description of the redistricting process that models the relationship between bias and responsiveness under different contexts, see id at 31–43 (cited in note 58).

[61] If voter partisanship were evenly distributed, the placement of district lines would have no effect.

composition of the delegation is polarized. As the above explanation demonstrates, in order to increase bias the party in control of redistricting generally has to spread itself more thinly across seats that it hopes to win (in order to lower the number of wasted votes cast in its favor). But the ideological polarization of an individual representative is often thought to be related to how much interparty competition there is for the representative's seat: safe seats produce more polarized representatives because, by definition, the median voter in a district that is closely divided between the two major parties is more centrist than the median voter in a district dominated by one party. Thus, depending on what one thinks the favored party's districts would look like absent the existence of a partisan gerrymander, it may be that representatives elected from many of the favored party's districts will be *less* polarized than they otherwise would have been. While the representatives elected from the packed disfavored party's districts will likely be more polarized (because those districts are likely to be dominated by supermajorities of voters from the disfavored party), it is difficult to know whether the end product of the gerrymander will be to increase or decrease the aggregate level of polarization within the congressional delegation.

In contrast, bipartisan gerrymanders should predictably lead to greater polarization in congressional delegations. Such gerrymanders aim to increase the number of safe, noncompetitive seats, and as explained above these less competitive seats are likely to produce more polarized legislators. Thus, whether political gerrymanders actually have a polarizing effect depends on the type of partisan manipulation undertaken. Nonetheless, because bipartisan gerrymanders should polarize representation (and, more to the point, because most partisan gerrymanders reflect an effort both to introduce bias and to depress competition), this obstacle is not fatal to the polarization account.

Even if congressional political gerrymanders do lead to polarization within congressional delegations in some contexts, however, one would need an independent normative account of why the polarization of a state's congressional delegation was harmful. The central difficulty with developing such an account is that one immediately runs into the same problem encountered in Part II: existing discussions of the consequences and concerns flowing from the polarization of representation typically focus on the risk of polarization in the legislature as a whole. Thus, shifting the focus from bias or competitiveness to the potential harm of polarization likely does not solve the central problem that plagues the conventional harm accounts; like those accounts, the polarization account describes a potential electoral consequence of redistricting that is typically conceptualized at the institutional level of the legislature, rather than at the level of some subset of the legislature.

The reasons for the legislature-wide focus are the same ones we have already seen. Scholars are interested in the concept of polarization because they care about the relationship between the composition of the electorate and the overall structure of representation in legislative institutions. This focus leads naturally to a systemwide institutional perspective. In addition, it is difficult to see how the concept of polarization could have much purchase at lower institutional levels. The polarization account is difficult to square with a district-level perspective for the same reason as the anticompetition account: districted elections tend to produce (and are often considered desirable because they produce) different levels of interparty competition in different districts. As a result, it is too much to expect that every district will produce fairly centrist legislators. And as with the anticompetition account, once one abandons the district-level inquiry, it is difficult to explain why it would matter if a few districts that produced ideological legislators were in close geographic proximity. For this reason, discussions of polarization typically measure and evaluate polarization at the level of the legislature as a whole. Because the polarization account adopts a legislature-wide perspective, the polarizing effect of one state's congressional gerrymander can only be determined by reference to what happens in other states. Thus, this account of partisan gerrymandering's harm cannot save the delegation-specific focus.

As with bias and competition, it is plausible that polarization caused by congressional political gerrymanders will accumulate across states and thereby increase the level of polarization in Congress. This would not salvage the delegation-specific polarization injury, but it would create the possibility of a Congress-wide injury that courts could attempt to remedy by intervening on a state-by-state basis. I discuss in Part IV the potential judicial strategy of intervening at the congressional delegation level to police a legislature-wide injury. My central point here is only that the polarization account does not justify judicial efforts to *identify* the injury by examining a single state's congressional rejecting scheme.

I should note, however, that intervening to prevent Congress as a whole from becoming more polarized would still require a theory about why greater polarization in Congress is harmful. One possibility is that such polarization is harmful because it alters the policy choices that Congress enacts. It is not clear, however, exactly how greater polarization will alter the content of the laws that Congress enacts. The effects of greater polarization on the legislative dynamics of Congress are quite complex. A median voter model of legislative behavior might predict that polarization would have no effect on legislative outcomes, because greater polarization would simply increase the dispersion of legislators without altering the position of the median legislator. In contrast, more deliberative models of congressional behavior might predict that greater polarization would lower the quality of deliberation, resulting in different legislative outcomes. In any event, even if one could demonstrate that polarization altered outcomes, one would need to explain why the outcomes produced by the more polarized Congress are worse. After all, a certain degree of polarization might help curb certain deliberative pathologies that can affect group decision making.[62] Moreover, the idea that the ideological positions of legislators should mirror the ideological positions of voters represents an implicit commitment to a certain conception of representation and a certain set of theories about how democratic decision making should best be structured to produce good outcomes.[63] The question of how representation of centrist attitudes should be traded off against representation of more extreme viewpoints in a legislative assembly is simply not subject to an easy answer.[64]

---

[62] See, for example, Cass Sunstein, *Deliberative Trouble? Why Groups Go to Extremes*, 110 Yale L J 71, 74, 109–10, 114–15 (2000) (explaining that, when groups of like-minded individuals deliberate, they may "predictably move toward a more extreme point in the direction indicated by the members' predeliberation tendencies"). See also Heather Gerken, *Second-Order Diversity and Democracy*, 118 Harv L Rev (forthcoming 2005). Polarization, which increases the difference between the viewpoints of those engaged in deliberation, may, of course, also lead to deliberative pathologies. See Sunstein, 110 Yale L J at 104–05. The point is just that one would need to know more to determine whether increased polarization would be better or worse in particular congressional decision-making contexts.

[63] See generally Hanna F. Pitkin, *The Concept of Representation* (California, 1967).

[64] Note also that it may be a mistake to analyze the polarization of a legislative assembly like Congress in isolation. Polarization in Congress might be counteracted by other voter

My point is not to argue that polarization is unproblematic or affirmatively good. Rather, I just mean to question the easy assumption—an assumption no doubt facilitated by the pejorative connotation to the term itself—that any polarizing effect of congressional gerrymandering is harmful.[65] More fundamentally, polarization, like partisan bias and anticompetitive effects, is a potential democratic harm that is consistently conceptualized at the institutional level of the legislature. The polarization account therefore does not save the effort to identify partisan gerrymandering's harm at the level of individual congressional delegations.

B. THE ILLEGITIMATE PURPOSE ACCOUNT

Another way to rehabilitate the possibility that partisan gerrymandering produces meaningful delegation-specific injuries is to move away from the first-order electoral consequences of such gerrymanders and to focus instead on the process by which redistricting plans are produced.[66] Perhaps the most plausible process-based account of partisan gerrymandering's harm is the illegitimate purpose account. On this view, partisan gerrymanders

---

behavior within our democratic decision-making structure. There is evidence, for example, that increased polarization may strengthen public support for divided government, which can moderate the effects of polarization between the parties or within one institution of the legislative process. See Gary Jacobson, *Party Polarization in National Politics: The Electoral Connection*, in Jon R. Bond and Richard Fleisher, eds, *Polarized Politics: Congress and the President in a Partisan Era* 28–29 (Cong Quarterly, 2000) (*Polarized Politics*).

[65] For the claim that it is harmful or bad for elected officials to be more polarized than the "population as a whole," see Issacharoff, 46 Wm & Mary L Rev at 423–25 (cited in note 56). As I indicated above, it is a bit unclear whether Issacharoff is concerned with polarization itself or with the possibility that increased polarization will reduce the responsiveness of representatives to constituent preferences. See note 56. For some skepticism about this connection, see Richard Fleisher and Jon R. Bond, *Polarized Politics: Does It Matter?* in *Polarized Politics* at 193 (cited in note 64) ("There is little evidence to support a claim that members of Congress have become less responsive to constituent preferences.").

[66] While it might seem easy to describe this shift as a shift from consequentialist to anticonsequentialist theory, it is imprecise to describe the conceptual boundary in this fashion. A theory that does not focus on the direct electoral consequences of redistricting can still be consequentialist; it just does not turn on one particular consequence—the effect of the redistricting plan on the aggregation of votes. Consider Matthew Adler, *Rights Against Rules: The Moral Structure of the American Constitution*, 97 Mich L Rev 1 (1998) (laying out a consequentialist account of constitutional law that focuses on the reasons for government action). For example, consider the possibility that a purposeful but completely ineffectual effort to gerrymander a state's legislative districts would lead the public to see the political process as somehow less legitimate and thereby skew their incentives to participate. The injury would be rooted in the public's perception of the redistricting purpose, but the harm could be understood in consequentialist terms as a function of the changes in political participation that resulted from the loss of perceived legitimacy.

are harmful because it is simply impermissible for the government to undertake redistricting for the *purpose* of partisan gain.[67] This account salvages the possibility of a court determining whether an alleged congressional political gerrymander is harmful without paying attention to any other state's congressional redistricting.[68] (After all, if the harm of partisan gerrymandering does not turn on the electoral consequences of the redistricting plans, then there would be no need to evaluate the combined consequences of every state's congressional redistricting plans in order to determine whether the plans produced an injury.) It would also justify the Court's decision in *Vieth* to review alleged congressional and state legislative partisan gerrymanders in the same way.

There are a variety of theories of constitutional law that might underwrite the position that partisan gerrymandering's harm turns on the reasons for redistricting rather than on the direct electoral consequences of redistricting.[69] While the illegitimate purpose account can therefore supply a coherent explanation of partisan gerrymandering's harm that avoids the difficulties stemming from the disaggregated nature of congressional redistricting, the account remains conclusory. It asserts that partisan gain (or perhaps bipartisan entrenchment) is an impermissible reason for action in the redistricting context, but it does not justify that assertion.[70]

---

[67] Justice Stevens proposed just this conception of harm in *Vieth*. See *Vieth v Jubelirer*, 124 S Ct 1769, 1808–13 (2004).

[68] To be precise, this theory does not require reference to *any* set or subset of districts because its focus is on the process through which a state produces its districts, rather than on the districts produced by that process.

[69] See, for example, Paul Brest, *Palmer v. Thompson: An Approach to the Problem of Unconstitutional Legislative Motive*, 1971 Supreme Court Review 95 (providing a political process–based account of why governmental decisions should be unconstitutional when they are motivated by illegitimate purposes); Richard H. Pildes and Elizabeth S. Anderson, *Expressive Theories of Law: A General Restatement*, 148 U Pa L Rev 1503, 1531 (2000) (arguing that the government should be prohibited from undertaking actions for certain morally impermissible reasons because "state action should be wrong . . . when it expresses impermissible valuations, without regard to further concerns about its cultural or material consequences"); Adler, 97 Mich L Rev 1 (cited in note 66) (arguing that constitutional rights should be understood to be "rights against rules"—that is, as prohibitions on the government infringing upon certain interests for impermissible reasons, rather than as shields protecting certain actions from government regulation). To be clear, these theories do not always equate the reasons for government action with legislative purpose as it is conventionally understood. See, for example, Pildes and Anderson, 148 U Pa L Rev at 1524–25 (making clear that their concern is with the social meaning of government action). For present purposes, however, these distinctions are not important.

[70] For an argument that partisan gain is a perfectly acceptable goal in the redistricting process, see Daniel H. Lowenstein and Jonathan Steinberg, *The Quest for Legislative Districting in the Public Interest: Elusive or Illusory?* 33 UCLA L Rev 1, 73–75 (1986).

In fact, there is reason to think that would be extremely difficult to justify the conclusion that partisan gain is an impermissible reason for action in the redistricting context—that is, unless one was prepared to invalidate every redistricting plan enacted by a legislature.[71] So long as legislatures are principally responsible for redrawing districts in this country, partisan advantage-seeking will be an inevitable component of redistricting. The Supreme Court has repeatedly recognized this fact,[72] and in *Vieth* nearly every member of the Court rejected the notion that proving partisan purpose itself could be enough to demonstrate that a redistricting plan constituted an unconstitutional political gerrymander.[73] Only Justice Stevens suggested that purpose alone should be the touch-stone of the inquiry: he argued that where "the predominant motive of the legislators who designed [a district] . . . was a purpose to discriminate against a political minority, that invidious purpose should invalidate the district."[74]

To be fair, Justice Stevens does not appear to advocate invalidating every district drawn in part with an eye to the partisan consequences of redistricting. Instead, he concludes that a district should be unconstitutional only where political discrimination was the "predominant motive" of the legislators.[75] Stevens borrows the

---

[71] Moreover, one cannot bootstrap electoral consequences into this theory by arguing that it makes sense to prohibit partisan purpose on the ground that partisan purpose is likely to be accompanied by partisan effects. If reasons for action are really just a proxy for expected effects, the theory collapses back into the theories discussed in the previous part that were concerned with the electoral consequences of redistricting. To treat reasons (or purpose) as a proxy for effect requires that one identify the "effect" about which one cares, which simply reintroduces the problem of choosing an institutional level from which to identify those effects.

[72] See, for example, *Davis v Bandemer*, 478 US 109, 128–29 (1986). See also *Gaffney v Cummings*, 412 US 735, 753 (1973) ("The reality is that districting inevitably has and is intended to have substantial political consequences.").

[73] See *Vieth*, 124 S Ct at 1785–86 (plurality); id at 1796–97 (Kennedy concurring); id at 1817–19 (Souter, joined by Ginsburg, dissenting); id at 1823–25 (Breyer dissenting). See also *Davis v Bandemer*, 478 US 109, 127, 130 (1986) (holding that the plaintiffs were required to show both discriminatory purpose and effect in order to demonstrate the existence of an unconstitutional partisan gerrymander).

[74] *Vieth*, 124 S Ct at 1810 (Stevens dissenting); id at 1799 ("In my view, when partisanship is the legislature's *sole motivation* . . . the governing body cannot be said to have acted impartially."); id at 1801 (suggesting "purpose as the ultimate inquiry"); id at 1804 ("State action that discriminates . . . for the sole and unadorned purpose of maximizing the power of the majority plainly violates the decision-maker's duty to remain impartial."); id ("Thus, the critical issue in both racial and political gerrymandering cases is the same: whether a single non-neutral criterion controlled the districting process to such an extent that the Constitution was offended."). Consider also *Cox v Larios*, 124 S Ct 2806, 2808 (2004) (Stevens concurring).

[75] *Vieth*, 124 S Ct at 1810.

"predominant motive" test from the *Shaw v Reno*[76] strand of the Supreme Court's racial redistricting doctrine—the one other area of redistricting jurisprudence where the Court has stated that redistricting arrangements might be impermissible by virtue of the reasons that they were enacted, regardless of the effects of the redistricting schemes.[77] In *Shaw* and its progeny, the Court concluded that districts drawn for the predominant purpose of segregating voters by race are unconstitutional.[78] The electoral consequences of the district lines challenged in *Shaw* litigation are doctrinally irrelevant to their constitutionality.[79] But not every redistricting scheme drawn with race in mind is automatically invalid under the *Shaw* doctrine—only those districts drawn with race as a predominant purpose.[80]

While requiring that partisan gain be the "predominant purpose" does alleviate slightly the concern that the illegitimate purpose account would render unconstitutional every redistricting plan drawn by a legislative assembly, it introduces other significant problems. Perhaps the most serious is that it is extremely difficult to figure out how a court can distinguish between cases where partisanship simply plays a role in the redistricting process and cases where partisan gain is the "predominant purpose." This problem has plagued the *Shaw* jurisprudence from its outset. In fact, many commentators have argued that this difficulty renders *Shaw*'s predominant motive test completely unworkable, or perhaps even theoretically incoherent.[81]

---

[76] 509 US 630 (1993).

[77] *Vieth*, 124 S Ct at 1802–04.

[78] See *Miller v Johnson*, 515 US 900, 915–16 (1995).

[79] Because the *Shaw* injury focuses on legislative motivations, it is conceptually distinct from a vote dilution claim; in fact, the *Shaw* plaintiffs specifically declined to allege that their voting power had been reduced by the voting scheme. See *Shaw*, 509 US at 641 ("In their complaint, appellants did not claim that the General Assembly's reapportionment plan unconstitutionally 'diluted' white voting strength."). See also Adam B. Cox, *Citizenship, Standing, and Immigration Law*, 92 Cal L Rev 373, 399 n 116 (2004). That said, *Shaw* itself hints that the origins of the doctrine may have been connected to Justice O'Connor's concern that drawing a district principally on the basis of race would affect the political dynamics within that district. See *Shaw*, 509 US at 647–48 (discussing possible representational harm).

[80] In other words, purpose is treated as a continuous variable, rather than as a dichotomous variable.

[81] See, for example, Richard H. Pildes, *Principled Limitations on Racial and Partisan Redistricting*, 106 Yale L J 2505 (1997); Pamela S. Karlan, *Still Hazy After All These Years: Voting Rights in the Post-Shaw Era*, 26 Cumb L Rev 287 (1996). See also *Bush v Vera*, 517 US 952, 1059–62, 1069–71 (1996) (Souter dissenting).

Even if these difficulties could be overcome, a purely purposive account of partisan gerrymandering's harms runs counter to the predominant thrust of most contemporary redistricting scholarship, which focuses more and more today on functional, structural approaches to the constitutional regulation of the political process.[82] For example, such a functional approach appears to be at the heart of Pildes and Issacharoff's antitrust theory of political process regulation. That approach seeks to "invert the focus of constitutional doctrine from the foreground of rights and equality to the background rules that structure partisan political competition"—that is, to focus attention on the actual electoral consequences of rules that regulate the political process.[83] As I described above, Issacharoff has argued that this functional focus should guide partisan gerrymandering jurisprudence, with courts invalidating redistricting schemes that are likely to have anticompetitive effects on political representation. And in other areas legal scholars have advocated a similar focus on electoral consequences: Nathaniel Persily, for example, has defended political party autonomy in primary elections on the ground that such autonomy preserves political competition.[84] While these approaches are certainly not logically incompatible with reason-for-action-based approaches that do not focus on electoral consequences,[85] they do highlight the extent to which this alternative conception of injury is atypical in the literature today.

In short, while the illegitimate purpose account of partisan gerrymandering's harm does make it possible to rehabilitate the attempts in *Vieth* to identify the injuries of congressional partisan gerrymandering by reference to individual states, moving toward such an account would require a fairly substantial about-face in

---

[82] Of course, this contemporary trend is by no means limited to the political process domain of constitutional law.

[83] Pildes and Issacharoff, 50 Stan L Rev at 648 (cited in note 43).

[84] Nathaniel Persily, *Toward a Functional Defense of Political Party Autonomy*, 76 NYU L Rev 750, 752 (2001).

[85] It is possible, for example, to be concerned both about the structural consequences of a law as well as its expressive significance. Richard Pildes, for example, appears to hold both commitments. He is a principal advocate for policing expressive harms through the constitutional regulation of the political process, see, for example, Richard H. Pildes and Richard G. Niemi, *Expressive Harms, "Bizarre Districts," and Voting Rights: Evaluating Election-District Appearances After Shaw v. Reno*, 92 Mich L Rev 483 (1993), and is also concerned about policing laws that have anticompetitive effects on the political process, see, for example, Pildes and Issacharoff, 50 Stan L Rev at 644–52 (cited in note 43).

both the academy and the courts. It would also risk calling into question the constitutionality of nearly every districting plan in the country.

C. DEFINING PARTISAN "GROUPS"

Finally, one might try to save *Vieth*'s focus on individual congressional delegations by contesting the definition of the relevant partisan groups. Up to this point, I have focused principally on the effects of redistricting for the electoral prospects of the two major parties—Democrats and Republicans. This focus is common in the literature. One might claim, however, that it is wrong to treat Democrats and Republicans as monolithic groups. Perhaps it is more appropriate to disaggregate the political parties state by state. Treating the parties in each state as distinct would make it possible for a court in one state to compare the relative effects of a redistricting plan on the political parties in that state without reference to the treatment of other states' parties. For example, a court could evaluate a single state's congressional redistricting plan to determine whether the plan contained partisan bias in favor of one state party or the other. By definition, it might seem, this would solve the disaggregation problem and restore the delegation-specific focus.

This is all true so far as it goes. But there are two substantial difficulties with this line of argument. First is the problem that the same criticism could be leveled against the claim that a state-level focus is appropriate. Republicans or Democrats from any single state are far from monolithic, so this line of argument runs the risk of an infinite regress, the conclusion of which is that there is no way of talking sensibly about partisan groups—or at least that the institutional level from which one defines such groups is arbitrary.

The threat of a regress shows that there is no "natural" institutional level from which partisan representation must always be defined.[86] In part, this point reinforces the central thesis of this article, which is that it is a mistake for courts or scholars unquestioningly to adopt a state-level institutional perspective for eval-

---

[86] For a general theoretical argument that voters should care about the composition of legislative assemblies, rather than the composition of some subpart of such assemblies, see Jean-Pierre Benoit and Lewis A. Kornhauser, *Assembly-Based Preferences, Candidate-Based Procedures, and the Voting Rights Act*, 68 S Cal L Rev 1503 (1995).

uating the partisan consequences of congressional redistricting. My point, however, is not to develop a comprehensive theory about how to define the boundaries of partisan groups in all circumstances. Nor is my point that the focus of congressional redistricting must necessarily be on national, rather than local, representation. My modest point is simply that the existing accounts about why we should care about partisan gerrymandering define the injuries that they identify by reference to characteristics of the system as a whole.

More important, the delegation-specific focus cannot be saved by redefining the relevant partisan groups because it is the theory of injury, and not the scope of the relevant partisan groups, that determines the appropriate institutional level of focus. Even if it is correct that the best account of partisan groups would disaggregate those groups into state-party units, such disaggregation is not sufficient to support the claim that the injuries caused by congressional gerrymandering are delegation specific. Consider, for example, the conventional injury of partisan bias. This account of redistricting is concerned with the effect of redistricting on the relative ability of parties to translate electoral support into power in the legislative assembly. Defining the parties as state party units rather than as national parties does not change this focus; it just increases from two to one hundred the number of (major) parties whose legislative power is at issue. In other words, disaggregating the parties would, on the partisan bias account of injury, increase the number of dimensions in the bias calculation, rather than decreasing the institutional level of inquiry.[87] Certainly, one would care about whether Democrats from Texas were disadvantaged relative to Republicans from Texas in their ability to translate electoral support into power in Congress. But one would also care about whether Democrats from Texas were disadvantaged relative to Democrats from Michigan in this respect.[88] For that reason, a

---

[87] For one explanation of how bias can be calculated in situations where there are more than two parties, see King, 15 Legis Stud Q at 161–67 (cited in note 33).

[88] In the post-Founding period, when the major parties were not the same across states, there was just this sort of interstate conflict between the power of parties from small and large states. Small states tended to use at-large congressional elections during this period, while large states used districted elections. The different electoral procedures affected the composition of the states' congressional delegations, because while the minority party tends to be overwhelmed in an at-large election, it stands a greater chance of success in districted elections. Thus, during this period the "small states sent more politically unified delegations to Congress than did large states. . . . [And because the small states' more

court evaluating Texas's redistricting scheme would still need to refer to Michigan's districting scheme, as well as the districting arrangement in every other state, in order to determine whether the system contained partisan bias. Disaggregating the parties does not, therefore, define away the institutional-level problem.

IV. RETHINKING VIETH

The Court's approach to the central justiciability question in *Vieth* was therefore misguided. The Justices in *Vieth* disagreed sharply about the answer to the question whether claims of congressional partisan gerrymandering should be justiciable. But they all approached the question in roughly the same fashion: nearly all of the Justices focused exclusively on whether a test could be developed that would identify the constitutional harms flowing from an individual state's putative congressional partisan gerrymander.[89] As I have shown, this approach is unlikely to succeed. To the extent that the harm of congressional gerrymanders can only be identified from a legislature-wide institutional perspective, the Court will inevitably fail if it tries to pin the injury on individual congressional redistricting plans.[90]

---

unified delegations tended to vote more frequently] as a bloc, they exercised an influence disproportionate to their numbers in the lower house." Rosemarie Zagarri, *The Politics of Size* 126–27 (1987). This difference between the power of political parties from small and large states led to repeated efforts in Congress to require districted elections throughout the country. See id at 128–31. In 1842, Congress finally adopted such a requirement, which remains on the books today. See 2 USC § 2c.

[89] The one partial exception is Justice Kennedy, who appeared to acknowledge that the aggregate consequences of congressional redistricting in several states might be relevant to the constitutional inquiry. See text accompanying note 26. While his opinion in *Vieth* has been perhaps the most widely derided, therefore, it may be the only opinion that points toward the shift in institutional perspective that the Court needs to make if it is to successfully police congressional partisan gerrymanders.

[90] Note that I am arguing only that courts should approach congressional and state legislative partisan gerrymanders differently because the former present special problems for any effort to *identify* the existence of the relevant constitutional injury. There is, of course, another reason why it might be that courts should treat these two types of gerrymanders differently: one type might pose a greater constitutional danger than the other because of the different political contexts in which they occur. For example, it might be that courts should police state legislative redistricting more closely because it involves self-interested state legislators drawing *their own* districts, while congressional redistricting does not. As I have noted elsewhere, the perception that state legislative redistricting presents a more direct conflict of interest may explain in part why more states have stripped their legislatures of authority over state legislative redistricting than over congressional redistricting. See Cox, 79 NYU L Rev at 793 (cited in note 12). See also id (questioning whether this distinction makes much sense in the contemporary political climate, where there is evidence of strong national political party influence over state parties in the redistricting arena). But this different set of potential reasons for distinguishing between

If the Court were to adopt a nationwide perspective in congressional partisan gerrymandering cases and give up on its efforts to figure out whether individual states' congressional redistricting schemes did or did not produce constitutionally cognizable harms, it would be left with three options: develop tests to measure directly the harm of congressional gerrymanders at the legislature-wide level; give up on trying to develop criteria for measuring the harm directly and focus instead on developing constitutional rules that reduce the *risk* that state redistricting efforts will combine to produce a Congress-wide injury; or abandon judicial review of congressional partisan gerrymanders altogether.

The first option is wholly impractical. Federal courts would have an extremely difficult time testing for Congress-wide harms, because doing so would require courts to evaluate every state's congressional redistricting plan simultaneously. Such an approach would be thwarted by a number of serious coordination problems both among courts and within the states that produce congressional redistricting plans. For these reasons, a shift toward risk-based regulation is a more attractive option. Federal courts can, in theory, reduce the risk of Congress-wide injuries by intervening at the state level. But the possibility that courts can intervene state by state to police congressional partisan gerrymanders does not mean that decisions about justiciability and doctrinal structure can remain identical for state legislative and congressional redistricting. To the contrary, the disaggregated nature of congressional redistricting leads to unique justiciability questions and has important practical implications for how judicial review of congressional gerrymanders will have to differ from the review of state legislative gerrymanders.

A. THE IMPRACTICALITY OF NATIONWIDE REVIEW

Federal courts probably cannot develop tests to identify directly the existence of Congress-wide harms produced by congressional gerrymanders. Doing so would require either that many courts coordinate their review of redistricting plans, or that an individual court review every state's redistricting plan simultaneously—neither of which is a particularly plausible option.

Congressional partisan gerrymandering lawsuits have histori-

---

state legislative and congressional redistricting (which are also overlooked by the Court) is not the focus of this article.

cally been framed as challenges to a single state's redistricting plan.[91] Unsurprisingly, courts in such litigation have focused only on the redistricting scheme before them.[92] As the above discussion makes clear, however, if federal courts continue this practice they will be incapable of identifying the presence of any legislature-wide injuries produced by the decennial congressional redistricting process. That harm can be identified only by reference to the districting plans of all other states in addition to the state whose redistricting plan the court is evaluating. Under the current judicial practices for reviewing redistricting schemes, therefore, federal courts will not be capable of identifying the injuries that have been the primary focus of the partisan gerrymandering literature.

Although partisan gerrymandering litigation is not currently structured to enable courts to evaluate legislature-wide injuries caused by congressional redistricting, this does not mean that such review is impossible. Courts could modify their review of partisan gerrymandering claims in an effort to identify such injuries. (Or, to put it from the perspective of litigation strategy, lawyers could reframe their partisan gerrymandering challenges.) In order to evaluate congressional redistricting plans for Congress-wide injuries, courts could do one of two things: First, one court could evaluate every state's congressional redistricting plan simultaneously to determine whether the plans, in the aggregate, biased the composition of Congress, depressed competition, or caused some other injury to the structure of representation in Congress as a whole. Alternatively, multiple courts could coordinate their review of individual states' redistricting plans in some fashion that would permit each court to review only one state's plan while ensuring that the conclusions drawn about each state's plan were aggregated to determine whether the plans in combination caused an impermissible harm.[93]

---

[91] See, for example, *Martinez v Bush*, 234 F Supp 2d 1275 (SD Fla 2002); *Badham v Eu*, 694 F Supp 664 (1988). See also note 27.

[92] See, for example, cases cited in notes 27, 91.

[93] Note that review of congressional redistricting does not present the same kind of coordination problem that often arises when a decentralized judiciary regulates a national activity—or, to be more precise, any activity that extends across multiple judicial districts. There, the difficulty is caused by the disaggregated nature of judicial review and can be solved by consolidating judicial review in one body, either initially (as with statutory rules that force all legal challenges to certain statutes into the district court for the District of Columbia) or on appeal (as with the Judiciary Act's rules of appellate jurisdiction that give the Supreme Court final say over most questions of federal law). With respect to con-

The second possibility seems extremely far-fetched. There are currently no mechanisms that would facilitate that sort of complex coordination between Article III courts. The first possibility seems superficially more plausible, but in practice it would present substantial problems as well. The evidentiary complexity of the task itself might tax judicial competence. Under the conventional injury accounts, for example, a court would have to evaluate the redistricting plans from all fifty states in order to determine whether congressional redistricting around the country had introduced partisan bias or anticompetitive effects.

Sheer complexity aside, simultaneously evaluating the congressional districts from every state poses its own set of coordination problems. The difficulty arises because different states' congressional districting plans are not created at the same time and do not remain stable over time. Although states are required to redraw their congressional districts following the release of each census,[94] states undertake the task of redistricting at somewhat different times.[95] (At least one state—Maine—does not revise its district lines until more than two years after the census.)[96] Moreover, the redistricting plans that states initially adopt are often challenged under the Voting Rights Act, the federal Constitution, state law, or some combination of all three. The districts are thus often in flux, which would introduce substantial uncertainty into any attempt to evaluate every state's congressional redistricting scheme simultaneously: at any point, one or more districting schemes could be either invalidated or revised, further complicating the

---

gressional redistricting, however, the difficulty is caused by the disaggregated nature of the government action being reviewed, not by the disaggregated nature of the federal judiciary.

[94] See *Georgia v Ashcroft*, 539 US 461, 489 n 2 (2003); *Reynolds v Sims*, 377 US 533, 583–84 (1964). See also Cox, 79 NYU L Rev at 758 n 36, 801 (cited in note 12) (explaining that this requirement originated as a presumption and grew into an apparently prophylactic requirement).

[95] States ordinarily must redistrict in time to have a new districting plan in place for the first round of elections following the release of the Census. See *Growe v Emison*, 507 US 25, 35–37 (1993). See also Cox, 79 NYU L Rev at 758 n 37, 778 n 102 (cited in note 12).

[96] Maine Const, Art IV, pt 1, § 2 ("The Legislature which convenes in 1983 and every 10th year thereafter shall cause the State to be divided into districts for the choice of one Representative for each district."); id Art IV, pt 2, § 2 ("The Legislature which shall convene in the year 1983 and every tenth year thereafter shall cause the State to be divided into districts for the choice of a Senator from each district, using the same method as provided in Article IV, Part First, Section 2 for apportionment of Representative Districts.").

efforts of a court to evaluate the state plans in the aggregate. And unfortunately, this difficulty cannot be avoided simply by delaying review of partisan gerrymandering claims until other legal challenges are resolved, because litigation over a state's redistricting scheme has been known to stretch over the course of the entire decade.[97] Solving this problem, therefore, would require radically revising the entire contemporary redistricting regulatory structure.

Finally, either of the two above approaches poses an additional problem at the remedial stage of litigation. Even if one of the approaches made it possible for a court (or courts) to identify the existence of a legislature-wide harm caused by the partisan gerrymandering of congressional delegations, there would remain the question of how to remedy that harm. Because each state's redistricting plan would have contributed to the harm, it would be incoherent to conclude that only state X or Y was the cause of the injury and therefore that only state X or Y should have its redistricting plan invalidated. Joint causation precludes the possibility of easily assigning blame to any particular state. Relatedly, it would often be possible to remedy the harm in a number of different ways, each of which would require revising the districts in a different state or set of states.[98] Accordingly, there would be no obvious way to figure out which states' plans to invalidate or revise at the remedial stage of litigation. And absent a theory about how to make this choice, the decision would be essentially arbitrary.

B.   RISK-BASED REGULATION AND STATE-LEVEL REVIEW

While courts are unlikely to be able to simultaneously evaluate the effect of multiple congressional redistricting plans, this does not necessarily mean that *Vieth*'s justiciability holding was wrong and that courts should get out of the business of policing congressional partisan gerrymanders. The question remains whether

---

[97] See, for example, *Hunt v Cromartie*, 121 S Ct 1452 (2001). Moreover, there are additional reasons that delay might be disfavored. Perhaps most obviously, delay might mean that elections would be conducted under gerrymandered congressional redistricting maps that were later determined to cause an impermissible harm.

[98] Heather Gerken has identified a similar dilemma in the context of racial vote dilution litigation. See Heather K. Gerken, *Understanding the Right to an Undiluted Vote*, 114 Harv L Rev 1663, 1700–02 (2001).

courts can police the nationwide harms of congressional gerrymandering by intervening state by state. If this is possible, then
the prescription that would follow from recognizing the disaggregated nature of congressional redistricting would be that the
Court should shift its focus—away from *Vieth*'s effort to develop
a test for directly measuring the harms of congressional gerrymanders, and toward an approach that reduces the risk that individual states' redistricting plans combine to produce cognizable
harms.[99]

In theory, courts can reduce the risk of Congress-wide injuries
through state-by-state intervention. Whether they can do so in
practice is another matter, precisely because of the differences
between state legislative and congressional redistricting. First,
whether intervention is worthwhile in the congressional context
turns on questions that are irrelevant in the state context—such
as whether the effects of congressional redistricting in each state
tend to combine to produce nationwide harms or, instead, tend
to cancel out. Perhaps more important, the disaggregated nature
of congressional redistricting has implications for how judicial
intervention should (and should not) be structured—beyond the
preliminary question whether judicial intervention is at all warranted. In particular, some doctrinal rules courts might use to
police state legislative gerrymanders would not be effective at policing congressional gerrymanders and might even make matters
worse.

1. *The theoretical possibility of risk-based regulation.* State-by-state
judicial intervention can in theory reduce the possibility of the
legislature-wide injuries described by the conventional accounts
of partisan gerrymandering's harms. Consider, for example, the
partisan bias account of injury. As a theoretical matter, it is clear
that judicial intervention at the state level could reduce the probability that a significant level of bias would accumulate across state
plans (so long as judicial intervention actually had the effect of
reducing partisan bias in congressional delegations). Imagine, for
example, that without judicial intervention each state's redistricting process produces some variable amount of state-level bias in
favor of one party or another. There is some probability that these

---

[99] Given the extent to which the Supreme Court has struggled to supply a coherent
partisan gerrymandering jurisprudence, setting judicial review of congressional gerrymanders on more solid theoretical footing would itself represent an important step forward.

state-level biases will accumulate to produce an objectionable national level bias, rather than essentially canceling out. The greater the average amount of bias generated by each state, the greater the probability of getting an unacceptable level of national bias.[100]

Thus, if courts could reduce the amount of bias in each state's plan from some positive amount to zero, judicial intervention would essentially eliminate the possibility of impermissible national bias.[101] Of course, producing this outcome would require perfect policing by courts—an unlikely scenario. Even absent perfect policing, however, judicial intervention can lower the likelihood that an unacceptable level of bias will accumulate.[102] So long as courts reduce the level of bias in each state congressional plan in some relatively uniform fashion,[103] they will decrease the probability that the state-level biases will accumulate into an unacceptable level of national bias.[104]

---

[100] This is because the higher levels of bias in each state will stretch out the distribution of bias across states. The fatter this distribution, the higher the statistical likelihood that aggregating across states will yield a high level of national bias. To see this more clearly, consider the skinny limiting case—where every state's bias equals zero. In that case, there is no chance that the state-level biases will accumulate to produce a national-level bias.

[101] See note 100.

[102] For an example of a risk-based regulatory approach that should lower the likelihood of high levels of national bias, consider Cox, 79 NYU L Rev 751 (cited in note 12) (discussing a prohibition on states redistricting more than once per decennial redistricting cycle).

[103] The caveat "relatively uniform" is necessary because if courts differ dramatically in how effective they are at lowering bias in congressional delegations then it is not clear that judicial intervention in every state will lower the likelihood of partisan bias in Congress. To see this, take the extreme case in which only one or two courts were at all effective at policing bias in congressional delegations. "Successful" intervention in one or two states may be worse than no intervention at all. See text accompanying notes 113–18.

[104] The same analysis holds for the anticompetition injury described in Part II. It might be tempting to argue that the analysis of anticompetitive effects should be different on the ground that such effects, by their nature, will only accumulate (rather than cancel out) across districts. After all, one might argue, the effects are *anticompetitive*—never *pro*-competitive. But such an argument engages in definitional sleight of hand. The fact that the literature does not talk about a baseline for competition in the same way that it does a baseline for partisan bias does not mean that there is no baseline; it just means that the baseline is unspecified. Accordingly, the aggregation of competition-based effects can in theory be modeled in the same way as bias effects, with some state plans favoring competition and some disfavoring it in the same way that some state plans favor Democrats while some disfavor them (by favoring Republicans). It may be true, of course, that no state plans favor competition—though more would need to be said about the appropriate competitiveness baseline in order to determine this. Even if this is true, however, the question remains whether the state-by-state effects accumulate to produce an objectionable Congress-wide anticompetitive effect. The distribution of state plans around the baseline will affect our predictions about the likelihood of this occurring (in the same way that our predictions about the possibility of bias accumulating would be different if we were

2. *The practice of risk-based regulation.* While courts can in theory use state-by-state intervention to police congressional gerrymanders, this does not mean that partisan gerrymandering jurisprudence can continue to be the same for both state legislative and congressional redistricting. Judicial intervention in the congressional context will still need to differ in potentially substantial ways from intervention in the state legislative context.

First, whether judicial intervention is worthwhile in the congressional context turns on questions that are irrelevant in the state legislative context. Judicial intervention can in theory lower the probability that state redistricting schemes combine to produce Congress-wide injuries. But if that probability is low in the first place, judicial intervention becomes less appealing.[105] Moreover, intervention is less attractive if state-by-state intervention can only reduce that probability by a small amount. Without knowing anything about the likelihood that harm will accumulate or about the extent to which courts can reduce this likelihood, therefore, we cannot meaningfully evaluate the value of judicial intervention.

Thus, the correctness of *Vieth*'s ultimate conclusion that courts should continue to police congressional partisan gerrymanders turns importantly on the answer to empirical questions—about how likely it is that injuries will aggregate substantially, and how likely it is that courts will improve the situation. These questions are underexplored. With respect to the partisan bias account, for example, the legal literature rarely asks whether state-by-state manipulation regularly leads to substantial levels of national partisan bias. While the political science literature has engaged the question a bit more directly, it is somewhat divided on the answer. For many years empirical work on this question reported "relatively moderate partisan effects state by state, which cumulate into even smaller net national effects."[106] More recent work, however, raises

---

told that the Democrats controlled the redistricting process in all fifty states), but the basic question remains the same.

[105] There is, of course, always the problem of setting a threshold above which systemwide bias should be considered substantial or unacceptable. But this difficulty is present whether one seeks to police partisan bias at the delegation- or Congress-wide level. Therefore, the debate about what degree of deviation from partisan symmetry the system should accept without intervention is orthogonal to the question of which institutional level is the appropriate one from which to evaluate partisan symmetry.

[106] Cox and Katz, *Elbridge Gerry's Salamander* at 21 (cited in note 58). See also id at 21 ("The view now prevailing in the literature is that redistricting is unlikely to produce any net partisan gains at the national level . . . ."); Butler and Cain, *Congressional Redistricting* at 8 (cited in note 57) (noting that "the electoral system has little or no systematic partisan

the possibility that state-by-state effects can aggregate to produce substantial national effects.[107]

The question of what courts should do in the face of this uncertainty—until better evidence is available—turns on a variety of institutional concerns that are well beyond the scope of this paper.[108] The important point, however, is that these questions about the risk-based approach all bear on whether it is even worth regulating congressional partisan gerrymanders. But they are irrelevant to this threshold determination in the state legislative context.

Beyond the question whether intervention is warranted, the disaggregated nature of congressional redistricting alters the type of state-level intervention that will be effective at policing congressional gerrymanders. Courts will not necessarily be able to apply identical doctrinal rules in the state legislative and congressional context, because some doctrinal rules that might work in the state legislative context simply will not work in the congressional context. An example of such a rule is the one that Justice Breyer proposed in *Vieth*. Breyer proposed that the Court invalidate redistricting plans that improperly enable a minority of voters to capture a majority of the state's seats.[109] He selected this rule to preserve legislative majoritarianism.[110] As I explained earlier, the rule does preserve legislative majoritarianism when it is applied to state legislative gerrymanders, but it does not directly protect that principle when it is applied to congressional gerrymanders.[111] In the congressional context, the rule only directly ensures majority control of an individual congressional delegation. And while it is perhaps easy to think that applying this rule, state by state, to congressional redistricting would have the indirect effect of

---

bias and that the net gains nationally from redistricting for one part over the other are very small").

[107] See Cox and Katz, *Elbridge Gerry's Salamander* at 51–54 (cited in note 58) (providing evidence that congressional redistricting produced a substantial pro-Republican bias in Congress before the reapportionment revolution in the 1960s). See also Hirsch, 2 Election L J at 190–95 (cited in note 33) (arguing that the last round of congressional redistricting produced a nationwide bias in favor of the Republicans of something like twenty-five seats).

[108] For an extended discussion of judicial decision making in the context of uncertainty, see Adrian Vermeule, *Judging Under Uncertainty: An Institutional Account of Legal Interpretation* (unpublished manuscript).

[109] See *Vieth v Jubelirer*, 124 S Ct 1769, 1825 (2004) (Breyer dissenting). See also text accompanying notes 37–42.

[110] See *Vieth*, 124 S Ct at 1825. See also text accompanying notes 37–42.

[111] See text accompanying note 42.

preserving legislative majoritarianism in Congress, it would not. Striking down congressional plans that allowed a minority of voters in the state to capture control of the delegation would not have the cumulative national effect of guarding against the possibility that a minority of voters nationwide could control a majority of seats in Congress.[112] If the Court were to adopt Breyer's goal of preserving legislative majoritarianism, therefore, it should not attempt to advance that goal by applying Breyer's rule in both contexts.

There are, of course, some rules for state-level intervention that might work well in both the state legislative and congressional contexts.[113] Even with respect to such rules, however, courts have to be attentive to an additional coordination problem in the congressional context that is not present in the state legislative context. The idea that state-by-state intervention can substitute in some cases for simultaneously assessing every state's redistricting plan depends crucially on reviewing courts' adopting the same rules for intervention and then applying those rules in roughly the same fashion. In other words, the possibility of risk-based regulation is contingent on the reviewing courts' coordinating around a set of rules to apply when they review congressional redistricting.[114] For federal courts this would require that myriad lower courts speak with a fairly uniform voice—which may be possible only on an overly optimistic view of federal courts.[115] And in the absence of

---

[112] An electoral minority can capture a majority of seats within a particular jurisdiction where two conditions obtain: the presence of partisan bias and the existence of a (relatively) closely divided electorate. In order to reduce the possibility of minority control in the congressional context, therefore, courts would need a rule designed to lower the national level of partisan bias. But applying Breyer's rule state by state would not do this. It would only strike down biased plans in states where the electorate was closely divided. Other states, however, might contain much larger levels of bias but be valid under his rule, either because the state was not closely divided or because the bias favored the electoral majority rather than the electoral minority. For example, a congressional redistricting plan in which partisan bias made it possible for a small electoral *majority* to capture essentially all of the seats in the state would be sustained under his proposed rule.

[113] As I mentioned above, a rule prohibiting redistricting more than once each decade might be such a rule.

[114] This is a different coordination problem than the one discussed in Part IV.A. That section was concerned with the difficulty courts would have coordinating their *review* of congressional redistricting in order to assess the combined effects of every state's congressional redistricting scheme. If courts adopt a risk-based regulatory strategy they will not have to coordinate their review. But they will have to coordinate around a set of doctrinal rules.

[115] See Adrian Vermeule, *The Judiciary is a They, Not an It: Interpretation and the Fallacy of Division*, J Contemp Legal Issues (forthcoming 2005).

effective coordination, the nonuniform application of the rules in federal courts could make an otherwise attractive risk-based regulatory strategy ineffectual or counterproductive.[116]

This coordination problem highlights an overlooked shortcoming of one of the most popular post-*Vieth* reform proposals. Following the Supreme Court's refusal in *Vieth* to police partisan gerrymandering more vigorously, a number of commentators have called on state courts to interpret their state constitutions to endorse more aggressive judicial oversight of partisan redistricting.[117] These commentators have uniformly assumed that state court oversight is a good substitute for federal court intervention. But state courts may be inferior in the context of congressional redistricting. If the success of state-by-state intervention depends on there being a uniform, nationwide rule for such intervention, then the piecemeal adoption of congressional partisan gerrymandering doctrines by different state courts might be ineffective. Such intervention could be ineffective if it were adopted in only a limited number of states, and could also be ineffective if different states adopted markedly different rules for intervention.

In fact, the decision by any given state court to read its state constitution to endorse broad oversight of congressional partisan gerrymanders could potentially even exacerbate the problem. If a state court in a large, predominantly Democratic state stepped in and disarmed the legislature's capacity to engage in congressional partisan gerrymandering, that court might inadvertently facilitate pro-Republican bias if the courts in large Republican-dominated states chose not to interpret their state constitutions in the same fashion.[118] Thus, the existing commentary on *Vieth* oversimplifies

---

[116] This conclusion also highlights a potential cost of adopting the approach that Justice Kennedy appears to favor in *Vieth*. Kennedy expressed hope that greater lower court experimentation in partisan gerrymandering cases could help courts tease out workable rules for policing partisan gerrymanders. During this period of experimentation, the different strategies applied to congressional redistricting by isolated lower courts may well be ineffective—even if the strategy itself is sound—simply because strategy is applied only to a small number of redistricting plans. This does not mean that experimentation is unwarranted; the benefits of experimentation might be sufficient to justify the approach. It does suggest, however, that in the interim this strategy may do little to lower the risk that congressional partisan gerrymanders combine to harm the structure of representation in Congress.

[117] See, for example, James A. Gardner, *A Post-Vieth Strategy for Litigating Partisan Gerrymandering Claims*, 2 Election L J 643 (2004).

[118] This point also suggests that there could be some unanticipated costs to another popular idea for reform—the proposal that voters use states' initiative processes to transfer

when it treats state court intervention as a simple fix for federal court impotence in congressional gerrymandering cases.

CONCLUSION

Congressional political gerrymanders pose different analytic, normative, and constitutional questions than do state legislative gerrymanders. The latter implicate the composition of the whole legislative body, while the former affect only a part. This difference, generally overlooked by courts and commentators, reveals that the Supreme Court's general approach in *Vieth v Jubelirer*—of treating the case as a referendum on *Davis v Bandemer*—is incomplete and misguided.

In contrast to state legislative partisan gerrymanders, congressional partisan gerrymanders produce harms that are most plausibly located at the *national*, not the state or individual district level. This aspect of the harm complicates the judicial review of congressional partisan gerrymanders, introducing a different set of empirical questions that bear on whether intervention is worthwhile, and highlighting the importance of judicial coordination for any successful intervention. While these new complications are significant, my aim is not to suggest that they are intractable and counsel swift judicial retreat. Rather, my goal is to refocus the discussion about congressional partisan gerrymanders on those issues that are central to evaluating the appropriateness of judicial intervention.

---

authority to draw congressional district lines from legislatures to nonpartisan or bipartisan commissions. If such efforts were successful in only a few states (or if there were a consistent partisan alignment among the states most likely to enact such reforms by initiative), the use of commissions might exacerbate certain harms. In this vein, it is interesting to note that Arnold Schwarzenegger is reportedly eyeing the possibility of backing an initiative in California to give redistricting authority to a group of retired judges. See Peter Nicholas, *Governor Considers a Special Election*, LA Times A1 (Dec 2, 2004).